P9-BYB-608

The **Rough Guide** to

Scottish Highlands and Islands

written and researched by

Rob Humphreys and Donald Reid

with additional contributions from
Helena Smith

ROUGH
GUIDES

www.roughguides.com

Contents

The great outdoors
colour section
following p.152

Wild Scotland
colour section
following p.312

◄◄ Red deer stag, Inverness ◄ Sanna Bay, Ardnamurchan peninsula

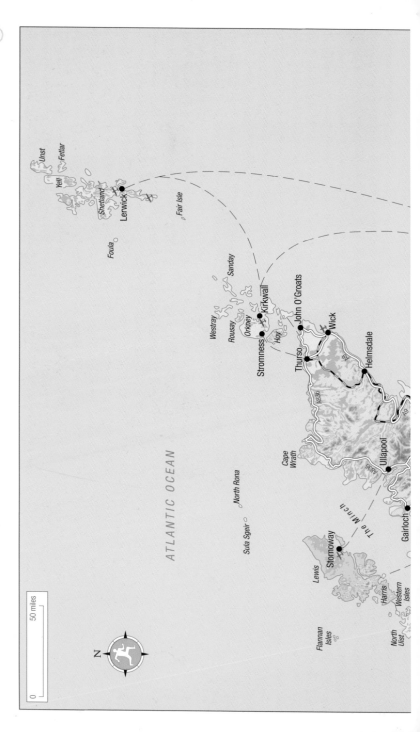

ATLANTIC OCEAN

Unst
Yell
Fetlar
Shetland
Lerwick

Foula

Fair Isle

Sanday
Westray
Rousay
Orkney
Kirkwall
Hoy
Stromness
John O'Groats
Thurso
Wick
A9
Helmsdale
A836
Cape
Wrath
A838
Ullapool
North Rona
Sula Sgeir
The Minch
A835
Gairloch
Lewis
Stornoway
Harris
Flannan
Isles
Western
Isles
North
Uist

N

50 miles
0

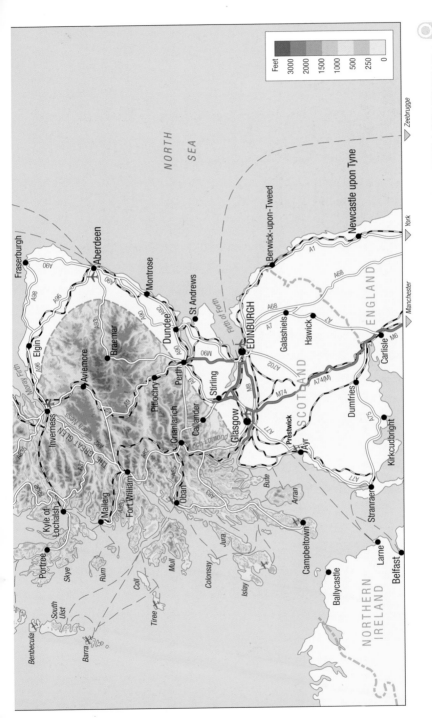

Feet
3000
2000
1500
1000
500
250
0

NORTH
SEA

Zeebrugge

Fraserburgh

Aberdeen

Montrose

A90

A98

A96

A93

A90

A94

A92

St Andrews

Dundee

Firth of Forth

Braemar

A9

A90

Aviemore

Pitlochry

Perth

M90

A9

Stirling

EDINBURGH

Elgin

A96

Moray Firth

Inverness

THE GREAT GLEN

A82

Loch Ness

Crianlarich

Callander

A9

M9

Glasgow

M8

A702

Galashiels

A7

Hawick

A68

Berwick-upon-Tweed

A1

Newcastle upon Tyne

York

Kyle of
Lochalsh

A87

A830

Fort William

A82

Oban

Loch Lomond

A85

A83

Bute

M74

A71

Prestwick

Ayr

SCOTLAND

A74(M)

Dumfries

A75

Kirkcudbright

Manchester

A68

Carlisle

M6

ENGLAND

Mallaig

A861

Portree

Skye

Rum

Coll

Tiree

Mull

Jura

Colonsay

Islay

Arran

Campbeltown

A77

Stranraer

Larne

Belfast

Ballycastle

NORTHERN
IRELAND

South
Uist

Benbecula

Barra

5

■

Introduction to

Scottish
Highlands & Islands

Rugged and weather-beaten, the Scottish Highlands and Islands are far removed from either the rural charms or the cosmopolitanism of much of Britain. Stuck out on the northwest fringe of Europe, this is a land where the elements play an important part in everyday life, where the shipping forecast is more than simply a form of sleep therapy. The landscape is raw, shaped over thousands of years by geological shifts, scouring glaciers and the hostile weather systems of the North Atlantic, to create magnificent land- and seascapes. It's a region with a wild, romantic glint in its eye, too, with a regular supply of glorious sunsets that turn the sea lochs gold, and with more deserted beaches than the entire Mediterranean. Sure, the roads can be tortuous, the weather sometimes grim and the midges a pain, but, when the mood is on, the Highlands and Islands rarely fail to seduce.

Despite all its dramatic beauty, it's impossible to travel in the Highlands and Islands without being touched by the fragility of life here. While the Jacobite defeat at Culloden in 1746 was a blow to Scottish pride, it was an unmitigated disaster for the Highlands and Islands, signalling the destruction of the Highland clan system, and ultimately the entire Highland way of life. The Clearances that followed in the nineteenth century more than halved the population, and even today the Highland landscape is littered with the crumbling shells of

Fact file

- Covering over 15,000 square miles, the Highlands and Islands region houses less than 400,000 inhabitants – a population density of 25 people per square mile, compared to Scotland's average of 166. The largest centre and only city in the region, Inverness has a population of little more than 66,000.

- The coastline of the Highlands and Islands region is nearly 7000 miles long, and Scotland has approximately 790 islands, 130 of which are inhabited.

- The highest mountain in the Highlands is Ben Nevis (4406ft), while the bottom of Loch Morar is 1017ft below sea level. The highest point of any island is Sgurr Alasdair in the Cuillin on Skye (3258ft). The highest point on the Shetland and Orkney islands is Ronas Hill (a streamlined 1476ft).

- Almost half of the 130,000 tons of salmon farmed annually is exported, mainly to Europe.

- The Highlands and Islands region is represented by fifteen MSPs (Members of the Scottish Parliament) in Edinburgh, and seven MPs (Members of Parliament) at Westminster.

pre-Clearance crofting communities. Depopulation remains a constant threat, particularly on the islands, and in many cases only the arrival of settlers from outside the region has stemmed the dwindling numbers. The economy, too, struggles, even with government and European Union subsidies. The traditional Highland industries of farming, crofting, fishing and whisky distilling are no longer enough to provide jobs for the younger generation, and have been supplemented by forestry, fish-farming and the oil industry. However, all three of these have a detrimental effect on the environment, whose health is of paramount importance to the region's other important industry – tourism. In the end, it's a tricky juggling act balancing the importance of seizing new opportunities with the will to maintain traditional values.

Tradition and the sense of the past may be vital elements of the Highlands and Islands, but the region is by no means entombed by them. Today visitors come not just to clamber over castles and wrap themselves in tartan nostalgia but to hike up hills or photograph puffins, meditate by standing stones or scuba-dive among shipwrecks. You don't have to look too far to find old assumptions being challenged in many aspects of Highland life – these days gourmets steer clear of tearooms serving short-bread to seek out wild venison and west-coast shellfish, landowning lairds are as likely to be Hollywood stars or Formula One racing drivers as titled aristocrats, while even in the remotest corners there are crofters looking after websites as well as shaggy Highland cattle.

Where to go

There's little to be gained in trying to rush round the Highlands and Islands. Travelling in these parts is time-consuming: distances on land are greater than elsewhere in Britain (and there are no motorways), while getting to the islands means coordinating with ferry or plane timetables and hoping the weather doesn't intervene and spoil your plans. Having said that, the journeys themselves – by spectacular train lines, small aircraft scudding over tiny islands, inter-island ferries or winding, scenic roads – are often memorable.

The most accessible parts of the region are not far from Glasgow and Edinburgh: you can be by the banks of Loch Lomond in half an hour, or Highland Perthshire in a little over an hour. As a result, **Loch Lomond**

▼ Tossing the caber, Highland Games

Ceilidhs

Highlanders have a deserved reputation for knowing how to throw a good party; if you hear rumour of a ceilidh (pronounced "kay-lee") happening nearby, change your plans to make sure you're there. From the Gaelic for "a visit", a ceilidh has its roots in an informal, homespun gathering of music, song, poetry and dance. These days, often helped along by a dram or two of whisky, they're lively events in the local pub or village hall. The main activity is dancing, to traditional set patterns, with music provided by a fiddler and an accordionist. While the whirling reels or jigs appear fiendishly complex, the popular ones aren't hard to pick up and the fun is infectious.

and the neighbouring hills and wooded glens of the **Trossachs** tend to be busier than other parts of the Highlands, and to escape the day-trippers you need to head further north into **Perthshire** and the **Grampian hills** of Angus and Deeside where the Highland scenery is at its richest. South of Inverness the mighty **Cairngorm** massif hints at the raw wilderness Scotland can still provide. To reach the lonely north and western Highlands, you'll have to cross the **Great Glen**, an ancient geological fissure which cuts across the country from **Ben Nevis** to **Loch Ness**, a moody stretch of water choked with tourists hoping for a glimpse of its monster. Meanwhile, the area with arguably the most memorable scenery of all is the jagged west coast, stretching from **Argyll** north to **Wester Ross** and the looming hills of **Assynt**.

Alongside the grand splendour of the Highlands, the islands, scattered like jigsaw pieces off the west and north coasts, are an essential complement. Assorted in size, flavour and accessibility, the long chain of rocky Hebrides which necklace Scotland's Atlantic shoreline include **Mull** and the nearby pilgrimage centre of **Iona**; **Islay** and **Jura**, famous for their wildlife and whisky; **Skye**, the most-visited of the Hebrides, where the Cuillin ridge rises up from the sea; and the **Western Isles**, an elongated archipelago that remains a bastion of Gaelic language and culture. Off the north coast, **Orkney** and **Shetland**, both with a rich Norse heritage, differ not only from each other, but also from mainland Scotland in dialect and culture – far-flung islands buffeted by wind and sea that offer some of the country's wildest scenery, finest birdwatching and best archeological sites.

A wee dram...

The Scots like a drink. Somehow, a Scot who doesn't like (or, worse, can't handle) a dram of "Scotch" – although whisky is rarely described as such in Scotland – isn't wholly credible. No Highland village would be complete without its cosy, convivial pub – and no pub complete without its array of amber-tinged bottles, the spirit within nurtured by a beguiling and well-marketed mix of soft Scottish rain, glistening Highland streams, rich peaty soil and tender Scots craftsmanship.

But not only is whisky the national drink, it's often regarded as the national pastime too, lubricating any social gathering from a Highland ceilidh to a Saturday night session. While it can be drunk neat, the truth is that a splash of water releases the whisky's flavours. It's no surprise, then, that the canny Scots also turn a healthy profit bottling the country's abundant spring water and selling it around the world.

When to go

The weather is probably the single biggest factor to put you off visiting the Highlands and Islands. It's not so much that the weather's always bad, it's just unpredictable and changeable: in the islands they say you can experience four seasons in one day. However, even if the weather's not necessarily good, it's generally interesting, exhilarating, dramatic and certainly photogenic – well suited, in fact, to the landscapes over which it plays such an important role.

The **summer** months of June, July and August are the high season, with local school holidays making July and early August the busiest period. The days are generally mild or warm, but the weather is often variable. Daylight hours are long, however, and, in the far north, darkness hardly falls during midsummer. The warmer weather does have its drawbacks, however: most significantly, the clouds of **midges**, tiny biting insects which frequently appear around dusk, dawn and in dank conditions, and which can drive even the most committed outdoors type scurrying indoors.

▶ Eilean Donan Castle

11

Commonly, **May** and **September** throw up weather as good as, if not better than, the months of high summer. You're less likely to encounter crowds, and the mild temperatures combined with the changing **colours** of nature mean both are great for outdoor activities, particularly hiking. May is also a good month for watching nesting **sea birds**; September, however, is stalking season for deer, which can disrupt **access** to the countryside.

The months of **April** and **October** bracket the season for many parts of rural Scotland. Many attractions, tourist offices and guesthouses open for business at Easter and close after the school half-term in October. If places do

Passing places

Whether marked by a stripy black-and-white pole or a simple white diamond, the first sighting of a passing place is genuine proof that you've escaped the rat race. You can't hurry a passing place: drive too fast and you'll only have to reverse back to the nearest one or dive into a verge. Drivers are forced to acknowledge and even cooperate with one another. Visitors soon get into the swing of it, thanking fellow travellers with a full, cheerful wave, or by raising a finger nonchalantly from the steering wheel. More experienced students of passing-place etiquette learn to pull over to allow vehicles to overtake – a gesture that will endear you to the locals more than any amount of vigorous waving.

stay open through the winter, it's normally with reduced opening hours; the October-to-March period is also the best time to pick up **special offers** at hotels and guesthouses. Note, too, that public transport will often operate on a reduced winter timetable.

Winter days, from November to March, although occasionally crisp and bright, are more often cold, gloomy and all too brief. Nevertheless, **Hogmanay** and **New Year** has traditionally been a time to visit Scotland for partying and warm hospitality. On a clear night in winter, visitors in the far

▲ Scots thistle

north might be treated to a celestial display from the **aurora borealis**, while a fall of snow in the Highlands will prompt plenty of activity around the **ski** resorts.

Average temperatures and rainfall

	Jan	Feb	Mar	Apr	May	Jun	Jul	Aug	Sep	Oct	Nov	Dec
Oban												
°C/°F	6/43	7/45	9/48	11/52	14/57	16/61	17/63	17/63	15/59	12/54	9/48	7/45
mm	146	109	83	90	72	87	120	116	141	169	146	172
inches	5.8	4.3	3.3	3.5	2.8	3.4	4.7	4.6	5.6	6.7	5.8	6.8
Braemar												
°C/°F	4/39	4/39	6/43	9/48	13/55	16/61	17/63	17/63	14/57	11/52	6/43	5/41
mm	93	59	59	51	65	55	58	76	73	87	87	96
inches	3.7	2.3	2.3	2	2.6	2.2	2.3	3	2.9	3.4	3.4	3.8
Fort William												
°C/°F	6/43	7/44	9/47	11/52	14/58	17/62	17/63	17/63	15/60	13/55	9/48	7/45
mm	200	132	152	111	103	124	137	150	199	215	220	238
inches	7.8	5.1	5.9	4.3	4	4.8	5.3	5.9	7.8	8.4	8.6	9.3
Shetland												
°C/°F	5/41	5/41	6/42	8/46	10/50	13/55	14/57	14/57	13/55	10/50	7/45	6/42
mm	127	93	93	72	64	64	67	78	113	119	140	147
inches	5	3.7	3.7	2.8	2.5	2.5	2.6	3	4.5	4.7	5.5	5.8

things not to miss

It's not possible to see everything that the Highlands and Islands have to offer in one trip – and we don't suggest you try. What follows is a selective taste of the highlights: natural wonders and outstanding sites, plus the best activities and experiences. They're arranged in five colour-coded categories, which you can browse through to find the very best things to see and do. All highlights have a page reference to take you straight into the Guide, where you can find out more.

01 **Wester Ross** Page **238** • Where the mountains meet the sea – the sparkling jewel of Highland scenery.

02 Mountain biking Page 48
• Scotland offers fabulous off-road cycling from gentle runs for the kids to championship-level trails.

03 St Magnus Cathedral
Page **354** • A medieval cathedral in miniature, built by the Vikings using beautiful red and yellow sandstone.

04 West Highland Railway Page **229** • One of the great railway journeys of the world.

06 Loch Fyne Oyster Bar
Page **66** • Pick up a picnic or enjoy fine dining at Scotland's top smokehouse and seafood outlet, located just outside Inveraray.

05 Whale-watching, Mull
Page **85** • Close encounters with a very different type of Highland wildlife.

07 Mousa, Shetland Page 393 • The mother of all Iron Age brochs, on an island off the coast of Shetland.

08 Pubs Page 38 • Forget the great outdoors and install yourself in one of Scotland's cosy and convivial hostelries.

09 **Kinloch Castle, Rùm** Page **298** • Stay in the servants' quarters of this Edwardian hideaway or in one of its few remaining four-poster beds.

10 **The Cairngorm mountains** Page **170** • Beguiling natural splendour mixed with terrific outdoor activities.

11 **Highland Games** Page **42** • An entertaining blend of summer sports day and traditional clan gathering, held in locations across the Highlands.

13 **Gearrannan, Lewis** Page **318** • Stay in the thatched blackhouse hostel in this beautifully restored, former crofting village.

12 **Caledonian forest** Page **171** • The few gnarled survivors of the great ancient Highland forests are majestic characters.

14 Tobermory Page **83** • Tobermory is the archetypal picturesque fishing village, with colourful houses ranged around a sheltered harbour and backed by steep hills.

15 Whisky tasting, Islay Page **121** • This Hebridean island boasts no fewer than eight distilleries, each offering guided tours.

16 Shetland Folk Festival Page **389** • Shetland is the place to experience traditional folk music, and the annual folk festival is the best time to do it.

17 **Glen Coe** Page **198** • Moody, poignant and spectacular glen within easy reach of Fort William.

18 **Flying above Orkney** Page **343** • Take an exhilarating aerial tour of the archipelago in an eight-seater plane.

19 **Jarlshof, Shetland** Page **395** • An exceptional archeological site taking in Iron Age, Bronze Age, Pictish, Viking and medieval remains.

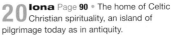

20 **Iona** Page **90** • The home of Celtic Christian spirituality, an island of pilgrimage today as in antiquity.

21 **South Harris beaches** Page **325** • Take your pick of deserted golden beaches in South Harris, or further south in the Uists.

22 Maes Howe, Orkney Page **347** • Amazingly preserved, this five-thousand-year-old burial chamber also contains Viking graffiti.

23 Staffa and the Treshnish Isles Page **87** • View the basalt columns of Staffa's Fingal's Cave from the sea, and then picnic amidst the puffins on the Isle of Lunga.

24 Birdwatching see *Wild Scotland* **colour section** • From wintering geese and cute puffins to the iconic golden eagle, the Highlands and Islands are twitcher heaven.

25 **Loch Shiel** Page **228** • Among Scotland's myriad lochs, Shiel stands out for its serene beauty and compelling history.

26 **Calanais, Lewis** Page **319** • Prehistoric standing stones that occupy a serene lochside setting in the Western Isles.

27 **Skye Cuillin** Page **287** • The most spectacular mountain range on the west coast, for viewing or climbing.

28 Eigg Page **300** • Perfect example of a tiny, friendly Hebridean island, with a golden beach to lie on, a hill to climb and stunning views across the sea to its neighbour, Rùm.

29 Up Helly-Aa Page **386** • Pack your thermals and head to Shetland in January for this spectacular Viking fire festival.

Basics

Basics

Getting there

There are numerous ways of getting to the Scottish Highlands and Islands. For most, the quickest and easiest way is by plane. Inverness is an obvious gateway for much of the region, but you'll get a wider selection of flights to Scotland's three main international airports – Glasgow, Edinburgh and Aberdeen – each of which is only a short hop from most areas of interest.

With most airlines nowadays, how much you pay depends on how far in advance you book and how much demand there is during that period – the earlier you book, the cheaper the prices.

If you're coming from elsewhere in Britain, from Ireland or even northwest Europe, you can reach Scotland easily enough by **train**, **bus** or **ferry** – it probably won't work out cheaper or faster than flying, but it's undoubtedly better for the environment.

From England and Wales

If you're heading out to the Highlands and Islands, **flying** is the quickest way to travel. If your ultimate destination is Argyll, Loch Lomond or the Hebrides, Glasgow is the natural gateway; for Perthshire and the Cairngorms, Edinburgh or Glasgow are good; for anywhere further north, Inverness is the best hub. Airfares on popular routes such as London or Birmingham to Edinburgh and Glasgow, can cost as little as £50 return (journey time just over 1hr). However, once you add on the cost of taxes and getting to and from the airport, the savings on the same journey overland are often minimal – and then, of course, there's the environmental impact to consider.

Flying may be quick, but the **coach and train** fares can be pretty competitive. If you book far enough in advance, **train** fares can cost as little as £70 for a London to Inverness return (journey time from 8hr), or £40 for a Manchester to Inverness (journey time 7hr). A more flexible or last-minute fare will obviously cost two or three times that amount. Another option is the overnight **Caledonian Sleeper** run by ScotRail from London Euston (daily except Sat; journey time around 7hr); again, if you book in advance, single overnight fares cost around £20, though most return fares are more like £100 return.

The **coach** takes longer than the train, but costs less, with a London or Birmingham to Inverness overnight return starting for as little as £30 return (journey time from 12hr 30min).

From Ireland

Travel from Ireland is quickest by plane, with **airfares** from either Belfast or Dublin to Glasgow Prestwick from as little as €40 return. There are also good **ferry** links with Northern Ireland and the train and ferry fares are very competitive: Belfast to Glasgow (via Stranraer) is just £50 return (journey time 5hr). P&O Irish Sea runs several sea crossings daily from Larne to Cairnryan (1hr) and Troon (2hr) and Stena Line operates services daily from Belfast to Stranraer (2hr 10min).

From the US and Canada

If you fly **nonstop to Scotland** from North America, you'll arrive in either Glasgow or Edinburgh. The majority of cheap fares, however, route through London, Manchester, Dublin or Paris. To reach any other Scottish airport, you'll definitely need to go via London, Glasgow or Edinburgh.

Figure on six to seven hours' flight time nonstop from the east coast to Glasgow, or seven hours to London plus an extra hour and a quarter from London to Glasgow or Edinburgh (not including stopover time). Add three or four hours more for travel from the west coast.

Return fares (including taxes) for nonstop flights to Glasgow from New York are $700–800; for nonstop flights from Toronto return fares are Can$700–800.

From Australia and New Zealand

Flight time from Australia and New Zealand to Scotland is at least 22 hours. There's a wide variety of routes, with those touching down in Southeast Asia the quickest and cheapest on average. To reach Scotland, you usually have to change planes either in London – the most popular choice – or in another European gateway such as Paris or Amsterdam. Given the length of the journey involved, you might be better off including a night's stopover in your itinerary, and indeed some airlines include one in the price of the flight.

The cheapest direct scheduled flights to London are usually to be found on one of the Asian airlines. Average **return fares** (including taxes) from eastern gateways to London are Aus$1500–2000 in low season, Aus$2000–2500 in high season. Fares from Perth or Darwin cost around Aus$200 less.

Return fares from Auckland to London range between NZ$2000 and NZ$3000 depending on the season, route and carrier.

From South Africa

There are **no direct flights** from South Africa to Scotland, so you must change planes en route. The quickest and cheapest route to take is via London, with flight time around eleven hours, usually overnight. **Return fares** from Cape Town to London are ZAR7500–10,000; you'll save money if you buy the next leg of your journey to Scotland online – see p.27 for details.

From mainland Europe

Ferries run by DFDS Seaways go overnight from IJmuiden, near Amsterdam to Newcastle (daily; 16–17hr), less than an hour's drive south of the Scottish border. High season return fares start at around €300, for a passenger with a car and an

---

Six steps to a better kind of travel

At Rough Guides we are passionately committed to travel. We feel strongly that only through travelling do we truly come to understand the world we live in and the people we share it with – plus tourism has brought a great deal of **benefit** to developing economies around the world over the last few decades. But the extraordinary growth in tourism has also damaged some places irreparably, and of course **climate change** is exacerbated by most forms of transport, especially flying. This means that now more than ever it's important to **travel thoughtfully** and **responsibly**, with respect for the cultures you're visiting – not only to derive the most benefit from your trip but also to preserve the best bits of the planet for everyone to enjoy. At Rough Guides we feel there are six main areas in which you can make a difference:

- Consider what you're contributing to the **local economy**, and how much the services you use do the same, whether it's through employing local workers and guides or sourcing locally grown produce and local services.
- Consider the **environment** on holiday as well as at home. Water is scarce in many developing destinations, and the biodiversity of local flora and fauna can be adversely affected by tourism. Try to patronize businesses that take account of this.
- Travel with a purpose, not just to tick off experiences. Consider **spending longer** in a place, and getting to know it and its people.
- Give thought to how often you **fly**. Try to avoid short hops by air and more harmful night flights.
- Consider **alternatives to flying**, travelling instead by bus, train, boat and even by bike or on foot where possible.
- Make your trips "**climate neutral**" via a reputable carbon offset scheme. All Rough Guide flights are offset, and every year we donate money to a variety of charities devoted to combating the effects of climate change.

overnight berth. Direct Ferries (@www .directferries.co.uk) has a very useful website that gives you the latest information on crossings and allows you to compare all the options.

Airlines

Aer Arann @www.aerarann.com
Aer Lingus @www.aerlingus.com
Air Canada @www.aircanada.com
Air New Zealand @www.airnewzealand.com
Air Transat @www.airtransat.com
American Airlines @www.aa.com
Asiana Airlines @www.flyasiana.com
bmi @www.flybmi.com
bmibaby @www.bmibaby.com
British Airways @www.ba.com
Cathay Pacific @www.cathaypacific.com
Continental Airlines @www.continental.com
Delta @www.delta.com
Eastern Airways @www.easternairways.com
easyJet @www.easyjet.com
Flybe @www.flybe.com
Gulf Air @www.gulfair.com
KLM @www.klm.com
Lufthansa @www.lufthansa.com
Malaysia Airlines @www.malaysiaairlines.com
Qantas @www.qantas.com
Royal Brunei @www.bruneiair.com
Ryanair @www.ryanair.com
Scandinavian Airlines @www.flysas.com
ScotAirways @www.scotairways.com
Singapore Airlines @www.singaporeair.com
Thai Airways @www.thaiair.com
United Airlines @www.united.com
US Airlines @www.usairways.com
Virgin Atlantic @www.virgin-atlantic.com
Widerøe @www.wideroe.no

Agents and operators

ebookers @www.ebookers.com. Low fares on an extensive selection of scheduled flights and package deals.

North South Travel @www.northsouthtravel .co.uk. Friendly, competitive travel agency, offering discounted fares worldwide. Profits are used to support projects in the developing world, especially the promotion of sustainable tourism.
STA Travel @www.statravel.com. Worldwide specialists in independent travel; also student IDs, travel insurance, car rental, rail passes and more. Good discounts for students and under-26s.
Trailfinders @www.trailfinders.com. One of the best-informed and most efficient agents for independent travellers.
Travel CUTS @www.travelcuts.com. Canadian youth and student travel firm.
USIT @www.usit.ie. Ireland's main student and youth travel specialists.

Train and coach information

East Coast @www.eastcoast.co.uk Trains to Edinburgh, Glasgow, Aberdeen and Inverness.
Man in Seat 61 @www.seat61.com The best train information website on the internet.
National Express @www.nationalexpress.com Coaches to Scotland.
National Rail enquiries @www.nationalrail .co.uk. Information and fares for all train services and companies.
ScotRail @www.scotrail.co.uk Caledonian Sleeper train to Glasgow, Edinburgh, Aberdeen, Inverness and Fort William.
Virgin @www.virgintrains.co.uk. Trains to Edinburgh and Glasgow.

Ferry companies

P&O Irish Sea @www.poirishsea.com Ferries from Ireland.
Stena Line @www.stenaline.co.uk Ferries from Ireland.
DFDS Seaways @www.dfdsseaways.com Ferries from Europe.

Getting around

There's no getting away from the fact that getting around the Highlands and Islands is a time-consuming business: off the main routes, public transport services are few and far between, particularly in more remote parts of Argyll, the Highland region and the islands. With careful planning, however, practically everywhere is accessible and you'll have no trouble getting to the main tourist destinations. And in most parts of Scotland, especially if you take the scenic backroads, the low level of traffic makes driving wonderfully unstressful.

By train

The **railway** network in the Highlands is skeletal but spectacular, with a number of the lines counted as among the great scenic routes of the world. There are four main lines all run by ScotRail: the two on the west coast depart Glasgow Queen Street and terminate at Oban and Mallaig (via Fort William); the main line divides at Inverness, one branch going to Kyle of Lochalsh and the other to Thurso.

You can buy train **tickets** at most stations, but if the ticket office at the station is closed, or the automatic machine isn't working, you may buy your ticket on board from the inspector using cash or a credit card. Those eligible for a **national rail pass** (£26) can obtain discounted tickets, with up to a third off most fares. These include the **16–25 Railcard**, for full-time students and those aged between 16 and 25, and the **Senior Railcard** for people over 60. Alternatively, a **Family & Friends Railcard** entitles up to four adults, and up to four children a reduction.

In addition, ScotRail offers several regional passes. The most flexible is the **Freedom of Scotland Travelpass**, which gives unlimited train travel within Scotland. It's also valid on all CalMac ferries and various buses in the remoter regions. The pass costs £114 for four days' travel in an eight-day period, or £153 for eight days' travel in a fifteen-day period. The **Highland Rover** allows unlimited train travel within the Highlands including the West Highland Line; it costs £74 for four out of eight consecutive days.

BritRail passes (@www.britrail.com) are only available to visitors not resident in the UK and must be purchased before you leave your home country. The pass is available in a wide variety of types; for example the adult pass allows unlimited train travel for eight days and costs US$359. If you've been resident in a European country other than the UK for at least six months, an **InterRail** pass, allowing unlimited train travel within Britain might be worth it, if Scotland is part of a longer European trip. For more details, visit @www.interrailnet.com. Note that **Eurail** passes are not valid in the UK.

On most ScotRail routes **bicycles** are carried free, but since there are only between two and six bike spaces available, it's a good idea to reserve ahead and a requirement on longer journeys.

Useful rail contacts

ScotRail @www.scotrail.co.uk. For booking tickets and seats on all trains within Scotland, and sleeper trains from London to Scotland.
National Rail Enquiries ☎0845/748 4950, @www.nationalrail.co.uk. Gives details of timetables, fares and other information on rail travel throughout the UK.

By coach and bus

The main centres of the Highlands are served by a few long-distance bus services, known across Britain as **coaches**. Scotland's national operator is **Scottish Citylink** (☎0871/266 3333, @www.citylink.co.uk). On the whole, coaches are cheaper than trains and, as a result, are very popular, so for longer journeys it's advisable to book ahead.

There are various **discounts** on offer for those with children, those under 26 or over

Hebridean Whale Cruises
Gairloch

ORCA 1
The Nº 1 whale-watching
boat in Scotland!*

Advance booking essential
☎ **01445 712468**
*Sea Watch Foundation data

Pier Road, Gairloch, IV21 2BQ
www.hebridean-whale-cruises.com

CASTLE
TOURS

Welcome to Scotland's
Castle & Whisky
Wonderland

Full day sightseeing
tours departing daily
from Aberdeen
and Inverness
see full
schedule
online

book online today!
www.castle-tours.co.uk
07525 865348
info@castle-tours.co.uk

60 and full-time students (contact Scottish Citylink for more details), as well as an **Explorer Pass**, which gives unlimited travel throughout Scotland; the £79 pass gives you 8 days' travel over a sixteen-day period. Overseas passport holders can buy a **Brit Xplorer pass** (in 7-, 14- or 28-day versions) in the UK, from National Express (Ⓦwww .nationalexpress.com), or at major ports and airports; the seven-day pass costs £79, though you'd have to do a lot of bus travelling to make it worth your while.

Local bus services are run by a bewildering array of companies, many of which change routes and timetables frequently. Local tourist offices can provide free timetables or you can contact **Traveline Scotland** (☎0871/200 2233, Ⓦwww.travelinescotland .com), which provides a reliable service both online and by phone. Some areas in the Highlands and Islands are only served by a **postbus**, vehicles carrying mail and a handful of fare-paying passengers. They set off early in the morning, usually around 8am and, though sociable, can be excruciatingly slow. You can view routes and timetables on the **Royal Mail website** (☎0845/774 0740, Ⓦwww.royalmail.com/postbus).

By car

In order to **drive** in Scotland you need a current full driving licence. If you're bringing your own vehicle into the country you should also carry your vehicle registration, ownership and insurance documents at all times.

In Scotland, as in the rest of the UK, you **drive on the left**. Speed limits are 20–40mph in built-up areas, 70mph on motorways and dual carriageways (freeways) and 60mph on most other roads. As a rule, assume that in any area with street lighting, the limit is 30mph.

In the Highlands and Islands, there are still plenty of **single-track roads** with passing places; in addition to allowing oncoming traffic to pass at these points, you should also let cars behind you overtake. In remoter regions, the roads are dotted with sheep which are entirely oblivious to cars, so slow down and edge your way past; should you kill or injure one, it is your duty to inform the local farmer.

The AA (Ⓦwww.theaa.com, ☎0800/ 887766), RAC (Ⓦwww.rac.co.uk, ☎0844/891 3111) and Green Flag (Ⓦwww.green flag.co.uk, ☎0845/246 2766) all operate

Minibus tours

Minibus tours that operate out of Edinburgh (and Glasgow) and head off into the Highlands are popular with backpackers who want a quick taste of Scotland. Aimed at the youth market, they adopt an upbeat and irreverent approach to sightseeing, as well as offering a good opportunity to get to know fellow travellers.

The current leading operator, **Haggis** (℡0131/557 9393, ⊛www.haggisadventures .com), has bright yellow minibuses setting off daily on whistlestop tours lasting between one and six days, in the company of a live-wire guide. A three-day trip round Skye starts from £99 (food and accommodation not included).

Several other companies offer similar packages, including **Macbackpackers** (℡0131/558 9900, ⊛www.macbackpackers.com), which runs tours linking up their own hostels round the country, and **Wild in Scotland** (℡0131/478 6500, ⊛www .wild-in-scotland.com), which takes in the Outer Hebrides or Orkney. The popular **Rabbie's Trail Burners** tours (℡0131/226 3133, ⊛www.rabbies.com) don't aim squarely at the backpacker market and have a rather more mellow outlook.

24-hour **emergency breakdown** services. You may be entitled to free assistance through a reciprocal arrangement with a motoring organization in your home country. If not, you can make use of these emergency services by joining at the roadside, but you will incur a hefty surcharge. In remote areas, you may have a long wait for assistance.

Renting a car

Car rental in Scotland is expensive. Most firms charge £25–50 per day, or around £130–200 a week. The major chains are mostly confined to the big cities, so it may be cheaper to use small **local agencies** – we've highlighted some in the account. Remember, too that **fuel** in Scotland is expensive – petrol (gasoline) and diesel cost well over £1.20 per litre. **Automatics** are rare at the lower end of the price scale – if you want one, you should book well ahead. **Camper vans** are another option; rates start at £400 a week in the high season, but you'll save on accommodation – visit ⊛www.walkhighlands.co.uk to view a range of options. Few companies will rent to drivers with less than one year's experience and most will only rent to people over 21 or 25 and under 70 or 75 years of age.

UK car rental companies

Arnold Clark ℡0141/237 4374, ⊛www
.arnoldclarkrental.co.uk
Avis ℡0844/581 0147, ⊛www.avis.co.uk
Budget ℡01344/484100, ⊛www.budget.co.uk
easyCar ℡0871/050 0444, ⊛www.easycar.com

Europcar ℡0871/384 9847, ⊛www.europcar
.co.uk
Hertz ℡0870/844 8844, ⊛www.hertz.co.uk
Holiday Autos ℡0871/472 5229, ⊛www
.holidayautos.co.uk
National ℡0871/384 3504, ⊛www.nationalcar
.co.uk
Thrifty ℡01494/751500, ⊛www.thrifty.co.uk

By ferry

Scotland has over sixty inhabited islands, and nearly fifty of them have scheduled **ferry** links. Most ferries carry cars and vans, and the vast majority can – and should – be booked as far in advance as possible.

CalMac has a virtual monopoly on services on the River Clyde and to the Hebrides, sailing to 22 islands and four peninsulas. They aren't quick – no catamarans or fast ferries – or cheap, but they do have two types of reduced-fare pass. If you're taking more than one ferry, ask for one of the discounted **Island Hopscotch** tickets. If you're going to be taking a lot of ferries, you might be better off with an **Island Rover**, which entitles you to eight or fifteen consecutive days' unlimited ferry travel. It does not, however, guarantee you a place on any ferry, so you still need to book ahead. Prices for the eight-day/fifteen-day pass are around £50/£70 for passengers and around £230/£350 for cars.

Car ferries to **Orkney and Shetland** are run by Northlink Ferries. Pentland Ferries also run a car ferry to Orkney, and John O'Groats Ferries run a summer-only passenger service to Orkney. The various Orkney islands are linked to each other by Orkney Ferries; Shetland's inter-island ferries are mostly council-run so the local tourist board is your best bet for information. There are also numerous **small operators** round the Scottish coast that run fast RIB taxi services, day-excursion trips and even the odd scheduled service; their contact details are given in the relevant chapters of this guide.

Ferry companies

CalMac ℡0800/066 5000, 🌐www.calmac.co.uk
John O'Groats Ferries ℡01955/611353, 🌐www.jogferry.co.uk
NorthLink Ferries ℡0845/600 0449, 🌐www.northlinkferries.co.uk
Orkney Ferries ℡01856/872044, 🌐www.orkneyferries.co.uk
Pentland Ferries ℡01856/831226, 🌐www.pentlandferries.co.uk

By plane

Aside from the international airport at Inverness, there are numerous minor **airports** around the Scottish Highlands and Islands, some of which are little more than gravel airstrips. Airfares fluctuate enormously depending on demand – if you book early enough you can fly from Glasgow to Islay for £50 one way, but leave it to the last minute and it could cost you more than twice that. Most flights within Scotland are operated by flybe (🌐www.flybe.com), or its franchise partner Loganair (🌐www.loganair.co.uk). For inter-island flights in Shetland, you need to book direct through Directflight (℡01595/840246). Competition emerges from time to time, with Eastern Airways (🌐www.easternairways.com) currently offering flights from Aberdeen to Stornoway and Wick.

Accommodation

In common with the rest of Britain, accommodation in the Highlands and Islands is expensive. Budget travellers are well catered for with numerous hostels and those with money to spend will relish the more expensive country-house hotels. In the middle ground, however, the standard of many B&Bs, guesthouses and hotels can be disappointing. Welcoming, comfortable, well-run places do, of course, exist in all parts of the country – and you'll find the best ones listed in the guide.

Booking hotels, guesthouses and B&Bs

VisitScotland, the country's tourist board, operates a system for grading accommodation, which is updated annually. However, by no means every establishment participates, and you shouldn't assume that a particular B&B is no good simply because it's not on VisitScotland's lists. The tourist board uses star awards, from one to five, which are supposed to reflect the quality of welcome, service and hospitality – though it's pretty clear that places without en-suite toilets, a TV in every room, matching fabrics or packets of shortbread on the sideboard are likely to be marked down.

Most **tourist offices** will help you find accommodation and **book a room** directly, for which they normally charge a flat fee of £4. If you take advantage of this service, it's worth being clear as to what kind of place you'd prefer, as the tourist office quite often selects something quite randomly across the whole range of their membership. Bear in mind that in the Highlands and Islands many places are only open for the summer season, roughly from Easter to October; you'll always find somewhere to stay outside this period, but the choice will be more limited.

Hotels

Hotels come in all shapes and sizes. At the upper end of the market, they can be huge country houses and converted castles offering a very exclusive and opulent experience. Most will have a licensed bar and offer both breakfast and dinner, and often lunch as well. In the cities the increasing prevalence of modern budget hotels and travel lodges run by national (and international) chains may not win any prizes for aesthetics or variety, but they are competitively priced and for the most part meet criteria for clean, smart, serviceable accommodation. Also making a bit of a comeback are inns (in other words, pubs), or their modern equivalent, "restaurants with rooms". These will often only have a handful of rooms, but their emphasis on creating an all-round convivial atmosphere as well as serving up top-quality food often make them worth seeking out.

Over 100 award-winning camp sites

If you love camping as much as we do, you'll love staying on one of The Camping and Caravanning Club's 108 UK Club Sites. Each of our sites are in great locations and are an ideal base for exploring.

There's just one thing: once you've discovered the friendly welcome, the excellent facilities and clean, safe surroundings, you'll probably want to join anyway!

To book your adventure or to join the Club call
0845 130 7633
quoting code **2857** or visit
www.thefriendlyclub.co.uk

The **Camping** and **Caravanning Club**
The Friendly Club

Guesthouses and B&Bs

Guesthouses and B&Bs offer the widest and most diverse range of accommodation. VisitScotland uses the term "guesthouse" for a commercial venture that has four or more rooms, at least some of which are en suite, reserving "B&B" for a predominantly private family home that has only a few rooms to let. In reality, however, most places offer en-suite facilities, and the different names often reflect the pretensions of the owners and the cost of the rooms more than differences in service: in general, guesthouses cost more than B&Bs.

Some guesthouses and B&Bs have decor that can be quite challenging to those who aren't keen on chintz, but the location, and the chance to get an insight into the local way of life; can be some compensation. Many B&Bs, even the pricier ones, have only a few rooms, so **advance booking** is recommended, especially in the Islands.

Hostels

There's an ever-increasing number of **hostels** in the Highlands and Islands to cater for travellers – youthful or otherwise – who are unable or unwilling to pay the rates charged by hotels, guesthouses and B&Bs. Most hostels are clean and comfortable, sometimes offering doubles (more often twins) and even singles as well as dormitory accommodation. Others concentrate more on keeping the price as low as possible, simply providing a roof over your head and a few basic facilities. Whatever type of hostel you stay in, expect to pay £8–15 per night.

SYHA hostels

The **Scottish Youth Hostels Association** (Ⓦwww.syha.org.uk), referred to throughout the Guide as "SYHA hostels", run the longest-established hostels in the Highlands and Islands. While these places sometimes occupy handsome buildings, many retain an institutionalized air. Bunk-bed accommodation in single-sex dormitories, lights out before midnight and no smoking/no alcohol policies are the norm outside the big cities. Breakfast is not normally included in the price, though most hostels have self-catering facilities.

Accommodation price codes

Throughout this book, accommodation prices have been graded with the **codes** below, corresponding to the cost of the least expensive double room in high season. The bulk of our recommendations fall in categories ❷ to ❺; those in the highest categories are limited to places that are especially attractive. Bear in mind that many of the chain hotels slash their tariffs at the weekend, and that a cheaper establishment may also have a selection of more expensive rooms. Price codes are not given for **campsites**, most of which charge less than £10 per person. Almost all **hostels** and **bunkhouses** charge between £10 and £15 per person per night; the few exceptions to this rule have their prices quoted in the review.

❶ £49 and under	❹ £70–79	❼ £120–149
❷ £50–59	❺ £80–99	❽ £150–199
❸ £60–69	❻ £100–119	❾ £200 and over

If you're not a **member** of one of the hostelling organizations affiliated to **Hostelling International** (HI), you can pay your £10 joining fee at most hostels. **Advance booking** is recommended, and essential at Easter, Christmas and from May to August. You can book online, by phone, post and sometimes fax, and your bed will be held until 6pm on the day of arrival.

Other hostels

The **Gatliff Hebridean Hostels Trust** or GHHT (www.gatliff.org.uk) is allied to the SYHA and rents out very simple croft accommodation in the Western Isles. Accommodation is basic, and you can't book ahead, but it's unlikely you'll be turned away. Elsewhere in the Highlands and Islands, these places tend to be known as **bothies** or bunkhouses, and are usually independently run. In Shetland, **camping böds**, operated by the Shetland Amenity Trust (www.camping-bods.co.uk), offer similarly plain accommodation: you need all your usual camping equipment to stay at one (except, of course, a tent). For more details about Gatliff hostels and camping böds, see the relevant chapters in the Guide.

There are also loads of **independent hostels** (sometimes known as "bunkhouses") across Scotland. These are usually laidback places with no membership, fewer rules, mixed dorms and no curfew. You can find most of them in the annually updated *Independent Hostel Guide* (www.independenthostelguide.co.uk). Many of them are also affiliated to the Independent Backpackers Hostels of Scotland (www.hostel-scotland.co.uk), which has a programme of inspection and lists members in their *Blue Hostel Guide,* available for free online.

Camping and self-catering

There are hundreds of **caravan and camping parks** around Scotland, most of which are open from April to October. The more expensive sites charge about £10–15 for two people to pitch a tent, and are usually well equipped, with shops, a restaurant, a bar and, occasionally, sports facilities. Most of these, however, are principally aimed at caravans, trailers and motorhomes, and generally don't offer the tranquil atmosphere and independence that those travelling with just a tent are seeking.

That said, **informal sites** of the kind tent campers relish do exist, and are described throughout this guide, though they are few and far between. Many **hostels** allow camping, and farmers will usually let folk camp on their land for free or for a nominal sum. Scotland's relaxed land access laws allow **wild camping** in open country. The basic rule is "leave no trace", but for a guide to good practice, visit www.outdooraccess-scotland.com.

The great majority of **caravans** are permanently moored nose-to-tail in the vicinity of some of Scotland's finest scenery; others are positioned singly in back gardens or amidst farmland. Some can be booked for self-catering, and with prices starting at around £100 a week, this can work out as

Remote getaways

We make it easy for you
to discover rustic Scotland

Hostelling
Scotland

w: **hostellingscotland.com**
t: **0845 293 73 73** (from the UK)
    +441786 891 375 (from outside the UK)
e: **reservations@syha.org.uk**

Experience
Hostelling
Experience
Scotland

Scottish Youth Hostels Association (also known as SYHA or Hostelling Scotland) is a
registered Scottish charity No.SCO13138 and a company limited by guarantee, registered in Scotland.
No. SC310841. Registered Office 7 Glebe Crescent, Stirling, FK8 2JA.

one of the cheapest options if you're travelling with kids in tow.

If you're planning to do a lot of camping at
official camping and caravanning sites, it
might be worthwhile joining the **Camping
and Caravanning Club** (Ⓦ www.campingand
caravanningclub.co.uk). Membership costs
around £37 and entitles you to pay only a
per-person fee, not a pitch fee, at CCC sites.
Those coming from abroad can get the same
benefits by buying an international camping
carnet, available from home motoring organizations or a CCC equivalent.

Self-catering

A huge proportion of visitors to the Highlands
and Islands opt for **self-catering**, booking a
cottage or apartment for a week and often
saving themselves a considerable amount of
money by doing so. In most cases, the
minimum period of let is a week, and therefore
isn't a valid option if you're aiming to tour
round the country. The least you can expect
to pay in the high season is around £250 per
week for a place sleeping four, but something
special or somewhere in a popular tourist area
might cost £500 or more. Such is the number
and variety of self-catering places on offer that

we've mentioned very few in the Guide. A
good source of information is VisitScotland's
self-catering guide, updated annually and
listing over 1200 properties, or one of the
websites listed below.

Cottages and Castles Ⓦ www.cottages-and
-castles.co.uk. A range of self-catering properties,
mainly in mainland Scotland.

Cottages4you Ⓦ www.cottages4you.co.uk.
Hundreds of reasonably priced properties all over
Scotland.

Ecosse Unique Ⓦ www.uniquescotland.com.
Carefully selected cottages across mainland Scotland,
plus a few in the Hebrides and Orkney.

Landmark Trust Ⓦ www.landmarktrust.org.uk.
A very select number of unforgettable, upmarket
historical properties; first, however, you must buy the
brochure (£13, refundable on first booking).

Mackay's Agency Ⓦ www.mackays-self
-catering.co.uk. A whole range of properties in every
corner of mainland Scotland (plus Skye and Orkney),
from chalets and town apartments to remote stone-
built cottages.

National Trust for Scotland Ⓦ www.nts.org
.uk. The NTS lets around forty of its converted historic
cottages and houses.

Scottish Country Cottages Ⓦ www.scottish
-country-cottages.co.uk. Superior cottages with lots
of character scattered across the Scottish mainland,
plus some of the Inner Hebrides.

Food and drink

The remoteness of parts of the Highlands and Islands will inevitably restrict your eating and drinking choices. It's often a good idea to plan meal locations ahead as you might find serving times restrictive or popular restaurants booked out, particularly in summer. Stocking up on picnic food from a good deli is also worthwhile.

Breakfast

In most hotels and B&Bs you'll be offered a **Scottish breakfast**, similar to its English counterpart of sausage, bacon and egg, but typically with the addition of black pudding (blood sausage) and potato scones. Porridge is another likely option, and fish in the form of kippers, smoked haddock or even kedgeree. Scotland's staple drink, like England's, is **tea**, drunk strong and with milk, though **coffee** is just as readily available everywhere. However, while designer coffee-shops are now a familiar feature in the cities, execrable versions of espresso and cappuccino, as well as instant coffee, are still all too familiar.

Lunches and snacks

The most common lunchtime fare in Scotland remains the **sandwich**. A bowl or cup of hearty **soup** is a typical accompaniment, particularly in winter. A **pub lunch** is often an attractive alternative. Bar menus generally have standard filling but unambitious options including soup, filled sandwiches, scampi and chips or steak pie

and chips, with vegetarians suffering from a paucity of choice. Having said that, some bar food is freshly prepared and filling, equalling the à la carte dishes served in the adjacent hotel restaurant. Pubs or hotel bars are among the cheapest options when it comes to eating out – in the smallest villages, these might be your only option.

Restaurants are often, though not always, open at lunchtimes. They tend to be less busy and generally offer a shorter menu compared with their evening service, which can make for a more pleasant and less expensive experience. For morning or afternoon snacks, as well as light lunches, **tearooms** are a common feature; you will often find decent home-baking.

As for **fast food**, chip shops, or **chippies**, abound, the best often found in coastal towns within sight of the fishing boats. Deep-fried battered fish is the standard choice – when served with chips it's known as a "fish supper", even if eaten at lunchtime – though everything from hamburgers to haggis suppers is normally on offer, all deep-fried, of course. Scotland is even credited with inventing the **deep-fried Mars Bar**, the

Classic Scottish dishes

Arbroath smokies Powerful smoked haddock.

Cullen skink Rich soup made from smoked haddock, potatoes and cream.

Haggis Rich sausage meat made from minced, spiced liver, offal, oatmeal and onion, and cooked inside a bag made from a sheep's stomach. Tasty and satisfying, particularly when eaten with its traditional accompaniments "bashed neeps" (mashed turnips) and "chappit tatties" (mashed potatoes).

Porridge A common offering at breakfast, though the quality is often variable: it's properly made with oatmeal and water and cooked with a pinch of salt, then eaten with a little milk, though some folk like to add honey, fruit or sugar as well.

Scots broth Hearty soup made with stock (usually mutton), vegetables and barley.

definitive badge of a nation with the worst heart-disease statistics in Europe.

Evening meals

If you're travelling in remoter parts of the Highlands and Islands, or staying at a B&B or guesthouse in the countryside, ask advice about nearby options for your **evening meal**. Many B&Bs and guesthouses will cook you dinner, but you must book ahead and indicate any dietary requirements.

In general, however, eating out in the evening means heading for a **restaurant**, pub or hotel bar. Standards vary enormously, but Scotland has an increasing number of small, independent restaurants using good-quality local produce, some offering accommodation too (see p.33). Less predictable are hotel restaurants, including those which serve non-residents; the food can be very ordinary despite the highfaluting menu descriptions.

There's no doubt that, as with the rest of the UK, eating out in Scotland is expensive. Our restaurant listings include a mix of high-quality and budget establishments. **Wine** in restaurants is marked up strongly, so you'll often pay £15 for a bottle selling for £5 in the shops; house wines generally start around the £10 mark.

Food shopping

Most Scots get their supplies from supermarkets, but you're increasingly likely to come across good delis, farm shops and specialist **food shops**. Many stock local produce alongside imported delicacies, as well as organic fruit and veg, specialist drinks such as locally brewed beer, freshly baked bread and sandwiches and other snacks for takeaway. Look out too for **farmers' markets** (ⓦ www.scottishfarmersmarkets .co.uk), which take place on Saturday and Sunday mornings; local farmers and small

producers from pig farmers to cheese-makers and small smokeries set up stalls to sell their specialist lines.

Scotland is notorious for its sweet tooth, and **cakes and puddings** are taken very seriously. Bakers with extensive displays of iced buns, cakes and cream-filled pastries are a typical feature of any Scottish high street, while home-made shortbread, scones or tablet (a hard, crystalline form of fudge) are considered great treats.

Drinking

As in the rest of Britain, Scottish **pubs**, which originated as travellers' hostelries and coaching inns, are the main social focal points of any community. Pubs in Scotland vary hugely, from old-fashioned inns with open fires and a convivial atmosphere to raucous theme-pubs with jukeboxes and satellite TV. Out in the islands, pubs are few and far between, with most drinking taking place in the local hotel bar. In some larger towns, traditional pubs are being supplemented by modern café-bars.

The national drink is **whisky**, though you might not guess it from the prodigious amount of "alcopops" (bottles of sweet fruit drinks laced with vodka or gin) consumed on a Friday and Saturday night. Similarly, Scotland produces some exceptionally good cask-conditioned real ales, yet lager is much more popular. In our listings, we've tended to steer folk towards pubs that take their beer and whisky seriously, rather than those hell-bent on getting punters drunk as quickly as possible.

As far as **soft drinks** go, lurid orange Irn Bru is Scotland's version of coke, and is renowned as a sugar-boosted hangover cure. The country produces its own bottled mineral water, notably Highland Spring, though everywhere tap water is more than acceptable.

Meal times

Unfortunately, in many parts of Scotland outside the cities, inflexible **meal times** mean that you have to keep a close eye on your watch if you don't want to miss out on eating. B&Bs and hotels will frequently serve breakfast only until 9am at the latest, lunch is usually over by 2pm, and, despite the long summer evenings, pub and hotel kitchens often stop serving dinner as early as 8pm.

Scotland has very relaxed licensing laws. Pub **opening hours** are generally 11am to 11pm, but some places stay open later. Whatever time the pub closes, "last orders" will be called by the bar staff about fifteen minutes before closing time to allow "drinking-up time". In general, you have to be 16 to enter a pub unaccompanied, though some places are easy about having folk with children in, or have special family rooms and beer gardens where the kids can run free. The legal drinking age is 18.

Whisky

Whisky – *uisge beatha*, or the "water of life" in Gaelic – has been produced in Scotland since the fifteenth century, but only really took off in popularity after the 1780 tax on claret made wine too expensive for most people. The taxman soon caught up with whisky distilling, however, and drove the stills underground. Today, many distilleries operate on the site of simple cottages that once distilled the stuff illegally. In 1823, Parliament revised its Excise Laws, in the process legalizing whisky production, and today the drink is Scotland's chief export.

Despite the dominance of the blended whiskies such as Johnnie Walker, Bell's, Teacher's and The Famous Grouse, **single malt whisky** is infinitely superior, and, as a result, a great deal more expensive. Single malts vary in character enormously depending on the amount of peat used for drying the barley, the water used for mashing, and the type of oak cask used in the maturing process. Malt whisky is best drunk with a splash of water to release its distinctive flavours.

The two most important **whisky regions** are Speyside (see p.182), home of famous varieties such as Glenlivet, Glenfiddich and Macallan, and Islay (see p.121), which produces distinctively peaty whiskies such as Laphroaig, Lagavulin and Ardbeg. Many distilleries offer **guided tours** that range from slick and streamlined to small and friendly. All offer visitors a "wee dram" as a finale, and distilleries that charge an entrance fee often give a discount if you buy a bottle at the end, though prices are no lower at source than in the shops – between £20 and £30 for the average 70cl bottle.

Beer

Traditional Scottish beer is a thick, dark ale known as **heavy**, served at room temperature in pints or half-pints, with a full head. Quite different in taste from English "bitter", heavy is a more robust, sweeter beer with less of an edge. Scottish beers are graded by the shilling in a system used since the 1870s to indicate the level of potency: the higher the shilling mark (/-), the stronger or "heavier" the beer.

All of Scotland's biggest-name breweries – McEwan's, Tennents, Belhaven and Caledonian – produce a reasonable selection of heavies. However, if you really want to discover Scottish beer, look out for the products of small local breweries such as Aviemore, the Black Isle, Arran, Fyne Ales, Skye, Orkney or Shetland. Look out, too, for Fraoch, mostly available in bottles, a very refreshing, lighter-coloured ale made from heather according to an ancient recipe.

The media

When you're up in the Highlands and Islands, the UK's national media may seem London-based and London-biased. Most locals prefer to listen to Scottish radio programmes, read local newspapers, and – albeit to a much lesser extent – watch Scottish TV.

The press

Provincial dailies are more widely read in the Highlands and Islands than anywhere else in Britain. The biggest-selling regional title is Aberdeen's famously parochial *Press and Journal*, which has special editions for each area of the Highlands and Islands. For an insight into local life, there's the staid **weekly** *Oban Times*. More entertaining and radical is the campaigning weekly *West Highland Free Press*, printed on Skye. All carry articles in Gaelic as well as English. Further north, the lively *Shetland Times* and Orkney's sedate *Orcadian* are essential weekly reads for anyone living in or just visiting those islands.

Given the distances in the Highlands and Islands, you shouldn't always expect to find a daily newspaper arriving with your early morning cup of tea, though unless you're in a particularly remote spot or bad weather is affecting transport links, the papers are normally around by mid-morning. Most easily obtained are **Scottish newspapers**. Principal among these are the two serious dailies – *The Scotsman*, based in Edinburgh, and *The Herald*, published in Glasgow, both offering reasonable coverage of the current issues affecting Scotland, along with British and foreign news, sport, arts and lifestyle pages. You should also be able to find a selection of popular tabloids, including Scotland's biggest-selling daily, the downmarket *Daily Record*, along with various national titles – from the reactionary *Sun* to the vaguely left-leaning *Daily Mirror* – which appear in specific Scottish editions.

Many **Sunday newspapers** published in London have a Scottish edition, although again Scotland has its own offerings – *Scotland on Sunday*, from the *Scotsman* stable, and the *Sunday Herald*, complementing its eponymous daily. Far more fun and widely read is the anachronistic *Sunday Post*, published by Dundee's mighty D.C. Thomson publishing group. It's a wholesome paper, uniquely Scottish, and has changed little since the 1950s, since which time its two long-running cartoon strips, *Oor Wullie* and *The Broons*, have acquired cult status.

Scottish **monthlies** include the *Scottish Field*, a lowbrow version of England's *Tatler*, and the widely read *Scots Magazine*, an old-fashioned middle-of-the-road publication which promotes family values and lots of good fresh air.

TV and radio

In Scotland there are five main 'terrestrial' **TV channels** (ie not specifically produced for cable or satellite services): the state-owned BBC1 and BBC2, and the independent commercial channels, ITV1, Channel 4 and Five. **BBC Scotland** produces news programmes and a regular crop of local-interest lifestyle, current affairs, drama and comedy shows which slot into the schedules of both BBC channels. In northwest Scotland there are also regular programmes broadcast by BBC Gaelic TV. A plethora of satellite and cable channels is also available; the dominant force is Rupert Murdoch's **Sky** organization, which offers, among other channels, blanket sports coverage that plays wall-to-wall in pubs the length of the country.

The **BBC radio** network broadcasts six main channels in Scotland, five of which are national stations originating largely from London: Radio 1 (pop and dance music), Radio 2 (mainstream pop, rock and light music), Radio 3 (classical music), Radio 4 (current affairs, arts and drama) and Radio Five Live (sports, news and live discussions and phone-ins). BBC Radio Scotland offers a Scottish perspective on news, politics, arts, music, travel and sport, as well as providing a Gaelic network in the Highlands with local programmes in Shetland and Orkney.

A web of local **commercial radio** stations covers the country, mostly mixing rock and pop music with news bulletins, but a few tiny community-based stations such as Lochbroom FM in Ullapool – famed for its daily midge count – transmit documentaries and discussions on local issues. The most populated areas of Scotland also receive UK-wide commercial stations such as Classic FM, Virgin Radio and TalkSport. With a special DAB **digital radio**, you can get all the main stations crackle-free along with a range of other digital-only ones, most of which can also be picked up on cable or satellite-equipped TVs.

Some Scottish radio stations

BBC Radio Scotland 92–95FM, 810MW Ⓦwww .bbc.co.uk/radioscotland. Nationwide news, sport, music, current affairs and arts.

BBC Radio nan Gaidheal 103.4FM Ⓦwww.bbc .co.uk/scotland/alba. An opt-out from Radio Scotland, with Gaelic-language news, phone-ins and great traditional-music shows.

Lochbroom FM 102.2 & 96.8FM Ⓦwww .lochbroomfm.co.uk. One of Britain's smallest radio stations, broadcasting to the northwest coast from Ullapool.

Moray Firth 97.4FM, 1107MW Ⓦwww.mfr.co .uk. Mainstream rock and pop for the youth of the Inverness area.

Nevis Radio 96.6 & 102.3FM Ⓦwww.nevisradio .co.uk. From the slopes of Ben Nevis, all that's happening in Fort William and its surrounds.

SIBC 96.2FM Ⓦwww.sibc.co.uk. Shetland's own independent station.

Events and spectator sports

There's a huge range of organized annual events on offer in the Highlands and Islands, reflecting both vibrant contemporary culture and well-marketed heritage. Many tourists will want to home straight in on Highland Games and other tartan-draped theatricals, but there's more to Scotland than this: numerous regional celebrations perpetuate ancient customs, and music both traditional and new is alive and kicking in places such as the Hebrides and the Northern Isles. A few of the smaller, more obscure events, particularly those with a pagan bent, do not welcome the casual visitor.

The tourist board publishes a weighty list of all Scottish events twice a year called *What's On in Scotland*: it's free and you can get it from area tourist offices or direct from their headquarters. Full details are at Ⓦwww .visitscotland.com.

Events calendar

Dec 31 and Jan 1 Hogmanay and Ne'er Day. Traditionally more important to the Scots than Christmas, known for the custom of "first-footing", when groups of revellers troop into neighbours' houses at midnight bearing gifts. More popular these days are huge and highly organized street parties in the larger towns.

Jan 1 Kirkwall Boys' and Men's Ba' Games, Orkney. Mass, drunken football game through the streets of the town, with the castle and the harbour the respective goals. As a grand finale the players jump into the harbour.

Last Tues in Jan Up-Helly-Aa, Lerwick, Shetland Ⓦwww.shetlandtourism.com. Norse fire festival culminating in the burning of a specially built Viking longship. Visitors will need an invite from one of the locals, or you can buy a ticket for the Town Hall celebrations.

Jan 25 Burns Night. Scots worldwide get stuck into haggis, whisky and vowel-grinding poetry to commemorate Scotland's greatest poet, Robert Burns.
Feb Fort William Mountain Festival ⓦwww .mountainfilmfestival.co.uk. Films, lectures, guided walks and music sessions in celebration of mountain culture.
April O'Neill Coldwater Classic ⓦwww.oneill.com /cwc/scotland. A top-grade surf event on the famous Thurso East break attracting professional surfers from around the world.
Early May Spirit of Speyside Whisky Festival ⓦwww.spiritofspeyside.com. Four-day binge with pipe bands, gigs and dancing as well as distillery crawls. Shetland Folk Festival ⓦwww .shetlandfolkfestival.com. One of the liveliest and most entertaining of Scotland's round of folk festivals.
Late May Atholl Highlanders Parade at Blair Castle, Perthshire ⓦwww.blair-castle.co.uk. The annual parade and inspection of Britain's last private army by their colonel-in-chief, the Duke of Atholl, on the eve of their Highland Games.
June Beginning of the Highland Games season across the Highlands and Argyll; St Magnus Festival, Orkney ⓦwww.stmagnusfestival.com. A classical and folk music, drama, dance and literature festival celebrating the islands. Rock Ness ⓦwww .rockness.co.uk. A big outdoor electronic, rock and dance festival on the shores of Loch Ness.
July Mendelssohn on Mull ⓦwww.mullfest.org .uk. Celebrating classical music. Hebridean Celtic Festival, Stornoway ⓦwww.hebceltfest.com. International Celtic music festival that takes place over four days in Stornoway in the Outer Hebrides. Tarbert Seafood Festival ⓦwww.seafood-festival .com. This weekend of gorging on seafood also sees live music and dance events around Tarbert's sheltered harbour.
Late July West Highland Yachting Week ⓦwww .whyw.co.uk. A week of yacht racing and shore-based partying which moves en masse from Oban to Tobermory and back again.
Aug Connect ⓦwww.connectmusicfestival.com. Acclaimed, new boutique outdoor pop/rock festival in grounds of Inveraray Castle.
Early Sept The Ben Nevis Race (for amateurs) Involves running to the top of Scotland's highest mountain and back again; Shinty's Camanachd Cup final ⓦwww.shinty.com, the climax of the season for Scotland's own stick-and-ball game, normally held in one of the main Highland towns; Blas ⓦwww .blas-festival.com the premier Gaelic and traditional-music festival, at venues across the Highlands.
Late Sept Annual World Stone Skimming Championships ⓦwww.stoneskimming.com, Easdale Island, near Oban. The John Lennon

Northern Lights Festival, Durness ⓦwww .northhighlandsscotland.com/festival. Music and poetry inspired by the Beatle who spent boyhood holidays in the northern Highlands.
Oct The National Mod ⓦwww.the-mod.co.uk Held over nine days at a different venue each year. It's a competitive festival and features all aspects of Gaelic performing arts. The Golden Spurtle World Porridge Making Championships, Carrbridge, Speyside ⓦwww.goldenspurtle.com; The Tour of Mull car rally ⓦwww.2300club.org; Tiree Wave Classic ⓦwww.tireewaveclassic.com. Annual event attracting windsurfers from around the world to the breezy Hebridean island.
Late Oct Glenfiddich Piping and Fiddle Championships ⓦwww.blairatholl.org.uk. Held at Blair Atholl for the world's top ten solo pipers.
Nov 30 St Andrew's Day. Celebrating Scotland's patron saint.

Highland Games

Despite their name, **Highland Games** are held all over Scotland between May and mid-September, varying in size and the range of events they offer, and although the most famous are at Oban, Cowal and especially Braemar, the smaller events are often more fun. The Games probably originated in the fourteenth century as a means of recruiting the best fighting men for the clan chiefs, and were popularized by Queen Victoria to encourage the traditional dress, music, games and dance of the Highlands; indeed, various royals still attend the Games at Braemar. The most distinctive events are known as the **heavies** – tossing the caber, putting the stone and tossing the weight over the bar – all of which require prodigious strength and skill. Tossing the caber is the most spectacular, when the athlete must run carrying an entire tree trunk and attempt to heave it end over end in a perfect, elegant throw. Just as important as the sporting events are the **piping** competitions – for individuals and bands – and **dancing** competitions, where you'll see girls as young as 3 tripping the quick, intricate steps of dances such as the Highland Fling.

Football

While **football** (soccer) is far and away Scotland's most popular spectator sport, its popularity in the Highlands and Islands is a little muted in comparison to the game's following in the Central Belt of the country. The strength of the Highland League (Ⓦ www.highlandfootballleague.com) was, however, recognized in the mid-1990s with the inclusion of Inverness Caledonian Thistle and Ross County in the Scottish Leagues. Inverness Caledonian Thistle have subsequently risen to Scotland's top division, the Scottish Premier League, and as a result the Caledonian Stadium on the shores of the Moray Firth regularly hosts the multinational stars of Glasgow's and Edinburgh's top teams. The **season** begins in early August and ends in mid-May, with most matches taking place on Saturday afternoons at 3pm, and also often on Sunday afternoons and Wednesday evenings. Tickets for Scottish League games are around the £10 mark, but less for Highland League fixtures.

Shinty

Played throughout Scotland but with particular strongholds in the West Highlands and Strathspey, the game of **shinty** (the Gaelic *sinteag* means "leap") arrived from Ireland around 1500 years ago. Until the latter part of the nineteenth century, it was played on an informal basis and teams from neighbouring villages had to come to an agreement about rules before matches could begin. However, in 1893, the **Camanachd Association** – the Gaelic word for shinty is *camanachd* – was set up to formalize the rules, and the first Camanachd Cup Final was held in Inverness in 1896.

Today, shinty is still fairly close to its Irish roots in the game of hurling, with each team having twelve players and a goalkeeper, and each goal a point. The game, which bears s an undisciplined version of hockey the faint-hearted; it's played at a pace, with sticks – called camans cammocks – flying alarmingly in all directions. Support is enthusiastic and vocal, and if you're in the Highlands during the season, which has recently changed to run from March to October to avoid the perils of midwinter, it's well worth trying to catch a match: check with tourist offices or the local paper, or go to Ⓦ www.shinty.com.

Curling

The one winter sport which enjoys a strong Scottish identity is **curling** (Ⓦ www.royalcaledoniancurlingclub.org), occasionally still played on a frozen outdoor rink, or "pond", though most commonly these days seen in indoor ice rinks. The game, which involves gently sliding smooth-bottomed 18kg discs of granite called "stones" across the ice towards a target circle, is said to have been invented in Scotland, although its earliest representation is in a sixteenth-century Flemish painting. Played by two teams of four, it's a highly tactical and skilful sport, enlivened by team members using brushes to furiously sweep the ice in front of a moving stone to help it travel further and straighter. If you're interested in seeing curling being played, go along to the ice rink in places such as Perth, Pitlochry or Inverness on a winter evening.

door activities

...cape that, weather conditions apart, is extremely attrac-
...and legislation enacted by the Scottish Parliament has
...ht of access to hills, mountains, lochs and rivers. Within
...ties are two national parks, remote wilderness areas and
vast stretches of glens and moorland, while sea-kayakers, sailors and surfers can
enjoy excellent conditions along the rugged but beautiful coastline.

Walking and climbing

The whole of Scotland offers superb opportunities for **hill walking** and the freedom to roam responsibly in wilder parts of the countryside, with some of the finest Highland climbing areas in the ownership of bodies such as the National Trust for Scotland and the John Muir Trust (ⓦwww.jmt.org); both permit year-round access. Bear in mind, though, restrictions may be in place during lambing and deerstalking seasons. See ⓦwww.snh.org.uk/hillphones for information about **hiking safely** during the stalking season. In addition, the green signposts of the Scottish Rights of Way Society point to established paths and routes all over the country.

There are several **Long-Distance Footpaths** (LDPs), such as the well-known West Highland Way, which take between three to seven days to walk, though you can, of course, just do a section of them. Paths are generally well signposted and well supported, with services from bunkhouses to baggage-carrying services.

Numerous short walks (from accessible towns and villages) and several major walks are touched on in this guide and "The Great Outdoors" colour section. However, you should only use our notes as general outlines, and always in conjunction with a good map. Where possible, we have given details of the best maps to use – in most cases one of the excellent and reliable **Ordnance Survey** (OS) series (see p.53), usually available from local tourist offices, which can also supply other local maps, safety advice and guidebooks/leaflets. We've listed a couple of good walking guidebooks in the "Books" section of Contexts (p.434). These, as well as a wide range of maps, are available from good outdoor stores (most notably Tiso), which are normally staffed by experienced climbers and walkers, and are a good source of advice about equipment and favourite hiking areas.

For relatively gentle walking in the company of knowledgeable locals, look out for guided walks offered by rangers at many National Trust for Scotland, Forest Enterprise and Scottish Natural Heritage sites. These often focus on local **wildlife**, and the best can lead to some special sightings, such as a badger's sett or a golden eagle's eyrie.

Useful contacts for walkers

General information

ⓦ**www.snh.org.uk/hillphones** Daily information for hill walkers about deerstalking activities (July–Oct).
ⓦ**www.outdooraccess-scotland.com** All you need to know about the Scottish Outdoor Access Code.
ⓦ**wildlife.visitscotland.com** Highlights the fauna and flora you may spot on a walk.
ⓦ**www.walkingwild.com** Official site from VisitScotland, with good lists of operators, information on long-distance footpaths, details of deerstalking restrictions and contact phone numbers.

Clubs and associations

Mountain Bothies Association ⓦwww.mountainbothies.org.uk. Charity dedicated to maintaining huts and shelters in the Scottish Highlands.
Mountaineering Council of Scotland ☎01738 /4 93942, ⓦwww.mcofs.org.uk. The representative body for all mountain activities, with detailed information on access and conservation issues.

Midges and ticks

Despite being only just over a millimetre long, and enjoying a life span on the wing of just a few weeks, the **midge** (genus: *culicoides*) – a tiny biting fly prevalent in the Highlands (mainly the west coast) and Islands – is considered to be second only to the weather as the major deterrent to tourism in Scotland. There are more than thirty varieties of midge, though only half of these bite humans. Ninety percent of all midge bites are down to the female *Culicoides impunctatus* or **Highland midge** (the male does not bite), which has two sets of jaws sporting twenty teeth each; she needs a good meal of blood in order to produce eggs.

These persistent creatures can be a nuisance, but some people also have a violent allergic reaction to midge bites. The easiest way to avoid midges is to visit in the **winter**, since they only appear between April and October. Midges also favour still, damp, overcast or shady conditions and are at their meanest around sunrise and sunset, when clouds of them can descend on an otherwise idyllic spot. Direct sunlight, heavy rain, noise and smoke discourage them to some degree, though wind is the most effective means of dispersing them. If they appear, cover up exposed skin and get your hands on some kind of repellent. Recommendations include Autan, Eureka, Jungle Formula (widely available from pharmacists) and the herbal remedy citronella. An alternative to repellents for protecting your face, especially if you're walking or camping, is a **midge net**, a little like a beekeeper's hat; though they appear ridiculous at first, you're unlikely to care as long as they work. The latest deployment in the battle against the midge is a gas-powered machine called a "midge magnet" which sucks up the wee beasties and is supposed to be able to clear up to an acre; each unit costs £400 and upwards, but there's been a healthy take-up by pubs with beer gardens and by campsite owners.

If you're walking through long grass or bracken, there's a possibility you may receive attention from **ticks**, tiny parasites no bigger than a pin head, which bury themselves into your skin. Removing ticks by dabbing them with alcohol, butter or oil is now discouraged; the medically favoured way of extracting them is to pull them out carefully with small tweezers. There is a very slight risk of catching some very nasty diseases, such as encephalitis, from ticks. If flu-like symptoms persist after a tick bite, you should see a doctor immediately.

Ramblers Association Scotland ⓦwww
.ramblers.org.uk/scotland, ☎01577/861222.
Campaigning organization with network of local groups and news on events and issues.
Scottish Mountaineering Club ⓦwww.smc.org
.uk. The largest mountaineering club in the country. A well-respected organization which publishes a popular series of mountain guidebooks.

Outdoor pursuits operators

Adventure Scotland ☎08702/402676, ⓦwww
.adventure-scotland.com. Highly experienced operator providing a wide range of courses and one-day adventures, from telemark skiing to climbing, kayaking and biking.
Bespoke Highland Tours ☎01854/612628,
ⓦwww.scotland-inverness.co.uk/bht-main.htm.
Offers five–twelve-day self-led treks with a detailed itinerary along routes such as the Great Glen Way and

West Highland Way, organizing baggage transfer and accommodation en route.
Cape Adventure International ☎01971/521006,
ⓦwww.capeadventure.co.uk. From a wonderfully remote northwest location near Kinlochbervie, Cape offers day, weekend and week-long individual and family adventure experiences including wilderness trips, climbing, sea-kayaking and walking.
C-N-Do Scotland ☎01786/445703, ⓦwww
.cndoscotland.com. Prides itself on offering the "best walking holidays in Scotland". Munro-bagging for novices and experts with qualified leaders.
G2 Outdoor ☎07946/285612, ⓦwww.g2outdoor
.co.uk. Personable, highly qualified adventure specialists offering gorge, hill walking, rock climbing, canoeing and telemark skiing in the Cairngorms.
Glenmore Lodge ☎01479/861256, ⓦwww
.glenmorelodge.org.uk. Based within the Cairngorm National Park, and internationally recognized as a leader in outdoor skills and leadership training.

Munro-bagging

In recent years hill walking in Scotland has become synonymous with "**Munro-bagging**". Munros are the hills in Scotland over 3000ft in height, defined by a list first drawn up by Sir Hugh Munro in 1891. You "bag" a Munro by walking to the top of it, and once you've bagged all 284 you can call yourself a Munroist and let your chiropodist retire in peace.

Sir Hugh's challenge is an enticing one: 3000ft is high enough to be an impressive ascent but not so high that it's for expert mountaineers only. Nor do you need to aim to do them all – at heart, Munro-bagging is simply about appreciating the great Scottish outdoors. Munros are found across the Highlands and on two of the islands (Mull and Skye), and include many of the more famous and attractive mountains in Scotland.

However, while the Munros by definition include all the highest hills in Scotland, there isn't any quality control, and one of the loudest arguments of critics of the game (known by some as "de-baggers") is that Munro-seekers will plod up a boring pudding of a mountain because it's 3000ft high and ignore one nearby that's much more pleasing but a few feet short of the requisite mark.

Judgement is also required in a few other ways. You do have to be properly equipped, and be aware what you're tackling before you set off – the hills are hazardous in all seasons. But for many the trickiest part of Munro-bagging is getting to grips with the Gaelic pronunciation of some of the hill names. However, as it's bad form not to be able to tell the folk in the pub at the end of the day which hills you've just ticked off, beginners are encouraged to stick to peaks such as Ben Vane or Ben More, and resign themselves to the fact that Beinn Fhionnlaidh (pronounced "Byn Yoonly") and Beinn an Dothaidh (pronounced "Byn an Daw-ee") are for the really experienced.

If you want some training, you can set about the **Corbetts** (hills between 2500 and 2999ft) or even the **Donalds** (lowland hills above 2000ft).

Hebridean Pursuits ☎01631/563594, 🕸www .hebrideanpursuits.com. Established in 1989, offering hill walking, winter and rock climbing in the Hebrides and West Highlands, as well as surf-kayaking and sailing trips.

Nae Limits ☎08450/178177, 🕸www.naelimits .co.uk. This excellent Perthshire-based operator offers everything from wet 'n' wild rafting to bug canyoning and cliff jumping.

North-West Frontiers ☎01854/612628, 🕸www .nwfrontiers.com. Based in Ullapool, offering guided mountain trips with small groups in the northwest Highlands, Hebrides and even the Shetland Islands. April–Oct.

Rua Reidh Lighthouse Holidays ☎01445/771263, 🕸www.ruareidh.co.uk. From its spectacular northwest location, this company offers guided walks highlighting wildlife, rock climbing courses and week-long treks into the Torridon hills.

Vertical Descents ☎01855/821593, 🕸www .verticaldescents.com. Ideally located for the Glencoe and Fort William area, activities and courses include canyoning, funyakking (a type of rafting) and climbing.

Wilderness Scotland ☎0131/625 6635, 🕸www .wildernessscotland.com. Guided, self-guided and customized adventure holidays and trips that focus on exploring the remote and unspoiled parts of Scotland by foot, bike, sea-kayak, yacht and even on skis.

Winter sports

Skiing and **snowboarding** take place at five different locations in Scotland – Glen Coe, the Nevis Range beside Fort William, Glen Shee, the Lecht and the Cairngorms near Aviemore. The resorts can go for months on end through the winter with insufficient snow, then see the approach roads suddenly made impassable by a glut of the stuff. When the conditions are good, Scotland's ski resorts have piste and off-piste areas that will challenge even the most accomplished alpine or cross-country skier.

Expect to pay up to £28 for a standard day-pass at one of the resorts, or around £110 for a five-day pass; rental of skis or snowboard comes in at around £25 per day, with reductions for multiday rents. At

Staying safe in the hills

Due to rapid weather changes, the mountains are potentially extremely dangerous and should be treated with respect. Every year, in every season, climbers and walkers lose their lives in the Scottish hills.

- Wear sturdy, ankle-supporting footwear and wear or carry with you warm, brightly coloured and waterproof layered clothing, even for what appears to be an easy expedition in apparently settled weather.
- Always carry adequate maps, a compass (which you should know how to use), food, water and a whistle. If it's sunny, make sure you use sun protection.
- Check out a weather forecast before you go. If the weather looks as if it's closing in, get down from the mountain fast.
- Always leave word with someone of your route and what time you expect to return, and remember to contact the person again to let them know that you are back.
- In an emergency, call mountain rescue on ☎999.

weekends, in good weather with decent snow, expect the slopes to be packed with trippers from the central belt, although midweek usually sees queues dissolving. For a comprehensive rundown of all the resorts, including ticket prices and conditions, visit Ⓦski.visitscotland.com.

Cross-country skiing (along with the related telemark or Nordic skiing) is becoming increasingly popular in the hills around Braemar near Glenshee and the Cairngorms. The best way to get started or to find out about good routes is to contact an outdoor pursuits company that offers telemark or Nordic rental and instruction; in the Aviemore area try Adventure Scotland or G2 Outdoor (see p.173). Also check out the Huntly Nordic and Outdoor Centre in Huntly, Aberdeenshire (☎01466/794428, Ⓦwww.nordicski.co.uk/hnoc). For equipment hire, sales or advice for Nordic and ski mountaineering equipment, contact Mountain Spirit (☎01479/811788, Ⓦwww.mountainspirit.co.uk) located at the southern entrance to Aviemore village.

Pony trekking and horse riding

There are approximately sixty pony-trekking or riding centres across the country, most approved by either the Trekking and Riding Society of Scotland (TRSS; Ⓦwww.ridinginscotland.com) or the British Horse Society (BHS; Ⓦwww.bhs.org.uk). As a rule, any centre will offer the option of **pony trekking** (leisurely ambles on sure-footed Highland ponies), **hacking** (for experienced riders who want to go for a short ride at a fastish pace) and **trail riding** (over longer distances, for riders who feel secure at a canter). In addition, a network of special horse-and-rider B&Bs means you can ride independently on your own horse.

Cycling and mountain biking

Cycle touring is a great way to see some of the remoter parts of Scotland and quickly navigate city streets. You'll find cycle shops in towns but few dedicated cycle lanes. Out in the countryside it can be tricky finding spare parts unless you are within the proximity of one of Scotland's purpose-built mountain-bike trail centres.

For up-to-date information on long-distance routes, including the **Great Glen Cycle Way**, along with a list of publications detailing specific routes, contact the cyclists campaigning group Sustrans (Ⓦwww.sustrans.co.uk), as well as some of the organizations listed on pp.48–49.

Another option is to shell out on a cycling holiday package. Britain's biggest cycling organization, the **Cycle Touring Club**, or CTC, provides lists of tour operators and rental outlets in Scotland, and supplies members with touring and technical advice, as well as insurance. As a general introduction, VisitScotland's *Cycling in Scotland* brochure (Ⓦcycling.visitscotland.com) is worth getting hold of, with practical advice and suggestions for itineraries around the country. The tourist board's "Cyclists Welcome" scheme gives guesthouses and B&Bs around the country a chance to advertise that they're cyclist-friendly, and able to provide such things as an overnight laundry service, a late meal or a packed lunch.

Mountain biking

Scotland is now regarded as one of the world's top destinations for **off-road mountain biking**. The Forestry Commission has worked with communities as far apart as Sutherland and the Isle of Arran as well as at the World Cup venue outside Fort William to establish well in excess of 1150 miles of excellent off-road routes. These are detailed in numerous *Cycling in the Forest* leaflets (available from Forest Enterprise offices, see below). Alternatively, get hold of the *Scottish Mountain Biking Guide* from tourist information centres. Some of the tougher routes are best attempted on full-suspension mountain bikes although the easier (blue/green) trails can be ridden on a standard mountain or road bike.

Travelling with bikes

Bikes are allowed free on mainline GNER and Virgin Intercity trains, as well as ScotRail trains, but always subject to available space, so you should book the space as far in advance as possible. Bus and coach companies, including National Express and Scottish Citylink, rarely accept cycles unless they are dismantled and boxed; one notable exception is the excellent service operated by Dearman Coaches (☎01349/883585, ⓦwww.timdearmancoaches.co.uk) between Inverness and Durness via Ullapool (May–Sept Mon–Sat, 1 daily). Most large towns and tourist centres will offer bike rental. Expect to pay £12–25 per day; most outlets also give good discounts for multiday rents.

Useful contacts for cyclists

Cyclists' Touring Club ☎01483/417217, ⓦwww.ctc.org.uk. Britain's largest cycling organization, and a good source of general advice; their handbook has lists of cyclist-friendly B&Bs and cafés in Scotland. Annual membership £36.
Forest Enterprise ☎0845/367 3787, ⓦwww.forestry.gov.uk/mtbscotland. The best source of

Enjoy Scotland's outdoors responsibly

Everyone has the right to be on most land and inland water providing they act responsibly. Your access rights and responsibilities are explained fully in the Scottish Outdoor Access Code.

Whether you're in the outdoors or managing the outdoors, the key things are to:

- **take responsibility for your own actions**
- **respect the interests of other people**
- **care for the environment**

Access in Scotland is different from that in England and Wales.

SCOTTISH **OUTDOOR ACCESS** CODE

KNOW THE CODE BEFORE YOU GO
outdooraccess-scotland.com

information on Scotland's extensive network of forest trails – ideal for mountain biking at all levels of ability.

Full On Adventure ☎07885/835838, ⓦwww .fullonadventure.co.uk. Among its many offerings, provides fully guided mountain-bike tours of Highland trails.

Highland Wildcat Trails ⓦwww.highlandwildcat .com. Scotland's most northerly, dedicated mountain-bike centre complete with one of the country's longest downhill tracks.

MBHI Bikes ☎07780/940342, ⓦwww.mbhi .co.uk. Whether for bike hire or a guided trip, this Cromarty-based operator is ideal if touring the east coast above Inverness.

Nevis Range ⓦwww.ridefortwilliam.co.uk. For information on all the trails around Fort William, including the home of Scotland's World Cup downhill and cross-country tracks (May–Oct) at Nevis Range.

Scottish Cycle Safaris ☎0131/556 5560, ⓦwww.cyclescotland.co.uk. Fully organized cycle tours at all levels, from camping to country-house hotels, with a good range of bikes available for rent, from tandems to children's bikes.

Scottish Cycling ☎0131/652 0187, ⓦnew .britishcycling.org.uk/scotland. Produces an annual handbook and calendar of cycling events – mainly road, mountain-bike and track races.

Wild Adventures ☎01479/851374, ⓦwww.wild -adventures.co.uk. A Speyside operator offering skills courses and biking holidays.

WolfTrax Mountain Bike Centre ☎01528/544786, ⓦwww.forestry.gov .uk/wolftrax. This Central Highland bike centre near Newtonmore has over ten miles of routes for every standard of rider, bike hire and an excellent café.

Air sports

Whether you're a willing novice or an expert **paraglider** or **sky diver**, there are centres just outside Glasgow, Edinburgh and Perth which will cater to your needs. There are also opportunities to try ballooning and gliding. The following are just a selection of operators who will help you spread your wings.

British Gliding Association ☎0116/253 1051, ⓦwww.gliding.co.uk. Governing body for gliding enthusiasts and schools across the UK with information on where to find many clubs in Scotland.

Flying Fever ☎01770/303899, ⓦwww .flyingfever.net. Based on the stunning Isle of Arran, forty miles southwest of Glasgow. From March–Oct, fully accredited paragliding courses and tandem flights can be enjoyed for around £100.

Skydive Strathallan ☎01764 662572, ⓦwww .skydivestrathallan.co.uk. Located just outside Auchterarder, this non-commercial school operates year-round. Tandem jump from around £250.

Golf

There are over four hundred golf courses in Scotland, where the game is less elitist and more accessible than anywhere else in the world. **Golf** took shape in the fifteenth century on the dunes of Scotland's east coast, and today you'll find some of the oldest courses in the world on these early coastal sites, known as "links". It's often possible just to turn up and play, though it's sensible to phone ahead; booking is essential for the championship courses.

Public courses are owned by the local council, while **private courses** belong to a club. You can play on both – occasionally the private courses require that you are a **member** of another club, and the odd one asks for introductions from a member, but these rules are often waived for overseas visitors and all you need to do is pay a one-off fee. The cost of a round will set you back around £10 on a small nine-hole course, and more than £50 on many good-quality eighteen-hole courses. In remote areas the courses are sometimes unstaffed; just put the admission fee into the honesty box.

Scotland's championship courses, which often host the British Open, are renowned for their immaculately kept greens and challenging holes and, though they're favoured by serious players, anybody with a valid handicap certificate can enjoy them. The most famous course in the Highland region is at **Royal Dornoch** in Sutherland (ⓦwww.royaldornoch.com; £75). Otherwise, see ⓦwww.scotlands-golf-courses.com.

Fishing

Scotland's serrated coastline – with the deep sea lochs of the west, the firths of the east and the myriad offshore islands – ranks among the cleanest coasts in Europe. Combine this with an abundance of salmon, sea trout, brown trout and pike, and you have a wonderful location for game-, coarse- or sea-**fishing**,

No licence is needed to fish in Scotland, although nearly all land is privately owned and its fishing therefore controlled by a landlord/lady or his/her agent. Permission, however, is usually easy to obtain: permits can be bought at local tackle shops, rural post offices or through fishing clubs in the area – if in doubt, ask at the nearest tourist office. Salmon and sea trout have strict **seasons**, which vary between districts but usually stretch from late August to late February. Individual tourist offices will know the precise dates, or get hold of Visit Scotland's excellent *Fish Scotland* brochure (Ⓦwww.fishpal.com/VisitScotland). See also Ⓦwww.fishscotland.co.uk.

Water sports

Opportunities for **sailing** are outstanding, tainted only by the unreliability of the weather. Even in summer, the full force of the North Atlantic can be felt, and changeable conditions combined with tricky tides and rocky shores demand good sailing and navigational skills.

Yacht charters are available from various ports, either bareboat or in yachts run by a skipper and crew; contact Sail Scotland (Ⓦwww.sailscotland.co.uk) or the Associated Scottish Yacht Charters (Ⓦwww.asyc.co.uk).

An alternative way to enjoy Scotland under sail is to spend a week at one of the sailing schools. Many schools, as well as small boat-rental operations dotted along the coast, rent sailing dinghies by the hour or day, as well as **windsurfers**, though the chilly water means you'll always need a wet suit. The Hebridean island of Tiree is internationally renowned for its beaches and waves and has an excellent surf, windsurfing and kite-surfing school, Wild Diamond Watersports (Ⓦwww.surfschoolscotland.co.uk).

In recent years **sea-kayaking** has witnessed an explosion in popularity, with operators across the country offering sea-kayaking lessons and expeditions. Canoe Scotland (Ⓦwww.canoescotland .org) can offer useful advice, while Glenmore Lodge (Ⓦwww.glenmorelodge .org.uk), Canoe Hebrides (Ⓦwww.canoe hebrides.com), Uist Outdoor Centre (Ⓦwww.seakayakouterhebrides.co.uk) and

Skyak Adventures (Ⓦwww.skyak adventures.com) are highly reputable for either training or tours.

Surfing

Scotland is fast gaining a reputation as a **surfing** destination. However, given its northern coastline lies on the same latitude as Alaska and Iceland, water temperature rarely exceeds 15°C, and in winter can drop to as low as to 7°C. The one vital accessory, therefore, is a good wet suit (ideally a 5/3mm steamer), wet suit boots and, outside summer, gloves and a hood, too.

Many of the best spots are surrounded by stunning scenery, and you'd be unlucky to encounter another surfer for miles. However, this isolation – combined with the cold water and big, powerful waves – means that many of the best locations can only be enjoyed by experienced surfers. If you're a beginner, be aware of your limitations and consider a lesson with a BSA-qualified coach.

The popularity of surfing in Scotland has led to a spate of surf shops opening up, all of which rent or sell equipment and provide good information about the local breaks and events on the surfing scene (the likes of Tempest Surf in Thurso also offer surfing lessons). Two further sources of information are *Surf UK* by Wayne "Alf" Alderson (Fernhurst Books; £14.95), with details on over four hundred breaks around Britain, and the British Surfing Association (Ⓦwww .britsurf.co.uk).

Surf information, shops and schools

Granite Reef 45 The Green, Aberdeen ☎01224/252752, Ⓦwww.granitereef.com. Sales, hire and lessons.

Tempest Surf Riverside Road, Thurso ☎01847/892500. At the harbourside, you'll find lessons, a shop and a café that may tempt you to remain snug indoors!

Wild Diamond Watersports Isle of Tiree, ☎07793/063849, Ⓦwww.surfschoolscotland .co.uk. Professional instruction and hire for surfing, windsurfing, kite-surfing and kayaking.

Travel essentials

Costs

Scotland is a relatively **expensive** place to visit, with travel, food and accommodation costs higher than the EU average. The minimum expenditure for two people travelling on public transport, self-catering and camping, is in the region of £30 each a day, rising to around £50 a day if you're staying at hostels and eating the odd meal out. Staying at budget B&Bs, eating at unpretentious restaurants and visiting the odd tourist attraction, will raise the costs to £75 each per day; if you're renting a car, staying in comfortable B&Bs or hotels and eating well, you should reckon on at least £100 a day per person.

Crime and personal safety

The crime rate in the Scottish Highlands and Islands is very low indeed. Even the largest urban centre, Inverness, sees very few offences committed. Out on the islands, the situation is often even more tranquil: the last reported crime on the Isle of Muck (population 40) was the theft of two wine bottles in 1960.

Discounts

Most attractions in Scotland offer **concessions** for senior citizens, the unemployed,

full-time studen[...]
with under-5s [...]
everywhere – [...]
required in mos[...]
often available if y[...]

Once obtained, **youth/student ID cards** soon pay for themselves in savings. Full-time students are eligible for the International Student Identity Card or **ISIC** (@www.isiccard.com), which costs around £10 and entitles the bearer to special air, rail and bus fares, and discounts at museums, theatres and other attractions. If you're not a student, but you're 25 or younger, you can get an International Youth Travel Card or **IYTC**, which costs the same as the ISIC and carries the same benefits.

Electricity

The current is the EU standard of approximately 230v AC. All sockets are designed for British three-pin plugs, which are totally different from the rest of the EU. North American appliances need a transformer and **adapter**; Australasian appliances need only an adapter.

Emergencies

For **police**, **fire** and **ambulance** services phone ☏999.

Entry requi[...]
Citizens of all E[...]
Albania, B[...]
Serbia [...]
(othe[...]

BASICS | T[...]

| essentials

Historic Scotland and National Trust for Scotland

Many of Scotland's most treasured sights – from castles and country houses to islands, gardens and tracts of protected landscape – come under the control of the privately-run **National Trust for Scotland** (@www.nts.org.uk) or the state-run **Historic Scotland** (@www.historic-scotland.gov.uk); we've quoted **"NTS"** or **"HS"** respectively for each site reviewed in this guide. Both organizations charge an admission fee for most places, and these can be quite high, especially for the more grandiose NTS estates. If you think you'll be visiting more than half a dozen NTS properties, or more than a dozen HS ones, it's worth taking annual membership, which costs around £40 (HS) or £46 (NTS), and allows free admission to their properties. In addition, both the NTS and HS offer short-term passes: the NTS has the **Discovery Ticket**, which costs between £20 for an adult ticket lasting three days to £60 for a family ticket lasting fourteen days; and the HS's **Explorer Pass**, ranging from £22 for three days (out of five) to £63 for seven days (out of fourteen) for a family.

...ements

...uropean countries – except
...snia, Macedonia, Montenegro,
...and all the former Soviet republics
...than the Baltic states) – can enter
...itain with just a **passport**, for up to three
months (indefinitely if you're from the EU).
US, Canadian, Australian and New Zealand
citizens can stay for up to six months,
providing they have a return ticket and
adequate funds to cover their stay. Citizens
of most other countries require a **visa**,
obtainable from the British consulate or
mission office in the country of application.

Note that visa regulations are subject to
frequent changes, so it's always wise to
contact the nearest British embassy or high
commission before you travel. If you visit
Ⓦwww.ukvisas.gov.uk, you can download
the full range of **application forms** and
information leaflets and find out the contact
details of your nearest embassy or
consulate. In addition, an independent
charity, the Immigration Advisory Service or
IAS (Ⓦwww.iasuk.org), offers free and confi-
dential advice to anyone applying for entry
clearance into the UK.

If you want to **extend your visa**, you
should contact the UK Border Agency
(Ⓦwww.ukba.homeoffice.gov.uk), a month
before the expiry date given in your
passport.

Gay and lesbian travellers

While there's no gay scene as such out in
the Highlands and Islands, nearly three-
quarters of Scots have a positive opinion of
gay and lesbian people. In more remote
areas, and in particular in those areas where
religious observance is high, attitudes tend
to be more conservative and gay and lesbian
locals are extremely discreet about their
sexuality.

Health

Pharmacists (known as chemists in
Scotland) can dispense only a limited range
of drugs without a doctor's prescription.
Most pharmacies are open standard shop
hours; local newspapers carry lists of late-
opening pharmacies, or you can contact the
local police for current details.

If your condition is serious enough, you
can turn up at the Accident and Emergency
(A&E) department of local **hospitals** for
complaints that require immediate attention.
Obviously, if it's an absolute emergency, ring
for an ambulance (☏999). These services
are free to all. You can also get free medical
advice from NHS Direct, the health service's
24-hour helpline (☏0845/4647, Ⓦwww
.nhsdirect.nhs.uk).

Insurance

Even though EU healthcare privileges apply
in the UK, it's as well to take out **travel
insurance** before travelling to cover against
theft, loss and illness or injury. For non-EU
citizens, it's worth checking whether you are
already covered before you buy a new
policy. If you need to take out insurance, you
might want to consider the travel insurance
deal we offer.

Internet

Internet cafés as such aren't that common
around the Highlands and Islands, but there

Rough Guides travel insurance

Rough Guides has teamed up with WorldNomads.com to offer great **travel
insurance** deals. Policies are available to residents of over 150 countries, with
cover for a wide range of **adventure sports**, 24hr emergency assistance, high
levels of medical and evacuation cover and a stream of **travel safety information**.
Roughguides.com users can take advantage of their policies online 24/7, from
anywhere in the world – even if you're already travelling. And since plans often
change when you're on the road, you can extend your policy and even claim online.
Roughguides.com users who buy travel insurance with WorldNomads.com can also
leave a positive footprint and donate to a community development project. For
more information go to Ⓦ**www.roughguides.com/shop**.

are plenty of places from local shops to sports centres where you can get online. Tourist offices and your accommodation hosts should be able to help – some will have an access point themselves – and public libraries often provide cheap or free access.

If you have your own laptop or smart phone, it's actually relatively easy to find a café, bar, restaurant, B&B or hotel that offers **wi-fi**, either for a fee or for free. The site ⓦwww.kropla.com gives useful details of how to plug in your laptop when abroad, phone country codes around the world and information about electrical systems in different countries.

Laundry

Coin-operated **laundries** can still be found in Scottish towns, but are becoming less and less common. A wash followed by a spin or tumble dry costs about £3; a "service wash" (having your laundry done for you in a few hours) costs about £2 extra. In the remoter regions, you'll have to rely on your accommodation's laundry facilities or a dry-cleaner.

Mail

A **stamp** for a first-class letter to anywhere in the British Isles currently costs 41p and should arrive the next day; second-class letters cost 32p, taking three days. Note that there are now size restrictions: letters over 240 x 165 x 5mm are designated as "Large letters" and are correspondingly more expensive to send. **Postcards** and **airmail letters** of less than 10g cost 60p to the rest of Europe and should get there within three days; to the rest of the world they cost 67p and should get there within five days. Note, however, that in many parts of the Highlands and Islands there will only be one or two mail collections each day, often at lunchtime or even earlier. Stamps can be bought at post-office counters or from newsagents and local shops, although they usually only sell books of four or ten stamps.

For general postal enquiries phone ⓣ0845/774 0740 (Mon–Fri 8am–6pm, Sat 8am–1pm), or visit the website ⓦwww.royalmail.com. Main **post offices** are open Monday to Friday 9am to 5.30pm, Saturday 9am to noon. However, in small communities you'll find post office counters operating out of a shop, shed or even a private house and these will often keep extremely restricted hours.

Maps

The most comprehensive **maps** of Scotland are produced by the Ordnance Survey or OS (ⓦwww.ordnancesurvey.co.uk), renowned for their accuracy and clarity. Scotland is covered by 85 maps in the 1:50,000 (pink) **Landranger** series which shows enough detail to be useful for most walkers and cyclists. There's more detail still in the full-colour 1:25,000 (orange) **Explorer** series, which covers Scotland in around 170 maps. The full Ordnance Survey range is only available at a few big-city stores or online, although in any walking district of Scotland you'll find the relevant maps in local shops or tourist offices. If you're planning a walk of more than a couple of hours in duration, or intend to walk in the Scottish hills at all, it is strongly recommended that you carry the relevant OS map and familiarize yourself with how to navigate using it.

Virtually every service station in Scotland stocks at least one large-format **road atlas**, covering all of Britain at around three miles to one inch, and generally including larger-scale plans of major towns. For an overview of the whole of Scotland on one map, Estate Publications' *Scotland* (1:500,000) is produced in cooperation with various local tourist boards and is designed to highlight places of interest. They also produce regional maps that mark all the major tourist sights as well as youth hostels and campsites, perfect if you're driving or cycling round one particular region. These are available from just about every tourist office in Scotland.

Money

The basic unit of **currency** in the UK is the pound sterling (£), divided into 100 pence (p). Coins come in denominations of 1p, 2p, 5p, 10p, 20p, 50p, £1 and £2. Bank of England £5, £10, £20 and £50 banknotes are legal tender in Scotland; in addition the Bank of Scotland (HBOS), the Royal Bank of Scotland (RBS) and the Clydesdale Bank issue their own banknotes in all the same denominations, plus a £100 note. All Scottish notes are legal tender throughout the UK, no matter what shopkeepers south of the border might say. In general, few people use £50 or £100 notes, and shopkeepers are likely to treat them with suspicion, since forgeries are widespread. At the time of going to press, £1 was worth around $1.60, €1.15, C$1.60, A$1.60 and NZ$2.15. For the most up-to-date exchange rates, check the useful website ⓦwww.xe.com.

Cards, ATMs and banks

Credit/debit cards are by far the most convenient way to carry your money, and most hotels, shops and restaurants in Scotland accept the major brand cards. In every sizeable town in Scotland, and in some surprisingly small places too, you'll find a branch of at least one of the big Scottish high-street **banks**, usually with an **ATM** attached. However, on some islands, and in remoter parts, you may find there is only a **mobile bank** that runs to a timetable (usually available from the local post office). General **banking hours** are Monday to Friday from 9 or 9.30am to 4 or 5pm, though some branches are open until slightly later on Thursdays. Post offices charge **no commission**, have longer opening hours, and are therefore often a good place to change money and cheques. Lost or stolen credit/debit cards should be reported to the police and the following numbers: Mastercard ⓣ0800/964767; Visa ⓣ0800/891725

Opening hours and public holidays

The **tourist season** in the Highlands and Islands runs from Easter to October, and outside this period many visitor attractions are shut, though ruins, parks and gardens are normally accessible year-round. Note that last entrance can be an hour (or more) before the published closing time. Traditional shop hours in Scotland are Monday to Saturday 9am to 5.30 or 6pm. In the bigger towns, supermarkets and other food shops typically stay open until 8pm or 10pm and also open on Sundays. However, there are still plenty of towns and villages in the Highlands and Islands where you'll find precious little open on a Sunday, with many small towns also retaining an "early closing day" – often Wednesday – when shops close at 1pm.

Phones

Public **payphones** are found in the Highlands and Islands, though with the ubiquity of mobile phones they're now less common and less assiduously maintained. Payphones take all coins from 10p upwards, some take only phonecards and credit cards, and others take all three – the minimum charge is usually 60p. Phonecards are available from post offices and newsagents, but discount call-cards with a PIN number are generally cheaper for international calls.

If you're taking your **mobile/cell phone** with you to Scotland, check with your service provider whether your phone will work abroad and what the call charges will be. Unless you have a tri-band phone, it's unlikely that a mobile bought for use in the US will work outside the States and vice versa. Mobiles in Australia and New Zealand generally use the same system as the UK so should work fine. All the main UK networks cover the Highlands and Islands, though you'll still find many places in among the hills or out on the islands where there's no signal at all. If you're in a rural area and having trouble with reception,

Public holidays

Official **bank holidays** in Scotland operate on: January 1 and 2; the Friday before Easter; the first and last Monday in May; Christmas Day (Dec 25); and Boxing Day (Dec 26); in addition, all Scottish towns have one-day holidays in spring, summer and autumn – dates vary from place to place but normally fall on a Monday. While many local shops and business close on these days, few tourist-related businesses observe the holidays, particularly in the summer months.

Operator services

Domestic operator ☎100
International operator ☎155
Domestic directory assistance
☎118 500
International directory assistance
☎118 505

simply ask a local where the strongest signals are found nearby.

Throughout this guide, every phone number is prefixed by the **area code**, which is separated from the number by an oblique slash. You don't have to dial the code if you're calling from within the same area, unless you're using a mobile phone. Any number with the prefix ☎0800, ☎0808 and ☎0500 are free of charge from land lines (but not necessarily mobiles). Beware of premium-rate numbers, which are common for prerecorded information services – and usually have the prefix ☎09.

Time

Greenwich Mean Time (GMT) – equivalent to Co-ordinated Universal Time (UTC) – is used from the end of October to the end of March; for the rest of the year the country switches to **British Summer Time** (BST), one hour ahead of GMT.

Tipping

There are no fixed rules for **tipping**. If you think you've received good service, particularly in restaurants or cafés, you may want to leave a tip of ten percent of the total bill (unless service has already been included). It's not normal, however, to leave tips in pubs, although bar staff are sometimes offered drinks, which they may accept in the form of money. The only other occasions when you'll be expected to tip are in

hairdressers, taxis and upmarket hotels where porters, bellboys and table waiters rely on being tipped to bump up their often dismal wages.

Tourist information

The official tourist board, VisitScotland (ⓦwww.visitscotland.com), runs **tourist offices** (often called Visitor or Tourist Information Centres, or even "TICs") in virtually every Scottish town. Opening hours are often fiendishly complex and often change at short notice; consequently, we've simply put the days and months in which the offices are open in the relevant sections throughout the book. Beware that phone enquiries are often directed to a central call centre in Livingstone, where the staff have no knowledge of local information other than what appears on their computer screen. Consequently, we've only given telephone numbers for tourist offices where you've got a good chance of getting through to that specific office.

As well as being stacked full of souvenirs and other gifts, most TICs have a decent selection of leaflets, displays, maps and books relating to the local area. The staff are usually helpful and will do their best to help with enquiries about accommodation, local transport, attractions and restaurants, although it's worth being aware that they're reluctant to divulge information about local attractions or accommodation which are not paid-up members of VisitScotland – and a number of perfectly decent guesthouses and the like choose not to pay the fees.

Travellers with disabilities

Scottish attitudes towards travellers with **disabilities** still lag behind advances towards independence made in North America and Australia. Access to many public buildings has improved, with legislation ensuring that

Phoning home

To Australia ☎0061 + area code without the zero + number
To Ireland ☎00353 + area code without the zero + number
To New Zealand ☎0064 + area code without the zero + number
To South Africa ☎0027 + area code without the zero + number
To US and Canada ☎001 + area code + number

all new buildings have appropriate facilities. It's worth keeping in mind, however, that installing ramps, lifts, wide doorways and disabled toilets is impossible or inappropriate in many of Scotland's older and historic buildings. Most **trains** in Scotland have wheelchair lifts and assistance is, in theory, available at all manned stations – for more, go to ⓦwww.scotrail.co.uk and click on "Facilities". Wheelchair users and blind or partially sighted people are automatically given thirty to forty percent reductions on train fares, and people with other disabilities are eligible for the Disabled Persons Railcard (£18 per year; ⓦwww.disabledpersons -railcard.co.uk), which gives a third off most tickets. There are no bus discounts for the disabled. **Car rental** firm Avis will fit their cars with Lynx Hand Controls for free as long as you give them a few days' notice. As for accommodation, modified suites for people with disabilities do exist, but are often available only at higher-priced establishments and perhaps the odd B&B.

Websites

Throughout the Guide, we've included **websites** for specific accommodation, museums, galleries, transport, entertainment venues and other attractions. If you're looking for more general information about Scotland, or just a different take on things, then the list below is a useful starting-point.

ⓦ adventure.visitscotland.com Tourist-board site cataloguing various Scottish adventure-holiday options, everything from pony trekking to mountain biking.

ⓦ www.ceolas.org/ceolas.html A very informative Celtic music site, both historical and contemporary, with lots of music to listen to.

ⓦ www.geo.ed.ac.uk/home/scotland /scotland.html Edinburgh University's Geography Department gives you an introduction to Scottish history, geography and politics, with a myriad of links.

ⓦ www.met-office.gov.uk The nation's favourite topic, the weather, discussed in detail with full regional (and shipping) forecasts.

ⓦ sco.wikipedia.org Wikipedia in the Scots vernacular.

ⓦ www.scottish-islands-federation.co.uk Lots of information and useful links for the Scottish islands from Arran to Shetland.

ⓦ shetlopedia.com Shetland's very own version of Wikipedia.

ⓦ www.stonepages.com/scotland Strangely compelling website for those hooked on cairns and stone circles.

Working in Scotland

All Swiss nationals and EEA citizens (except those from Bulgaria and Romania) can work in Scotland without a permit, although citizens of the Czech Republic, Estonia, Hungary, Latvia, Lithuania, Poland, Slovakia or Slovenia must register under the Worker Registration Scheme. Other nationals need a **work permit** in order to work legally in the UK, with eligibility worked out on a points-based system. There are exceptions to the above rules, although these are constantly changing, so for the latest regulations visit ⓦwww.ukvisas.gov.uk.

Guide

Guide

Argyll

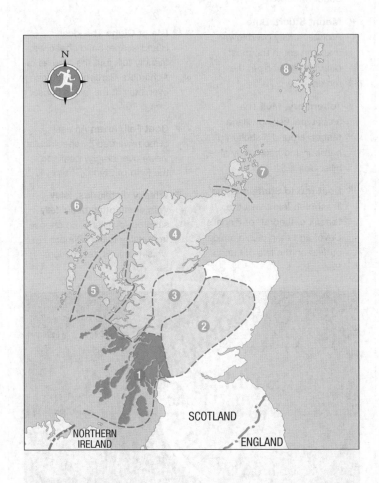

CHAPTER 1　　Highlights

✳ **Loch Fyne Oyster Bar, Cairndow** Dine in or take away at Scotland's finest smokehouse and seafood outlet. See p.66

✳ **Mount Stuart, Bute** Architecturally overblown mansion set in the most beautiful grounds in the region. See p.70

✳ **Tobermory, Mull** The archetypal fishing village ranged around a sheltered harbour and backed by steep hills. See p.83

✳ **Boat trip to Staffa and the Treshnish Isles** Visit the "basalt cathedral" of Fingal's Cave, and then picnic amidst puffins on the Isle of Lunga. See p.87

✳ **Golden beaches** Kiloran Bay on Colonsay is one of the most perfect sandy beaches in Argyll, but there are plenty more on Islay, Coll and Tiree. See p.98

✳ **Isle of Gigha** The ideal island-scape: sandy beaches, friendly folk and the azaleas of Achamore Gardens – you can even stay at the laird's house. See p.107

✳ **Goat Fell, Arran** An easy climb rewarded by spectacular views over craggy peaks to the Firth of Clyde. See p.117

✳ **Whisky distilleries, Islay** With eight, often beautifully situated, distilleries to choose from, Islay is the ultimate whisky-lover's destination. See p.121

▲ Laphroaig distillery, Islay

Argyll

C ut off for centuries from the rest of Scotland by the mountains and sea lochs that characterize the region, **Argyll** remains remote, its scatter of offshore islands forming part of the Inner Hebridean archipelago (the remaining Hebrides are dealt with in chapters 5 and 6). Geographically as well as culturally, this is a transitional area between Highland and Lowland, boasting a rich variety of scenery, from lush, subtropical gardens warmed by the Gulf Stream to flat and treeless islands on the edge of the Atlantic. It's in the folds and twists of the countryside, the interplay of land and water and the views out to the islands that the strengths and beauties of mainland Argyll lie.

Overall, the population is tiny (just ninety thousand); even **Oban**, Argyll's chief ferry port, has just eight thousand inhabitants, while the prettiest settlement, **Inveraray**, boasts only five hundred. Much of mainland Argyll comprises remote peninsulas separated by a series of long sea lochs. The first peninsula you come to from Glasgow is **Cowal**, cut off from the rest of Argyll by a series of mountains including the Arrochar Alps. Nestling in one of Cowal's sea lochs is the **Isle of Bute**, whose capital, Rothesay, is probably the most appealing of the old Clyde steamer resorts. **Kintyre**, the long finger of land that stretches south towards Ireland, is less visually dramatic than Cowal, though it does provide a stepping stone for several islands, including Arran.

Arran, Scotland's most southerly big island – now strictly speaking part of North Ayrshire – is justifiably popular, with spectacular scenery ranging from the granite peaks of the north to the Lowland pasture of the south. Of Argyll's Hebridean islands, mountainous **Mull** is the most visited, though it's large enough to absorb the crowds, many of whom are only passing through en route to the tiny isle of **Iona**, a centre of Christian culture since the sixth century, or to **Tobermory**, the island's impossibly picturesque port (aka "Balamory"). Islay, best known for its distinctive malt whiskies, is fairly quiet even in the height of summer, as is neighbouring **Jura**, which offers excellent walking opportunities. And, for those seeking further solitude, there's the island of **Colonsay**, with its beautiful golden sands, and the windswept islands of **Tiree** and **Coll**, which also boast great beaches and enjoy more sunny days than anywhere else in Scotland.

If you can, avoid July and August, when the **crowds** on Mull, Iona and Arran are at their densest – there's no guarantee the weather will be any better than during the rest of the year, and you might have more chance of avoiding the persistent Scottish midge (for more on which, see p.45). **Public transport** throughout Argyll is minimal, though buses do serve most major settlements, and the train line reaches all the way to Oban. In the remoter parts of the region and on the islands you'll have to rely on a combination of walking, hitching, bike rental, shared taxis and the postbus. If you're planning to take a car across to one of the islands, it's

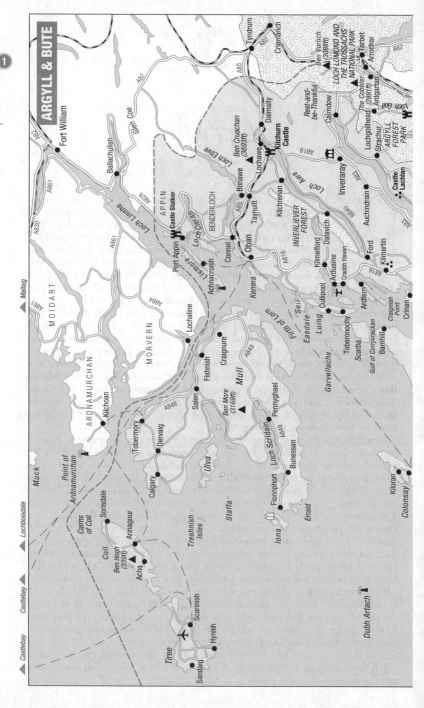

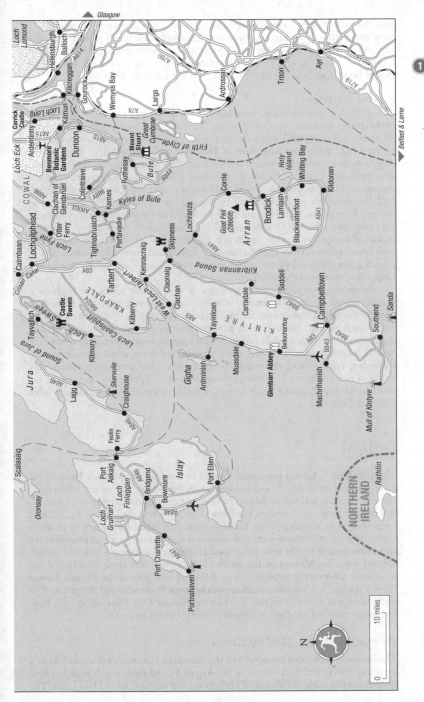

Glasgow

Loch Lomond
Helensburgh
Balloch
A814
Kilcreggan
Gourock
Wemyss Bay
Largs
Ardrossan
Troon
Ayr
A719
A78
A760

Belfast & Larne

Carrick Castle
Loch Long
Kilmun
Dunoon
A815
Ardentinny
Benmore Botanic Gardens
Loch Eck
COWAL
A886
Colintraive
Clachan of Glendaruel
A8003
Kames
Tighnabruaich
Portavadie
Kyles of Bute
Mount Stuart
Great Cumbrae
Rothesay
Bute
A844
Holy Island
Corrie
Lochranza
Goat Fell (2866ft)
Arran
Brodick
Lamlash
Whiting Bay
Kildonan
Blackwaterfoot
A841

Loch Fyne
Lochgilphead
Cairnbaan
Crinan Canal
A83
Otter Ferry
Tarbert
Kennacraig
Skipness
Kilbrannan Sound
West Loch Tarbert
Claonaig
Clachan
KNAPDALE
B8024
Kilberry
Castle Sween
Loch Sween
Tayvallich
Kilmory
Loch Caolisport
Tayinloan
Carradale
Saddell
B842
KINTYRE
Campbeltown
Southend
B842
Sanda
Glenbarr Abbey
Bellochantuy
A83
A842

Skervuile
Jura
A846
Lagg
Craighouse
Feolin Ferry
Gigha
Ardminish
Muasdale
Machrihanish
B843
Mull of Kintyre

Scalasaig
Oronsay

Port Askaig
A846
Loch Finlaggan
Bridgend
Bowmore
Islay
Port Ellen
Port Charlotte
A847
Portnahaven
Loch Gruinart

NORTHERN IRELAND
Rathlin

N

0   10 miles

essential to book ahead as early as possible. Lastly, a word on **accommodation**: a large proportion of visitors to this part of Scotland come here for a week or two and stay in self-catering cottages. On some islands and in more remote areas, this is often the most common form of accommodation available – in peak season, you should book months in advance (for more on self-catering, see p.36).

Some history

The earliest man-made sites preserved in Argyll are the cluster of **Celtic** and **prehistoric remains** near Kilmartin. The region's name, however, means "Boundary of the Gaels", and refers to the Irish Celts who settled here in the fifth century AD, and whose **Kingdom of Dalriada** embraced much of what is now Argyll. Known to the Romans as *Scotti* – hence "Scotland" – it was the Irish Celts who promoted Celtic Christianity, and whose Gaelic language eventually became the national tongue. After a period of Norse invasion and settlement, the islands (and the peninsula of Kintyre) fell to the immensely powerful Somerled, who became King of the Hebrides and Lord of Argyll in the twelfth century. Somerled's successors, the MacDonalds, established Islay as their headquarters, but were in turn dislodged by Robert the Bruce. Of Bruce's allies, it was the **Campbells** who benefited most from the MacDonalds' demise and eventually, as the dukes of Argyll, gained control of the entire area – even today, they remain one of the largest landowners in the region.

In the aftermath of the Jacobite uprisings, Argyll, like the rest of the Highlands, was devastated by the **Clearances**, with thousands of crofters evicted from their homes in order to make room for profitable sheep farming – "the white plague" – and cattle rearing. More recently forestry plantations have dramatically altered the landscape of Argyll, while purpose-built marinas have sprouted all around the heavily indented coastline. Today the traditional industries of fishing and farming are in deep crisis, leaving the region ever more dependent on tourism and a steady influx of new settlers to keep things going, while Gaelic, once the language of the majority in Argyll, retains only a tenuous hold on the outlying islands of Islay, Coll and Tiree.

Cowal

The claw-shaped **Cowal** peninsula, formed by Loch Fyne and Loch Long, is the most-visited part of Argyll, and has been since the nineteenth century when rapid steamer connections brought hordes of Glaswegian holidaymakers to its shores. It's still quicker to get to Cowal via the ferries that ply across the Clyde – by car, it's a long, though exhilarating, drive through some rich Highland scenery in order to reach the same spot. Beyond the old-fashioned coastal towns such as **Dunoon**, the largest settlement in the area, the Cowal landscape is extremely rich and varied, ranging from the Munros of the north to the gentle, low-lying coastline of the southwest. One way to explore it is to follow at least part of the 47-mile **Cowal Way**, a waymarked long-distance footpath between Portavadie and Ardgartan. The western edge of Cowal is marked by the long, narrow Loch Fyne, famous for both its kippers (smoked herring) and, more recently, oysters (see p.66).

Arrochar to Cairndow

The boundaries of Loch Lomond and the Trossachs National Park extend quite a long way into Cowal, incorporating the **Argyll Forest Park** which stretches west from Arrochar along the shores of Loch Long and south as far as Holy Loch. The area has the peninsula's most grandiose scenery, including the ambitiously named **Arrochar Alps**, whose peaks offer some of the best climbing in Argyll: Ben Ime (3318ft) is the tallest of the range, while Ben Arthur or "The Cobbler" (2891ft), named after the anvil-like rock formation at its summit, is the most distinctive. At the other end of the scale there are several gentle forest walks clearly laid out by the Forestry Commission and helpful leaflets are available from tourist offices.

Arrochar and around

Approaching by road from Glasgow, the entry point to Cowal is **ARROCHAR**, at the head of Loch Long. The village itself is ordinary enough, but the setting is dramatic, and it makes a convenient base for exploring the nearby Alps and forests. There's a **train station** a mile or so east, just off the A83 to Tarbet (see p.141). For **accommodation**, try *Ben Bheula* (℡01301/702184, ⓦwww.benbheula.co.uk; ❷), a clean B&B in nearby Succoth, set back from the head of the loch and run by a very friendly couple, or *Fascadail* (℡01301/702344, ⓦwww.fascadail.com; ❸), a Victorian guesthouse with a glorious garden situated in the quieter southern part of the village. If you need a bite **to eat**, head for the *Village Inn*, which has tables outside overlooking the loch as well as a cosy real-ale bar.

Two miles west at **ARDGARTAN**, there's a well-maintained lochside Forestry Commission **campsite** (℡01301/702293, ⓦwww.forestholidays.co.uk; April–Oct), and, a little further down the road, in the Ardgartan Visitor Centre is a **tourist office** (April–Oct daily; ℡01301/702432), which doubles as a forestry office and has occasional organized walks. **Bike rental** is available and there are waymarked **walks and bike trails** starting from here.

Heading west from Arrochar, you climb **Glen Croe**, a strategic hill-pass whose saddle is called – for obvious reasons – **Rest-and-be-Thankful**. Here the road forks, with the single-track B828 heading down to **LOCHGOILHEAD**, an isolated village overlooking Loch Goil, where the majority of houses are holiday homes. A road tracks the west side of the loch, petering out after five miles at the picturesque ruins of **Carrick Castle**, a classic tower-house castle built around 1400 and used as a hunting lodge by James IV. Facing this across the water is a hilly peninsula known as **Argyll's Bowling Green** – no ironic nickname, but an English corruption of the Gaelic *Baile na Greine* (Sunny Hamlet).

Cairndow and around

Continuing west towards Inveraray along the A83 you come to **CAIRNDOW**, at the head of Loch Fyne. Just behind the village, off the main road, you'll find the **Ardkinglas Woodland Gardens** (daily dawn–dusk; £3.50; ℡01499/600261, ⓦwww.ardkinglas.com), which contains exotic rhododendrons, azaleas and a superb collection of conifers, one of which is, at 210ft, the tallest tree in Britain.

Climbing The Cobbler

The jagged, triple-peaked ridge of Ben Arthur (2891ft) – better known as **The Cobbler** because it is supposed to look like a cobbler bent over his work – is the most enticing of the peaks within the Argyll Forest Park. It's surprisingly accessible, with the most popular route starting from the car park at Succoth, on the road to Ardgartan. Skirting the woods, you join the Allt a' Bhalachain, which climbs steeply up to the col between the northern peak (known as The Cobbler's Wife) and The Cobbler itself. Traversing the ridge in order to ascend one or all of the three peaks is a tricky business, and the final scramble should only be attempted by experienced hikers. The total distance of the climb is only five miles, but the return trip will probably take you between five and six hours. For more on safety precautions, see p.47.

In the southern part of the gardens stands **Ardkinglas House** (April–Oct guided tour last Fri of month 2pm; £6), a particularly handsome Scottish Baronial mansion, built in 1907 by Robert Lorimer for the Noble family – book ahead if you want to join a guided tour. In Cairndow itself, the *Stagecoach Inn* is good for a pint and inexpensive pub food, but for something a bit special continue a mile or so further along on the A83 to the famous ⚓ **Loch Fyne Oyster Bar and Shop** (℡01499/600236, ⓦ www.loch-fyne.com), which sells more oysters than anywhere else in the country, plus lots of other fish and seafood treats. You can assemble a gourmet picnic in the shop or stock up on provisions, and the moderately expensive **restaurant** is excellent, though booking is advisable at busy times.

Dunoon

The principal entry-point into Cowal by sea is **DUNOON**. In the nineteenth century it grew from a village to a major Clyde seaside resort and favourite holiday spot for Glaswegians, but nowadays there's really little to tempt you to stay, particularly with attractive countryside beckoning just beyond.

The centre of town is dominated by a grassy lump of rock known as **Castle Hill**, crowned by Castle House, built in the 1820s by a wealthy Glaswegian and the subject of a bitter dispute with the local populace over closure of the common land around his house. The people eventually won, and the grounds remain open to the public to this day, as does the house, which is home to the **Castle House Museum** (Easter–Oct Mon–Sat 10.30am–4.30pm, Sun 2–4.30pm; £2; ⓦ www.castlehousemuseum.org.uk). There's some good hands-on nature stuff for kids, an excellent section on the Clyde steamers as well as details about "Highland Mary", betrothed to Robbie Burns (despite the fact that he already had a pregnant wife), who died of typhus before the pair could see through their plan to elope to the West Indies. A statue of her is in the grounds.

Practicalities

Dunoon's **tourist office**, the principal one in Cowal, is located on Alexandra Parade (open daily all year round; ⓦ www.visitcowal.co.uk). There are two **ferry** crossings across the Clyde from Gourock to Dunoon; the shorter, more frequent service is on Western Ferries to Hunter's Quay, a mile north of the town centre; CalMac's boats, though, arrive at the main pier, and have better transport connections if you're on foot.

Despite the enormous supply of accommodation, it's a good idea to book ahead since availability can be a problem in the summer. For hotels, try *Abbot's Brae*, a beautiful family-run Victorian villa, set in woods above West Bay with lovely views over the Clyde (℡01369/705021, ⓦ www.abbotsbrae.co.uk; ➎), or the smart *Dhailling Lodge* (℡01369/701253, ⓦ www.dhaillinglodge.com; ➍), another attractive villa closer to town on Alexandra Parade, run by a very welcoming Glaswegian couple. *Chatters*, 58 John St (℡01369/706402, ⓦ www.chattersdunoon.co.uk; Wed–Sat only), is Dunoon's best restaurant by far, offering delicious Scottish fare, while the nicest café is the bright, modern *Perk Up* (closed Sun), up Ferry Brae from the main street.

For **bike rental**, head for the Highland Stores on Argyll Street; for **pony trekking**, contact the Velvet Path Trekking and Riding Centre (℡01369/830580) at Inellan, four miles south of town. The 1950s Queen's Hall, on the seafront, hosts frequent gigs, and Dunoon boasts a two-screen **cinema** (a rarity in Argyll) on John Street, but the town's most famous entertainment is the **Cowal Highland Gathering** (ⓦ www.cowalgathering.com), the largest of its kind in the world, held here on the last weekend in August, and culminating in the awesome spectacle of the massed pipes and drums of more than 150 bands marching through the streets.

Holy Loch and Benmore Botanic Garden

Immediately north of Dunoon lies **Holy Loch**, the former site of a US nuclear submarine base which closed in 1992. On the northern shores of the loch is the elongated settlement of **KILMUN**, which harbours the fascinating **St Munn's Church** (May–Sept Tues & Thurs 1.30–4.30pm; free), with a mausoleum where many a Duke of Argyll is buried, several good stained-glass windows and an organ driven by tap water. There's also an **arboretum** at Kilmun, through which the Forestry Commission has laid out several pleasant walks.

Just three miles north of Holy Loch along the A815 is **Benmore Botanic Garden** (daily: March & Oct 10am–5pm; April–Sept 10am–6pm; £5), at the foot of Loch Eck, a narrow freshwater loch squeezed between steeply banked hills. An offshoot of Edinburgh's Royal Botanic Garden, the beautifully laid-out garden occupies 120 acres of lush hillside; the mild, moist climate of Argyll allows a vast range of unusual plants to grow here, with different sections devoted to rainforest species native to places as exotic as China, Chile and Bhutan. The gardens boast 300 species of rhododendron and a memorably striking avenue of Great Redwoods, planted in 1863 and now over 150ft high.

If you need something to eat, there's a pleasant, inexpensive **café** (April–Oct daily; Nov–March Wed–Sun) by the entrance. It's also possible to combine a visit to Benmore with one of the local **forest walks**, the most popular being a leisurely stroll up the rocky ravine of **Puck's Glen** (1hr 30min round-trip), which begins from the car park a mile south of the gardens. There are two **pubs** on the eastern shores of Loch Eck itself: the *Coylet Inn* and, further north, the *Whistlefield Inn* (T01369/860440, Wwww.whistlefield.com; ②). Both are good for a pint, but the *Whistlefield* is the place to go for food and **accommodation**, with both comfortable en-suite rooms and a **bunkhouse** to choose from.

Southwest Cowal

The mellower landscape of **southwest Cowal**, which stands in complete contrast to the bustle of Dunoon or the Highland grandeur of the Argyll Forest Park, becomes immediate as soon as you head into the area. And there are few more beautiful sights in Argyll than the **Kyles of Bute**, the slivers of water that separate Cowal from the bleak bulk of the Isle of Bute and constitute some of the best sailing territory in Scotland. **COLINTRAIVE**, on the eastern Kyle, marks the narrowest point in the area – barely more than a couple of hundred yards across – and is where the CalMac car ferry departs to Bute. The *Colintraive Hotel* (T01700/841207, Wwww.colintraivehotel.com; ⑤), hidden away south of the ferry slipway, is well worth seeking out; a favourite with yachties, it serves up delicious fresh dishes and has some lovely rooms, too.

The most popular spot from which to appreciate the Kyles is along the A8003 as it rises dramatically above the sea lochs before descending to the peaceful, lochside village of **TIGHNABRUAICH**, best known for its excellent **sailing school** (T01700/811717, Wwww.tssargyll.co.uk). You can stay at the impressive *An Lochan* by the waterside (T01700/811239, Wwww.anlochan.co.uk; ⑥), which serves exceptionally good seafood bar meals and has wonderful views over the Kyles; not quite so grand, but justifiably popular with sailors and walkers, is the wood-panelled bar in the *Kames Hotel* (T01700/811489, Wkames-hotel.com; ⑤) in neighbouring **KAMES**. You can get B&B at *Ardeneden* (T01700/811354; ③), a lovely Victorian guesthouse run by the same people who look after the excellent *Burnside Restaurant* in the village. If you're driving to Kintyre, Islay or Jura, you can avoid the long haul around Loch Fyne – some seventy miles or so – by using the **ferry** to Tarbert from **Portavadie**, three miles southwest of Kames.

In contrast to the Kyles, Cowal west coast, overlooking Loch Fyne, is more or less deserted. The road meets the loch shore at **OTTER FERRY**, which has a small shingle beach, a wonderful pub and an oyster restaurant, *The Oystercatcher*, with outside tables in good weather. Further north, overlooking the romantic ruin of **Castle Lachlan**, ⚘ *Inver Cottage* (☎01369/860537, ⓦwww.inver cottage.co.uk) is a contemporary and relaxed restaurant which serves a delicious seafood soup, Argyll venison burgers and peat-smoked haddock. One of the most picturesque **campsites** in Cowal is *Glendaruel Caravan Park* (☎01369/820267, ⓦwww.glendaruelcaravanpark.co.uk; April–Oct), set in the lovely mature grounds of a former stately home. For **accommodation**, head for *Thistle House* (☎01369/302209, ⓦwww.thistlehouseguesthouse.com; ❸), a really top-notch guesthouse overlooking Loch Fyne, situated between Strachur and Cairndow.

Isle of Bute

The island of **Bute** (ⓦwww.isle-of-bute.com) is in many ways simply an extension of the Cowal peninsula, from which it is separated by the narrow Kyles of Bute. Thanks to its mild climate and its ferry link with Wemyss Bay, Bute has been a popular holiday and convalescence spot for Clydesiders for over a century. Its chief town, **Rothesay**, rivals Dunoon as the major seaside resort on the Clyde, easily surpassing it thanks to some splendid Victorian architecture, decent accommodation and eating options and the chance to visit **Mount Stuart**, one of Scotland's most singular aristocratic piles. Bute's inhabitants live around the two wide bays on the island's east coast, which resembles one long seaside promenade. To escape the crowds head for the sparsely populated west coast, which, in any case, has the sandiest beaches.

Rothesay

Bute's only town, **ROTHESAY** is a handsome Victorian resort, set in a wide sweeping bay, backed by green hills, with a classic palm-tree promenade and 1920s pagoda-style pavilion originally built to house the **Winter Gardens**. Though often busy with day-trippers from Glasgow, there's plenty that's attractive about the place, with some handsome buildings, a prominent Art Deco pavilion and occasional flourishes of wrought-ironwork. Its **Victorian toilets** (daily: Easter–Sept 8am–7.45pm; Oct–Easter 9am–4.45pm; 20p), built in 1899 by Twyfords, are a feast of marble, ceramics and brass so ornate that they're now one of the town's most celebrated sights. The Victorians didn't make provision for ladies' conveniences, so the women's half is a modern add-on, but if the coast is clear the attendant – attired in a neat burgundy waistcoat – will allow ladies a tour of the gents.

Rothesay also boasts the militarily useless, but architecturally impressive, moated ruins of **Rothesay Castle** (April–Sept daily 9.30am–5.30pm; Oct–March Mon–Wed, Sat & Sun 9.30am–4.30pm; HS; £4.20), hidden amid the town's backstreets. Built around the twelfth century, it was twice captured by the Vikings; such vulnerability was the reasoning behind the unusual, almost circular, curtain wall, with its four big drum-towers, only one of which remains fully intact.

In rainy weather you could hide inside the **Bute Museum** (April–Sept Mon–Sat 10.30am–4.30pm, Sun 2.30–4.30pm; Oct–March Tues–Sat 2.30–4.30pm; £2; ⓦwww.butemuseum.org) behind the castle, a classic local-history museum,

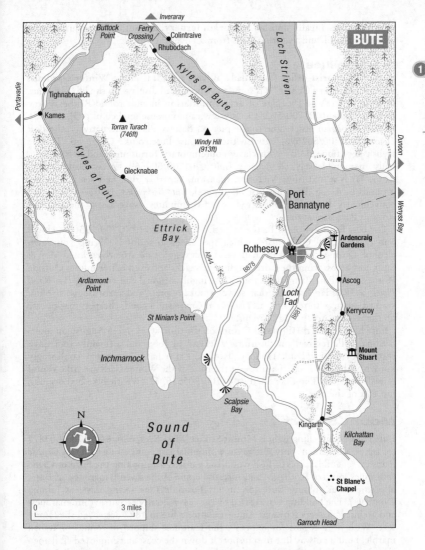

Within the map:

Inveraray

Buttock Point

Ferry Crossing

Colintraive

Rhubodach

Kyles of Bute

Loch Striven

Portavadie

Tighnabruaich

Kames

Torran Turach (746ft)

A886

Windy Hill (913ft)

Kyles of Bute

Glecknabae

Dunoon

Wemyss Bay

Port Bannatyne

Ettrick Bay

Rothesay

A844

B878

Ardencraig Gardens

Ardlamont Point

St Ninian's Point

Loch Fad

Ascog

B881

Kerrycroy

Inchmarnock

Mount Stuart

N

Scalpsie Bay

Kingarth

A844

Kilchattan Bay

Sound of Bute

St Blane's Chapel

0   3 miles

Garroch Head

purpose-built in 1926, with everything from Pictish stones to bits of local shipwrecks. More interesting, though, is the fourteenth-century **St Mary's Chapel**, beside the High Kirk at the top of town up the High Street in the direction of Loch Fad; it houses a couple of impressive monumental medieval tombs.

On the fringes of Rothesay heading east along the coast, not far from Craigmore Pier, you'll come to **Ardencraig Gardens** (May–Sept Mon–Fri 10am–4.30pm; Sat & Sun 1–4.30pm; free), a small riot of colour in summer, with a series of Victorian hothouses and an aviary full of exotic birds surrounding a lovingly tended hillside garden. A mile or so further down the coastal road is the **Ascog Hall Gardens** (Easter–Oct Wed–Sun 10am–5pm; £4; Ⓦascoghallfernery.co.uk), which features a really unusual **Victorian fernery**, a beautiful, dank place, sunk into the ground, and featuring ferns from all over the world.

Practicalities

Rothesay's **tourist office** (open daily all year round) is in the **Winter Gardens**, whose "Discovery Centre" has some well-presented displays on the life and times of Bute. There's no shortage of **accommodation** in and around Rothesay: try *Cannon House* (℡01700/502819, ⓦwww.cannonhousehotel.co.uk; ④), a really elegant Georgian hotel close to the pier on Battery Place; alternatively, the *Boat House* (℡01700/502696, ⓦwww.theboathouse-bute.co.uk; ③) at no. 15 is a stylish "boutique B&B" with classy contemporary furnishings and decor; for a truly memorable stay, ⚘ *Balmory Hall* (℡01700/500669, ⓦwww.balmoryhall .com; ⑦) is a luxurious Victorian mansion, superbly run, and set in its own grounds in Ascog. Bute has just one **hostel**, *Bute Backpackers* (℡01700/501876), conveniently located at 36 Argyle St, five minutes' walk along the seafront towards Port Bannatyne.

The best **food** option in Rothesay is the *Squat Lobster* (℡01700/503603; closed Sun & Mon), 29 Gallowgate, which specializes in seafood – bring your own alcohol. During the day, the small but stylish veggie café, *Musicker* (closed Mon & Sun), just across from the castle has decent snacks and even better music. Outside Rothesay, in Port Bannatyne, there's the highly original and engaging *Port Royal Hotel*, a "Russian Tavern" that serves smoked sprats and razorfish with blini, washed down with real ales, or *The Pier at Craigmore*, a good, cheaper, snacky café on the road to Ardencraig Gardens.

Bute holds its own **Highland Games** on the third weekend in August, an international **folk festival** on the third weekend in July, and a (mainly trad) **jazz festival** over May Bank Holiday. Rothesay also has a **cinema** – confusingly known as the Discovery Theatre – at the back of the Winter Gardens. **Bike rental** is available from The Bike Shed (℡01700/505515, ⓦwww.thebikeshed.org.uk), just east of the pier.

Mount Stuart

Bute's most compelling sight is **Mount Stuart** (May–Sept, phone ℡01700/503877 for times; £8, gardens only £4; ⓦwww.mountstuart.com), a huge, fantasy Gothic mansion set amidst acres of lush woodland gardens overlooking the Firth of Clyde four miles south of Rothesay, and ancestral home of the seventh marquess of Bute, also known as Johnny Bute (or, in his Formula One racing days, as Johnny Dumfries). The building was created by the marvellously eccentric third marquess and architect Robert Rowand Anderson after a fire in 1877 destroyed the family seat. With little regard for expense, the marquess shipped in tonnes of Italian marble, built a railway line to transport it down the coast and employed craftsmen who had worked with William Burges on the marquess's other medieval concoction, Cardiff Castle.

Mount Stuart's sleek modern **visitor centre** contains an excellent **café/restaurant** serving light lunches and giving great views into the trees. The house itself is a fifteen-minute walk through the grounds (daily 10am–6pm). The *pièce de resistance* is the columned **Marble Hall**, its vaulted ceiling and stained-glass windows decorated with the signs of the zodiac, reflecting the marquess's taste for mysticism. He was equally fond of animal and plant imagery; hence you'll find birds feeding on berries in the dining-room frieze and monkeys reading (and tearing up) books and scrolls in the library. Look out also for the unusual heraldic ceiling in the drawing room. After all the heavy furnishings, seek aesthetic relief in the vast **Marble Chapel**, built entirely out of dazzling white Carrara marble, with a magnificent cosmati floor pattern. Upstairs, along with three impressive bathrooms, check out the **Horoscope Room**, where you can see a fine astrological ceiling and adjacent observatory/conservatory.

Before you leave Mount Stuart, take a look at the planned village of **Kerrycroy**, just beyond the main exit, built by the second Marquess in the early nineteenth century for the estate workers. Semi-detached houses – alternately mock-Tudor and whitewashed stone – form a crescent that overlooks a pristine village green and, beyond, the sea.

Around Bute

The Highland–Lowland dividing line passes through Bute, which is all but sliced in two by the freshwater Loch Fad. As a result, the northern half of the island is hilly and uninhabited, while the southern half is made up of Lowland-style farmland. The two highest peaks on the island are **Windy Hill** (913ft) and **Torran Turach** (746ft), both in the north; from the latter, there are fine views of the Kyles, but for a gentler overview of the island you can simply walk up to the **viewpoint**, in the midst of the golf course, on Canada Hill just east of Rothesay.

Six miles south of Rothesay, east-facing **Kilchattan Bay** has a lovely arc of sand overlooked by a row of grand Victorian houses, including *Kingarth Hotel*, which has a very convivial bar.

Over on the west coast, **St Blane's Chapel** is a twelfth-century ruin beautifully situated in open countryside amidst the foundations of an earlier Christian settlement established in the sixth century by St Catan, uncle to the local-born St Blane. From the road it's a short uphill walk through farmland; over the brow of a hill you come upon a well-built churchyard wall surrounded by mature trees; the ruined chapel sits amid a rather peculiar two-tier graveyard, the upper area reserved for the men of the parish while the women were consigned to the lower one.

Four miles up the coast is the sandy strand of **Scalpsie Bay**, while further on, beyond the village of Straad, lies **St Ninian's Point**, where the ruins of a sixth-century chapel overlook another fine sandy strand and the uninhabited island of **Inchmarnock** – to which, according to tradition, alcoholics were banished in the nineteenth century. Bute's finest sandy beach is further north at **Ettrick Bay**, which has a tearoom (April–Oct) and basic camping site at its north end – a path along the island's former tramway links the bay with Port Bannatyne.

Inveraray

The traditional county town of Argyll, and a classic example of an eighteenth-century planned town, **INVERARAY** was built in the 1770s by the Duke of Argyll, in order to distance his newly rebuilt castle from the hoi polloi in the town and to establish a commercial and legal centre for the region. Inveraray has changed very little since and remains an absolute set-piece of Scottish Georgian architecture, with a truly memorable setting, the brilliant white arches of Front Street reflected in the still waters of Loch Fyne.

The Town

Despite its picture-book location, there's not much more to Inveraray than its distinctive **Main Street** (perpendicular to Front St), flanked by whitewashed terraces, characterized by black window casements. At the top of the street, the road divides to circumnavigate the town's Neoclassical church: originally the southern half served the Gaelic-speaking community, while the northern half served those who spoke English.

East of the church is **Inveraray Jail** (daily: April–Oct 9.30am–6pm; £8.25; Nov–March 10am–5pm; Ⓦwww.inverarayjail.co.uk), whose attractive Georgian courthouse and grim prison blocks ceased to function in the 1930s. The jail is now a thoroughly enjoyable museum, which graphically recounts prison conditions from medieval times to the twentieth century. You can try out the minute "Airing Yards" where the prisoners got to exercise for an hour a day, and also sit in the semicircular courthouse, with its great views over the loch, and listen to a re-enactment of a trial of the period.

Moored at the town pier is the **Arctic Penguin** (daily 10am–4pm; £5 Ⓦwww .inveraraypier.com), a handsome, triple-masted schooner built in Dublin in 1911. It has some nautical knick-knacks and displays on the maritime history of the Clyde, with the odd puffer berthed alongside, but is only really worth exploring if you're a marine enthusiast.

A ten-minute walk north of Main Street, **Inveraray Castle** (April–Oct daily 10am–5.45pm; £9; Ⓦwww.inveraray-castle.com) remains the family home of the Duke of Argyll, head of the powerful Campbell clan. Built in 1745, it was given a touch of the Loire in the nineteenth century with the addition of dormer windows and conical corner spires. Inside, the most startling feature is the armoury hall, whose displays of weaponry – supplied to the Campbells by the British government to put down the Jacobites – rise through several storeys; otherwise, the interior's pretty ordinary, with the exception of Rob Roy's rather sad-looking sporran and dirk handle.

Gracing the extensive **castle grounds** (daily dawn to dusk; free) is an attractive Celtic cross from Tiree, and one of three elegant bridges built during the reland-scaping of Inveraray (the other two are on the road from Cairndow). Of the walks marked out in the grounds, the most strenuous takes you to the tower atop **Dùn na Cuaiche** (813ft), from where there's a spectacular view over the castle, town and loch.

Practicalities

Inveraray's **tourist office** is on Front Street (open daily all year round; ℡01499/302063), as is the town's chief **hotel**, the *Argyll*, formerly the *Great Inn*, where Dr Johnson and Boswell once stayed. A better **place to stay**, however, is *Rudha-Na-Craige* (℡01499/302668, Ⓦwww.rudha-na-craige.f2s.com; ❺), a beautifully restored Scottish Baronial house on the southern edge of town. Other options include *Newton Hall* (℡01499/302484, Ⓦwww.newtonhallinveraray .com; ❹), a nearby former church, now a B&B with views over the loch, and *Creag Dhubh* (℡01499/302430, Ⓦwww.creagdhubh.com; Feb–Nov; ❸), set in a large garden overlooking Loch Fyne down the A83 to Lochgilphead. The SYHA **hostel** (℡0870/004 1125, Ⓦwww.syha.org.uk; mid-March to Oct) is in a modern building a short walk up the A819, while the old Royal Navy base, two miles down the A83 to Lochgilphead, has been converted into the excellent, fully equipped *Argyll Caravan Park* (℡01499/302285, Ⓦwww.argyllcaravanpark.com; April–Oct). *Brambles*, on Main Street, does classic café fare, plus home-made cakes, while the **bar** of the *George Hotel*, opposite, is the town's liveliest spot, and also serves decent bar **meals**. To sample Loch Fyne's delicious fresh fish and seafood, though, you should head for the restaurant of the nearby *Loch Fyne Oyster Bar* (see p.66).

Oban and around

The solidly Victorian resort of **OBAN** (Ⓦwww.oban.org.uk) enjoys a superb setting – the island of Kerrera to the southwest providing its bay with a natural shelter – distinguished by a bizarre granite amphitheatre, dramatically lit at night, on the hilltop above the town. Despite a population of just eight thousand, it's by far the largest port in northwest Scotland, the second-largest town in Argyll, and the main departure point for ferries to the Hebrides. If you arrive late, or are catching an early boat, you may have to spend the night here (there's no real need otherwise); if you're staying elsewhere, it's a useful location for wet-weather activities and shopping, and it's a great place to eat fresh seafood.

Oban lies at the centre of the coastal region known as Lorn, named after the Irish Celt Loarn, who, along with his brothers Fergus and Oengus, settled here around 500 AD. The mainland is very picturesque, although its beauty is no secret – to escape the crowds, head off and explore the nearby islands, like **Lismore** or **Kerrera**, just offshore, or to the peninsula of Appin or quiet freshwater Loch Awe.

Arrival and information

Arriving in Oban **by car** can be a bit of a nightmare in the summer, when traffic chokes the main drag. If you're heading straight for the ferry, make sure you leave an extra hour to allow for sitting in the tailbacks. If you're just coming in to town to look around, use one of the non-central or supermarket car parks. The CalMac **ferry terminal** (Ⓣ01631/566688, Ⓦwww.calmac.co.uk) for the islands is on Railway Pier, a stone's throw from the **train station**, which is itself adjacent to the bus stops on Station Square. Six miles north of town, tiny **Oban Airport** (Ⓣ0845/805 7465, Ⓦwww.hebrideanair.co.uk) in North Connel has flights to Coll, Tiree, Islay and Colonsay; the nearest train station to the airport is Connel Ferry, or take bus #405 from Oban to Barcaldine.

The **tourist office** (open daily year round; Ⓣ01631/563122) is housed in a converted church on Argyll Square, and has heaps of leaflets and books as well as internet access. For **car** and **bike rental** go to Flit on Glencruitten Road (Ⓣ01631/566553, Ⓦwww.flitselfdrive.co.uk). If you fancy taking the plunge and trying your hand at some **diving** contact the Puffin Dive Centre, based a mile south of Oban at Port Gallanach (Ⓣ01631/566088, Ⓦwww.puffin.org.uk).

Accommodation

Oban is positively heaving with **hotels** and **B&Bs**, most of them very reasonably priced and many on or near the quayside.

Hotels and B&Bs

Alt na Craig House Glenmore Rd
Ⓣ01631/564524, Ⓦwww.guesthouseinoban.com.
A handsome Victorian house just south of town, with a woodland garden, beautifully furnished rooms and views of the bay. ❻
Dungallan House Hotel Gallanach Rd
Ⓣ01631/563799, Ⓦwww.dungallanhotel-oban .co.uk. Solid Victorian villa hotel with a dozen rooms set in its own woodland grounds, hidden away on the Gallanach Rd, with great views across the Sound of Kerrera. No under-12s. ❽

Hawthornbank Guest House Dalriach Rd
Ⓣ01631/562041. Decent, traditional guesthouse in the lower backstreets of Oban, just across the road from the swimming pool. ❸
Kilchrenan House Corran Esplanade
Ⓣ01631/562663, Ⓦwww.kilchrenanhouse.co.uk. A bright and hospitable home located near the cathedral, with ten rooms, most of which have sea views. ❸
Lerags House Lerags Ⓣ01631/563381, Ⓦwww.leragshouse.com. A super special option located four miles south of Oban – *Lerags House* is a Georgian mansion somewhere between

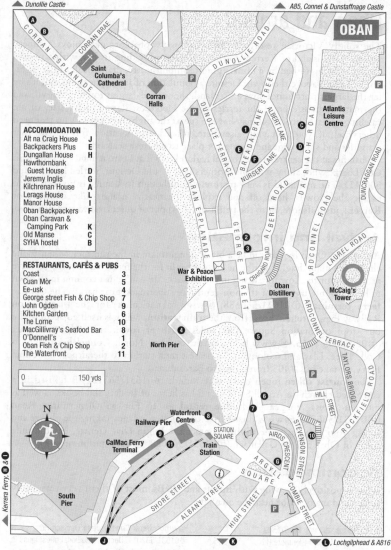

Dunollie Castle
A85, Connel & Dunstaffnage Castle
OBAN
CORRAN ESPLANADE
CORRAN BRAE
Saint Columba's Cathedral
Corran Halls
DUNOLLIE ROAD
DUNOLLIE TERRACE
BREADALBANE STREET
ALBERT LANE
DALRIACH ROAD
Atlantis Leisure Centre
NURSERY LANE
ALBERT ROAD
DUNCRAGGAN ROAD
ARDCONNEL ROAD
GEORGE STREET
LAUREL ROAD
CRAIGARD ROAD
War & Peace Exhibition
Oban Distillery
McCaig's Tower
ARDCONNEL TERRACE
North Pier
TAYLORS BRIDGE
ROCKFIELD ROAD
HILL STREET
STEVENSON STREET
AIRDS CRESCENT
Waterfront Centre
Railway Pier
STATION SQUARE
CalMac Ferry Terminal
Train Station
ARGYLL SQUARE
COMBIE STREET
SHORE STREET
ALBANY STREET
HIGH STREET
South Pier
Kerrera Ferry, H & I
J
K
L, Lochgilphead & A816
N
0
150 yds
ACCOMMODATION
Alt na Craig House J
Backpackers Plus E
Dungallan House H
Hawthornbank Guest House D
Jeremy Inglis G
Kilchrenan House A
Lerags House L
Manor House I
Oban Backpackers F
Oban Caravan & Camping Park K
Old Manse C
SYHA hostel B
RESTAURANTS, CAFÉS & PUBS
Coast 3
Cuan Mòr 5
Ee-usk 4
George street Fish & Chip Shop 7
John Ogden 9
Kitchen Garden 6
The Lorne 10
MacGillivray's Seafood Bar 8
O'Donnell's 1
Oban Fish & Chip Shop 2
The Waterfront 11

a B&B and a country house hotel with chic decor and excellent food – the tariff includes dinner. 8

Manor House Hotel Gallanach Rd ⓣ01631/562087, ⓦwww.manorhouseoban.com. Beautiful eighteenth-century manor house, peacefully located on the fringes of town by the shores of the Sound of Kerrera, with a top-notch restaurant attached. 9

Old Manse Dalriach Rd ⓣ01631/564886, ⓦwww.obanguesthouse.co.uk. Spotlessly clean guesthouse run by a very welcoming couple, with a beautiful garden and lovely views over the sea. 3

Hostels and campsites

Jeremy Inglis 21 Airds Crescent ⓣ01631/565065. Halfway between a hostel and a B&B, with an eccentric proprietor who also runs *McTavish's Kitchens*. Located near the train station, with shared rooms, doubles or family rooms available, plus kitchen facilities; it's the cheapest bed in town, with breakfast included. 1

Oban Backpackers Breadalbane St
☎01631/562107, ⓦwww.obanbackpackers.com.
Friendly and central Oban hostel, with a pool table,
real fire, internet access and breakfast included.
March–Oct & Christmas–New Year. Round the
corner, *Backpackers Plus* is slightly more expensive
and is good for couples on a budget as it has
doubles, as well as rooms for small groups. ❷
Oban Caravan & Camping Park Gallanach Rd
☎01631/562425, ⓦwww.obancaravanpark.com.

Huge site with lots of camping space and great
views, with a good chance of a breeze to blow the
midges away. A mile and a half from Oban up a
pretty glen. Open April–Oct.
SYHA hostel Corran Esplanade ☎01631/562025,
ⓦwww.syha.org.uk. Converted Victorian house,
with a quieter, modern annexe behind, both a fair
trek with a backpack from the ferry terminal along
the Corran Esplanade. Two-, three- and four-bed
en-suite rooms available. ❶

The Town

Apart from the setting and views, the only truly remarkable sight in Oban is the
town's landmark, **McCaig's Tower**, a stiff ten-minute climb from the quayside.
Built in imitation of Rome's Colosseum, it was the brainchild of a local
businessman a century ago, who had the twin aims of alleviating off-season
unemployment among the local stonemasons and creating a museum, art gallery
and chapel. Originally, the plan was to add a 95-foot central tower, but work
never progressed further than the exterior granite walls before McCaig died. In his
will, McCaig gave instructions for the lancet windows to be filled with bronze
statues of the family, though no such work was ever undertaken. Instead, the folly
has been turned into a sort of walled garden which is a popular rendezvous for
Oban's youth after dark, but for the rest of the time simply provides a wonderful
seaward panorama, particularly at sunset.

Down in the centre of town, you can pass a few hours admiring the boats in the
harbour and looking out for scavenging seals in the bay. If the weather's bad, the
best option is to sign up for one of the excellent guided tours around **Oban
Distillery** (Feb Mon–Fri 12.30–4pm; March–Dec Mon–Fri 9.30am–5pm; June–
Oct also Sat 9.30am–4.30pm; July & Aug also Sun 12.30–4.30pm; £7), slap in the
centre of town off George Street. The tour ends with a generous dram of Oban's
lightly peaty malt. Another refuge is the **War and Peace Exhibition** (March–
April & Oct daily 10am–4pm; May–Sept Mon–Sat 10am–6pm, Sun 10am–4pm;
free; ⓦwww.obanmuseum.org.uk) in the old *Oban Times* building beside the
Art-Deco *Regent Hotel* on the Esplanade; stuffed full of memorabilia and staffed by
enthusiasts, it tells the story of the intriguing wartime role of the area around
Oban as a flying-boat base, mustering point for Atlantic convoys and as a training
centre for the D-Day landings.

Eating, drinking and nightlife

Oban has become a terrific place to get good fresh seafood. If you're only here to
catch a ferry, grab a quick langoustine sandwich or dressed fresh crab from John
Ogden's excellent ⅓ **takeaway** seafood shack near the CalMac terminal, or head
to nearby *MacGillivray's Seafood Bar*, another alfresco harbour place which serves
pan-fried scallops and lobster tails. Of course, there's always fish and chips, from
Oban Fish & Chip Shop & Restaurant at 116 George St, or the *George Street Fish &
Chip Shop* by the seafront.

You should be able to catch some **live music** at the weekend at *O'Donnell's* Irish
pub, underneath an incongruously flash bar called *Paparazzi* on Breadalbane Street,
or in *The Lorne*, a more attractive and popular pub on Stevenson Street which also
serves real ales, forty malts and local seafood.

Cafés and restaurants

Coast 104 George St ☎01631/569900, ⓦwww
.coastoban.com. A slick place with a metropolitan
atmosphere, serving acclaimed and original fish,
game and meat dishes. Mains start at £15.

Cuan Mòr 60 George St ☎01631/565078,
ⓦwww.cuanmor.co.uk. Contemporary bistro-pub
with lots of fish and seafood dishes, plus
bangers and mash, baguettes and salads, all for
under £12.

Ee-usk North Pier ☎01631/565666, ⓦwww
.eeusk.com. A lively restaurant with plenty of glass
that makes the most of the harbour views. They
serve glistening seafood platters, fresh fish dishes

and lighter snacks such as Thai fish cakes (£12.95)
or mussels (£6.95). Moderate–expensive.

Kitchen Garden 14 George St ☎01631/566332,
ⓦwww.kitchengardenoban.co.uk. Impressive,
central deli and licensed café offering all-day
breakfast and delicious snacks on the mezzanine,
open in the evenings in peak season.

The Waterfront 1 Railway Pier ☎01631/563110,
ⓦwww.waterfrontoban.co.uk. Despite the unprepossessing exterior, this is a great place with an
open kitchen rustling up impressive dishes using
scallops, langoustine and the best of the daily
catch. Mains average £15, or you can get fish and
chips for under a tenner.

Isle of Kerrera

One of the best places to escape from the crowds that plague Oban is the low-lying
island of **Kerrera**, which shelters Oban Bay from the worst of the westerly winds.
Measuring just five miles by two, the island is easily explored on foot. The most
prominent landmark is the **Hutcheson's Monument**, best viewed, appropriately
enough, from the ferries heading out of Oban, as it commemorates David
Hutcheson, one of the Victorian founders of what is now Caledonian MacBrayne.
The most appealing vistas, however, are from Kerrera's highest point, **Càrn
Breugach** (620ft), over to Mull, the Slate Islands, Lismore, Jura and beyond.

The ferry lands roughly halfway down the east coast, at the north end of
Horseshoe Bay, where King Alexander II died in 1249. If the weather's good and
you feel like lazing by the sea, head for the island's finest sandy beach, **Slatrach
Bay**, on the west coast, one mile northwest of the ferry jetty. Otherwise, there's a
very rewarding trail down to **Gylen Castle**, a clifftop ruin enjoying a majestic
setting on the south coast, built in 1582 by the MacDougalls and burnt to the
ground by the Covenanter General Leslie in 1647. You can head back to the ferry
via the Drove Road, where cattle from Mull and other islands were once herded to
be swum across the sound to the market in Oban.

The passenger and bicycle **ferry** crosses regularly (summer every 30min; winter
every 1–2hr; ☎01631/563665; £5) through the day from the mainland two miles
down the Gallanach road from Oban. In summer, **bus** #431 from Oban train
station connects with the ferry once a day. Kerrera has a population of around
thirty – and no shop, so if you're planning to self cater then bring food. However,
you can eat home-made veggie **snacks** at the *Kerrera Teagarden* (Easter–Sept Wed–
Sun only), located in a nice spot at Lower Gylen, a 45-minute walk from the ferry.
Right beside this is the seven-bed *Kerrera Bunkhouse* (☎01631/570223, ⓦwww
.kerrerabunkhouse.co.uk), a converted eighteenth-century stable building, with a
byre living space for hire by the evening in order to watch films. They also rent a
room in the farmhouse for B&B (❶). For more **B&B** or self-catering accommodation enquire at *Ardentrive Farm* (☎01631/567180, ⓔdavid@ardentrive.fsnet.co
.uk; ❶), at the north of the island.

North of Oban

Just beyond the northern satellite suburbs of Oban, on a strategic promontory
overlooking the important water crossroads at the mouth of Loch Etive, lie the
ruins of **Dunstaffnage Castle** (April–Sept daily 9.30am–5.30pm; Oct daily
9.30am–4.30pm; Nov–March Mon–Wed, Sat & Sun 9.30am–4.30pm; HS;

£3.70). Originally built as a thirteenth-century MacDougall fort, garrisoned by government forces during the 1745 rebellion, and briefly a prison for Flora McDonald, the castle's most impressive feature is its vast curtain-wall.

A couple of miles further up the A85, at the straggling village of **CONNEL**, you can't fail to admire the majestic, steel cantilever **Connel Bridge**, built in 1903 to take the old branch railway line across the sea cataract at the mouth of Loch Etive, north to Fort William. The name "Connel" comes from the Gaelic *conghail* ("tumultuous flood"), created by tidal streams rushing over a ledge of rock. Known as the Falls of Lora, this is one of the few tidal waterfalls in the country and looks as menacing as it does spectacular. If you want to stay out here in Connel as a mellower alternative to Oban, *Ards House* (℡01631/710255, www.ardshouse .com; ●), a whitewashed Victorian villa by the main road overlooking the water, is a pleasant option, while a good place to admire the kayakers tackling the tidal falls is modern *Strumhor* guesthouse (℡01631/710167, www.strumhor.co.uk; ●), whose proprietors run sea-kayaking courses from beginners upwards (www .seafreedomkayak.co.uk). The *Wide-Mouthed Frog* (℡01631/567005, www .widemouthedfrog.com; mid-Feb to Dec), on the way to Oban at Dunstaffnage Marina, serves pub grub and has tables outside with views over to the castle.

On the north side of the Connel Bridge lies the hammerhead peninsula of **Benderloch** (from *beinn eadar da loch*, "hill between two lochs"), which harbours three of Argyll's more interesting **places to stay**. Standing on its own, right above the beach just west of the village of Benderloch, A *Dun Na Mara* (℡01631/720233, www.dunnamara.com; ●) is a fine Arts and Crafts–style holiday home where highly stylish contemporary decor is complemented by the warm hospitality (and lavish breakfasts) of its two young architect owners. Further up the A828 you can stay at *Barcaldine House* (℡01631/720219, www.barcaldinehouse.co.uk; ●), a stylish, early Georgian house built for the Campbells of Barcaldine. If you have an unlimited budget you might like to stay at the area's most exclusive hotel, the *Isle of Eriska*, a luxury, turreted, Scottish Baronial place with a spa, pool and upmarket dining room. It's run by the Buchanan-Smiths on their own three-hundred-acre island off the northern point of Benderloch (℡01631/720371, www.eriska -hotel.co.uk; ●).

Since the weather in this part of Scotland can be bad at almost any time of the year, it's as well to know about the **Scottish Sea Life Sanctuary** (daily 10am–5pm, with earlier closing time in winter; £12.50 though cheaper if bought online; www.sealsanctuary.co.uk), which is to be found on the A828, along the southern shores of Loch Creran. Here you can see loads of sea creatures at close quarters, touch the (non-)stingrays, do a bit of rockpool dipping, keep a look out for the resident otters and learn about how common seal orphan pups are rescued and returned to the wild.

Appin

The next peninsula after Benderloch is **Appin**, best known as the setting for Robert Louis Stevenson's *Kidnapped*, a fictionalized account of the "Appin Murder" of 1752, when Colin Campbell was shot in the back, allegedly by one of the disenfranchised Stewart clan.

The name Appin derives from the Gaelic *abthaine*, meaning "lands belonging to the abbey", in this case the one on the island of Lismore (see p.78), which is linked to the peninsula by passenger ferry from **PORT APPIN**, a pretty little fishing village at the peninsula's westernmost tip. Overlooking a host of tiny little islands dotted around Loch Linnhe, with Lismore and the mountains of Morvern and Mull in the background, this is, without doubt, one of Argyll's most picturesque

spots. The *Pierhouse Hotel* (℡01631/730302, ⓦwww.pierhousehotel.co.uk; ⑥),
nicely situated right by the ferry, has a popular bar and an expensive seafood
restaurant.

Framed magnificently as you wind along the single-track road to Port Appin is
one of Argyll's most romantic ruined castles, the much-photographed sixteenth-
century ruins of **Castle Stalker** (open irregular hours; ℡01631/740315 or
730354, ⓦwww.castlestalker.com). Offering one of the best outlooks over the
castle, the pleasant, modern *Castle Stalker View* **café** and shop (daily except Nov–
Dec Thurs–Sun, closed Jan) is a short distance up the road to Ballachulish. **Bike
rental** is available from Port Appin Bikes (℡01631/730391) and it's worth noting
that bicycles travel for free on the passenger ferry to Lismore (see below). For other
outdoor pursuits, head for the Linnhe Marine Water Sports Centre
(℡07721/503981; May–Sept) in Lettershuna (just north of Castle Stalker), which
rents out boats of all shapes and sizes, offers sailing and windsurfing lessons, not to
mention water-skiing, clay-pigeon shooting and even pony trekking.

Isle of Lismore

Lying in the middle of Loch Linnhe, to the north of Oban, and barely rising above
a hillock, the narrow island of **Lismore** (ⓦwww.isleoflismore.com) offers
wonderful gentle walking and cycling opportunities, with unrivalled views, in fine
weather, across to the mountains of Morvern, Lochaber and Mull. Legend has it
that St Columba and Moluag both fancied the skinny island as a missionary base,
but as they raced towards it Moluag cut off his finger and threw it ashore ahead of
Columba, claiming the land for himself. Of Moluag's sixth-century foundation
nothing remains, but from 1236 until 1507 the island served as the seat of the
bishop of Argyll. Lismore is one of the most fertile of the Inner Hebrides – its
name, coined by Moluag himself, derives from the Gaelic *lios mór*, meaning "great
garden" – and before the Clearances (see p.426) it supported nearly 1400 inhabitants; the population today is only 180, half of them over 60.

Lismore is about ten miles long and a mile wide, and the ferry from Oban lands
at **ACHNACROISH**, roughly halfway along the eastern coastline. To get to
grips with the history of the island and its Gaelic culture, follow the signs to the
Heritage Centre, **Ionad Naomh Moluag** (May–Sept daily 11am–5pm; March,
April & Oct to mid Nov daily noon–3pm; £3.50), a turf-roofed, timber-clad
building with a permanent exhibition on Lismore, a reference library, a gift shop
and a **café** with an outdoor terrace. Your ticket also covers entry to the nearby
restored nineteenth-century cottar's (landless tenant's) cottage, **Tigh Iseabal
Dhaibh**, with its traditionally built stone walls, birch roof timbers and thatched
roof. In **CLACHAN** you'll find the diminutive, whitewashed fourteenth-
century **Cathedral of St Moluag**, whose choir was reduced in height and
converted into the parish church in 1749; inside you can see a few of the original
seats for the upper clergy, a stone basin in the south wall and several medieval
doorways. Due east of the church – head north up the road and take the turning
signposted on the right – the circular **Tirefour Broch**, over two thousand years
old, occupies a commanding position and boasts walls almost 10ft thick in
places. West of Clachan are the much more recent ruins of **Castle Coeffin**, a
twelfth-century MacDougall fortress once believed to have been haunted by the
ghost of Beothail, sister of the Norse prince Caiffen. A few other places worth
exploring are **Sailean**, an abandoned quarry village further south along the west
coast, with its disused kilns and cottages; the ruins of **Achanduin Castle**, in the
southwest, where the bishops are thought to have resided; and Barr Mór (416ft),
the island's highest point.

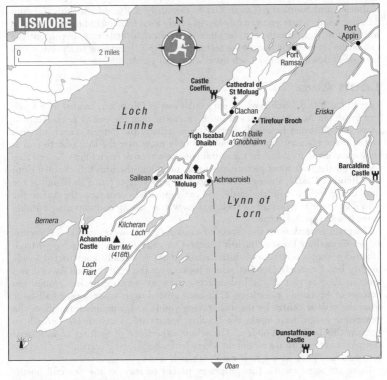

▼ *Oban*

Practicalities

Two **ferries** serve Lismore: a small CalMac car ferry from Oban to Achnacroish (Mon–Sat 4–5 daily, 2 on Sun; 50min), and a shorter passenger- and bicycle-only crossing from Port Appin to Point, the island's north point (daily hourly; 10min). **Accommodation** on the island is extremely limited: try the budget B&B at the *Schoolhouse* (☎01631/760262; ➊), north of Clachan, which also serves evening meals; or Elizabeth Kilmurray's popular B&B in Achnacroish (☎01631/760260 or 07760/260008). **Bike rental** is available from Lismore Bike Hire (☎01631/760213) – they'll deliver to the ferry if asked.

Taynuilt and Loch Etive

TAYNUILT, seven miles east of Connel, at the point where the River Awe flows into the sea at **Loch Etive**, is a small but sprawling village, best known for its iron-smelting works. To reach this industrial heritage site, follow the signpost off the A85 to **Bonawe Iron Furnace** (April–Sept daily 9.30am–5.30pm; HS; £4.20), which was originally founded by Cumbrian ironworkers in 1753. A whole series of buildings in various states of repair are scattered across the factory site, which employed six hundred people at its height, and eventually closed down in 1876.

From the pier beyond the iron furnace, **boat cruises** (Easter to Christmas 3 sailings: 10am [2hr], noon [2hr], 2pm [3hr]; £10/£15) check out the local seals and explore the otherwise inaccessible reaches of Loch Etive; phone Loch Etive Cruises (☎01866/822430) for more details. A mile or so east up the A85 from Taynuilt, a sign invites you down a minor road to visit the tucked-away **Inverawe**

Fisheries and Smokery (Easter–Oct & Dec daily 8.30am–5pm; Nov Fri–Sun 8.30am–5pm), where you can buy lots of lovely local food including traditionally smoked fish and mussels, eat the same in their casual little café, check out the exhibition on traditional smoking techniques (£1.50), learn how to fly-fish, or go for a stroll down to nearby Loch Etive with your picnic.

Loch Awe

Legend has it that **Loch Awe**, twenty miles east of Oban, was created by a witch and inhabited by a monster even more gruesome than the one at Loch Ness. At more than 25 miles in length, Loch Awe is actually the longest stretch of fresh water in the country, but most travellers only encounter the loch's north end as they speed along its shores by car or train on the way to or from Oban. Several tiny islands on the loch sport picturesque ruins, including the fifteenth-century ruins of **Kilchurn Castle**, strategically situated on a rocky spit (once an island) at the head of the loch; to visit the castle, you can approach by foot from the A85 to the east. The castle is essentially a shell, but its watery setting and imposing outlines make it well worth a detour.

The main attraction on the shores of Loch Awe is, however, rather less picturesque. **Cruachan Power Station** (Easter–Oct daily 9.30am–5pm; Nov–March 10am–3.45pm; £6; Ⓦ www.visitcruachan.co.uk) is actually constructed inside mighty Ben Cruachan (3693ft), which looms over the head of Loch Awe; it was built in 1965 as part of the hydroelectric network which generates around ten percent of Scotland's electricity. Half-hour guided tours set off every half-hour from the **visitor centre** by the loch, taking you to a viewing platform above the generating room deep inside the "hollow mountain", a cavern big enough to contain the Tower of London. The whole experience of visiting an industrial complex hidden within a mountain is very James Bond, and it certainly pulls in the tour coaches. They have a basic **café** with loch views.

There are some terrific though pricey **places to stay** on the peaceful north-western shores of Loch Awe around the hamlet of **KILCHRENAN**, reached by a back road from Taynuilt. The *Taychreggan Hotel* (Ⓣ01866/833211, Ⓦwww .taychregganhotel.co.uk; Ⓞ) is an old drovers' inn by the loch now plumped up into an upmarket retreat, while the *Ardanaiseig Hotel* (Ⓣ01866/833333, Ⓦwww .ardanaiseig.com; Ⓞ; closed Jan) is a wonderfully secluded, romantic escape set in a palatial Scottish Baronial pile four miles to the northeast down a dead-end track. Both these hotels have superb, though expensive, restaurants, and the *Ardanaiseig* also boasts its own glorious **gardens** (daily 9.30am–dusk), home of rare species of azalea and rhododendron, worth visiting even if you're not staying here. *Roineabhal Country House* is a superior B&B (Ⓣ01866 833207, Ⓦwww.roineabhal.com, minimum 2-night booking; Ⓞ), very stylish and comfortable and serving fine dinners as well as breakfast.

Isle of Mull

The second largest of the Inner Hebrides, **Mull** (Ⓦwww.holidaymull.co.uk) is by far the most accessible: just forty minutes from Oban by ferry. As so often, first impressions largely depend on the weather – it is the wettest of the Hebrides (and that's saying something) – for without the sun the large tracts of moorland, particularly around the island's highest peak, Ben More (3169ft), can appear bleak and unwelcoming. There are, however, areas of more gentle pastoral scenery around **Dervaig** in the north and **Salen** on the east coast, and the indented west coast varies from the sandy beaches around **Calgary** to the cliffs of Loch na Keal. The most common mistake is to try and "do" the island in a day or two: flogging up the main road to the picturesque capital of **Tobermory**, then covering the fifty-odd miles between there and Fionnphort, in order to visit **Iona**. Mull is a place that will grow on you only if you have the time and patience to explore.

Historically, crofting, whisky distilling and fishing supported the islanders (*Muileachs*), but the population – which peaked at ten thousand – decreased dramatically in the late nineteenth century due to the Clearances and the 1846 potato famine. On Mull, it is a trend that has been reversed, mostly owing to the large influx of settlers from elsewhere in the country, which has brought the current population up to over 2500. One of the main reasons for this resurgence is, of course, tourism – more than half a million visitors come here each year. Mull makes particular efforts to draw visitors to **special events** through the year: these annual events include a wildlife week in May, the Mendelssohn on Mull Festival in July, which commemorates the composer's visit here in 1829, and a rally car event around the island's winding roads in October.

Arrival and transport

Craignure is the main ferry terminal, with a frequent daily **car ferry** link to Oban (booking ahead advisable). A smaller and less-expensive car ferry crosses daily from Lochaline on the Morvern peninsula (see p.226) to Fishnish, six miles northwest of Craignure. Another even smaller car ferry connects Kilchoan on the Ardnamurchan peninsula (see p.227) with Tobermory, the island capital. **Public transport** on Mull is not too bad on the main A849, but there's more or less no service along the west coast. If **driving**, note that the roads are still predominantly single-track, with passing places, which can slow journeys down considerably. If

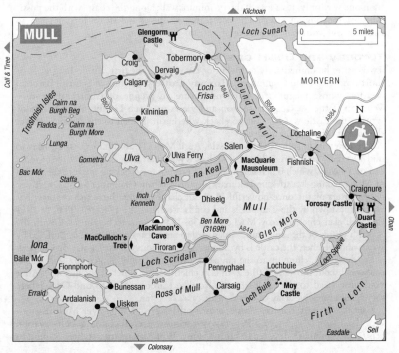

you're looking to rent a cottage on Mull, Ⓦ www.isleofmullcottages.com and Ⓦ www.islandholidaycottages.com feature some good rustic options.

Craignure and around

CRAIGNURE is little more than a scattering of cottages, though there is a small shop, a bar, some toilets and a CalMac ticket and **tourist office** – the only one on the island open daily all year round – situated opposite the pier. The eiteheenth-century whitewashed *Craignure Inn* (Ⓣ 01680/812305, Ⓦ www.craignure-inn .co.uk; ❹), just a minute's stroll up the road towards Fionnphort, is a snug **pub** to hole up in, with decent rooms and food. Along the side road leading to Mull Rail, there's also a well-equipped **campsite** run by Shieling Holidays (Ⓣ 01680/812496, Ⓦ www.shielingholidays.co.uk; April–Oct) set above a shingle beach with good views over to the Morvern shore. The campsite also offers accommodation in "shielings" (large, furnished, hard-top tents), and has boats, canoes and bikes for rent. Another pleasant place to camp is the well-equipped *Balmeanach Park* site (Ⓣ 01680/300342; April–Oct), five miles up the A849 at Fishnish, which has a small tearoom attached. There are several B&Bs in the area, but the best **guesthouse** is the *Old Mill Cottage* (Ⓣ 01680/812442, Ⓦ www.oldmillmull.com; ❹), a sensitively converted mill, three miles south on the A849 in Lochdon; they also provide attractive self-catering accommodation.

The most memorable mode of transport available at Craignure is the diminutive, narrow-gauge Mull & West Highland Railway, commonly known as **Mull Rail** (Easter–Oct; £5 return; Ⓣ 01680/812494, Ⓦ www.mullrail.co.uk), built in the 1980s and the only working railway in the Scottish islands. The Craignure station is situated beyond the Shieling Holidays campsite, and the line stretches southeast for about a mile and a half to Torosay Castle (see below). If you prefer to take the train one way only, it's a lovely thirty-minute walk along the coast (with the possibility of spotting an otter). The company uses diesel and steam locomotives, so ring ahead if you want to be sure of a steam-driven train.

Torosay and Duart castles

Two castles lie immediately southeast of Craignure. The first, a mile-long walk or short train-ride from Craignure, is **Torosay Castle**, a full-blown Scottish Baronial creation whose magnificent **gardens** feature an avenue of eighteenth-century Venetian statues, a Japanese section and views up Loch Linnhe. At the time of writing the castle was for sale; to check whether it is open to the public, contact the tourist office in Craignure.

Very different in style is **Duart Castle** (April Mon–Thurs 10.30am–4pm; May to mid-Oct daily 10.30am–5.30pm; £5.30; Ⓦ www.duartcastle.com), a couple of miles east of Torosay, which is perched on a rocky promontory sticking out into the Sound of Mull, making it a striking landmark from the Oban–Craignure ferry. Duart was headquarters of the once-powerful MacLean clan from the thirteenth century, but was burnt down by the Campbells and confiscated after the 1745 rebellion. In 1911 the 26th clan chief, Fitzroy MacLean (1835–1936) – not to be confused with the Scottish writer of the same name – managed to buy it back and restore it. Buffeted by winds and weather, the castle is by no means a luxurious country seat: you can peek at the dungeons, climb up to the ramparts, study the family photos and learn about the world scout movement (the 27th clan chief became Chief Scout in 1959). After your visit, head to the castle's pretty, barnlike tearoom (May to mid-Oct), where there's an impressive array of home-made cakes on offer.

A short way past Torosay Castle, a turn-off leads to **Wings over Mull** (Easter–Oct 10.30am–5.30pm; £4.50; Ⓦ www.wingsovermull.com), a conservation centre and sanctuary devoted to birds of prey. While keen birdwatchers coming to

Mull have an excellent chance of seeing some of Britain's finest birds of prey in the wild, the visitors' centre here, based in a converted steading, has lots of background information about all kinds of owls, hawks, falcons and eagles, as well as details about the work done at the centre to rescue and preserve these species. More memorably, you can take a close look at around forty different birds housed in cages and pens nearby. They're not cooped up all the time, however, with flying displays taking place at noon, 2pm and 4pm each day.

Tobermory

Mull's chief town, **TOBERMORY**, at the northern tip of the island, is easily the most attractive fishing port on the west coast of Scotland, its clusters of brightly coloured houses and boats sheltering in a bay backed by a steep bluff. Founded in 1788 by the British Society for Encouraging Fisheries, it never really took off as a fishing port and only survived due to the steady influx of crofters evicted from other parts of the island during the Clearances. With a population of more than 800, it is the most important settlement on Mull, and if you're staying any length of time on the island you're bound to want to visit, not least because it has a Womble named after it (or, if you're under 10, because it's the setting for the children's TV show *Balamory*).

Information and accommodation

The **tourist office** (April–Oct daily) is in the same building as the CalMac ticket office on the pier at the far end of Main Street. If you want to **rent a bike**, head to Archibald Brown, the endearingly old-fashioned ironmongers on Main Street (℡01688/302020, ⓦwww.browns-tobermory.co.uk). At the large whitewashed Harbour Visitor Centre you can book a variety of **boat outings**, from a half-hour seal trip (£6) to an all-day Whalewatch Explorer Cruise (£59) with an island landing for lunch.

The small, friendly SYHA **hostel** is on Main Street (℡0870/004 1151, ⓦwww .syha.org.uk; March–Oct) and has internet and laundry facilities. The nearest **campsite** is spruce *Newdale* (℡01688/302624, ⓦwww.tobermory-campsite .co.uk; April–Oct), nicely situated one and a half miles uphill from Tobermory on the B8073 to Dervaig.

Baliscate Guest House Salen Rd ℡01688/ 302251, ⓦwww.baliscate.co.uk. Good-quality self-catering apartments in an imposing white-washed Victorian guesthouse with a large garden, set back from the road to Salen on the edge of Tobermory. ❺

Glengorm Castle Near Tobermory ℡01688/302321, ⓦwww.glengorm castle.co.uk. Fairy-tale, rambling Baronial mansion in a superb, secluded setting, five miles northwest of Tobermory, with incredible coastal views, lovely gardens and local walks. Guests get use of the castle's wood-panelled library and lounge; the bedrooms are large and full of splendid features and there are self-catering cottages available too. ❼

Highland Cottage Breadalbane St ℡01688/302030, ⓦwww.highlandcottage.co.uk. Super-luxury B&B run by a very welcoming couple in a quiet street high above the harbour; the outstanding four-course Scottish menu in the restaurant costs around £40 a head. ❽

Sonas House Upper town, by the golf course ℡01688 302304, ⓦwww.sonashouse.co.uk. Fairly plain but comfortable rooms with terrific views over the Sound of Mull; they have a small swimming pool. ❼

Strongarbh House Upper Tobermory ℡01688/302319, ⓦwww.strongarbh.com. A super-stylish but friendly B&B in a large Victorian villa, with a library, boardgames and wi-fi. Two rooms have four-posters. ❺

Tobermory Hotel Main St ℡01688/302091, ⓦwww.thetobermoryhotel.com. Smallish, fairly smart and comfortable hotel converted from fisher-mens' cottages, with fifteen rooms situated right on the harbourfront. ❺

Western Isles Hotel Above the harbour ℡01688/302012, ⓦwww.westernisleshotel.com. The decor – moth-eaten stag heads and floral drapes – isn't for everyone, but the *Western Isles* is undergoing gradual renovation. The setting above town is impressive, and the hotel has a glamorous pedigree as a location for the Powell and Press-burger classic *I Know Where I'm Going*. ❺

The Town

The harbour – known as **Main Street** – is one long parade of multicoloured hotels, guesthouses, restaurants and shops, and you could happily spend an hour or so meandering around. A good wet-weather retreat is the **Mull Museum** (Easter to mid-Oct Mon–Fri 10am–4pm, Sat 10am–1pm; free), further along Main Street, a tiny room with a great deal of information and artefacts – including a few objects salvaged from the *San Juan de Sicilia*, a ship from the Spanish Armada which lies at the bottom of Tobermory harbour.

A stiff climb up Back Brae will bring you to the island's main arts centre, **An Tobar** (March–Dec Mon–Sat 10am–5pm; May–Sept also Sun 1–4pm; free; Ⓦwww.antobar.co.uk), housed in a converted Victorian schoolhouse. The small but attractive centre hosts exhibitions and a variety of live events, and contains a café with comfy sofas set before a real fire. The rest of the upper town, laid out on a classic grid-plan, merits a stroll, if only for the great views over the bay.

Alternatively, there's the minuscule **Tobermory Distillery** (Easter–Oct Mon–Fri 10am–4/5pm; £3.50) at the south end of the bay, founded in 1795 but closed down three times since then. Today, it's back in business and offers a pretty desultory guided tour, rounded off with a dram. Meanwhile, five miles northwest of town, along a dead-end single-track road, lies **Glengorm Castle**, a Scots Baronial pile overlooking the sea which offers accommodation (see p.83) and also has an attractively converted steading, housing a café, well-stocked farm shop, craft shop and art gallery (Easter to mid-Oct). You can walk around their attractive walled garden or make for the longer forest, archeological and coastal trails.

Eating

Main Street heaves with **places to eat**, including a highly rated *Fish & Chip Van* (Mon–Sat) on the old pier which serves up scallops and chips alongside more traditional fish suppers. Fine **picnic** fodder, fresh bread and goodies can be found at the excellent Tobermory Bakery, also on the harbourfront.

Café Fish The Pier ☎01688/301253, Ⓦwww.thecafefish.com. Great little place above the tourist office, which cooks up the best of the catch from their own boat. Inexpensive–moderate.

The Glassbarn Tearooms Glengorm Rd ☎01688/302235. The prettiest eating option on Mull – a spacious glasshouse with sofas and wooden furniture serving good coffee, snacks and cakes. Walk through the cottage garden to visit the farmshop of the Isle of Mull dairy.

Highland Cottage Breadalbane St ☎01688/302030, Ⓦwww.highlandcottage.co.uk. B&B restaurant that serves dishes such as Tobermory scallops with parsnip mash and roast saddle of Ardnamurchan venison for around £37 for four courses. Expensive.

Mull Pottery Salen Rd ☎01688/302347. This pleasant café/bistro above Mull Pottery is a good option for imaginatively prepared meals using Mull produce including beef, venison and seafood. Inexpensive.

Water's Edge Main St ☎01688/302091, Ⓦwww.thetobermoryhotel.com. Restaurant in the *Tobermory Hotel* which serves up elegant seafood dishes. Expensive.

Pubs, live music and entertainment

The lively bar of the *Mishnish Hotel* on Main Street has been the most popular local **drinking** hole for many years, and features live music at the weekend. On the opposite side of the bay, near the distillery, is *MacGochan's*, a purpose-built, though pleasant enough, pub, which also offers occasional live music. For the latest **events** in Tobermory (or anywhere else on Mull), pick up the free monthly newsletter *Round & About*, and/or buy a copy of *Am Muileach*, the monthly island newspaper. An Tobar (see above) is an excellent venue for concerts and ceilidhs, while the **Mull Theatre** (☎01688/302828, Ⓦwww.mulltheatre.com) performs around the island and has a box office at the far end of Main Street.

Wildlife boat trips around Mull

Boat trips leave from several different places around Mull, with prices ranging from around £6 for a half-hour seal cruise to £59 for a full day **whale-watching**. Sea Life Surveys (Easter–Oct; ℡01688/302916, Ⓦwww.sealifesurveys.com), linked to the Hebridean Whale and Dolphin Trust, focuses on seeking out the whales (minke and even killer whales are the most common), porpoises, dolphins and basking sharks that spend time in the waters around the Hebrides. Based in the Harbour Visitor Centre in Tobermory, the same outfit also operates friendly Ecocruz, which sticks to coastal waters, and is particularly good for families. Rather more sedate are the wildlife cruises with Hebridean Adventure (mid-May to Sept Mon–Sat ℡01688/302044, Ⓦwww.hebrideanadventure.co.uk; half-day £35, full day £70), which head out of Tobermory harbour; they also do a dinner cruise.

Dervaig and Calgary

The gently undulating countryside west of Tobermory, beyond the freshwater Mishnish lochs, provides some of the most beguiling scenery on the island. Added to this, the road out west, the B8073, is exceptionally dramatic, with fiendish switchbacks much appreciated during the annual Mull Rally, which takes place each October. Loch Frisa, a long slash in the landscape south of the road, is an established nesting place for **white-tailed (or sea) eagles**. There's a well-placed hide which has close-up, live CCTV pictures of the nest; if you're here between April and July, when the birds are nesting, guided access to the hide is available through the RSPB (£3; bookings on ℡01688/302038).

The only village of any size on this side of the island is **DERVAIG**, which nestles beside narrow Loch Chumhainn, just eight miles southwest of Tobermory, distinguished by its unusual pencil-shaped church spire and single street of dinky whitewashed cottages and old corrugated-iron shacks. Dervaig has a shop, a bookshop/café and a wide choice of **places to stay**. At the upper end of the scale, Victorian *Druimard Country House* (℡01688/400345, Ⓦwww.druimard.co.uk; ④), located on the fringe of Dervaig, is a pleasant, comfy place serving good dinners. Local food is also served at the *Druimnacroish Hotel* (℡01688/400274, Ⓦwww.druimnacroish.co.uk; March–Nov; ③), a lovely country house in a rural setting two miles out on the Salen road, though you need to book in advance. There are several pleasant B&Bs, including the excellent *Cuin Lodge* (℡01688/400346, Ⓦwww.cuinlodgemull.co.uk; ④), an old shooting lodge overlooking the loch, to the northwest of the village. There's also a modern **bunkhouse** (℡01688/4004291 or 07919/870664) in the village hall, with bedding provided and disabled facilities, while the *Bellachroy*, a rugged early seventeenth-century **inn** with an attractive whitewashed interior, serves good seafood and real ales and offers six plain but cosy rooms (℡01688/400314, Ⓦwww.bellachroyhotel.co.uk; ⑤).

The cross-country road takes you on to *Am Birlinn* (℡01688/400619, Ⓦwww.ambirlinnw5.com), a contemporary chalet-like **restaurant** serving up elegant food: lobster, scallops, venison and mussels feature. Beyond here is **CALGARY**, once a thriving crofting community, now a quiet glen which opens out onto Mull's finest sandy bay, backed by low-lying dunes and machair, with wonderful views over to Coll and Tiree. A few hundred yards back from the beach is the delightful 🎋 *Calgary Farmhouse* (℡01688/400256, Ⓦwww.calgary.co.uk), providing glamorous self-catering accommodation and an art-filled daytime **café**. A sculpture trail winds through the wooded hills behind the farm; you can buy a map (£1) at the entrance gate to help identify the artworks amongst the trees. Down by the beach itself, there's spectacular and very popular spot for **camping** rough; the only facilities are the basic public toilets. For the record: the city of Calgary in Canada does indeed take its name from this little village, though it was not so named by Mull emigrants, but by one Colonel McLeod of the North West Mounted Police, who once holidayed here.

Salen and around

SALEN, on the east coast halfway between Craignure and Tobermory, lies at the narrowest point on Mull, and is not a bad place to base yourself. **Accommodation** choices range from the hostel-style *Arle Lodge* (℡01680/300299, Ⓦwww .arlelodge.co.uk; ❸), with twin and family rooms four miles north of Salen on the road to Tobermory, to the pretty Victorian *Gruline Home Farm* **B&B** (℡01680/300581, Ⓦwww.gruline.com; ❺), a former farmhouse four miles southwest near the shores of Loch Na Keal, which serves up excellent and elaborate dinners (nonresidents must reserve). Simpler, less expensive B&B is available next door at *Barn Cottage* (℡01680/300451, Ⓦwww.barncottagemull .co.uk; ❷). Salen itself has a great place to **eat**: *Mediterranea* (℡01680/300200, Ⓦwww.mull-cuisine.co.uk; lunch Thurs–Sun, dinner nightly), which mixes engaging Scottish hospitality with Sicilian cooking. You can **rent bikes** from On Yer Bike (℡01680/300501), which has mountain bikes, hybrids and child trailers to rent.

Isle of Ulva

A chieftain to the Highlands bound/Cries "Boatman, do not tarry!/And I'll give thee a silver pound/To row us o'er the ferry!"/"Now who be ye, would cross Lochgyle/This dark and stormy water?"/"O I'm the chief of Ulva's isle,/And this, Lord Ullin's daughter."

Lord Ullin's Daughter by Thomas Campbell (1777–1844)

Around the time poet laureate Campbell penned this tragic poem, the population of **Ulva** (from the Norse *ulv øy*, or "wolf island") was a staggering 850, sustained by the huge quantities of kelp which were exported for glass and soap production. That was before the market for kelp collapsed and the 1846 potato famine hit, after which the remaining population was brutally evicted. Nowadays around fifteen people live here, and the island is littered with ruined crofts, not to mention a church, designed by Thomas Telford, which would once have seated over three hundred parishioners. It's great walking country, however, with several clearly marked paths crisscrossing the native woodland and the rocky heather moorland interior – and you're almost guaranteed to spot some of the abundant wildlife: at the very least deer, if not buzzards, golden eagles and even sea eagles, with seals and divers offshore. If you like to have a focus for your wanderings, head for the ruined crofting villages and basalt columns similar to those on Staffa along the island's southern coastline; for the island's highest point, Beinn Chreagach (1027ft); or along the north coast to Ulva's tidal neighbour, Gometra, off the west coast.

To **get to Ulva**, which lies just a hundred yards or so off the west coast of Mull, follow the signs for "Ulva Ferry" west from Salen or south from Calgary – if you've no transport, a postbus can get you there, but you'll have to make your own way back. From **Ulva Ferry**, a small bicycle/passenger-only ferry (£5 return) is available on demand (Mon–Fri 9am–5pm; June–Aug also Sun; at other times by arrangement on ℡01688/500226). ⚥ *The Boathouse*, near the ferry slip on the Ulva side, serves as a licensed **tearoom** selling soup, cakes, snacks, Guinness and Ulva oysters. You can learn more about the history of the island from the exhibition upstairs, and pop into the newly restored thatched smiddy nearby, housing **Sheila's Cottage**, which has been restored to the period when islander Sheila MacFadyen lived there in the first half of the last century. There's no accommodation, but with permission from the present owners (℡01688/500264, ©ulva @mull.com) you can **camp** rough overnight.

Isle of Staffa and the Treshnish Isles

Five miles southwest of Ulva, **Staffa** is one of the most romantic and dramatic of Scotland's many uninhabited islands. On its south side, the perpendicular rockface features an imposing series of black basalt columns, known as the Colonnade, which have been cut by the sea into cathedralesque caverns, most notably **Fingal's Cave**. The Vikings knew about the island – the name derives from their word for "Island of Pillars" – but it wasn't until 1772 that it was "discovered" by the world. Turner painted it, Wordsworth explored it, but Mendelssohn's *Die Fingalshöhle* (the lovely *Hebrides Overture*), inspired by the sounds of the sea-wracked caves he heard on a visit here in 1829, did most to popularize the place – after which Queen Victoria gave her blessing, too. The polygonal basalt organ-pipes were created some sixty million years ago when a huge mass of molten basalt burst forth onto land and, as it cooled, solidified into hexagonal crystals. The same phenomenon produced the Giant's Causeway in Northern Ireland and Celtic folk tales often link the two with rival giants Fionn mac Cumhail (Irish) and Fingal (Scottish) throwing rocks at each other across the Irish Sea.

Northwest of Staffa lie the **Treshnish Isles**, an archipelago of uninhabited volcanic islets, none more than a mile or two across. The most distinctive is **Bac Mór**, shaped like a Puritan's hat and popularly dubbed the Dutchman's Cap. **Lunga**, the largest island is a summer nesting-place for hundreds of sea birds, in particular guillemots, razorbills and puffins, as well as a breeding ground for seals. The two most northerly islands, **Cairn na Burgh More** and **Cairn na Burgh Beag**, have the remains of ruined castles, the first of which served as a lookout post

---

Whales and dolphins

Watching whales, dolphins and porpoises – collectively known as cetaceans – is a growing tourist industry in Scotland. The Moray Firth (see p.216) is one of the best places in the UK to watch **bottlenose dolphins**, but the waters around the Inner Hebrides have, if anything, a wider variety of cetaceans on offer. Although there are several operators who offer whale-watching boat trips from Oban and Tobermory (see p.85), it is quite possible to catch sight of marine mammals from the shore, or from a ferry. The chief problem is trying to identify what you've seen.

The most common sightings are of **harbour porpoises**, the smallest of the marine mammals, which are about the size of an adult human and have a fairly small dorsal fin. Porpoises are easily confused with dolphins; however, if you see it leap out of the water, then you can be sure it's a dolphin, as porpoises only break the surface with their backs and fins. If you spot a whale, the likelihood is that it's a **minke whale**, which grows to about 30ft in length, making it a mere tiddler in the whale world, but a good four or five times bigger than a porpoise. Minkes are baleen whales, which is to say they have no teeth; instead, they gulp huge quantities of water and sift their food through plates of whalebone. Whales do several things dolphins and porpoises can't do, such as blowing water high into the air, and breaching, which is when they launch themselves out of the water and belly-flop down. The two other whale species regularly seen in Hebridean waters are the **killer whale** or orca, distinguished by its very tall, pointed, dorsal fin, and the **pilot whale**, which is even smaller than the minke, has no white on it, and no throat grooves.

for the Lords of the Isles and was last garrisoned in the Civil War; Cairn na Burgh Beag hasn't been occupied since the 1715 Jacobite uprising.

From April to October several operators offer **boat trips** to Staffa and the Treshnish Isles. Long-established Turus Mara (☎0800/085 8786, ⓦwww .turusmara.com) sets out from Ulva Ferry and is a classy outfit, charging around £50 return, as does Gordon Grant Marine (☎01681/700338, ⓦwww.staffatours .com), who depart from Fionnphort. If you just want to go to Staffa, try Iolaire (☎01681/700358, ⓦwww.staffatrips.f9.co.uk), who charge around £20 for passage from Fionnphort.

Ben More and the Ardmeanach peninsula

From the southern shores of Loch na Keal, which almost splits Mull in two, rise the terraced slopes of **Ben More** (3169ft) – literally "big mountain" – a mighty extinct volcano, and the only Munro in the Hebrides outside of Skye. It's most easily climbed from Dhiseig, halfway along the loch's southern shores, though an alternative route is to climb up to the col between Beinn Fhada and A'Chioch, and approach via the mountain's eastern ridge. Further west along the shore the road carves through spectacular overhanging cliffs before heading south past the Gribun rocks which face the tiny island of **Inch Kenneth**, where Unity Mitford lived until her death in 1948. There are great views out to Staffa and the Treshnish Isles as the road leaves the coast behind, climbing over the pass to Loch Scribain, where it eventually joins the equally dramatic Glen More road (A849) from Craignure.

If you're properly equipped for walking, however, you can explore the **Ardmeanach peninsula**, to the west of the road, on foot. On the north coast, a mile or so from the road, is **Mackinnon's Cave** – at 100ft high, one of the largest caves in the Hebrides, and accessible only at low tide. As so often, there's a legend attached to the cave, which tells of an entire party, led by a lone piper, who were once devoured here by evil spirits. On the south coast of the peninsula, it's a longer, rougher six-mile hike from the road to **MacCulloch's Tree**, a forty-foot-high conifer that was engulfed by a lava flow some fifty million years ago and is now embedded in the cliffs at Rubha na h-Uambha. You'll need a good map, sturdy boots and, again, you need to time your arrival with a falling tide. The area is NTS-owned and there is a car park just before *Tiroran House* (☎01681/705232, ⓦwww.tiroran.com; ⑥ including afternoon tea), a beautiful secluded **hotel** with six rooms, cosy lounges, good home-cooking and a lovely, lush, south-facing garden.

The Ross of Mull

Stretching for twenty miles west as far as Iona is Mull's rocky southernmost peninsula, the **Ross of Mull**, which, like much of Scotland, appears blissfully tranquil in good weather, and desolate and bleak in bad climes. Most visitors simply drive through the Ross en route to Iona, but if you have the time it's definitely worth considering exploring, or even staying, in this little-visited part of Mull.

The most scenic spots on the Ross are hidden away on the south coast. If you're approaching the Ross from Craignure, the first of these (to Lochbuie) is signposted even before you've negotiated the splendid Highland pass of **Glen More**, which brings you to the Ross itself. The road to **LOCHBUIE** skirts Loch Spelve, a sheltered sea loch, followed by freshwater loch Uisg, which is fringed by woodland, before emerging, after eight miles, on a fertile plain beside the sea. The bay here is rugged and wide, and overlooked by the handsome peak of Ben Buie (2352ft), to the northwest. Hidden behind a patch of Scots pine are the ivy-strewn ruins of **Moy**

Castle, an old MacLean stronghold; in the fields to the north is one of the few **stone circles** in the west of Scotland, dating from the second century BC, the tallest of its stones about 6ft high. The best **accommodation** in the vicinity is at *Barrachandroman* (℡01680/814220, Ⓦwww.barrachandroman.co.uk; ❹), a converted stone barn in Kinlochspelve, overlooking the sea loch. A popular and fairly easy walk is the five-mile hike west from Lochbuie along the coastal path to Carsaig (see below).

The main A849 road, single-track (for the most part), hugs the northern coastline of the Ross, passing, first off, the tiny settlement of **PENNYGHAEL**, home to the *Pennyghael Hotel* (℡01681/704288, Ⓦwww.pennyghaelhotel.com; ❺), which has a good restaurant serving island produce including crab, mussels, pork and Tobermory cheeses. A cheaper option is the rustic *Smithy* B&B (℡01681/704034, Ⓦwww.mull-bedandbreakfast.com; ❷), which also has a pretty waterside location and a view of Ben More. A rickety single-track road heads south four miles to **CARSAIG**, which enjoys an idyllic setting, looking south out to Colonsay, Islay and Jura. Most folk come here either to walk east to Lochbuie, or west under the cliffs, to the **Nuns' Cave**, where nuns from Iona are alleged to have hidden during the Reformation, and then, after four miles or so, at Malcolm's Point, the spectacular **Carsaig Arches**, formed by eroded sea-caves, which are linked to basalt cliffs.

Meanwhile, the main road continues for another eleven miles to **BUNESSAN**, the largest village on the peninsula, roughly two-thirds of the way along the Ross. Bunessan has a few useful shops and a reasonable pub, *The Argyll Arms Hotel*. A road connects Bunessan with the sandy bays of the south coast. A couple of miles out of the village, modern *Ardachy House Hotel* (℡01681/700505, Ⓦwww .ardachy.co.uk; March–Oct; ❻) overlooks the wide expanse of **Ardalanish Bay**. Just beyond the hotel, drop in at Ardalanish Weavers (daily tour 1pm; ℡01681/700265, Ⓦwww.ardalanishfarm.co.uk), where beautiful durable organic tweed is produced on Victorian looms originally from Torosay Castle. The tweed is snapped up by upmarket high-street stores, and is used for the elegant couture collection displayed in the small shop; you can also buy smaller items such as scarves, and balls of wool. The road continues to the more sheltered bay of sand and granite outcrops at neighbouring **UISKEN**, a mile to the east. The beach is a wonderful spot for wild **camping**, but ask permission first at *Uisken Croft* (℡01681/700307), just up the hill. From Uisken, the Lorn Ferry Service (April–Oct; ℡01951/200320) runs an occasional **passenger-only ferry** to Colonsay.

Fionnphort

The road ends at **FIONNPHORT**, facing Iona, probably the least attractive place to stay on the Ross. Partly to ease congestion on Iona, and to give their neighbours a slice of the tourist pound, Fionnphort was chosen as the site for the little-visited **Columba Centre** (Easter–Sept daily 10am–1pm & 2–5.30pm; free), whose small but well-presented exhibition outlines Iona's history, tells a little of Columba's life, and has a few facsimiles of the illuminated manuscripts produced by the island's monks.

For **B&B** in Fionnphort, try the sandstone Victorian villa of *Seaview* (℡01681/700235, Ⓦwww.seaview-mull.co.uk; ❸) or whitewashed *Staffa House* (℡01681/700677, Ⓦwww.staffahouse.co.uk; ❸), both of which are close to the ferry and the local pub, the *Keel Row*, which serves reasonable meals. For a treat, head to stylish and upmarket ⚓ *Ninth Wave* (℡01681/700757, Ⓦwww.ninth waverestaurant.co.uk) just outside the village, where the owner catches and then serves up crab and lobster; veggies are supplied from their kitchen garden. The simple *Fidden Farm* **campsite** (℡01681/700427; April–Sept), a mile or so south of Fionnphort, is a lovely place to camp, with direct access to the golden sands of

Fidden beach. Fidden beach looks out to the **Isle of Erraid**, where Robert Louis Stevenson is believed to have written *Kidnapped* while staying in one of the island's cottages; *Kidnapped*'s hero, David Balfour, is shipwrecked on the **Torran Rocks**, out to sea to the south of Erraid, beyond which lies the remarkable, stripy **Dubh Artach lighthouse**, built by Stevenson's father in 1862. In the book, Balfour spends a miserable time convinced that he's stranded on Erraid, which can, in fact, be reached across the sands on its eastern side at low tide. The island is now in Dutch ownership, and cared for by the Findhorn Community. **Bikes** can be rented from *Seaview* B&B.

Isle of Iona

Less than a mile off the southwest tip of Mull, **IONA** (ⓦ www.isle-of-iona.com) – just three miles long and not much more than a mile wide – has been a place of pilgrimage for several centuries, and a place of Christian worship for more than 1400 years. For it was to this flat Hebridean island that St Columba fled from Ireland in 563 and established a monastery which was responsible for the conversion of more or less all of pagan Scotland as well as much of northern England. This history and the island's splendid isolation have lent it a peculiar religiosity; in the much-quoted words of Dr Johnson, who visited in 1773, "That man is little to be envied…whose piety would not grow warmer among the ruins of Iona." Today, however, the island can barely cope with the constant flood of day-trippers, so to appreciate the special atmosphere and to have time to see the whole island, including the often overlooked west coast, you should plan on staying at least one night.

Some history

Whatever the truth about Columba's life (see below), in the sixth and seventh centuries Iona enjoyed a great deal of autonomy from Rome, establishing a specifically **Celtic Christian** tradition. Missionaries were sent out to the rest of Scotland and parts of England, and Iona quickly became a respected seat of learning and

St Columba

Legend has it that **St Columba** (Colum Cille), born in Donegal some time around 521, was a direct descendant of the semi-legendary Irish king, Niall of the Nine Hostages. A scholar and soldier priest, who founded numerous monasteries in Ireland, he is thought to have become involved in a bloody dispute with the king when he refused to hand over a copy of *St Jerome's Psalter,* copied illegally from the original owned by St Finian of Moville. This, in turn, provoked the Battle of Cúl Drebene (Cooldrumman) – also known as the **Battle of the Book** – at which Columba's forces won, though with the loss of over 3000 lives. The story goes that, repenting this bloodshed, Columba went into exile with twelve other monks, eventually settling on Iona in 563, allegedly because it was the first island he encountered from which he couldn't see his homeland. The bottom line, however, is that we know very little about Columba, though he undoubtedly became something of a cult figure after his death in 597. He was posthumously credited with miraculous feats such as defeating the Loch Ness monster – it only had to hear his voice and it recoiled in terror – and casting out snakes (and, some say, frogs) from the island. He is also famously alleged to have banned women and cows from Iona, exiling them to Eilean nam Ban (Woman's Island), just north of Fionnphort, for, as he believed, "Where there is a cow there is a woman, and where there is a woman there is mischief."

artistry; the monks compiled a vast library of intricately **illuminated manuscripts** – most famously the *Book of Kells* (now on display in Trinity College, Dublin) – while the masons excelled in carving peculiarly intricate crosses. Two factors were instrumental in the demise of the Celtic tradition: a series of Viking raids, the worst of which was the massacre of 68 monks on the sands of Martyrs' Bay in 806; and relentless pressure from the established Church, beginning with the Synod of Whitby in 664, which chose Rome over the Celtic Church, and culminated in its suppression by King David I in 1144.

In 1203, Iona became part of the mainstream Church with the establishment of an **Augustinian nunnery** and a **Benedictine monastery** by Reginald, son of Somerled, Lord of the Isles. During the Reformation, the entire complex was ransacked, the contents of the library burnt and all but three of the island's 360 crosses destroyed. Although plans were drawn up at various times to turn the abbey into a Cathedral of the Isles, nothing came of them until 1899, when the (then) owner, the eighth Duke of Argyll, donated the abbey buildings to the **Church of Scotland**, who restored the abbey church for worship over the course of the next decade. Iona's modern resurgence began in 1938, when **George MacLeod**, a minister from Glasgow, established a group of ministers, students and artisans to begin rebuilding the remainder of the monastic buildings. What began as a mostly male, Gaelic-speaking, strictly Presbyterian community is today a lay, mixed and ecumenical retreat. The entire abbey complex has been successfully restored, and is now looked after by Historic Scotland, while the island, apart from the church land and a few crofts, is in the care of the NTS.

Baile Mór

The passenger ferry from Fionnphort drops you off at the island's main village, **BAILE MÓR** (literally "Large Village"), which is in fact little more than a single terrace of cottages facing the sea. Just inland lie the extensive pink-granite ruins of the **Augustinian nunnery**, disused since the Reformation. A beautifully maintained garden now occupies the cloisters, and if nothing else the complex gives you an idea of the state of the present-day abbey before it was restored. Across the road to the north, housed in a manse built, like the nearby parish church, by the ubiquitous Thomas Telford, is the **Iona Heritage Centre** (Easter–Oct Mon–Sat 10.30am–4.30pm; £3), with displays on the social history of the island over the last 200 years, including the Clearances, which nearly halved the island's population of 500 in the mid-nineteenth century. At a bend in the road, just south of the manse and church, stands the fifteenth-century **MacLean's Cross**, a fine, late medieval example of the distinctive, flowing, three-leaved foliage of the Iona school.

Iona Abbey

No buildings remain from Columba's time: the present **abbey** (daily: April–Sept 9.30am–5.30pm; Oct–March 9.30am–4.30pm; HS; £4.70) dates from the arrival of the Benedictines in around 1200; it was extensively rebuilt in the fifteenth and sixteenth centuries, and restored virtually wholesale last century. Iona's oldest building, the plain-looking eleventh-century **St Oran's Chapel**, lies south of the abbey, to your right. Legend has it that the original chapel could only be completed through human sacrifice. Oran apparently volunteered to be buried alive, and was found to have survived the ordeal when the grave was opened a few days later. Declaring that he had seen hell and it wasn't all bad, he was promptly reinterred for blasphemy. Oran's Chapel stands at the centre of Iona's sacred burial ground, **Reilig Odhráin** (Oran's Cemetery), which is said to contain the graves of sixty kings of Norway, Ireland, France and Scotland, including Duncan and Macbeth.

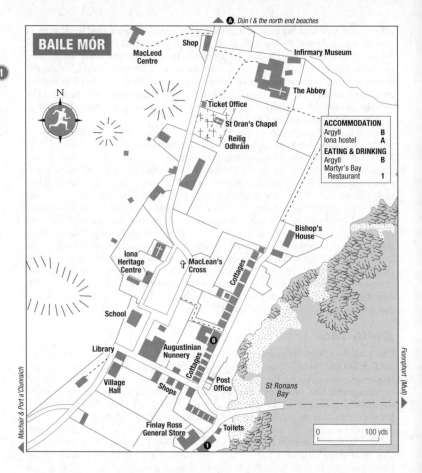

Approaching the abbey itself, from the ticket office, you cross an exposed section of the evocative medieval **Street of the Dead**, whose giant pink-granite cobbles once stretched from the abbey, past St Oran's Chapel, to the village. Beside the road stands the most impressive of Iona's Celtic high crosses, the eighth-century **St Martin's Cross**, smothered with figural scenes – the Virgin and Child at the centre, Daniel in the lion's den, Abraham sacrificing Isaac, and David with musicians in the shaft below. The reverse side features Pictish serpent-and-boss decoration. Standing directly in front of the abbey are the base of St Matthew's Cross (the rest of which is in the Infirmary Museum) and, to the left, a concrete cast of the eighth-century **St John's Cross**, decorated with serpent-and-boss and Celtic spiral ornamental panels. Before you enter the abbey, take a look inside **St Columba's Shrine**, a small steep-roofed chamber to the left of the main entrance. Columba is believed to have been buried either here or under the rocky mound to the west of the abbey, known as Tórr an Aba.

The **Abbey** itself has been simply and sensitively restored to incorporate the original elements. You can spot many of the medieval capitals in the south aisle of the choir and in the south transept, where the white-marble effigies of the eighth Duke of Argyll and his wife, Ina, lie in a side-chapel – an incongruous piece of

Victorian pomp in an otherwise modest and tranquil place. The finest pre-Reformation effigy is that of John MacKinnon, the last abbot of Iona, who died around 1500, and now lies on the south side of the choir steps. For reasons of sanitation, the **cloisters** were placed, contrary to the norm, on the north side of the church (where running water was available); entirely reconstructed in the late 1950s, they now shelter lots of medieval grave-slabs. There are free daily guided tours of the abbey (the times are posted up at the ticket office).

The rest of the island

Not many day-visitors get further than the village and abbey, but it's perfectly possible to walk to the stunning sandy beaches and turquoise seas at the **north end** of the island, or up to the highest point, **Dún I**, a mere 328ft above sea level but with views on a clear day to Skye, Tiree and Jura. Alternatively, it takes about half an hour to walk over to the **machair**, or common grazing land, on the west side of Iona (also used as a rough golf course). On the edge of this are a series of pretty sandy beaches, the largest of which is the evocatively named **Camus Cúl an t-Saimh** ("Bay at the Back of the Ocean"), a crescent of pebble and shell-strewn sand with a spouting cave to the south. Those with more time (2–3hr) might hike over to the **south** of the island, where Port a'Churaich ("Bay of the Coracle", also known as St Columba's Bay), the saint's traditional landing place on Iona, is filled with smooth round rocks and multi-coloured pebbles and stones. A short distance to the east is the **disused marble quarry** at Rubha na Carraig Geire on the south-easternmost point of Iona, finally closed down in 1914.

Practicalities

There's no **tourist office** on Iona, and as demand far exceeds supply you should organize **accommodation** well in advance; otherwise, if you're stuck, an information board just up from the jetty lists all the options. Of the island's two **hotels**, the stone-built *Argyll* (℡01681/700334, ⓦwww.argyllhoteliona.co.uk; Feb–Nov; ❺), in the village's terrace of cottages overlooking the Sound of Iona, is by far the nicer. As for **B&Bs**, try *Clachan Corrach* (May–Oct; ℡01681/700323; ❷), a croft in the middle of the island. For **camping** head to the *Cnoc-Oran* site (℡01681/700112) a fifteen-minute walk beyond *Martyr's Bay Restaurant*. There's a terrific ⚑**hostel** (℡01681/700781, ⓦwww.ionahostel.co.uk) at the north of the island, where the main room is filled with lovely wooden furniture and there are views out to the Treshnish Isles; to reach it, follow the road past the abbey for half a mile. If you want to stay with the **Iona Community** (℡01681/700404, ⓦwww.iona.org.uk), either in the abbey itself or the *MacLeod Centre* (popularly known as "The Mac"), you must be prepared to participate fully in the daily activities, prayers and religious services.

Eating options aren't bad: the restaurant at the *Argyll* uses home-grown vegetables and organic produce, whenever possible, and they have a pretty tea garden by the water. The pub grub at the bar adjoining the *Martyr's Bay Restaurant* by the jetty is reasonable too, often serving the freshest possible seafood. For something lighter during the day, head for the **tearoom** beside the Heritage Centre, which serves home-made soup and tasty cakes and has an idyllic garden setting.

Visitors are not allowed to bring cars onto the island, but **bikes** can be rented in Fionnphort (see p.89) or from the Finlay Ross general store in the village (℡01681/700357, ⓦwww.finlayrossiona.co.uk; ❷); they also do basic B&B. There's also a taxi on the island (℡01681/700776). Mark Jardine's Alternative Boat Hire (℡01681/700537, ⓦwww.boattripsiona.com), based on Iona, takes the lovely wooden gaff-rigged sailing boat *Freya* on short trips to some of the less-visited spots around the Sound of Iona and Erraid. There are also trips to Staffa (℡01681/700358) and whale-watching and wildlife outings (℡01681/700362, ⓦwww.volanteiona.com)

Coll and Tiree

Coll and **Tiree** are among the most isolated of the Inner Hebrides, and if anything have more in common with the outlying Western Isles than with their closest neighbour, Mull. Each is roughly twelve miles long and three miles wide, both are low-lying, treeless and exceptionally windy, with white sandy beaches and the highest sunshine records in Scotland. Like most of the Hebrides, they were once ruled by Vikings, and didn't pass into Scottish hands until the thirteenth century.

In the 1830s Coll's population peaked at 1440, Tiree's at a staggering 4450, but both were badly affected by the Clearances, which virtually halved their populations in a generation. Coll was fortunate to be in the hands of the enlightened MacLeans, but they were forced to sell in 1856 to the Stewart family, who sold two-thirds of the island to a Dutch millionaire in the 1960s. Tiree was ruthlessly cleared by its owner, the Duke of Argyll, who sent in the marines in 1885 to evict the crofters. Both islands have strong Gaelic roots, but the percentage of English-speaking newcomers is rising steadily.

Throughout the summer, the CalMac **ferry** from Oban calls daily at Coll (2hr 40min) and Tiree (3hr 40min). On Thursdays – though the day may change – the ferry continues to Barra in the Western Isles, and calls in at Tiree on the way back, making a **day-trip from Oban** possible; a minibus tour of the island is thrown in as part of the package. Tiree also has an **airport** with daily flights (Mon–Sat) to and from Glasgow. The majority of visitors on both islands stay for at least a week in self-catering accommodation (see p.36), though there are B&Bs and hotels on the islands – advance booking is essential (and that goes for the ferry crossing, too).

Isle of Coll

The fish-shaped rocky island of **Coll** (ⓦwww.visitcoll.co.uk), with a population of around a hundred, lies less than seven miles off the coast of Mull. The ferry docks at Coll's only real village, **ARINAGOUR**, whose whitewashed cottages line the western shore of Loch Eatharna, a popular safe anchorage for boats. Half the island's population lives in the village, and it's here you'll find the island's hotel and pub, post office, churches and a couple of shops; two miles northwest along the Arnabost road, there's even a golf course. The island's petrol pump is also in Arinagour, and is run on a volunteer basis – it's basically open when the ferry arrives.

On the southwest coast there are two edifices, both confusingly known as **Breachacha Castle**, and both built by the MacLeans. The older, at the head of Loch Breachacha, is a fifteenth-century tower house with an additional curtain wall, now used by Project Trust overseas-aid volunteers (ⓦwww.projecttrust.org .uk). The less attractive "new castle", to the northwest, is made up of a central block built around 1750 and two side-pavilions added a century later, now converted into holiday cottages. It was here that Dr Johnson and Boswell stayed in 1773 after a storm forced them to take refuge en route to Mull. Much of the surrounding area is now owned by the RSPB, in the hope of protecting the island's corncrakes. To the west are some **giant sand dunes**, with two glorious golden sandy bays stretching for over a mile on either side. At the far western end is *Caolas*, where you can get a cup of tea and home-baked goodies.

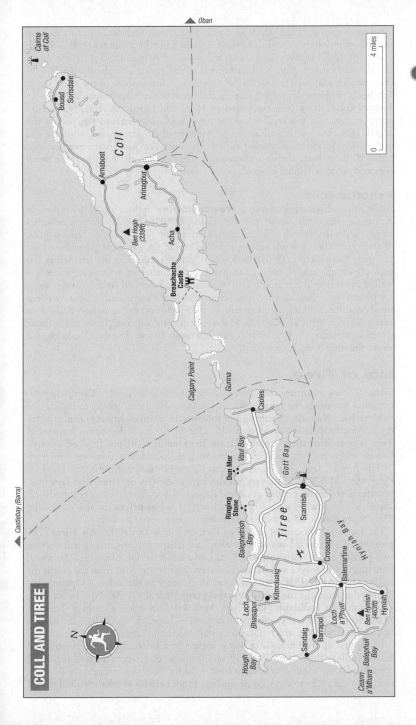

COLL AND TIRE

▲ Oban

Cairns of Coll

Sorisdale
Bousd

Arnabost

Coll

Arinagour

Ben Hogh
(339ft) ▲

Acha

Breachacha
Castle ⌘

Calgary Point

Gunna

▲ Castlebay (Barra)

Caoles

Vaul Bay

Dun Mor

Gott Bay

**Ringing
Stone**

Balephetrish
Bay

Tiree

Scarinish

HYnish Bay

Kilmoluaig

Loch
a'Phuill

Crossapol

Balemartine

Loch
Bhasapol

Sandaig

Barrapol

Ben Hynish
(463ft) ▲

Hynish

Hough
Bay

Balephuil
Bay

Ceann
a'Mhara

N

0   4 miles

For an overview of the whole island, and a fantastic Hebridean panorama, you can follow in Johnson's and Boswell's footsteps and take a wander up **Ben Hogh** – at 339ft, Coll's highest point – two miles west of Arinagour, close to the shore. On the summit is a giant boulder known as an "erratic", perilously perched on three small boulders. The island's northwest coast boasts some of the finest sandy beaches in the Hebrides, which take the full brunt of the Atlantic winds. When the Stewart family took over the island in 1856, and raised the rents, the island's population moved wholesale from the more fertile southeast to this part of the island. However, overcrowding led to widespread emigration; a few of the old crofts in Bousd and Sorisdale, at Coll's northernmost tip, have more recently been restored. From here, there's an impressive view over to the headland, the Small Isles and the Skye Cuillin beyond.

Practicalities

Aside from self-catering cottages, **accommodation** options are very limited. In Arinagour, the small, family-run *Coll Hotel* (℡01879/230334, Ⓦwww.collhotel .com; ❺) provides decent accommodation, or else there's *Tigh-na-Mara* (℡01879/230354, Ⓦwww.sturgeon.dircon.co.uk; ❷), a modern guesthouse near the pier. *Garden House* (℡01879/230374), down a track on the left before the turn-off for the castles, runs a **campsite** in the shelter of what was formerly a walled garden; wild camping is also possible behind the *Coll Hotel* – contact them for permission. The *Coll Hotel* doubles as the island's social centre, does excellent **meals** and has a dining-room overflow. Another good eating option is the *First Port of Coll* café (℡01879/230488, Ⓦwww.firstportofcoll.com), in the old harbour stores overlooking the bay, which offers hot meals all day. The three-bedroom flat above the shop is available to rent.

Isle of Tiree

Tiree (Ⓦwww.isleoftiree.com), as its Gaelic name *tir-iodh* (Land of Corn) suggests, was once known as the breadbasket of the Inner Hebrides, thanks to its acres of rich machair. Nowadays, crofting and tourism are the main sources of income for the resident population of around 750. One of the most distinctive features of Tiree is its **architecture**, in particular the large numbers of "pudding" or "spotty" houses, where only the mortar is painted white. In addition, there are numerous "white houses" (*tigh geal*) and traditional "black houses" (*tigh dubh*); for more on these, see p.317. **Wildlife**-lovers can also have a field day on Tiree, with lapwings, wheatears, redshank, greylag geese and large, laid-back brown hares in abundance. Tiree's sandy beaches attract large numbers of **windsurfers** for the week-long Tiree Wave Classic (Ⓦwww.tireewaveclassic.com) every October.

The CalMac ferry calls at Gott Bay Pier, now best known for **An Turas** (The Journey), Tiree's award-winning "shelter", an artistic extravaganza which features two parallel white walls connected via a black felt section to a glass box which punctures a stone dyke and frames a seaview. Just up the road from the pier is the village of **SCARINISH**, home to a post office, some public toilets, a supermarket, the butcher's and the bank, with a petrol pump back at the pier. Also in Scarinish you'll find **An Iodhlann** (June–Sept Mon–Fri 9am–5pm; Oct–May Tues–Fri 11am–5pm; £3; Ⓦwww.aniodhlann.org.uk) – "haystack" in Gaelic – the island's two-roomed archive, which puts on exhibitions in the summer.

To the east of Scarinish, **Gott Bay** is backed by a two-mile stretch of sand, and just one mile to the north is Vaul Bay, on the north coast, where the well-preserved remains of a dry-stone broch, **Dun Mor** – dating from the first century BC – lie hidden in the rocks to the west of the bay. From here it's another two miles west along the coast to the *Clach a'Choire* or **Ringing Stone**, a huge glacial boulder decorated with mysterious prehistoric markings, which when struck with a stone gives out a metallic sound, thus giving rise to the legend that inside is a crock of gold. The story goes that, should the Ringing Stone ever be broken in two, Tiree will sink beneath the waves. A mile further west you come to lovely **Balephetrish Bay**, where you can watch waders feeding in the breakers, and look out to sea to Skye and the Western Isles.

The most intriguing sights, however, lie in the bulging western half of the island, where Tiree's two landmark hills rise up. The higher of the two, **Ben Hynish** (463ft), is unfortunately occupied by a "golf-ball" radar station, which tracks incoming transatlantic flights; the views from the top, though, are great. Below Ben Hynish, to the east, is **HYNISH**, with its recently restored **harbour**, designed by Alan Stevenson in the 1830s to transport building materials for the magnificent 140-foot-tall **Skerryvore Lighthouse**, which lies on a sea-swept reef some twelve miles southwest of Tiree. The harbour features an ingenious reservoir to prevent silting and, up on the hill behind, beside the row of lightkeepers' houses, a stumpy granite signal-tower. The tower, whose signals used to be the only contact the lighthouse keepers had with civilization, now houses a **museum** telling the history of the herculean effort required to erect the lighthouse.

On the other side of Ben Hynish, a mile or so across the golden sands of Balephuil Bay, is the spectacular headland of **Ceann a'Mhara** (pronounced "kenavara"). The cliffs here are home to thousands of sea birds, including fulmar, kittiwake, guillemot, razorbill, shag and cormorant, with gannet and tern feeding offshore; the islands of Barra and South Uist are also visible on the northern horizon. In the scattered west-coast settlement of **SANDAIG**, to the north of Ceann a'Mhara, three thatched white houses in a row have been turned into the **Taigh Iain Mhoir** (June–Sept Mon–Fri 2–4pm; free), which gives an insight into how the majority of islanders lived in the nineteenth century.

Practicalities

If you're arriving at the **airport**, about three miles west of Scarinish, you should arrange for your hosts to collect you (most will). Tiree has a Ring'n'Ride **minibus** service (Mon–Sat 7am–6pm, Tues until 10pm; ☏01879/220419) which will take you anywhere on the island; **bike rental** (☏01879/220428) or MacLennans **car rental** (☏01879/220555) are the other options.

The island has two **hotels**, with the *Scarinish* (☏01879/220308, ⓦwww.tiree scarinishhotel.com; ④), overlooking the old harbour, the better of the two. Other options include *Kirkapol House* (☏01879/220729, ⓦwww.kirkapoltiree .co.uk; ④), a friendly **B&B** in a tastefully converted kirk, a mile or so east of Scarinish along Gott Bay; *Glebe House* (☏01879/220758, ⓦwww.glebehouse tiree.co.uk; ③), the renovated former manse overlooking the pier in Scarinish; and the very welcoming *Cèabhar* (☏01879/220684, ⓦwww.ceabhar.com; ④), a guesthouse and **restaurant** in Sandaig. Great **hostel** accommodation is available at *Millhouse* (☏01879/220435, ⓦwww.tireemillhouse.co.uk), a converted barn near Loch Bhasapol, in the northwest of the island. For **camping**, contact **Wild Diamond Watersports** (☏01879/220399, ⓦwww.wilddiamond.co.uk) who operate a site in the southwest of the island; their watersport **activities centre** around Loch Bhasapol.

As for **eating**, the bar meals at both hotels are good, and local goodies such as crab, lobster and langoustine are served at the homey *Elephant's End* (☏01879/220 694, ⓦwww.elephantsend.com) in Kirkapol. For a **map** of the island and the daily papers, you need to go to the supermarket at Crossapol.

Isle of Colonsay

Isolated between Mull and Islay, **Colonsay** (ⓦ www.colonsay.org.uk) – measuring just eight miles by three – is nothing like as bleak and windswept as Coll or Tiree. Its craggy, heather-backed hills even support the occasional patch of woodland, plus a bewildering array of plant and birdlife, wild goats and rabbits, and a very fine quasi-tropical garden. The population of around a hundred is down from a pre-Clearance peak of nearly a thousand. With only one hotel and infrequent ferry links with the mainland, there's no fear of mass tourism taking over.

The ferry terminal is at **SCALASAIG**, on the east coast, where there's a post office/shop, a petrol pump, a brewery, a café and the island's hotel. Two miles north is **Colonsay House**, built in 1722 by Malcolm MacNeil. In 1904, the island and house were bought by Lord Strathcona, who made his fortune building the Canadian Pacific Railway (and whose descendants still own the island). He was also responsible for the house's romantically dilapidated woodland **gardens** (April–Sept Wed & Fri noon–5pm; £2.50), which shelter the strange eighth-century **Riasg Buidhe Cross**, decorated with an unusually lifelike mug shot (possibly of a monk) – ask for directions from the tearoom.

To the north of Colonsay House is the island's finest sandy beach, the breath-taking **Kiloran Bay**, where spectacular breakers roll in from the Atlantic. There's another unspoilt sandy beach backed by dunes at Balnahard, two miles northeast along a rough track; en route, you might spot wild goats, choughs and even a golden eagle. The island's west coast forms a sharp escarpment, quite at odds with the gentle undulating landscape that characterizes the rest of the island. Due west of Colonsay House around **Beinn Bhreac** (456ft), the cliffs are at their most spectacular, and in their lower reaches provide a home to hundreds of sea birds, among them kittiwake, cormorant and guillemot in spring and early summer.

Isle of Oronsay

Whilst on Colonsay, it's worth taking a day out to visit the **Isle of Oronsay**, half a mile to the south, with its ruined Augustinian priory. The two islands are separated by "The Strand", a stretch of tidal mud flats, which act as a causeway for two hours either side of low tide (check locally for timings); you can drive over to the island at low tide, though most people park their cars and walk across. Legends (and etymology) link saints Columba and Oran with Colonsay and Oronsay, although the ruins only date back to the fourteenth century. You can, neverthe-less, still make out the original church and tiny cloisters, abandoned since the Reformation and now roofless. The highlight, though, is the **Oronsay Cross**, a superb example of late medieval artistry from Iona which, along with thirty or so beautifully carved grave-slabs, can be found in the restored side-chapel. It takes about an hour to walk from the tip of Colonsay across The Strand to the priory (wellington boots are a good option).

Practicalities

CalMac **ferries** run from Oban (daily except Tues & Sat; 2hr 20min) and once a week from Kennacraig via Islay (Wed; 3hr 35min), when a day-trip is possible, giving you around six hours on the island. There are also scheduled **flights** from Oban (Tues & Thurs, plus Fri & Sun during school terms) run by Hebridean Air (℡ 01631/524568). There's no public transport, but a **minibus** meets the Wednesday ferry and takes folk on a tour of the island – Archie McConnel (℡ 01951/200355) will rent out **bikes**.

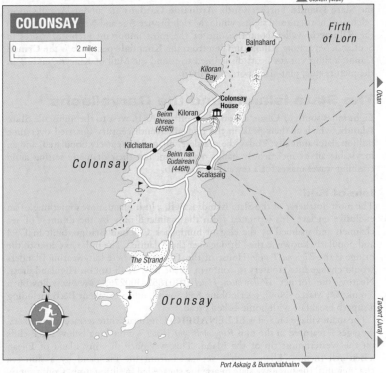

A short stroll from the pier in Scalasaig is the island's only **hotel**, *The Colonsay* (℡01951/200316, Ⓦwww.thecolonsay.com; ⑤). A cosy eighteenth-century inn at heart, it has transformed itself into a really stylish, comfortable place to stay; there's a good restaurant, it serves very decent bar snacks and acts as the island's social centre. There are also a couple of modern **B&Bs** to choose from, though most visitors rent **self-catering** accommodation, the majority of which is run by the estate. Note that self-catering cottages tend to be booked from Friday to Friday, because of the ferries. Wild **camping** is, of course, an option, or you can sleep at the Colonsay Estate's *Backpackers' Lodge* (℡01951/200312, Ⓦwww.colonsayestate.co.uk), a very comfortable **hostel** with a real fire, overlooking Loch Fada. An alternative to **eating out** at the hotel bar is *The Pantry*, above the pier in Scalasaig, which offers simple home-cooking as well as tea and cakes (phone ahead for evening meals; ℡01951/200325). Colonsay organizes its own annual, small (but very popular), four-day **folk festival**, Ceòl Cholasa (Ⓦwww.ceolcholasa.com), in mid-September.

Mid-Argyll

Mid-Argyll loosely describes the central wedge of land south of Oban and north of Kintyre. **Lochgilphead**, on Loch Fyne, is the chief town in the area, but has little to offer beyond its practical uses. The highlights of this gently undulating scenery lie along the sharply indented and remote western coastline. Closest to Oban are the melancholy former slate-mining settlements known collectively as the **Slate Islands**. Further south, **Arduaine Gardens** are among Argyll's most celebrated horticultural sights, while the rich Bronze Age and Neolithic remains in the **Kilmartin** valley comprise one of the most important prehistoric sites in Scotland. Separating Kilmartin Glen from the **Knapdale** peninsula is the **Crinan Canal**, a short cut for boats disinclined to round the Mull of Kintyre, ending in the picturesque, pint-sized port of **Crinan**.

The Slate Islands and the Garvellachs

Eight miles south of Oban, a road heads off the A816 west to the miniscule **Slate Islands**, which at their peak in the mid-nineteenth century quarried over nine million slates annually. Today the old slate villages are sparsely populated, and an inevitable air of melancholy hangs over them, but their dramatic setting amid crashing waves makes for a rewarding day-trip.

Isle of Seil

The most northerly of the Slate Islands is **Seil**, a lush island, now something of an exclusive enclave. It's separated from the mainland only by the thinnest of sea channels and spanned by the elegant humpback **Clachan Bridge**, built in 1793 and popularly known as the "Bridge over the Atlantic". The **pub** next door to the bridge is the *Tigh na Truish* (House of the Trousers), where kilt-wearing islanders would change into trousers to conform to the post-1745 ban on Highland dress. Nearby, the former *Willowburn Hotel* (℡ 01852/300276, ⓦ www.willowburn .co.uk; ❹; March–Nov), overlooking Seil Sound, offers excellent **B&B** including a superb breakfast with home-baked bread.

The main village on Seil is **ELLENABEICH**, its neat white terraces of workers' cottages – featured in the film *Ring of Bright Water* – crouching below black cliffs on the westernmost tip of the island. This was once the tiny island of Eilean a'Beithich (hence "Ellenabeich"), separated from the mainland by a slim sea channel until the intensive slate quarrying succeeded in silting it up. Confusingly, the village is often referred to by the same name as the nearby island of Easdale, since they formed an interdependent community based exclusively around the slate industry. The **Slate Islands Heritage Centre** (April–Oct daily 10.30am– 1pm & 2–5pm; free; ⓦ www.slateislands.org.uk), in one of the little white cottages, has a model of the slate quarry as it would have been in its heyday.

For home-made pasties, seafood and real ale, pop inside the snug wood-panelled bar of the *Oyster Brewery* (℡ 01852/300121, ⓦ www.seilislandpub.co.uk), on the way to the ferry. High-adrenalin **boat trips** are offered by Sea.fari (℡ 01852/300003, ⓦ www.seafari.co.uk), who are based at the Ellenabeich jetty; the boats are rigid inflatables (RIBs) and travel at some speed round the offshore islands and through the Corrievrechan Whirlpool (see box opposite).

Isle of Easdale

Easdale (ⓦ www.easdale.org) remains an island, though the few hundred yards that separate it from Ellanabeich have to be dredged to keep the channel open. On the eve of a great storm in 1881, Easdale, less than a mile across at any one point, supported an incredible 452 inhabitants. That night, waves engulfed the island and flooded the quarries. The island never really recovered, slate quarrying stopped in 1914, and by the 1960s the population dwindled to single figures.

Recently many of the old workers' cottages have been restored: some as holiday homes, others sold to new residents. One of the cottages houses the interesting **Easdale Folk Museum** (daily: April–June, Sept & Oct 11am–4.30pm; July & Aug 11am–5pm; £2.50; ⓦ www.easdalemuseum.org), near the main square, selling a useful historical map of the island, which you can walk round in about half an hour.

The **ferry** from Ellenabeich runs more or less on demand (press the buttons in the ferry shed or phone ☎01852/300559), and there's *The Puffer* **bar/tearoom** (☎01852/300022, Ⓦwww.pufferbar.com) if you've failed to put together a picnic.

With lots of wonderfully flat stones freely available, Easdale makes the perfect venue for the annual **World Stone Skimming Championships** (Ⓦwww.stone skimming.com), held on the last Sunday of September.

Isle of Luing

South of Seil, across the narrow, treacherous Cuan Sound, lies **Luing** (Ⓦwww .isleofluing.co.uk) – pronounced "Ling" – a long, thin, fertile island which once supported more than six hundred people, but now has a third of that. During the Clearances, the population was drastically reduced to make way for cattle; Luing is still renowned for its beef and for the chocolate-brown crossbreed named after it. A council-run car **ferry** crosses the Cuan Sound every half-hour or so during the day.

CULLIPOOL, a mile or so southwest of the ferry slipway, is the main village, its whitewashed cottages (mostly built by the slate company) dotted along the shore facing Scarba and Mull. Luing's only other village, **TOBERONOCHY**, lies on the more sheltered east coast, three miles southeast, and boasts the same distinctive white cottages. Only self-catering **accommodation** is available on the island and the only shop is in Cullipool.

Arduaine and Craignish

A great spot at which to stop and have a picnic on the A816 from Oban to Lochgilphead is **Arduaine Garden** (daily 9.30am–dusk; NTS; £5.50; Ⓦwww.arduaine -garden.org.uk), overlooking Asknish Bay and the islands of Shuna, Luing, Scarba

Whirlpools, witches and monks

Scarba is the largest of the islands around Luing, a brooding 1500-foot hulk of slate, a couple of miles wide, inhospitable and wild – most of the fifty or so inhabitants who once lived here had left by the mid-nineteenth century. To the south, between Scarba and Jura, is the raging **Corrievrechan Whirlpool** (Ⓦwww.whirlpool-scotland.co.uk), one of the world's most spectacular whirlpools, thought to be caused by a rocky pinnacle some 100ft below the sea. Exactly how the whirlpool appears depends on the tide and wind, but there's a potential tidal flow of over eight knots, which, when accompanied by gale-force winds, can create standing waves up to 15ft high. Inevitably there are numerous legends about the place – known as *coire bhreacain* (speckled cauldron) in Gaelic – concerning *Cailleach* (Hag), the Celtic storm goddess.

The string of uninhabited islands visible west of Luing are known collectively as the **Garvellachs**, after the largest, **Garbh Eileach** (Rough Rock), which was inhabited as recently as sixty years ago. The most northerly, **Dún Chonnuill**, contains the remains of an old fort thought to have belonged to Conal of Dalriada, and **Eileach an Naoimh** (Holy Isle), the most southerly, is where the Celtic missionary Brendan the Navigator founded a community in 542, twenty years before Columba landed on Iona. Nothing survives from Brendan's day, but there are a few ninth-century remains, among them a double-beehive cell and a grave enclosure. One school of thought has it that the island is Hinba, Columba's legendary secret retreat, where he founded a monastery before settling on Iona.

From the land, the best place from which to view it is the northern tip of Jura (see p.126). If you're interested in taking a **boat trip** to Scarba, Corrievrechan or the nearby Garvellach islands, contact Sea.fari (☎01852/300003, Ⓦwww.seafari.co.uk), based at Easdale, or Craignish Cruises (☎07747/023038, Ⓦwww.craignishcruises.co.uk), in Ardfern.

and Jura. The gardens are stupendous, particularly in May and June, and have the feel of an intimate private garden, with immaculately-mowed lawns, lily-strewn ponds, mature woods and spectacular rhododendrons and azaleas. For good bar meals, a great view, or pristine **accommodation** for the night, look no further than the *Loch Melfort Hotel* (℡01852/200233, ⓦwww.lochmelfort.co.uk; ❼), adjacent to the garden; for something a bit less pricey and more secluded, head for *Glenmore* B&B (℡01852/200314, ⓦwww.glenmorecountryhouse.co.uk; ❺), a handsome country house set in its own grounds just outside Kilmelford. For superb, formal dining, head for the *Shower of Herring* **restaurant** (℡01852/200345), situated a little further north in Melfort village itself.

A couple of miles south, on the far side of Asknish Bay, is **CRAOBH HAVEN**, a slightly surreal purpose-built holiday village and marina that's reminiscent of a soap opera set. However, there's a range of self-catering and B&B **accommodation** close by, in the rambling Baronial pile of *Lunga* (℡01852/500237, ⓦwww .lunga.com; ❸), run by an eccentric laird. There's also **food** to be had at either the *Lord of the Isles* pub or the *Cabin* bistro café opposite.

There's a fine walk from Craobh Haven along the spine of the **Craignish peninsula** to the southernmost tip five miles away. Alternatively, you can simply head over to **ARDFERN**, on the sheltered shores of Loch Craignish, a favourite anchorage for yachts. Ardfern is everything Croabh Haven isn't and boasts a real **pub**, the *Galley of Lorne*. Opposite is *The Crafty Kitchen* (℡01852/500303; closed Mon), a small, popular daytime restaurant (and craftshop), which serves up home-made soups, beef burgers and puddings.

Kilmartin Glen

Kilmartin Glen – on the road between Oban to Lochgilphead – is the most important prehistoric site on the Scottish mainland. The most remarkable relic is the **linear cemetery**, where several cairns are aligned for more than two miles, to the south of Kilmartin village. These are thought to represent the successive burials of a ruling family or chieftains, but nobody can be sure. The best view of the cemetery's configuration is from the Bronze Age **Mid-Cairn**, but the Neolithic **South Cairn**, dating from around 3000 BC, is by far the oldest and the most impressive, with its large chambered tomb roofed by giant slabs.

Close to the Mid-Cairn, the two **Temple Wood stone circles** appear to have been the architectural focus of burials in the area from Neolithic times to the Bronze Age. Visible to the south are the impressively cup-marked **Nether Largie standing stones**, the largest of which looms over 10ft high. **Cup- and ring-marked rocks** are a recurrent feature of prehistoric sites in the Kilmartin Glen and elsewhere in Argyll. There are many theories as to their origin: some see them as Pictish symbols, others as primitive solar calendars. The most extensive markings in the entire country are at Achnabreck, off the A816 towards Lochgilphead.

Kilmartin

Situated on high ground to the north of the cairns is the tiny village of **KILMARTIN**, where the old manse adjacent to the village church now houses a **Museum of Ancient Culture** (March–Oct daily 10am–5.30pm; £4.60; ⓦwww .kilmartin.org), which is both enlightening and entertaining. Not only can you learn about the various theories concerning prehistoric crannogs, henges and cairns, but you can practise polishing an axe, examine different types of wood, and listen to a variety of weird and wonderful sounds (check out the Gaelic bird imitations).

Nearby **Kilmartin church** shelters several richly sculptured graves and crosses, while a separate enclosure in the graveyard houses a large collection of medieval

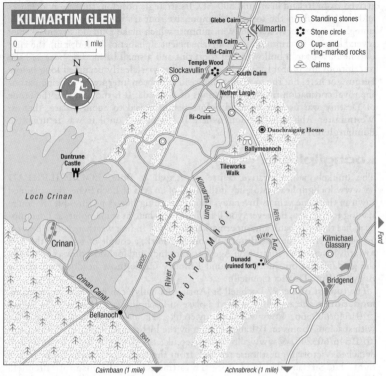

KILMARTIN GLEN

0   1 mile

N

	Standing stones
	Stone circle
	Cup- and ring-marked rocks
	Cairns

Glebe Cairn
Kilmartin
North Cairn
Mid-Cairn
Temple Wood
Slockavullin   South Cairn
Nether Largie
Ri-Cruin
Dunchraigaig House
Ballymeanoch
Tileworks Walk
Duntrune Castle
Loch Crinan
Kilmartin Burn
Móine Mhór
A816
River Add
Kilmichael Glassary
Crinan
River Add
Dunadd (ruined fort)
Ford
B8025
Crinan Canal
Bridgend
Bellanoch
B841

Cairnbaan (1 mile) ▼   *Achnabreck (1 mile)* ▼

grave-slabs of the Malcolms of Poltalloch. Kilmartin's own castle is ruined beyond recognition; head instead for the much less ruined **Carnasserie Castle**, built in the 1560s on a high ridge a mile up the road towards Oban. Architecturally, the castle is interesting, too, as it represents the transition between fully fortified castles and later mansion houses, and has several original finely carved stone fireplaces and doorways, as well as numerous gun-loops and shot holes.

For something to eat, try the museum's *Glebe Cairn* **café**, with home-baked produce on offer – it's open in the evening too (Thurs–Sat). The nearest **B&B** is at ✈ *Dunchraigaig House* (☎01546/605209, ⓦ www.dunchraigaig.co.uk; ❹), a large detached Victorian house situated opposite the Ballymeanoch standing stones, where you can have home-made clootie dumpling for breakfast.

Mòine Mhór and Dunadd

To the south of Kilmartin, beyond the linear cemetery, lies the raised peat-bog of **Mòine Mhór** (Great Moss), now a nature reserve and home to remarkable plant, insect and birdlife. To get a close look at the sphagnum moss and wetlands, head for the **Tileworks Walk**, just off the A816, which includes a short boardwalk over the bog.

Mòine Mhór is best known as home to the Iron Age fort of **Dunadd**, one of Scotland's most important Celtic sites, occupying a distinctive 176ft rocky knoll once surrounded by the sea but currently stranded beside the winding River Add. It was here that Fergus, the first King of Dalriada, established his royal seat, having arrived from Ireland in around 500 AD. Its strategic position, the craggy defences and the view from the top are all impressive, but it's the **stone carvings** (now fibreglass copies) between the twin summits which make Dunadd so remarkable: several lines of inscription in ogham (an ancient alphabet of Irish origin), the faint outline of a boar, a hollowed-out footprint and a small basin. The boar and the inscriptions are probably Pictish, since the fort was clearly occupied long before Fergus got here, but the footprint and basin have been interpreted as being part of the royal coronation rituals of the kings of Dalriada. It is thought that the Stone of Destiny was used at Dunadd before being moved to Scone Palace, then to Westminster Abbey in London, where it languished until it was returned to Edinburgh in 1996.

Lochgilphead

The unlikely administrative centre of Argyll & Bute, **LOCHGILPHEAD** (Ⓦwww.lochgilphead.info), lies at the head of an arm of Loch Fyne. It's a planned town in the same vein as Inveraray, though nothing like as picturesque. If you're staying in the area, however, you'll find yourself here at some point, as Lochgilphead has the only bank and supermarket for miles. In fine weather, you're best off going for a stroll round **Kilmory Woodland Park**, a couple of miles up the A83 towards Inveraray, with its Iron Age fort, bird hide and lochside views, and take in the gardens laid out in 1830 around Kilmory Castle (now headquarters of the Argyll & Bute District Council).

The **tourist office**, 27 Lochnell St (April–Oct daily), can help find you **accommodation** in the area. If you need a place in Lochgilphead itself, try *The Corran* (Ⓣ01546/603866, Ⓦwww.lamonthoy.co.uk; ❸), an attractive Victorian villa with spacious rooms on Poltalloch Street by the lochside; otherwise, *Allt-na-Craig* (Ⓣ01546/603245, Ⓦwww.allt-na-craig.co.uk; ❺) is a very handsome, stylish, detached Victorian guesthouse set back from the road to Ardrishaig. Those on a tight budget should head for the attractive **bunkhouse** at Brenfield (Ⓣ01546/603274, Ⓦwww.brenfield.co.uk), a horsey farm three miles south. The nicest **café** in town is *The Smiddy*, on Smithy Lane (closed Sun), which does simple café fare. For high-class picnic provisions, call in at *Cockles*, a smart deli on the main street that also sells fresh and smoked fish and delicious home-made bread. **Bike rental** is available from Crinan Cycles, 34 Argyll St (Ⓣ01546/603511, Ⓦwww.crinancycles.co.uk; closed Sun).

Knapdale

Forested **Knapdale** – from the Gaelic *cnap* (hill) and *dall* (field) – forms a buffer zone between the Kintyre peninsula and the rest of Argyll, bounded to the north by the Crinan Canal and to the south by West Loch Tarbert and consisting of three fingers of land, separated by Loch Sween and Loch Caolisport.

Crinan Canal

In 1801 the nine-mile-long **Crinan Canal** opened, linking Loch Fyne, at Ardrishaig south of Lochgilphead, with the Sound of Jura, thus cutting out the long and treacherous journey around the Mull of Kintyre. John Rennie's original design, although an impressive engineering feat, had numerous faults, and by 1816 Thomas Telford was called in to take charge of the renovations. The canal runs parallel to the sea for quite some way before cutting across the bottom of Mòine Mhór and hitting a flight of locks either side of **CAIRNBAAN** (there are fifteen in total); a walk along the towpath is both picturesque and pleasantly unstrenuous. A useful pit-stop can be made at the *Cairnbaan Hotel* (Ⓣ01546/603668), an eighteenth-century coaching inn overlooking the canal that has a decent restaurant and bar meals featuring local seared scallops and Stornoway black pudding.

There are usually one or two yachts passing through the locks, but the most relaxing place from which to view the canal in action is **CRINAN**, the pretty little fishing port at the western end of the canal. Crinan's tiny harbour is, for the moment at least, still home to a small fishing fleet; a quick burst up through Crinan Wood to the hill above the village will give you a bird's-eye view of the sea lock and its setting. It's worth having a pint or an excellent **bar meal** at the *Crinan Hotel* as it enjoys one of the most beautiful views in Scotland, especially at sunset, when the myriad islets and the distinctive Paps of Jura are reflected in the waters of the loch. Down on the lockside there is a cheaper, cheerful **café** called the *Coffee Shop* (Easter–Oct), serving mouthwatering home-made cakes and wonderful clootie dumplings. For **accommodation**, it's best to head out to *Bellanoch House* (☎01546/830149, ⓦwww.bellanochhouse.co.uk; ❺), a grand old schoolhouse with stripped pine floors and lots of character, right on the canal, a mile or so before Crinan.

Knapdale Forest and Loch Sween

South of the canal, **Knapdale Forest** stretches virtually uninterrupted from coast to coast, across hills sprinkled with tiny lochs – it's here that **beavers** are being reintroduced into Scotland, though your chances of actually seeing one of these elusive creatures is pretty slim. There are several waymarked walks in the area to choose from: a circular, mile-long path will take you deep into the forest just past **ACHNAMARA**, a three-mile route around **Loch Coille-Bharr**, and a two-and-a-half mile path which runs along the canal and ascends **Dunardry** (702ft). If you need somewhere to stay, *The Stables* (☎01546/850276, ⓦwww.thestablesbandb .co.uk; ❸; March–Nov), part of an old hunting lodge in Achnamara, is the best B&B for miles around.

Continuing down the western finger of Knapdale you come to **TAYVALLICH** (ⓦwww.tayvallich.com), with its attractive horseshoe bay, after which the peninsula splits again. The western arm leads to the medieval **Chapel of Keills**, housing a display of late medieval carved stones, and the remains of a small port where cattle used to be landed from Ireland. There's also a fine view of the **MacCormaig Islands**, the largest of which, Eilean Mór (owned by the Scottish National Party), was once a retreat of the seventh-century Saint Cormac. If you want to eat or drink round here, then head for the *Tayvallich Inn* (☎01546/870282), in the village of the same name. You can currently catch a **passenger ferry to Jura** from Tayvallich (see p.126).

Six miles south of Achnamara on the eastern shores of **Loch Sween** is the "Key of Knapdale", the eleventh-century **Castle Sween**, the earliest stone castle in Scotland but in ruins since 1647. The tranquillity and beauty of the setting is spoilt by the nearby caravan park, an eyesore which makes a visit pretty depressing. You're better off continuing south to the thirteenth-century **Kilmory Chapel**, also ruined but with a new roof protecting the medieval grave-slabs and the well-preserved MacMillan's Cross, an eight-foot fifteenth-century Celtic cross showing the Crucifixion on one side and a hunting scene on the other.

The bulk of Knapdale is isolated and fairly impenetrable, but it's worth persevering the fourteen miles of single-track road in order to reach **KILBERRY**, where you can **camp** at *Port Bàn* (☎01880/770224, ⓦwww.portban.com; April–Oct), and enjoy the fantastic sunsets and views over Jura, or **stay the night** in comfort and style at the ⚘ *Kilberry Inn* (☎01880/770223, ⓦwww.kilberryinn .com; April–Oct Tues–Sun ❽); the inn's **food** is superb – from the home-smoked mackerel to the Loch Fyne queenies, much of the menu is sourced from the local area. There's also a church worth viewing in Kilberry and a small collection of carved medieval grave-slabs. Look out, too, for the **concerts** put on at *Crear* (℡01880/770369, Ⓦwww.crear.co.uk), a barn a mile from the village that's been transformed into an artists' retreat, studio and concert hall – they manage to pull in top classical musicians to perform there.

Kintyre

But for the mile-long isthmus between West Loch Tarbert and the much smaller East Loch Tarbert, the little-visited, sparsely-populated peninsula of **KINTYRE** (Ⓦwww.kintyre.org) – from the Gaelic *ceann tire*, "land's end" – would be an island. Indeed, in the eleventh century, when the Scottish king, Malcolm Canmore, allowed Magnus Barefoot, King of Norway, to lay claim to any island he could circumnavigate by boat, Magnus dragged his boat across the Tarbert isthmus and added the peninsula to his Hebridean kingdom. During the Wars of the Covenant, the majority of the population and property was wiped out by a combination of the 1646 potato blight and the destructive attentions of the Earl of Argyll. Kintyre remained a virtual desert until the earl began his policy of transplanting Gaelic-speaking Lowlanders to the region. They probably felt quite at home here, as the southern third of the peninsula lies on the Lowland side of the Highland Boundary Fault. Despite its relative proximity to Scotland's Central Belt, Kintyre remains quiet and unfashionable; its main towns of **Tarbert** and **Campbeltown** have few obvious attractions, but that's part of their appeal. In many ways, it's a peninsula in a kind of time warp, where you can hole up for a week in perfect solitude.

There are regular daily **buses** from Glasgow to Campbeltown, via Tarbert and the west coast, and even a skeleton service down parts of the east coast. Bear in mind, though, if you're driving, that the new west-coast road is extremely fast, whereas the single-track east-coast road takes more than twice as long.

Tarbert

A distinctive rocket-like church steeple heralds the fishing village of **TARBERT** (in Gaelic *an tairbeart*, meaning "isthmus"), sheltering an attractive little bay backed by rugged hills. Tarbert's herring industry was mentioned in the *Annals of Ulster* as far back as 836 AD, though right now the local fishing industry is down to its lowest level ever. Ironically, it was local Tarbert fishermen, who, in the 1830s, pioneered the method of herring-fishing known as trawling, seining or ring-netting, which eventually wiped out the Loch Fyne herring stocks. Tourism is now an increasingly important source of income, as is the money that flows through the town during the last week in May, when the **yacht races** of the famous Scottish Series take place, and in the first weekend in July, when traditional boats and a seafood festival hit town.

Tarbert's harbourfront is really quite pretty, and is best appreciated from Robert the Bruce's fourteenth-century **castle** above the town to the south. Only the ivy-strewn ruins of the keep remain, though the view from the overgrown rubble makes the stroll up here worthwhile. There are steps up to the castle and a red-waymarked path from beside the bookshop and gallery on the south side of the harbour. Longer walks are also marked out, including the newly marked out **Kintyre Way** (Ⓦwww.kintyreway.com), an 89-mile walk that zigzags its way down the peninsula to Southend. The shortest stroll of all, though, is to the far end of Pier Road, where there's a tiny, but very lovely, shell beach.

Tarbert's **tourist office** (April–June, Sept & Oct Mon–Fri 10am–5pm, Sat & Sun 11am–5pm; July & Aug Mon–Sat 9am–6pm, Sun 10am–5pm) is on the harbour. The **ferry** from Portavadie on the Cowal peninsula arrives at the southeastern corner of the harbour, a fifteen-minute walk from town. There's no shortage of **accommodation**: try *The Knap* (℡01880/820015, ⓦwww.knapguesthouse.co.uk; ❸), a thoughtfully refurbished Victorian townhouse right in the centre of Tarbert, or *Struan House* (℡01880/820190, ⓦwww.struan-house-lochfyne.co.uk; ❸), built in 1846 as a small hotel, overlooking the harbour a short distance along Harbour Street. The *Ca'Dora* is the café to head for on the seafront, while *The Anchor* pub, also overlooking the harbour, is a good option for a seafood lunch. The best **food** is to be had courtesy of the French chef at the ⚲ *Corner House Bistro* (℡01880/820263), just by the side of the *Corner House* pub.

Isle of Gigha

Gigha (ⓦwww.gigha.org.uk) – pronounced "Geeya", with a hard "g" – is a low-lying, fertile island, with a population of around 150, just three miles off the west coast of Kintyre. The island's Ayrshire cattle produce over a quarter of a million gallons of milk a year, though the island's distinctive (occasionally fruit-shaped) cheese is actually produced on the mainland. Like many of the smaller Hebrides, Gigha was bought and sold numerous times after its original lairds, the MacNeils, sold up, before being bought by the islanders themselves in 2002. The most visible sign of the island's regeneration are the three community-owned wind turbines – the "Dancing Ladies" of Faith, Hope and Charity – at the southern tip of the island, which supply Gigha's electricity needs and feed the surplus into the national grid.

The ferry from Tayinloan, 23 miles south of Tarbert, deposits you at the island's only village, **ARDMINISH**, where you'll find the post office and shop and the all-denominations island church with some interesting stained-glass windows, including one to Kenneth MacLeod, composer of the well-known ditty *Road to the Isles*. The main attraction on the island is the **Achamore Gardens** (daily 9am–dusk; £4), a mile south of Ardminish. Established by the first postwar owner, Sir James Horlick of hot drink fame, their spectacularly colourful displays of azaleas are best seen in early summer. Achamore House itself is now home to an American who runs a flower-essence business. To the southwest of the gardens, the ruins of the thirteenth-century **St Catan's Chapel** are floored with weathered medieval gravestones; the ogham stone nearby is the only one of its kind in the west of Scotland. The real draw of Gigha, however, apart from the peace and quiet, are the white sandy beaches – including one at Ardminish itself – that dot the coastline.

Gigha is small – six miles by one mile – and most visitors come here just for the day; CalMac **ferries** depart more or less hourly from Tayinloan for the twenty-minute crossing. However, it's a great place to **stay** too: contact *Tighnavinish* (℡01583/505378, ⓦwww.gigha.net; ❷), a modern crofthouse B&B half a mile north of the post office, or the *Gigha Hotel* (℡01583/505254, ⓦwww.gigha.org .uk; ❺), the social centre of the island and a very welcoming place to stay, just to the south of the post office. And if you want to stay in the style of a laird, book into one of the grand rooms at *Achamore House* (℡01583/505400, ⓦwww .achamorehouse.com; ❺), the beautiful house in the midst of Achamore Gardens. For advice about **camping**, you should contact the *Gigha Hotel*. The licensed *Boathouse* (April–Oct; ⓦwww.boathouse-bar.com), by the pier, is the place to go for delicious **food** and, occasionally, live music and quiz nights. **Bike rental** is available from the post office, and there's a nine-hole **golf course**.

The west coast

Kintyre's bleak **west coast** ranks among the most exposed stretches of coastline in Argyll. Atlantic breakers pound the rocky shoreline, while the persistent westerly wind forces the trees against the hillside. However, when the weather's fine and the wind not too fierce, there are numerous deserted sandy beaches to enjoy with great views over to Gigha, Islay, Jura and even Ireland.

There are several campsites to choose from along the stretch of coast around **TAYINLOAN**, ranging from the big, well-equipped *Point Sands Caravan Park* (℡01583/441263, ⓦwww.pointsands.co.uk; April–Oct), two miles to the north, set back a long way from the main road near a long stretch of sandy beach, to the smaller, more informal *Muasdale Holiday Park*, three miles to the south (℡01583/421207, ⓦwww.muasdaleholidays.com; April–Oct), squeezed between the main road and the beach.

Machrihanish

The only major development along the entire west coast is **MACHRIHANISH**, at the southern end of Machrihanish Bay, the longest continuous stretch of sand in Argyll. There are two approaches to the **beach**: from Machrihanish itself, or from Westport, at the north end of the bay, where the A83 swings east towards Campbeltown; either way, the sea here is too dangerous for swimming. Machrihanish itself was once a thriving salt-producing and coal-mining centre – you can still see the miners' cottages at neighbouring Drumlemble – with a light railway link to Campbeltown, but now survives solely on tourism. The main draw, apart from the beach, is the exposed championship **golf links** (ⓦwww.machgolf.com) between the beach and Campbeltown airport on the nearby flat and fertile swath of land known as the Laggan. There's also a tiny **sea-bird observatory** (Easter–Oct daily; ⓦwww.machrihanishbirds.org.uk) at Uisaed Point, ten minutes' walk west of the village, though it's best visited in the migration periods, when it provides a welcome shelter for ornithologists trying to spot a rare bird blown off-course.

Several of the imposing, detached Victorian townhouses overlooking the bay in Machrihanish, such as *Ardell House* (℡01586/810235; ❸; March–Oct), offer **accommodation**; there's also a large, fully equipped and very exposed family-run **campsite** (℡07570/670012, ⓦwww.campkintyre.co.uk; Feb–Oct & Dec) overlooking the golf links, which even has an array of heated wooden "wigwams" (❶). In the evening, *The Beachcomber* bar is the liveliest place in Machrihanish.

Campbeltown

CAMPBELTOWN's best feature is its setting, in a deep bay sheltered by Davaar Island and the surrounding hills. With a population of around five thousand, it is also one of the largest towns in Argyll and, if you're staying in the southern half of Kintyre, you may need to come here to stock up on supplies. Originally known as Kinlochkilkerran (*Ceann Loch Cill Chiaran*), the town was renamed in the seventeenth century by the Earl of Argyll – a Campbell – when it became one of the main points for immigration from the Lowlands. As is evident from the architecture, Campbeltown's heyday was the Victorian era, when **shipbuilding** was going strong, **coal** was shipped by canal from Drumlemble, there was a light-railway connection with Machrihanish, the **fishing** fleet was vast and Campbeltown Loch was said to be made of **whisky**. The decline of all its old industries has left the town permanently depressed, and unemployment and underemployment remain persistent problems.

The Town

Nineteenth-century visitors to Campbeltown frequently found the place engulfed in a thick fog of pungent peat smoke from the town's 34 **whisky distilleries** – today, only a handful are left to maintain this regional subgroup of single malt whiskies. If you're at all interested in whisky, pop into **Cadenhead's** whisky shop at 7 Bolgam St (℡01586/551710), which runs parallel with Longrow, where you can sign up for a guided tour of the nearby **Springbank distillery**, (Ⓦwww .springbankwhisky.com; Mon–Fri 10am & 2pm, Sat & Sun by appointment; £6–20 depending on the tour), a deeply traditional, family-owned business that does absolutely everything from malting to bottling, on its own premises, and produces three different single malts.

The **Campbeltown Cross**, a fourteenth-century blue-green cross with figural scenes and spirals of Celtic knotting, presides over the main roundabout on the quayside. Further along the palm-tree-dotted waterfront is the **Wee Pictures**, a dinky Art Deco cinema on Hall Street, built in 1913, community-owned and run, and still going strong (daily except Fri; ℡01586/553899, Ⓦwww.weepictures .co.uk). Next door is the **Burnett Building** (Mon–Fri 9am–5pm; free), built in red sandstone as the town library in 1897, crowned by a distinctive lantern and decorated with four relief panels depicting the town's main industries at the time. The building harbours a very old-fashioned one-room local museum, and also boasts the **Linda McCartney Memorial Garden**, which you should approach from Shore Street. Here, you'll find a slightly ludicrous bronze statue of Linda holding a lamb, commissioned by the ex-Beatle, who spent many happy times with Linda and the kids on the farm he owns near Campbeltown.

It used to be said that Campbeltown had almost as many churches as it did distilleries, and even today the townscape is dominated by its church spires – in particular, the top-heavy crown spire of **Longrow Church**. The former Lorne Street Church, with its stripy bell-cote and pinnacles, is now the **Campbeltown Heritage Centre** (April–Sept Mon–Sat 11.30am–4.30pm, Sun 2–4.30pm; £2). A beautiful wooden skiff from 1906 stands where the main altar once was, and there's plenty on the town's whisky and fishing industries, plus a model of the Victorian harbour front with the light railway running along Hall Street.

Campbeltown's most popular attraction is the **Scottish Owl Centre** (April–June & Sept Wed–Sat 1.30–4.30pm; July & Aug Mon–Sat 1.30–4.30pm; £6; Ⓦwww .scottishowlcentre.com), signposted off the B842 to Machrihanish, five minutes' walk out of town. As well as being actively involved in conservation work, the centre has a huge collection of owls spread out in terraced aviaries, ranging from the tiny Scops Owl to the world's largest, the Eurasian Eagle Owl. Try and time your visit with the daily flight display at 2.30pm.

Practicalities

Campbeltown's **tourist office** is on the Old Quay (April Mon–Sat; May–Oct daily; Nov–March Mon–Fri; ℡01586/552056), and will happily hand out a free map of the town. The **airport** (℡01586/553797) lies three miles west, towards Machrihanish; there's a bus connection, but you need to phone ahead to book it (℡01586/552319) – it's part of Campbeltown's **Ring'n'Ride** service, which also operates around the town and to Southend.

There's a good choice of **accommodation** in Campbeltown from *Redknowe* (℡01586/550374, Ⓦwww.redknowe.co.uk; ❶), a very welcoming sandstone B&B on the edge of town up the B842, to the very well-run *Ardshiel Hotel* (℡01586/552133, Ⓦwww.ardshiel.co.uk; ❼), a former whisky distiller's Victorian mansion situated on a lovely leafy square, just a block or so back from the harbour front. Another place worth considering is 🍴 *Oatfield House* (℡01586/551551, www.oatfield.org; ⑤), a beautifully renovated whitewashed laird's house set in its own grounds, three miles down the B842 to Southend.

As for **places to eat**, the *Gallery 10*, on Longrow South (closed Sun & Mon), serves up the best coffee and tea in town, plus an excellent "smoked platter". The best bar meals are to be found at the *Ardshiel Hotel*, while the *Commercial Inn* on Cross Street is a good drinking-hole. There are a couple of good **mountain-bike trails** in Beinn Ghuilean Forest, to the south of town; **bike rental** is available from the Cycle Shop, Longrow (℡01586/554443). If you're here in the middle of August, be prepared for the **Mull of Kintyre Music & Arts Festival** (www.mokfest.com), which pulls in a few old rock bands, plus some good traditional Irish and Scottish bands.

Southend and the Mull of Kintyre

The bulbous, hilly end of Kintyre, to the south of Campbeltown, features some of the most spectacular scenery on the whole peninsula, mixed with large swathes of Lowland-style farmland. **SOUTHEND** itself, a bleak, blustery spot, comes as something of a disappointment, though it does have a golden sandy beach. Below the cliffs to the west of the beach, a ruined thirteenth-century chapel marks the alleged arrival-point of St Columba prior to his trip to Iona, and on a rocky knoll nearby a pair of footprints carved into the rock are known as **Columba's footprints**, though only one is actually of ancient origin. Jutting out into the sea at the east end of the bay is **Dunaverty Rock**, where a force of three hundred Royalists was massacred by the Covenanting army of the Earl of Argyll in 1647, despite having surrendered voluntarily. A couple of miles out to sea lies **Sanda**, a privately owned island containing the remains of St Ninian's chapel, plus two ancient crosses, a holy well, an unusual lighthouse comprised of three sandstone towers and lots of sea birds. If you're looking for even nicer beaches head further west to Carskey Bay, or Macharioch Bay, three miles east, looking out to distant Ailsa Craig in the Firth of Clyde.

Most people venture south of Campbeltown to make a pilgrimage to the **Mull of Kintyre**, made famous by the mawkish number-one hit by sometime local resident Paul McCartney, with the help of the Campbeltown Pipe Band. It's also infamous as the site of the **RAF's worst peacetime accident** when, on June 2, 1994, a Chinook helicopter on its way from Belfast to Inverness crashed, killing all 29 on board. The Ministry of Defence blamed the pilots and, despite the findings of a Scottish enquiry and the opinions of a cross-party select committee, still maintains there were no technical problems with the helicopter. A small memorial can be found on the hillside, not far from the **Gap** (1150ft) – after which no vehicles are allowed. The Mull is the nearest Britain gets to Ireland, just twelve miles away, and the Irish coastline appears remarkably close on fine days. There's nothing specifically to see, but the trek down to the lighthouse, itself 300ft above the ocean waves, is challengingly tortuous. It's about a mile from the "Gap" to the lighthouse (and a long haul back up), though there's a strategic viewpoint just ten-minutes' walk from the car park.

Southend's derelict Art Deco *Keil Hotel* cuts a forlorn figure, set back from the bay, but you can stay in the simple, but clean rooms above the *Argyll Arms* (℡01586/830622, www.argyllarmshotel; ②), the local **pub**, unremarkable except for the fact that it has a post office inside it. Alternatively, you can stay at *Ormsary Farm* (℡01586/830665, www.holidaymullofkintyre.co.uk; April–Sept; ②), a small working dairy farm up Glen Breakerie, northwest of Southend. **Camping** is possible in the field right by Southend beach, run by *Machribeg Farm* (℡01586/830249; Easter–Sept).

The east coast

The **east coast** of Kintyre is gentler than the west, sheltered from the Atlantic winds and in parts strikingly beautiful, with stunning views across to Arran. However, be warned that there's no bus service between Carradale and Skipness and, if you're driving the thirty or so miles up to Skipness on the slow, winding, single-track B842, you'll need a fair amount of time.

The ruins of **Saddell Abbey**, a Cistercian foundation thought to have been founded by Somerled in 1148, lie ten miles up the coast from Campbeltown, set at the lush, wooded entrance to Saddell Glen. The abbey fell into disrepair in the sixteenth century and, though the remains are not exactly impressive, there's a good collection of medieval grave-slabs decorated with full-scale relief figures of knights housed in a new shelter in the grounds. Standing by the privately owned shoreline there's a splendid memorial to the last Campbell laird to live at Saddell Castle, which he built in 1774.

Carradale

Further north lies the fishing village of **CARRADALE**, the only place of any size on the east coast north of Campbeltown, and "popular with those who like unsophisticated resorts", as one 1930s guide put it. The village itself is rather drab, but the tiny, very pretty harbour with its small fishing fleet, and the wide, sandy beach to the south, make up for it. On the east side of the beach is Carradale Point, a wildlife reserve with feral goats and a good example of a vitrified fort built more than two thousand years ago on a small tidal island off the headland (best approached from the beach). There are several pleasant walks with good views across to Arran laid out in the woods around Carradale, for which the best starting-point is the car park at Port na Storm on the road into the village.

Carradale also has a couple of good wet-weather retreats. First, there's **Network Carradale Heritage Centre** (April–Sept daily except Thurs 10am–5.30pm; Oct–March daily except Wed & Thurs 11am–4pm; free), by the aforementioned car park. The displays trace the demise of the local herring fleet and the puffers that used to bring tourists, and the rise of forestry; it's small in scale but informative, and there's good home-baking to be had in the tearoom.

The bar of the *Carradale Hotel* is the hub of village social life, but if you want **accommodation**, head for *Ashbank Hotel* (℡01583/431650, ⓦwww.ashbankhotel .com; ❹), a dinky little place in the heart of the village run by two very welcoming sisters. Another option is to head out to *Dunvalanree* (℡01583/431226, ⓦwww .dunvalanree.com; ❻), the big Victorian house overlooking the sheltered little bay of Port Righ, towards Carradale Point, which also serves up great food. The nearest **campsite** is the superbly equipped *Carradale Bay Caravan Park* (℡01583/431665, ⓦwww.carradalebay.com; March–Oct), right by the sandy beach. Carradale boasts a real bakery, too – try the treacle scones or cookie pudding (known as bread-and-butter pudding south of the border).

Skipness

The B842 ends twelve miles north of Carradale at **Claonaig**, little more than a slipway for the small summer car ferry to Arran. Beyond here, a dead-end road winds its way along the shore a few miles further north to the tiny village of **SKIPNESS**, where the considerable ruins of the enormous thirteenth-century **Skipness Castle** and a chapel look out across the Kilbrannan Sound to Arran. You can sit outside and admire both, whilst enjoying fresh oysters, delicious queenies (queen scallops), mussels and home-baked cakes from the excellent **seafood cabin** (late May to Sept daily except Sat). There are several gentle walks laid out in the nearby mixed woodland, up the glen.

Isle of Arran

Shaped like a kidney bean and occupying centre stage in the Firth of Clyde, **Arran** (Ⓦ www.visitarran.net) is the most southerly (and therefore the most accessible) of all the Scottish islands. The Highland–Lowland dividing line passes right through its centre – hence the cliché about it being like "Scotland in miniature" – leaving the northern half sparsely populated, spectacularly mountainous and forbidding, while the lush southern half enjoys a much milder climate. The population of around 5000 – many of whom are incomers – tend to stick to the southeastern quarter of the island, leaving the west and the north relatively undisturbed.

There are two big crowd-pullers on Arran: **geology** and **golf**. The former has fascinated rock-obsessed students since Sir James Hutton came here in the late eighteenth century (see box below). As for golf, Arran boasts seven courses, including three of the eighteen-hole variety at Brodick, Lamlash and Whiting Bay, and a unique twelve-hole course at Shiskine, near Blackwaterfoot; an Arran Golf Pass is available for £105, giving you a round on each course.

Arran geology

Arran is a top destination for the country's geology students. First, this small island is split in two by the **Highland Boundary Fault**, and therefore contains a superb variety of rock formations, typical of both the Highlands and the Lowlands. And, second, it is the place where **Sir James Hutton** (1726–97), the "father of modern geology" came in 1787, in order to lay down research for his epic work, *A Theory of the Earth*.

Even if you know very little about geology, it is possible to appreciate some of the island's more obvious features. The most famous location is just beyond **Newton Point**, on the north shore of Loch Ranza, where Allt Beithe stream runs into the sea. Here, two types of rocks by the shore are set virtually at right angles to one another, the older Cambrian schist dipping towards the land, while the younger Devonian sandstone slopes into the sea. This phenomenon became known as **Hutton's Unconformity**.

At **Imachar Point**, between Pirnmill and Dougarie, you can view in miniature the geological process known as **folding**, which affected the ancient Cambrian schist around a hundred million years ago, and, on a larger scale, resulted in the formation of mountain ranges such as those of north Arran. Another classic, more recent geological formation to be seen on Arran is **raised beaches**, formed at the end of the last Ice Age, some fifteen thousand years ago, when the sea level was much higher, and then left high and dry when the sea level dropped. The road that wraps itself around Arran runs along the flat ground that subsequently emerged from the sea. One of the best locations to observe this is at the **King's Cave**, north of Blackwaterfoot (see p.117), where you can see huge sea caves stranded some distance from today's shoreline.

Down on the south coast, the shoreline below **Kildonan** reveals some superb examples of **dolerite dykes**, formed when molten rock erupted through cracks in the sedimentary sandstone rocks above, around sixty million years ago. The molten rock solidified and, being harder, now stands above the surrounding sandstone, forming strange, rocky piers jutting out into the sea.

There are numerous other interesting features to look out for, such as **solidified sand dunes** and huge granite boulders, known as **erratics**, on Corrie beach in the northeast of the island, classic **glacial valleys** such as Glen Sannox, and **felsite sills** such as the one at Drumadoon, near Blackwaterfoot, in the southwest. If any of the above whets your appetite, start by getting hold of the geological booklet, *Arran and the Clyde Islands*, produced by Scottish Natural Heritage.

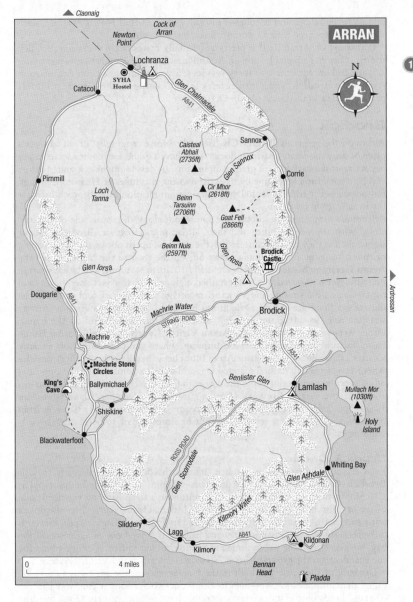

Although **tourism** is now by far its most important industry – forty percent of the island's housing is holiday accommodation – Arran, at twenty miles in length, is large enough to have a life of its own. While the island's post-1745 history and the Clearances (set in motion by the local lairds, the Hamiltons) are as depressing as elsewhere in the Highlands, in recent years Arran's population has actually increased, in contrast with more remote islands. Once a county in its own right (along with Bute), Arran was left out of Argyll & Bute in the latest county boundary shake-up, and is coupled instead with mainland North Ayrshire, with which it enjoys year-round transport links, but little else.

Transport on Arran itself is pretty good: daily **buses** circle the island (Brodick tourist office has timetables and an Arran Rural Rover day-ticket costs just under £5) and link in with the two **ferry services**: a year-round one from Ardrossan in Ayrshire to **Brodick**; and a smaller ferry from Claonaig on the Kintyre peninsula to **Lochranza** in the north (April–Oct).

Brodick

Although the resort of **BRODICK** (from the Norse *breidr vik*, "broad bay") is a place of only moderate charm, it does at least have a grand setting in a wide, sandy bay set against a backdrop of granite mountains. Its development as a tourist resort was held back for a long time by its elitist owners, the dukes of Hamilton, though nowadays, as the island's capital and main communication hub, Brodick is by far the busiest town on Arran.

Brodick's shops and guesthouses are spread out along the south side of the bay, along with the tourist office and the CalMac pier. However, Brodick's tourist sights, such as they are, are clustered on the west and north side of the bay, a couple of miles from the ferry terminal. First off, on the road to the castle, there's the **Arran Heritage Museum** (April–Oct daily 10.30am–4.30pm; £3; ⓦ www.arran museum.co.uk), housed in a whitewashed eighteenth-century crofter's farm, and containing an old smiddy and a Victorian cottage with box bed and range. In the old stables there are lots of agricultural bits and bobs, plus material on Arran's wartime role, its intriguing geology, and a Neolithic skull found on the island. Other wet-weather options in the **Arran Visitor Centre**, in neighbouring Home Farm, include the **Island Cheese Company**, where you can see the soft, creamy Crofter's Crowdie or the piquant Arran Blue cheese being made; Arran Aromatics where you can watch natural soapmaking; and Creelers smokehouse (see opposite) offers succulent seafood. Round the corner in Cladach, right by the castle, you can also visit the **Arran Brewery** (April to mid-Sept Mon–Sat 10am–5pm, Sun 12.30–5pm; mid-Sept to March daily except Tues & Sun; £2; ⓦ www.arran brewery.com) and take a self-guided tour or simply quaff some of their award-winning beers.

Brodick Castle

Even if you're not based in Brodick, it's worth coming here in order to visit **Brodick Castle** (daily: April–Sept 11am–4.30pm; Oct 11am–3.30pm; NTS; £10.50), former seat of the dukes of Hamilton on a steep bank on the north side of the bay. Just before the entrance, there's a little sandstone jetty where the duke's wine and ice from Canada was landed. It used to serve the village, but the eleventh duke thought the tenants unsightly and had them moved out of sight round the bay. He also closed the barytes mine at Sannox, a vital source of employment for the islanders, on the grounds that it "spoilt the solemn grandeur of the scene".

The bulk of the castle was built in the nineteenth century, giving it a domestic rather than military look, and the **interior** – once you've fought your way past the 87 stags' heads on the stairs – is comfortable but undistinguished. Don't miss the portrait of the eleventh duke's faithful piper, who injured his throat on a grouse bone, was warned never to pipe again, but did so and died. Probably the most atmospheric room is the copper-filled Victorian kitchen, which conjures up a vision of the sweating labour required to feed the folk upstairs.

Much more attractive, however, are the walled **gardens** (daily 9.30am–dusk; gardens and country park only £5.50) and extensive grounds, a treasury of exotic plants and trees enjoying the favourable climate (including one of Europe's finest collections of rhododendrons), and commanding a superb view across the bay. There is an adventure playground for kids, but the whole area is a natural playground, with waterfalls, a giant pitcher-plant that swallows thousands of midges daily, and a maze of paths. Buried in the grounds there is a bizarre Bavarian-style **summerhouse** lined entirely with pine cones, one of three built by the eleventh duke to make his wife, Princess Marie of Baden, feel at home. For the energetic there's also a **country park** with scenic walks and mountain bike trails, starting from a small, informative, hands-on nature centre. In summer there are guided walks with the rangers, but at any time you can be surprised by red squirrels, nightjars and the abundance of fungi. The castle **tearoom** serves light snacks and home-made cakes and scones.

Practicalities

Brodick's **tourist office** (March–May & Oct Mon–Sat; June–Sept daily; ☎01770/303776) is by the CalMac pier, and has reams of information on every activity from pony trekking to paragliding. Unless you've got to catch an early-morning ferry, however, there's little reason to stay in Brodick, though there's a decent choice of accommodation should you need to. The best **rooms** close to the ferry terminal are at the excellent *Dunvegan Guest House* on Shore Road (☎01770/302811, ⓦwww.dunveganhouse.co.uk; ⑤); for somewhere cheaper and more peaceful, head out to *The Barn* (☎01770/303615, ⓦwww.arranbarn .co.uk; ③), a charming B&B with real style and character on the southwest edge of Brodick in Glencloy. Finally, the luxury option is the elegant and secluded *Kilmichael Country House Hotel* (☎01770/302219, ⓦwww.kilmichael.com; ⑨), originally built in the seventeenth century and still retaining lots of period features; a four-course dinner here is around £40 a head, but it's one of the best you'll get on the island. The nearest **campsite** is *Glen Rosa* (☎01770/302380, ⓦwww.glenrosa.com), a lovely, but very basic, farm site (cold water only and no showers), two miles from town off the B880 to Blackwaterfoot.

For **food**, apart from dinner at the aforementioned *Kilmichael*, the only place that really stands out is the seafood restaurant *Creelers* (☎01770/302797, ⓦwww .creelers.co.uk; Easter–Oct), which has its own smokehouse, by the museum on

---

Outdoor activities on Arran

Arran has a highly developed tourist industry, and there are a number of outfits ready and willing to help you enjoy the great outdoors. For **hiking** in the mountains in the northern half of the island, all you need is a good map and the right gear – see p.47 for safety in the hills, while the walks are described in more detail on p.118. The Forestry Commission (☎01770/302218, ⓦwww.forestry.gov.uk) has laid out several more gentle **woodland walks** in its various plantations, as well as a network of **mountain-bike trails** (ⓦwww.arranbikeclub.com) on their forestry roads; they also organize various guided forest-walks in the summer. **Bike rental** is available from the Boathouse (☎01770/302377), 300yd from the pier in Brodick. **Horse riding**, from hourly treks in the morning to afternoon hacks for experienced riders, can be sorted out at Cairnhouse Riding Centre in Blackwaterfoot (☎01770/860466) or North Sannox Pony Trekking Centre (☎01770/810222). For **boat rental**, contact Lamlash Boat Hire (☎01770/600998), who are based on the pier in Lamlash. High-adrenalin sports can be organized by Arran Adventure (☎01770/302244, ⓦwww.arranadventure.com), who also arrange sea kayaking; the Arran Quad Centre, near Blackwaterfoot, offers quad-biking (☎01770/860596, ⓦwww.arranquadcentre.co.uk; closed Mon & Sat); and for the truly mad, there's the chance to go paragliding with Flying Fever (☎01770/303899, ⓦwww.flyingfever.net; April–Oct), based in Kildonan.

the road to the castle. Nearer to the ferry terminal, the bar snacks (lunch only) at *Mac's Bar* in the *McLaren Hotel* make a cheaper option and there's real ale too. If you want to find out about any other events taking place on Arran, pick up a copy of the island's **weekly newspaper**, the *Arran Banner*.

The south of Arran

The **southern half of Arran** is less spectacular, and less forbidding than the north; it's more heavily forested and the land is more fertile, and for that reason the vast majority of the population lives here. The tourist industry has followed them, though with considerably less justification.

Lamlash, Holy Island and Whiting Bay

With its distinctive Edwardian architecture and mild climate, **LAMLASH**, four miles south of Brodick, epitomizes the sedate charm of southeast Arran. Lamlash Bay has in its time sheltered King Haakon's fleet in 1263 before the Battle of Largs and, more recently, served as a naval base in both world wars. The major drawback for the visitor, however, is that its beach is made not of sand but of boulder-strewn mud flats. The monument on the village green marks the spot on which a farewell sermon was given to the eleven families, victims of the Clearances, who, in 1829, sailed from here to Canada. In 2008 a section of the bay became Scotland's first No Take Zone (an area of sea and seabed from which no marine life can be removed by any fishing method).

The best reason for coming to Lamlash is to visit the slug-shaped hump of **Holy Island**, which shelters the bay. The island is owned by a group of Tibetan Buddhists who have established a long-term retreat at the lighthouse on the island's southern tip and built a Peace Centre at the north end of the island. Providing you don't dawdle, it's possible to scramble up to the top of Mullach Mór (1030ft), the island's highest point, and still catch the last ferry back. En route, you might well bump into the island's most numerous residents: feral goats, Eriskay ponies, Soay sheep and rabbits. The Holy Island ferry runs more or less hourly (April–Oct daily; Nov–March Tues & Fri only; ☎01770/600998; £8 return), and you can stay at the *Peace Centre* (☎01387/373232, Ⓦwww.holyisland.org; full vegetarian board ❸), in a single, twin or dorm bed. The centre puts on a range of courses on yoga, meditation and relaxation throughout the season.

If you want to **stay** in Lamlash, head for the comfortable *Lilybank* (☎01770/600230, Ⓦwww.lilybank-arran.co.uk; Easter–Oct; ❸), overlooking the bay and offering good home-made food, or try out the stylishly refurbished rooms of the *Glenisle Hotel* (☎01770/600559, Ⓦwww.glenislehotel.com; ❼). The best food option is the **bar meals** at the friendly *Drift Inn*, which has tables by the shore. For something more upmarket, head for the stylish modern restaurant in the *Glenisle Hotel*. On the subject of eating, it was a Lamlash man, Donald McKelvie, who made Arran potatoes world-famous, breeding in the rich soil of the island: Arran Pilot, Arran Chief and Arran Victory, of which Maris Piper is a modern descendant.

An established Clydeside resort for over a century now, **WHITING BAY**, four miles south of Lamlash, is spread out along a very pleasant bay, though it doesn't have quite the distinctive architecture of Lamlash. It's a good base for walking, with the gentle hike up to the **Glenashdale Falls** probably the most popular excursion; the waterfall can be reached via a pretty woodland walk that sets off from the southern end of the bay (2hr return). Whiting Bay also has a good choice of simple **B&Bs**, such as *Mingulay* (☎01770/700346; ❷), and its neighbour *Ellan-gowan* (☎01770/700784; ❷) on Middle Road. The **food** is very good, though expensive, at the *Burlington Hotel* on Shore Road, but for home-made cakes and fresh-cooked snacks with scrumptious chips head for *The Coffee Pot* further along the road.

Kildonan to Lagg

Access to the sea is tricky along the south coast, but worth the effort, as the sandy beaches here are among the island's finest. One place you can get down to the sea is at **KILDONAN**, an attractive small village south of Lamlash, set slightly off the main road, with a good sandy beach, which you share with the local wildlife, and views out to the tiny flat island of Pladda, with its distinctive lighthouse and, in the distance, the great hump of Ailsa Craig. Kildonan has a nice, laid-back **campsite** (☎01770/820320) right by the sea next to the nicely refurbished *Kildonan Hotel* (☎01770/820207, ⓦwww.kildonanhotel.co.uk; ⑤). A short stroll west along the shore road is ⚵ *Mare* (☎01770/820375, ⓦwww.mare-arran .co.uk; ⑤), a tastefully furnished modern B&B offering superb breakfasts and stunning sea views.

Five miles west of Kildonan is the picturesque village of **LAGG**, nestling in a tree-filled hollow by Kilmory Water; you can **stay** at the comfortable ⚵ *Lagg Hotel* (☎01770/870255, ⓦwww.lagghotel.com; ⑤), an old-fashioned eighteenth-century inn beside the main road, with real fires and good food.

Blackwaterfoot and Machrie

BLACKWATERFOOT, on the western end of the String Road, which bisects the island, has some lovely sandy beaches, but is dominated, not to say somewhat spoilt, by the presence of the island's largest hotel, the *Kinloch*. A gentle two-mile walk north along the coast will bring you to the **King's Cave**, one of several where Robert the Bruce is said to have encountered the famously patient arachnid, while hiding during his final bid to free Scotland in 1306. If you want **to stay**, best place to hole up is *Lochside Guest House* (☎01770/860276, ⓦwww.lochside-arran .co.uk; ❷), a great B&B just half a mile south along the main road, set beside its very own trout loch.

North of Blackwaterfoot, the wide expanse of **Machrie Moor** boasts a wealth of Bronze Age sites. No fewer than six **stone circles** sit east of the main road and, although many of them barely break the peat's surface, the tallest surviving monolith is over 18ft high. The most striking configuration is at Fingal's Cauldron Seat, with two concentric circles of granite boulders; legend has it that Fingal tied his dog to one of them while cooking at his cauldron. If you're feeling peckish, the Machrie golf-course **tearoom** (April to mid-Oct) is a welcome oasis in this sparsely populated area.

The north of Arran

The **north half of Arran** – effectively the Highland part – features wonderful bare granite peaks, the occasional golden eagle and miles of unspoilt scenery, within reach only to those prepared to do some hiking. Arran's most accessible peak is also the island's highest, **Goat Fell** (2866ft) – take your pick from the Gaelic, *goath*, meaning "windy", or the Norse, *geit-fjall*, "goat mountain" – which can be ascended in just three hours from Brodick or from Corrie (return journey 5hr), though it's a strenuous hike (for the usual safety precautions, see p.47).

Corrie and Sannox

Arran's prettiest little seaside village is **CORRIE**, six miles north of Brodick, where a procession of picturesque cottages lines the road to Lochranza and wraps

Walking in North Arran

Ordnance Survey Explorer map no. 361

The ferociously jagged and barren outline of the mountains of **north Arran** is on a par with that of the Cuillin of Skye. None of the peaks is a Munro, but they are spectacular, nevertheless, partly because they rise up so rapidly from sea level and, in fine weather, offer such wonderful views over sea and land.

One of the most popular walks is the circuit of peaks that surround Glen Rosa. The walk begins with the relatively straightforward ascent of **Goat Fell** (2866ft), which is normally approached from the grounds of Brodick Castle, to the south. From Goat Fell, you can follow a series of rocky ridges that spread out in the shape of an "H". In order to keep to the crest of the ridge, head north to the next peak of **North Goat Fell** (2657ft), and then make the sharp descent to the Saddle, a perfect spot for a rest, before making the ascent of **Cir Mhòr** (2618ft), by far the most exhilarating peak in the whole range, and the finest viewpoint of all. The next section of the walk, southwest across the knife's-edge ridge of **A'Chir**, is quite tricky due to the Bad Step, a lethal gap in the ridge, which you can avoid by dropping down slightly on the east side. Beyond A'Chir, the ascent of **Beinn Tarsuinn** (2706ft) and **Beinn Nuis** (2597ft) is relatively simple. A path leads down from the southeast face of Beinn Nuis to Glen Rosa and back to Brodick. If you don't fancy attempting A'Chir, or if the weather closes in, you can simply descend from the Saddle, or from the southwest side of Cir Mhor, to Glen Rosa.

The walk described above covers a total distance of eleven miles, with over 4600ft of climbing, and should take between eight and ten hours to complete. All walks should be approached with care, and the usual **safety precautions** should be observed (see p.47).

itself around an exquisite little harbour and pier. If you want to use Corrie as a base for hiking, book ahead at the *North High Corrie Croft*, a **bunkhouse** (℡01770/810218), ten-minutes' steep climb above the village on a raised beach; it has one large room for group bookings, and an annexe with eight beds. The red-sandstone *Corrie Hotel*, at the centre of the village, does bar **meals**, and the tearoom in the *Corrie Golf Club*, confusingly in Sannox, offers good-value food all day in summer.

At **SANNOX**, two miles north, the road leaves the shoreline and climbs steeply, giving breathtaking views over to the scree-strewn slopes around Caisteal Abhail (2735ft). If you make this journey around dusk, be sure to pause in **Glen Chalmadale**, on the other northern side of the pass, to catch a glimpse of the red deer that come down to pasture by the water. Another possibility is to turn off to North Sannox, where you can park and walk along the shore to the **Fallen Rocks**, a major rock-fall of Devonian sandstone.

Lochranza

On fair Lochranza streamed the early day,
Thin wreaths of cottage smoke are upward curl'd
From the lone hamlet, which her inland bay
And circling mountains sever from the world.

The Lord of the Isles by Sir Walter Scott

The ruined castle which occupies the mud flats of the bay, and the brooding north-facing slopes of the mountains which frame it, make for one of the most spectacular settings on the island – yet **LOCHRANZA**, despite being the only place of any size in this sparsely populated area, attracts far fewer visitors than Arran's southern resorts. The castle is worth a brief look inside, but Lochranza's main tourist attraction now is the island's modern whisky **distillery** (mid-March to Oct Mon–Sat 10am–6pm; Sun 11am–6pm; Nov & Dec phone ☎ 01770/830264; £3.50; ⓦ www.arranwhisky.com), distinguished by its pagoda-style roofs at the south end of the village. The tours are entertaining and slick, and end with a free sample of the island's single malt.

The finest **accommodation** is to be had at the superb ⚘ *Apple Lodge* (☎ 01770/830229; ❺), the old village manse where you'll get excellent home-cooking, or at the unusual *Castlekirk* (☎ 01770/830202, ⓦ www.castlekirk .co.uk; ❷), a converted church that retains lots of original features including a rose window in the breakfast room. Lochranza also has a friendly and well-equipped SYHA **hostel** (☎ 01700/830631; mid-Feb to Oct), situated halfway between the distillery and the castle, with views over the bay, and a well-equipped **campsite** (☎ 01770/830273, ⓦ www.arran.net/lochranza; April-Oct), beautifully placed by the golf course on the Brodick road, where red deer come to graze in the early evening. The campsite has a friendly **tearoom** serving all-day breakfasts and light snacks; the bar of the *Lochranza* is the centre of the local social scene and its **bar meals** are very popular with hungry walkers. If you're just passing through, or need a **packed lunch**, there's the takeaway *Sandwich Station*, close to the CalMac slipway.

Isle of Islay

The fertile, largely treeless island of **ISLAY** (pronounced "eye-la") is famous for one thing – single malt **whisky**. The smoky, peaty, pungent quality of Islay whisky is unique, recognizable even to the untutored palate, and all eight of the island's distilleries will happily take visitors on a guided tour, ending with the customary complimentary tipple. Yet, despite the fame of its whiskies, Islay still remains relatively undiscovered, especially when compared with Arran, Mull or Skye. Part of the reason may be the expense of the two-hour ferry journey from Kennacraig on Kintyre. If you do make the effort, however, you'll be rewarded with a genuinely friendly welcome from islanders proud of their history, landscape and Gaelic culture.

In medieval times, Islay was the political centre of the Hebrides, with **Finlaggan**, near Port Askaig, the seat of the MacDonalds, Lords of the Isles. The picturesque, whitewashed villages you see on Islay today, however, date from the planned settlements founded by the Campbells in the late eighteenth and early nineteenth centuries. Apart from whisky and solitude, the other great draw is the **birdlife** – there's a real possibility of spotting a golden eagle, or the rare crow-like chough, and no possibility at all of missing the white-fronted and barnacle geese that winter here in their thousands. In late May, the **Fèis Ìle**, or Islay Festival of Music and Malt (ⓦ www.theislayfestival.co.uk), takes place, with whisky tasting, piping recitals, folk dancing and other events celebrating the island's Gaelic roots.

CalMac **ferries** from Kennacraig on Kintyre connect with both Port Ellen and Port Askaig and the island's airport has regular **flights** to and from Glasgow. Public transport will get you from one end of the island to the other, but if you're thinking of bringing your own vehicle, it's worth considering **car hire** on the island itself and saving on ferry fares – Islay Car Hire (☎ 01496/810544, ⓦ www.islaycarhire.co.uk) will deliver to both ferry terminals. For a local point of view and news of upcoming events, pick up a copy of the fortnightly *Ileach* (ⓦ www.ileach.co.uk); the island also has its own website ⓦ www .islayinfo.com.

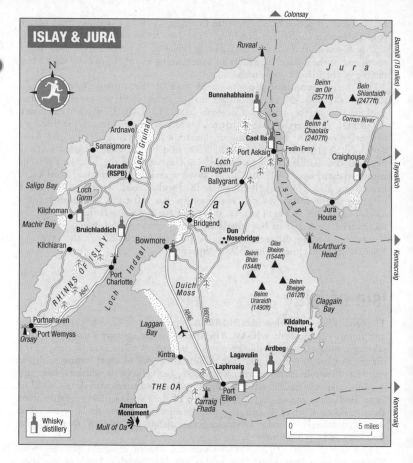

Port Ellen and around

Laid out as a planned village in 1821 by Walter Frederick Campbell, and named after his wife, **PORT ELLEN** is the chief port on Islay, with the island's largest fishing fleet and main CalMac ferry terminal. The neat whitewashed terraces which overlook the town's bay of golden sand are pretty enough, but the strand to the north, up Charlotte Street, is dominated by the modern maltings, whose powerful odours waft across the town. Arriving at Port Ellen by boat, it's impossible to miss the unusual, square-shaped **Carraig Fhada lighthouse**, at the western entrance to the bay, erected in 1832 in memory of Walter Frederick Campbell's aforementioned wife. Just beyond the lighthouse is the prettiest bay on the island's south coast, Traigh Bhán, or the **Singing Sands**, a perfect sandy beach peppered with jagged rocky extrusions.

For **accommodation** in Port Ellen itself, the most central place is *Caladh Sona* (☎01496/302694, Ⓔhamish.scott@lineone.net; ❸), a detached house at 53 Frederick Crescent. On the west side of the bay near the Carraig Fhada lighthouse, *Samhchair* (☎01496/302596, Ⓦwww.samhchair.co.uk; ❺) is an expertly-run bungalow B&B which serves up superb breakfasts. For somewhere really special, though, opt for the *Glenegedale House Hotel* (☎01496/300400, Ⓦwww.glenegedalehouse.co.uk; ❻), the whitewashed guesthouse opposite the airport, for delicious home-cooking and fantastic breakfasts. There's also the *Kintra Farm* **campsite** (℡01496/302051, Ⓦwww.kintrafarm.co.uk; April–Sept; ❸), which enjoys a great situation at the southern tip of sandy Laggan Bay, three miles northwest of Port Ellen; the farm also offers B&B.

Islay whisky

Islay has woken up to the fact that its **whisky distilleries** are a major tourist attraction. Nowadays, every distillery offers guided tours, traditionally ending with a generous dram, and a refund (or discount) for your entrance fee if you buy a bottle in the shop. Phone ahead to make sure there's a tour running, as times do change frequently.

Ardbeg ℡01496/302244, Ⓦwww.ardbeg.com. Ardbeg is traditionally considered the saltiest, peatiest malt on Islay (and that's saying something). Bought by Glenmorangie in 1997, the distillery has been thoroughly overhauled and restored, yet it still has bags of character inside. The *Old Kiln Café* is excellent (June–Aug daily 10am–5pm; Sept–May Mon–Fri 10am–5pm). Guided tours regularly 10.30am, noon & 3pm; £4.

Bowmore ℡01496/810671, Ⓦwww.bowmore.co.uk. Bowmore is the most touristy of the Islay distilleries, too much so for some. However, it is by far the most central (with unrivalled disabled access), and also one of the few still doing its own malting and kilning. Daily guided tours Easter–June Mon–Sat 9am–5pm; July to mid-Sept Mon–Sat 9am–5pm, Sun noon–4pm; mid-Sept to Easter Mon–Fri 9am–5pm, Sat 9am–noon; £4.

Bruichladdich ℡01496/850190, Ⓦwww.bruichladdich.com. Rescued in 2001 by a group of whisky fanatics, this independent distillery offers regular guided tours and is currently planning to build a new distillery in Port Charlotte. Guided tours: Easter–Oct Mon–Fri 10.30, 11.30am & 2.30pm, Sat 11.30am & 2.30pm; Nov–Easter Mon–Fri 11.30am & 2.30pm, Sat 11.30am; £4.

Bunnahabhain ℡01496/840646, Ⓦwww.bunnahabhain.com. A visit to Bunnahabhain (pronounced "Bunna-have-in") is really only for whisky obsessives. The road from Port Askaig is windy, the whisky the least characteristically Islay and the distillery itself only in production for a few months each year. Guided tours April–Oct Mon–Fri 10.30am, 2 & 3.15pm; Nov–March by appointment; £4.

Caol Ila ℡01496/302760, Ⓦwww.discovering-distilleries.com. Caol Ila (pronounced "Cull-eela"), just north of Port Askaig, is a modern distillery, the majority of whose lightly peaty malt goes into blended whiskies. Guided tours April–Oct Mon–Fri 9.30 & 10.45am, 1.45 & 3.15pm, Sat 1.45 & 3.15pm; at other times by appointment; £6 (joint ticket with Lagavulin).

Kilchoman ℡01496/850011, Ⓦwww.kilchomandistillery.com. Established in 2005 as the first new distillery on Islay for over a century, Kilchoman is a very welcoming, tiny, farm-based enterprise that grows its own barley, as well as distilling, maturing and bottling its whisky on site. The first single malt has appeared (and sold out) and it's peaty. The café serves good coffee, plus home-made soup and baking (Mon–Sat 10am–5pm). Guided tours April–Oct Mon–Sat 11am & 3pm; Nov–March Mon–Fri 11am & 3pm; £4.50.

Lagavulin ℡01496/302730, Ⓦwww.discovering-distilleries.com. Lagavulin probably is the classic, all-round Islay malt, with lots of smoke and peat. The distillery enjoys a fabulous setting and is extremely busy all year round. Guided tours April–Oct Mon–Fri 9.30 & 11.15am, 2.30 & 3.45pm, Sat 9.30 & 11.15am; Nov–March Mon–Fri 9.30 & 11.15am; £6 (joint ticket with Caol Ila).

Laphroaig ℡01496/302418, Ⓦwww.laphroaig.com. Another classic smoky, peaty Islay malt, and another great setting. One bonus at Laphroaig is that you get to see the malting and see and smell the peat kilns. Guided tours March–Oct Mon–Fri 10 & 11.30am & 2 & 3.30pm; free.

Along the coast to Kildalton

From Port Ellen, a dead-end road heads off east along the coastline, passing three distilleries in as many miles. First comes **Laphroaig**, which, as every bottle tells you, is Gaelic for "the beautiful hollow by the broad bay", and, true enough, the whitewashed distillery is indeed in a gorgeous setting by the sea – it even has its own railway for transporting peat to the distillery. Laphroaig also has the stamp of approval from Prince Charles, who famously paid a flying visit to the island in 1994, crashing an airplane of the Queen's Flight in the process. A mile down the road lies **Lagavulin** distillery, beyond which stands **Dunyvaig Castle** (*Dún Naomhaig*), a romantic ruin on a promontory looking out to the tiny isle of Texa. Another mile further on, **Ardbeg** distillery sports the traditional pagoda-style kiln roofs, and has recently been brought back to life by Glenmorangie. In common with all Islay's distilleries, the above three offer guided tours (for more on which, see the box, p.121).

Six miles beyond Ardbeg, slightly off the road, the simple thirteenth-century **Kildalton Chapel** boasts a wonderful eighth-century Celtic ringed cross made from the local "bluestone", which is a rich blue-grey. The quality of the scenes matches any to be found on the crosses carved by the monks on Iona: the Virgin and Child are on the east face, with Cain murdering Abel to the left, David fighting the lion on the top, and Abraham sacrificing Isaac on the right; on the west side amidst the serpent-and–boss work are four elephant-like beasts.

The Oa

The most dramatic landscape on Islay is to be found in the nub of land to the southwest of Port Ellen known as **The Oa** (pronounced "O"), a windswept and inhospitable spot, much loved by illicit whisky distillers and smugglers over the centuries. Halfway along the road, a ruined church is visible to the south, testament to the area's once large population dispersed during the Clearances – several abandoned villages lie in the north of the peninsula, near **Kintra**. The chief target for most visitors to The Oa, however, is the gargantuan **American Monument**, built in the shape of a lighthouse on the clifftop above the Mull of Oa. It was erected by the American National Red Cross in memory of those who died in two naval disasters that took place in 1918. The first occurred when the troop transporter SS *Tuscania*, carrying over two thousand American army personnel, was torpedoed by a German U-boat seven miles offshore in February 1918. As the lifeboats were being lowered, several ropes broke and threw the occupants into the sea, drowning 266 of those on board. The monument also commemorates those who drowned when the HMS *Otranto* was shipwrecked off Kilchoman (see p.124) in October of the same year. The memorial is inscribed with the unusual sustained metaphor: "On Fame's eternal camping ground, their silent tents are spread, while glory keeps with solemn round, the bivouac of the dead." If you're driving, you can park in a car park, just before Upper Killeyan farm, and follow the duckboards across the soggy peat. En route, look out for choughs, golden eagles and other birds of prey, not to mention feral goats and, down on the shore, basking seals; for a longer walk, follow the coast five miles round to or from Kintra.

Bowmore

On the other side of the monotonous peat bog of Duich Moss, on the southern shores of the tidal Loch Indaal, lies **BOWMORE**, Islay's administrative capital, with a population of around eight hundred. It was founded in 1768 to replace the village of Kilarrow, which was deemed by the local laird to be too close to his own residence. It's a striking place, laid out in a grid plan rather like Inveraray, with the whitewashed terraces of Main Street climbing up the hill in a straight line from the pier on Loch Indaal to the town's crowning landmark, the **Round Church** (Ⓦwww.theroundchurch.org.uk), whose central tower looks uncannily like a lighthouse. Built in the round, so that the devil would have no corners in which to hide, it has a plain, wood-panelled interior, with a lovely tiered balcony and a big central mushroom pillar. A little to the west of Main Street is **Bowmore distillery** (see p.121), the first of the legal Islay distilleries, founded in 1779, and still occupying its original whitewashed buildings by the loch.

Islay's only **tourist office** is in Bowmore (April–Oct daily; Nov–March Mon– Fri; Ⓣ01496/810254); it can help you find **accommodation** anywhere on Islay or Jura. In Bowmore itself, head for one of the town's better B&Bs, such as *Lambeth House* (Ⓣ01496/810597, Ⓔlambethguesthouse@tiscali.co.uk; ❸), on Jamieson Street, just off Main Street, or the *Bowmore Hotel* (Ⓣ01496/810416, Ⓦwww.bowmorehotel.com; ❺), which has been totally refurbished, and is also on Jamieson Street. **Bike rental** is available from the craft shop beside the post office on Main Street.

At the *Harbour Inn* on Main Street, you can warm yourself by a peat fire in the **pub**, where they also do lunchtime bar snacks. At the other end of the scale, there's a decent **bakery** on Main Street, and, further up on the same side of the street, *The Cottage* (closed Sun), a cheap and friendly greasy spoon.

Loch Gruinart to Kilchoman

Between mid-September and the third week of April, it's impossible to miss the island's staggeringly large wintering population of **Greenland Barnacle** and **Greater White-fronted geese**. During this period, the geese dominate the landscape, feeding incessantly off the rich pasture, strolling by the shores, and flying in formation across the winter skies. In the spring, the geese hang around just long enough to snap up the first shoots of new grass, in order to give themselves enough energy to make the 2000-mile journey to Greenland, where they breed in the summer. Understandably, many local farmers are not exactly very happy about the geese feeding off their land, and some receive compensation for the inconvenience.

You can see the geese just about anywhere on the island – there are an estimated 15,000 white-fronted and 40,000 barnacles here (and rising) – though they are usually at their most concentrated in the fields between Bridgend and Ballygrant. In the evening, they tend to congregate in the tidal mud flats and fields around **Loch Gruinart**, which is an **RSPB nature reserve**. The nearby farm of **Aoradh** (pronounced "oorig") is run by the RSPB, and one of its outbuildings contains a **visitor centre** (daily 10am–5pm; free), housing an observation point with telescopes and a CCTV link with the mud flats; there's also a hide across the road looking north over the salt flats at the head of the loch. From the hide, you're more likely to see reed bunting, redshank, lapwing, pintail, wigeon, teal and other waterfowl rather than geese.

The road along the western shores of Loch Gruinart to Ardnave is a good place to spot **choughs**, members of the crow family, distinguished by their curved red beaks and matching legs. Halfway along the road, there's a path off to the ruins of **Kilnave Chapel**, whose working graveyard contains a very weathered, eighth-century Celtic cross. The road ends at Ardnave Loch, beyond which lie numerous sand dunes, where seals often sun themselves, and otters sometimes fish offshore. Anyone interested in **birding** or **bushcraft** should get in touch with Islay Birding (Ⓣ01496/850010, Ⓦwww.islaybirding.co.uk), based in Port Charlotte, who organize all sorts of adventures and activities.

Without doubt the best **sandy beaches** on Islay are to be found on the isolated northwest coast, in particular, the lovely golden beach of **Machir Bay**, which is backed by great white-sand dunes. The sea here has dangerous undercurrents, however, and is not safe to swim in (the same goes for the much smaller **Saligo Bay**, to the north). At the nearby settlement of **KILCHOMAN**, set back from Machir Bay, beneath low rocky cliffs, where fulmars nest inland, the church is in a sorry state of disrepair. Its churchyard, however, contains a beautiful fifteenth-century cross, decorated with interlacing on one side and the Crucifixion on the other; at its base there's a wishing stone that should be turned sunwise when wishing. Across a nearby field towards the bay lies the **sailors' cemetery**, containing just 75 graves of the 400 or so who were drowned when the armed merchant cruiser SS *Otranto* collided with another ship in its convoy in a storm in October 1918. The ship was carrying 1000 army personnel (including 665 Americans), the majority of whom made it safely to a ship which came to their aid; of the 400 who had to try and swim ashore, only 16 survived. The sailors' graves lie in three neat rows, from the cook to the captain, who has his own, much larger gravestone.

Another poignant memorial stands at **SANAIGMORE**, at the end of a road three miles due west of Loch Gruinart, commemorating 241 Irish emigrants, fleeing the potato famine, drowned when the *Exmouth of Newcastle* was wrecked off the coast in April 1847 – another beautiful sandy beach lies a short walk north of the settlement.

Port Charlotte

PORT CHARLOTTE, founded in 1828 by Walter Frederick Campbell and named after his mother, is generally agreed to be Islay's prettiest village. Known as the "Queen of the Rhinns" (derived from the Gaelic word for a promontory), its immaculate whitewashed cottages cluster around a sandy cove overlooking Loch Indaal. On the northern fringe of the village, in a whitewashed former chapel, the imaginative **Museum of Islay Life** (April–Oct Mon–Sat 10.30am–4.30pm; Nov–March Mon–Sat 10am–4pm; £3; Ⓦ www.islaymuseum.org) has a children's corner, quizzes, a good library of books about the island, and tantalizing snippets about eighteenth-century illegal whisky distillers. The **Wildlife Information Centre** (Easter–Oct daily except Sat 10am–4pm; June–Aug also Sat 10am–4pm; £2.50), housed in the former distillery warehouse, is also worth a visit for anyone interested in the island's fauna and flora. As well as an extensive library to browse, there's lots of hands-on stuff for kids: microscopes, a touch table full of natural goodies, a sea-water aquarium, a bug world and owl pellets to examine. Tickets are valid for a week, allowing you to go back and identify things you've seen on your travels.

Port Charlotte is the perfect place in which to base yourself on Islay. The welcoming *Port Charlotte Hotel* (Ⓣ 01496/850360, Ⓦ www.portcharlottehotel .co.uk; ❽) has the finest **accommodation** – the seafood lunches served in the bar are very popular, and there's a good, more expensive restaurant. For B&B, you're actually better off heading out along the road to Portnahaven as far as Nerabus. There, you'll find *The Monachs* (Ⓣ 01496/850049, Ⓦ www.islayguest house.co.uk; ❻), a spacious new luxury villa B&B with stupendous sea views, and the excellent *Octofad Farm* (Ⓣ 01496/850594, Ⓦ www.octofadfarm.com; ❸; April–Oct). Port Charlotte itself is also home to Islay's SYHA **hostel** (Ⓣ 0870/004 1128, Ⓦ www.syha.org.uk; April–Sept), housed in an old bonded warehouse, by the sea, next door to the Wildlife Information Centre. In addition, there's now a community-run **campsite** at the Port Mòr Centre (Ⓣ 01496/850441, Ⓦ www .islandofislay.co.uk), with sea views and tip-top facilities, just outside the village on the road to Portnahaven. For inexpensive food, there's a choice between the *Croft Kitchen* (☎01496/850230; April–Oct), opposite the museum, and the café in the Port Mòr Centre. The **bar** of the *Port Charlotte* is very easygoing, while the crack (and occasional live music) goes on at the *Lochindaal Inn*, down the road, where you can also tuck into a very good local-bred steak. **Bike rental** is available from 33 Main St (☎01496/850488), opposite the hotel.

Portnahaven and Port Wemyss

The main coastal road culminates seven miles south of Port Charlotte at **PORTNAHAVEN**, a fishing and crofting community since the early nineteenth century. The familiar whitewashed cottages wrap themselves prettily around the steep banks of a deep bay, where seals bask on the rocks in considerable numbers; in the distance, you can see Portnahaven's twin settlement, **PORT WEMYSS**, a mile south. The communities share a little whitewashed church, located above the bay in Portnahaven, with separate doors for each village. For a drink, head for *an tigh seinnse* in Portnahaven, a tiny **pub** where you can sit outside and enjoy the view in fine weather. A short way out to sea are two islands, the largest of which, Orsay, sports the **Rhinns of Islay Lighthouse**, built by Robert Louis Stevenson's father in 1825; ask around locally if you're keen to visit the island.

Finlaggan

Just beyond Ballygrant, on the road to Port Askaig, a narrow road leads off north to **Loch Finlaggan**, site of a number of prehistoric crannogs (artificial islands) and, for four hundred years from the twelfth century, headquarters of the Lords of the Isles, semi-autonomous rulers over the Hebrides and Kintyre. The site is evocative enough, but there are, in truth, very few remains beyond the foundations. Remarkably, the palace that stood here appears to have been unfortified, a testament perhaps to the prosperity and stability of the islands in those days. Unless you need shelter from the rain, or are desperate to see the head of the commemorative medieval cross found here, you can happily skip the **information centre** (April–Sept Mon–Sat 10.30am–4.30pm, Sun 1.30–4.30pm; £3; ⓦ www.finlaggan.com), to the northeast of the loch, and simply head on down to the site itself (access at any time), which is dotted with interpretive panels. Duckboards allow you to walk out across the reed beds of the loch and explore the main crannog, **Eilean Mor**, where several carved gravestones are displayed under cover in the chapel, all of which seem to support the theory that the Lords of the Isles buried their wives and children, while having themselves interred on Iona. Further out into the loch is another smaller crannog, **Eilean na Comhairle**, originally connected to Eilean Mor by a causeway, where the Lords of the Isles are thought to have held meetings of the Council of the Isles.

Port Askaig

Islay's other ferry connection with the mainland, and its sole link with Colonsay and Jura, is from **PORT ASKAIG**, a scattering of buildings which tumble down a little cove by the narrowest section of the Sound of Islay or Caol Ila. The only real reason to come here is to catch one of the ferries or go to the hotel bar; if you've time to kill, you can wander round the island's RNLI lifeboat station or through the nearby woods of Dunlossit House. Whisky fanatics might want to head half a mile north of Port Askaig to the distilleries of **Caol Ila** and **Bunnahabhain**, a couple of miles further on; both enjoy idyllic settings, overlooking the

Sound of Islay, though they are no beauties in themselves (see p.121 for details of their tours).

This part of Islay has several superb **places to stay**. First, there's *Skerrols House* (℡01496/810520, Ⓦwww.skerrolshouse.com; Ⓖ), a lovely whitewashed house a mile or so out of Bridgend off the A846 to Port Askaig. Further along the road, just southwest of Ballygrant is another fine whitewashed farmhouse ⅍ *Kilmeny Farmhouse* (℡01496/840668, Ⓦwww.kilmeny.co.uk; Ⓖ), a place which richly deserves all the superlatives it regularly receives, its rooms furnished with antiques and its dinners (Tues & Thurs only) worth the extra £35 a head. The *Ballygrant Inn* is a good **pub** in which to grab a pint (and a bar meal), while the *Port Askaig Hotel* enjoys a wonderful position by Port Askaig pier, with views over to the Paps of Jura. For high-adrenalin **boat trips**, contact Islay Sea Safari (℡01496/840510, Ⓦwww.islayseasafari.co.uk), which is based in Port Askaig and best known for whizzing round the distilleries in a rigid inflatable. It's also possible to take a **day-trip to Colonsay** (see p.98) on a CalMac ferry on Wednesday.

Isle of Jura

Twenty-eight miles long and eight miles wide, the long whale-shaped island of **Jura** is one of the wildest and most mountainous of the Inner Hebrides, its entire west coast uninhabited and inaccessible except to the dedicated walker. The distinctive **Paps of Jura** – so called because of their smooth breast-like shape, though there are, in fact, three of them – seem to dominate every view off the west coast of

---

Walking the Paps of Jura

Ordnance Survey Explorer map no. 355

Perhaps the most popular of all the hillwalks on Jura is an ascent of any of the island's famous **Paps of Jura** – Beinn an Oir (2571ft), Beinn a'Chaolais (2407ft) and Beinn Shiantaidh (2477ft) – which cluster together in the south half of the island. It's possible to do a round trip from Craighouse itself, or from the Feolin Ferry, but the easiest approach is from the three-arched bridge on the island's main road, three miles north of Craighouse. From the bridge, keeping to the north side of the Corran River, you eventually reach Loch an t'Siob. If you only want to climb one Pap, then simply climb up to the saddle between Beinn an Oir and Beinn Shiantaidh and choose which one (Beinn an Oir is probably the most interesting), returning to the bridge the same way. The trip to and from the bridge should take between five and six hours; it's hard going and care needs to be taken, as the scree is unstable.

If you want to try and bag all three Paps, you need to attack Beinn Shiantaidh via its southeast spur, leaving the loch at its easternmost point. This makes for a more difficult ascent, as the scree and large lumps of quartzite are tough going. Descending to the aforementioned saddle, and climbing Beinn an Oir is straightforward enough, but make sure you come off Beinn an Oir via the south spur, before climbing Beinn a'Chaolais, as the western side of Beinn an Oir is dangerously steep. Again, you can return via the loch to the three-arched bridge.

Every year, in the last bank-holiday weekend in May, hundreds of masochists take part in a fell race up the Paps, which the winner usually completes in three hours. Given the number of deer on Jura, it's as well to be aware of the **stalking season** (July–Feb), during which you should check with the Jura Hotel before heading out. At all times of year, you should take all the usual **safety precautions** (see p.47); beware, too, of adders, which are quite numerous on Jura. If you want a guide to help you seek out the wildlife, contact Exploration Jura (℡07899/912116).

George Orwell on Jura

In April 1946, Eric Blair (better known by his pen name of **George Orwell**), intending to give himself "six months' quiet" in which to complete his latest novel, moved to a remote farmhouse called **Barnhill**, at the northern end of Jura, which he had visited for the first time the previous year. He appears to have relished the challenge of living in Barnhill, fishing almost every night, shooting rabbits, laying lobster pots, and even attempting a little farming. Along with his adopted 3-year-old son Richard, and later his sister Avril, he clearly enjoyed his spartan existence. The book Orwell was writing, under the working title *The Last Man in Europe*, was to become *1984* (the title was arrived at by simply reversing the last two digits of the year in which it was finished – 1948). During his time on Jura, however, Orwell was suffering badly from tuberculosis, and eventually he was forced to return to London, where he died in January 1950.

Barnhill, 23 miles north of Craighouse, is as remote today as it was in Orwell's day. The road deteriorates rapidly beyond Lealt, where vehicles must be left, leaving pilgrims a four-mile walk to the house itself. Alternatively, the Richardsons of Kinauachdrachd (☎07899/912116) can organize a taxi and guided walk, and also run a bunkhouse. Orwell wrote most of the book in the bedroom (top left window as you look at the house); the place is now a self-catering cottage (☎01786/850274). If you're keen on making the journey out to Barnhill, you might as well combine it with a trip to the nearby **Corrievrechan Whirlpool** (see box, p.101), which lies between Jura and Scarba, to the north. Orwell nearly drowned in the whirlpool during a fishing trip in August 1947, along with his three companions (including Richard): the outboard motor was washed away, and they had to row to a nearby island and wait for several hours before being rescued by a passing fisherman. The best place to view the whirlpool from Jura is Carraig Mhòr, seven miles from Lealt.

Argyll, their glacial rounded tops covered in a light dusting of quartzite scree. The island's name is commonly thought to derive from the Norse *dyr-oe* (deer island) and, appropriately enough, the current deer population of 6000 outnumbers the 180 humans 33 to 1; other wildlife to look out for include mountain hares and eagles. With just one road, which sticks to the more sheltered eastern coast of the island, and only one hotel, a couple of B&Bs and some self-catering cottages, Jura is an ideal place to go for peace and quiet and some great walking.

If you're just coming over for the day from Islay, pop into the **Feolin Research Centre** (daily; free), near the ferry slipway, which has information and displays on the island, and then head off, five miles up the road, to the lovely wooded grounds of **Jura House** (daily 9am–5pm; £2.50; ⓦwww.jurahouseandgardens.co.uk), originally built by the Campbells in the early nineteenth century. Pick up a booklet at the entrance to the grounds, and follow the path which takes you down to the sandy shore, a perfect picnic spot in fine weather. Closer to the house itself, there's an idyllic **walled garden**, divided in two by a natural rushing burn that tumbles down in steps. The garden specializes in antipodean plants, which flourish in the frost-free climate; in season, you can buy some of the garden's organic produce or take tea in the **tea tent** (June–Aug Mon–Fri 11am–5pm).

Anything that happens on Jura happens in the island's only real village, **CRAIGHOUSE**, eight miles up the road from Feolin Ferry. The village enjoys a sheltered setting, overlooking Knapdale on the mainland – so sheltered, in fact, that there are even a few palm trees thriving on the seafront. There's a shop/post office, the island hotel and a tearoom, plus the tiny **Isle of Jura distillery** (☎01496/820601, ⓦwww.isleofjura.com), which is very welcoming to visitors and offers free guided tours.

The family-run *Jura Hotel* in Craighouse is the island's one and only **hotel** (☎01496/820243, ⓦwww.jurahotel.co.uk; ❹), not much to look at from the outside, but warm and friendly within, and centre of the island's social scene. The hotel does the usual bar meals, and has a shower block and laundry facilities round the back for those who wish to **camp** in the hotel gardens. For **B&B**, try *Sealladh na Mara* (☎01496/820349, ⓦwww.isleofjura.net; ❷), a modern croft house four miles north of Craighouse. If you're planning to explore the north end of the island, it's worth knowing about the **bunkhouse** at Kinauachdrachd (☎07899/912116). Jura has its own (unlicensed) bistro **restaurant**, *The Antlers* (☎01496/820123; closed Mon eve), which serves up burgers, sandwiches and salads for lunch, and beautifully presented Jura lamb, pork and salmon in the evening.

Very occasionally a **minibus** (☎01496/820314) meets the **car ferry** (☎01496/840681) from Port Askaig – phone ahead to check times. The ferry itself will not run if there's a strong northerly or southerly wind, so bring your toothbrush if you're coming for a day-trip. There's also a **passenger ferry** service (☎07768/450000, ⓦwww.jurapassengerferry.com) from Tayvallich, on the Argyll mainland, to Craighouse.

Travel details

Trains

Glasgow (Queen St) to: Arrochar and Tarbert (Mon–Sat 3–4 daily, Sun 1–3 daily; 1hr 15min); Dalmally (Mon–Sat 3–4 daily, Sun 1–3 daily; 2hr 15min); Oban (Mon–Sat 3–4 daily, Sun 1–3 daily; 3hr).

Mainland buses

Arrochar to: Carrick Castle (Mon–Sat 1–2 daily; 50min); Inveraray (3 daily, 2 on Sun; 35min); Lochgilphead (3 daily; 1hr 30min); Lochgoilhead (Mon–Sat 1–2 daily; 40min).
Campbeltown to: Carradale (Mon–Sat 4–5 daily, 2 on Sun; 45min); Machrihanish (Mon–Sat 9 daily, 3 on Sun; 20–30min); Saddell (Mon–Sat 4–5 daily, 2 on Sun; 25min); Southend (Mon–Sat 4–5 daily, 2 on Sun; 25min).
Colintraive to: Dunoon (2 daily; 1hr); Tighnabruaich (Mon–Thurs 1–2 daily; 35min).
Dunoon to: Colintraive (2 daily; 1hr); Inveraray (Mon–Sat 3 daily, Sun 0–3 daily; 1hr 10min); Lochgoilhead (Mon–Sat 3 daily; 1hr).
Glasgow to: Arrochar (3–5 daily; 1hr 5min); Campbeltown (3 daily; 4hr 5min); Dalmally (Mon–Sat 4 daily, 2 on Sun; 2hr 20min); Inveraray (4–6 daily; 2hr); Kennacraig (Mon–Sat 2 daily, 1 on Sun; 3hr 30min); Lochgilphead (3 daily; 2hr 40min); Oban (Mon–Sat 4 daily, 2 on Sun; 3hr); Tarbert (3 daily; 3hr 15min); Taynuilt (Mon–Sat 4 daily, 2 on Sun; 2hr 45min).

Inveraray to: Dalmally (Mon–Sat 3 daily, 2 on Sun; 25min); Dunoon (3 daily; 1hr 10min); Lochgilphead (2–3 daily; 40min); Oban (Mon–Sat 3 daily, 2 on Sun; 1hr 5min); Tarbert (2–3 daily; 1hr 30min).
Kennacraig to: Claonaig (Mon–Sat 3 daily; 15min); Skipness (Mon–Sat 3 daily; 20min).
Lochgilphead to: Campbeltown (4–7 daily; 1hr 45min); Crinan (Mon–Sat 3–4 daily; 20min); Kilmartin (Mon–Sat 2–5 daily; 15min); Tarbert (Mon–Fri 7–10 daily, Sat & 3 on Sun; 30min); Tayvallich (3–4 daily; 25min).
Oban to: Appin (Mon–Sat 2–3 daily; 30min); Benderloch (Mon–Sat hourly; 20min); Connel (Mon–Sat hourly; 10–15min); Ellenabeich (Mon–Sat 4–5 daily; 50min); Fort William (Mon–Sat 4 daily; 1hr 30min); Kilmartin (Mon–Sat 2–4 daily; 1hr 20min); Lochgilphead (Mon–Sat 2–4 daily; 1hr 20min); Mallaig (April–Oct daily; 2hr 30min).
Tarbert to: Campbeltown (Mon–Sat 4 daily, 2 on Sun; 1hr 15min); Claonaig (Mon–Sat 3 daily; 30min); Kennacraig (3–6 daily; 15min); Skipness (Mon–Sat 3 daily; 30min); Tayinloan (3–6 daily; 30min).
Tighnabruaich to: Portavadie (Mon–Sat 3–4 daily; 25min); Rothesay (Mon–Thurs 1–2 daily; 1hr).

Island buses

Arran

Brodick (Arran) to: Blackwaterfoot (Mon–Sat 8–10 daily, 4 on Sun; 30min); Corrie (3–5 daily;

20min); Kildonan (4–6 daily; 40min); Lagg (3–5 daily; 50min); Lamlash (Mon–Sat hourly, 4 on Sun; 10–15min); Lochranza (3–5 daily; 45min); Whiting Bay (Mon–Sat hourly, 4 on Sun; 25min).

Bute

Rothesay to: Kilchattan Bay (Mon–Sat 4 daily, 3 on Sun; 30min); Mount Stuart (every 45min; 15min); Rhubodach (Mon–Fri 1–2 daily; 20min).

Islay

Bowmore to: Port Askaig (Mon–Sat 6–8 daily, 4 on Sun; 25min); Port Charlotte (Mon–Sat 5–6 daily, 3 on Sun; 25min); Port Ellen (Mon–Sat 10 daily, 4 on Sun; 20–30min); Portnahaven (Mon–Sat 6 daily, 3 on Sun; 50min).

Mull

Craignure to: Fionnphort (Mon–Sat 3–4 daily, 1 on Sun; 1hr 10min); Fishnish (1–4 daily; 10min); Salen (3–6 daily; 20min); Tobermory (3–6 daily; 45min).
Tobermory to: Calgary (Mon–Sat 2–3 daily; 45min); Dervaig (Mon–Sat 2–4 daily; 25min); Fishnish (2–4 daily; 40min).

Ferries

Car ferries
Summer timetable only.
To Arran: Ardrossan–Brodick (5–6 daily; 55min); Claonaig–Lochranza (8–9 daily; 30min).
To Bute: Colintraive–Rhubodach (frequently; 5min); Wemyss Bay–Rothesay (every 45min–1hr; 30min).
To Coll: Barra–Coll (Thurs 1 daily; 4hr); Oban–Coll (daily except Wed & Fri; 2hr 40min).
To Colonsay: Kennacraig–Colonsay (Wed 1 daily; 3hr 40min); Oban–Colonsay (1 daily except Tues & Sat; 2hr 15min); Port Askaig–Colonsay (Wed 1 daily; 1hr 10min).

To Dunoon: Gourock–Dunoon (hourly; 20min); McInroy's Point–Hunter's Quay (every 30min; 20min).
To Gigha: Tayinloan–Gigha (hourly; 20min).
To Islay: Colonsay–Port Askaig (Wed 1 daily; 1hr 10min); Kennacraig–Port Askaig/Port Ellen (3–4 daily; 2hr 5min–2hr 20min).
To Jura: Port Askaig–Feolin (Mon–Sat hourly, Sun 7–8 daily; 10min); Tayvallich–Craighouse (2 daily except Wed, 1 on Sun; 1hr).
To Kintyre: Portavadie–Tarbert (hourly; 25min).
To Lismore: Oban–Achnacroish (Mon–Sat 4–5 daily, 2 on Sun; 50min).
To Luing: Cuan Ferry (Seil)–Luing (every 30min; 5min).
To Mull: Kilchoan–Tobermory (Mon–Sat every 2hr; May–Aug daily; 35min); Lochaline–Fishnish (daily hourly; 15min); Oban–Craignure (daily every 2hr; 45min).
To Tiree: Barra–Tiree (Thurs 1 daily; 2hr 45min); Oban–Tiree (1 daily; 3hr 40min).

Passenger-only ferries
Summer timetable only.
To Iona: Fionnphort–Iona (daily frequently; 5min).
To Kerrera: Gallanach–Kerrera (every 30min; 10min).
To Lismore: Port Appin–Lismore (hourly; 5min).

Flights

Glasgow to: Campbeltown (Mon–Fri 2 daily; 40min); Islay (Mon–Fri 2–3 daily, Sat & 1 on Sun; 40min); Tiree (Mon–Sat 1 daily; 45min).
Oban to: Coll (Mon & Wed 2–3 daily; 30min); Colonsay (Tues & Thurs 2 daily, Fri & 1 on Sun; 30min); Islay (Tues & Thurs 2 daily; 40min); Tiree (Mon & Wed 2 daily; 1hr).

2

The Central Highlands

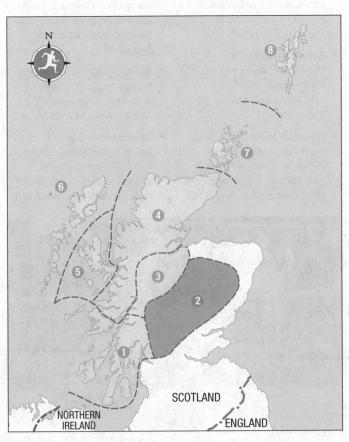

CHAPTER 2 # Highlights

* **Mountain biking in the Trossachs** Pocket Highlands with shining lochs, wooded glens and noble peaks, and some superb forest trails. See p.144

* **Folk music** Join in a session at the bar of the *Taybank Hotel* in the dignified town of Dunkeld. See p.148

* **Schiehallion** Scale Perthshire's "fairy mountain" for the views over lochs, hills, glens and moors. See p.154

* **Rannoch Moor** One of the most inaccessible places in Scotland, where hikers can discover a true sense of remote emptiness. See p.155

* **The castles of Deeside and the Don Valley** A trail of some of Scotland's finest castles, from stately piles to moody ruins. See p.162

* **The Cairngorms** Scotland's grandest mountain massif, a place of wild animals, ancient forests, inspiring vistas – and terrific outdoor activities. See p.170

* **Shinty** A wild mix between hockey and golf; watch a game at Kingussie or Newtonmore. See p.178

* **Speyside Way** Walking route taking in Glenfiddich, Glenlivet and Glen Grant, with the chance to drop in and taste their whiskies too. See p.180

▲ Shinty match

The Central
Highlands

The **Central Highlands** lie right in the heart of Scotland, bounded by the country's two major geological fissures: the Highland Fault, which runs along a line drawn approximately from Arran to Aberdeen and marks the southern extent of Scotland's Highlands, and the Great Glen, the string of lochs that run on a similar southwest–northeast axis between Fort William and Inverness. The appeal of the region is undoubtedly its landscape, a concentrated mix of mountain, glen, loch and moorland that responds to each season with a dramatic blend of colour and mood, combined with the outdoor activities the landscape inspires. It's also an area with a rich history, stemming in large part from the fact that along the geological divide of north and south is a significant cultural and social shift, and it is no surprise that the region is littered with castles, battlefields and monuments from the centuries of power struggle between the Highlanders and the Sassenachs, whether from lowland Scotland or south of the border.

Northwest of Glasgow, the elongated teardrop of **Loch Lomond** is at the heart of Scotland's first national park. The magnificent scenery around the loch continues east into the fabled mountains and lochs of the **Trossachs**, where hikers and mountain-bikers are drawn to explore the forested glens and fugitive Highlanders such as **Rob Roy** once roamed. North of the Trossachs, the massive county of **Perthshire** lies right at the heart of the Central Highlands, with **lochs Tay** and **Rannoch** stacked up across the middle of the region, each surrounded by impressive hills and progressively more remote countryside.

Further to the east are the **Grampian Mountains**. Within this range the **Angus glens**, immediately north of Perth and Dundee, are renowned for their prettiness and easy accessibility, while closer to Aberdeen the river valleys of **Deeside** and **Donside** combine the drama of peaks such as **Lochnagar** with the richly wooded glens and dramatic castles which so enchanted Queen Victoria. The northern side of the Grampians are dominated by the dramatic **Cairngorm** massif, the largest area of land over 2500ft in Britain and epicentre of Scotland's second national park. These hills, with their deserved reputation for superb outdoor sports in both summer and winter, are complemented by the atmospheric ancient woodlands of **Strathspey**. A little way downstream is the whisky-producing region of **Speyside**, where various trails lead you to the distilleries, home of some of the world's most famous single malts.

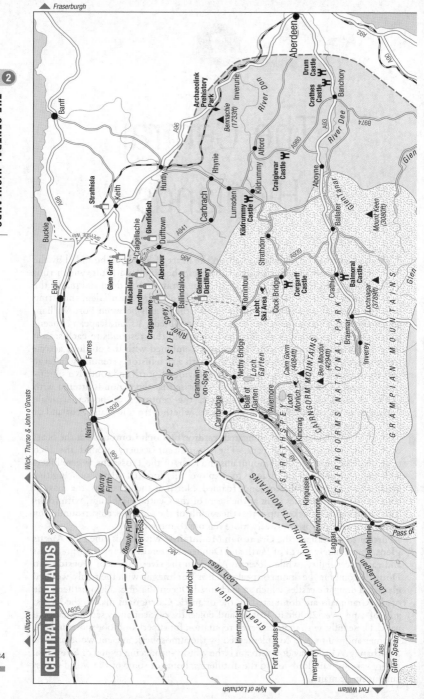

CENTRAL HIGHLANDS

▲ Fraserburgh

Aberdeen

Inverurie

Banff

Archaeolink Prehistory Park

Drum Castle

Crathes Castle

Banchory

River Don

Bennachie (1733ft)

River Dee

Glen

A96

Huntly

Rhynie

Alford

Aboyne

Ballater

Keith

Strathisla

Carbrach

Lumsden

Kildrummy

Craigievar Castle

Mount Keen (3080ft)

Glen Tanar

Glenfiddich

Dufftown

Kildrummy Castle

Glen

Craigellachie

Strathdon

Buckie

Glen Grant

Aberlour

A95

Glenlivet Distillery

Tomintoul

Corgarff Castle

Balmoral Castle

Elgin

Macallan

Cardhu

Ballindalloch

Lecht Ski Area

Crathie

Cragganmore

River Spey

Cock Bridge

Lochnagar (3789ft)

SPEYSIDE WAY

SPEYSIDE

Nethy Bridge

Braemar

Inverey

Forres

Grantown-on-Spey

Loch Garten

Cairn Gorm (4084ft)

CAIRNGORM MOUNTAINS

Ben Macdui (4294ft)

GRAMPIAN MOUNTAINS

Nairn

A939

Carrbridge

Boat of Garten

Aviemore

Loch Morlich

Kincraig

CAIRNGORMS NATIONAL PARK

Moray Firth

STRATHSPEY

Kingussie

Newtonmore

Beauty Firth

Inverness

MONADHLIATH MOUNTAINS

Laggan

Dalwhinnie

Pass of

A82

A9

Loch Ness

Great Glen

Drumnadrochit

Loch Laggan

Loch Ericht

Invermoriston

Fort Augustus

Invergarry

Glen Spean

▲ Ullapool

▲ Wick, Thurso & John o'Groats

▲ Kyle of Lochalsh

▲ Fort William

134

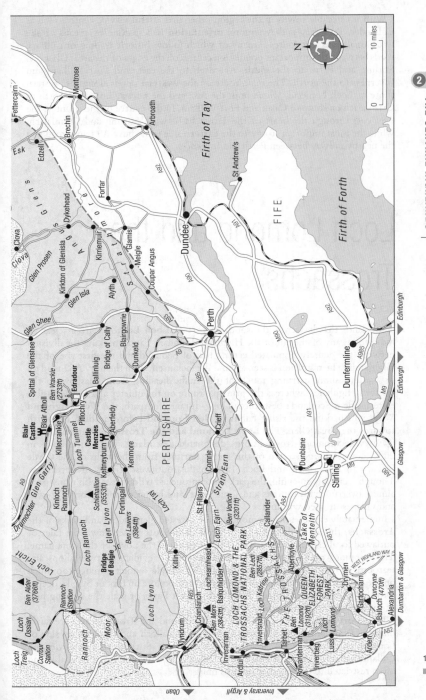

N

0   10 miles

Fettercairn
Montrose
Brechin
Edzell
Esk
Arbroath
Firth of Tay
St Andrew's
Forfar
Clova
Glen Prosen
Glen Clova
Dykehead
Kirriemuir
FIFE
Firth of Forth
Kirkton of Glenisla
Glamis
Meigle
Dundee
Glen Isla
Alyth
Coupar Angus
Glen Shee
Blairgowrie
Bridge of Cally
Perth
Dunkeld
Edinburgh
Spittal of Glenshee
Ballinluig
Dunfermline
Edradour
Ben Vrackie (2757ft)
PERTHSHIRE
Blair Castle
Blair Atholl
Pitlochry
Killiecrankie
Loch Tummel
Castle Menzies
Aberfeldy
Kenmore
Crieff
Edinburgh
Drumochter
Glen Garry
Kinloch Rannoch
Schiehallion (3553ft)
Keltneyburn
Fortingall
Dunblane
Glasgow
Loch Rannoch
Glen Lyon
Ben Lawers (3984ft)
Loch Tay
Comrie
St Fillans
Strath Earn
Stirling
Bridge of Balgie
Rannoch Station
Loch Earn
Ben Vorlich (3201ft)
Loch Eicht
Rannoch Moor
Loch Lyon
Killin
Lochearnhead
Balquhidder
Callander
Lake of Menteith
Ben Alder (3766ft)
Ben Ledi (2857ft)
Crianlarich
Ben More (3843ft)
LOCH LOMOND & THE TROSSACHS NATIONAL PARK
THE TROSSACHS
Aberfoyle
Loch Ossian
Tyndrum
Invervar
Inversnaid
Loch Katrine
Corrour Station
Loch Treig
Inverarnan
Ardlui
Ben Lomond (3192ft)
QUEEN ELIZABETH FOREST PARK
Drymen
Rowardennan
Inverbeg
Loch Lomond
Gartmore
Duncryne (470ft)
Luss
Arden
Balloch
Tarbet
WEST HIGHLAND WAY
Alexandria
Inveraray & Argyll
Oban
Dumbarton & Glasgow

With no sizeable towns in the region other than useful service centres such as Callander, Pitlochry and Aviemore, **orientation** is best done by means of the traditional transport routes – many of which follow historic trading or military roads between the important population centres on the edges of the area: Glasgow, Stirling and Perth to the south, Aberdeen to the east, and Fort William and Inverness to the north. The main route on the **western** side is along the western shore of Loch Lomond, where both the A82 and the railway line wind north to Crianlarich en route to Oban and Fort William. In the **centre** of the country, the A84 cuts through the heart of the Trossachs between Stirling and Crianlarich, while the most important route to the **eastern** side is the busy A9 trunk road and the nearby railway between Perth and Inverness.

Loch Lomond and the Trossachs

The islands that lie across the southern part of **Loch Lomond** are as clear an indicator as any of the cut of the Highland Boundary Fault, marking the division between the densely populated central belt of Scotland and the first rise of the Highlands. The transition is seen around the loch itself, with the busy A82 road on its western shore carrying much of the traffic heading from Glasgow to the western Highlands, whereas the principal route on the quieter and less accessible eastern side is Scotland's best-known long-distance footpath, the **West Highland Way**, which skirts the rising flanks of **Ben Lomond** before heading off north towards the Great Glen. The **Loch Lomond and the Trossachs National Park** (Ⓦ www.lochlomond-trossachs.org), designated as Scotland's first national park in 2002, covers a large stretch of this scenic territory from the lochs of the Clyde Estuary to Loch Earn and Loch Tay, on the southwest fringes of Perthshire. Though scenically splendid, the park is no untouched wilderness, with many parts almost overrun with tourists and some large (and by no means beautiful) towns and villages situated within it.

Immediately east of Loch Lomond are the forested glens, lochs and peaks of the **Trossachs**, the area which inspired **Sir Walter Scott** to set down the tales of outlawed local clansman **Rob Roy (MacGregor)** in the novel of the same name. The trappings of tourism first sparked by Scott – evident in twee shops and tearooms in towns such as **Callander** and **Aberfoyle** – don't impinge too much on the experience, particularly if you're ready to explore on foot or by bike deeper into the well-managed **Queen Elizabeth Forest Park**, or scale the striking hills of the area such as **Ben Ledi** or **Ben A'an**.

Transport links to and within the Loch Lomond and Trossachs area are fairly limited. Trains and buses run from Glasgow to Balloch and the western side of Loch Lomond and there are regular buses from Stirling to Aberfoyle and Callander. Services to other parts of the Trossachs, however, are less reliable and often restricted to the summer months only.

Loch Lomond

The largest stretch of fresh water in Britain (23 miles long and up to five miles wide), **Loch Lomond** is the epitome of Scottish scenic splendour, thanks in large part to the ballad that fondly recalls its "bonnie, bonnie banks". The song was said to have been written by a Jacobite prisoner captured by the English, who, sure of his fate, wrote that his spirit would return to Scotland on the low road much faster than his living compatriots on the high road.

Loch Lomond is undoubtedly the centrepiece of the national park, and the most popular gateway into the park is **Balloch**, the town on the southern tip of Loch Lomond; with Glasgow city centre just nineteen miles away, both Balloch and the southwest side of the loch around **Luss** are often packed with day-trippers and

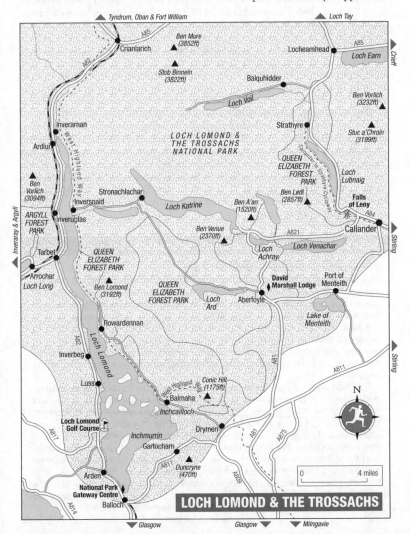

LOCH LOMOND & THE TROSSACHS

tour coaches. Many of these continue up the western side of the loch, though the fast A82 road isn't ideal for a leisurely lochside drive.

Very different in tone, the eastern side of the loch, abutting the Trossachs, operates at a different pace with wooden ferryboats puttering out to a scattering of tree-covered islands off the village of **Balmaha**. Much of the eastern shore can only be reached by boat or foot, although the West Highland Way long-distance footpath (see p.140) and the distinctive peak of **Ben Lomond** ensure that even these parts are well travelled in comparison to many other areas of the Highlands.

Balloch

The main settlement by Loch Lomond is **BALLOCH** at its southwestern corner, where the water channels into the River Leven for its short journey south to the sea in the Firth of Clyde. Surrounded by housing estates and overstuffed with undistinguished guesthouses, Balloch has few redeeming features and is little more than a suburb of the factory town of Alexandria. Accessible from Glasgow by both car and train, it's the site of a large development, **Loch Lomond Shores** (Ⓦwww .lochlomondshores.com), with a "retail crescent" of shops including branches of Edinburgh's venerable department store, Jenners, and of the city's best deli, Valvona & Crolla. The centre can be accessed from town on a miniature train, or by the lakeside path. Alongside, **Drumkinnon Tower** is a striking, stone-built, cylindrical building housing an aquarium (daily 10am–5pm; £12; Ⓣ01389/721000).

There are a number of **activities** available, including nature walks, canoe, bike and even pedalo rental with Can You Experience (Ⓣ01389/602576, Ⓦwww .canyouexperience.com), based right beside Drumkinnon Tower; they also organize "aquaphering" in summer, allowing kids to literally walk on water, in large plastic balls. A short stroll away, restored 1950s **paddle steamer** *The Maid of the Loch* is permanently moored at the pier (11am–4pm: May–Sept daily; Oct–April Sat & Sun; free); aboard you can find out about her glory days sailing the loch and have a cup of tea in the onboard café.

High roads and low roads around Loch Lomond

Ordnance Survey Explorer Map nos. 347 & 364

The popularity of hiking and biking within **Loch Lomond and the Trossachs National Park** has been recognized in an initiative entitled "4Bs" which aims to co-ordinate and enhance the links between boats, boots (ie walking), bikes and buses around the park. Good signposting and information is an increasing facet of the park, with new cycle paths and trails being set out all the time, in addition to enhanced provision for walking and nature trails. Indeed, with a seaplane and wooden mail boats operating on Loch Lomond as well as a 100-year-old steamship on Loch Katrine, getting around the park is very much part of the experience.

For those keen to take to the high road there are three obvious targets offering different levels of challenge. Most prominent of all, **Ben Lomond** (3192ft) is the most southerly of the "Munros" (see p.46) and one of the most popular hills in Scotland, its commanding position above Loch Lomond affording amazing views of both the Highlands and Lowlands. The well-signposted route to the summit and back from Rowardennan takes five to six hours. If you're looking for an easier climb, but an equally impressive view over Loch Lomond, start at Balmaha for the ascent of **Conic Hill** (1175ft), a two-to-three-hour walk through forest and open hillside.

Finally, you need less than an hour to complete the ascent of **Duncryne** (470ft), a small conical hill beside Gartocharn to the east of Balloch on the south side of the loch. The route up is undemanding and the view wonderfully rewarding.

In the centre of town near the bridge, Sweeney's Cruises (℡01389/752376, ⓦwww.sweeney.uk.com) make **loch trips**, including a two-hour sailing to Luss. Otherwise, head across the river to the extensive mature grounds of **Balloch Castle Country Park**, and enjoy various shore-side and sylvan walks.

Practicalities

Balloch has a direct **train** connection with Glasgow Queen Street. Opposite the train station is a small **tourist office** (daily). There's really little point in basing yourself in Balloch, although you could make an exception for one of Scotland's most impressive SYHA **hostels** (℡0870/004 1136, ⓦwww.syha.org.uk; April–Oct); this grand country house with turrets, stained-glass windows and walled gardens two miles northwest of the train station, just off the A82. If you're travelling by Citylink's coach services from Glasgow to Oban, Fort William or Campbeltown, ask to be dropped off.

The exclusive DeVere *Cameron House* resort (℡01389/755565, ⓦwww.cameron house.co.uk; ⑨), just north of Balloch, has its own spa and championship golf course as well as the area's best **restaurant**, an offshoot of Edinburgh's *Martin Wishart*. At Loch Lomond Shores, *Café Zest* is useful for a daytime snack, while *Cucina* and *Sarti's*, near the tourist office on Balloch Road, are both lively, family-run Italian places though unprepossessing from the outside.

The eastern shore of Loch Lomond and the islands

The tranquil **eastern shore** is far better for walking and appreciating the loch's natural beauty than the overcrowded western side. The dead-end B837 from Drymen will take you halfway up the east bank to Rowardennan, as far as you can get by car or bus (#309 from Balloch and Drymen runs to Balmaha every 2hr), while the West Highland Way sticks close to the shores for the entire length of the loch, beginning at the tiny lochside settlement of **BALMAHA**, perched on the Highland Boundary Fault. If you stand on the viewpoint above the pier, you can see the fault line clearly marked by the series of woody islands that form giant stepping stones across the loch. Many of the loch's 37 **islands** are privately owned, and rather quaintly an old wooden mail boat still delivers post to four of them. It's possible to join the **mail boat cruise**, which is run by MacFarlane & Son; from the jetty at Balmaha (May–June & Sept Mon, Thurs & Sat 11.30am, returns 2pm; July & Aug daily 11.30am, returns 2pm; Oct–April Mon & Thurs 10.50am, returns 12.50pm; £9; ℡01360/870214, ⓦwww .balmahaboatyard.co.uk). The timetable allows a one-hour stop on Inchmurrin Island, which has just ten permanent residents; it has the ruins of a monastery and castle, and food is served in the bar of the *Inchmurrin Hotel* (℡01389/850245).

If you're looking for an island to explore, however, a better bet is **Inchcailloch**, owned by Scottish Natural Heritage and the closest to Balmaha. There's a two-mile-long signposted nature trail round the island, which was extensively planted with oaks to provide bark for the local tanning industry. Along the way you'll encounter the ruins of a fourteenth-century nunnery and associated burial ground, and there's a picnic and camping site at Port Bawn on the southwestern side, near a pleasant sandy beach. Until the mid-seventeenth century parishioners on the far (western) shore of Loch Lomond used to row across to Inchcailloch for Sunday services at the church linked to the nunnery. You can row here yourself using a boat rented from MacFarlane & Son (from £10/hr or £30/day), or use their on-demand ferry service (£5 return).

The West Highland Way

Opened in 1980, the spectacular **West Highland Way** was Scotland's first long-distance footpath, stretching some 95 miles from Milngavie (pronounced "mill-guy"), six miles north of central Glasgow, to Fort William, where it reaches the foot of Ben Nevis, Britain's highest mountain. Today, it is by far the most popular such footpath in Scotland, and while for many the range of walking and nearby facilities make it a classic route, others find it a little too busy in high season, particularly in comparison with the isolation of many other parts of the Highlands.

The route follows a combination of ancient **drove roads**, along which Highlanders herded their cattle and sheep to market in the lowlands, military roads built by troops to control the Jacobite insurgency in the eighteenth century, old coaching roads and disused railway lines. In addition to the stunning scenery, which is increasingly dramatic as the path heads north, walkers may see some of Scotland's rarer **wildlife**, including red deer, feral goats – descendants of those left behind after the Highland clearances – and, soaring over the highest peaks, golden eagles.

Passing through the lowlands north of Glasgow, the route runs along the eastern shores of Loch Lomond, over the Highland Boundary Fault Line, then round Crianlarich, crossing open heather moorland across the **Rannoch Moor** wilderness area. It passes close to **Glen Coe** (see p.199) notorious for the massacre of the MacDonald clan, before reaching **Fort William** (see p.191). Apart from a stretch between Loch Lomond and Bridge of Orchy, when the path is within earshot of the main road, this is wild, remote country: north of Rowardennan on Loch Lomond, the landscape is increasingly exposed, and you should be well prepared for sudden and extreme weather changes.

Though this is emphatically not the most strenuous of Britain's long-distance walks – it passes between lofty mountain peaks, rather than over them – a moderate degree of fitness is required as there are some steep ascents. If you're looking for an added challenge, you could work a climb of Ben Lomond or Ben Nevis into your schedule. You might choose to walk individual sections of the Way (the eight-mile climb from Glen Coe up the Devil's Staircase is particularly spectacular), but to tackle the whole thing you need to set aside at least seven days; avoid a Saturday start from Milngavie and you'll be less likely to be walking with hordes of people, and there'll be less pressure on accommodation. Most walkers tackle the route from south to north, and manage between ten and fourteen miles a day, staying at hotels, B&Bs and bunkhouses en route. Camping is permitted at recognized sites.

Although the path is clearly waymarked, you may want to check one of the many maps or guidebooks published: the **official guide**, published by Mercat Press (£16.99), includes a foldout map as well as descriptions of the route, with detailed cultural, historical, archeological and wildlife information. Further details about the Way, including a comprehensive accommodation list, can be found at Ⓦwww.west -highland-way.co.uk, which also has links to tour companies and transport providers, who can take your luggage from one stopping point to the next.

Balmaha gets very busy in summer, not least with day-trippers on the West Highland Way. Beside the large car park is a **National Park Centre** (daily: April– Sept 9.30am–4pm) where you can find out about local forest walks and occasional wildlife workshops. You can **stay** at the well-run *Oak Tree Inn* (Ⓣ01360/870357, Ⓦwww.oak-tree-inn.co.uk), set back from the boatyard, in one of its en-suite double rooms (❹) or bunk-bed quads (❸). There's also a convivial pub with all-day **food**. A cheaper, more basic option is the *Balmaha Bunkhouse Lodge* (Ⓣ01360/870084) just down and across the road, while the idyllically located *Passfoot Cottage* **B&B** (Ⓣ01360/870324, Ⓦwww.passfoot.com; ❸) is set in a whitewashed toll cottage with a lochside garden. **Camping** is available two miles north, on the water at

Milarrochy Bay (☎01360/870236; March–Oct), or, a couple of miles or so further up the road, at Cashel, a lovely, secluded Forestry Commission campsite also on the shores (☎01360/870234; mid-March to Oct).

Public transport ends at Balmaha, but another seven miles north through the woods brings you to the end of the road at **ROWARDENNAN**, a scattered settlement that sits below Ben Lomond (see p.138). Passenger ferries (Easter–Sept 2 daily; ☎01301/702356, ⓦwww.cruiselochlomond.co.uk) cross from Tarbet, on the west shore, and **accommodation** is available at the newly refurbished *Rowardennan Hotel* (☎01360/870273, ⓦwww.rowardennanhotel.co.uk; ❹), and, half a mile beyond, at a wonderfully situated SYHA **hostel** (☎0870/004 1148, ⓦwww.syha.org.uk; March–Oct), a classic turreted Scots Baronial lodge with lawns running down to the shore. Nightlife centres around the hotel's *Clansman Bar*, with open fires and weekend live music.

Only walkers can continue further north up the lochside, where the only other settlement is seven miles north of Rowardennan at **INVERSNAID**, made famous by a poem of the same name by Gerard Manley Hopkins about a frothing waterfall nearby ("This darksome burn, horseback brown/His rollrock highroad roaring down…"). Though remote, the *Inversnaid Hotel* (☎01877/386223; ❹) by the shore is mainly used by coach tours, who arrive via the only road in, the remote B829 from Aberfoyle, though walkers can sometimes snap up any free rooms. It's also possible to get to or from Inversnaid by **ferry** (£4 one-way/£5 return), which crosses from Inveruglas, directly opposite on the western shore. You'll have to phone the *Inversnaid Hotel* to make arrangements.

The western shore of Loch Lomond

Despite the roar of traffic hurtling along the upgraded A82, the **west bank** of Loch Lomond is an undeniably beautiful stretch of water. **LUSS** is without doubt the prettiest village in the region, with its prim, identical sandstone and slate cottages garlanded in rambling roses, and its narrow sand-and-pebble strand. However, its charms are no secret, and its streets and beach can become crowded in summer. If you want to escape the hordes, pop into the parish **church**, which is a haven of peace and has a lovely ceiling made from Scots pine rafters and some fine Victorian stained-glass windows. You can pick up local information at the neighbouring **Luss Visitor Centre**. The modern *Lodge on Loch Lomond* (☎01436/860201, ⓦwww.loch-lomond.co.uk; ❼), just north of town, has a string of **rooms** with balconies and views over the loch, and serves decent meals in its restaurant, *Colquhoun's*. The *Coach House* **tearoom** is a must, a spruce and lively little place serving a range of teas, cakes, ciabattas, Orkney ice cream and its own take on haggis.

Ten miles north of Luss is the small settlement of **TARBET**, where the West Highland **train** – the line from Glasgow to Fort William and Mallaig, with a branch line to Oban – reaches the shoreline at the point where the A83 heads off west into Argyll; the A82 continues north along the banks of the loch towards Crianlarich. Tarbet has a small **tourist office** (April–Oct daily; ☎01301/702260). At the pier over the road from the prominent *Tarbet Hotel* you can hop on a **cruise** run by Cruise Loch Lomond (90min; £8.50; ☎01301/702356, ⓦwww.cruise lochlomond.co.uk). The same operator also offers trips to Inversnaid and Rowardennan on the eastern side.

North of Tarbet, the A82 turns back into the narrow, winding road of old, making for slower but much more interesting driving. There's one more **train station** on Loch Lomond at **Ardlui**, at the mountain-framed head of the loch, but most travellers continue a couple of miles further north to **Inverarnan**, where the 🕱 *Drover's Inn* (☎01301/704234, ⓦwww.thedroversinn.co.uk; ❹) is, arguably, the most idiosyncratic **hotel** in Scotland. The bar has a roaring fire, barmen dressed in kilts, weary hillwalkers sipping pints and bearded musicians banging out folk songs. Down the creaking corridors, past moth-eaten stuffed animals, are a number of supposedly haunted and resolutely old-fashioned rooms.

Crianlarich and Tyndrum

CRIANLARICH, some eight miles north of the head of Loch Lomond, is an important staging post on various transport routes, including the West Highland Railway which divides here, one branch heading due west towards Oban, the other continuing north over Rannoch Moor to Fort William. The West Highland Way long-distance footpath (see box, p.140) also trogs past. Otherwise there's little reason to stop here, unless you're keen on tackling some of the steep-sided hills that rise up from the glen.

Five miles further north from here on the A82/A85, the village of **TYNDRUM** owes its existence to a minor (and very short-lived) nineteenth-century gold rush, but today supports little more than a busy service station and several characterless hotels. Right beside Tyndrum Lower railway station is a good campsite and small bunkhouse at *By The Way Hostel and Campsite* (℡01838/400333, ⓦwww.tyndrumbytheway.com), and for a refreshingly different roadside dining experience, it's well worth trying the airy *Real Food Café* (daily until 10pm) on the main road for fresh, fast food that's locally sourced and cooked to order. At Tyndrum the road divides, with the A85 heading west to Oban, and the A82 heading for Fort William via Glen Coe.

The Trossachs

Often described as the Highlands in miniature, the **Trossachs** area boasts a magnificent diversity of scenery, with distinctive peaks, silvery lochs and mysterious, forest-covered slopes. It is country ripe for stirring tales of brave kilted clansmen, a role fulfilled by Rob Roy Macgregor, the seventeenth-century outlaw whose name seems to attach to every second waterfall, cave and barely discernible path. Strictly speaking, the name "Trossachs", normally translated as either "bristly country" or "crossing place", originally referred only to the wooded glen between **Loch Katrine** and Loch Achray, but today it is usually taken as being the whole area from **Callander** right up to the eastern banks of Loch Lomond, with which it has been grouped as one of Scotland's national parks.

The Trossachs' high tourist profile was largely attributable in the early days to Sir Walter Scott, whose novels *Lady of the Lake* and *Rob Roy* were set in and around the area. According to one contemporaneous account, after Scott's *Lady of the Lake* was published in 1810, the number of carriages passing Loch Katrine rose from fifty the previous year to 270. Since then, neither the popularity nor beauty of the region has waned, and in high season the place is jam-packed with coaches full of tourists as well as walkers and mountain-bikers taking advantage of the easily accessed scenery. Autumn is a better time to come, when the hills are blanketed in rich, rusty colours and the crowds are thinner. In terms of where to stay, **Aberfoyle** has a rather dowdy air while **Callander** feels somewhat overrun, and you're often better off seeking out one of the guesthouses or B&Bs tucked away in secluded corners of the region.

If you're not driving, try **Demand Responsive Transport** (DRT), which offers a taxi-type service for the price of a bus fare (℡0844/567 5670, ⓦwww.aberfoylecoaches.com); you're advised to book 24 hours in advance.

Rob Roy

A member of the outlawed Macgregor clan, **Rob Roy** (meaning "Red Robert" in Gaelic) was born in 1671 in Glengyle, just north of Loch Katrine, and lived for some time as a respectable cattle farmer and trader, supported by the powerful duke of Montrose. In 1712, finding himself in a tight spot when a cattle deal fell through, Rob Roy absconded with £1000, some of it belonging to the duke. He took to the hills to live as a brigand, his feud with Montrose escalating after the duke repossessed Rob Roy's land and drove his wife from their house. He was present at the Battle of Sheriffmuir during the earlier Jacobite uprising of 1715, ostensibly supporting the Jacobites but probably as an opportunist: the chaos would have made cattle-raiding easier. Eventually captured and sentenced to transportation, Rob Roy was pardoned and returned to **Balquhidder**, northeast of Glengyle, where he remained until his death in 1734.

Rob Roy's status as a local hero in the mould of Robin Hood should be tempered with the fact that he was without doubt a bandit and blackmailer. His life has been much romanticized, from Sir Walter Scott's 1818 novel *Rob Roy* to the 1995 film starring Liam Neeson, although the tale does serve well to dramatize the clash between the doomed clan culture of the Gaelic-speaking Highlanders and the organized feudal culture of lowland Scots, which effectively ended with the defeat of the Jacobites at Culloden in 1746. His **grave** in Balquhidder, a simple affair behind the ruined church, is one of the principal sights on the unofficial Rob Roy trail, though the peaceful graveyard is mercifully underdeveloped and free of the tartan trappings that plague parts of the Trossachs, predictably dubbed "Rob Roy Country" by the tourist board.

Aberfoyle and the Lake of Menteith

Each summer the sleepy little town of **ABERFOYLE**, twenty miles west of Stirling, dusts itself down for its annual influx of tourists. Though of little appeal itself, Aberfoyle's position in the heart of the Trossachs is ideal, with **Loch Ard Forest** and **Queen Elizabeth Forest Park** stretching across to Ben Lomond and Loch Lomond to the west, the long curve of Loch Katrine and Ben Venue to the northwest, and Ben Ledi to the northeast.

Don't come here for lively nightlife or entertainment, but for a good, healthy blast of the outdoors. From Aberfoyle you might like to wander north of the village to **Doon Hill**: cross the bridge over the Forth, continue past the cemetery and then follow signs to the **Fairy Knowe** (knoll). A toadstool marker points you through oak and holly trees to the summit of the Knowe where there is a pine tree said to contain the unquiet spirit of the Reverend Robert Kirk, who studied local fairy lore and published his inquiries in *The Secret Commonwealth* (1691). Legend has it that, as punishment for disclosing supernatural secrets, he was forcibly removed to fairyland where he has languished ever since, although his mortal remains can be found in the nearby graveyard. This short walk should preferably be made at dusk, when it is at its most atmospheric.

Practicalities

Regular **buses** from Stirling pull into the car park on Aberfoyle's Main Street. The adjacent **tourist office** (daily; ℡0870/720 0604) has full details of local accommodation, sights and outdoor activities. The nearby **Scottish Wool Centre** (daily: May–Sept 9.30am–5.30pm; Oct–April 10am–5pm; free) – a popular stop-off point with tour buses – is a glorified country knitwear shop selling all the usual jumpers and woolly toys as well as featuring daily seasonal displays of sheep gathering and shearing.

Hiking and biking in the Trossachs

The Trossachs are ideal for exploring on **foot** or on a **mountain bike**. This is partly because the terrain is slightly more benign than the Highlands proper, but much is due to the excellent management of the **Queen Elizabeth Forest Park**, a huge chunk of the national park that lies between Loch Lomond and Loch Lubnaig. The main visitor centre for the area, David Marshall Lodge (see opposite), is just outside Aberfoyle, and is well worth a visit.

For **hillwalkers**, the prize peak is Ben Lomond (3192ft), best accessed from Rowardennan (see p.141). Other highlights include Ben Venue (2370ft) and Ben A'an (1520ft) on the shores of Loch Katrine, as well as Ben Ledi (2857ft), just northwest of Callander, which all offer relatively straightforward but very rewarding climbs and, on clear days, stunning views. Walkers can also choose from any number of waymarked routes through the forests and along lochsides; pick up a map of these at the visitor centre.

Mountain bikers are served by a network of forest paths and one of the more impressive stretches of the National Cycle Network cutting through the region from Loch Lomond to Killin. If you don't have your own bike, head for the best **rental** place in the area, Wheels Cycling Centre (℡01877/331100, ⓦwww.scottish-cycling.com), next to *Trossachs Tryst Backpackers* (see p.146) a mile and a half southwest of Callander; it stocks front or full suspension models, baby seats and children's cycles. Try also the *Trossachs Holiday Park* (see below) on the A81 two miles south of Aberfoyle, and Mounter Bikes (℡01877/331052, ⓦwww.callandercyclehire.co.uk) beside the visitor centre in the centre of Callander (see p.146).

Accommodation options in Aberfoyle itself aren't all that inspiring. Head a mile west out of the town to *Creag-Ard House* (℡01877/382297, ⓦwww .creag-ard.co.uk; ❺; Easter–Oct), which serves lovely breakfasts in a Victorian house overlooking Loch Ard. The **Lake of Menteith** (see below) is another beautiful place to stay: the *Lake of Menteith Hotel* (℡01877/385258, ⓦwww.lake -hotel.com; ❼) at Port of Menteith has a lovely waterfront setting next to the Victorian Gothic parish church, as well as a classy restaurant. Near the lake in a beautiful hillside setting is *Inchie Farm*, a farmstay/B&B (℡01877/385233, ⓦinchiefarm.co.uk; ❷).

For **camping**, a couple of miles south of Aberfoyle, off the A81 and on the edge of Queen Elizabeth Forest Park, there's *Cobleland* (℡01877/382392, ⓦwww .forestholidays.co.uk; mid-March to mid-Jan), run by the Forestry Commission, which covers five acres of woodland by the River Forth (little more than a stream here). Further south, the excellent family-run *Trossachs Holiday Park* (℡01877/382614, ⓦwww.trossachsholidays.co.uk; March–Oct) is twice the size and has **bikes** for rent.

The Lake of Menteith

About four miles east of Aberfoyle towards Doune, the **Lake of Menteith** is a superb fly-fishing centre and Scotland's only lake (as opposed to loch), so named due to a historic mix-up with the word *laigh*, Scots for "low-lying ground", which applied to the whole area. To rent a **fishing boat** or a rod contact the Lake of Menteith Fisheries (℡01877/385664; April–Oct). There are also some nice secluded spots along the shore for picnics and swims.

From the northern shore of the lake, you can take a little ferry out to the **Island of Inchmahome** (daily: April–Sept 9.30am–4.30pm; Oct 9.30am–3.30pm; HS; £4.70 including ferry) to explore the lovely ruined Augustinian abbey. Founded in 1238, **Inchmahome Priory** is the most beautiful island monastery in Scotland, its remains rising tall and graceful above the trees. The masons employed to build the priory are thought to be those who built Dunblane Cathedral; certainly the western entrance there resembles that at Inchmahome. The nave of the church is roofless, but in the choir are preserved the graves of important families from the surrounding area. Most touching is a late thirteenth-century double effigy depicting Walter, the first Stewart earl of Menteith, and his countess, Mary, who, feet resting on lion-like animals, turn towards each other and embrace.

Also buried here is the adventurer and scholar Robert Bontine Cunninghame Graham, once a pal of Buffalo Bill and Joseph Conrad, and first president of the National Party of Scotland. Five-year-old Mary, Queen of Scots was hidden at Inchmahome in 1547 before being taken to France, and there's a formal garden in the west of the island, known as Queen Mary's Bower, where legend has it she played. Traces remain of an orchard planted by the monks, but the island is thick now with oak, ash and Spanish chestnut. Visible on a nearby but inaccessible islet is the ruined castle of **Inchtalla**, the home of the earls of Menteith in the sixteenth and seventeenth centuries.

Aberfoyle to Callander

North of Aberfoyle, the A821 road to Loch Katrine winds its way into the Queen Elizabeth Forest, snaking up **Duke's Pass** (so called because it once belonged to the Duke of Montrose). You can walk or drive the short distance from Aberfoyle to the park's excellent **visitor centre** at **David Marshall Lodge** (daily: March–June, Sept & Oct 10am–5pm; July & Aug 10am–6pm; Nov & Dec 10am–4pm; Jan Sat & Sun 10am–4pm; Feb Thurs–Sun 10am–4pm; car park £2; ℡01877/382258), where you can pick up maps of the walks and cycle routes in the forest, get background information on the area's flora and fauna (there's a video-relay to the nests of local peregrine falcons, pine martens and ospreys) or settle into the café with its splendid views out over the tree tops. Adjacent to the centre is the **Go Ape adventure course** (April–Oct daily 9am–5pm; Feb & March Sat & Sun 9am–5pm; £30; bookings ℡0870/428 2710, ⓦwww.goape.co.uk), which involves an extended series of 40ft-high rope bridges, tarzan swings and high-wire slides though the forest. The only road in the forest open to cars is the **Achray Forest Drive**, just under two miles further on from the centre, which leads through the park and along the western shore of **Loch Drunkie** before rejoining the main road.

Loch Katrine

Heading down the northern side of the Duke's Pass you come first to **Loch Achray**, tucked under Ben A'an. Look out across the loch for the small **Callander Kirk** in a lovely setting alone on a promontory. At the head of the loch a road follows the short distance through to the southern end of **Loch Katrine** at the foot of Ben Venue (2370ft), from where the elegant Victorian passenger **steamer**, the SS *Sir Walter Scott* (April–Oct daily; £12 return; ℡01877/376315, ⓦwww .lochkatrine.co.uk), has been plying the waters since 1900, chugging up to the wild country of Glengyle. It makes various cruises each day, but only the first (departing at 10.30am) stops off at Stronachlachar most days, though on Wednesdays and weekends there's a second trip to Stronachlachar departing at 2.30pm; the shorter one-hour cruises don't make any stops (£11). A popular combination is to **rent a bike** from the Katrinewheelz (℡01877/376366, ⓦwww.katrinewheelz .co.uk) hut by the pier, take the steamer up to Stronachlachar, then cycle back on the road around the north side of the loch.

From Loch Katrine the A821 heads due east past the tiny village of **Brig o'Turk**, where it's worth looking in on the ⌂ *Byre Inn*, a tiny pub and classy restaurant set in an old stone barn with wooden pews and a welcoming open fire; it's the starting point for waymarked walks to lochs Achray, Drunkie and Venachar. The cosy, wooden-clad *Brig o' Turk Tea-Room* (Easter–Sept 11am–4pm) is also a good place to refresh after a walk or cycle. From here, carry on along the shores of Loch Venachar, where you'll find a stylish new building, *Venacher Lochside* (T01877/330011, W www.trossachs-leisure.co.uk), which houses an attractive café serving meals on the lochside terrace and a fishing centre offering boat rental and fly-fishing tuition.

Callander and around

CALLANDER, on the eastern edge of the Trossachs, sits on the banks of the River Teith at the southern end of the **Pass of Leny**, one of the key routes into the Highlands. Significantly larger than Aberfoyle, it suffers in high season for being right on the main tourist trail from Stirling through to the west Highlands. Callander first came to fame during the "Scottish Enlightenment" of the eighteenth and nineteenth centuries, with the glowing reports of the Trossachs given by Sir Walter Scott and William Wordsworth. Development was given a further boost when Queen Victoria chose to visit, and then by the arrival of the train line – long since closed – in the 1860s. Tourists have arrived in throngs ever since, as the plethora of restaurants, tearooms, gift shops and shops selling woollens and crafts testifies.

Callander's **tourist office** is situated in a converted church at Ancaster Square on the main street (March–Oct daily; T0870/720 0628); there's **bike rental** at Mounter Bikes (T01877/331052, W www.callandercyclehire.co.uk), also on Ancaster Square.

Accommodation

Arden House Bracklinn Rd T01877/330235, W www.ardenhouse.org.uk. A grand Victorian guesthouse in its own gardens with good views and woodland walks from the back door. April–Oct. **4**

Burnt Inn House Brig o'Turk T01877/376212, W www.burntinnhouse.co.uk. Simple, farmhouse-style B&B right in the heart of the Trossachs countryside: a good alternative to staying in Callander. **2**

Callander Meadows 24 Main St T01877/330 181, W www.callandermeadows.co.uk. Centrally located rooms in an attractive townhouse that boasts three comfortable

en-suite rooms and a decent restaurant. Full board available. **4**

Roman Camp Country House Hotel Main St T01877/330003, W www.romancamphotel.co.uk. The town's upmarket option is this romantic, turreted seventeenth-century hunting lodge in twenty-acre gardens on the River Teith. **7**

Trossachs Tryst Invertrossachs Rd T01877/331200, W www.scottish-hostel .com. A friendly, well-equipped and comfortable 32-bed hostel and activity centre with self-catering dorms and family rooms, a mile southwest of town down a turn-off from the A81 to Port of Menteith. Bike rental available. **1**

Eating and drinking

Despite Callander's tourist throngs, the town itself has few **restaurants** worth recommending. *Callander Meadows* (see above; restaurant closed Mon & Tues) serves up decent, freshly cooked lunches and dinners. Also on the main drag, at no.75, *Mhor Fish* is one of a new breed of fish and chip shops; it has a sustainable fish policy, daily specials and everything from snacks to bistro-style seafood dishes – the takeaway section serves fish suppers, burgers, pies and haggis. For coffee, cheeses and other deli items head for cheerful *Deli Ecosse*, beside the church on Ancaster Square. There's **pub food** at the convivial *Lade Inn* in Kilmahog, a mile west of Callander, where the owners are particularly keen on real ales, with an on-site shop selling bottled beers from all over Scotland.

North of town, you can walk or ride the scenic six-mile Callander to Strathyre (Route 7) Cycleway, which forms part of the network of cycleways between the Highlands and Glasgow. The route is based on the old Caledonian train line to Oban, which closed in 1965, and runs along the western side of Loch Lubnaig.

Beyond the northern end of Loch Lubnaig is tiny **BALQUHIDDER**, most famous as the site of the **grave of Rob Roy**, which you'll find in the small yard behind the ruined church. Refreshingly, considering the Rob Roy fever that plagues the region, his grave – marked by a rough stone carved with a sword, cross and a man with a dog – is remarkably understated. The village's tiny wood-panelled library – built by the laird as a distraction to the pub across the road – is now a tearoom (Easter–Oct daily 10am–5pm) serving freshly baked scones to passing cyclists and walkers. Avoid the plethora of Rob Roy-themed **accommodation** in Balquhidder, and drive six miles beyond the village to the award-winning ⚓ *Monachyle Mhor* hotel (☎01877/384622, ⓦwww.monachylemhor.com; ❼), an eighteenth-century farmhouse with stylish modern rooms and a terrific restaurant (open to non-residents, but book ahead) specializing in locally sourced food – much of it from the family's farm and bakery – and with the added bonus of lovely views over Loch Voil. On the road to the hotel is the unexpected sight of the Dhanakosa Buddhist retreat centre (☎01877/384213, ⓦwww.dhanakosa.com) – they run weekend or week-long retreats here, with courses ranging from t'ai chi to hillwalking.

North of Balquhidder the busy A84 slides past Lochearnhead, at the western end of Loch Earn, and Killin, at the western end of Loch Tay, before swinging west towards Crianlarich (see p.142) and the west coast.

Perthshire

Genteel **Perthshire** is, in many ways, the epitome of well-groomed rural Scotland. First settled over eight thousand years ago, it was occupied by the Romans and then the Picts before Celtic missionaries established themselves, enjoying the amenable climate, fertile soil and ideal defensive and trading location. North and west of the county town of Perth, there are some magnificent landscapes to be discovered – snow-capped peaks falling away to forested slopes and long, deep lochs – topography which inevitably controls transport routes, influences the weather and tolerates little development. The various mountains, woods and lochs provide terrific walking and water sports, particularly through the **Strath Tay** area, dominated by Scotland's longest river, the **Tay**, which flows from **Loch Tay** past the attractive towns of **Dunkeld** and **Aberfeldy**. Further north, the countryside of **Highland Perthshire** becomes more sparsely populated and more spectacular, especially around the towns of **Pitlochry** and **Blair Atholl** and the wild expanses of **Rannoch Moor** to the west.

Transport connections in the region are at their best if you head straight north from Perth, along the main A9 road and train line to Inverness, but buses – albeit often infrequent – also serve the more remote areas. Keep asking at bus stations for details of services, as the further you get from the main villages, the less definitive timetables become.

Strath Tay to Loch Tay

Heading due north from Perth, both the railway and main A9 trunk road carry much of the traffic heading into the Highlands, often speeding straight through some of Perthshire's most attractive countryside in its eagerness to get to the bleaker country to the north. Perthshire has been dubbed **Big Tree Country** by the tourist board in recognition of some magnificent woodland in the area, including a number of individual trees that rank among Europe's oldest, tallest and certainly most handsome specimens. Many of these are found around the valley – or "strath" – of the River Tay as it heads towards the sea from attractive **Loch Tay**, set up among the high Breadalbane mountains which include the striking peak of **Ben Lawers**, Perthshire's highest, and the hills which enclose the long, enchanting **Glen Lyon**. Studded around Loch Tay are remains of crannogs, ancient dwellings built on man-made islands, which are brought to life at the **Crannog Centre** beside the village of Kenmore. Not far downriver is the prosperous small town of **Aberfeldy**; from here the Tay drifts southeast between the unspoilt twin villages of **Dunkeld** and **Birnam** before meandering its way past Perth.

Dunkeld and Birnam

DUNKELD, twelve miles north of Perth on the A9, was proclaimed Scotland's ecclesiastical capital by Kenneth MacAlpine in 850. Its position at the southern boundary of the Grampian Mountains made it a favoured meeting-place for Highland and Lowland cultures, and the town is one of the area's most pleasant communities, with handsome whitewashed houses, appealing arts-and-crafts shops and a charming cathedral. The **tourist office** is at The Cross in the town centre (April–Oct daily; ☎01350/727688).

Dunkeld's partly ruined **cathedral** (daily: May–Sept 9.30am–6.30pm; Oct–April 9.30am–4pm; free; ⓦwww.dunkeldcathedral.org.uk) is on the northern side of town, in an idyllic setting amid lawns and trees on the east bank of the Tay. Construction began in the early twelfth century and continued throughout the next two hundred years, but the building was more or less ruined at the time of the Reformation. The present structure consists of the fourteenth-century choir and the fifteenth-century nave; the choir, restored in 1600 (and several times since), now serves as the parish church, while the nave remains roofless apart from the clock tower. Inside, note the leper's peep near the pulpit in the north wall, through which lepers could receive the sacrament without coming into contact with the congregation. Also look out for the great effigy of the **Wolf of Badenoch**, Robert II's son, born in 1343. The Wolf acquired his name and notoriety when, after being excommunicated for leaving his wife, he took his revenge by burning the towns of Forres and Elgin and sacking the latter's cathedral.

Birnam

Dunkeld is linked to its sister community, **BIRNAM**, by Thomas Telford's seven-arched bridge of 1809. This little village has a place in history thanks to Shakespeare, for it was on Dunsinane Hill, to the southeast of the village, that Macbeth declared: "I will not be afraid of death and bane/Till Birnam Forest come to Dunsinane".

The **Birnam Oak**, a gnarly old character propped up by crutches that can be seen on the waymarked riverside walk, is inevitably claimed to be a survivor of the infamous mobile forest. Several centuries after Shakespeare, another literary personality, Beatrix Potter, drew inspiration from the area, recalling her childhood holidays here when penning the Peter Rabbit stories. A Potter-themed exhibition and garden can be found in the impressive barrel-fronted **Birnam Institute** (daily 10am–4.30pm; £1; Ⓦwww.birnaminstitute.com), a lively theatre, arts and community centre.

Practicalities

Dunkeld is well served by **public transport**: by train between Perth and Inverness, and bus from Perth #23 (Stagecoach) and #957 (Scottish Citylink). There are several large **hotels** in Dunkeld and Birnam, including the central *Royal Dunkeld*, Atholl Street (Ⓣ01350/727322, Ⓦwww.royaldunkeld.co.uk; ❺), which also has cheaper twin rooms in an annexe (❷). Priciest is the rather corporate *Dunkeld House Hilton* (Ⓣ01350/727771, Ⓦwww.hilton.co.uk/dunkeld; ❽ dinner, B&B), a vast country estate house on the banks of the Tay to the north of town, with a spa, swimming pool and excellent facilities for outdoor pursuits. Local **B&Bs** include the *Waterbury Guest House* (Ⓣ01350/727324, Ⓦwww.waterbury-guesthouse.co .uk; ❸) in a turreted Victorian villa on Murthly Terrace in Birnam, and *The Pend* (Ⓣ01350/727586, Ⓦwww.thepend.com; ❹), an elegantly furnished option just off the main street in Dunkeld.

The central ⚡ *Taybank Hotel* (Ⓣ01350/727340, Ⓦwww.thetaybank.com; ❷) is a characterful beacon for music fans, who come for the regular live sessions in the convivial bar. There are decent bar **meals** at the *Taybank* (the stovies are a speciality); coffee, cakes and light meals at the *Foyer Café* in the Birnam Institute; and snacks, sandwiches, Scottish beers and fresh fruit at the *Robert Menzies* deli in Dunkeld, where there's also a tiny café.

Around Dunkeld

Dunkeld and Birnam are surrounded by some lovely countryside, both along the banks of the Tay and in the deep surrounding forest. One of the most rewarding walks is the mile and a half from Birnam to **The Hermitage**, set in a grandly wooded gorge of the plunging River Braan. Here you'll find a pretty eighteenth-century folly, also known as Ossian's Hall, which was once mirrored to reflect the water – the mirrors were smashed by Victorian vandals and the folly was more tamely restored. The hall, appealing yet incongruous in its splendid setting, neatly frames a dramatic waterfall. Nearby you can crane your neck to look up at a Douglas fir that claims the title of tallest tree in Britain – last time the tape was out it managed 212ft.

Two miles east of Dunkeld, the **Loch of the Lowes** is a nature reserve that offers a rare chance to see breeding **ospreys** and other wildfowl; the visitor centre (April–Sept 10am–5pm; £3; Ⓣ01350/727337) has video-relay screens and will point you in the direction of the best vantage points. If the surroundings seem appealing enough to warrant lingering a day or two, you could head for the mellow *Wester Caputh Independent Hostel* (Ⓣ01738/710449, Ⓦwww.westercaputh .co.uk), four miles downstream along the Tay from Dunkeld, which has small dorms and makes for a great base with a relaxing and welcoming atmosphere; there's also a self-catering house.

Aberfeldy and around

From Dunkeld the A9 runs north alongside the Tay for eight miles to Ballinluig, a little place marking the turn-off along the A827 to **ABERFELDY**, a prosperous settlement of large stone houses that acts as a service centre for the wider Loch Tay area. The **tourist office** (daily; Ⓣ01887/820276) at The Square in the town centre is good for advice on local accommodation and details of nearby walking trails. If you want to **rent a bike**, head to Girvans outdoor store (Ⓣ01887/820254), behind the filling station on your way into town from the east.

Aberfeldy sits at the point where the Urlar Burn – lined by the silver birch trees celebrated by Robert Burns in his poem *The Birks of Aberfeldy* – flows into the River Tay. The Tay is spanned by the humpbacked, four-arch **Wade's Bridge**, built by General Wade in 1733 during his efforts to control the unrest in the Highlands, and one of his more impressive pieces of work. Overlooking the bridge from the south end is the **Black Watch Monument**, depicting a pensive, kilted soldier, erected in 1887 to commemorate the first muster of the Highland regiment gathered as a peacekeeping force by Wade in 1740.

The main set-piece attraction in town is **Dewar's World of Whisky** at the Aberfeldy Distillery (April–Oct Mon–Sat 10am–6pm, Sun noon–4pm; Nov–March Mon–Sat 10am–4pm; £6.50; ⊛ www.dewarswow.com), which puts on an impressive show of describing the making of whisky. A **Deluxe Tour** (£18) and **Signature Tour** (£30) are available for connoisseurs, giving a more in-depth look around the distillery and a chance to taste (or "nose") the whisky at different stages in its life. The rest of the small town centre is a busy mixture of craft and tourist shops, the most interesting by far being ⅍ **The Watermill** on Mill Street (Mon–Sat 10am–5pm, Sun noon–5pm; ⊛ www.aberfeldywatermill.com), an inspiring bookshop, contemporary art gallery and café located in the town's superbly restored early nineteenth-century mill.

Practicalities

For accommodation there's ⅍ *Guinach House* (☎ 01887/820251, ⊛ www .guinachhouse.co.uk; ⊙) by The Birks, a tastefully decorated guesthouse/holiday rental in well-tended grounds; while the stylish and unpretentious *Balnearn Guest House* (☎ 01887/820431, ⊛ www.balnearnhouse.com; ❸) is on Crieff Road. The closest **bunkhouse** is *Adventurer's Escape* (☎ 01887/820498, ⊛ www.adventurers -escape.co.uk), a brightly painted lodge right next to the *Weem Hotel* on the road to Castle Menzies. As you'd expect, it's well tuned into the many adventure sports and outdoor pursuits that are available locally.

Aberfeldy isn't short on cafés and tearooms; the best bet for a good cup of coffee, a bowl of lunchtime soup or afternoon tea is the relaxed **café** in The Watermill (see above), with its pretty riverside garden. Decent **bar** meals can be found over the Wade Bridge in Weem at the *Ailean Chraggan Inn*.

Castle Menzies and around

One mile west of Aberfeldy, across Wade's Bridge, **Castle Menzies** (April to mid-Oct Mon–Sat 10.30am–5pm, Sun 2–5pm; £3.50; ⊛ www.menzies.org) is an imposing, Z-shaped, sixteenth-century tower house which, until the middle of the last century, was the chief seat of the Clan Menzies (pronounced "Ming-iss"). With the demise of the line, the castle has been taken over by the Menzies Clan Society, which since 1971 has been involved in the lengthy process of restoring it. Much of the interior is on view, most of it refreshingly free of fixtures and fittings, displaying an austerity that is much more true to medieval life than many grander, furnished castles elsewhere in the country.

A mile or so further along the road by the hamlet with the unfortunate name of **Dull** is Highland Adventure Safaris (☎ 01887/820071, ⊛ www.highland adventuresafaris.net), where you can join Land Rover trips into the heather-clad hills nearby in search of wildlife such as eagles, red deer and grouse. At the lodge try your hand at gold and mineral panning (£4), a big hit with kids; there's also a deer park, play area and a good farm shop/café. Shortly after this point the road splits: you can strike out for the hills of Glen Lyon (see p.152), or head north past the striking mountain Schiehallion to Loch Tummel (see p.154).

Loch Tay

Aberfeldy grew up around a crossing point on the River Tay, which leaves it six miles adrift of Loch Tay, a fourteen-mile-long stretch of fresh water connecting the western and eastern Highlands. Guarding the northern end of the loch is **KENMORE**, where whitewashed estate houses and well-tended gardens cluster around the gate to the extensive grounds of **Taymouth Castle**, built by the Campbells of Glenorchy in the early nineteenth century. The rocket-like eighteenth-century **church** contains an ancient "poor box", and memorials to soldiers of the Black Watch Regiment. The main attraction here, though, is the **Scottish Crannog Centre** (daily: April–Oct 10am–5.30pm; Nov 10am–4pm; £6.50; ⓦwww.crannog.co.uk). Crannogs are Iron Age loch dwellings built on stilts over the water, with a gangway to the shore which could be lifted up to defy a hostile intruder, whether animal or human. Following underwater excavations in Loch Tay, the team here has superbly reconstructed a crannog, and visitors can now walk out over the loch to the thatched wooden dwelling, complete with sheepskin rugs, wooden bowls and other evidence of the way life was lived 2500 years ago.

The nicest place to **stay** in town is the pleasant and well-run *Kenmore Hotel* on the village square (Ⓣ01887/830205, ⓦwww.kenmorehotel.com; ❼); established in 1572, it's Scotland's oldest inn. Two miles to the west, ⚑ *Rock House* (Ⓣ01887/830336, ⓦwww.lochtay.co.uk; ❼) is a wonderfully swish B&B overlooking the loch, while *Culdees* (Ⓣ01887/830519, ⓦwww.culdeesbunk house.co.uk; ❶), four miles along the loch's north shore at Fearnan, has family-friendly bunkhouse and B&B accommodation on a farm with an emphasis on permaculture and spiritual values. For something to **eat**, head to *The Courtyard* (Ⓣ01887/830756, ⓦwww.taymouthcourtyard.com) beside the Kenmore golf course, comprising a smart restaurant, large bar and deli/gift shop.

Killin

The **mountains of Breadalbane** (pronounced "bred-albin", from the Gaelic "braghaid Albin" meaning high country of Scotland) loom over the southern end of Loch Tay. Glens Lochay and Dochart curve north and south respectively from the small town of **KILLIN**, right in the centre of which the River Dochart comes

---

Climbing the Ben Lawers group

Ordnance Survey Explorer map no. 378

Dominating the northern side of Loch Tay is moody **Ben Lawers** (3984ft), Perthshire's highest mountain; from the top there are incredible views towards both the Atlantic and the North Sea. The ascent – which, despite the well-marked footpath, should not be tackled without all the right equipment (see p.47) – takes around three hours from the NTS **visitor centre** (May–Sept daily 10.30am–5pm; Ⓣ01567/820397), which is located at 1300ft and reached by a signposted road off the A827. The centre has an audiovisual show (£2), slides of the mountain flowers – including the rare alpine flora found here – and a nature trail with accompanying descriptive booklet.

The Ben Lawers range offers rich pickings for Munro-baggers, with nine hills over 3000ft in close proximity. The whole double-horseshoe-shaped ridge from Meall Greigh in the east to Meall a'Choire Leith in the northwest is too much for one day, though the eastern section from Meall Greigh (3284ft) to Beinn Ghlas (3619ft), taking in Ben Lawers, can be walked in eight to ten hours in good conditions. Standing on its own a little to the east is perhaps the prettiest of the lot, **Meall nan Tarmachan** ("The Hill of the Ptarmigan"); at 3427ft, a less arduous but rewarding four-hour round-trip from the roadside, a mile or so further on from the visitor centre.

rushing down over the frothy **Falls of Dochart** before disgorging into Loch Tay. A short distance west of Killin the A827 meets the A85, linking the Trossachs with Crianlarich (see p.142), an important waypoint on the roads to Oban, Fort William and the west coast.

There's little to do in Killin itself, but it makes a convenient base for some of the area's best walks. The **tourist office** (April–Oct daily; ℡01567/820254) is located on the ground floor of the old watermill by the falls; upstairs is the **Breadalbane Folklore Centre** (same times; £2.95). The centre explores the history and mythology of Breadalbane and holds the 1300-year-old "healing stones" of St Fillan, an early Christian missionary who settled in Glen Dochart.

Killin is littered with **B&Bs**, including *Fairview House*, halfway along Main Street (℡01567/820667, ⓦwww.fairview-killin.co.uk; ❷), a Victorian villa with decent rooms and breakfasts. At the eastern edge of town behind the large *Killin Hotel* you'll find the friendly but shambolic *Braveheart Backpackers*, with timber-lined en-suite dorms and family rooms (℡01567/829089; ❶). The place to grab a bite to **eat** is the *Falls of Dochart Inn*, an attractive stone-walled pub right above the famous rapids; a café adjoins the pub, supplying coffee and cakes. If you're interested in **outdoor activities**, make for the helpful and enthusiastic Killin Outdoor Centre and Mountain Shop (℡01567/820652, ⓦwww.killinoutdoor.co.uk) on Main Street, which rents out mountain bikes, canoes and tents.

Glen Lyon

North of Breadalbane, the mountains tumble down into **Glen Lyon** – at 34 miles long, the longest enclosed glen in Scotland – where, legend has it, the Celtic warrior Fingal built twelve castles. The narrow single track road through the glen starts at **Keltneyburn**, near Kenmore at the northern end of the loch, although a road does struggle over the hills past the Ben Lawers visitor centre (see p.151) to **Bridge of Balgie**, halfway down the glen, where the post office does good tea and scones (April–Oct). Either way, it's a long, winding journey. A few miles on from Keltneyburn, the village of **FORTINGALL** is little more than a handful of pretty thatched cottages, though locals make much of their 5000-year-old yew tree – believed (by them at least) to be the oldest living thing in Europe. The venerable tree can be found in the churchyard, with a timeline nearby listing some of the events the yew has lived through. One of these, bizarrely, is the birth of Pontius Pilate, reputedly the son of a Roman officer stationed near Fortingall. If you're taken by the peace and remoteness of Glen Lyon, you can **stay** at the attractive, upmarket *Fortingall Hotel* (℡01887/830367, ⓦwww.fortingallhotel.com; ❼), with its Arts and Crafts heritage, eleven bedrooms and excellent restaurant; it organizes fishing and walking packages.

Highland Perthshire

North of the Tay Valley, Perthshire doesn't discard its lush richness immediately, but there are clear indications of the more rugged, barren influences of the Highlands proper. The principal settlements of **Pitlochry** and **Blair Atholl**, both just off the A9, are separated by the narrow gorge of Killiecrankie. Though there are reasons to stop in both places, inevitably the greater rewards are to be found further from the main drag, most notably in the winding westward road along the shores of **Loch Tummel** and **Loch Rannoch** past the distinctive peak of **Schiehallion**, which eventually leads to the remote wilderness of **Rannoch Moor**.

The great outdoors

For outdoor enthusiasts, Scotland provides a wonderfully rugged and diverse landscape where you can take a bracing walk through an ancient oak forest or practise ice-climbing for the Himalayas a thousand feet up. Hillwalkers take to picking off Munros (hills over 3000ft in height), mountain bikers get muddy and if you're into watersports, there's white water, waves and wind a plenty. And while it's always tempting to postpone your outdoor foray on account of the unreliable weather, it's worth keeping in mind that the poorer the conditions, the cosier the pub at the end of the day.

To the hills

Walking in Scotland needn't necessarily mean uphill, though it is hard to go far without encountering a slope. The Highlands and Islands are remarkably well suited to **hill walking**: access is generally free, though there may be restricted access during lambing (April and May) and deerstalking seasons (July 1 to October 20); there are a range of good paths or forest tracks; and, despite the popularity of walking, the hills aren't nearly as busy as, say, the Lake District in northern England. Serious hillwalkers usually aim for the spectacular and tough ranges around **Glen Coe** or **Torridon**, though for many the ultimate challenge remains the dragon-back **Cullin** ridge on Skye.

Buachaille Etive, Glen Coe ▲

Road sign, Kilmartin Valley ▼

Long-distance trails

West Highland Way This five-day, 95-mile trek along well-marked paths between north Glasgow and Fort William, via Loch Lomond and Rannoch Moor, is the doyen of Scotland's official long-distance footpaths. See p.140.

Great Glen Way You can choose to detour up a couple of Munros, but otherwise, this is a straightforward, low-level 73-mile hike from Fort William to Inverness. See p.191.

Speyside Way A gentle, 65- to 84-mile wander (depending on the route chosen) through whisky country from the Cairngorms to the sea. See p.180.

Cateran Trail Perthshire's very own regional footpath is a 64-mile circular route starting and finishing in Blairgowrie. See p.157.

Cowal Way Argyll's regional footpath is a fairly gentle, 57-mile walk from Portavadie in the southwest of the peninsula to Inveruglas on Loch Lomond. See p.64.

On your bike

Scotland is one of the world's top five mountain-bike destinations, with over a thousand miles of remote terrain to challenge even the most accomplished cyclist. Dedicated mountain-bike centres, such as those on the Black Isle, provide waymarked trails designed for every level of rider, with experiences on offer ranging from white-knuckle black runs to leisurely rides through national parks and Forestry Commission areas. A number of long-distance routes, including The Great Glen Cycle Way (see p.191), have been established in Scotland using a combination of specially built cycle paths and quieter back roads. The rural roads are infinitely more enjoyable, particularly in the gentler landscapes of Argyll and the Hebrides, where generally amiable gradients and the dearth of traffic make the area perfect for cycle touring.

Worth a surf

One thing Scotland isn't short of is water, so it's no surprise that watersports are popular on inland lochs and around the coast. The Outer Hebrides in particular are regarded as world class for sea-kayaking, with their innumerable skerries, sea caves and remote white-sand beaches; yacht racing and sailing are excellent on the protected Firth of Clyde, while cruising is the main focus on the west coast. And though the climate can't quite match Bondi or Malibu, serious surfers will tell you that it's not the sun but the waves that count. There are world-class breaks near Thurso, in the Moray Firth and on the islands Coll, Tiree and Islay. Other remote spots include the Outer Hebrides and the Mull of Kintyre. Just pack some cocoa with the surf wax.

▲ Mountain biking, Great Glen
▼ Sea-kayaking, Staffa

The crazy stuff

Scotland's long-standing image as a place to play a testing but well-mannered round of golf, or to pull on your waders and tweed cap to spend a relaxing day fishing, is fast being overtaken by the lycra and neon blur of adrenaline-junkies revelling in the wild conditions the country has to offer. Near Fort William there's a purpose-built downhill **mountain-bike track** that descends 1800ft in little over two miles – it's used for world championships and is definitely not one for Sunday riders. Out in Tiree there's also first-class sporting action in the annual **windsurfing Wave Classic**, while each year sailors and fell-runners team up for the exhausting **Scottish Islands Peak Race** to the top of the highest summits on the islands of Mull, Jura and Arran. In winter, there's downhill and cross-country **skiing** action in places such as Cairngorm National Park, Glen Shee and Ben Nevis, while Glencoe is popular with **ice-** and **rock-climbers** training for international high-altitude expeditions; in recent years some of the world's finest indoor facilities for both sports have been built at the likes of Kinlochleven near Fort William. Thrill-seekers in Scotland aren't put off by the weather – it merely sets the agenda. A fresh breeze has **kite-surfers** and power-, buggy- or blo-karters scurrying for stretches of sand such as the gloriously empty flat strands of the Outer Hebrides. A good dump of rain, on the other hand, will see whitewater **rafters** and **canoeists** heading for frothing white rivers such as the Tay, Tummel, Orchy and Etive. Finally, if you're looking to stretch yourself to the limit, why not enter for the **Hebridean Challenge**, Europe's most extreme endurance race, which involves five days of running, cycling, swimming and kayaking around a 400-mile course in the Outer Hebrides?

Ice climbing, Aonach Mhòr ▲

Windsurfers at the Tiree Wave Classic ▼

Pitlochry

PITLOCHRY is undoubtedly a useful place to find somewhere to stay or eat en route to or from the Highlands. However, there's little charm to its main street, with crawling traffic and endless shops selling cut-price woollens and knobbly walking sticks. The one attraction with some distinction is the **Edradour Distillery** (Jan & Feb Mon–Sat 10am–4pm; March & April, Nov & Dec Mon–Sat 10am–4pm, Sun noon–4pm; May & Oct Mon–Sat 10am–5pm, Sun noon–5pm; June–Sept Mon–Sat 9.30am–5pm, Sun noon–5pm; £5; Ⓦwww.edradour .co.uk), Scotland's smallest, tucked into the hills a couple of miles east of Pitlochry on the A924. Although the tour itself isn't out of the ordinary, the lack of industrialization and the fact that the whole traditional process is done on site gives Edradour more personality than many of its rivals.

On the western edge of Pitlochry, just across the river, lies Scotland's renowned "Theatre in the Hills", the modern **Pitlochry Festival Theatre** (Ⓣ01796/484626, Ⓦwww.pitlochry.org.uk). A variety of productions – mostly mainstream theatre from the resident repertoire company, along with regular music events – are staged in the summer season (May–Oct) and on ad hoc dates the rest of the year. By day it's worth coming here to wander around **Explorers: the Scottish Plant Hunters' Garden** (April–Oct daily 10am–5pm; £4, tours £1 extra; Ⓦwww .explorersgarden.com), a garden and forest area beside the theatre that pays tribute to Scottish botanists and collectors who roamed the world in the eighteenth and nineteenth centuries in search of new plant species. An open-air amphitheatre is sometimes used for outdoor performances.

A short stroll upstream from the theatre is the **Pitlochry Power Station and Dam**, a massive concrete wall that harnesses the water of the artificial Loch Faskally, just north of the town, for hydroelectric power. The **visitor centre** (April–Oct Mon–Fri 10.30am–5.30pm; £3) offers a pretty thorough rundown on how hydro schemes work, but what draws most attention is the **salmon ladder**, a staircase of murky glass boxes through which you might see some nonplussed fish making their way upstream past the dam.

Practicalities

Pitlochry is on the main **train** line to Inverness, and the regular **buses** from Perth stop near the train station on Station Road, five minutes' walk up the main street from the **tourist office**, 22 Atholl Rd (April–Oct daily; Nov–March closed Sun; Ⓣ01796/472215). The office can sell you a guide to walks in the surrounding area (50p) and also offers an accommodation-booking service. For **bike rental**, advice on local cycling routes, and general outdoor gear, try Escape Route, 3 Atholl Rd (Ⓣ01796/473859, Ⓦwww.escape-route.biz).

Pitlochry is packed with grand houses converted into good-quality **accommodation**. The *Moulin Hotel* (Ⓣ01796/472196, Ⓦwww.moulinhotel.co.uk; ❹), at Moulin on the outskirts along the A924, is a pleasant old travellers' inn with a great bar and its own brewery, while *Craigatin House and Courtyard* (Ⓣ01796/472478, Ⓦwww.craigatinhouse.co.uk; ❹) on the northern section of the main road through town, is an attractive, contemporary **B&B** with large beds, soothing decor and a pretty garden; *Beinn Bhracaigh*, Higher Oakfield, is similarly chic (Ⓣ01796/470355, Ⓦwww.beinnbhracaigh.com; ❹). Otherwise, try *Ferryman's Cottage*, Port-na-Craig (Ⓣ01796/473681, Ⓦwww.ferrymanscottage.co.uk; ❷), a traditional and welcoming B&B in a beautiful position next to the River Tummel and the theatre. Right in the centre is *Pitlochry Backpackers Hotel*, 134 Atholl Rd (Ⓣ01796/470044, Ⓦwww.pitlochrybackpackershotel.com; March–Oct), a **hostel** based in a former hotel offering dorms along with around ten twin and double rooms (❶).

Ordnance Survey Explorer map no. 368

Pitlochry is surrounded by good walking country. The biggest lure has to be **Ben Vrackie** (2733ft), which provides a stunning backdrop for the town and deserves better than a straight up-and-down walk; however, the climb should only be attempted in settled weather conditions and if you're properly prepared (see p.47).

The direct route up the hill follows the course of the Moulin burn past the inn of the same name. Alternatively, a longer but much more rewarding circular route heads north out of Pitlochry, along the edge of Loch Faskally, then up the River Garry to go through the **Pass of Killiecrankie**. This is looked after by the NTS, which has a visitor centre (April–Oct daily 10am–5.30pm) detailing the famous battle here as well as the abundant natural history of the gorge. From the centre follow the route past Old Faskally to reach the main track at Loch a'Choire.

Other worthwhile walks in the area include the trip right round **Loch Faskally**, or you could follow the walk above but turn back from Killiecrankie. A lovely short hill walk from the south end of Pitlochry follows a path through oak forests along the banks of the **Black Spout** burn; when you emerge from the woods it's a few hundred yards further uphill to the lovely Edradour Distillery (see p.153).

Pitlochry is the domain of the tearoom and you have to hunt to find decent **places to eat**; *The Old Armoury* (℡01796/474281, Ⓦwww.theoldarmouryrestaurant .com) on a back road between the train station and dam is a civilized restaurant serving expensive meals in the evening, and also has a secluded tea garden. There's more moderately priced bistro food in the *Strathgarry Hotel* in the centre of town; the same owners run the *Port-na-craig Inn* which has a beautiful riverside location near the theatre. The best bet for traditional **pub grub** is the *Moulin Inn*, handily placed at the foot of Ben Vrackie, while *Food for Thought*, 8 West Moulin Rd, is a good **deli**, serving sandwiches and coffee.

Loch Tummel and Loch Rannoch

West of Pitlochry, the B8019/B846 makes a memorably scenic, if tortuous, traverse of the shores of **Loch Tummel** and then **Loch Rannoch**. These two lochs and their adjoining rivers were much changed by the massive hydroelectric schemes built in the 1940s and 1950s, yet this is still a spectacular stretch of countryside and one that deserves leisurely exploration. **Queen's View** at the eastern end of Loch Tummel is an obvious vantage point, looking down the loch to the misty peak of **Schiehallion** (3553ft) from the Gaelic meaning "Fairy Mountain". It's a popular, fairly easy and inspiring mountain to climb (3–4hr), with views on a good day to the massed ranks of Highland peaks; the path starts at Braes of Foss, just off the B846 that links Aberfeldy with Kinloch Rannoch. You'll get a good view of the mountain from cosy *Loch Tummel Inn* (℡01882/634272, Ⓦwww.lochtummelinn.co.uk; ❺), about halfway along Loch Tummel, which serves real ale, local venison and salmon.

Beyond Loch Tummel, marking the eastern end of Loch Rannoch, the small community of **KINLOCH RANNOCH** doesn't see a lot of passing trade – fishermen and hillwalkers are the most common visitors. Otherwise, the only real destination here is Rannoch Station, a lonely outpost on the Glasgow–Fort William West Highland train line (see opposite), sixteen miles further on. The road goes no further. Here you can contemplate the bleakness of **Rannoch Moor** (see box opposite), a wide expanse of bog, heather and wind-blown pine tree that stretches right across to the imposing entrance to Glen Coe (see p.199). A local bus service (Broons Bus #85) from Kinloch Rannoch and a postbus from Pitlochry (#223; Mon–Sat 8am) provide connections to the railway station.

In Kinloch Rannoch, *Bunrannoch House* (☏01882/632407, ⓦwww.bunrannoch .co.uk; ❹), a former Victorian shooting lodge, with lovely views, is a good choice for **accommodation** (and evening meals). Otherwise, there's the *Dunalastair Hotel* (☏01882/632323, ⓦwww.dunalastair.co.uk; ❼), which dominates the main square of the village and boasts a cosy pub, bar brasserie and formal dining room, as well as a linked activity centre (ⓦwww.activityscotland.com) that caters for most pursuits, from whitewater rafting to quad biking.

North of Pitlochry

Four miles north of Pitlochry, the A9 cuts through the **Pass of Killiecrankie**, a breathtaking wooded gorge that falls away to the River Garry below. This dramatic setting was the site of the **Battle of Killiecrankie** in 1689, when the Jacobites crushed the forces of General Mackay. Legend has it that one soldier of the Crown, fleeing for his life, made a miraculous jump across the 18ft **Soldier's Leap**, an impossibly wide chasm halfway up the gorge. Queen Victoria, visiting 160 years later, contented herself with recording the beauty of the area in her diary. Exhibits at the slick NTS **visitor centre** (April–Oct daily 10am–5.30pm; parking £2) recall the battle and examine the gorge in detail. The surroundings here are thick, mature forest, full of interesting plants and creatures – the local ranger leads **guided walks** from the visitor centre which are well worth joining.

Blair Atholl

Three miles north of Killiecrankie, the village of **BLAIR ATHOLL** makes for a much quieter and more idiosyncratic stop than Pitlochry. At the **Atholl Estates Information Centre** (April–Oct daily 9am–4.45pm; ☏01796/481646, ⓦwww .athollestatesrangerservice.co.uk) you can get details of the extensive network of

Rannoch Moor

Rannoch Moor occupies roughly 150 square miles of uninhabited and uninhabitable peat bogs, lochs, heather hillocks, strewn lumps of granite and a few gnarled Caledonian pines, all of it over 1000ft above sea level. Perhaps the moor's most striking feature is its inaccessibility: one road, between Crianlarich and Glen Coe, skirts its western side, while another struggles west from Pitlochry to reach its eastern edge at Rannoch Station. The only regular form of transport is the **West Highland Railway**, which stops at **Rannoch** and, a little to the north, Corrour station, which has no road access at all. There is a simple tearoom in the station building at Rannoch, as well as a pleasant small hotel, the *Moor of Rannoch* (☏01882/633238, ⓦwww.moorofrannoch.co.uk; mid-Feb to Oct; ❺), but even these struggle to diminish the feeling of isolation. **Corrour**, meanwhile, stole an unlikely scene in the film *Trainspotting* when the four central characters headed here for a taste of the great outdoors; a wooden SYHA hostel is located a mile away on the shores of **Loch Ossian** (☏0870/004 1139, ⓦwww.syha.org.uk; April–Oct) and is only accessible on foot, making the area a great place for hikers seeking somewhere genuinely off the beaten track. From Rannoch Station it's possible to catch the train to Corrour and walk the nine miles back; it's a longer slog west to the *Kingshouse Hotel* (see p.200) at the eastern end of Glen Coe, the dramatic peaks of which poke up above the moor's western horizon. Determined hillwalkers will find a clutch of Munros around Corrour, including remote Ben Alder (3765ft), high above the forbidding shores of **Loch Ericht**.

local walks and bike rides as well as information on surrounding flora and fauna. Rent **bikes** locally from Base Camp Bikes (pre-booking required; ☎01796/481256, ⓦwww.basecamp-bikes.co.uk). Right beside the Estates Info Centre, the modest **Atholl Country Life Museum** (May–Sept daily 1.30–5pm, July & Aug from 10am Mon–Fri; £3; ☎01796/481232, ⓦwww.athollcountrylifemuseum.org) offers a homespun and nostalgic look at the history of life in the local glens; in among the old photos and artefacts the star attraction is a stuffed, full-size Highland cow. The grand but reasonably priced *Atholl Arms Hotel* (☎01796/481205, ⓦwww.athollarms.co.uk; ④) is the best place in town for a drink or a bar meal. Nearby, you can wander round the ⚒**Water Mill** on Ford Road (April–Oct daily 10.30am–5.30pm; ⓦwww.blairathollwatermill.co.uk), which dates back to 1613, and watch flour being milled; better still, you can enjoy home-baked scones and light lunches in its pleasant timber-beamed tearoom.

Blair Castle

Seat of the Atholl dukedom and dating from 1269, whitewashed, turreted **Blair Castle** (April–Oct daily 9.30am–last admission 4.30pm; Nov–March Tues & Sat 9.30am–12.30pm; £8.75, grounds only £4.75; ⓦwww.blair-castle.co.uk), presents an impressive sight as you approach up the drive. A piper may be playing in front of the castle, one of the Atholl Highlanders, a select group retained by the duke as his private army – a unique privilege afforded to him by Queen Victoria, who stayed here in 1844.

Thirty or so rooms display a selection of paintings, antique furniture and plaster-work that is sumptuous in the extreme. Highlights are the soaring **entrance hall**, with every spare inch of wood panelling covered in weapons of some description, and the vast **ballroom**, with its timber roof, antlers and mixture of portraits.

As impressive as the castle's interior are its parkland surroundings: Highland cows graze the ancient landscaped grounds and peacocks strut in front of the castle. There is a **riding stable** from where you can take treks, and formal woodland walks lead you to various parts of the castle grounds, including the walled water garden and the towering giant conifers of Diana's Grove. There is also a busy but attractive caravan and **camping** park (☎01796/481263, ⓦwww .blaircastlecaravanpark.co.uk; April–Nov) in the grounds.

The Grampian Highlands

The high country in the northern part of the county of **Angus**, east of the A9 and north of the Firth of Tay, holds some of the Central Highlands' most pleasant scenery and is relatively free of tourists, most of whom tend to bypass it on their way north. Here the long fingers of the **Angus glens** – heather-covered hills tumbling down to rushing rivers – are overlooked by the southern peaks of the Grampian Mountains. Each has its own feel and devotees, **Glen Clova** being, deservedly, one of the most popular, along with **Glen Shee**, which attracts large numbers of people to its ski slopes. Handsome market towns like **Kirriemuir** and **Blairgowrie** are good bases for the area, while the tiny village of **Meigle** at the southern end of Glen Isla has Scotland's finest collection of carved Pictish stones.

North of the Angus glens and west of the city of Aberdeen, **Deeside** is a fertile yet ruggedly attractive area made famous by the royal family, who have favoured the estate at **Balmoral** as a summer holiday retreat ever since Queen Victoria fell in love with the region back in the 1840s. Hemmed in by imposing mountains, Deeside and the **Don Valley** to the north boast a terrific collection of **castles**, some elegant residences but many the sparse, functional garrisons which were used to guard the routes into the high country of the Cairngorms, often blocked by snow in winter and remote and desolate at any time of year.

The Angus glens

Immediately north of Dundee, the low-lying Sidlaw Hills divide the city from the rich agricultural region of **Strathmore**, whose string of tidy market towns lies on a fertile strip along the southernmost edge of the heather-covered lower slopes of the Grampian Mountains. These towns act as gateways to the **Angus glens** (Ⓦ www.angusglens.co.uk), a series of tranquil valleys penetrated by single-track roads and offering some of the most rugged and majestic landscapes in northeast Scotland. It's a rain-swept, windblown, sparsely populated area, whose roads become impassable with the first snows, sometimes as early as October, and where the summers see clouds of ferocious midges. Nevertheless, most of the glens, particularly **Glen Clova**, are well and truly on the tourist circuit, with the rolling hills and dales attracting hikers, birdwatchers and botanists in the summer, grouse shooters and deer hunters in autumn and a growing number of skiers in winter. The most useful road through the glens is the A93, which cuts through **Glen Shee**, linking Blairgowrie to Braemar on Deeside (see p.167). It's pretty dramatic stuff, threading its way over Britain's highest main-road pass, the **Cairnwell Pass** (2199ft).

Public transport in the region is limited: to get up the glens you'll have to rely on the **postbuses** from Blairgowrie (for Glen Shee) and Kirriemuir (for glens Clova and Prosen).

Blairgowrie and Glen Shee

The upper reaches of **Glen Shee**, the most dramatic and best known of the Angus glens, are dominated by its **ski fields**, ranged over four mountains above the Cairnwell mountain pass. During the season (Dec–March), ski lifts and tows give access to gentle beginners' slopes, while experienced skiers can try the more intimidating Tiger run. In summer it's all a bit sad, although there are some excellent hiking and mountain-biking routes.

To get to Glen Shee from the south you'll pass through the well-heeled little town of **BLAIRGOWRIE**, set among raspberry fields on the glen's southernmost tip and a good place to pick up information and plan your activities. Strictly two communities, Blairgowrie and **Rattray**, set on either side of the River Ericht, the town's modest claim to fame is that St Ninian once camped at Wellmeadow, a pleasant grassy triangle in the town centre. If you've time to kill here, wander up the leafy riverbank past a series of old mill buildings. Altogether more ambitious is the 64-mile **Cateran Trail** (Ⓦ www.caterantrail.org), a long-distance footpath that starts in Blairgowrie, then heads off on a long loop into the glens to the north following some of the drove roads used by caterans, or cattle thieves. It's a four- to five-day tramp, though of course it's possible to walk shorter sections of the way.

Blairgowrie's friendly **tourist office** (April–Oct daily; Nov–March Tues–Sat; ☎01250/872960, Ⓦ www.perthshire.co.uk) on the high side of Wellmeadow can

Skiing at Glen Shee

Scotland's **ski resorts** may not amount to much more than gentle training slopes in comparison with those of the Alps or North America, but they all make for a fun day out for beginners to experienced skiers. The strongest card of all the resorts is probably their scenic surroundings, and given that **Glen Shee** is both the most extensive and the most accessible of Scotland's ski areas, just over two hours from both Glasgow and Edinburgh, it's as good an introduction as any to the sport in Scotland.

For information, contact Ski Glenshee (☎013397/41320, ⓦwww.ski-glenshee.co.uk), which also offers ski rental and lessons, as does Cairnwell Mountain Sports (☎01250/885255, ⓦwww.cairnwellmountainsports.co.uk), at the Spittal of Glenshee. For the latest snow and **weather conditions**, phone Ski Glenshee or check out the Ski Scotland website (ⓦski.visitscotland.com). For **cross-country** skiing, there are some good touring areas in the vicinity; contact Cairnwell Mountain Sports (see above) or Braemar Mountain Sports (☎013397/41242, ⓦwww.braemarmountainsports.com) for information and equipment rental.

help with **accommodation**. A number of Blairgowrie's grand houses offer B&B, among them *Heathpark House* (☎01250/870700, ⓦwww.heathparkhouse.com; ④) on the Coupar Angus Road. Otherwise, try the airy and comfortable rooms at *West Freuchies* in the village of Glenisla (☎01575/582716, ⓦwww.glenisla-westfreuchies .co.uk; ③). **Camping** is available at the year-round *Blairgowrie Holiday Park* on Rattray's Hatton Road (☎01250/876666), within walking distance of Wellmeadow.

Blairgowrie boasts plenty of places to **eat**: *Cargills* (☎01250/876735, ⓦwww .cargillsbistro.com) by the river on Lower Mill Street serves inexpensive formal meals and civilized coffee and cakes; *Antiquary* (☎01250/873232), along the same road, provides more upmarket dining; while the inexpensive *Dome Restaurant*, just behind the tourist office, is a cheery place serving hearty platefuls of traditional grub. On Reform Street, pop into Blairgowrie Farm Shop for jams, vegetables, organic breads and deli items, while for a good local **pub** try the convivial and historic *Ericht Alehouse* on Wellmeadow. Alternatively, head six miles north of town on the A93 to the welcoming *Bridge of Cally Hotel* (☎01250/886231, ⓦwww.bridgeofcallyhotel .com; ⑤), which serves food all day, plus real ale by an open fire. Back in Blairgowrie you can rent **bikes** from Scottish Cycling Holidays, 87 Perth St (☎01250/876100).

Nearly twenty miles north of Blairgowrie, the small settlement of **SPITTAL OF GLENSHEE** (the name derives from the same root as "hospital", indicating a refuge), though ideally situated for skiing, has little to commend it other than the busy *Gulabin Bunkhouse* (①) on the A93, run by Cairnwell Mountain Sports (see above). Tucked away among the hills behind Spittal, *Dalmunzie House* (☎01250/885224, ⓦwww.dalmunzie.com; ⑦) is a lovely Highland retreat in a magnificent turreted mansion, with first-class dining and over sixty malt whiskies. From Spittal the road climbs another five miles or so to the ski centre at the crest of the Cairnwell Pass.

Blairgowrie is well linked by hourly **bus** #57 to both Perth and Dundee whilst the #71 runs at least twice daily (Mon–Sat) to Pitlochry via Bridge of Cally. To travel up Glen Shee, you'll have to rely on the **postbus**, which leaves town at 7.30am (not Sun) and returns from the Spittal of Glenshee at 12.30pm.

Meigle and Glen Isla

Fifteen miles north of Dundee on the B954 lies the tiny settlement of **MEIGLE**, home to Scotland's most important collection of early Christian and Pictish inscribed stones. Housed in a modest former schoolhouse, the **Meigle Museum** (April–Sept daily 9.30am–5.30pm; HS; £3.20) displays some thirty pieces dating from the seventh to the tenth centuries, all found in and around the nearby churchyard. The majority are either gravestones that would have lain flat, or cross slabs inscribed with the sign of the cross, usually standing. Most impressive is the seven-foot-tall great cross slab, said to be the gravestone of Guinevere, wife of King Arthur. The exact purpose of the stones and their enigmatic symbols is obscure, as is the reason why so many of them were found at Meigle. The most likely theory suggests that Meigle was once an important ecclesiastical centre that attracted secular burials of prominent Picts.

Glen Isla

Three miles north of Meigle is **Alyth**, near which, legend has it, Guinevere was held captive by Mordred. The sleepy village lies at the south end of **Glen Isla**, which runs parallel to Glen Shee and is linked to it by the A926. Dominated by Mount Blair (2441ft), Glen Isla suffers from an excess of angular conifers alongside great bald chunks of hillside waiting to be planted. Heading north along the B954, the River Isla narrows and then plunges some 60ft into a deep gorge to produce the classically pretty waterfall of **Reekie Linn**, or "smoking fall", so called because of the water-mist produced when the fall hits a ledge and bounces a further 20ft into a deep pool known as the Black Dub. Just after this, a side road leads east to the pleasant Loch of Lintrathen while, back into the glen proper, you'll come to the tiny hamlet of **KIRKTON OF GLENISLA** ten miles or so up the glen. Here, the cosy *Glenisla Hotel* (T 01575/582223, W www.glenisla-hotel.com; ④) is good for classy home-made bar food and convivial drinking. There are some relatively easy **hiking** trails in the nearby Glenisla forest, while just before Kirkton, a turn-off on the right-hand side leads northeast up a long bumpy road to the *Glenmarkie Guesthouse Health Spa and Riding Centre* (T 01575/582295, W www.glenmarkie.co.uk; ②), where the treats include reiki, massage and the chance to fish or pony trek.

Transport connections into the glen are limited: Alyth is on the main bus routes linking Blairgowrie with Dundee and Kirriemuir, while hourly bus #57 from Dundee to Perth passes through Meigle. Transport up to Kirkton is limited to a postbus that leaves Blairgowrie at 7am (not Sun) and travels via Alyth to arrive around 10.35am.

Kirriemuir and glens Prosen, Clova and Doll

The sandstone town of **KIRRIEMUIR**, known locally as Kirrie, is set on a hill six miles northwest of Forfar on the cusp of glens Clova and Prosen. Despite the influx of hunters up for the "season", it's still a pretty special place, a haphazard confection of narrow closes, twisting wynds and steep braes. The main cluster of streets have all the appeal of an old film set, with their old-fashioned bars, tiled butcher's shop, tartan outlets and haberdasheries somehow managing to avoid being contrived and quaint.

Kirrie was the birthplace of **J.M. Barrie**: a local handloom-weaver's son, Barrie first came to notice with his series of novels about "Thrums", a village based on his home town, in particular *A Window in Thrums* and his third novel, *The Little Minister*. The story of Peter Pan, the little boy who never grew up, was penned by Barrie in 1904 – some say as a response to a strange upbringing dominated by the memory of his older brother, who died as a child. **Barrie's birthplace**, a plain little whitewashed cottage at 9 Brechin Rd (April–June & Sept–Oct Mon–Wed &

Sat noon–5pm, Sun 1–5pm; July & Aug daily 11am–5pm; NTS; £5.50, includes entrance to the camera obscura), has a series of small rooms decorated as they would have been during Barrie's childhood, as well as displays about his life and works. The wash house outside was apparently the model for the house built by the Lost Boys for Wendy in Never-Never Land. Despite being offered a prestigious plot at London's Westminster Abbey, Barrie chose to be buried in Kirrie, and the unassuming family grave can be seen in the town cemetery, a short walk from the **camera obscura** (April–June Sat & Sun noon–5pm; July–Sept Mon–Sat noon–5pm, Sun 1–5pm; NTS; £3 or £5.50 combined with Barrie's Birthplace), in the old cricket pavilion above town just off West Hill Road. This unexpected treasure was donated to the town in 1930 by Barrie, and offers splendid views of Strathmore and the glens. Another local son who attracts a handful of rather different pilgrims is **Bon Scott** of the rock band AC/DC, who was born and lived here before emigrating to Australia.

There's more on Scott at Kirriemuir's **Gateway to the Glens Museum** (April–Sept Mon–Sat 10am–5pm; Oct–March Mon, Wed & Fri–Sat 10am–5pm, Thurs 1–5pm; free), in the old Town House on the main square. The oldest building in Kirrie, it has seen service as a tollbooth, court, jail, post office, police station and chemist; these days you can find two floors of interactive displays and exhibits on the town and the Angus Glens, including a scale model of Kirrie in 1604.

Reasonable **accommodation** is available at the attractive, inn-styled *Airlie Arms*, St Malcolm's Wynd (℡01575/572847, ⓦwww.theairliearms.co.uk; ❹), while on the edge of town, and offering a taste of the rolling countryside, is *Muirhouses Farm* (℡01575/573128, ⓦwww.muirhousesfarm.co.uk; ❸), a working cattle farm with bright plain rooms. Six miles from town towards Glen Isla, the cosy and luxurious *Falls of Holm* guesthouse (℡01575/575867, ⓦwww .fallsofholm.com; ❷) offers an attractive alternative. Back in town by the square, *Visocchi's* is great for daytime **snacks** and ice cream, while *Hook's Hotel* on Bank Street serves good food in the evening. The hourly #20 bus runs from Kirriemuir High Street to Forfar and Dundee.

Glen Prosen

Five miles north of Kirrie, and past Memus where *The Drovers Inn* serves good- value bar lunches, the low-key hamlet of **DYKEHEAD** marks the point where **Glen Prosen** and Glen Clova divide. A mile or so up Glen Prosen, you'll find the house where Captain Scott and fellow explorer Doctor Wilson planned their ill-fated trip to Antarctica in 1910–11, with a roadside **stone cairn** commemorating the expedi- tion. From here on, Glen Prosen remains essentially a quiet wooded backwater, with all the wild and rugged splendour of the other glens but without the crowds. To explore the area thoroughly you need to go on foot, but a good road circuit can be made by crossing the river at the tiny village of **GLENPROSEN** and returning to Kirriemuir along the western side of the glen via Pearsie. Alternatively, the reason- ably easy four-mile **Minister's Path** links Prosen with Clova. It is clearly marked and leaves from near the church in the village.

Glen Clova and Glen Doll

With its stunning cliffs, heather slopes and valley meadows, **Glen Clova** – which in the north becomes **Glen Doll** – is one of the loveliest of the Angus glens. Although it can get unpleasantly congested in peak season, the area is still remote enough to enable you to leave the crowds with little effort. Wildlife is abundant, with deer on the mountains, wild hares and even grouse and the occasional buzzard. The meadow flowers on the valley floor and arctic plants (including great splashes of white and purple saxifrage) on the rocks make it a botanist's paradise.

Walks from Glen Doll

Ordnance Survey Explorer maps nos. 388 & 387

These **walks** are some of the main routes across the Grampians from the Angus glens to Deeside, many of which follow well-established old drovers' roads. All three either fringe or cross the royal estate of Balmoral, and Prince Charles's favourite mountain – **Lochnagar** – can be seen from all angles. The walks all begin from the car park at the end of the tarred road where Glen Clova meets Glen Doll; all routes should always be approached with care, and you should follow the usual safety precautions.

Capel Mounth to Ballater (15 miles; 7hr). Initially, the path zigzags its way up fierce slopes before levelling out to a moorland plateau, leading to the eastern end of Loch Muick. It then follows the River Muick to Ballater.

Capel Mounth round-trip (15 miles; 8hr). Follows the above route to Loch Muick, doubling back along the loch's southern shore. The dramatic Streak of Lightning path that follows Corrie Chash leads to a ruined stables below Sandy Hillock; the descent passes the waterfall by the bridge at Bachnagairn, where a gentle burn-side track leads back to Glen Doll car park.

Jock's Road to Braemar (14 miles; 7hr). A signposted path leads below Cairn Lunkhard and along a wide ridge towards the summit of Crow Craigies (3018ft). From here, the path bumps down to Loch Callater then follows the Callater Burn, eventually hitting the A93 two miles short of Braemar.

The B955 from Dykehead and Kirriemuir divides at the Gella bridge over the swift-coursing River South Esk. Six miles north of Gella, the two branches of the road join up once more at the hamlet of **CLOVA**, little more than the hearty *Glen Clova Hotel* (℡01575/550350, Ⓦwww.clova.com; ❺), which also runs a bunkhouse and a private fishing loch. The restaurant serves up traditional Scottish food, such as venison casserole and haggis. An excellent, if fairly strenuous, four-hour walk from behind the old school at the back of the hotel leads up into the mountains and around the lip of **Loch Brandy**.

North from Clova village, the road turns into a rabbit-infested lane coursing along the riverside for four miles to the car park, a useful starting point for numerous superb **walks** (see box above). There are no other facilities beyond the village.

Edzell and Glen Esk

Travelling around Angus, you can hardly fail to notice the difference between organic settlements and planned towns that were built by landowners who forcibly rehoused local people in order to keep them under control, especially after the Jacobite uprisings. One of the better examples of the latter, **EDZELL**, five miles north of Brechin on the B966 (and linked to it by buses #21, #29 and #30), was cleared and rebuilt with Victorian rectitude a mile to the west of its original site in the 1840s. Through the Dalhousie Arch at the entrance to the village the long, wide and ruler-straight main street is lined with prim nineteenth-century buildings, which now do a roaring trade as genteel teashops and antiques emporia.

The original village (identifiable from the cemetery and surrounding grassy mounds) lay immediately to the west of the wonderfully explorable red-sandstone ruins of **Edzell Castle** (April–Sept daily 9.30am–5.30pm; Oct–March Mon–Wed, Sat & Sun 9.30am–4.30pm; HS; £4.70), itself a mile west of the planned village. The main part of the old castle is a good example of a comfortable tower house, where luxurious living became a priority rather than defence. However it's the formal **garden** (or "pleasance") overlooked by the castle tower that makes a visit to Edzell essential, especially in late spring and early to mid-summer. The garden was built by Sir David Lindsay in 1604, at the height of the optimistic Renaissance, and its refinement and extravagance are evident. The walls contain sculpted images of erudition: the Planetary Deities on the east side, the Liberal Arts on the south and, under floods of lobelia, the Cardinal Virtues on the west wall. In the centre of the garden, low-cut box hedges spell out the family mottoes and enclose voluminous beds of roses.

Four miles southwest of Edzell, lying either side of the lane to Bridgend which can be reached either by carrying on along the road past the castle or by taking the narrow road at the southern end of Edzell village, are the **Caterthuns**, twin Iron Age hill forts that were probably occupied at different times. The surviving ramparts on the White Caterthun (978ft) – easily reached from the small car park below – are the most impressive, and this is thought to be the later fort, occupied by the Picts in the first few centuries AD.

Just north of Edzell, a fifteen-mile road climbs alongside the River North Esk to form **Glen Esk**, the most easterly of the Angus glens and, like the others, sparsely populated. Ten miles along the Glen, the excellent **Glenesk Retreat, Folk Museum and Restaurant** (Easter–Sept daily noon–6pm; ℡01356/648070, Ⓦwww.gleneskretreat.btik.com) brings together records, costumes, photographs, maps and tools from the Angus glens, depicting the often harsh way of life for the inhabitants. The museum (£2) is housed adjacent to a former shooting lodge known as The Retreat, and is run independently and enthusiastically by the local community. Sunday hikers who labour up the winding glen will be heartened to find tasty and inexpensive home-baking, haggis and steak pies in the restaurant. There are some excellent **hiking** routes further up the glen (see Ⓦwww.visit cairngorms.com), including one to Queen Victoria's Well in Glen Mark and another up Mount Keen, Scotland's most easterly Munro.

In Edzell, *Alexandra Lodge*, Inveriscandye Road (℡01356/648266, Ⓦwww .alexandralodge.co.uk; April–Oct; ❸), is a friendly **B&B** located in a little Edwardian lodge. The best of the **hotels** in town is the *Panmure Arms* (℡01356/648950, Ⓦwww.panmurearmshotel.co.uk; ❹), at the far end of the main street near the turn-off to the castle, offering sizeable rooms and predictable bar meals. Further up the glen, one and a half miles north of the village, you can **camp** at the small, child-friendly *Glenesk Caravan Park* (℡01356/648565; April–Oct).

Deeside

More commonly known as **Royal Deeside**, the land stretching west from Aberdeen along the River Dee revels in its connections with the Royal Family, who have regularly holidayed here, at **Balmoral**, since Queen Victoria bought the estate. Eighty thousand Scots turned out to welcome her on her first visit in 1848. Victoria adored the place and the woods were said to remind Prince Albert of Thuringia, his homeland.

Deeside is undoubtedly handsome in a fierce, craggy, Scottish way, and the royal presence has helped keep a lid on any unattractive mass development. The villages strung along the A93, the main route through the area, are well heeled and have something of an old-fashioned air. Facilities for visitors hereabouts are first-class, with a number of bunkhouses and hostels, some decent hotels and plenty of castles and grounds to snoop around. It's also an excellent area for **outdoor activities**,

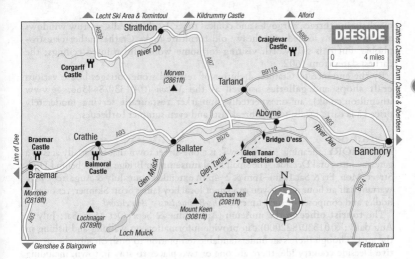

with hiking routes into both the Grampian and Cairngorm mountains, alongside good mountain biking, horseriding and skiing.

Stagecoach Bluebird **buses** #201, #202 and #203 from Aberdeen regularly chug along the A93, serving most of the towns on the way to Braemar.

Drum Castle to Glen Tanar

West of Aberdeen, you'll pass through low-lying land of mixed farming, forestry and suburbs. Easily reached from the main road are the castles of **Drum** and **Crathes**, both interesting fortified houses with pleasant gardens, while the uneventful town of **Banchory** serves as gateway to the heart of Royal Deeside. Further west, **Glen Tanar** is a great example of the area's attractive blend of forest, river and mountain scenery.

Drum Castle and Crathes Castle

Ten miles west of Aberdeen on the A93, **Drum Castle** (April–June & Sept to end-Oct Mon & Thurs–Sun 11am–5pm; July & Aug daily 11am–5pm; Garden of Historic Roses April–Oct daily 10am–6pm; NTS; £8.50, grounds only £3) stands in a clearing in the ancient **woods of Drum**, made up of the splendid pines and oaks that covered this whole area before the shipbuilding industry precipitated mass forest clearance. The castle itself combines a 1619 Jacobean mansion with Victorian extensions and the original, huge thirteenth-century keep, which has been restored and reopened. Given by Robert the Bruce to his armour-bearer, William de Irvine, in 1323 for services rendered at Bannockburn, the castle remained in Irvine hands for 24 generations until the NTS took over in 1976. The main part of the house is Victorian in character, with grand, antique-filled rooms and lots of family portraits. The finest room is the library, within the ancient tower; you'll get an even better sense of the medieval atmosphere of the place by climbing up to the upper levels of the tower, with the battlements offering views out over the forest.

Further along the A93, four miles west of Drum Castle, **Crathes Castle** (Jan–March & Nov–Dec Sat & Sun 10.30am–3.45pm; April–May & Sept–Oct daily except Fri 10.30am–4.30pm; June–Aug daily 10.30am–5pm; NTS; £10.50) is a splendid sixteenth-century granite tower house adorned with flourishes such as overhanging turrets, gargoyles and conical roofs. Its thick walls, narrow windows and tiny rooms loaded with heavy old furniture make Crathes rather claustrophobic, but it is still worth visiting for some wonderful painted ceilings; the earliest dates from 1602.

By the entrance to Crathes, a cluster of restored stone cottages house various **craft shops** and **galleries** as well as the *Milton* (T01330/844566, Wwww .themilton.co.uk), an unexpectedly upmarket **restaurant** serving moderately priced à la carte meals, terrific breakfasts and even summer barbecues.

Banchory

BANCHORY, meaning "fair hollow", is a one-street town that essentially acts as a gateway into rural Deeside. The small local **museum** on Bridge Street, behind High Street (Mon, Fri & Sat 11am–1pm & 2–4pm; extended hours July & Aug; free), may warrant half an hour or so if you're a fan of local boy James Scott Skinner, renowned fiddler and composer of such tunes as *The Bonnie Lass o' Bon Accord*.

The **tourist office** in the museum (April–June & Sept–Oct Mon–Sat; July & Aug daily; T01330/822000) can provide information on walking and fishing in the area. Though there's an understandable temptation to push on into the attractive Deeside countryside, there are one or two places **to stay** in town, including the smart *Tor-Na-Coille Hotel* (T01330/822242, Wwww.tornacoille.com; ●), once a retreat for Charlie Chaplin and his family. *Raemoir House* (T01330/824884, Wwww.raemoir.com; ●), 5km to the north, is a glamorous country-house hotel option set in spacious parkland. The Dee Larder on Watson Lane, off the main street, is a good deli; for memorable home-baking, drop into the *Shieling* coffee shop on Dee Street.

Aboyne and Glen Tanar

Twelve miles west of Banchory on the A93, **ABOYNE** is a typically well-mannered Deeside village at the mouth of **Glen Tanar**, which runs southwest from here for ten miles or so deep into the Grampian hills. The glen, with few steep gradients and some glorious stands of mature Caledonian pine, is ideal for walking, mountain biking or horseriding; the ranger information point two miles into the glen off the B976 has details of suitable routes, while the Glen Tanar Equestrian Centre (T01339/886448, Wwww.glentanar.co.uk) offers one- and two-hour **horserides** (from £25). Alternative activities hereabouts include **flights** from the Deeside Gliding Club (T01339/853339, Wwww.deesideglidingclub .co.uk), while a handful of family-oriented thrills from year-round sledging to go-karts can be found at the **Deeside Activity Park** (daily 9am–5pm; T01339/883536, Wwww.deesideactivitypark.com), signposted off the A93 a couple of miles east of Aboyne, where there's also a farm shop and restaurant. Aboyne itself has some handy retreats for **food**: the excellent *Sign of the Black Faced Sheep* coffee shop just off the main road serves home-baking and light lunches, while the *Boat Inn* on Charlestown Road, right beside the bridge over the Dee, does good-quality pub grub.

Ballater and Balmoral

Ten miles west of Aboyne is the neat and ordered town of **BALLATER**, attractively hemmed in by the river and fir-covered mountains. The town was dragged from obscurity in the nineteenth century when it was discovered that waters from the local Pannanich Wells might be useful in curing scrofula. Deeside water is now back in fashion, though these days it's bottled and sold far and wide as a natural mineral water.

Ordnance Survey Explorer map no. 395

Lying to the south of the Deeside town of Aboyne, the easily navigated forest tracks of **Glen Tanar** offer a taste of the changing landscape of the northeastern Highlands, passing through relatively prosperous farmland along the River Dee, through ancient woodland and then to remote grouse moors and bleak hillsides in the heart of the Grampian Mountains. Flatter than, and without the vehicle traffic of, Glen Muick to the west, Glen Tanar is a great place to explore on mountain bike, although there is plenty of opportunity for walking and there's also an **equestrian centre** (☎01339/886448) in the glen, offering riding trips lasting from one hour to all day on riverside, mountain and forest horse-trails.

Leave the south Deeside road (B976) at **Bridge o'Ess**, one and a half miles southwest of Aboyne, and carry on along a tarred road on the west side of the Water of Tanar for two miles to a car park and the Braeloine Visitor Centre and **ranger information point** (10am–5pm: April–Sept closed Tues; Oct–March closed Tues or Wed; ☎01339/886072). Here you can pick up details on the various routes in the glen, as well as some background on the flora and fauna of the area including efforts to protect the habitat of the rare caipercaillie. If you're on **foot**, the best idea is to strike out along the clear forest tracks that follow both sides of the river, connected at various points by attractive stone bridges, allowing for easy round-trips. Most of the time you are surrounded by superb old pine woodland, some of which is naturally seeded remnants of ancient Caledonian forest, with broadleafs in evidence along the river, as are wild flowers and fungi in season. The end of the glen, at **Shiel of Glentanar**, is eight miles from the car park, from where you can either retrace your path or take to the hills: **Mount Keen** (3081ft), the most easterly of Scotland's 3000ft-high mountains, looms ahead. The more ambitious can pick up the Mounth road at Shiel of Glentanar, which heads up and over Mount Keen to Invermark at the head of Glen Esk (see p.162).

It was in Ballater that Queen Victoria first arrived in Deeside by train from Aberdeen back in 1848; she wouldn't allow a station to be built any closer to Balmoral, eight miles further west. Although the line has long been closed, the town's rather self-important royalism is much in evidence at the restored **train station** in the centre (daily: July & Aug 9am–6pm; rest of year 10am–5pm). The local shops that supply Balmoral with groceries and household basics also flaunt their connections, with oversized "By Appointment" crests.

If you prefer to discover the fresh air and natural beauty that Victoria came to love so much, Ballater is an excellent base for local **walks and outdoor activities**. There are numerous hikes from Loch Muik (pronounced "mick"), nine miles southwest of town, including the Capel Mount drovers' route over the mountains to Glen Doll (see p.160), and a well-worn but strenuous all-day trek up and around Lochnagar (3789ft), the mountain much painted and written about by the current Prince of Wales. Good-quality **bikes** can be rented from Cabin Fever (☎013397/54004; £15/day), beside the station on Station Square, or Cycle Highlands (☎013397/55864, ⓦwww.cyclehighlands.com; £16/day, or £30/day for full suspension) at 16 Bridge St.

Practicalities

The **tourist office** (daily; ☎013397/55306) is in the renovated train station. Good-quality **bunkhouse** accommodation with breakfast is available at the *Schoolhouse*, Anderson Road (☎013397/56333, ⓦwww.theschool-house.eu; ❷), complete with ghost walks and storytelling, or at the excellent and well-equipped *Habitat*

@*Ballater* on Bridge Square (℡013397/53752, Ⓦwww.habitat-at-ballater.com; ❶). There are plenty of reasonable **B&Bs** in town, including *Inverdeen House* on Bridge Square (℡013397/55759, Ⓦwww.inverdeen.com; ❷), which offers a wide choice of breakfasts, most involving local produce and home-baking. Another choice is the welcoming *Deeside Hotel* on the main road through town at 45 Braemar Rd (℡013397/55420, Ⓦwww.deesidehotel.co.uk; ❸). For **camping**, head for *Anderson Road Caravan Park* (℡013397/55727; Easter–Oct) down towards the river.

There are numerous **places to eat**, from smart hotel restaurants to bakers and coffee shops. The *Green Inn Restaurant*, 9 Victoria Rd, has comfortable en-suite rooms attached (❻). *The Auld Kirk* is, as the name suggests, based in a renovated church (℡01339/755762, Ⓦwww.theauldkirk.co.uk; ❻), and is pricey but excellent with locally sourced game on the menu, while *La Mangiatoia* (℡013397/55999), on Bridge Square, is a cheaper and cheerful family pizza/pasta place. A couple of miles east of Ballater at Cambus O'May there's also the *Crannach Coffee Shop and Gallery* (closed Mon), a cultured spot offering good coffees, snacks and light meals, as well as superb cakes and bread from its in-house organic bakery. For a **dram** with the locals, try the back bar (entrance down Golf St) of the Prince of Wales, which faces the main square and the nearby *Coilacreich Inn*.

Balmoral Estate and Crathie Church

Originally a sixteenth-century tower house built for the powerful Gordon family, **Balmoral Castle** (April–July daily 10am–5pm; £8.70; ℡013397/42534, Ⓦwww .balmoralcastle.com) has been a royal residence since 1852, when it was converted to the Scottish Baronial mansion that stands today. The Royal Family traditionally spend their summer holidays here each August, but despite its fame it can be something of a disappointment even for a dedicated royalist. For the three months when the doors are nudged open, the general riffraff are permitted to view only the ballroom, an exhibition room and the grounds. With so little of the castle on view, it's worth making the most of the grounds and larger estate by following some of the country walks, heading off on a Land Rover safari (£45 per person for 3hr) or joining a two-hour ranger-led walk of the estate (April–July Wed 2pm; included in entrance price to castle).

Opposite the castle's gates on the main road, the otherwise dull granite church of **Crathie**, built in 1895 with the proceeds of a bazaar held at Balmoral, is the royals'

Deeside and Donside Highland Games

Royal Deeside is the home of the modern **Highland Games**, claiming descent from gatherings organized by eleventh-century Scottish king Malcolm Canmore to help him recruit the strongest and fittest clansmen for his army. The most famous of the local games is undoubtedly the **Braemar Gathering**, held on the first Saturday in September, which can see crowds of 15,000 and usually a royal or two as guest of honour. Vying for celebrity status in recent years has been the **Lonach** gathering in nearby Strathdon on Donside, held the weekend before Braemar, where local laird Billy Connolly dispenses drams of whisky to marching village men and has been known to invite some Hollywood chums along – Steve Martin has appeared dressed in kilt and jacket, while Robin Williams has competed in the punishing hill race. For a true flavour of the spirit of Highland gatherings, however, try to get to one of the events that take place in other local towns and villages at weekends throughout July and August, where locals outnumber tourists and the competitions are guaranteed to be hard-fought and entertaining. Local tourist offices and the tourist board website (Ⓦwww.aberdeen-grampian.com) should be able to tell you what's happening where.

local church. A small **tourist office** operates in the car park by the church on the main road (daily; ☎013397/42414).

Braemar

Continuing westwards for another few miles, the road rises to 1100ft above sea level in the upper part of Deeside and the village of **BRAEMAR**, situated where three passes meet and overlooked by an unremarkable **castle**. It's an invigorating, outdoor kind of place, well patronized by committed hikers, but probably best known for its Highland Games, the annual **Braemar Gathering**, on the first Saturday of September (Ⓦwww.braemargathering.org). Since Queen Victoria's day, successive generations of royals have attended and the world's most famous Highland Games have become rather an overcrowded, overblown event. You're not guaranteed to get in if you just turn up; the website has details of how to book tickets in advance.

A pleasant diversion from Braemar is to head six miles west to the end of the road and the **Linn of Dee**, where the river plummets savagely through a narrow rock gorge. From here there are countless walks into the surrounding countryside or up into the heart of the Cairngorms (see p.170), including the awesome Lairig Ghru pass which cuts all the way through to Strathspey.

Practicalities

Braemar's **tourist office** is in the modern building known as the Mews, in the middle of the village on Mar Road (daily; ☎013397/41600). **Accommodation** is scarce in Braemar in the lead-up to the Games, but at other times there's a wide choice. *Clunie Lodge Guest House*, Clunie Bank Road (☎013397/41330, Ⓦwww .clunielodge.com; ❸), on the edge of town, is a good **B&B** with lovely views up Clunie Glen, and there's a large SYHA **hostel** at Corrie Feragie, 21 Glenshee Rd (☎01339/741659, Ⓦwww.syha.org.uk; Jan–Oct). Cheery *Rucksacks*, an easygoing bunkhouse that's well equipped for walkers and backpackers, is just behind the Mews complex (☎013397/41517) while the *Invercauld Caravan Club Park* (☎013397/41373), just south of the village off Glenshee Road, has thirty **camping** pitches. A quarter of a mile south of town on Glenshee Road, you'll also find the cosy *Braemar Lodge Bunkhouse* (☎013397/41627, Ⓦwww.braemarlodge .co.uk).

For **food**, avoid the large hotels, which tend to be filled with coach parties, and try either *Taste*, a coffee shop and moderately priced contemporary restaurant on the road out to the Linn of Dee, or *The Gathering Place* bistro (☎013397/41234, Ⓦwww.the-gathering-place.co.uk) in the heart of the village (by Braemar Mountain Sports) where for lunch or dinner you'll find mouthwatering, though pricey, freshly prepared Scottish-based cuisine.

Advice on **outdoor activities**, as well as ski, mountain-bike and climbing equipment rental, is available from Braemar Mountain Sports (daily 8.30am–6pm; Ⓦwww.braemarmountainsports.com).

The Don Valley

The quiet countryside around the **Don Valley**, once renowned for its illegal whisky distilleries and smugglers, lies at the heart of Aberdeenshire's prosperous agricultural region. From Aberdeen, the River Don winds northwest through **Inverurie**, where it takes a sharp turn west to **Alford**, then continues past ruined castles through the **Upper Don Valley** and the heather moorlands of the eastern

Highlands. This remote and under-visited area is positively littered with ruined castles, Pictish sites, stones and hillforts.

Inverurie is served by the regular Aberdeen to Inverness **train** and various **bus** services up the A96. Stagecoach Bluebird buses #210, #215, #217 and #220 link Aberdeen with Alford, but getting any further by public transport is all but impossible.

Inverurie and around

Some seventeen miles northwest of Aberdeen, the prosperous – if largely unexciting – farming town of **INVERURIE** lies fairly central to the numerous relics and castles in the area as well as the **Glen Garioch distillery** in Old Meldrum (Mon–Sat 10am–4pm; ☎01651/873450, ⊛www.glengarioch.com; £4). The **tourist office** (April–Oct Mon–Sat; ☎01467/625800) shares space with a bookshop at 18 High St, not far from the station.

Bennachie and Archaeolink

The granite hill **Bennachie**, five miles west of Inverurie, is possibly the site of Mons Graupius, Scotland's first-ever recorded battle, when the Romans defeated the Picts in 84 AD. At 1733ft, this is one of the most prominent tors in the region, with tremendous views, and it makes for a stiff two-and-a-half-hour walk. The best route starts from the **Bennachie Centre** (Tues–Sun: April–Oct 10.30am–5pm; Nov–March 9.30am–4pm), a countryside ranger station and interactive interpretation centre located two miles south of **Chapel of Garioch** (pronounced "geery"). A mile immediately west of Chapel of Garioch is one of the region's most notable Pictish standing stones, the **Maiden Stone**, a 10ft-high slab inscribed with marine monsters, an elephant-like beast and the mirror and comb for which it's named.

A further four miles northwest of Chapel of Garioch on the B9002 at Oyne, the **Archaeolink Prehistory Park** (April–Oct daily 10am–5pm; £6.10; ⊛www .archaeolink.co.uk) gives an insight into the area's Pictish heritage. An ambitious attraction, it includes a reconstructed Iron Age farm, a hillside archeological site and an innovative grass-roofed building containing lively audiovisual displays and hands-on exhibits.

Craigievar Castle

Six miles south of Alford on the A980, **Craigievar Castle** (noon–5.30pm: May–June & Sept Mon, Tues & Fri–Sun; July & Aug daily; NTS; £10; ☎08444/932174) is a fantastic pink confection of turrets, gables, balustrades and cupolas bubbling over from its top three storeys. It was built in 1626 by a Baltic trader known as Willy the Merchant, who evidently allowed his whimsy to run riot. The **grounds** are open all year (9.30am to sunset; £1).

Lumsden and Rhynie

The A944 heads west from Alford, meeting the A97 just south of the tiny village of **LUMSDEN**, an unexpected hot spot of Scottish sculpture. A contemporary **Sculpture Walk** – heralded by a fabulous skeletal black horse at its southern end – runs parallel to the main road, coming out near the premises of the widely respected **Scottish Sculpture Workshop** (Mon–Fri 9am–5pm, or by arrangement; ⊛www.ssw.org.uk), very much an active workshop rather than a gallery, at the northern end of the village.

The village of **RHYNIE**, folded beautifully into the hills three miles further north up the A97, is forever associated with one of the greatest Pictish memorials, the **Rhynie Man**, a remarkable 6ft-high boulder discovered in 1978, depicting a rare whole figure, clad in a tunic and holding what is thought to be a ceremonial axe. The original is in Woodhill House in Aberdeen, but there's a cast on display at the school in Rhynie, across the road from the church. A further claim to fame for the village is that the bedrock lying deep beneath it, known as **Rhynie Chert**, contains plant and insect fossils up to 400 million years old, making them some of the earth's oldest. A mile or so from the village, along the A941 to Dufftown, a car park gives access to a path up the looming **Tap O'Noth**, Scotland's second-highest Pictish hill fort (1847ft), where substantial remnants of the wall around the lip of the summit show evidence of vitrification (fierce burning), probably to fuse the rocks together.

The Upper Don Valley

Travelling west from Alford, settlements become noticeably more scattered and remote as the countryside takes on a more open, familiarly Highland appearance. Ten miles from Alford stand the impressive ruins of the thirteenth-century **Kildrummy Castle** (April–Sept daily 9.30am–5.30pm; HS; £3.70), where Robert the Bruce sent his wife and children during the Wars of Independence. The castle blacksmith, bribed with as much gold as he could carry, set fire to the place and it fell into English hands. Bruce's immediate family survived, but his brother was executed and the entire garrison hanged, drawn and quartered. Meanwhile, the duplicitous blacksmith was rewarded for his help by having molten gold poured down his throat. The sixth earl of Mar used the castle as the headquarters of the ill-fated Jacobite risings in 1715, but after that, Kildrummy became redundant and it fell into disrepair. Beside the ruins, the separate **Kildrummy Castle Gardens** (April–Oct daily 10am–5pm; £3.50) are quite a draw, boasting everything from swathes of azaleas in spring to Himalayan poppies in summer.

Ten miles further west, the A944 sweeps round into the parish of **STRATHDON**, little more than scattered buildings by the roadside. Four miles north of here, up a rough track leading into Glen Nochty, lies the unexpected **Lost Gallery** (daily except Tues 11am–5pm; Ⓦwww.lostgallery.co.uk), which shows work by some of Scotland's leading modern artists in a wonderfully remote and tranquil setting. A further eight miles west, just beyond the junction of the Ballater road, lies **Corgarff Castle** (April–Sept daily 9.30am–5.30pm; Oct–March Sat & Sun 9.30am–4.30pm; HS; £4.70), an austere tower house with an unusual star-shaped curtain wall – and an eventful history. Built in 1537, it was turned into a barracks by the Hanoverian government in 1748 in the aftermath of Culloden in order to track down local Jacobite rebels; a century later, English redcoats were stationed here with the unpopular task of trying to control whisky smuggling. Today the place has been restored to resemble its days as a barracks, with stark rooms and rows of hard, uncomfortable beds – authentic touches which also extend to graffiti on the walls and peat smoke permeating the building from a fire on the upper floor.

Leading to the castle from the south is the old military road, which, unusually, hasn't been covered over by the present road and is fairly clear for about three miles. A mile or so along this from the castle, approached from the main road by the track beside Rowan Tree Cottage, is ⚑ *Jenny's Bothy* at **Dellachuper** (☎019756/51449, Ⓦwww.jennysbothy.co.uk), a beautifully remote and simple **bunkhouse** with a cosy wood-burning stove. You'll have to bring your own supplies, but it's a great base for hiking, cycling and skiing, or just detaching yourself from the madding crowd for a day or two. Another bunkhouse, along with standard **B&B** accommodation and good-value bar meals can be found at the *Allargue Arms Hotel* (☎019756/51410, Ⓦwww.allarguearmshotel.co.uk; ❷), an old wayside inn overlooking Corgarff Castle and a cosy base for skiing, fishing or hiking trips.

The **Lecht Road**, crossing the area of bleak but wonderfully empty high country to the remote mountain village of Tomintoul (see p.184), passes the Lecht ski centre at 2090ft above sea level, but is frequently impassable in winter due to snow.

The Cairngorms and Speyside

Rising high in the heather-clad hills above remote Loch Laggan, forty miles due south of Inverness, the **River Spey**, Scotland's second longest river, drains northeast towards the Moray Firth through one of the Highlands' most spell-binding valleys. Famous for its ancient forests, salmon fishing and ospreys, the area around the upper section of the river, known as **Strathspey**, is dominated by the sculpted **Cairngorms**, Britain's most extensive mountain massif, unique in supporting subarctic tundra on its high plateau. Though the area has been admired and treasured for many years as one of Scotland's prime natural assets, the Cairngorms National Park was only declared in 2004. Outdoor enthusiasts flock to the area to take advantage of the superb hiking, biking, watersports and winter snows, aided by the fact that the area is easily accessible by road and rail from both the central belt and Inverness.

A string of villages along the river provide useful bases for setting out into the wilder country, principal among them **Aviemore**, a rather ugly straggle of housing and hotel developments which nevertheless has a lively, youthful feel to it. A little way north, **Grantown-on-Spey** is more attractive, with solid Victorian mansions but much less vitality, while smaller settlements such as **Boat of Garten** and **Kincraig** are quieter, well-kept villages.

Downriver, Strathspey gives way to the area known as **Speyside**, famous as the heart of Scotland's **malt whisky** industry. In addition to the Malt Whisky Trail which leads round a number of well-known distilleries in the vicinity of villages such as **Dufftown** and **Craigellachie**, the lesser-known **Speyside Way**, another of Scotland's long-distance footpaths, offers the chance to enjoy the scenery of the region, as well as its whiskies, on foot.

Strathspey

Of Strathspey's scattered settlements, **Aviemore** absorbs the largest number of visitors, particularly in midwinter when it metamorphoses into the UK's busiest ski resort. Despite significant recent redevelopment, the village still struggles to reflect the charm of its surrounding area, but it's a good first stop for information, to sort out somewhere to stay or to find out about nearby outdoor activities, which are likely to seem very enticing after a glimpse of the stunning mountain

The **Cairngorms National Park** (⊛ www.cairngorms.co.uk) covers some 1500 square miles and incorporates the **Cairngorms massif**, the largest mountainscape in the UK and the only sizeable plateau in the country over 2500ft. It's the biggest national park in Britain, and while Aviemore and the surrounding area are regarded as the main point of entry, particularly for those planning outdoor activities, it's also possible to access the eastern side of the park from both Deeside and Donside in Aberdeenshire (see p.162). Crossing the range is a significant challenge: by road the only connection is the A939 Tomintoul to Cock Bridge, frequently impassable in winter due to snow, while on foot the only way to avoid the high peaks is to follow the old cattle drovers' route called the **Lairig Ghru**, a very long day's walk between Inverdruie at the edge of Rothiemurchus and the Linn of Dee, near Inverey.

The name Cairngorm comes from the Gaelic *An Carrn Gorm*, meaning "the blue hill" after the blueish-tinged stones found in the area, and within the park there are 52 summits over 2953ft, as well as a quarter of Scotland's native woodland and a quarter of the UK's threatened wildlife species. The conservation of the landscape's unique flora and fauna is, of course, one of the principal reasons national park status was conferred. However, an important role for the park is to consider the needs of an estimated 17,000 people living and working within its boundaries and integrate the array of outdoor activities enjoyed by visitors.

Vegetation in the area ranges from one of the largest tracts of ancient **Caledonian pine and birch forest** remaining in Scotland at Rothiemurchus, to subarctic tundra on the high plateau, where **alpine flora** such as starry saxifrage and the star-shaped pink flowers of moss campion peek out of the pink granite in the few months of summer that the ground is free of snow. In the pine forests of the river valleys, strikingly coloured **birds** such as crested tits, redwings and goldfinches can be observed, along with rarely seen **mammals** such as the red squirrel and pine marten. On the heather slopes above the forest, red and black grouse are often encountered, though their larger relative, the capercaillie, is a much rarer sight, having been reintroduced in 1837 after dying out in the seventeenth century. Birds of prey you're most likely to see are **osprey**, best seen at the osprey observation centre (see p.176) at Loch Garten or fishing on the lochs around Aviemore, though golden eagles and peregrine falcons can occasionally be seen higher up. Venturing up to the plateau you'll have the chance of seeing the shy **ptarmigan**, another member of the grouse family, which nests on bare rock and has white plumage during winter, or even the dotterel and snow bunting, rare visitors from the Arctic, along with mountain (blue) hares, which also turn white in winter and are best seen in spring as they scurry across patches of brown hillside where the snow has melted.

scenery provided by the 4000ft-summit plateau of the Cairngorms. The planned Georgian town of **Grantown-on-Spey** makes a good alternative base for summer visitors, but while it has more charm than Aviemore, there are fewer facilities. Further upriver, the sedate villages of **Newtonmore** and **Kingussie** are older-established holiday centres, popular more with anglers and grouse hunters than canoeists and climbers. The whole area boasts a wide choice of good-quality accommodation, particularly in the budget market, with various easygoing hostels run by and for outdoor enthusiasts.

Aviemore and around

The once-sleepy village of **AVIEMORE** was first developed as a ski and tourism resort in the mid-1960s and, over the years, fell victim to profiteering developers with scant regard for the needs of the local community. More

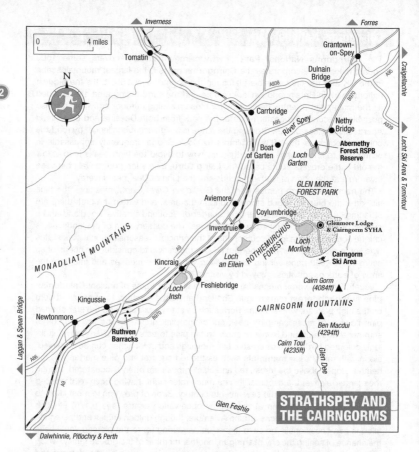

Inverness   Forres

Tomatin

Grantown-on-Spey

Dulnain Bridge

A938

River Spey

Carrbridge

A95

Nethy Bridge

Boat of Garten

Loch Garten

Abernethy Forest RSPB Reserve

GLEN MORE FOREST PARK

Aviemore

Coylumbridge

Inverdruie

ROTHIEMURCHUS FOREST

Glenmore Lodge & Cairngorm SYHA

Loch Morlich

Cairngorm Ski Area

Loch an Eilein

Kincraig

Cairn Gorm (4084ft) ▲

Feshiebridge

Loch Insh

CAIRNGORM MOUNTAINS

Ben Macdui (4294ft) ▲

Kingussie

Newtonmore

Ruthven Barracks

Cairn Toul (4235ft) ▲

Glen Dee

Glen Feshie

Laggan & Spean Bridge

A86

A9

B970

Monadliath Mountains

A9

0   4 miles

N

STRATHSPEY AND THE CAIRNGORMS

Craigellachie

A95

Lecht Ski Area & Tomintoul

A939

Dalwhinnie, Pitlochry & Perth

recently, an ambitious hotel and spa development has finally replaced most of the glaring planning eyesores, but to all but its most loyal defenders the town remains a soulless hotchpotch of retail outlets, café bars and characterless housing developments. That said, Aviemore is undeniably well equipped with services and facilities for visitors and is the most convenient base for the Cairngorms.

The main attractions of Aviemore are its **outdoor pursuits**, though train enthusiasts are drawn to the restored **Strathspey Steam Railway**, which chugs the short distance between Aviemore and Broomhill, just beyond Boat of Garten village, four times daily through the summer (June–Sept; less regular service at other times; ☎01479/810725, ⊛www.strathspeyrailway.co.uk). The more energetic can head for the fabulous Aviemore Indoor Climbing Wall (daily 9am–5pm; Tues & Thurs till 10pm; £8; ☎01479/812466). The most useful local **bus** route is the #34, which runs hourly from Aviemore to the Cairngorm Mountain Railway via Rothiemurchus and Loch Morlich. The same service runs regularly (5 daily) to Grantown via the Osprey Centre at Boat of Garten.

Aviemore's businesslike **tourist office** is in the heart of things at 7 The Parade, Grampian Road (daily; ☎01479/810930). It offers an accommodation booking service and reams of leaflets on local attractions.

Summer activities

In summer, the main activities around Aviemore are **walking** (see box, p.175) and **water sports**, and there are great opportunities for mountain biking, pony trekking and fly-fishing. Two centres offer sailing, windsurfing and canoeing: the Loch Morlich Watersports Centre (℡01479/861221, ⓦ www.lochmorlich .com), seven miles east of Aviemore, and the Loch Insh Watersports Centre (℡01540/651272, ⓦ www.lochinsh.com), six miles up-valley near Kincraig. The latter also rents mountain bikes, boats for fishing, runs boat-based wildlife tours (May–Sept) and gives ski instruction on a 200ft-long dry slope. If you want still more action, G2 Outdoor (℡01479/811008, ⓦ www.g2outdoor .co.uk) will take you kayaking and canyoning whilst Full On Adventure (℡07885/835838, ⓦ www.fullonadventure.com) runs **whitewater rafting** trips on the Findhorn River.

Riding and **pony trekking** are on offer up and down the valley: try Alvie Stables near Kincraig (℡07831/495397, ⓦ www.alvie-estate.co.uk), or Strathspey Highland Ponies (Easter to end Oct; ℡01479/812345), where you can ride this ancient Highland breed on hacks and treks from Rothiemurchus Visitor Centre at Inverdruie. **Fishing** is very much part of the local scene; you can fish for trout and salmon on the River Spey, and the Rothiemurchus Estate (℡01479/810703, ⓦ www.rothiemurchus.com) has a stocked rainbow-trout-fishing loch (June–Aug 9am–9pm; Sept–May 9am–5pm; 1hr introductory package £13) at **Inverdruie**, where success is virtually guaranteed. The Abernethy Angling Association (ⓦ www.river-spey.com) is a good source of information for the seasons, locations and costs of renting a rod and tackle. The Aviemore tourist office provides a brochure outlining the permits required.

For both the adventurous and novice cyclist, the entire region is great for **mountain biking**. The Rothiemurchus Estate has several excellent (and non-technical) way-marked trails running through its extensive lands. However, for the best advice including guiding, maps and high-quality (front suspension) bike rental (£15/half day, £20/day) stop in at Bothy Bikes (℡01479/810111, ⓦ www.bothybikes.co.uk) beside the tennis courts at Inverdruie. To buy (and, in some instances, rent) other outdoor equipment, in particular **climbing** and **hill-walking** gear, pop into the friendly and professional Mountain Spirit (℡01479/811788) shop at 62 Grampian Rd or try Cairngorm Mountain Sports in the centre of Aviemore (℡01479/810903).

Winter activities

Scottish **skiing** on a commercial level first really took off in Aviemore. By continental European and North American standards it's all on a tiny scale, but occasionally snow and sun coincide to offer beginner and expert alike a great day on the pistes. February and March are usually the best times, but there's a chance of decent snow at any time between mid-November and April. Several places sell or rent standard equipment though The Ski School (ⓦ www.theskischool.co.uk) in the Day Lodge at Corie Cas on Cairngorm mountain is your best bet for ski/ board rental and lessons. For ski mountaineering/cross-country rental, Mountain Spirit in Aviemore (see above) is the place to go, while the experts at G2 Outdoor (see above) will provide one-to-one tuition in the art of telemarking and back country skiing. For an overview of skiing in the area check out ⓦ www.ski .visitscotland.com.

The **Cairngorm Ski Area** (℡01479/861319, ⓦ www.cairngormmountain.com), nine miles southeast of Aviemore, above Loch Morlich in Glenmore Forest Park, is well served during winter by buses from Aviemore. From here, the year-round **funicular railway** is the principal means of getting to the top of the ski slopes.

For a crash course in surviving Scottish winters, you could do worse than try a week at the National Outdoor Training Centre at *Glenmore Lodge* (see below) in the heart of the Glenmore Forest Park at the east end of Loch Morlich. This superbly equipped and organized centre (complete with cosy après-ski bar) offers winter and summer courses in hillwalking, mountaineering, alpine ski-mountaineering, avalanche awareness and much more. To add to the winter scene, there's a herd of reindeer at the **Cairngorm Reindeer Centre** by Loch Morlich (daily 10am–5pm; guided excursions 11am & 2.30pm, July & Aug also 3.30pm; £9.50; ☎01479/861228, ⓦwww.reindeer-company.demon.co.uk), while between Loch Morlich and Inverdruie the **Cairngorm Sleddog Adventure Centre** (☎07767/270526, ⓦwww.sled-dogs.co.uk), the UK's only sleddog centre, has a small museum (£8), as well as two- to three-hour trips on a wheeled or ski-based sled pulled by ten dogs (Oct–April only; £60 per person).

Accommodation

There's a good range of accommodation in Aviemore, and no shortage of **campsites**: two of the best are *Rothiemurchus Caravan Park*, among the tall pine trees at Coylumbridge on the way to Loch Morlich (☎01479/812800, ⓦwww .rothiemurchus.net), and the Forestry Enterprise site beside the banks of Loch Morlich (☎01479/861271).

Hotels and B&Bs

🏃 **Corrour House Hotel** Inverdruie, 2 miles southeast of Aviemore ☎01479/810220, ⓦwww.corrourhousehotel.co.uk. A secluded small hotel with a distinctly upmarket atmosphere. ④

Glenmore Lodge 8 miles east of Aviemore ☎01479/861256, ⓦwww.glenmorelodge.org.uk. Specialist outdoor pursuits centre with excellent accommodation in twin rooms (with shared facilities) and self-catered lodges – guests can make use of the superb facilities, which include a pool, weights room, sauna and indoor climbing wall. ②

Macdonald Aviemore Highland Resort Aviemore ☎0845/608 3734, ⓦwww.macdonaldhotels.co.uk /aviemore. A huge resort incorporating four separate hotels, self-catering chalets, several restaurants, a spa, luxury boutique shopping and a golf course. Modern and rather soulless. ⑥

Ravenscraig Guest House Grampian Rd ☎01479/810278. A handy central location and a welcoming and family-friendly B&B. ③

Rowan Tree Country Hotel 3 miles south of Aviemore, overlooking Loch Alvie ☎01479/810207, ⓦwww.rowantreehotel.com. A relaxed, comfortable alternative to staying in town. ⑤

Hostels

Aviemore Bunkhouse Dalfaber Rd ☎01479/811181, ⓦwww.aviemore-bunkhouse .com. A large modern place beside the *Old Bridge Inn* within walking distance from the station; a family room and a double. ①

Aviemore SYHA 25 Grampian Rd ☎0870/004 1104, ⓦwww.syha.org.uk. Aviemore's large and well-equipped SYHA hostel is within walking distance of the centre of the village.

Cairngorm Lodge ☎0870/004 1137. A SYHA hostel towards the Cairngorms at Loch Morlich, located in an old shooting lodge. Jan–Oct.

Eating

All along Aviemore's main drag are bistros, hotels and takeaways serving fairly predictable, run-of-the-mill **food**. One exception is the reasonably priced 🏃 *Mountain Café* (☎01479/812473), above Cairngorm Mountain Sports (see p.173), which serves an all-day menu of wholesome snacks and freshly prepared meals, often using local produce. Nearby, *RD's* (☎01479/811633) is a safe bet for good-value dinners, while *The Einich* (☎01479/812334), tucked away at the Rothiemurchus Visitor Centre at Inverdruie, is a delight and open for tasty home-bakes and lunches every day, and moderately priced evening meals from Wednesday to Saturday. Alternatively, *The Old Bridge Inn* on the east side of the railway on Dalfaber Road dishes up decent Scottish dinners, tasty pub grub and

Walks around Aviemore

Ordnance Survey Explorer Maps nos. 402 & 403 or *OS Outdoor Leisure Map no. 3*
Walking of all grades is a highlight of the Aviemore area, though you should heed the usual safety guidelines (see p.47). These are particularly important if you want to venture into the subarctic climatic zone of the Cairngorms. However, as well as the high mountain trails, there are some lovely and well-signposted **low-level walks** in the area. It takes an hour or so to complete the gentle circular walk around pretty **Loch an Eilean** (with its ruined castle) in the Rothiemurchus Estate, beginning at the end of the back road that turns east off the B970 a mile south of Inverdruie. The helpful estate **visitor centres** at the lochside and by the roadside at Inverdruie provide more information on other woodland trails.

Another good, shortish (half-day) walk leads along a well-surfaced forestry track from Glenmore Lodge up towards the **Ryvoan Pass**, taking in An Lochan Uaine, known as the "Green Loch" and living up to its name, with amazing colours that range from turquoise to slate grey depending on the weather. The **Glenmore Forest Park Visitor Centre** by the roadside at the turn-off to Glenmore Lodge is the starting point for the three-hour round-trip climb of Meall a' Bhuachaillie (2654ft), which offers excellent views and is usually accessible year-round. The centre has information on other trails in this section of the forest.

real ales in a mellow, cosy setting, while *Café Mambo*, adjacent to Aviemore Shopping Centre on Grampian Road, has a cheerful burger'n'chips-style menu.

Cairn Gorm mountain

From Aviemore, a road leads past Inverdruie and Loch Morlich and winds its way up into the Cairngorms, reaching the Coire Cas car park at a height of 2150ft. Here there's the base station for the ski area and the departure point for the **Cairn Gorm Mountain Railway** (daily 10am–5pm, last train up 4.20pm; every 20min; £9.75; ⓦ www.cairngormmountain.com), a two-car funicular system that runs to the top of the ski area. A highly controversial £15 million scheme that was bitterly opposed by conservationists, the railway whisks skiers in winter, and tourists throughout the year, along a mile and a half of track to the top station at an altitude of 3600ft, not far from the summit of Cairn Gorm mountain. The top station incorporates an exhibition/interpretation area and a café/restaurant from which spectacular views can be had on clear days; there is no access beyond the confines of the top station and its open-air viewing terrace unless you're embarking on winter skiing, so anyone wanting to walk on the subarctic Cairngorm plateau will have to trudge up from the car park at the bottom.

At the base station there's a **ranger office** (daily: April–Oct 9am–5pm; Nov–March 8.30am–4.30pm) where you can find out about various trails and even join occasional guided walks, as well as check the latest weather report. The simplest of the walks is around a **Mountain Garden Trail**, which features shrubs and trees native to the Cairngorms. The *Ptarmigan* **restaurant** at the top station offers self-service meals through the day and, in summer (July–Sept), more formal three-course "sunset dining" on Friday and Saturday evenings, as well as a three-course meal and ceilidh on Thursday evenings (July & Aug only); pre-booking is required for both (ⓣ 01479/861341).

Carrbridge

Worth considering as an alternative to Aviemore – particularly as a skiing base – **CARRBRIDGE** is a pleasant, quiet village about seven miles north. Look out for the spindly Bridge of Carr at the northern end of the village, built in 1717 and still making a graceful stone arch over the River Dulnain. The main attraction in the village is the **Landmark Forest Heritage Park** (daily: April to mid-July 10am–6pm; mid-July to Aug 10am–7pm; Sept–March 10am–5pm; £11.55; Ⓦwww.landmark -centre.co.uk), which offers families a host of excellent outdoor and indoor activities including forest walks, nature trails, water fun rides and Britain's highest wooden tower. For local **accommodation** both *Carrmoor Guest House*, Carr Road (Ⓣ01479/841244, Ⓦwww.carrmoorguesthouse.co.uk; ❸), and the very friendly *MellonPatch* B&B (Ⓣ01479/841592, Ⓦwww.mellonpatch.com; ❷) on Station Road are good options. The cosy, basic *Carrbridge Bunkhouse* (Ⓣ01479/841250, Ⓦwww .carrbridge-bunkhouse.co.uk), a timber-lined cabin with a wood-burning stove, is a good base for walkers; it's half a mile or so north of the village on the Inverness road.

Loch Garten and around

The **Abernethy Forest RSPB Reserve** on the shore of **LOCH GARTEN**, seven miles northeast of Aviemore and eight miles south of Grantown-on-Spey, is famous as the nesting site of one of Britain's rarest birds. A little over fifty years ago, the **osprey**, known in North America as the fish hawk, had completely disappeared from the British Isles. Then, in 1954, a single pair of these exquisite white-and-brown raptors mysteriously reappeared and built a nest in a tree half a mile or so from the loch. One year's eggs fell victim to thieves, and thereafter the area became the centre of an effective high-security operation. There are now believed to be up to 150 pairs nesting across the Highlands. The best time to visit is between April and August, when the ospreys return from West Africa to nest and the RSPB opens an **observation centre** (daily 10am–6pm; £3; Ⓣ01479/831476), complete with powerful telescopes and CCTV monitoring of the nest. The reserve is also home to several other rare species, including the Scottish crossbill, capercaillie, whooper swan and red squirrel; once-weekly **guided walks** leave from the observation centre (Wed 9.30am), while during the spring lekking season (April to mid-May) when male capercaillie gather and joust with each other, the centre opens very early for "Caperwatch" (daily 5.30–8am; £3). Rent two-wheeled transport from Cairngorm Bike and Hike by the station (Ⓣ01479/831745, Ⓦww.cairngormbikeandhike.co.uk), from where **steam trains** run to Aviemore.

Loch Garten is about a mile and a half west of **BOAT OF GARTEN** village: from the village, cross the Spey then take the Grantown road and the reserve is signposted to the right. An attractive wee place, Boat of Garten has a number of good **accommodation** options, the most elegant being the *Boat Hotel and Restaurant* (Ⓣ01479/831258, Ⓦwww.boathotel.co.uk; ❺). *Fraoch Lodge*, 15 Deshar Rd (Ⓣ01479/831331, Ⓦwww.scotmountain.co.uk; ❶), is an excellent hostel with four twin rooms and a family room sleeping four, and provides high-quality home-cooked meals along with good facilities such as a purpose-built drying room. It's enthusiastically run by experienced mountaineers, who also offer guided walking holidays and instruction in mountain skills. Alternatively, the *Old Ferryman's House* (Ⓣ01479/831370; ❷), just across the Spey, is a wonderfully homely, hospitable B&B, with no TVs, lots of books and delicious evening meals and breakfasts. *Anderson's* **restaurant** on Deshar Road is a homely and attractive place serving creative dishes based on local ingredients (closed Tues).

Kincraig

At **KINCRAIG**, six miles southwest of Aviemore on the B9152 towards Kingussie, there are a couple of unusual encounters with animals which offer a memorable diversion if you're not setting off on outdoor pursuits. The captive animals of the **Highland Wildlife Park** (daily: June–Aug 10am–6pm; April, May, Sept & Oct 10am–5pm; Nov–March 10am–4pm; last entry 2hr before closing; £13.50; ☎01540/651270, ⓦwww.highlandwildlifepark.org), will not appeal to everyone; it is a charity run by the Royal Zoological Society of Scotland where you can see wolves and bison, as well as many rarely seen natives, including pine martens, capercaillie, wildcat and eagles. Nearby, the engrossing **Working Sheepdogs** demonstrations at Leault Farm (May–Oct Sun–Fri 4pm; ☎01540/651310, ⓦwww.leaultworkingsheepdogs.co.uk; £5) afford the rare opportunity to see a champion shepherd herd a flock of sheep with up to eight dogs, using whistles and other commands. The fascinating hour-long display also includes a chance to see traditional hand-shearing, duck-herding and collie-pup training. Meanwhile, the Loch Insh Watersports Centre (see below) runs a **wildlife passenger boat trip** around Loch Insh and into Inchmarsh RSPB reserve (daily May & June 11am, 2pm & 4pm; also 6pm July & Aug; £8).

There are some good low-price **accommodation** options nearby. The Loch Insh Watersports Centre (☎01540/651272, ⓦwww.lochinsh.com) has basic but practical en-suite B&B rooms (❷) as well as a decent waterfront café/restaurant (☎01540/651394). At the remote *Glen Feshie Hostel* at Balachroick (☎01540/651323, ⓦwww.glenfeshiehostel.co.uk), three miles from Loch Insh down beautiful Glen Feshie, the price includes as much porridge as you like for breakfast.

Grantown-on-Spey

Buses run from Aviemore and Inverness to the small town of **GRANTOWN-ON-SPEY**, about fifteen miles northeast of Aviemore and another alternative base for exploring the Strathspey area. Life is concentrated around the central square, with its attractive Georgian architecture; the **tourist office** is on the High Street (March–Oct daily).

As with much of Speyside, there's a decent choice of **accommodation**. There's top-notch **B&B** in luxury organic ⚘*Eden House*, outside of town in the village of Cromdale (☎01479/872112, ⓦwww.theedenhouse.co.uk). In Grantown itself, *Parkburn Guest House* (☎01479/873116, ⓦwww.parkburnguesthouse.co.uk; ❷) on the High Street is welcoming; if you're after something more upmarket head for the large seventeenth-century *Garth Hotel*, at the north end of the square (☎01479/872836, ⓦwww.garthhotel.com; ❺) where the restaurant serves respectable, traditional meat-based dinners. There's also the smart *Muckrach Lodge Hotel and Restaurant* (☎01479/851257, ⓦwww.muckrach.co.uk; ❺), three miles southeast of Grantown by Dulnain Bridge.

In the budget range, you'll find a **bunkhouse** at Ardenbeg Outdoor Centre (☎01479/872824, ⓦwww.ardenbeg.co.uk), on Grant Road, parallel to the High Street, a base for courses in hillwalking, climbing, canoeing and skiing, while a mile or two south of town at Nethy Bridge, between Grantown and Boat of Garten, is the tiny, eight-bed *Lazy Duck Hostel* (☎01479/821642, ⓦwww.lazyduck.co.uk), a peaceful and comfortable retreat with woodland **camping** and great moorland walking on its doorstep. For **bike rental**, head just south of town to Craggan Outdoor Centre (☎01479/873283; £25/day) by the Craggan Golf Course.

To **eat** out in grand style, *Muckrach Lodge* offers a thoughtfully prepared and moderately pricey menu whilst within Grantown itself, the *Glass House* restaurant on Grant Road (☎01479/872980, ⓦwww.theglasshouse-grantown.co.uk) serves excellent, moderate-to-expensive contemporary Scottish food in a relaxed conservatory dining room. You can watch red squirrels at play over a coffee and tremendous cakes at the beautiful 350-acre *Revack Highland Estate and Adventure Park* (☎01479/872234), located just a mile out of town.

Newtonmore, Kingussie and Laggan

Twelve miles southwest of Aviemore, close neighbours **NEWTONMORE** and **KINGUSSIE** (pronounced "king-*yoos*-ee") are pleasant villages at the head of the Strathspey Valley separated by a couple of miles of farmland. On the **shinty** field their peaceful coexistence is forgotten and the two become bitter rivals; in recent years Kingussie has been dominant in the game, a fierce, indigenous sport from which ice hockey and golf evolved. Otherwise, the excellent **Highland Folk Museum** at Newtonmore (April–Aug daily 10.30am–5.30pm; Sept & Oct 11am–4.30pm; donation; ⓦwww.highlandfolk.com) is the chief attraction here. The outdoor site is a living history museum, with an old vintage bus offering a jump-on/jump-off tour round reconstructions of a working croft, a water-powered sawmill and a church where recitals on traditional Highland instruments are given.

Kingussie is also notable for the ruins of **Ruthven Barracks** (free access), standing east across the river on a hillock. The best-preserved garrison built to pacify the Highlands after the 1715 rebellion, it makes for great exploring by day and is impressively floodlit at night.

Eight miles southwest of Newtonmore on the A86, just beyond the junction with the A889 from Dalwhinnie, **Laggan Wolftrax mountain-bike centre** (£20/day; ☎01528/544786, ⓦwww.basecampmtb.com) is a superb facility boasting a café and over nine miles of trails to suit all abilities.

Practicalities

In Newtonmore, the best place for local **tourist information** is the Craft Centre (Feb–Dec Mon–Sat) opposite the Co-op supermarket. The Wildcat Centre (April–Sept Mon–Fri 9.30am–12.30pm & 2–5pm, Sat 9.30am–12.30pm; Oct–March Wed–Sat 9.30am–12.30pm; ☎01540/673131) also offers local information and details of some well-organized walking trails in the area.

One of the most appealing places **to stay** in the whole of Speyside is the relaxed but stylish ⚘ *The Cross* "restaurant with rooms" (☎01540/661166, ⓦwww .thecross.co.uk; ❻) located in a converted tweed mill on the banks of the River Gynack in Kingussie. On the edge of Newtonmore, *Coig Na Shee* (☎01540/670109, ⓦwww.coignashee.co.uk; ❹) is a soothingly decorated **B&B** in an Edwardian hunting lodge. Newtonmore boasts a number of good **hostels** including *Newtonmore Hostel* (☎01540/673360, ⓦwww.highlandhostel.co.uk), a welcoming and well-equipped place. In Kingussie, you'll find a comfortable, cheap bed in *The Laird's Bothy* (☎01540/661334, ⓦwww.thetipsylaird.co.uk). The most convenient accommodation for Laggan is *The Pottery Bunkhouse* and coffee shop (☎01528/544231, ⓦwww.potterybunkhouse.co.uk), which offers convenient, comfortable rooms and even an outdoor hot tub. For camping, those with transport will find good amenities at the *Invernahavon Holiday Park* (☎01540/673534) three miles south of Newtonmore.

The most ambitious **food** in the area is served at *The Cross* (see above; restaurant closed Sun & Mon), where the meals, though expensive, make imaginative use of local ingredients, complemented by a vast wine list. Cheaper food is available at several cafés and pubs in both towns – *Gilly's Kitchen* on the main street in Kingussie is open during the day (Tues–Sat 10am–5pm; ⓦwww.gillyskitchen .com) for simple home-made soup and light lunches. Also on High Street, the *Tipsy Laird* (☎01540/661334) is a good spot for a light lunch or an inexpensive, evening meal.

Speyside

Strictly speaking, the term **Speyside** refers to the entire region surrounding the River Spey, but to most people the name is synonymous with the **whisky triangle**, stretching from just north of Craigellachie, down towards Tomintoul in the south and east to Huntly. Indeed, there are more whisky distilleries and famous brands (including Glenfiddich, Glenlivet and Macallan) concentrated in this small area than in any other part of the country. Running through the heart of the region is the River Spey, whose clean, clear, fast-running waters play a vital part in the whisky industry and are also home to thousands of salmon, making it

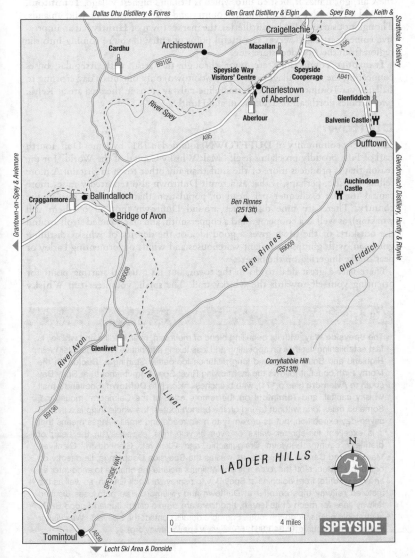

one of Scotland's finest angling locations. Obviously fertile, the tranquil glens of the area have none of the ruggedness of other parts of the Highlands; tourism blends into a local economy kept healthy by whisky and farming, rather than dominating it.

At the centre of Speyside is the quiet market town of **Dufftown**, full of solid, stone-built workers' houses and dotted with no fewer than nine whisky distilleries. Along with the well-kept nearby villages of **Craigellachie** and **Aberlour**, it makes the best base for a tour of whisky country, whether on the official Malt Whisky Trail or more independent explorations. Fewer visitors take the chance to discover the more remote glens, such as **Glenlivet**, which push higher up towards the Cairngorm massif, nestled into which is Britain's highest village, **Tomintoul**, situated on the edge of both whisky country and a large expanse of wild uplands. Though not surrounded by distilleries, the market town of **Huntly** has an impressive ruined castle and serves as a useful point of entry if you're coming into the region from the Aberdeenshire side.

Transport connections are poor through the area, with irregular buses connecting the main villages and (from Grantown) only one bus a day crossing to Ballater via Tomintoul. The only mainline railway stops in the area are at Keith, twelve miles northeast of Dufftown, and Huntly.

Dufftown

The cheery community of **DUFFTOWN**, founded in 1817 by James Duff, fourth Earl of Fife, proudly proclaims itself "Malt Whisky Capital of the World" for the reason that it produces more of the stuff than any other town in Britain. A more telling statistic, perhaps, is that as a result Dufftown also reportedly raises more capital for the exchequer per head of population than anywhere else in the country. There are nine distilleries around Dufftown (not all of them still working), as well as a cooperage and a coppersmith, and an extended stroll around the outskirts of the town gives a good idea of the density of whisky distilling going on, with glimpses of giant warehouses and whiffs of fermenting barley or peat smoke lingering on the breeze.

There isn't a great deal to do in the town, but it's a useful starting point for orienting yourself towards the whisky trail. The small, volunteer-run **Whisky**

The Speyside Way

The **Speyside Way**, with its beguiling blend of mountain, river, wildlife and whisky, is fast establishing itself as an appealing and less taxing alternative to the popular West Highland and Southern Upland long-distance footpaths. Starting at **Buckie** on the Moray Firth coast, it follows the fast-flowing River Spey from its mouth at Spey Bay south to **Aviemore** (see p.171), with branches linking it to **Dufftown**, Scotland's malt whisky capital, and **Tomintoul** on the remote edge of the Cairngorm mountains. Some 65 miles long without taking on the branch routes, the whole thing is a five- to seven-day expedition, but its proximity to main roads and small villages means that it is excellent for shorter walks or even bicycle trips, especially in the heart of **distillery** country between Craigellachie and Glenlivet: Glenfiddich, Glenlivet, Macallan and Cardhu distilleries, as well as the Speyside Cooperage, lie directly on or a short distance off the route. Other highlights include the chance to encounter an array of **wildlife**, from dolphins at Spey Bay to ospreys at Loch Garten, as well as the restored **railway** trips on offer at Dufftown and Aviemore. The path uses disused railway lines for much of its length, and there are simple campsites and good B&Bs at strategic points along the route. For more details contact the Speyside Way Visitor Centre at Aberlour (☎01340/881266, ⓦwww.speysideway.org).

Museum at 24 Fife St (mid-June to Sept Mon–Fri 1–4pm; free) has a slightly disorganized collection of illicit distilling equipment, books and old photographs. On the edge of town along the A941 is the town's largest working distillery, Glenfiddich (see box, p.182), as well as the old Dufftown train station, which has been restored by enthusiasts in recent years and is now the departure point for the Keith & Dufftown Railway (April–Sept 3 trips Sat & Sun, June–Aug also Fri; 40min; £9.50 return; ☎01340/821181, ⓦwww.keith-dufftown-railway.co.uk for journey times), which uses various restored diesel locomotives to chug through whisky country to Keith, home of the Strathisla distillery (see box, p.182). Beside the platform at Dufftown a permanent buffet car serves coffee, tea, soup and home-baked cakes.

Practicalities

Dufftown's four main streets converge on its main square, scene of a lively annual party on Hogmanay when free drams are handed out to revellers. The official tourist office is located inside the handsome clock tower at the centre of the square (April–Oct daily; ☎01340/820501), though an informal information and accommodation booking service has developed at The Whisky Shop (☎01340/821097, ⓦwww.whiskyshopdufftown.co.uk) across the road, boasting an array of six hundred malts and umpteen beers, produced not just on Speyside but all over Scotland. Nosings and other special events are regularly organized here, most notably the twice-yearly Spirit of Speyside Whisky Festival (ⓦwww.spiritofspeyside.com), which draws whisky experts and enthusiasts to the area in late April and late September.

There's a handful of places to stay in Dufftown itself, although you may choose to look elsewhere in Speyside where you will feel a bit closer to the attractive countryside. The only hostel accommodation nearby is the small self-catering Swan Bunkhouse (☎01542/810334) located at Drummuir, which has facilities suitable for wheelchair users. Located three miles northeast of Dufftown, it's possible to camp (£5), rent kayaks (£12) and fish (£18) at the Loch Park Adventure Centre (☎01542/810334, ⓦwww.lochpark.co.uk), one mile away; though unfortunately, there's no public transport this far. In town, Morven, on the main square (☎01340/820507, ⓦwww.morvendufftown.co.uk; ❷), offers simple, inexpensive B&B. Tannochbrae and Restaurant, 22 Fife St (☎01340/820541, ⓦwww.tannochbrae.co.uk; ❸), is a pleasant, enthusiastically run former provost's house with a lovely restaurant and bike rental (£15/day).

The smartest of Dufftown's restaurants are the expensive (and child friendly) La Faisanderie, on the corner of The Square and Balvenie Street (☎01340/821273; closed Tues), which serves local produce such as trout and game in a French style, and Taste of Speyside, 10 Balverie St (☎01340/820860; closed Mon), just off The Square, where you'll pay around £20 for three courses of Scottish cuisine. Alternatively, the rustic setting of Noah's Ark Bistro and Café (☎01542/821428) on Balvenie Street offers good value and wholesome daytime home-bakes, lunches and dinners. Whisky isn't in short supply in the local pubs and hotels, but for a choice of over seven hundred different whiskies you have to head to the Grouse Inn at Cabrach, tucked among the hills six miles out along the A941 to Rhynie.

Craigellachie

Four miles north of Dufftown, the small settlement of CRAIGELLACHIE (pronounced "Craig-ell-ach-ee") sits above the confluence of the sparkling waters of the Fiddich and the Spey. From the village, you can look down on a beautiful iron bridge over the Spey built by Thomas Telford in 1815. The local distillery isn't open to the public, though Glen Grant (see box, p.182) with its attractive

Speyside is the heart of Scotland's **whisky** industry, with over fifty distilleries testimony to a unique combination of clear, clean water, benign climate and gentle upland terrain. Yet for all the advertising-influenced visions of timeless traditions, whisky is a multi million-pound business dominated by huge corporations, and to many working distilleries visitors are an afterthought, if not a downright nuisance. Having said that, plenty are located in attractive historic buildings that now go to some lengths to provide an engaging experience for visitors. Mostly this involves a tour around the essential stages in the whisky-making process, though a number of distilleries now offer pricier connoisseur tours with a tutored tasting (or **nosing**, as it's properly called) and in-depth studies of the distiller's art. Some tours have restrictions on children.

There are eight distilleries on the official **Malt Whisky Trail** (Ⓦwww.maltwhiskytrail .com), a clearly signposted seventy-mile meander around the region. Unless you're seriously interested in whisky, it's best to just pick out a couple that appeal. All offer a guided tour (some are free, others charge but then give you a voucher redeemable against a bottle of whisky from the distillery shop), with a tasting to round it off; if you're driving you'll often be offered a miniature to takeaway. You could cycle or walk parts of the route, using the Speyside Way (see box, p.180). The following are selected highlights:

Cardhu, on the B9102 at Knockando (April–June Mon–Fri 10am–5pm; July–Sept Mon–Sat 10am–5pm, Sun noon–4pm; Oct–April Mon–Fri 11am–3pm; tours at 11am, 1pm & 2pm; £4 including voucher). Established over a century ago, when the founder's wife would raise a red flag to warn crofters if the authorities were on the lookout for their illegal stills. With attractive, pagoda-topped buildings, it sells rich, full-bodied whisky with distinctive peaty flavours that comes in an attractive bulbous bottle.

Glen Grant, Rothes (mid-Jan to mid-Dec Mon–Sat 9.30am–5pm; Sun noon–5pm; £3.50 including voucher). A well-known, floral whisky aggressively marketed to the younger customer. The highlight here is the attractive Victorian gardens, a mix of well-tended lawns and mixed, mature trees which include a tumbling waterfall and a hidden whisky safe.

Glenfiddich, on the A941 just north of Dufftown (Jan to mid-Dec Mon–Sat 9.30am–4.30pm, Sun noon–4.30pm; free). The biggest and slickest of all the Speyside distilleries, despite the fact that it's still owned by the same Grant family who

gardens is only a few miles up the road at Rothes, and, for an unusual alternative to a distillery tour, the **Speyside Cooperage** (Mon–Fri 9.30am–4pm; £3.30) is well worth a visit. After a short exhibition explaining the ancient and skilled art of cooperage, you're shown onto a balcony overlooking the large workshop where the oak casks for whisky are made and repaired.

For somewhere **to stay** in the village there's an extremely welcoming and tasteful B&B attached to the 🎨 *Green Hall Gallery* on Victoria Street (☎01340/871010, Ⓦwww.aboutscotland.com/greenhall; ④) while just along the road, the grand *Craigellachie Hotel* (☎01340/881204, Ⓦwww.craigellachie.com; ⑦) is the epitome of sumptuous "tartan-draped" Scottish hospitality, with classy cuisine and a bar lined with whisky bottles. In Archiestown, a few miles west of Craigellachie, the pleasant, traditional *Archiestown Hotel* (☎01340/810218, Ⓦwww.archiestown hotel.co.uk; ⑦) serves good evening **meals** and has some comfy rooms upstairs. In good weather, it's also a fine spot for al fresco dining. There's moderately priced pub grub in the busy *Highlander Inn* (☎01340/881446, Ⓦwww.whiskyinn.com; ⑤) on Victoria Street in Craigellachie, which has five smallish rooms and also hosts frequent folk **music sessions**. The tiny *Fiddichside Inn*, on the A95 just outside Craigellachie, is a wonderfully original and convivial **pub** with a garden by the

founded it in 1887. It's a light, sweet whisky packaged in triangular bottles – unusually, the bottling is still done on the premises and is part of the tours (offered in various languages).

Glenlivet, on the B9008 to Tomintoul (April–Oct Mon–Sat 9.30am–4pm, Sun noon–4pm; free). A famous name in a lonely hillside setting. This was the first licensed distillery in the Highlands, following the 1823 act that aimed to reduce illicit distilling and smuggling. The Glenlivet 12-year-old malt is a floral, fragrant, medium-bodied whisky. The Speyside Way passes through the distillery grounds.

Strathisla, Keith (April–Oct Mon–Sat 9.30am–4pm, Sun noon–4pm; £5). A small, old-fashioned distillery claiming to be Scotland's oldest (1786); it's certainly one of the most attractive, with classic pagoda-shaped buildings and the River Isla rushing by. Inside there's an old-fashioned mashtun and brass-bound spirit safes. The malt itself has a rich, almost fruity taste and is pretty rare, but is used as the heart of the better-known Chivas Regal blend. You can arrive here on one of the restored trains of the Keith & Dufftown Railway (see p.181).

The **Speyside Cooperage** at Craigellachie (see p.182) is also part of the official trail, with fascinating glimpses of a highly skilled and vital part of the industry.

Other distilleries, not on the official trail, include:

Aberlour, in Aberlour (April–Oct daily 10.30am & 2pm; Nov & Dec Mon–Fri; £7.50; booking essential ☎01340/881249). The twice-daily tours are quite specialized, with a tutored nosing and the chance to buy and fill your own bottle of cask-strength single malt.

Cragganmore, at Ballindalloch (tours April–Sept Mon–Fri 11.30am & 2pm; £4; booking essential ☎01479/874700). Offers a personalized, exclusive tour by appointment.

Glendronach, 8 miles northeast of Huntly (Mon–Sat 10am–4.30pm, Sun noon–4pm; £3). An isolated distillery that makes much of the fact that, uniquely, the stills are heated in the traditional method by coal fires.

Macallan, near Craigellachie (April–Oct Mon–Sat 9.30am–4.30pm; Nov–March Mon–Fri 11am–3pm; ☎01340/872280). Small tours, and a classy whisky aged in sherry casks to give it a rich colour and flavour.

river; quite unfazed by the demands of fashion, it has been in the hands of just two landladies (mother and daughter) for the last seventy years or so.

Aberlour

Two miles southwest from Craigellachie is **ABERLOUR**, officially "Charlestown of Aberlour". Founded in 1812 by Charles Grant, its long main street, neat, flower-filled central square and well-trimmed lawns running down to the Spey have all the markings of a planned village. Though you can visit the distillery here, it's another local produce – **shortbread** – that is exported in greater quantity around the world, mostly in tartan tins adorned with kilted warriors. A local baker, **Joseph Walker**, set up shop here at the turn of the twentieth century, quickly gaining a reputation for the product which seems to epitomize the Scottish sweet tooth. If you're keen, you can join the coachloads who visit the factory shop on the outskirts of the village.

Aberlour is just a few miles from the extensive **Moray Monster (Mountainbike) Trails** at Ben Aigen (ⓦwww.moraymountainbikeclub.co.uk). The town is also right on the Speyside Way (see box, p.180) and the **visitor centre** occupies half of the old train station, just back from the main square (May–Oct daily; Nov–April open when ranger in office; ℡01340/881266, Ⓦwww.speysideway.org). The centre has detailed information boards about natural history and other aspects of the way, and there's a wee tearoom next door (June–Sept Mon–Sat 10am–noon & 2–4.30pm, Sun 2–4.30pm). Though the **campsite** here, *Aberlour Gardens Caravan Park* (℡01340/871586, Ⓦwww.aberlourgardens.co.uk; March–Dec), is the most pleasant in the area, it's a walk of a mile and a half from either Aberlour or Craigellachie. Alternatively, there's a reasonable **B&B** at *Knockside* (℡01340/881561, Ⓦwww.speyside.moray.org/Aberlour/knockside.html; ❷). The best place to **eat and drink** is the *Mash Tun* (℡01340/881771, Ⓦwww.mashtun-aberlour.com), a pleasant, traditional pub at 8 Broomfield Square that serves up freshly prepared bar meals, real ales and all the local whiskies in the heart of Aberlour near the Spey; it also has cosy rooms and a luxury suite (❺). There's a range of deli produce at the Spey Larder, right by the village square.

Glenlivet

Beyond Aberlour, the Spey and the main road both head generally southwest to Ballindalloch and, a dozen miles beyond that, Grantown-on-Spey, at the head of the Strathspey region (see p.177). South from Ballindalloch are the quieter, remote glens of the Avon (pronounced "*A'an*") and Livet rivers. Allegedly, in the days of the despised tax excisemen, the Braes of Glenlivet once held over one hundred illicit whisky stills. The (legal) distillery at **GLENLIVET**, founded in 1824 by George Smith, is one of the most famous on Speyside, and certainly enjoys one of the more attractive settings. You can **stay** in George Smith's former house, right beside the distillery: ⚘ *Minmore House* (℡01807/590378, Ⓦwww.minmorehouse hotel.com; ❼), which has a lovely country-house feel with antique furniture and a wood-panelled bar. The owner is a chef and the superb **meals**, including a cake-laden afternoon tea by the open fire, are available to nonresidents if they book ahead.

Tomintoul

South of Glenlivet, deep into the foothills of the Cairngorms, **TOMINTOUL** (pronounced "*tom*-in-towel") is, at 1150ft, the highest village in the Scottish Highlands, and the northern gateway to the **Lecht** ski area (see box opposite). Its long, thin layout is reminiscent of a Wild West frontier town; Queen Victoria wrote that it was "the most tumble-down, poor looking place I ever saw". A spur of the Speyside Way connects Ballindalloch through Glenlivet to Tomintoul, and there are plenty of other terrific walking opportunities in the area, as well as some great routes for mountain biking. Many of these are on the Glenlivet Crown Estate (Ⓦwww.crownestate.co.uk/glenlivet), an extensive tract of carefully managed land abutting Tomintoul; information and useful maps about its wildlife (including reindeer) and numerous paths and bike trails are available from the tourist office or the estate **ranger's office** at the far end of the long main street (℡01807/580283). Land Rover and walking safaris are offered locally by Glenlivet Wildlife (℡01807/590241, Ⓦwww.glenlivet-wildlife.co.uk), including trips out to see black grouse, birds of prey and roe deer.

In the central square, the helpful **tourist office** (April–June, Sept & Oct Mon–Sat; July & Aug daily; ℡01807/580285) also acts as the local **museum** (same times; free), with mock-ups of an old farm kitchen and a smithie. It is possible to **camp** beside the Glenlivet Estate ranger's office, though there are no facilities here. There's a good SYHA **hostel** situated in the old schoolhouse on Main Street (℡0870/004 1152; mid-May to mid-Sept). Of the **B&Bs**, try *Findron Farmhouse*, a working farm half a mile south of town on the Braemar road (℡01807/580734,

Skiing and go-karting at the Lecht

The Lecht is the most remote of Scotland's ski areas, but it works hard to make itself appealing with a range of winter and summer activities. While its twenty runs include some gentle beginners' slopes there's little really challenging for experienced skiers other than a Snowboard Fun Park, with specially built jumps and ramps. Snow-making equipment helps extend the snow season beyond January and February, while there are also various summer activities, including quad bikes (£10) and "Deval karts" (£6) – go-karts with balloon tyres imported from the Alps which you can use to speed down the slopes from the top of the chairlift. A day's ski pass is £25; ski rental costs £17 a day from the ski school at the base station. For information on skiing and road conditions, call the base station ⌦01975/651440 or check ⓦwww.lecht.co.uk or ⓦski.visitscotland.com. There's also a lovely café at the base station with views across the pistes.

ⓦwww.ballindalloch-guesthouse.com; ❶), while the *Glenavon* (⌦01807/580218, ⓦwww.glenavon-hotel.co.uk; ❸) is the most convivial of the **hotels** gathered around the main square.

Travel details

Trains

Aberdeen to: Dundee (every 30min; 1hr 15min); Edinburgh (1–2 hourly; 2hr 35min); Forres (Mon–Sat 10 daily, 5 on Sun; 1hr 45min); Glasgow (hourly; 2hr 35min); Inverness (Mon–Sat 10 daily, 5 on Sun; 2hr 15min); London (Sun–Fri sleeper service; 10hr).
Aviemore to: Edinburgh (Mon–Sat 9 daily, 5 on Sun; 2hr 30min); Glasgow (9 daily, 5 on Sun; 2hr 30min); Inverness (Mon–Sat 9 daily, 5 on Sun; 1hr).
Balloch to: Glasgow (every 30min; 40min).
Crianlarich to: Fort William (3-4 daily; 1hr 50min); Glasgow Queen Street (6–8 Mon–Sat, 1–3 Sun; 1hr 50min); Oban (3–4 Mon–Sat, 1–3 Sun; 1hr 10min).
Dundee to: Aberdeen (every 30min; 1hr 15min); Edinburgh (1–2 hourly; 1hr 15min); Glasgow (1–2 hourly; 1hr 30min).
Kingussie to: Edinburgh (Mon–Sat 9 daily, 5 on Sun Sun; 2hr 30min); Glasgow (Mon–Sat 9 daily, 5 on Sun; 2hr 30min); Inverness (Mon–Sat 9 daily, 5 on Sun; 1hr).
Perth to: Aberdeen (hourly; 1hr 40min); Blair Atholl (3–7 daily; 45min); Dundee (hourly; 25min); Dunkeld (3–7 daily; 20min); Edinburgh (every 1–2hr; 1hr 25min); Glasgow Queen Steet (hourly; 1hr); Inverness (4–9 daily; 2hr); Pitlochry (4–9 daily; 30min); Stirling (hourly; 30min).
Rannoch to: Corrour (3–4 daily; 12min); Fort William (3–4 daily; 1hr); Glasgow Queen Steet (3–4 daily; 2hr 45min); London Euston (sleeper service; Sun–Fri daily; 11hr).
Stirling to: Aberdeen (hourly; 2hr 5min); Dundee (hourly; 55min); Edinburgh (every 30min; 1hr); Falkirk (every 30min; 15min); Glasgow Queen Street (every 20min; 30min); Inverness (3–5 daily; 2hr 55min); Perth (hourly; 30min).

Buses

Aberdeen to: Ballater (hourly; 1hr 45min); Banchory (every hour; 55min); Braemar (at least once every 2hr; 2hr 10min); Crathie for Balmoral (at least once every 2hr; 1hr 55min); Dundee (hourly; 2hr); Forres (hourly; 4hr).
Aberfeldy to Perth (6 daily; 1hr 20min).
Aberfoyle to: Callander (late June–mid-Oct 4 Thurs–Tues; 25min); Port of Menteith (late June–mid-Oct 4 Thurs–Tues; 10min).
Aviemore to: Cairngorm ski area (hourly; 30min); Edinburgh (5 daily; 2hr 30min–3hr 30min); Glasgow (7 daily; 3hr 30min); Grantown-on-Spey (Mon–Sat twice hourly; 35min); Inverness (Mon–Sat 6 daily, 5 on Sun; 45min).
Balloch to: Balmaha (every 2hr; 25min); Luss (hourly; 15min).
Callander to Loch Katrine (late June–mid-Oct 4 Thurs–Tues; 55min).
Dufftown to: Aberlour (Mon–Sat hourly; 5 on Sun; 15min;); Elgin (Mon–Sat hourly; 5 on Sun; 50min).

Dundee to: Aberdeen (hourly; 1hr 20min); Blair-gowrie (7 daily; 50min); Kirriemuir (5 daily; 55 min); Meigle (hourly; 40min).

Kingussie/Newtonmore to: Edinburgh and Glasgow (Mon–Fri 5 daily, Sat & 3 on Sun; 2hr 30min–3hr 30min); Inverness (Mon–Fri 6 daily, Sat & 5 on Sun; 1hr).

Kinloch Rannoch to: Pitlochry (3 daily; 50min); Rannoch Station (4 daily; 40min).

Luss to Tarbet (hourly; 10min).

Perth to: Aberfeldy (10 daily; 1hr 15min); Dundee (hourly; 45min); Dunkeld (hourly; 30min); Edinburgh (hourly; 1hr 20min); Glasgow (hourly; 1hr 35min); Inverness (hourly; 2hr 45min); Pitlochry (hourly; 45min); Stirling (hourly; 50min).

Stirling to: Aberfoyle (4 daily; 45min); Callander (1–2 hourly; 45min); Dundee (hourly; 1hr 30min); Edinburgh (hourly; 1hr); Glasgow (hourly; 50min); Inverness (every 2hr; 3hr 20min); Perth (hourly; 50min); St Andrews (every 2hr; 1hr 55min).

Flights

Aberdeen to: Belfast (1 daily, 1hr 15min); Birmingham (Mon–Fri 5 daily, Sat & 2 on Sun; 1hr 30min); Dublin (1 daily; 1hr 5min); East Midlands (3 daily Mon–Fri; 1 Sun; 1hr 25min); Exeter (1 daily; 1hr 50min); Kirkwall, Orkney (1 daily; 55min); Liverpool (1 daily, 1hr; London Gatwick (min 3 daily; 1hr 35min); London Heathrow (Mon–Fri, min 7 daily, Sat & Sun min 2; 1hr 30min); London Luton (2 daily; 1hr 30min); Manchester (Mon–Fri 6 daily, Sat & 2 on Sun; 1hr 20min); Newcastle (Mon–Fri 5 daily, Sat & 1 on Sun; 55min); Sumburgh, Shetland (Mon–Fri 5 daily, Sat & 2 on Sun; 1hr).

Dundee to London City (Mon–Fri 4 daily, Sat 1 daily, 2 on Sun; 1hr 25min).

3

The Great Glen

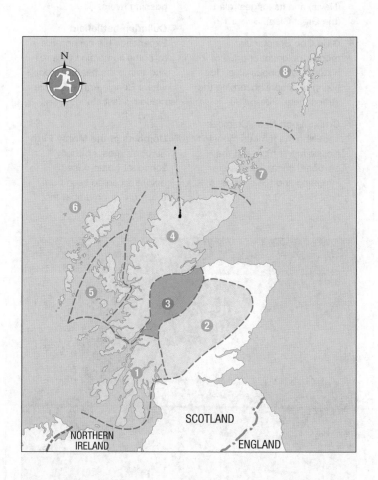

CHAPTER 3   # Highlights

✳ **Commando Memorial** An exposed but dramatic place to take in sweeping views over Scotland's highest ben (Nevis) and its longest glen (the Great Glen). See p.197

✳ **Glen Coe** Spectacular, moody, poignant and full of history – a glorious place for hiking or simply absorbing the atmosphere. See p.198

✳ **Cruise Loch Ness** Chances of seeing the famous monster Nessie aren't high, but the on-board sonar images are intriguing and the scenery's fine. See p.202

✳ **Glen Affric** Some of Scotland's best hidden scenery, with ancient Caledonian forests and gushing rivers. See p.206

✳ **Culloden battlefield** Experience the cannon-fire in a "battle immersion theatre" and tramp the heather moor where Bonnie Prince Charlie made his last stand. See p.213

✳ **Dolphins of the Moray Firth** Europe's most northerly school of bottle-nosed dolphins can be seen from the shore or on a boat trip. See p.216

▲ Commando Memorial near Ben Nevis

The Great Glen

The **Great Glen**, a major geological faultline cutting diagonally across the Highlands from Fort William to Inverness, is the defining geographic feature of the north of Scotland. A huge rift valley was formed when the northwestern and southeastern sides of the fault slid in opposite directions for more than sixty miles, while the present landscape was shaped by glaciers that retreated only around 8000 BC. The glen is impressive more for its sheer scale than its beauty, but the imposing barrier of loch and mountain means that no one can travel into the northern Highlands without passing through it. With the two major service centres of the Highlands at either end, it makes an obvious and rewarding route between the west and east coasts.

Of the Great Glen's four elongated lochs, the most famous is **Loch Ness**, home to the mythical monster; lochs **Oich**, **Lochy** and **Linnhe** (the last of these a sea loch) are less renowned though no less attractive. All four are linked by the Caledonian Canal. The southwestern end of the Great Glen is dominated by the town of **Fort William**, the self-proclaimed "Outdoor Capital of the UK". Situated at the heart of the Lochaber area, it is a utilitarian base, with plenty of places to stay and excellent access to a host of adventure sports. While the town itself is charmless, the surrounding countryside is a magnificent blend of rugged mountain terrain and tranquil sea loch. Dominating the scene to the south is **Ben Nevis**, Britain's highest peak, best approached from scenic Glen Nevis. The most famous glen of all, **Glen Coe**, lies on the main A82 road half an hour's drive south of Fort William, the two separated by the coastal inlet of **Loch Leven**. Nowadays the whole area is unashamedly given over to tourism, with Fort William swamped by bus tours throughout the summer, but, as ever in the Highlands, within a thirty-minute drive you can be totally alone.

At the northeastern end of the Great Glen is the capital of the Highlands, **Inverness**, a sprawling city with some decent places to eat; it's most often used as a springboard to remoter areas further north. Inevitably, most transport links to the northern Highlands, including Ullapool, Thurso and the Orkney and Shetland islands, pass through Inverness.

The region has a turbulent and bloody **history**. Founded in 1655 and named in honour of William III, Fort William was successfully held by government troops during both of the Jacobite risings; the country to the southwest is inextricably associated with Bonnie Prince Charlie's flight after **Culloden**. Glen Coe is another historic site with a violent past, renowned as much for the infamous massacre of 1692 as for its magnificent scenery.

Transport

The main **A82** road runs the length of the Great Glen, although relatively high traffic levels mean that it's not a fast or particularly easy route to drive. The area is reasonably well served by **buses**, with several daily services between Inverness and Fort William, and a couple of extra buses covering the section between Fort William and Invergarry during school terms. However, the traditional and most rewarding way to travel through the Glen itself is by **boat**: a flotilla of kayaks, small yachts and pleasure vessels take advantage of the canal and its old wooden locks during the summer. Alternatively, an excellent **cycle path** traverses the Glen, as well as a long-distance footpath, the 73-mile **Great Glen Way**, which takes five to six days to walk in full (see box opposite).

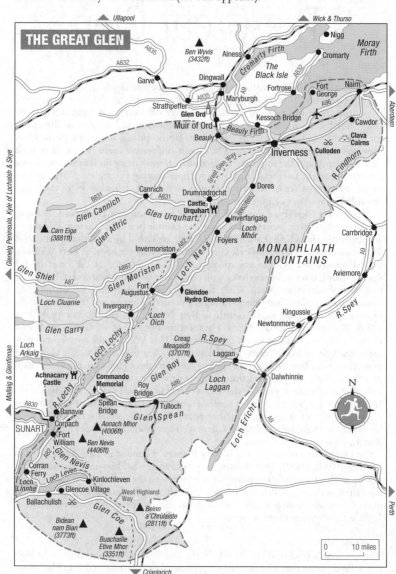

The 73-mile cleft of the Great Glen is the most obvious – and by far the flattest – way of traversing northern Scotland from coast to coast. The **Great Glen Way** long-distance footpath (ⓦwww.greatglenway.com) is a relatively undemanding five-to-six-day hike that uses a combination of canal towpath and forest- and hill-tracks between Fort William and Inverness. Accommodation is readily available all the way along the route in campsites, hostels, bunkhouses and B&Bs, though in high season you should book ahead and if you know you're going to arrive late somewhere it's worth checking that you can still get a meal either where you're staying or somewhere nearby. The maps you'll need to do the whole thing are *Ordnance Survey Landranger maps 41, 34* and *26*. Alternatively, *The Great Glen Way and Cycle Route* published by Footprint (£4.95) also maps out the way. There are various other guidebooks that describe the route, including *The Great Glen Way* published by Rucksack Readers (£10.99). A **cycle path** also traverses the Glen, offering a tranquil alternative to the hazardous A82. The path, which shares some of its route with the footpath but also utilizes stretches of minor roads, is well signposted and can be managed in one long day or two easier days, though of course you can tackle shorter sections. Bikes can be rented at Fort William, Banavie, Drumnadrochit and Inverness. The Forestry Commission publishes *Cycling in the Forest, The Great Glen*, a handy booklet highlighting the various sections of the route (ⓣ01320/366322 or 01397/702184, ⓦwww.forestry.gov.uk). The suggested **direction** for following both routes is from west to east – to take advantage of the prevailing southwesterly wind.

Fort William

With its stunning position on Loch Linnhe, tucked in below the snow-streaked bulk of Ben Nevis, **FORT WILLIAM** (known by the many walkers and climbers that come here as "Fort Bill") should be a gem. Sadly, the same lack of taste that nearly saw the town renamed "Abernevis" in the 1950s is evident in the ribbon bungalow development and ill-advised dual carriageway – complete with grubby pedestrian underpass – which have wrecked the waterfront. The main street and the little squares off it are more appealing, though occupied by some decidedly tacky tourist gift shops.

Arrival, information and accommodation

Just across the A82 dual carriageway from the north end of the High Street you'll find Fort William's **train station** (a stop on the scenic West Highland Railway direct from Glasgow; see p.229). Intercity **coaches** from Glasgow and Inverness stop outside here. The busy and very helpful **tourist office** is on the High Street (April–Sept daily; Oct–March Mon–Sat; ⓣ01397/701801, ⓦwww.visithighlands.com).

You'll find a host of outdoor-activity specialists in town. High-spec **mountain bikes** are available for rent at Off Beat Bikes, 117 High St (ⓣ01397/704008, ⓦwww.offbeatbikes.co.uk); they know the best routes, issue free maps and also have a branch open at the Nevis Range gondola base station (June–Sept; ⓣ01397/705825) – a location that boasts forest rides and a world-championship standard downhill track. Local **mountain guides** include Alan Kimber of *Calluna* (see p.192) and the **Snowgoose Mountain Centre** (ⓣ01397/772467, ⓦwww.highland-mountain -guides.co.uk), set beside *Smiddy Bunkhouse and Blacksmith's Hostel*, which offers instruction, rental and residential courses for activities such as mountaineering. For sea-kayak coaching, half-day and weekend trips, Rockhoppers in Corpach is a good bet (ⓣ07739/837344, ⓦwww.rockhopperscotland.co.uk).

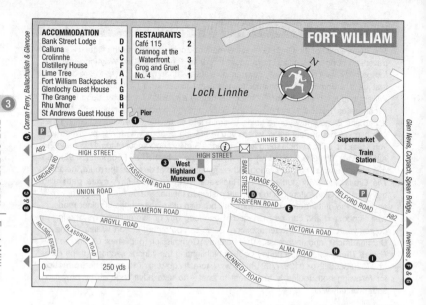

ACCOMMODATION
Bank Street Lodge   D
Calluna   J
Crolinnhe   C
Distillery House   F
Lime Tree   A
Fort William Backpackers   I
Glenlochy Guest House   G
The Grange   B
Rhu Mhor   H
St Andrews Guest House   E

RESTAURANTS
Café 115   2
Crannog at the
  Waterfront   3
Grog and Gruel   4
No. 4   1

FORT WILLIAM

Loch Linnhe

Corran Ferry, Ballachulish & Glencoe

Glen Nevis, Corpach, Spean Bridge, *Inverness*

This town itself isn't the most characterful place to base yourself, but Fort William's plentiful **accommodation** ranges from large luxury hotels to budget hostels and bunkhouses. Numerous B&Bs are also scattered across town, many of them in the suburb of Corpach on the other side of Loch Linnhe, three miles along the Mallaig road (served by regular buses), where you'll also find a couple of good hostels.

In-town accommodation

Hotels and B&Bs

Crolinnhe Grange Rd ☏01397/702709, ⓦwww .crolinnhe.co.uk. Beautifully appointed guesthouse overlooking Loch Linnhe. Quite grand and upmarket. ⑥

Distillery House North Rd ☏01397/700103, ⓦwww.stayinfortwilliam.co.uk. Very comfortable, well-equipped upper-range guesthouse a 10min walk north of the town centre near the Glen Nevis turn-off, with singles, doubles and "superior" rooms. ⑤

The Grange Grange Rd ☏01397/705516, ⓦwww.thegrange-scotland.co.uk. Top-grade accommodation in a striking old stone house, with log fires, views towards Loch Linnhe and luxurious en-suite doubles. Vegetarian breakfasts on request. Open April–Oct. ⑥

Lime Tree Achintore Rd ☏01397 /701806, ⓦwww.limetreefortwilliam. co.uk. A stylish and relaxing option in an old manse, with a great modern restaurant and an excellent gallery; they've also got the practicalities covered with a drying room, map room and bike storage. ⑤

Rhu Mhor Alma Rd ☏01397/702213, ⓦwww .rhumhor.co.uk. Congenial and characterful B&B, a 10min walk from the town centre, offering good breakfasts; vegetarians and vegans catered for on request. ③

St Andrews Guest House Fassifern Rd ☏01397/703038, ⓦwww.standrewsguesthouse .co.uk. Comfortable, central and very reasonable B&B in a converted granite choir-school featuring various inscriptions and stained-glass windows. ①

Hostels and campsites

Bank Street Lodge Bank St ☏01397/700070, ⓦwww.bankstreetlodge.co.uk. A clean and bright 43-bed hostel handy for transport and the town centre.

Calluna Heathercroft, Connachie Rd ☏01397/ 700451, ⓦwww.fortwilliamholiday.co.uk. Well-run self-catering and hostel accommodation a 10min walk from the centre of town, configured for individual, family and group stays. Free pick-up from town available, along with on-site laundry and mountain-guiding services (see ⓦwestcoast -mountainguides.co.uk).

Fort William Backpackers Alma Rd
☎01397/700711, ⓦwww.scotlands-top-hostels
.com. A busy 38-bed, rambling, archetypal
backpacker hostel a 5min walk up the hill from
town, with great views and large communal areas.

Out-of-town accommodation

Hotels and B&Bs

Achintee Farm Guest House Glen Nevis
☎01397/702240, ⓦwww.achinteefarm.com.
Friendly B&B with adjoining hostel and self-
catering cottage, right by the *Ben Nevis Inn* at the
start of the Ben Nevis footpath. ❹

Inverlochy Castle Torlundy, 2 miles north of
town on the A82 ☎01397/702177, ⓦwww
.inverlochycastlehotel.co.uk. Built on the site of a
thirteenth-century fortress, this is one of
Scotland's grandest and most luxurious country-
house hotels with fantastic accommodation and
Michelin-star food. ❾

Rhiw Goch Banavie ☎01397/772373, ⓦwww
.rhiwgoch.co.uk. Comfortable and welcoming B&B
overlooking Neptune's Staircase with great views
to Ben Nevis. For a super-healthy breakfast, try the
great fresh-fruit platter. Bike and canoe rental also
available. ❷

Hostels and campsites

Ben Nevis Inn Achintee, Glen Nevis
☎01397/701227, ⓦwww.ben-nevis-inn
.co.uk. A basic and cosy twenty-bed bunkhouse in

the basement of a lively 250-year-old pub, 500m
north of *Achintee Farm Guest House*. Terrific pub
grub and atmosphere.

Chase the Wild Goose Hostel Banavie
☎01397/772531, ⓦwww.great-glen-hostel.com.
A small, comfortable hostel close to Neptune's
Staircase and handy for the Great Glen Way.

Farr Cottage Lodge Corpach, on the main
A830 ☎01397/772315, ⓦwww.farrcottage.co.uk.
Well-equipped, lively place with range of dorms
and double/twin rooms (❶). Offers a multitude
of outdoor activities including canyoning and
sea-fishing; evening entertainment includes
whisky tastings.

Glen Nevis Caravan and Camping Park Glen
Nevis, 2 miles up the Glen Nevis road ☎01397/
702191, ⓦwww.glennevisholidays.co.uk. Offers a
range of lodges and rentable caravans as well as
camping pitches. Facilities include hot showers, a
shop and restaurant, and disabled facilities.

Glen Nevis SYHA hostel Glen Nevis, 2.5 miles up
the Glen Nevis road, opposite the start of the path
to the summit ☎01397/702336, ⓦwww.syha.org
.uk. Though far from town, this friendly hostel is an
excellent base for walkers. Very busy in summer.

Smiddy Bunkhouse and Blacksmith's Hostel
Snowgoose Mountain Centre, Station Rd, Corpach
☎01397/772467, ⓦwww.highland-mountain
-guides.co.uk. Alpine hostel and bunkhouse on the
site of an old blacksmith's workshop. It's four miles
from Ben Nevis at the southwestern end of the
Caledonian Canal.

The Town

Fort William's aesthetic decline started in the nineteenth century when the
original fort, which gave the town its name, was demolished to make way for the
train line. There's little to detain you except the splendid and idiosyncratic **West
Highland Museum**, on Cameron Square, just off the High Street (June–Sept
Mon–Sat 10am–5pm, July & Aug also Sun 10am–4pm; Oct–May Mon–Sat
10am–4pm; £4). Its collections cover virtually every aspect of Highland life and
the presentation is traditional, but very well done, making a refreshing change
from state-of-the-art heritage centres. There's a secret portrait of Bonnie Prince
Charlie and the long Spanish rifle used in the famous Appin Murder, and even a
550kg slab of aluminium, the stuff that's processed into silver foil just five miles
north of town, betrayed by the huge pipes running down the mountainside.

Excursions from town include the 84-mile round-trip to Mallaig (see p.232) on the
West Highland Railway Line aboard the **Jacobite Steam Train** (mid-May to Oct
Mon–Fri; July–Aug also Sat & Sun; depart Fort William 10.20am, return 2.10pm;
£31; ☎01524/737751 or 737753, ⓦwww.westcoastrailways.co.uk). Heading along
the shore of Loch Eil to the west coast via historic Glenfinnan (see p.229), the train
passes through some of the region's most spectacular scenery, though these days it's
as popular for its role as the locomotive used in the *Harry Potter* films. Several **cruises**
also leave from the town pier every day, offering the chance to spot the marine life

of Loch Linnhe, which includes seals and sea birds. Try Crannog Cruises (April to mid-Sept; 90min; £10; ☎01397/705589, ⓦwww.crannog.net) or Seaventures, who offer exhilarating fast boat trips (March–Nov; incl 90min Loch Linnhe trip; £10; ☎01397/701687, ⓦwww.seaventuresscotland.com).

Eating and drinking

Fort William has a reasonable range of places to **eat** and **drink**. If your budget won't stretch to the Michelin-starred fare at *Inverlochy Castle*, the pick of the bunch is the *Lime Tree Restaurant* (☎01397/701806, ⓦwww.limetreefortwilliam.co.uk) in the Old Manse on Achintore Road, which serves excellent contemporary Scottish food. At *Crannog at the Waterfront* (☎01397/705589, ⓦwww.oceanandoak.co.uk), located at the pier just off the bypass on entering Fort William, you'll find lochside views and fresh seafood, including lobster, oak-smoked salmon and langoustines, alongside a reasonable wine list. Another option is *No. 4* (☎01397/704222), at the top end of Cameron Square, with dishes including lamb, venison and a handful of traditional Scottish dishes. On the High Street, loud and friendly *Grog and Gruel* is a good bet for Scottish real ales, malts, entertainment and some traditional pub grub, while *Café 115* is decent for coffee.

Fort William and Glen Coe outdoor activities

In and around Fort William and Glen Coe you'll find a high concentration of **outdoor-activity** specialists who can help you make the most of the area's spectacular array of lochs, rivers and mountains. Most of the places and people listed below offer guiding, instruction and equipment rental. Other good places to go for **information** and advice are outdoor equipment stores – in Fort William the best is Nevisport, at the train-station end of High Street – or hostels and bunkhouses, many of which are run by outdoor enthusiasts.

Climbing For rock climbing or winter mountaineering, contact any of the mountain guides listed below under "Walking" or visit Ice Factor, the world's largest indoor ice-climbing wall, in Kinlochleven (see p.199).

Fishing For fly-fishing tuition and guiding, contact Jimmy Couts (see p.197) at Roy Bridge.

Horseriding Torlundy Farm Trout Fishery and Riding Centre (☎01397/703015), three miles north of Fort William on the A82, caters for experienced riders.

Mountain biking Contact Off Beat Bikes (see p.191) in Fort William, Nevis Range, or check out ⓦwww.ridefortwilliam.co.uk. For a guide see ⓦwww.nofussevents.co.uk.

Skiing Skiing opportunities are available at the Nevis Range Ski Centre (see p.197) and the Glen Coe Ski Centre ⓦwww.glencoemountain.com.

Walking Some of the best routes include the Great Glen Way (see p.192), walks in Glen Nevis and on Ben Nevis (see opposite), the Commando Trail (see p.198) and walks in Glen Coe (see p.198). If you're interested in tackling the more difficult peaks, traverses such as the Aonach Eagach ridge in Glen Coe, or want to improve your mountain skills, it's a good idea to hire a mountain guide, normally for £100–150 a day. Contact *Calluna* (see p.192), Snowgoose Mountain Centre (see p.191), or Ice Factor (see p.201).

Water sports For sea-kayaking instruction and half-day, day- and weekend-long expeditions, contact Rockhoppers Scotland (☎07739/837344, ⓦwww.rockhopper scotland.co.uk). Snowgoose Mountain Centre (see p.191) offers a number of water-based activities, with canyoning or fun-yakking (using inflatable two-man rafts-cum-kayaks), on local rivers.

Around Fort William

Any disappointment you harbour about the dispiriting flavour of Fort William town should be offset by the wealth of scenery and activities in its immediate vicinity. Most obvious – on a clear day, at least – is **Ben Nevis**, the most popular, though hardly the most rewarding, of Scotland's high peaks. The path up leaves from **Glen Nevis**, also a starting point for some other excellent walks of various lengths and elevations. The mountain abutting Ben Nevis is **Aonach Mhòr**, home of Scotland's most modern ski resort and an internationally renowned honey-pot for downhill mountain-bike enthusiasts. Some of the best views of these peaks can be had from **Corpach**, a small village opposite Fort William that marks the start of the **Caledonian Canal** (see p.204).

The main road travelling up the Great Glen from Fort William towards Inverness is the A82, ten miles along which is the small settlement of **Spean Bridge**, a good waypoint for getting to various remote and attractive walking areas with several backpacker hostels, notably glens **Spean** and **Roy**, found along the A86 trunk road, which links across the central highlands to the A9 and the Speyside region (see p.179).

Glen Nevis

A ten-minute drive south of Fort William, **GLEN NEVIS** is indisputably among the Highlands' most impressive glens: a classic U-shaped glacial valley hemmed in by steep bracken-covered slopes and swathes of blue-grey scree. With the forbidding mass of Ben Nevis rising steeply to the north, it's not surprising that the valley has served as a location in the films *Rob Roy* and *Braveheart*. Apart from its natural beauty, Glen Nevis is also the starting point for the ascent of Ben Nevis, and you can rent **mountain equipment** at the trailhead. One of the best maps is *Harvey's Ben Nevis Walkers Map and Guide*, available from Fort William's tourist office and most local bookshops and outdoor stores. Highland Country **bus** #42 (May to late Sept) runs from the bus station in Fort William via the SYHA hostel to the Lower Falls car park almost five miles up the Glen Nevis road.

A great **low-level walk** (six miles round-trip) runs from the end of the road at the top of Glen Nevis. The good but very rocky path leads through a dramatic gorge with impressive falls and rapids, then opens out into a secret hanging valley, carpeted with wild flowers, with a high waterfall at the far end. If you're really energetic (and properly equipped) you can walk the full twelve miles over Rannoch Moor to **Corrour Station** (see box, p.155), where you can pick up one of three daily trains to take you back to Fort William.

Of all the walks in and around Glen Nevis, the **ascent of Ben Nevis** (4406ft), Britain's highest summit, inevitably attracts the most attention. In high summer the trail is teeming with hikers – around 100,000 summit each year. However, this doesn't mean the mountain should be treated casually. It can snow at the summit any day of the year and people die on the slopes, so take the necessary precautions (see p.47); in winter, of course, the mountain should be left to the experts. The most obvious **route**, a Victorian pony-path up the whaleback south side of the mountain, built to service the observatory that once stood on the top, starts from the helpful Glen Nevis visitor centre (daily: Easter to mid-May & Oct 9am–5pm; mid-May to end Sept 9am–6pm) a mile and a half southeast of Fort William along the Glen Nevis road (bus #42 from Fort William). Ask here for the useful leaflet *Ben Nevis: Safety information for walking the mountain track*. Return via the main route or, if the weather is settled and you're confident enough, make a side-trip from the wide saddle into the **Allt a'Mhuilinn glen** for spectacular views of the great cliffs on Ben Nevis's north face. Allow a full day for the climb (8hr) and check the weather forecast at your accommodation before setting out.

Neptune's Staircase

In the suburb of **BANAVIE**, three miles north of the centre of Fort William along the A830 to Mallaig, the Caledonian Canal climbs 64ft in less than half a mile via a punishing but picturesque series of eight locks known as **Neptune's Staircase**. There are stunning views from here of Ben Nevis and its neighbours, and it's a popular point from which to walk or cycle along the canal towpath. *Moorings Hotel* near the staircase does decent pub food. Canoes (£25/day) can be rented from *Rhiw Goch* B&B (see p.193) a half-mile up the B8004 in Banavie, whilst the Snowgoose Mountain Centre in Corpach (℡01397/772467) also rents kayaks and canoes. If you do choose to cycle along the Caledonian Canal, look out for *The Eagle Inn* at Laggan Locks at the head of Loch Lochy, where fresh seafood and real ale are on offer aboard a wonderful 1920s Dutch barge (℡07789/858567 & 07811/956893; Easter–Oct).

Spean Bridge and around

Ten miles northeast of Fort William, the village of **SPEAN BRIDGE** marks the junction of the A82 with the A86 from Dalwhinnie and Kingussie (see p.178). If you're here, it's well worth heading a mile out of the village on the A82

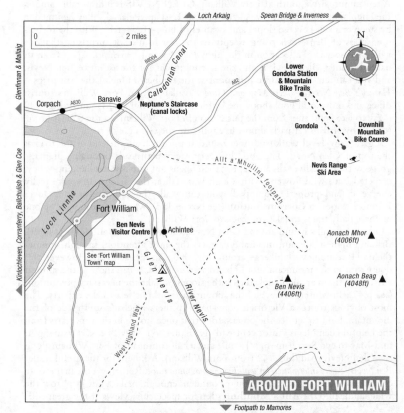

Situated seven miles northeast of Fort William by the A82, on the slopes of **Aonach Mhòr**, one of the high mountains abutting Ben Nevis, the **Nevis Range** (☏01397/705825, ⓦ www.nevis-range.co.uk) is Scotland's highest ski area. All year round, Highland Country bus #42 runs from Fort William at least five times a day (Mon–Sat; 3 on Sun) to the base station of the country's only **gondola** system (daily: 10am–5pm; July & Aug 9.30am–6pm; closed mid-Nov to mid-Dec; £10.50 return). The one-and-a-half-mile gondola trip (15min), rising 2000ft, gives an easy approach to some high-level walking as well as spectacular views from the terrace of the self-service restaurant at the top station. There's also a Discovery Centre here, providing insights into the mountain's geology and wildlife. From the top of the gondola station, you can experience a white-knuckle ride down Britain's only World-Cup standard **downhill mountain-bike course** (mid-May to mid-Sept 11am–3pm; £12 including gondola one-way; £19 multi-trip), a hair-raising 3km route that's not for the faint-hearted. There's also over 25 miles of waymarked off-road bike routes, known as the Witch's Trails, on the mountainside and in the Leanachan Forest, ranging from gentle paths to cross-country scrambles. Off Beat Bikes (Mon–Sat 9am–5.30pm, Sun 10am–5pm; £12/half-day, £17/day; ☏01397/704008, ⓦ www.offbeatbikes.co.uk) rents general mountain bikes as well as full-suspension ones for the downhill course from its shops in Fort William and at the gondola base station (mid-May to mid-Sept). The base station area also has a café and there's a play area and nature trail nearby.

towards Inverness to the **Commando Memorial**, a group of bronze soldiers commemorating the men who trained in the area during World War II. The statue looks out on an awesome sweep of moor and mountain that takes in the wider Lochaber area and the Ben Nevis massif. A few hundred yards from the memorial, on the minor B8004 to Gairlochy, is the welcoming and upmarket *Old Pines Hotel and Restaurant* (☏01397/712324, ⓦ www.oldpines.co.uk; ❽), where guests are treated to locally sourced game and shellfish as well as home-baking, pasta and ice cream.

Three miles east of Spean Bridge, a minor road turns off up **Glen Roy**. A couple of miles along the glen, you'll see the so-called "parallel roads": not roads at all, but ancient beaches at various levels along the valley sides, which mark the shorelines of a loch confined here by a glacial dam in the last Ice Age. Back on the A86 at **ROY BRIDGE**, four miles from Spean Bridge, you can enjoy some tasty home-made soup and bar food under the gaze of stag heads in the *Roy Bridge Hotel*, which runs the adjacent cosy *Grey Corrie Lodge* backpackers hostel (☏01397/712236, ⓦ www.roybridgehotel.co.uk). Just 500m further north, the *Stronlossit Inn* (☏01397/712253, ⓦ www.stronlossit.co.uk; ❺) serves standard bar food and has several real ales on tap. Two miles east of Roy Bridge, *Aite Cruinnichidh* (☏01397/712315, ⓦ www.highland-hostel.co.uk) is a comfortable wood-lined **bunkhouse** in a beautiful setting, with good facilities including family rooms and a sauna, as well as local advice for walkers and cyclists. The nearby Roy Bridge Store is handy for provisions while Jimmy Couts (☏01397/712812, ⓦ www.fishing-scotland.co.uk) is the man to call for **fly-fishing** tuition and excursions.

Five miles further east from *Aite Cruinnichidh*, the railway line and road part company at **TULLOCH**, and trains swing south to pass Loch Treig and cross Rannoch Moor (see p.155). The station building at Tulloch is now a friendly and well-equipped **hostel**, *Station Lodge* (☏01397/732333, ⓦ www.stationlodge.co .uk), which can provide breakfasts and dinners with advance notice. The Caledo-nian sleeper train from London stops right at the door. Further east, the A86 runs

The Commando Trail

From 1942 until the end of World War II, the Lochaber district around the southern part of the Great Glen was used as a training area by the elite **commando** units of the British army. A striking **memorial** depicting a group of bronze soldiers, sculpted in 1952 by Scott Sutherland, stands overlooking an awesome sweep of moor and mountain beside the A82 just to the north of Spean Bridge. Nearby, in a room inside the *Spean Bridge Hotel* (☎01397/712250, ⓦwww.speanbridgehotel.co.uk; ❹), the proudly assembled **Commando Exhibition** (April–Oct daily 9.15am–4.45pm; free) has impressive displays of photos, medals and memorabilia.

The soldiers' base was at **Achnacarry Castle**, hereditary seat of the Clan Cameron, around which there's an interesting five-mile **walk** retracing many of the places used by them during their training. To get here, follow the minor B8004 beside the memorial, which branches down to Gairlochy by the canalside at Loch Lochy's southern tip, then follow the signs for the small **Clan Cameron museum** (Easter to mid-Oct daily 1.30–5pm, July & Aug opens at 11am; £3.50; ⓦwww.clan-cameron .org), located in the old post office near the castle still occupied by the clan chief Cameron of Lochiel. The museum tells the clan history, including its involvement in the 1745 rebellion, and has memorabilia relating to the commandos' residency. You can park your car here and walk to the eastern end of **Loch Arkaig**, one of Scotland's most ruggedly wild and remote stretches of water, then walk down the tree-lined **Mile Dorcha**, or Dark Mile. Around here there are various caves and small bothies used by **Bonnie Prince Charlie** when he was on the run after Culloden, dodging government troops, and desperately hoping for the arrival of a French ship to carry him to safety. The road leads to the shores of **Loch Lochy**, where the commandos would practise opposed landings, often using live ammunition to keep them on their toes. After a mile by the lochside, turn right back along the road that leads to the Clan Cameron museum. A **leaflet** giving a fuller description of the trail and the commandos' activities can be obtained from tourist information offices in the area.

alongside the artificial **Loch Laggan** with the picturesque Ardverikie Castle on its southern shore and the attractive walking area of **Creag Meagaidh National Nature Reserve** to the north.

Glen Coe and around

Glen Coe, half an hour's drive south of Fort William on the main A82 road to Glasgow, is one of Scotland's most inspiring places. Arriving from the south across the desolate reaches of Rannoch Moor, you're likely to find the start of the glen – with **Buachaille Etive Mhòr** to the south and **Beinn a'Chrùlaiste** to the north – little short of forbidding. By the time you've reached the heart of the glen, with the three huge rock buttresses known as the **Three Sisters** on one side and the Anoach Eagach ridge on the other combining to close up the sky, you'll almost certainly want to stop. Added to the compelling emotional mix is the story of the notorious **massacre of Glen Coe** in 1692, nadir of the long-standing enmity between the clans MacDonald and Campbell. At its western end, Glen Coe meets Loch Leven: the main road goes west and over the bridge at **Ballachulish** en route to Fort William, while at the eastern end of the loch is the slowly reviving settlement of **Kinlochleven**, site of the world's largest indoor ice-climbing centre and a waypoint on the **West Highland Way** long-distance footpath (see box, p.140).

Glen Coe

Breathtakingly beautiful **Glen Coe** (literally "Valley of Weeping"), sixteen miles south of Fort William on the A82, is a spectacular mountain valley between velvety-green conical peaks, their tops often wreathed in cloud, their flanks streaked by cascades of rock and scree. In 1692 it was the site of a notorious massacre, in which the MacDonalds were victims of an abiding government desire to suppress the clans. Fed up with what they regarded as unacceptable lawlessness, and a groundswell of Jacobitism and Catholicism, the government offered a general pardon to all those who signed an oath of allegiance to William III by January 1, 1692. When clan chief **Alastair MacDonald** missed the deadline, a plot was hatched to make an example of "that damnable sept", and **Campbell of Glenlyon** was ordered to billet his soldiers in the homes of the MacDonalds, who for ten days entertained them with traditional Highland hospitality. In the early morning of February 13, the soldiers turned on their hosts, slaying around forty and causing more than three hundred to flee in a blizzard.

Beyond the small village of **GLENCOE** at the western end of the glen, the glen itself (a property of the NTS since the 1930s) is virtually uninhabited, and provides outstanding climbing and walking. The attractive NTS **visitor centre** (March daily 10am–4pm; April–Aug daily 9.30am–5.30pm; Sept & Oct daily 10am–5pm; Nov to mid-Dec, Jan & Feb Thurs–Sun 10am–4pm; NTS; £5.50) sits in woodland a mile south of the village, has a good exhibition with video giving a balanced account of the massacre, information about the area's natural history and conservation issues, and some entertaining material on rock- and hill-climbing through the years. There's also a cabin area providing information on the local weather and wildlife, and you may be able to join a ranger-led **guided walk**

Walks around Glen Coe

Ordnance Survey Explorer map no. 384
Flanked by the sheer-sided Munros, Glen Coe offers some of the Highlands' most challenging **hiking** routes, with long steep ascents over rough trails and notoriously unpredictable weather conditions that claim lives every year. The walks outlined below number among the glen's less-ambitious routes, but still require a map. It's essential that you take the proper precautions (see p.47), and stick to the paths, both for your own safety and the sake of the landscape, which has become badly eroded in places. For a broader selection of walks, get hold of the Ordnance Survey *Pathfinder Guide: Fort William and Glen Coe Walks*.

A good introduction to the splendours of Glen Coe is the half-day hike over the **Devil's Staircase**, which follows part of the old military road that once ran between Fort William and Stirling. The trail, part of the West Highland Way (see p.140), starts at the village of **Kinlochleven** and is marked by thistle signs, which lead uphill to the 1804ft pass and down the other side into Glen Coe.

Set right in the heart of the glen, the half-day **Allt Coire Gabhail** hike starts at the car park opposite the distinctive Three Sisters massif on the main A82. This explores the so-called "Lost Valley" where the Clan MacDonald fled and hid their cattle when attacked. Once in the valley, there are superb views of the upper slopes of Bidean nan Bian, Gearr Aonach and Beinn Fhada, which improve as you continue on to its head, another twenty-to-thirty-minute walk.

Undoubtedly one of the finest walks in the Glen Coe area that doesn't entail the ascent of a Munro is the **Buachaille Etive Beag** circuit, which follows the textbook glacial valleys of Lairig Eilde and Lairig Gartain, ascending 1968ft in only nine miles of rough trail. Park near the waterfall at **The Study** – the gorge part of the A82 through Glen Coe – and walk up the road until you see a sign pointing south to "Loch Etiveside".

(Easter & June–Sept). Unfortunately the café food doesn't live up to its nice-looking interior. Meanwhile, in Glencoe village, you can pay a visit to the delightful heather-roofed **Glencoe Folk Museum** (April–Oct Mon–Sat 10am–5.30pm; £3). Various games and activities for kids can be enjoyed within this cosy 1720 croft where items include a chair that reputedly once belonged to Bonnie Prince Charlie.

At the eastern end of Glen Coe beyond the looming massif of Buachaille Etive Mhòr, the landscape opens out onto vast Rannoch Moor. From the **Glen Coe Mountain Resort** (Jan–Oct & Dec daily; ☎01855/851226, ⓦwww.glen coemountain.com) a chairlift (£8) climbs 2400ft to Meall a Bhuiridh, giving spectacular views over Rannoch Moor and to Ben Nevis. At the base station, there's a simple but pleasant café.

Practicalities

To get to the heart of Glen Coe from Fort William, hop on the Glasgow-bound Scottish Citylink **coach** service (4 daily; 30min). The Highland County bus #44 from Fort William also stops at least five times a day (3 on Sun) at Glencoe village en route to Kinlochleven.

There's a good selection of **accommodation** in Glen Coe and the surrounding area. Basic options include an SYHA **hostel** (☎01855/811219, ⓦwww.syha.org .uk) on a back road halfway between Glencoe village and the *Clachaig Inn* (see below); a cheaper neighbouring **independent hostel** (☎01855/811906, ⓦwww .glencoehostel.co.uk) in rustic whitewashed buildings; the sylvan year-round *Red Squirrel* campsite nearby (☎01855/811256, ⓦwww.redsquirrelcampsite.co.uk; campfires permitted); and the *Caravanning and Camping Club* site (☎01855/811397; April–Oct) beside the NTS visitor centre on the main road.

Glencoe village has a few comfortable **B&Bs**, such as the secluded and friendly *Scorry Breac* (☎01855/811354, ⓦwww.scorrybreac.co.uk; ❷), while the best-known **hotel** in the area is the lively ⚔ *Clachaig Inn* (☎01855/811252, ⓦwww .clachaig.com; ❺), a great place to reward your exertions with cask-conditioned ales and heaped platefuls of food; it's three miles south of Glencoe village on the minor road off the A82, a stroll away from the campsite and hostels. The other famous hotel in the glen is the historic though run-down *Kingshouse Hotel* (☎01855/851259, ⓦwww.kingy.com; ❸), ten miles south of here on the edge of the empty wilds of Rannoch Moor. If nothing else, it's worth stopping for a pint at the atmospheric *Climber's Bar* within. Ten miles further south at Bridge of Orchy station is the cosy *West Highland Way Sleeper Hostel* (☎01838/400548, ⓦwww.westhighlandwaysleeper.co.uk). You can enjoy reasonably priced pub grub in the nearby *Bridge of Orchy Hotel*.

Ballachulish and Onich

From 1693 to 1955, the village of **BALLACHULISH**, just one mile west of Glencoe village, was a major centre for the quarrying of roofing slates, shipping out 26 million of them at the height of production in the mid-nineteenth century. There's a short, well-maintained footpath leading from directly opposite Balla-chulish tourist office into the now-disued slate quarry – a few information boards tell the history of the quarry, which, like many former industrial sites, has an eerie stillness to it. Ballachulish has two parts – the main village on the south of the loch and North Ballachulish on the other side of the road bridge, which spans the mouth of Loch Leven. Beyond North Ballachulish on the road to Fort William is the roadside settlement of **ONICH**, a mile or so on from which is **CORRAN**, from where a car ferry crosses the narrowest point of Loch Linnhe, providing access to the Morvern and Ardnamurchan peninsulas (see p.226).

Ballachulish's **tourist office** is on Albert Road, sharing space with a coffee and gift shop (daily; ℡01855/811866); you can use its freephone line to organize somewhere to stay. For a cheap bed, head to the *Corran Bunkhouse* (℡01855/821000, ⓦwww.corranbunkhouse.co.uk) by the ferry jetty at Corran, or welcoming *Inchree Lodge* (℡0800/310 1536, ⓦwww.inchreecentre.co.uk) at Onich, where accommodation is available in a bunkhouse or chalets and there's a decent real-ale **pub** and bistro, *The Four Seasons*. The excellent activity operator Vertical Descents (℡01855/821593, ⓦwww.verticaldescents.com) is also based at Onich; through them you can try a host of activities including wet and wild water sports and adrenaline-pumping canyoning (both around £55/half-day).

In Ballachulish village, *Fern Villa* (℡01855/811393, ⓦwww.fernvilla.org.uk; ❷) is a friendly **B&B**, while *Cuildorag House* (℡01855/821529, ⓦwww.cuildorag house.com; ❷) in Onich is a particularly pleasant vegetarian and vegan B&B, renowned for its great breakfasts. For **hotels**, the luxurious *Ballachulish Hotel* (℡0844/855 9133, ⓦwww.ballachulishhotel.com; ❽), just outside the village, offers sumptuous accommodation, pricey fine dining, terrific mountain views, its own nine-hole golf course and a fine dose of Scottish history (including a role in Robert Louis Stevenson's literary classic *Kidnapped*). Another option is the family-friendly *Isles of Glencoe Hotel* (℡01855/831800, ⓦwww.islesofglencoe.com; ❺), which has a swimming pool. At the adjacent Lochaber Watersports (℡01855/821391, ⓦwww.lochaberwatersports.co.uk) you can rent a small sailing dinghy, rowing boat or canoe from £12 per hour.

Kinlochleven

At the easternmost end of Loch Leven, the settlement of **KINLOCHLEVEN** is steadily reviving its fortunes after many years of being a tourism backwater best known as the site of a huge, unsightly aluminium smelter built in 1904. The tale of the area's industrial past is told in **The Aluminium Story** (Mon–Fri 10am–1pm & 2–5pm, Oct–March closed Fri afternoon; free), a small series of displays in the same building as the town library and tourist office. The disused smelter is now the home of an innovative indoor mountaineering centre called **The Ice Factor** (℡01855/831100, ⓦwww.ice-factor.co.uk). This impressive facility includes the world's largest artificial ice-climbing wall (13.5m) as well as a range of more tradi-tional climbing walls plus equipment rental, and a steam room and sauna. There's a bar upstairs and food is available. Alongside, another part of the aluminium smelter has been transformed into the **Atlas Brewery**, open for tours on summer evenings (groups can arrange tours at other times; ℡01855/831111, ⓦwww .atlasbrewery.com). As well as being close to Glen Coe, Kinlochleven stands at the foot of the Mamore hills, popular with Munro-baggers; it's also a convenient overnight stop on the **West Highland Way**, with Fort William a day's walk away.

For hikers looking to spend the night in Kinlochleven, the *Blackwater* **hostel** (℡01855/831253, ⓦwww.blackwaterhostel.co.uk) beside the river is decidedly upmarket, with TVs and en-suite facilities in dorms with two, three, four or eight beds, and a communal kitchen/dining area. For £5 per person you can also **camp** here. There's fine hospitality at the Edwardian-built *Edencoille Guest House* (℡01855/831358, ⓦwww.kinlochlevenbedandbreakfast.co.uk; ❷) where, with notice, you can organize packed lunches, evening meals and guided walking trips. There are also two decent **hotels** in Kinlochleven: *MacDonald Hotel* (℡01855/831539, ⓦwww.macdonaldhotel.co.uk; ❺), whose *Bothy Bar* is popular with walkers and where you can also camp (£4), and the *Tailrace Inn* on Riverside Road (℡01855/831777, ⓦwww.tailraceinn.com; ❹), offering reasonable rooms and food (including breakfast and packed lunches for nonresidents), along with regular entertainment. The best place to eat near here is the ♯ *Lochleven Seafood*

Café (℡ 01855/821048, ⓦ www.lochlevenseafoodcafe.co.uk; closed Mon & Tues), a relaxed restaurant with an attractive outdoor terrace specializing in local shellfish, located a few miles along the B836 following the north side of the loch.

Loch Ness and around

Twenty-three miles long, unfathomably deep, cold and often moody, **Loch Ness** is bounded by rugged heather-clad mountains rising steeply from a wooded shoreline and attractive glens opening up on either side. Its fame, however, is based overwhelmingly on its legendary inhabitant Nessie, the "Loch Ness monster", whose fame ensures a steady flow of hopeful visitors to the settlements dotted along the loch, in particular **Drumnadrochit**. Nearby, the impressive ruins of **Castle Urquhart** – a favourite monster-spotting location – perch atop a rock on the lochside and attract a deluge of bus parties during the summer. Almost as busy in high season is the village of **Fort Augustus**, at the more scenic southwest tip of Loch Ness, where you can watch queues of boats tackling one of the Caledonian Canal's longest flight of locks.

Away from the lochside, and seeing a fraction of Loch Ness's visitor numbers, the remote glens of **Urquhart** and **Affric** make an appealing contrast, with Affric in particular boasting narrow, winding roads, gushing streams and hillsides dotted with ancient Caledonian pine forests. The busiest of these glens to the north is the often bleak high country of **Glen Moriston**, a little to the southwest of Glen Affric, through which the main road between Inverness and Skye passes.

Although most visitors drive along the tree-lined A82 road, which runs along the western shore of Loch Ness, the sinuous single-track B862/B852 (originally a military road built to link Fort Augustus and Fort George) that skirts the eastern shore is quieter and affords far more spectacular views. However, buses from Inverness along this road only run as far south as **Foyers**, so you'll need your own transport to complete the whole loop around the loch, a journey which includes a most impressive stretch between Fort Augustus and the high, hidden **Loch Mhor**, overlooked by the imposing Monadhliath range to the south.

Fort Augustus

FORT AUGUSTUS, a tiny, busy village at the scenic southwestern tip of Loch Ness, was named after George II's son, the chubby lad who later became the "Butcher" duke of Cumberland of Culloden fame; it was built as a barracks after the 1715 Jacobite rebellion. Today, it's dominated by comings and goings along the Caledonian Canal, which leaves Loch Ness here, and by its large former **Benedictine abbey**, a campus of grey Victorian buildings founded on the site of the original fort in 1876. Until relatively recently this was home to a small but active community of monks, but it has now been converted into luxury flats. From its berth by the Clansman Centre, Cruise Loch Ness (March–Oct; 1hr; £11; ℡ 01320/366277, ⓦ www.cruiselochness.com) sails five miles up Loch Ness, using sonar technology to provide passengers with impressive live 3D imagery of the deep where underwater cave systems, salmon, cannibalistic trout (and, some would speculate, Nessie) are to be found.

Fort Augustus's very helpful **tourist office** (April–Sept daily; Oct–Dec & mid-Feb to March Sat & Sun; ℡ 01320/366779) hands out useful free walking leaflets and stocks maps of the Great Glen Way (see box, p.191). They'll also advise on fishing permits for the loch or nearby river. There's **hostel** accommodation at *Morag's Lodge* (℡ 01320/366289, ⓦ www.moragslodge.com) at Bunoich Brae on

The world-famous **Loch Ness monster**, affectionately known as **Nessie** (and by serious aficionados as *Nessiteras rhombopteryx*), has been a local celebrity for some time. The first mention of a mystery creature crops up in St Adamnan's seventh-century biography of **St Columba**, who allegedly calmed an aquatic animal that had attacked one of his monks. Present-day interest, however, is probably greater outside Scotland than within the country, and dates from the building of the road along the loch's western shore in the early 1930s. In 1934 the *Daily Mail* published London surgeon R.K. Wilson's sensational photograph of the head and neck of the monster peering up out of the loch, and the hype has hardly diminished since. Recent encounters range from glimpses of ripples by anglers to the famous occasion in 1961 when thirty hotel guests saw a pair of humps break the water's surface and cruise for about half a mile before submerging.

Photographic evidence is showcased in two separate exhibitions located at Drumnadrochit, but the most impressive of these exhibits – including the renowned black-and-white movie footage of Nessie's humps moving across the water, and Wilson's original head-and-shoulders shot – have now been exposed as fakes. Indeed, in few other places on earth has watching a rather lifeless and often grey expanse of water seemed so compelling, or have floating logs, otters and boat wakes been photographed so often and with such excitement. Yet while even high-tech sonar surveys carried out over the past two decades have failed to come up with conclusive evidence, it's hard to dismiss Nessie as pure myth. After all, no one yet knows where the unknown layers of silt and mud at the bottom of the loch begin and end: best estimates say the loch is over 750ft deep, deeper than much of the North Sea, while others point to the possibilities of underwater caves and undiscovered channels connected to the sea. What scientists have found in the cold, murky depths, including pure white eels and rare arctic char, offers fertile grounds for speculation, with different theories declaring Nessie to be a remnant from the dinosaur age, a giant newt or a huge visiting Baltic sturgeon. Technological advances have also expanded the scope for Nessie-watching: Ⓦwww.lochness.co.uk offers round-the-clock **webcams** for views across the loch, while Ⓦwww.lochnessinvestigation.org is packed with research information.

the Loch Ness side of town, where the atmosphere livens up with the daily arrival of backpackers' minibus tours, and at the well-equipped thirty-bed *Stravaigers Lodge* (Ⓣ01320/366257, Ⓦwww.highlandbunkhouse.co.uk) on Glendoe Road. *Abbey Cottage* (Ⓣ0845/471 8332, Ⓦwww.abbeycottagelochness.co.uk; ❷) is a nicely renovated **B&B** on the main street, and there's the spacious *Cumberlands Campsite* a five-minute walk from the loch (Ⓣ01320/366257, Ⓦwww.cumberlands-campsite .com). Of the **hotels**, try either the small, friendly *Caledonian* (Ⓣ01320/366256, Ⓦwww.thecaledonianhotel.com; ❹) or the distinctly upmarket *Lovat Hotel* opposite (Ⓣ0845/450 1100, Ⓦwww.thelovat.com; ❹), built on the site of the 1718 Kilwhimen Barracks and refurbished along ecofriendly principles.

Both of the above hotels provide decent **food**, or try the *Lock Inn* by the canal, with its attractive wood-panelled interior and upscale pub food. There are tables outside by the lock for summer days, and regular live-music events. *The Scots Kitchen* opposite the tourist office does moderately priced, home-cooked food including steak-and-ale pie or clootie dumpling. There are some good **cycling** routes locally, notably along the Great Glen cycle route. The best place to rent bikes or watersports equipment, including boats and canoes, is at Monster Activities (Ⓣ01809/501340, Ⓦwww.monsteractivities.com), South Laggan, eight miles or so southwest at the head of Loch Lochy.

Lots and lots of lochs and locks

Surveyed by James Watt in 1773, the **Caledonian Canal** was completed in the early 1800s by Thomas Telford to enable ships to pass between the North Sea and the Atlantic without having to navigate Scotland's treacherous northern coast. There are sixty miles between the west-coast entrance to the canal at Corpach, near Fort William, and its exit onto the Moray Firth at Inverness, although strictly speaking only 22 miles of it are bona fide canal – the other 38 exploit the Great Glen's natural string of **freshwater lochs** of Lochy, Oich and Ness.

The most famous piece of canal engineering in Scotland is the series of eight **locks** at Banavie, about a mile from the entrance at Corpach, known as Neptune's Staircase (see p.196). While the canal was originally built for freight-carrying ships and large passenger-steamers, these days it is almost exclusively used by small yachts and pleasure boats. Good spots to watch their leisurely progress are Neptune's Staircase and Fort Augustus, where four locks take traffic through the centre of the village into Loch Ness.

If you're interested in the **history of the waterway**, there's the small Caledonian Canal Visitor Centre (Easter–Oct daily 9.30am–5.30pm; free) in Ardchattan House, beside the locks in Fort Augustus. For more active encounters with the canal, you can set off along a section of the Great Glen Way footpath or Great Glen cycleway, both of which follow the **canal towpath** for part of their length (see box, p.191), or you can spend a week **cruising** through the canal on the barge *Fingal of Caledonia* (☎01397/772167, ✆www.fingal-cruising.co.uk), which organizes a wide range of activities from water sports to mountain biking along the way.

The east side of Loch Ness

The tranquil and scenic **east side** of Loch Ness is skirted by General Wade's old military highway, now the B862/B852. From Fort Augustus, the narrow single-track road swings up, away from the lochside through the near-deserted **Stratherrick** valley, dotted with tiny lochans. To the southeast of Fort Augustus you'll pass the massive earth workings of the new Glendoe Hydro Station. From here, the road drops down to rejoin the shores of Loch Ness at **FOYERS**, where there are numerous marked forest trails and an impressive waterfall. In Upper Foyers village you can find the *Red Squirrel Café*, which runs a live web-cam of red squirrels nesting (April–June) across the road, and the friendly *Foyers House* (☎01456/486405, ✆www.foyershouse-lochness.com; no children; ❹), located by the signposted waterfall. This secluded B&B has fabulous views of the loch from its terrace and a **restaurant** serving up game pie, venison and local salmon (daily 7–9pm Easter to Sept; ☎01463/711870).

Past **Inverfarigaig** – where a road up a beautiful, steep-sided river valley leads east over to Loch Mhor – is the sleepy village of **DORES**, nestled at the north-eastern end of Loch Ness, the whitewashed *Dores Inn* providing a pleasant pit-stop. Only nine miles southwest of Inverness, the old **pub** is popular with Invernessians, who trickle out here on summer evenings for a stroll along the grey pebble beach and some monster-spotting. Note that a local **bus** from Inverness runs down the east side of the loch to Foyers (Mon–Fri 3 daily; 2 on Sat).

Invermoriston and west

On the other shore, heading north from Fort Augustus along the main A82, **INVERMORISTON** is a tiny, attractive village situated just above the loch. Here you can follow well-marked woodland footpaths past a series of grand waterfalls, and a good stop for lunch or a drink is provided by the *Glenmoriston Arms Hotel* (☎01320/351206,

@ www.glenmoristonarms.co.uk), a whitewashed stone building with a popular bar. The A887 leads west from Invermoriston to the west coast (via the A87) on the main commercial route to the Skye Bridge. Rugged and somewhat awesome, the stretch through **Glen Moriston**, beside **Loch Cluanie**, has serious peaks on either side and little sign of human habitation. At the western end of the loch, you'll find the isolated *Cluanie Inn* (℡01320/340238, @ www.cluanieinn.com; ❼), a popular place with outdoor types serving good food in its real-fire pub; one of the bedrooms has a jacuzzi bath and a four-poster. West from here, the road drops gradually down **Glen Shiel** into the superb mountainscape of Kintail.

Drumnadrochit and around

Situated above a verdant, sheltered bay of Loch Ness fifteen miles southwest of Inverness, **DRUMNADROCHIT** is the southern gateway to remote Glen Affric and the epicentre of Nessie-hype, complete with a rash of tacky souvenir shops and two rival monster exhibitions whose head-to-head scramble for punters occasionally erupts into acrimonious exchanges, detailed with relish by the local press. Of the pair, the **Loch Ness Centre & Exhibition** (daily: Easter–May 9.30am–5pm; June & Sept 9am–6pm; July & Aug 9am–8pm; Oct 9.30am–5.30pm; Nov–Easter 10am–3.30pm; £6.50) is the better bet, offering an in-depth rundown of eyewitness accounts and information on various Nessie research projects. The **Nessieland Monster Centre** (daily: April–June & Sept–Nov 9am–5pm; July & Aug 9am–9pm; Dec–March 9am–4pm; £5) is a worthwhile stop if only for the in-house bakery in the adjacent hotel (❺) where guests can search for the resident ghost within the heavily wood-panelled and tartanized interior.

Cruises on the loch aboard Deep Scan Cruises run from the Loch Ness 2000 Exhibition (hourly; Easter–Sept 10am–6pm; 1hr; £10; ℡01456/450218), while the *Nessie Hunter* (hourly: Easter–Dec 9am–6pm; 50min; £10; ℡01456/450395, @ www.loch-ness-cruises.com) can be booked at the Nessieland Monster Centre; there's a decent little shop here where all the crafts are made in Scotland. If you want to turn your back on all the hype, you could opt for the well-run **pony trekking** available at Borlum Farm (℡01456/450220, @ www.borlum.co.uk; from £23/hr) just two minutes' drive north of Urquhart Castle.

Most photographs allegedly showing the monster have been taken a couple of miles east of Drumnadrochit, around the thirteenth-century ruined lochside **Castle Urquhart** (daily: April–Sept 9.30am–6pm; Oct–March 9.30am–5pm; HS; £6.50). Built as a strategic base to guard the Great Glen, the castle was taken by Edward I of England and later held by Robert the Bruce against Edward III, only to be blown up in 1692 to prevent it from falling to the Jacobites. Today it's one of Scotland's classic picture-postcard ruins, particularly splendid at night when it's floodlit and the crowds have gone. In the small visitor centre, a short film (in six languages) highlights the turbulent history of the castle. There's a footpath alongside the A82 road between Drumnadrochit and the castle, though the constant stream of cars, caravans and tour buses doesn't make it a particularly pleasant stroll.

Practicalities

Drumnadrochit's helpful **tourist office** (April, May, Sept & Oct Mon–Sat; June–Aug daily; ℡01456/459086) shares space with a Highland Council service point in the middle of the main car park in the village. There's a good range of **accommodation** around Drumnadrochit and in the adjoining village of Lewiston. A very welcoming **B&B** is *Gillyflowers* (℡01456/450641, @ www.cali.co.uk/freeway/gillyflowers; ❷), a renovated 1780s farmhouse on a country lane in Lewiston. Otherwise, try the cluster of cottage B&Bs on the village green. **Hotels** include the friendly and simply furnished *Benleva* (℡01456/450080, Ⓦwww.benleva.co.uk; ❹), also in Lewiston, with several real ales on tap and locally sourced game on the menu. Two miles west of Drumnadrochit along the Cannich road is a particularly relaxed country-house hotel, *Polmaily House* (℡01456/450343, Ⓦwww.polmaily.co.uk; ❻), a family-oriented option with a heated indoor swimming pool and hot tub. For **hostel** beds you can also head for the immaculate and friendly *Loch Ness Backpackers Lodge* (℡01456/450807, Ⓦwww.lochness-backpackers.com; ❶), at Coiltie Farmhouse in Lewiston; follow the signs to the left when coming from Drumnadrochit. As well as dorms, the hostel has one double and two family rooms and facilities include bike rental and pony trekking. A special Sunday bus into Glen Affric can be arranged. There's scenic **camping** at *Borlum Farm* (see p.205).

Most of the hotels in the area – the *Benleva* in particular – serve good bar **food**; in Drumnadrochit try the *Karasia* Indian restaurant (℡01456/450002) or the inexpensive *Glen Café* on the village green for reasonable lunches and snacks. Next door, the slightly more upmarket *Fiddlers' Café Bar* offers local steaks, salmon and hearty lunches.

Glen Affric

Due west of Drumnadrochit lies a vast area of high peaks, remote glens and few roads. The reason most folk head this way is to explore the picturesque native forests and grand mountains of **Glen Affric**, heaven for walkers, climbers and mountain-bikers. If you're driving, note that the nearest petrol stations are in Drumnadrochit and Beauly to the north. Coming by public transport, Ross's Minibus (℡07801/988491, Ⓦwww.ross-minibuses.co.uk) runs a handy Dial-a-Bus service, as well as scheduled buses; its vehicles will also carry bikes if given advance notice. It's worth getting your hands on the excellent Glen Affric and Strathglass tourist map (Ⓦwww.glenaffric.info), usually available from local businesses and tourist offices.

The approach to the glen is through the small settlement of **CANNICH**, fourteen miles west of Drumnadrochit on the A831. Keen mountain-bikers may want to stop off at the (free) **Balnain Bike Park** five miles west of Drumnadrochit where a variety of timber-based obstacles will test your riding ability. Look out for the Glen Urquhart Forestry Commission sign for access off the main road. Cannich is a quiet and uninspiring village, but it has an excellent campsite (℡01456/415364) where mountain bikes can be rented, and there's also the friendly neighbouring *Glen Affric Backpackers Hostel* (℡01456/415263), which offers inexpensive twin or four-bed rooms. For food, the best option is the chalet-like *Bog Cotton Café* (daily 9am–3pm) at the campsite. Otherwise, try the modest *Slaters Arms* or buy supplies from the village Spar shop.

Hemmed in by a string of Munros, Glen Affric is great for picnics and pottering. From the car park at the head of the single-track road along the glen, ten miles southwest of Cannich, there's a selection of **walks**: the trip around **Loch Affric** will take you a good five hours but allows you to appreciate the glen, its wildlife and Caledonian pine and birch woods in all their remote splendour. For details of **volunteer work** in Glen Affric helping with the restoration of the woodland, get in touch with Trees for Life (Ⓦwww.treesforlife.org.uk). You could also do some serious **hiking**. Munro-baggers (see p.47) are normally much in evidence, and it is possible to tramp 25 miles all the way through Glen Affric to Shiel Bridge, on the west coast near Kyle of Lochalsh. The utterly remote *Allt Beithe* SYHA hostel (℡0845/293 7373, Ⓦwww.syha.org.uk; April–Oct) near the head of Glen Affric,

makes a convenient if rudimentary stopover halfway. A wind ⸝
panels provide the hostel with electricity, but note that you'll
your own food: the nearest shop is 21 miles away.

Inverness

Straddling a nexus of major road and rail routes, **INVERNESS** is the busy hub of
the Highlands, and an inevitable port of call if you're exploring the region by
public transport. Over a hundred miles from any other major settlement yet with
a population rapidly approaching 100,000, Inverness is the only city in the
Highlands. Crowned by a pink crenellated **castle** and lavishly decorated with
flowers, the city centre still has some hints of its medieval street layout, though
unsightly concrete blocks do an efficient job of masking it. Within walking
distance of the centre are peaceful spots along by the Ness, leafy parks and friendly
B&Bs located in prosperous-looking stone houses.

The sheltered **harbour** and proximity to the open sea made Inverness an
important entrepôt and shipbuilding centre during medieval times. David I, who
first imposed a feudal system on Scotland, erected a castle on the banks of the Ness
to oversee maritime trade in the early twelfth century, promoting it to royal burgh
status soon after. Bolstered by receipts from the lucrative export of leather, salmon
and timber, the town grew to become the kingdom's most prosperous northern
outpost, and an obvious target for the marauding Highlanders who plagued this
remote border area. A second wave of growth occurred during the eighteenth
century as the Highland cattle trade flourished. The arrival of the **Caledonian
Canal** and **rail** links with the east and south brought further prosperity, heralding
a tourist boom that reached a fashionable zenith in the Victorian era, fostered by
the Royal Family's enthusiasm for all things Scottish.

Arrival, information and accommodation

Inverness **airport** (☎01667/464000) is at Dalcross, seven miles east of the city;
from here, bus #11 (every 30min; 20min; £2.90; ⓦwww.thejet.co.uk) goes into
town, while a taxi costs around £12. The **bus station** (☎01463/233371) and **train
station** both lie just off Academy Street to the northeast of the centre. The **tourist
office** (March–Nov daily; Dec–Feb Mon–Sat) is in an unsightly 1960s block on
Castle Wynd, just five minutes' walk from the train station. It stocks a wide range
of literature, including free maps of the city and its environs, and the staff can

---

Tours and cruises from Inverness

Inverness is the departure point for a range of **day-tours** and **cruises** to nearby
attractions, including Loch Ness and the Moray Firth. **Loch Ness cruises** typically
incorporate a visit to a monster exhibition at **Drumnadrochit** and **Urquhart Castle**
– try Jacobite Cruises (from £11.50; ☎01463/233999, ⓦwww.jacobite.co.uk) or
Cruise Loch Ness (from £11; ☎01320/366277, ⓦwww.cruiselochness.com).
Inverness is about the one place where transport connections allow you to embark
on a major **grand tour** of the Highlands or a round trip to Skye in a day. For exploring
the northwest, Dearman Coaches (April–Sept Mon–Sat, also Sun July–Aug; six-day
rover ticket £36; ☎01349/883585, ⓦwww.timdearmancoaches.co.uk) have a daily
service (bikes accepted) to **Ullapool**, **Lochinver**, **Durness** and back stopping at
several hostels en route.

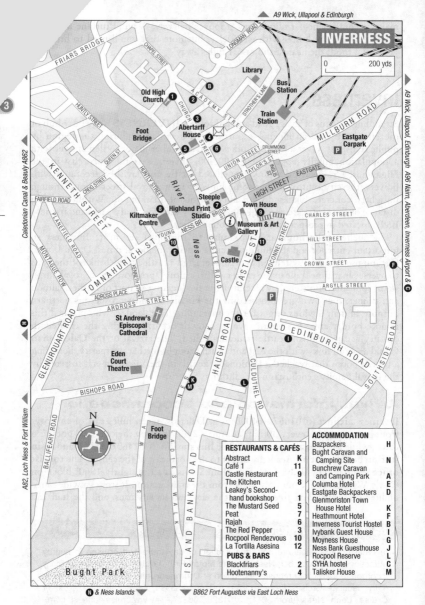

book local accommodation for a £4 fee. There's also a CalMac ferry booking office in the building.

Inverness is one of the few places in the Highlands where you're unlikely to have problems finding **accommodation**, although in July and August you'll have to book ahead. The city boasts several good **hotels**, and nearly every street in the older residential areas of town has a sprinkling of **B&Bs**. A good place to look is both banks of the river south of the Ness Bridge. There are several **hostels** in town, all reasonably central, and a couple of large **campsites**, one near the Ness Islands and the other further out to the west.

Hotels

Columba Hotel 7 Ness Walk ☎08444/146600, ⓦwww.oxfordhotelsandinns.com/OurHotels /Columba. A great location on the river and a handsome Victorian building make this a decent city-centre option. ❻

Glenmoriston Town House Hotel 20 Ness Bank ☎01463/223777, ⓦwww.glenmoristontownhouse .com. An upmarket, contemporary hotel by the riverside just a few minutes' walk from the town centre. Muted decor and a good dining experience at *Abstract*. ❼

Heathmount Hotel Kingsmill Rd ☎01463/235877, ⓦwww.heathmounthotel.com. Reasonably central boutique hotel with rather overstyled but comfort-able rooms. ❻

Loch Ness Country House Hotel Off the A82 Fort William road ☎01463/230512, ⓦwww.lochness countryhousehotel.co.uk. Luxurious country-house hotel, three miles west of central Inverness. Attrac-tive modern Scottish food, fine wines and over two hundred malts, as well as very comfortable and spacious rooms. ❽

Rocpool Reserve Culduthel Rd ☎01463/240089, ⓦwww.rocpool.com. Only a 10min walk south from the castle, this acclaimed boutique hotel and restaurant offers hip, chic and decadent rooms and upmarket modern dining. ❽

B&Bs

Ivybank Guest House 28 Old Edinburgh Rd ☎01463/232796, ⓦwww.ivybankguesthouse .com. A grand Georgian home just up the hill from the castle, with open fires and a lovely homey interior. ❷

Moyness House 6 Bruce Gardens ☎01463/233836, ⓦwww.moyness.co.uk. Warm, welcoming, upmarket B&B on the west side of Inverness, with original Victorian features and a nice walled garden. ❺

Ness Bank Guesthouse 7 Ness Bank ☎01463/232939, ⓦwww.nessbankguesthouse .co.uk. Five lovely, tasteful rooms in Grade II listed Victorian house on the river; good for large get-togethers. ❷

Talisker House 25 Ness Bank ☎01463/236221, ⓦwww.scotland-inverness.co.uk/talisker. Pleasant 1830s B&B in a riverside location just a 5min walk from the centre. ❹

Hostels

Bazpackers Top of Castle St ☎01463/717663, ⓦwww.bazpackershostel.co.uk. The most cosy and relaxed of the city's hostels, with over thirty beds including two doubles and a twin (❶); some dorms are mixed. Good location, great views and a garden, which is used for barbecues.

Eastgate Backpackers Hostel 38 Eastgate ☎01463/718756, ⓦwww.eastgatebackpackers .com. Well-maintained former hotel with single, twin and double rooms (❶). Bike rental, internet access and left-luggage storage.

Inverness Tourist Hostel 24 Rose St ☎01463/ 241962, ⓦwww.invernesshostel.com. A central, clean, well-equipped sixty-bed hostel offering top-notch amenities including wide-screen TVs and internet access.

SYHA hostel Victoria Drive, off Millburn Rd, about three-quarters of a mile east of the centre ☎01463/231771, ⓦwww.syha.org.uk. Well equipped with large kitchens and communal areas, and ten four-bed family rooms among the 166-bed total. However, it's quite far from the centre, and the building is devoid of character.

Campsites

Bught Caravan and Camping Site Bught Park ☎01463/236920, ⓦwww.invernesscaravanpark .com. Inverness's main campsite, south of the centre, on the west bank of the river near the sports centre. Good facilities, but it can get very crowded at the height of the season. Easter to mid-Sept.

Bunchrew Caravan and Camping Park Bunchrew, 3 miles west of Inverness on the A862 ☎01463/237802, ⓦwww.bunchrew -caravanpark.co.uk. Well-equipped site with lots of space for tents on the shores of the Beauly Firth, plus hot water, showers, laundry and a shop. Very popular with families. March–Nov.

The Town

Looming above the city and dominating the horizon is **Inverness Castle**, a predominantly nineteenth-century red-sandstone edifice perched above the river. The original castle formed the core of the ancient town, which had rapidly developed as a port trading with Europe after its conversion to Christianity by

St Columba in the sixth century. Robert the Bruce wrested the castle back from the English during the Wars of Independence, destroying much of the structure in the process, and while held by the Jacobites in both the 1715 and the 1745 rebellions, it was blown up by them to prevent it falling into government hands. Today's edifice houses the Sheriff Court and is not open to the general public. However, there are good views down the River Ness and various plaques and statues in the grounds including a small plinth marking the start of the 73-mile Great Glen Way.

Below the castle, the revamped **IMAG** (Inverness Museum and Art Gallery; Mon–Sat 10am–5pm, July & Aug Sun 1–5pm; free; ⓦ www.invernessmuseum .com) on Castle Wynd offers an insight into the social history of the Highlands,

The truth about tartan

To much of the world, **tartan** is synonymous with Scotland. It's the natural choice of packaging for Scottish exports from shortbread to Sean Connery, and when the Scottish football team travels abroad to play a fixture, the high-spirited "Tartan Army" of fans is never far behind. Tartan is big business for the tourist industry, yet the truth is that romantic fiction and commercial interest have enclosed this ancient Highland art form within an almost insurmountable wall of myth.

The original form of tartan, the kind that long ago was called **Helande**, was a fine, hard and almost showerproof cloth spun in Highland villages from the wool of the native sheep, dyed with preparations of local plants and with patterns woven by artist-weavers. It was worn as a huge single piece of cloth, or **plaid**, which was belted around the waist and draped over the upper body, rather like a knee-length toga. The natural colours of old tartans were clear but soft, and the broken pattern gave superb camouflage, unlike modern versions, where garish, clashing colours are often used to create impact.

The myth-makers were about four centuries ahead of themselves in dressing up the warriors of the film *Braveheart* in plaid: in fact tartan did not become popular in the Lowlands until the beginning of the eighteenth century, when it was adopted as the anti-Union badge of the **Jacobites**. After Culloden, a ban on the wearing of tartan in the Highlands lasted some 25 years; in that time it became a fondly held emblem for emigrant Highlanders in the colonies and was incorporated into the uniforms of the new Highland regiments in the British Army. Then Sir Walter Scott set to work glamorizing the clans, dressing George IV in a kilt (and, just as controversially, flesh-coloured tights) for his visit to Edinburgh in 1822. By the time Queen Victoria set the royal seal of approval on both the Highlands and tartan with her extended annual holidays at Balmoral, the concept of tartan as formal dress rather than rough Highland wear was assured.

Hand in hand with the gentrification of the kilt came "rules" about the correct form of attire and the idea that every clan had its own distinguishing tartan. To have the right to wear tartan, one had to belong, albeit remotely, to a clan, and so the way was paved for the "what's-my-tartan?" lists that appear in tartan picture-books and souvenir shops. Great feats of genealogical gymnastics were performed: where lists left gaps, a marketing phenomenon of themed tartans developed, with new patterns for different districts, companies and even football teams being produced.

Scotsmen today will commonly wear the **kilt** for weddings and other formal occasions; properly made kilts, however – comprising some four yards of one hundred percent wool – are likely to set you back £300 or more, with the rest of the regalia at least doubling that figure. If the contents of your sporran don't stretch that far, most places selling kilts will rent outfits on a daily basis. The best place to find better-quality material is a recognized Highland outfitter rather than a souvenir shop: in Inverness, try the Scottish Kiltmaker Visitor Centre at the Highland House of Fraser shop (see opposite).

with treasures from the times of the Picts and Vikings, taxidermy ex
"Felicity" the puma, caught in Cannich in 1980, and interactive fear
an introduction to the Gaelic language. It also has impressive
exhibitions.

Leading north from the castle, medieval **Church Street** is ho
oldest surviving buildings. On the corner with Bridge Street stands u.
(1791), whose spire had to be straightened after an earth tremor in 1816. The
High Church, founded in 1171 and rebuilt on several occasions since, stands just
along the street, hemmed in by a walled graveyard. Those Jacobites who survived
the massacre of Culloden were brought here and incarcerated prior to their
execution in the cemetery. If you look carefully you may see the bullet holes left
on gravestones by the firing squads.

Along the River Ness

Just across Ness Bridge from Bridge Street is the **Scottish Kiltmaker Visitor
Centre** in Highland House of Fraser (daily 9am–9pm, open later summer; £2).
Entered through the factory shop, this imaginative small attraction, complete with
the outfits worn by actors for the *Braveheart* and *Rob Roy* films, sets out everything
you ever wanted to know about tartan. There's an interesting seven-minute film
and on weekdays (9am–5pm) you can watch various tartan products being made in
the workshop. The finished products are, of course, on sale in the showroom
downstairs, along with all manner of Highland knitwear, woven woollies and
Harris tweed.

On the opposite bank, the new base of the **Highland Print Studio**
(T 01463/718999, W www.highlandprintstudio.co.uk) is well worth a visit, both
to browse the collection of prints for sale, or to improve your artistic skills: they
run courses in all types of printmaking, and have an impressive digital suite.

Rising from the west bank directly opposite the castle, **St Andrew's
Episcopal Cathedral** (built 1869) was intended by its architects to be one of
the grandest buildings in Scotland. However, funds ran out before the giant
twin spires of the original design could be completed. The interior is pretty
ordinary, too, though it does claim an unusual octagonal chapterhouse.
Alongside the cathedral, the **Eden Court Theatre and Cinema** (W www.eden
-court.co.uk) is a major multi-arts venue in Scotland and hub for theatrical
performances in the Highlands.

From here, you can wander a mile or so upriver to the peaceful **Ness Islands**, an
attractive, informal public park reached and linked by footbridges. Laid out with
mature trees and shrubs, the islands are the favourite haunt of local anglers. Half a
mile further upstream, the river runs close to the **Caledonian Canal**, designed by
Thomas Telford in the early nineteenth century as a link between the east and west
coasts, joining lochs Ness, Oich, Lochy and Linnhe. Today its main use is recrea-
tional, and there are cruises through part of it to Loch Ness (see box, p.207), while
the towpath provides relaxing walks with good views.

Three miles to the west of the town, on the top of **Craig Phadrig** hill, there's a
vitrified **Iron Age fort**, reputed to be where the Pictish king Brude received
St Columba in the sixth century. The walls of the fort were built of stone laced
with timber and, when the timber was set alight, some of the stone fused to glass,
becoming "vitrified". Waymarked forest trails start from the car parks at the
bottom of the hill and lead up to the fort, though only the outlines of its perimeter
defences are now visible, and tree planting is beginning to block some of the
views. Stagecoach bus #1 from Church Street (Mon–Sat every 30min) drops you
at the foot of Craig Dunain, right beside Craig Phadrig.

...verness has lots of places to eat, including a few excellent quality gourmet options, while for the budget-conscious there's no shortage of **pubs**, **cafés** and **restaurants** around the town centre. **Takeaways** cluster on Young Street, just across the river, and at the ends of Eastgate and Academy Street.

The liveliest **nightlife** revolves around the pubs and, on Friday and Saturday nights, in nightclubs such as *G's* on Castle Street. The *Iron Works* on Academy Street (Ⓦwww.ironworksvenue.com) hosts touring bands. The far end of Academy Street features a cluster of good **pubs**; there's a lively atmosphere at *Blackfriars*, where you can enjoy folk and ceilidh music five nights a week. *Hootananny's*, on Church Street, continues to be a popular and lively pub with excellent ceilidhs, real ale and tasty "Thai Tananny" bar food.

Cafés

Castle Restaurant 41 Castle St. There's little finery here but this long-established family-run café does a roaring trade in hearty breakfasts, meat pies and mean haggis. Open at 8am for breakfast; closed Sun.

Leakey's Second-Hand Bookshop Church St Ⓣ01463/239947. Prise yourself away from the old books and maps for delicious soup and open sandwiches.

The Red Pepper 74 Church St. Reasonable coffee-bar hangout with freshly made sandwiches. Takeaway available.

Restaurants

Abstract 20 Ness Bank Ⓣ01463/223777, Ⓦwww.abstractrestaurant.com. This award-winning French restaurant within *Glenmoriston Town House Hotel* (see p.209) serves delicious creations with panache; mains start at £14. Closed Mon. The *Contrast Brasserie* (Ⓣ01463/227889) is more affordable and relaxed but still good quality.

Café 1 75 Castle St Ⓣ01463/226200. Contemporary Scottish cooking including venison fillet and gateaux of haggis, served in a bistro-style

setting. Its "express" pre-theatre menu (until 6.45pm) is very good value (£9.50 for two courses). Closed Sun.

The Kitchen 15 Huntly St Ⓣ01463/259119, Ⓦwww.kitchenrestaurant.co.uk. Beneath a distinctive wavy roof, this stylish sister restaurant of *The Mustard Seed* has riverside views and thoughtfully prepared seafood and meat dishes (around £15).

La Tortilla Asesina 99 Castle St Ⓣ01463/709809. Simple but lively tapas restaurant, serving all the old favourites as well as some "tartan tapas" concentrating on local ingredients.

The Mustard Seed 16 Fraser St Ⓣ01463/220220, Ⓦwww.mustardseedrestaurant.co.uk. Airy, welcoming restaurant with great-value Mediterra-nean-style lunches and tasty, à la carte dining: a starter and a main will set you back around £25.

Rajah Post Office Ave Ⓣ01463/237190. One of a couple of decent and affordable Indian restaurants in town, tucked away in a backstreet basement.

Rocpool Rendezvous 1 Ness Walk Ⓣ01463/717274. Another of the city's excellent, smartish dining options, boasting a smart contemporary setting, attentive staff and delicious bistro food. Around £30 for a three-course meal.

Listings

Bike rental Fancy a Ride? (Ⓣ07902/242301, Ⓦwww.tickettoridehighlands.co.uk; from £20/day) will deliver bikes to you and also offer tours. For cycle kit try Bikes of Inverness, 39 Grant St Ⓣ01463/225965.

Bookshops Leakey's, Scotland's largest used bookshop, is located in a former church on Church St and filled with almost 100,000 secondhand books. A great spot to browse, with a warming wood stove in winter and a cosy, inexpensive café (see above). There's also Waterstones at 50–52 High St.

Car rental Aberdeen 4x4 Self-Drive, 15b Harbour Rd (Ⓣ01463/871083); Budget, Railway Terrace, behind

the train station (Ⓣ01463/713333); Focus Vehicle Rental, 36 Shore St (Ⓣ01463/709517);Turner Hire Drive, Lotland St (Ⓣ01463/716058).

Cinemas VUE, Inverness Retail Park, Eastfield Way Ⓣ08712/240240; Eden Court Theatre and Cinema, Bishops Rd Ⓣ01463/234234.

Dentist Contact the Scotland-wide National Health Service Line (Ⓣ08454/242424) for local and emergency dentists or The Dental Clinic within Optical Express on High St (Ⓣ01463/248871; Mon–Sat 9am–5pm).

Hospital Raigmore Hospital (Ⓣ01463/704000) on the southeastern outskirts of town close to the A9.

Internet Highland libraries provide 30min free internet access.

Laundry Young Street Laundrette, 17 Young St ✆01463/242507.

Left luggage Train-station lockers cost £3–5 for 24hr (can only deposit 8am–6.30pm); the left-luggage room in the bus station costs £1 per item per day (Mon–Sat 8.30am–6pm, Sun 12.30pm–6.30pm).

Library Inverness Library (Mon–Fri 9am–6.30pm, Sat 9am–5pm; ✆01463/236463), housed in a Neoclassical building on the northeast side of the bus station, has an excellent genealogical research unit (Mon–Fri 10am–1pm & 2–5pm; ext 9).

Outdoor supplies Macpherson's "traditional mountaineering shop", 34 Church St ✆01463/711427; Tiso, 41 High St ✆01463/716617; Tiso Outdoor Experience, 2 Henderson Rd, Longman Estate ✆01463/729171.

Pharmacy Boots, 1–11 Eastgate Sho, (Mon–Wed & Fri 8.45am–6pm, Thurs 8.4 Sat 8.30am–6pm, Sun 11am–5pm; ✆01463/225167).

Post office 14–16 Queensgate (Mon–Thurs 9am–5.30pm, Fri 9.30am–5.30pm, Sat 9am–1pm ✆01463/234111); also noon–5pm at Tesco's.

Public toilets Just behind tourist information on Castle St.

Radio The local radio station is Moray Firth Radio on 97.4FM and 1107AM.

Sports centre Inverness Sports Centre & Aquadome leisure pool (Mon–Fri 10am–8pm, Sat & Sun 9am–5pm; ✆01463/667502), a mile or so south of the town centre off the A82, has a large pool with flumes and waves, also gym, health suite and climbing wall.

Taxis Tartan Taxis ✆01463/222777. Expect to pay £14 from city centre to airport.

Around Inverness

A string of worthwhile sights punctuates the approach to Inverness along the main route from Aberdeen. The low-key resort of **Nairn**, with its long white-sand beaches and championship golf course, stands within striking distance of several monuments, including whimsical **Cawdor Castle**, best known for its role in Shakespeare's *Macbeth*, and **Fort George**, one of several impressive Hanoverian bastions erected in the wake of the Jacobite rebellion. The infamous battle and ensuing massacre that ended Bonnie Prince Charlie's uprising took place on the outskirts of Inverness at **Culloden**, where a brand-new visitor centre and memorial stones beside a heather-clad moor recall the gruesome events of 1746. The area's gentle, undulating green landscape is well tended and tranquil, a fertile contrast to the windswept moorland and mountains which almost surround it.

East of Inverness

East of Inverness lies the fertile, sheltered coastal strip of the **Moray Firth** and its hinterland, the pastoral countryside contrasting with the scenic splendours you'll encounter once you head further north into the Highlands. Primary target is **Culloden**, the most poignant battlefield-site in Scotland, where Bonnie Prince Charlie's Jacobites were routed in 1746. Further east are **Cawdor Castle** and **Fort George**, two of the best-preserved fortified structures in the Highlands. **Nairn**, the main town of the district, has a pretty harbour as well as appealing walks and cycle routes.

The overloaded A96 traverses this stretch and the region is well served by public transport, with all the historic sites and castles accessible on day-trips from Inverness, or en route to Aberdeen. Stagecoach buses (✆01463/239292) run from Inverness to Fort George, Cawdor Castle and Culloden.

Culloden

The windswept moorland of **CULLODEN** (site open all year; free), five miles east of Inverness, witnessed the last-ever battle on British soil when, on April 16, 1746,

was finally subdued – a turning point in the history of the

the Jacobite rebellion had begun on August 19, 1745, with the raising of S??s' standard at **Glenfinnan** on the west coast (see p.229). Shortly after, ??rgh fell into Jacobite hands, and Bonnie Prince Charlie began his march on ??don. The English had appointed the ambitious young duke of Cumberland to command their forces, and his pursuit, together with bad weather and lack of funds, eventually forced the Jacobites to retreat north. They ended up at Culloden, where, ill fed and exhausted after a pointless night march, they were hopelessly outnumbered by the English. The open, flat ground of Culloden Moor was totally unsuitable for the Highlanders' style of courageous but undisciplined fighting, which needed steep hills and lots of cover to provide the element of surprise, and they were routed. After the battle, in which 1500 Highlanders were slaughtered (many of them as they lay wounded on the battlefield), Bonnie Prince Charlie fled west to the hills and islands, where loyal Highlanders sheltered and protected him. He eventually escaped to France, leaving his supporters to their fate – and, in effect, ushering in the end of the clan system. The clans were disarmed, the wearing of tartan and playing of bagpipes forbidden, and the chiefs became landlords greedy for higher and higher rents. The battle also unleashed an orgy of violent reprisals on Scotland, as unruly English troops raped and pillaged their way across the region; within a century, the Highland way of life had changed out of all recognition.

The visitor centre and battlefield

Today, this historic site annually attracts over 200,000 visitors. Your first stop should be the superb ecofriendly **visitor centre** (daily: April–Oct 9am–6pm; Nov–March 10am–4pm; £10; NTS; Ⓦwww.nts.org.uk/culloden). The sleek building hosts costumed actors and state-of-the-art audiovisual and interactive technology, all employed to tell the tragedy of Culloden through the words, songs and poetic verse of locals and soldiers who experienced it. The *pièce de résistance* is the powerful "battle immersion theatre" where visitors are surrounded by lifelike cinematography and the sounds of the raging, bloody fight.

Go up to the rooftop platform to enjoy the elevated view across the actual battlefield before, armed with a nifty audio guide (free) that makes use of global positioning software, walking around the battle site on twenty-, forty-five- and sixty-minute routes with more evocative narrative. Flags mark out the positions of the two armies while simple headstones mark the **clan graves**. The **Field of the English**, for many years unmarked, is a mass grave for the fifty or so English soldiers who died. Half a mile east of the battlefield, just beyond the crossroads on the main road, is the **Cumberland Stone**, thought for many years to have been the point from where the duke watched the battle. It is more likely, however, that he was much further forward and simply used the stone for shelter. Elsewhere, the restored **Leanach cottage** marks the spot where thirty injured Jacobites were burnt alive.

Every April, on the Saturday closest to the date of the battle, there's a small commemorative service. The visitor centre has a reference library and will check for you if you think you have an ancestor who died here. The beautifully designed **café** serves good cooked meals, as well as snacks and cakes.

The Clava Cairns

If you're visiting Culloden with your own transport, it's worth making a short detour to the **Clava Cairns**, an impressive collection of prehistoric burial chambers clustered around the south bank of the River Nairn, a half-mile southeast of the battlefield. Erected some time before 2000 BC, the Bronze-Age cairns, which are encircled by standing stones in a spinney of mature beech trees, are of two different kinds: one large and one very small **ring-cairn**, and two **passage graves**, which have a narrow passageway from edge to centre. Though cremated remains have been found in both types of structure, and unburnt remains in the passage graves, little is known about the nomadic herdsmen who are thought to have built them. For refreshments, pop into the refurbished *Culloden Moor Inn* near the Cairns and Culloden battlefield.

Cawdor Castle

The pretty village of **CAWDOR**, eight miles east of Culloden, is the site of **Cawdor Castle** (May–Oct daily 10am–5.30pm; £8.30, £4.50 gardens and nature trails only; ⓦ www.cawdorcastle.com), a setting intimately linked to Shakespeare's *Macbeth*: the fulfilment of the witches' prediction that Macbeth was to become thane of Cawdor sets off his tragic desire to be king. Though visitors arrive here in their droves each summer because of the site's literary associations, the castle, which dates from the early fourteenth century, could not possibly have witnessed the grisly historical events on which the Bard's drama was based. However, the immaculately restored monument – a fairy tale affair of towers, turrets, hidden passageways, dungeons, gargoyles and crenellations whimsically shooting off from the original keep – is still well worth a visit.

Six centuries on, the Campbells of Cawdor still spend their winters here, and the castle feels like a family home, albeit one with tapestries, pictures and opulent furniture (all catalogued with mischievous humour). As you explore, look out for the **Thorn Tree Room**, a vaulted chamber complete with the remains of an ancient holly tree that has been carbon-dated to 1372 – an ancient pagan fertility symbol believed to ward off fairies and evil spirits. The **grounds** of the castle are impressive, with an attractive walled garden, a maze, small golf course, putting green and nature trails. It's also worth visiting the village for a drink or delicious meal at the traditional *Cawdor Tavern*. To get here, take **bus** #12 from Inverness.

Fort George

Eight miles of undulating coastal farmland separate Cawdor Castle from **Fort George** (daily: April–Sept 9.30am–5.30pm; Oct–March 9.30am–4.30pm; HS; £6.70), an old Hanoverian bastion with walls a mile long, considered by military architectural historians to be one of the finest fortifications in Europe. Crowning a sandy spit that juts into the middle of the Moray Firth, it was built between 1747 and 1769 as a base for George II's army, in case the Highlanders should attempt to rekindle the Jacobite flame. By the time of its completion, however, the uprising had been firmly quashed and the fort has been used ever since as barracks; note the armed sentries at the main entrance and the periodic crack of live gunfire from the nearby firing ranges.

Apart from the sweeping panoramic views across the Firth from its ramparts, the main incentive to visit Fort George is the **Regimental Museum** of the Queen's Own Highlanders. It displays a predictable array of regimental silver, coins, moth-eaten uniforms and medals, along with some macabre war trophies, ranging from blood-stained nineteenth-century Sudanese battle robes to Iraqi gas masks gathered in the first Gulf War. The **chapel** is also worth a look – squat and solid outside, and all light and grace within.

Walking on the northern, grass-covered casemates, which look out into the estuary, you may be lucky enough to see a school of bottle-nosed **dolphins** (see box, p.216) swimming in with the tide. This is also a good spot for birdwatching: a colony of kittiwakes occupies the fort's slate rooftops. Highland Country **bus** #11 from Queensgate in Inverness serves the fort.

3

Moray Firth, a great wedge-shaped bay forming the eastern coastline of the Highlands, is one of only three areas of UK waters that support a resident population of dolphins. Over a hundred of these beautiful, intelligent marine mammals live in the estuary, the most northerly breeding-ground in Europe for this particular species – the bottle-nosed dolphin (*Tursiops truncatus*) – and you stand a good chance of spotting a few, either from the shore or a boat.

One of the best places in Scotland, if not in Europe, to look for them is **Chanonry Point**, on the Black Isle (see p.265) – a spit of sand protruding into a narrow, deep channel, where converging currents bring fish close to the surface, and thus the dolphins close to shore; a rising tide is the most likely time to see them. **Kessock Bridge**, one mile north of Inverness, is another prime dolphin-spotting location. You can go all the way down to the beach at the small village of North Kessock, underneath the road bridge or stop above the village in a car park just off the A9 at the **Dolphin and Seal Visitor Centre** and listening post (June–Sept daily 9.30am–12.30pm & 1–4.30pm; free), run by the Whale and Dolphin Conservation Society (WDCS), where hydrophones allow you to eavesdrop on the clicks and whistles of underwater conversations.

In addition, several companies run dolphin-spotting **boat trips** around the Moray Firth. However, researchers claim that the increased traffic is causing the dolphins unnecessary stress, particularly during the all-important breeding period when passing vessels are thought to force calves underwater for uncomfortably long periods. So if you decide to go on a cruise to see the dolphins, which also sometimes provides the chance of spotting minke whales, porpoises, seals and otters, make sure the operator is a member of the Dolphin Space Programme's Accreditation Scheme (Ⓦ www.dolphinspace.org). Operators currently accredited include Phoenix, based in Nairn (Ⓣ01667/456078, Ⓦ www.phoenix-boat-trips.co.uk); Inverness Dolphin Cruises, Inverness (Ⓣ01463/717900, Ⓦ www.inverness-dolphin-cruises.co.uk); and the WDCS Wildlife Centre, Spey Bay (Ⓣ01343/820339). In addition, Dolphin Trips Avoch (Ⓣ01381/622383, Ⓦ www.dolphintripsavoch.co.uk) and the highly regarded Ecoventures, Cromarty (Ⓣ01381/600323, Ⓦ www.ecoventures.co.uk), are based on the Black Isle, on the northern side of the firth. Trips with all operators, most of which operate between April and October, cost from £10 for one hour. All these trips are very popular, so be sure to book them well in advance. To reach the dolphin sites, take bus #26 (Mon–Sat hourly, irregular Sun) from Inverness Union Street to Avoch, Rosemarkie and Cromarty. Bus #12 also stops in the village of North Kessock.

Nairn and around

One of the driest and sunniest places in the whole of Scotland, **NAIRN**, sixteen miles east of Inverness, began its days as a peaceful community of fishermen and farmers. The former spoke Gaelic, the latter English, allowing James VI to boast that a town in his kingdom was so large that people at one end of the main street could not understand those at the other end. Nairn became popular in Victorian times, when the train line offered a convenient link to its revitalizing sea air and mild climate, and today the 11,000-strong population still relies on tourism, with all the ingredients for a traditional seaside holiday – sandy beach, ice-cream shops and fish-and-chip stalls. It boasts two championship golf courses, and Thomas Telford's **harbour** is filled with leisure craft rather than fishing boats. The **Nairn Museum**, Viewfield House, King Street (May–Oct Mon–Fri 10am–4.30pm, Sat 10am–1pm; £3; Ⓦ www.nairnmuseum.co .uk), provides a general insight into the history and prehistory of the area; the **Fishertown Room** illustrates the parsimonious and puritanical life of the fishing families.

With a good map to help navigate the maze of minor roads, you can explore some pleasant countryside south of Nairn, particularly in the valley of the **River Findhorn**, with **Dulsie Bridge**, on the old military road linking Perth and Fort George, being a favourite local picnic spot. A few miles farther south, the waters of **Lochindorb** surround the ruined thirteenth-century castle used as a base by Alexander Stewart, the Wolf of Badenoch (see p.148). The relative flatness of the land makes these roads ideal for cycling; a bike is also a great way to explore **Culbin Forest**, an unusual area of coastal forest northeast of Nairn where Scots and Corsican pine trees were planted to stabilize an extensive area of sand dune. The forest, a Site of Special Scientific Interest, has a network of paths including a wheelchair-accessible route and a "Flowers of the Forest" trail, as well as a number of picnic spots. Wildlife abounds, including an array of migrating waterfowl at the adjacent RSPB reserve of Culbin Sands.

Nairn no longer has a tourist office but there is a freephone accommodation booking service within the main library at 68 High St. For **places to stay**, the pick of the bunch is the luxurious *Boath House Hotel and Spa* (℡01667/454896, Ⓦwww .boath-house.com; ❽) in the village of Auldearn just outside Nairn, a fine Georgian country house set in magnificent gardens where guests are lavished with attention and mouthwatering (if pricey) cooking that draws upon organic fare and regional dairy, fish and meat suppliers. For an affordable taste of such luxury, book a lunchtime table in the Michelin-starred restaurant. Alternatively, *Cawdor House* is a bright and attractive **B&B** (℡01667/455855, Ⓦwww.cawdorhousenairn .co.uk; ❹), while *Greenlawns*, 13 Seafield St (℡01667/452738, Ⓦwww.green lawns.uk.com; ❸), is a spacious friendly home where kedgeree and smoked salmon feature on the breakfast menu.

For a reasonably priced **meal** try the family-run Italian restaurant in the *Aurora Hotel*, 2 Academy St (℡01667/453551), while *The Classroom*, 1 Cawdor St, continues to be Nairn's most popular coffee shop serving tasty light bites, lunches and dinners (daily 11am–11pm). **Bike rental** is available from Bike and Buggy at 2 Leopold St (℡01667/455416, Ⓦwww.bikeandbuggy.co.uk). Delnies Wood, two miles west of Nairn, has an excellent campsite (April–Oct; ℡01667/455281).

West of Inverness

West of Inverness, the Moray Firth becomes the **Beauly Firth**, a sheltered sea loch bounded by the Black Isle in the north and the wooded hills of the Aird to the south. At the head of the firth is the medieval village of **Beauly**, seat of the colourful Lovat clan, with the small settlement of **Muir of Ord**, known for its whisky, close by. Most northbound traffic uses Kessock Bridge to cross the Moray Firth from Inverness, so this whole area is quieter, and the A862, which skirts the shoreline and the mud flats, offers a more scenic alternative to the faster A9.

Beauly

The self-confident stone-built village of **BEAULY** lies ten miles west of Inverness, at the point where the Beauly River – one of Scotland's most renowned salmon-fishing streams – flows into the Firth. It's arranged around a single main street that widens into a spacious marketplace, at the north end of which stand the skeletal red-sandstone remains of **Beauly Priory** (daily 9.30am–4.30pm; free). Founded in 1230 by the Bisset family for the Valliscaulian order, and later becoming Cistercian, it was destroyed during the Reformation and is now in ruins. Beside this, the refurbished **Beauly Centre** (daily 10am–6pm) provides local tourist information and a bookshop. Just outside of town, the **Kilmorack Gallery** (℡01463/783230, Ⓦwww.kilmorack gallery.co.uk) is based in a beautiful vaulted church, and shows changing exhibitions of contemporary Scottish art: a refreshing change from the more twee galleries hereabouts.

Beauly has a surprising number of **places to stay**. The most comfortable is the modern *Priory Hotel* (℡01463/782309, Ⓦwww.priory-hotel.com; ❻) on the

picturesque village square. The **Lovat Arms Hotel** (℡01463/782313, ⓦwww
.lovatarms.com; ❻), at the opposite end of the main street, is more traditional and
has a decent restaurant. Within the row of Victorian houses past the *Lovat Arms*
visitors will find several reasonable B&Bs including *Heathmount Guest House*
(℡01463/782411; ❷). For a bolthole in the tranquil hamlet of Struy in Strathglass, nine miles south on the A831, the rustic *Cnoc Hotel* (℡01463/761264,
ⓦwww.thecnochotel.co.uk; ❺) is a good bet for hearty food and a comfortable
bed. For daytime **eating** in Beauly, the *Corner on the Square* delicatessen on the
High Street offers tasty home-baked quiches and cakes (open till 10pm on Thurs).

Around Beauly

Muir of Ord, a sprawling village four miles north of Beauly, is notable only for
the **Glen Ord Distillery** (Jan–March & Oct–Dec Mon–Fri 11am–3pm; April–
Sept Mon–Fri 10am–5pm, July–Sept also Sat & Sun noon–4pm; £5 including
discount voucher; ⓦwww.discovering-distilleries.com/glenord) on its northern
outskirts. Here, as at other distilleries, the mysteries of whisky production are
explained with a tour that winds up in the cellars, where you get to sample the
12-year-old Glen Ord single malt. No buses stop outside the distillery, but it's a
ten-minute walk from Muir of Ord, which you can reach on **buses** #17, #18, #19
from Union Street in Inverness that travel several times a day via Beauly (Mon–Sat)
to Dingwall. More helpfully, the **train** from Inverness stops at Muir of Ord station
(Mon–Sat 6 daily; 2 on Sun; 20min).

You can also visit a family-run **winery** at **Moniack Castle** (April–Oct Mon–Sat
10am–5pm; Nov–March Mon–Fri 11am–4pm; £2), four miles east of Beauly, just
off the A862, where you can taste and buy over thirty different home-made
products, including silver-birch or meadowsweet wine, sloe-berry liqueur, juniper
chutney and rosehip jam.

Travel details

Trains

Fort William to: Crianlarich (Mon–Sat 3 daily, 2 on
Sun; 1hr 50min); Glasgow (Mon–Sat 3 daily, 2 on
Sun; 3hr 50min); London (1 daily, 2 nightly; 9hr
25min–12hr); Mallaig (Mon–Sat 3 daily, 2 on Sun;
1hr 25min).

Inverness to: Aberdeen (Mon–Sat 10 daily; 5 on
Sun; 2hr 15min); Aviemore (Mon–Sat 9 daily, 5 on
Sun; 40min); Edinburgh (Mon–Sat 5 daily, 3 on Sun;
3hr 30min); Glasgow (3 daily; 3hr 20min); Kyle of
Lochalsh (Mon–Sat 2–3 daily, 1 on Sun; 2hr 25min);
London (Mon–Fri & 4 on Sun, 1 nightly; 8hr
30min–11hr); Thurso (Mon–Sat 2 daily, 1 on Sun; 3hr
25min); Wick (Mon–Sat 3 daily, 1 on Sun; 4hr 20min).

Buses

Fort William to: Drumnadrochit (8 daily; 1hr 30min);
Edinburgh (4 daily; 4hr); Fort Augustus (5 daily; 1hr);
Glasgow (4 daily; 3hr); Inverness (6 daily; 2hr);
Mallaig (Mon–Fri 1 daily; 1hr 20min); Oban (Mon–Sat
4 daily; 1hr 30min); Portree, Skye (2 daily; 3hr).

Inverness to: Aberdeen (hourly; 3hr 40min);
Aviemore (Mon–Sat 6 daily, 5 on Sun; 45min);
Drumnadrochit (8 daily; 25min); Fort Augustus
(5 daily; 1hr); Fort William (6 daily; 2hr); Glasgow
(6 daily direct; 3hr 35min–4hr 25min); Kyle of
Lochalsh (3 daily; 2hr); Nairn (hourly; 50min); Perth
(10 daily; 2hr 35min); Portree (3 daily; 3hr); Thurso
(Mon–Sat 5 daily, 2 on Sun; 3hr 30min); Ullapool
(2 Mon, Tues, Thurs & Sat; 3 Wed & Fri; 2hr 25min);
Wick (Mon–Sat 3 daily, 2 on Sun; 3hr).

Flights

Inverness to: Dublin (Mon–Fri 2 daily, 1 Sun; 1hr
30min); Edinburgh (Mon–Fri 2 daily, 1 Sat; 45min);
Kirkwall (Mon–Fri 2 daily, 1 Sat & Sun; 45min);
London (Gatwick 4 daily Mon–Fri; 3 Sat & Sun;
Heathrow 1 daily; Luton Mon–Fri 1 daily; 2 daily
Sat & Sun; 1hr 30min); Manchester (Mon–Fri 2
daily, 1 Sun; 1hr 25min); Shetland (Mon–Fri 2 daily;
1 daily Sat & Sun; 1hr 40min); Stornoway (Mon–Fri
4 daily, Sat 2 daily, 1 on Sun; 40min).

The north and
northwest Highlands

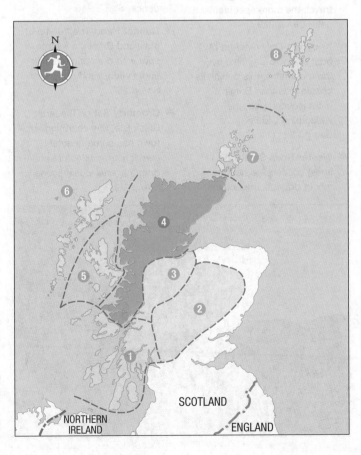

SCOTLAND

NORTHERN
IRELAND

ENGLAND

CHAPTER 4 # Highlights

✳ **Loch Shiel** This romantic, unspoilt loch is where Bonnie Prince Charlie first raised an army. See p.228

✳ **West Highland Railway** From Glasgow to Mallaig via Fort William; the further north you travel, the more spectacular it gets. See p.229

✳ **Knoydart** Only reached by boat or a two-day hike over the mountains, this peninsula boasts mainland Britain's most isolated pub, the welcoming Old Forge. See p.232

✳ **Wester Ross** Scotland's finest scenery – a heady mix of dramatic mountains, rugged sea lochs, sweeping bays, scattered islands and idyllic Applecross. See p.238

✳ **Ceilidh Place, Ullapool** The best venue for modern Highland culture, with evenings of music, song and dance. See p.246

✳ **Dunnet Head** The true tip of mainland Britain, a remote spot with dramatic red cliffs and a wide, sandy bay. See p.262

✳ **Cromarty** Set on the fertile Black Isle, this charming small town has some beautiful vernacular architecture and dramatic east-coast scenery. See p.265

▲ Ben More Assynt massif, Wester Ross

The north and northwest Highlands

The **north and northwest Highlands** – the area beyond the Great Glen – holds some of Scotland's most spectacular scenery: a classic combination of bare mountains, remote glens, dark lochs and tumbling rivers, surrounded on three sides by a magnificently rugged coastline. The inspiring landscape and the tranquillity and space that it offers are without doubt the main attractions of the region. You may be surprised at just how remote much of it still is: the vast peat bogs in the north, for example, are among the most extensive and unspoilt wilderness areas in Europe, while a handful of the west coast's crofting villages can still be reached only by boat.

Different weather conditions and cultural influences have given each of the three coastlines its own distinct character. The beautiful **west coast**, with its indented shoreline and the dramatic mountains of **Torridon** and **Assynt**, is a place whose charm and poetic scenery just about hold their own against the intrusions of the touring hordes in summer. West of Fort William lies the remote and tranquil **Ardnamurchan peninsula** and the "Road to the Isles" to the fishing port of **Mallaig**, railhead of the famous West Highland Railway. From Mallaig ferries cross to Skye and **Knoydart**, a magical peninsula with no road access that's home to the remotest pub in Britain. The more direct route to Skye is across the famous Skye Bridge at **Kyle of Lochalsh**, not far from which are charming coastal villages such as **Glenelg** and **Plockton**. Between Kyle of Lochalsh and

Getting around the Highlands

Unless you're prepared to spend weeks on the road, the Highlands are simply too vast to see in a single trip. Most visitors, therefore, base themselves in one or two areas, exploring the coast or hills on foot, and making longer hops across the interior by car, bus or train. Getting around the Highlands, particularly the remoter parts, is obviously easiest if you've got your own transport, but with a little forward planning you can see a surprising amount using **buses** and **trains**, especially if you fill in with **postbuses** (for which you can get timetables at most post offices, or see Ⓦwww .royalmail.com/postbus). It is worth remembering, however, that much of the Highlands comes to a halt on **Sundays**, when bus services are sporadic at best and you may well find most shops and restaurants closed.

THE NORTH & NORTHWEST HIGHLANDS

0 ____ 20 miles

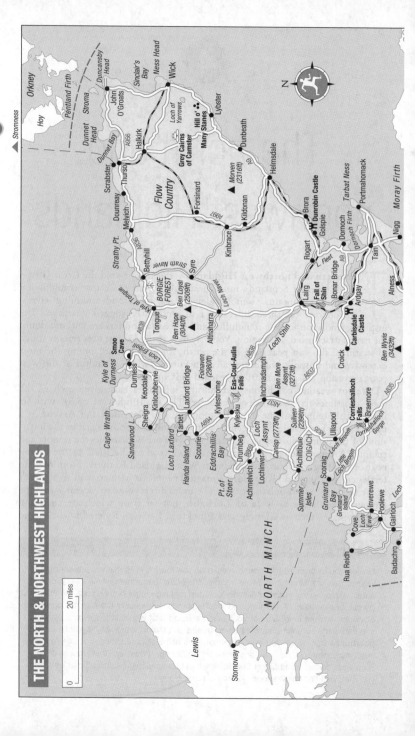

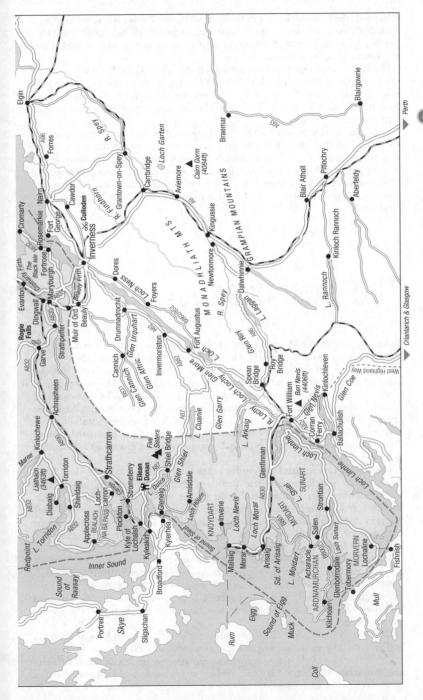

Ullapool, the main settlement in the northwest, lies **Wester Ross**, with quintessentially west-coast scenes of sparkling sea lochs, rocky headlands and sandy beaches set against some of Scotland's most dramatic mountains, with Skye and the Western Isles on the horizon.

The little-visited **north coast**, stretching from stormy **Cape Wrath**, at the very northwest tip of the mainland, to **John O'Groats**, is even more rugged than the west, its sheer cliffs and sand-filled bays bearing the brunt of frequently fierce Atlantic storms. The main settlement is **Thurso**, jumping-off point for the main ferry service to Orkney.

On the fertile **east coast** of the Highland region, stretching north from Inverness to the old herring port of **Wick**, green fields and woodland run down to the sweeping sandy beaches of the **Black Isle** and the **Cromarty** and **Dornoch firths**. This region is rich with historical sites, including the contentious **Sutherland Monument** by Golspie, **Dornoch**'s fourteenth-century sandstone cathedral, and a number of places linked to the **Clearances**, a tragic chapter in the story of the Highlands.

The west coast

For many people, the Highlands' starkly beautiful **west coast** – stretching from the **Morvern peninsula** (opposite Mull) in the south to wind-lashed **Cape Wrath** in the far north – is the finest part of Scotland. Cut by fjord-like sea lochs, the long coastline is scattered with windswept white-sand beaches and cliff-girt headlands, with rugged mountains sweeping up from the shoreline. The fast-changing weather rolling off the North Atlantic can be harsh, but when the sun shines, the sparkle of the sea, the richness of colour and the clarity of the views out to the scattered Hebrides are simply irresistible. This is the least populated part of Britain, with just two small towns, and yawning tracts of moorland and desolate peat bog.

The **Vikings**, who ruled the region in the ninth century, called it the "South Land", from which the modern district of Sutherland takes its name. After Culloden, the Clearances emptied most of the inland glens of the far north, however, and left the population clinging to the coastline, where a herring-fishing industry developed. Today, tourism, crofting, fishing and salmon farming are the mainstays of the local economy, supplemented by EU construction grants and subsidies to farm the sheep you'll encounter everywhere.

For visitors, **cycling**, **walking** and, increasingly, sea-kayaking are the obvious ways to make the most of the superb scenery, and countless lochans and crystal-clear rivers offer superlative trout and salmon **fishing**. The shattered cliffs of the far northwest harbour some of Europe's largest and most diverse **sea-bird colonies**, while the area's craggy mountaintops are the haunt of the elusive golden eagle.

The most visited part of the west coast is the stretch between Kyle of Lochalsh and Ullapool. Lying within easy reach of Inverness, this sector boasts the region's more obvious highlights: the awesome mountainscape of **Torridon**, **Gairloch**'s sandy beaches, the famous botanic gardens at **Inverewe** and **Ullapool** itself, a picturesque and bustling fishing town from where ferries leave for the Outer Hebrides. However, press on further north, or south, and you'll get a truer sense of the isolation that makes the west coast so special. Traversed by few roads, the remote northwest corner of Scotland is wild and bleak, receiving the full force of the North Atlantic's frequently ferocious weather. The scattered settlements of the far southwest tend to be more sheltered, but they are separated by some of the most extensive wilderness areas in Britain – lonely peninsulas with evocative Gaelic names like **Ardnamurchan**, **Knoydart** and **Glenelg**.

Practicalities

Tempered by the Gulf Stream, the west coast's **weather** ranges from stupendous to diabolical. Never count on a sunny morning meaning a fine day; it can rain here at any time, and go on raining for days. Beware, too, of the dreaded **midge**, which drives even the hardiest of locals to distraction on warm summer evenings.

Without your own vehicle, **transport** can be a problem. There's a reasonable **train** service from Inverness to Kyle of Lochalsh and from Fort William to Mallaig, and a useful **summer bus** service connects Inverness to Ullapool, Lochinver, Scourie and Durness. However, services peter out as you venture further afield, where you'll have to rely on **postbuses**, which go just about everywhere, albeit slowly and at odd times of day. **Driving** is a much simpler option: the roads aren't busy, though they are frequently single-track and scattered with sheep. Refuel whenever you can since pumps are few and far between, and make sure your vehicle is in good condition; in a crisis, even if you manage to reach the nearest garage, spares may well have to be sent over from Inverness.

Morvern to Knoydart: the "Rough Bounds"

The remote and sparsely populated southwest corner of the Highlands, from the empty district of **Morvern** to the isolated peninsula of **Knoydart**, is a dramatic, lonely region of mountain and moorland, its rocky, indented coast studded by stunning white beaches which enjoy wonderful views to Mull, Skye and other islands. Its Gaelic name, *Garbh-chiochan*, translates as the "**Rough Bounds**", implying a region geographically and spiritually apart. Even if you have got a car, you should spend some time here exploring on foot.

The southwest Highlands' main road is the A830, often described as "the Road to the Isles", which winds in tandem with the rail line through the glens from Fort William to the road- and railhead at **Mallaig**, a busy fishing-port with ferry connections to Skye. Along the way, the road passes **Glenfinnan**, the much-photographed spot at the head of stunning **Loch Shiel** where Bonnie Prince Charlie gathered the clans to start the doomed Jacobite uprising of 1745. There are regular buses and trains along the main road; elsewhere in the region you'll usually have to rely on daily post- or schoolbuses. If you have your own transport, the five-minute ferry crossing at **Corran Ferry** (every 20–30min; Mon–Sat 6.30am–9.20pm, Sun 8.45am–9.20pm; car and passengers £6.40, foot passengers and bicycles go free), a nine-mile drive south of Fort William down Loch Linnhe, provides a more direct point of entry for Morvern and the rugged **Ardnamurchan** peninsula. *The Inn at Ardgour* (☎01855/841225, Ⓦwww.ardgour.biz; ❹), on the Morvern side, is a pleasant stop for a drink or a bite to eat.

Morvern

Bounded on three sides by sea lochs and in the north by desolate Glen Tarbet, the large, mountainous **Morvern** peninsula lies at the southwest corner of the Rough Bounds region. The landscape can seem unremittingly bleak and empty – until, that is, you reach the coast, which reveals some lovely views over to Mull. Most visitors only travel through here to get to **LOCHALINE** (pronounced "loch-*aa*lin"), a remote community on the **Sound of Mull**, from where a small car ferry chugs to **Fishnish** – the shortest crossing from the mainland (and cheaper than the main Oban–Craignure crossing if you're taking a car onto Mull). Lochaline village, little more than a scattering of houses around a small pier, has a diving centre specializing in underwater archeology (℡01967/421627, ⓦwww.lochalinedivecentre.co.uk) and is a popular anchorage for yachts cruising the west coast.

For **accommodation**, the dive centre offers two self-catering options: a ten-bed facility in the *Old Post Office* and 24 beds in the *Dive Lodge*. You could also try the straightforward and friendly *Lochaline Hotel* (℡01967/421657; ❷). The best reason to stop here, however, is to **eat** at the superb ✻ *White House Restaurant* (℡01967/421777, ⓦwww.thewhitehouserestaurant.co.uk; closed Mon) which specializes in delicious, freshly prepared dishes using local meat and seafood, plus coffee and home-baked scones. You can also *Catch a Snack* in the wooden hut by the pier: they do a mean venison burger.

As you'd expect, **transport** links here (other than the Fishnish ferry) are extremely limited, with a bus running to and from Fort William on a Tuesday, Thursday and Friday only, plus a Saturday service in summer (check with Shiel Buses ℡01967/431272, ⓦwww.shielbuses.co.uk). By request, the bus goes as far as the road end at **Drimnin** at the northwest corner of Morvern, from where you can cross to Tobermory on Mull with Ardnamurchan Charters (℡01972/500208, ⓦwww.west-scotland-marine.com). Booking is essential, and trips depend on passenger numbers. The same company also runs wildlife excursions and trips to outlying islands.

Sunart and Ardgour

North of Morvern, the predominantly roadless regions of **Sunart** and **Ardgour** make up the country between Loch Shiel, Loch Sunart and Loch Linnhe. The heart of Jacobite support in the mid-eighteenth century, they're Catholic strongholds to this day. The area's only real village is sleepy **STRONTIAN**, grouped around a green on an inlet of Loch Sunart. In 1722, lead mines here yielded the first-ever traces of the element **strontium**, which was named after the village.

You can get to Strontian on the one **bus** a day (Mon–Sat; ℡01967/431272), which leaves Fort William at 1.25pm and reaches Strontian at 2.15pm before continuing to Kilchoan. Strontian's **tourist office** (Easter–Oct Mon–Sat; June–Sept also Sun; ℡01967/402382) is by the roadside as you pass through the village. The six-bedroom *Strontian Hotel* (℡01967/402029, ⓦwww.thestrontianhotel .co.uk; ❺) offers reasonable bar meals on the main road looking over the water. You can also cross the bridge heading north through the village and turn right for the *Ariundle Centre* (℡01967/402279), a wood-beamed café and craft centre with a plain but decent **bunkhouse**. **B&B** is available at the delightfully secluded *Craigrowan Croft* (℡01967/402253, ⓦwww.craigrowancroft.co.uk; ❷), a little way up the Ariundle turn-off. Six miles west of Strontian, only two miles before Salen, *Resipole Farm* (℡01967/431235, ⓦwww.resipole.co.uk; April–Oct) has a great set-up, with a **camping** and caravan park and (year-round) self-catering accommodation. The reception stocks basic foodstuffs. For dinner, drive a few minutes to the *Salen Hotel* (see opposite).

The Ardnamurchan peninsula

The tortuous single-track B8007 road winds west from Salen to the wild **Ardna-murchan peninsula**, the most westerly point on the British mainland. The unspoilt landscape is relatively gentle and wooded at the eastern end, with much of the coastline of long Loch Sunart fringed by ancient oakwoods. The further west you travel, however, the trees disappear and are replaced by a wild, salt-sprayed moorland. The peninsula, once ruled by Norse invaders, lost most of its inhabitants during the infamous Clearances, and only a handful of tiny crofting settlements cling to its jagged coastline.

Yet Ardnamurchan, with its pristine, empty beaches and wonderful sea vistas, can be an inspiring place. The peninsula harbours a huge variety of birds, mammals and wild flowers such as thrift and wild iris, making **walking** an obvious attraction. Over forty walks are detailed in a guide to the peninsula produced annually by the local community (available from tourist offices and most shops), while **guided walks** are also available at most of the nature reserves dotted along the Loch Sunart shoreline. For wildlife-spotting, stop off at the turf-roofed Garbh Eilean hide (free access), five miles west of Strontian on the A861, from where you can see seals, sea birds and the occasional eagle.

Salen to Glenborrodale

The coastal hamlet of **SALEN** marks the turn-off for Ardnamurchan Point: from here it's a further 25 miles of slow, scenic driving along the single-track road which follows the northern shore of Loch Sunart. Salen is a sheltered anchorage, and yachties often row ashore for a drink at the *Salen Hotel* (T 01967/431 1661 W www .salenhotel.co.uk; ❷), which has some neat rooms and serves good seafood bar meals. There's not much more until you get to the engaging **Ardnamurchan Natural History Centre** (April–Oct Mon–Sat 10.30am–5.30pm, Sun noon–5.30pm; £4 W www.ardnamurchannaturalhistorycentre.co.uk), an inspiring introduction to the diverse flora, fauna and geology of Ardnamurchan just west of the hamlet of **GLENBORRODALE**. The centre is housed in a sensitively designed timber structure complete with turf roof, bark floor and wildlife ponds. Live-cam record-ings show the comings and goings of heron, a pine marten's nest, and sea and golden eagles feeding nearby. The *Antler Tearoom* here dishes up sandwiches and good home-baked cakes, and evening meals are sometimes served in summer (T 01972/500209).

Kilchoan and Ardnamurchan Point

KILCHOAN, nine miles west of the Glenmore Centre, is Ardnamurchan's main village – a straggling but appealing crofting township overlooking the Sound of Mull. A **car ferry** runs from here to Tobermory (Mon–Sat 8am–6.40pm 3–4 daily, plus May–Aug Sun 10.15am–4.45pm 5 daily; 35min). The community centre in the village houses a **tourist office** (Easter–Oct daily; T 01972/510222, W www.ardnamurchan.com) that also serves coffee and lunchtime soup. For **boat trips** out of Kilchoan to observe wildlife, including dolphins, seals, whales and possibly the rare sea eagle, contact Ardnamurchan Charters (T 01972/500208, W www.west-scotland-marine.com). The only direct **bus** to Kilchoan leaves from Fort William at 3.20pm (Mon–Sat), travelling via the Corran Ferry and arriving three hours later.

The road continues beyond Kilchoan to the rocky, windy **Ardnamurchan Point** and its famous 36m-high **lighthouse**. The lighthouse buildings house a small café and an absorbing **exhibition** (daily April–Oct 10am–5pm; £5; T 01972/510210, W www.ardnamurchanlighthouse.com). Best of all is the chance to climb up the inside of the Egyptian-style tower; at the top, a guide will show you the lighting mechanism. Minke whales sometimes surface in the waters off the point.

Also worth exploring around the peninsula are the myriad coves, beaches and headlands along the long coastline. The finest of the sandy beaches is about three miles north of the lighthouse at **Sanna Bay**, a shell-strewn strand and series of dunes which offers unforgettable vistas of the Small Isles to the north, circled by gulls, terns and guillemots.

Practicalities

Accommodation isn't plentiful in Kilchoan, and in summer you're well advised to book far ahead. You can normally camp in the gardens of the *Kilchoan House Hotel*, and there's a good campsite with lovely coastal views by the Ardnamurchan Study Centre (℡07787 812084, Ⓦwww.ardnamurchanstudycentre.co.uk), about half a mile past the Ferry Stores. For B&B, try friendly *Doirlinn House* (℡01972/510209, Ⓔdoirlinnhouse@ardnamurchan-holidays.com; ❷; March–Oct) or nearby two-bedroom *Torrsolais* (℡01972/510389, Ⓦwww.ardnamurchan -holidays.co.uk; ❷). Both have lovely views over the bay and Sound of Mull.

Options for lunch and evening meals in the area are limited, with the Kilchoan community centre serving good-value snacks and lunches and *Kilchoan House Hotel* (℡01972/510200, Ⓦwww.kilchoanhousehotel.co.uk; ❹) the best bet for an evening meal – it also has half a dozen rooms, including some family rooms. The Ferry Stores in Kilchoan makes an impressive effort to carry fresh food and local produce when it's available.

Acharacle and around

At the eastern end of Ardnamurchan, just north of Salen where the A861 heads north towards the district of Moidart, the main settlement is **ACHARACLE**, an attractive ancient crofting village set back a few hundred yards from the seaward end of freshwater **Loch Shiel**. The pleasant *Loch Shiel House Hotel* (℡01967/431224, Ⓦwww.lochshielhotel.co.uk; ❷) is a comfortable, friendly place to stay, stop for a drink or eat, while *Ardshealach Lodge* (℡01967/431399, Ⓦwww.ardshealach -lodge.co.uk; ❹) serves lunch, afternoon tea and dinner in an attractive house in its own grounds with a great outlook over the loch and hills. The *Chimneys B&B* (℡01967/431528, Ⓦwww.chimneysmoidart.co.uk; ❷) is another option, and you can head to the *Blue Parrot Café* for daytime snacks and home-baking.

You can get to Acharacle by **boat** from Glenfinnan at the head of Loch Shiel with Loch Shiel Cruises (Wed only; Easter to mid-Oct; £15 single, £22 return; ℡01687/470322, Ⓦwww.highlandcruises.co.uk), or on infrequent **buses** from Mallaig or Fort William.

Castle Tioram

A mile north of Acharacle, a side road running north off the A861 winds for three miles or so past a secluded estuary lined with rhododendron thickets and fishing platforms to **Loch Moidart**, a calm and sheltered sea loch. Perched atop a rocky promontory jutting out into the loch is **Castle Tioram** (pronounced "cheerum"), one of Scotland's most atmospheric monuments. Reached via a sandy causeway that's only just above the high tide, the thirteenth-century fortress, whose Gaelic name means "dry land", was the seat of the MacDonalds of Clanranald until it was destroyed by their chief in 1715 to prevent it from falling into Hanoverian hands.

The Road to the Isles

The "**Road to the Isles**" (Ⓦwww.road-to-the-isles.org.uk) from Fort William to Mallaig, followed by the West Highland Railway and the narrow, winding A830, traverses the mountains and glens of the Rough Bounds before breaking out near

Arisaig onto a spectacularly scenic coast of sheltered inlets, stunning white beaches and wonderful views to the islands of Rùm, Eigg, Muck and Skye. This is country commonly associated with **Bonnie Prince Charlie**, whose adventures of 1745–46 began and ended on this stretch of coast, with his defiant gathering of the clans at **Glenfinnan**.

Glenfinnan

GLENFINNAN, nineteen miles west of Fort William at the head of lovely Loch Shiel, was where Bonnie Prince Charlie raised his standard to signal the start of the Jacobite uprising of 1745. Surrounded by no more than two hundred loyal clansmen, the young rebel prince waited here to see if the Cameron of Loch Shiel would join his army. The drone of this powerful chief's pipers drifting up the glen was eagerly awaited, for without him the Stuarts' attempt to claim the English throne would have been sheer folly. Despite strong misgivings, Cameron did decide to support the uprising, and arrived at Glenfinnan on a sunny August 19 with eight hundred men, thereby encouraging other clan leaders to follow suit. The prince raised his red-and-white silk colour, proclaimed his father as King James III of England and set off on the long march to London – from which only a handful of the soldiers gathered at Glenfinnan would return. The spot is marked by a **column** (now a little lopsided), crowned with a clansman in full battle dress, erected as a tribute by Alexander Macdonald of Glenaladale in 1815.

The West Highland Railway

Scotland's most famous railway line, and a train journey counted by many as among the world's most scenic, is the brilliantly engineered **West Highland Railway**, running from Glasgow to Mallaig via Fort William. The line is in two sections: the southern part travels from **Glasgow** Queen Street station along the Clyde estuary and up Loch Long before switching to the banks of Loch Lomond on its way to **Crianlarich**, where the train divides, with one section heading for Oban. After climbing around Beinn Odhar on a unique horseshoe-shaped loop of viaducts, the line traverses desolate **Rannoch Moor**, where the track had to be laid on a mattress of tree roots, brushwood and thousands of tons of earth and ashes. By this point the line has diverged from the road, and travels through country that can otherwise be reached only by long-distance footpaths. The train then swings into Glen Roy, passing through the dramatic **Monessie Gorge** and entering **Fort William** from the northeast.

The second leg of the journey, from Fort William to Mallaig, is arguably even more spectacular, and from mid-May to mid-October one of the scheduled services is pulled by the **Jacobite Steam Train** (Mon–Fri, also Sat & Sun July & Aug; departs Fort William 10.20am, departs Mallaig 2.10pm; day-return £28; book on ☏01524/737751, ⓦwww.steamtrain.info). Shortly after leaving Fort William the railway crosses the Caledonian Canal beside Neptune's Staircase by way of a swing bridge at **Benavie**, before travelling along the shores of Locheil and crossing the magnificent 21-arch viaduct at **Glenfinnan**, where the steam train, in its "Hogwarts Express" livery, was filmed for the *Harry Potter* movies. At Glenfinnan station there's a small **museum**, a restaurant and a bunkhouse (see p.230). Not long afterwards the line reaches the coast, with views of the Small Isles and Skye as it runs past the famous silver sands of **Morar** and up to **Mallaig**, where there are ferry connections to Armadale on Skye.

If you're planning on travelling the West Highland line, and in particular linking it to other train journeys (such as the similarly attractive route between Inverness and Kyle of Lochalsh), it's worth considering one of First ScotRail's multi-day **Highland Rover tickets**, details of which are given on p.30.

The **visitor centre** and run-of-the-mill café (daily: April, May, June, Sept & Oct 10am–5pm; July & Aug 9.30am–5.30pm; NTS; £3), opposite the monument, gives an account of the '45 uprising through to the rout at Culloden eight months later (see p.213). Loch Shiel Cruises (℡01687/470322, ⓦwww.highlandcruises.co.uk) run a number of **boat trips** on the loch, all offering a worthwhile opportunity to view the remote, beguiling scenery and occasionally a golden eagle. Cyclists can also disembark at the Polloch Pontoon and return by the lochside track to Glenfinnan.

Glenfinnan is one of the most spectacular parts of the **West Highland Railway** line (see box, p.229), not only for the glimpse it offers of the monument and graceful Loch Shiel, but also for the mighty 21-arched Loch nan Uamh **viaduct**, built in 1901 and one of the first-ever large constructions made out of concrete: it is now famed as a *Harry Potter* film location. You can learn more of the history of this section of the railway at the **Glenfinnan Station Museum** (June to mid-Oct daily 9am–5pm; 50p; ⓦwww.glenfinnanstationmuseum.co.uk) set in the old station booking office. Right beside the station, two old railway carriages have been pressed into use as a highly original **restaurant** and **bunkhouse**; the *Dining Car* (June–Sept daily 10am–5pm; ℡01397/722300) is open for light lunches and home-baking (phone ahead for evening meals), while the *Sleeping Car* (℡01397/722295; year-round), a converted 1958 camping coach, sleeps ten in bunk beds and makes for a memorable, if slightly restricted, place to stay. The best of the more conventional accommodation options is the *Lochailort Inn* (℡01687/470208, ⓦwww.lochailortinn.co.uk; ⑤), about ten miles on from Glenfinnan towards Arisaig (and also on the train line, although you have to request to stop here).

Arisaig

West of Glenfinnan, the A830 runs alongside captivating Loch Eilt in the district of **Morar**, through Lochailort – where it meets the road from Acharacle – and onwards to white sands, turquoise seas and rocky islets draped with orange seaweed. **ARISAIG**, scattered round a sandy bay at the west end of the Morar peninsula, makes a good base for exploring this area. A **bypass** now whizzes cars (and, more importantly, fish lorries) to Mallaig, but the slower coast road enjoys the best of the scenery.

The only specific attraction in Arisaig village is the **Land, Sea and Islands Centre** (Easter to mid-Oct Mon–Fri 10am–3pm, Sun 1–4pm; £2.50), a small, volunteer-run community project whose displays give intriguing detail on local events, including secret operations during World War II and background on local characters such as the man who inspired Robert Louis Stevenson's Long John Silver. There's a small seal colony at nearby **Rhumach**, reached via the single-track lane heading west out of Arisaig village along the headland. A **boat** also leaves from here (11am) daily during the summer for the Small Isles (see p.296), operated by Arisaig Marine (℡01687/450224, ⓦwww.arisaig.co.uk).

Accommodation in the village is plentiful: *Hilbre* (℡01687/450685, ⓦwww.road-to-the-isles.org.uk/hilbre.html; ❷; March–Oct) is modern and comfortable with fine sea views, while the more upmarket *Old Library Lodge and Restaurant* (℡01687/450651, ⓦwww.oldlibrary.co.uk; ⑤; April–Oct) has well-appointed rooms, though only two overlook the seafront. For **food**, the restaurant at the *Old Library* serves tasty if rather pricey fare, while meals and plain rooms are available at the characterless *Arisaig Hotel* (℡01687/450210, ⓦwww.arisaighotel.co.uk; ❻).

Morar

Stretching for eight miles or so north of Arisaig is a string of stunning white-sand **beaches** backed by flowery machair, with barren granite hills and moorland rising up behind, and wonderful seaward views of Eigg and Rùm. The next settlement of any significance is **MORAR**, where the famous beach scenes from *Local Hero* were shot. There are umpteen **campsites** along the coast road, and **B&B** at the home of adventurer Tom McClean, *Invermorar House* (℡01687/462274, ⓦwww .road-to-the-isles.org.uk/invermorar.html; ❷; July to mid-Sept only). He runs outdoor activities at Ardintigh, a ninety-minute sail up Loch Nevis.

Much closer is **Loch Morar** – rumoured to be the home of a monster called Morag, a lesser-known rival to Nessie – which runs east of Morar village into the heart of a huge wilderness area. For boat rental or to obtain a fishing permit for Loch Morar call ℡01687/462388. Delicious, freshly prepared Thai take-aways can be had in Morar from *Sunset* (℡01687/462259; closed Mon) on the main drag.

In the footsteps of Bonnie Prince Charlie

Along the Road to the Isles are various places that have great resonance whenever the romantic, tragic tale of **Bonnie Prince Charlie**'s failed rebellion is told. Having landed on the Western Isles (see p.333), he set foot on the Scottish mainland on the sparkling sands of **Borrodale** at Loch nan Uamh (Loch of Caves) near Arisaig on July 25, 1745. In his bid to claim the throne of Britain for his father, the Old Pretender, he had been promised 10,000 French troops; instead he arrived with only seven companions – the "Seven Men of Moidart", who are commemorated at Kinloch-moidart by a (now somewhat ravaged) line of beech trees. Having stayed a week at Kinlochmoidart, trying to ascertain what support he might muster, the prince took the old hill route (known as the General's Road) to **Dalilea**, on the north shore of Loch Shiel, and the next day, August 19, rowed from Glenalandale to the head of the loch at **Glenfinnan**. Here, surrounded by no more than two hundred loyal clansmen, he awaited the arrival of the clans loyal to the Jacobite cause. Most of the important local chiefs had turned their back on what they regarded as a desperate enterprise, and it was only when the prince persuaded two younger chiefs to join him late in the day that eight hundred more Highlanders arrived, the standard was raised, and the famous rebellion of 1745 was under way. The tall **Glenfinnan monument** (see p.229) at the head of Loch Shiel is a poignant memorial both to the inspiring symbolism of that day and the Highlanders who fought and died for the Prince.

If Charles's original encounter with the Arisaig and Moidart area had been filled with optimism and high ideals, his next visit was far less auspicious. By the summer of 1746 he was on the run, his armies had been routed at Culloden and a price of £30,000 was on his head. Despite this, none of the countless Highlanders the prince called on for food, favours or hiding turned him in, and his fortitude and bravery in those desperate months earned much respect. Fleeing from Culloden down the Great Glen, he passed through Arisaig again on his way to the Western Isles, desperately hoping for the arrival of a French ship to rescue him. It was on South Uist that Flora MacDonald extracted him from a tight situation (see p.293), but still on the run he landed back on the mainland again at **Mallaigvaig**, a short walk from Mallaig. The place was swarming with soldiers, and he went on to **Borrodale** once more, this time hiding in a large cave by the shore. From here Charles set off across Lochaber, dodging patrols and hiding in caves and shelters, including some near **Loch Arkaig** (see p.198) and on the slopes of Ben Alder, by **Loch Ericht** (see p.155). It was here that he got word that a French frigate, *L'Heureux*, was off the west coast, and he made a final dash to Arisaig, departing on September 19, 1746, from a promontory in **Loch nan Uamh**, half a mile east of the spot where he'd landed fourteen months before. Today, a cairn on the shores of the loch beside the A830, between Lochailort and Arisaig village, marks the spot.

The best place for evocative background on the prince's doomed campaign is at the site of his final defeat, Culloden (see p.213).

Mallaig

A cluttered, noisy port whose pebble-dashed houses struggle for space with great lumps of exposed granite, **MALLAIG**, 47 miles west of Fort William, is not pretty. Before the railway line reached here in 1901 it consisted of only a few cottages, but it's now bustling and, as the main ferry-stop for Skye, the Small Isles and Knoydart, always full of visitors. Once one of Europe's busiest herring ports, the continuing source of the village's wealth is its **fishing** industry.

Alongside the train station, apart from the daily hubbub of the harbour, the **Mallaig Heritage Centre** (April, May & Oct Mon–Sat 11am–4pm; June–Sept Mon–Fri 9.30am–4.30pm, Sat & Sun noon–4pm; £2; ℡01687/462085, Ⓦwww .mallaigheritage.org.uk) is worth a browse for its displays on the area's past, and for information about lifeboats, fishing and the ancient highland galleys that once plied the waters of the Inner Hebrides. The walking trail to **Mallaigmore** (1hr), a small cove with a white-sand beach and isolated croft, begins at the top of the harbour on East Bay; follow the road north past the tourist office and turn right when you see the signpost between two houses.

Practicalities

Mallaig is concentrated around the harbour, where you'll find the **tourist office** (April–Oct Mon–Sat; ℡01687/462064 for winter opening hours), and the **bus** and **train stations**. The CalMac ticket office (℡01687/462403), serving passengers for Skye and the Small Isles, is also nearby. You can arrange transport to Knoydart by calling Bruce Watt Cruises (℡01687/462320, Ⓦwww.knoydart -ferry.co.uk), which sail to Inverie, on the Knoydart peninsula, every morning and afternoon (mid-May to mid-Sept Mon–Fri; mid-Sept to mid-May Mon, Wed & Fri); the loch is quite sheltered, so crossings are rarely cancelled. To fish, spot dolphins and seals or be put ashore for a day as a "castaway", try fluent Gaelic speaker Ewen Nicholson (℡01687/462652).

There are plenty of **places to stay**. The *West Highland Hotel* (℡01687/462210, Ⓦwww.westhighlandhotel.co.uk; ❺) is a typically bland but comfortable Scottish Highland hotel; some rooms have excellent sea views. For **B&B**, head around the harbour to East Bay, where you'll find the cheery *Western Isles Guest House* (℡01687/462320, Ⓦwww.road-to-the-isles.org.uk/western-isles.html; ❸). *Sheena's Backpackers' Lodge* (℡01687/462764, Ⓦwww.mallaigbackpackers.co.uk), a refreshingly laid-back independent **hostel** overlooking the harbour, has mixed dorms and the (licensed) *Tea Garden Restaurant*, a great place to watch the world go by while you tuck into Cullen skink, a pint of prawns or home-made scones. Another fishy and slightly more upmarket **eating** option, though it's not much to look at, is the *Fishmarket Restaurant* across the road. Fresh fish and chips – or scallops and chips if you're feeling decadent – are served at the *Cornerstone*, across from the tourist office.

The Knoydart peninsula

Many people regard the **Knoydart peninsula** as mainland Britain's most dramatic and unspoilt wilderness area. Flanked by **Loch Nevis** ("Loch of Heaven") in the south and the fjord-like inlet of **Loch Hourn** ("Loch of Hell") to the north, Knoydart's knobbly green peaks – three of them Munros – sweep straight out of the sea. To get to the heart of the peninsula, you must catch a **boat** from Mallaig or Glenelg, or else **hike** for a couple of days across rugged moorland and mountains and sleep rough in old stone bothies (most marked on OS maps). Unsurprisingly, the peninsula attracts walkers, lured by well-maintained trails that wind east into the wild interior, where Bonnie Prince Charlie is rumoured to have hidden out after Culloden.

At the end of the eighteenth century, around a thousand people eked out a living from this inhospitable terrain through crofting and fishing. Evictions in 1853 began a dramatic decrease in the population, which continued to dwindle through the twentieth century as a succession of landowners ran the estate as a hunting and shooting playground, prompting a famous land raid in 1948 by a group of crofters known as the "Seven Men of Knoydart", who claimed ownership of portions of the estate. Although their bid failed, their cause was invoked when the crofters of Knoydart finally achieved a community buy-out in 1998. These days the peninsula supports around seventy people, most in the hamlet of **INVERIE**. Nestled beside a sheltered bay on the south side of the peninsula, it has a pint-sized post office and shop, a ranger post (with internet access) advising on local walks and wildlife, and mainland Britain's most remote pub, the *Old Forge*.

Bruce Watt Cruises' **boat** chugs into Inverie from Mallaig (see opposite). To arrange for a (passenger) boat crossing from Arnisdale on the Glenelg peninsula to the north coast of Knoydart or Kinloch Hourn, contact Billy Mackenzie (see below).

There are two main **hiking routes** into Knoydart. The trailhead for the first is **KINLOCH HOURN**, a crofting hamlet at the far east end of Loch Hourn which you can get to by road (turn south off the A87 six miles west of Invergarry). From Kinloch Hourn, a well-marked path winds around the coast to Barrisdale (where there's a year-round bothy and campsite; ⓦ www.barisdale.com) before continuing ten miles to Inverie. The second path into Knoydart starts west of Loch Arkaig, approaching the peninsula via Glen Dessary. Take wet-weather gear, a decent map, plenty of food, warm clothes and a good sleeping bag, and leave your name and expected time of arrival with someone when you set off.

You can rent **mountain bikes** from *The Pier House* and there are plans to develop cycle trails in the area. Your best source of information for walking and wildlife (including guided walks) is the ranger post (☎01687/462242) beside the *Old Forge*.

Accommodation

Most of Knoydart's surprisingly numerous **accommodation** options are concentrated in and around Inverie. If you want to wild camp, for a small donation to the ranger office you can pitch on "long beach" just ten minutes from the only pub.

Hotels and B&Bs

Doune Stone Lodges ☎01687/462667, ⓦ www.doune-knoydart.co.uk. Rebuilt from ruined crofts and offering pine-fitted en-suite doubles right on the shore, this place provides both total isolation and creature comforts, with delicious meals served in the dining room. Owner Martin gives advice about walks and provides OS maps and compasses for wild walks. It's not easy to get to Doune by land, but they'll pick you up by boat from Mallaig (£20pp). Minimum stay three nights. Full board ❼.

The Gathering Inverie ☎01687/460051, ⓦ www .thegatheringknoydart.co.uk. Situated in Inverie itself, this friendly B&B has some bunkbed options and beautiful wood furnishings. ❺

Knoydart Lodge Inverie ☎01687/460129, ⓦ www.knoydartlodge.co.uk. Beautifully located near the pub and the beach, this wooden lodge provides a warm welcome and elegant en-suite rooms. ❺

The Pier House Inverie ☎01687/462347, ⓦ www.thepierhouseknoydart.co.uk. This cosy abode, with fine views over the loch, is the most convenient option for the pub and ranger post. It has its own restaurant with dinner available to nonresidents. ❻

Hostels

Knoydart Foundation Bunkhouse Inverie ☎01687/462242, ⓦ www.knoydart-foundation .com. Simple and straightforward option, with adequate facilities in old steadings a 10min walk from the pub.

Torrie Shieling Inverie ☎01687/462669, ⓔ torrie@knoydart.org. Upmarket, independent hostel just east of the village on the side of the mountain, and offering top-notch self-catering facilities, comfortable wooden beds in four-person rooms and open fires in the convivial living-room. It also has a Land Rover and boat for ferrying guests around the peninsula, and to neighbouring lochs and islands.

Eating

The ⚔ *Old Forge* is one of Scotland's finer pubs, with a convivial atmosphere where visitors and locals mix. You'll find generous bar meals often featuring recently caught seafood, real ales, an open fire, terrific loch views and a good chance of live music of an evening. *The Pier House* (see p.233) is also a good option for eating.

Kyle of Lochalsh and around

As the main gateway to Skye, **Kyle of Lochalsh** used to be an important transit point though, with the construction of the Skye Bridge in 1995, it was left as merely the terminus for the train route from Inverness. Of much more interest to most visitors is nearby **Eilean Donan Castle**, perched at the end of a stone causeway on the shores of **Loch Duich**. It's not hard, however, to step off the tourist trail: remote **Glenelg** peninsula is just to the south side of Loch Duich. A few miles north of Kyle of Lochalsh, the delightful village of **Plockton** is a refreshing alternative to its utilitarian neighbour, with cottages grouped around a bay and Highland cattle wandering the streets. Plockton lies on the southern shore of **Loch Carron**, a long inlet which acts as a dividing line between Kyle of Lochalsh and the splendours of Wester Ross to the north.

Kyle of Lochalsh

KYLE OF LOCHALSH is not particularly attractive and with the building of the **Skye Bridge**, traffic has little reason to stop before rumbling over the channel a mile to the west. Just about the only reason to pause in Kyle is to take a ride on the *Atlantis* (Easter–Oct; ☎01471/822716 or 0800/980 4846, ⓦwww.seaprobeatlantis.com), the UK's only semi-submersible glass-bottomed **boat**, aboard which you can visit the protected seal and bird colonies on Seal Island (£12.50) or see the World War II wreck of HMS *Port Napier* (£15).

Buses run to Kyle of Lochalsh from Glasgow via Fort William and Invergarry (3 daily; 5hr) and from Inverness via Invermoriston (3 daily; 2hr 10min). You should book in advance for all of them (☎0870/550 5050, ⓦwww.citylink .co.uk). All continue at least as far as Portree on Skye. Buses also shuttle across the bridge to Kyleakin on Skye every thirty minutes or so. **Trains** run to Kyle of Lochalsh from Inverness (Mon–Sat 4 daily, 2 on Sun; 2hr 30min), curving north through Achnasheen and Glen Carron; the line is a rail-enthusiast's dream.

Kyle's helpful **tourist office** (April–Oct daily), on top of the small hill near the old ferry jetty, can book **accommodation** – a useful service as there are surprisingly few options. The best hotel is probably the welcoming *Kyle Hotel* in Main Street, with a menu including fresh seafood and game (☎01599/534204, ⓦwww .kylehotel.co.uk; ⑤). Spacious and comfortable *Ardenlea* on Church Street (☎01599/534630, ②) or nearby *A'Chomraich* (☎01599/534210; ②) are both good central B&B options. There's a simple bunkhouse in town, *Cúchulainn's* (☎01599/534492), above a pub across the main street from the tourist office, and you'll find tent pitches at pleasant *Reraig Caravan Park* at Balmacara, a few miles east of Kyle (☎01599/566215, ⓦwww.reraig.com). To **eat**, sample the fresh dishes and delicious home-made puddings of the tiny *Waverley Restaurant* on the main street (5.30–9.30pm, closed Thurs; ☎01599/534337), while for a snack visit *Sheila's Café* opposite the tourist office.

Loch Duich

Skirted on its northern shore by the A87, **Loch Duich**, the boot-shaped inlet just to the south of Kyle of Lochalsh, features prominently on the tourist trail, and buses from all over Europe thunder down the sixteen miles from **SHIEL BRIDGE** to Kyle of Lochalsh on their way to Skye. The main road, which connects to the Great Glen at Invermoriston (see p.204) and Invergarry, makes for a dramatic approach to the loch out of Glen Shiel, where, to the north, the **Five Sisters of Kintail** surge impressively up to heights of 3000ft. There's comfortable **accommodation** to be had in Shiel Bridge itself at the *Kintail Lodge Hotel* (☎01599/511275, ⓦwww.kintaillodgehotel.co.uk; ⑥); the hotel also offers dorm-style **hostel** accommodation in the appropriately named *Wee Bunkhouse* and in twins and singles in the *Trekkers' Lodge*. At **RATAGAN**, a mile or so up the southern shore from Shiel Bridge, the excellent SYHA **hostel** (☎01599/511243, ⓦwww.syha.org.uk; March–Oct) is popular with walkers newly arrived off the Glen Affric trek from Cannich (see p.206). However, for fine food, views and comfort, head for *Grants at Craigellachie* (☎01599/511331, ⓦwww.housebythe loch.co.uk; ⑥) in Ratagan. There's scenic camping at the *Shielbridge Caravan Park & Campsite* (☎01599/511221, ⓦwww.shielbridgecaravanpark.co.uk).

Eilean Donan Castle

After Edinburgh's hilltop fortress, **Eilean Donan Castle** (April to end Oct daily 10am–5pm; opens 9am July–Aug; £5.50; ⓦwww.eileandonancastle.com), ten miles north of Shiel Bridge on the A87, has to be Scotland's most photographed monument. Presiding over the once strategically important confluence of lochs Alsh, Long and Duich, the forbidding crenellated tower rises from the water's edge, joined to the shore by a narrow stone bridge and with sheer mountains as a backdrop. The castle was established in 1230 by Alexander II to protect the area from the Vikings. Later, during a Jacobite uprising in 1719, it was occupied by troops dispatched by the king of Spain to help the **"Old Pretender"**. In response, George I sent frigates to recapture the castle. The formidable walls withstood the bombardment for three days, only falling when the Hanoverian forces came ashore for an assault: having taken the castle, they lit its magazine, shattering its walls.

Hiking in Glen Shiel

Ordnance Survey Explorer map no. 414

The mountains of **Glen Shiel**, sweeping southeast from Loch Duich, offer some of the best hiking routes in Scotland. Rising dramatically from sea level to over 3000ft in less than a couple of miles, they are also exposed to the worst of the west coast's notoriously fickle weather. Don't underestimate either of these two routes. Tracing the paths on a map, they can appear short and easy to follow; nonetheless, walkers come unstuck here every year, often failing to allow enough time to get off the mountain by nightfall or suffering a sudden change in the weather. Only attempt them if you're confident in your walking experience, and have a map and a compass. A detailed trekking guide can also be very useful – *Hill Walks in Northwest Scotland* or *The Munros*, both published by SMC, are recommended. Also make sure to follow the usual safety precautions outlined on p.47.

Taking in a bumper crop of Munros, the **Five Sisters traverse** is deservedly the most popular trek in the area. Allow a full day to complete the whole route. The distinctive chain of mountains across the glen from the Five Sisters is the **Kintail Ridge**, with breathtaking views south across Knoydart and the islands of the west. It's another full-day trek, beginning from the *Cluanie Inn* (see p.204) on the A87.

Thereafter, it lay in ruins until John Macrae-Gilstrap had it rebuilt between 1912 and 1932. Eilean Donan has since featured in *Highlander*, *Entrapment* and the James Bond adventure *The World is Not Enough*. Three floors, including the banqueting hall, the bedrooms and the troops' quarters are open to the public, with various Jacobite and clan relics also on display.

There are a couple of places to **stay** less than a mile away from the castle, in the hamlet of **DORNIE**, though both trade on the location, so you may want to go further afield. There's whitewashed *Dornie Hotel*, Francis Street (☎01599/555205; ⑤), and the *Loch Duich Hotel* (☎01599/555213; ⑤), whose small **restaurant** serves bar snacks and evening meals. On Sunday nights a **folk music** session takes place in the bar. Along from the *Dornie Hotel*, reasonable bar meals and ales are offered at the *Clachan Pub*. However, to escape the hordes, head for the splendidly remote *Whitefalls Retreat* (☎01599/588205) bunkhouse in Camusluinie eight miles north.

The Glenelg peninsula

South of Loch Duich, the isolated and little-known **Glenelg peninsula**, jutting out into the Sound of Sleat, is the crofting area featured in Gavin Maxwell's otter novel *Ring of Bright Water*. Maxwell disguised the identity of this pristine stretch of coast by calling it "Camusfearnà", and it has remained a tranquil backwater in spite of the traffic that trickles through during the summer for the Kylerhea ferry to Skye (see p.284 for details of the museum at Eilean Bàn, once Maxwell's home).

The landward approach to the peninsula is from the east by turning off the fast A87 at Shiel Bridge on Loch Duich, from where a narrow single-track road climbs a tortuous series of switchbacks to the Mam Ratagan Pass (1115ft), affording spectacular views over the awesome **Five Sisters** massif. There's a terrific picnic stop halfway up the road. Following the route of an old drovers' trail, the road, covered by both the postbus and Skyeways bus service (both Mon–Fri) from Kyle of Lochalsh, drops down the other side through Glen More, with the magnificent Kintail Ridge visible to the southeast, towards the peninsula's main settlement, **GLENELG**, on the Sound of Sleat.

Glenelg itself is a row of picturesque whitewashed houses, surrounded by trees. The ⚡ *Glenelg Inn* (☎01599/522273, ⓦwww.glenelg-inn.com; ⓿) is a wonderful spot, boasting seven luxurious (en-suite) **rooms** overlooking the bay and offering moderately priced fresh food all day and occasional live music.

The community-run, six-car **Glenelg–Kylerhea ferry** (daily: Easter May & Sept–Oct 9am–6pm, June–Aug 10am–7pm; ☎01599/522313, ⓦwww.skyeferry .co.uk) shuttles to Skye every fifteen minutes across the Sound of Sleat, one of the fastest tidal races in the UK, from a jetty northwest of the village; minke whale and dolphin may be spotted. In former times, this choppy channel used to be an important drovers' crossing: eight thousand cattle each year were herded head to tail across from Skye to the mainland.

One and a half miles south of Glenelg village, a left turn up Glen Beag leads to the **Glenelg Brochs**, some of the best-preserved Iron Age monuments in the country. Standing in a sheltered stream valley, the circular towers – Dun Telve and Dun Troddan – are thought to have been erected around two thousand years ago to protect the surrounding settlements from raiders. About a third of each main structure remains, with the curving dry-stone walls and internal passages still impressively intact.

Arnisdale

A narrow backroad snakes its way southeast beyond Glenelg village through a scattering of old crofting hamlets and timber forests. The views across the Sound of Sleat to Knoydart grow more spectacular at each bend, reaching a high point at a windy pass that takes in a vast sweep of sea, loch and islands. Below the road at **Sandaig** is where Gavin Maxwell and his otters lived in the 1950s: the site of his house is now marked by a cairn.

Swinging east, the road winds down to the waterside again, following the north shore of Loch Hourn as far as **ARNISDALE**, departure point for the boat to Knoydart (see p.232). Arnisdale is made up of the two hamlets of **Camusbane** and **Corran**, the former consisting of a single row of old cottages ranged behind a long pebble beach, with a massive scree slope behind, while the latter, a mile along the road, is a minuscule whitewashed fishing hamlet at the water's edge. Aside from the arrival of electricity and a red telephone box, the only major addition to this gorgeous hamlet in the last hundred years has been Mrs Nash's friendly **B&B** and tea hut (T01599/522336; ●), with home-baking, breathtaking views and dinner options such as tasty fish pie (order in advance).

Unless you're prepared to walk the nine miles from Glenelg, reaching Arnisdale requires forward planning. With the demise of the postbus service, your only option is to use the MacRae community bus that links Kyle of Lochalsh with *Ratagan Youth Hostel* and Glenelg (plus Arnisdale on request). Book ahead on T01599/511384.

Billy Mackenzie's year-round fast-boat **passenger ferry** from Arnisdale across Loch Hourn to Barrisdale (and to Kinlochhourn) provides an excellent means for walkers and cyclists to explore the most inaccessible parts of the Knoydart peninsula (April–Sept; £12 single; T01599/522247, Wwww.arnisdaleferry.com). The boat can also be chartered for wildlife trips and fishing.

Plockton

A fifteen-minute train ride north of Kyle at the seaward end of islet-studded Loch Carron lies the unbelievably picturesque village of **PLOCKTON**: a chocolate-box row of cottages ranged around the curve of a tiny harbour and backed by a craggy landscape of heather and pine. Originally known as Am Ploc, the settlement was a crofting hamlet until the end of the eighteenth century, when a local laird transformed it into a prosperous fishery, renaming it "Plocktown". In high season it's packed with tourists, yachties and second-home owners, and the unique brilliance of the light has also made it something of an artists' hangout.

The *Haven Hotel*, on Innes Street (T01599/544223; ●), the almost adjacent family-run *Plockton Inn* (T01599/544222, Wwww.plocktoninn.co.uk; ●) and the *Plockton Hotel* on Harbour Street (T01599/544274, Wwww.plocktonhotel .co.uk; ●) all have comfortable **accommodation** within their respective atmospheric walls, live music in summer, and the last also offers terrific harbour and loch views. Of the fifteen or so B&Bs, try comfortable *Mackenzie's* on the main street (T01599/544306; ●) or, beyond the tiny post office, *Heron's Flight* (T01599/544220, Wwww.heronsflight.org; March–Nov ●), with loch views from its two upstairs bedrooms. At the cosy main-street retreat *An Caladh*, "the resting place on the shore" (T01599/544356, Wwww.plockton.uk.com; ●), guests have free use of two wooden sailing dinghies and can watch the owner sail in with his morning catch. On the outskirts of Plockton, meanwhile, opposite the railway station, the attractive *Station Bunkhouse* (T01599/544235) features four- and six-person dorms and an open-plan kitchen and living area; check in at friendly *Nessun Dorma*: the owners also do B&B (●). On the other side of the tracks, *Off the Rails* (T01559/544306, Wwww.plocktonstation.co.uk) provides self-catering accommodation in the delightful wood-panelled station building. Follow the road for Stromferry to *Duncraig Castle* (T01599/544295, Wwww .duncraigcastle.com; ●), which provides B&B in a Scots baronial pile romantically sited across the bay from Plockton.

For a small village, Plockton offers a number of good places to **eat**. Fresh seafood is a staple on the evening menus at *The Haven*, the *Plockton Inn* and the *Plockton Hotel*. The latter two sell local real ales, and it's hard to beat the views over the bay from the hotel. All of the above, plus the modern café/restaurant in *Plockton Stores* at the seafront, serve filling breakfasts, good-value lunches and dinner. For fish and chips, pizza and so on, try the tiny *Harbour* takeaway. Calum's Seal Trips (Easter–Oct daily; £8; free if no seals; ℡01599/544306 or 07761/263828) provides an interesting one-hour excursion as well as a two-hour dolphin trip; Calum also rents out canoes (£10/hr). **Bike rental** (£14/day) is available from Gordon Mackenzie at Plockton Cottages. Call ℡01599/544255 or 07922/934630.

Strathcarron and Kishorn

The sea lochs immediately north of Plockton are the dual inlets of **Loch Kishorn**, so deep it was once used as an oil-rig construction site, and **Loch Carron**, which cuts inland to **STRATHCARRON**, a useful link between Kyle of Lochalsh and Torridon to the north. Strathcarron has a station on the Kyle–Inverness line and provides a postbus connection to Shieldaig (for Applecross) and Torridon (Mon–Sat 10am). Right by Strathcarron station, housed in the old station building, is the helpful Strathcarron **tourist information, shop and post office** (Mon–Sat; ℡01520/722218). A mile south, along the road to Kyle, the *Carron Pottery, Crafts and Restaurant* (℡01520/722488) serves fresh home-made meals and you can browse local crafts. Another mile or so south, **Alladale** (Mon–Sat 10am–5.30pm) is an attractive "artist's garden" with sculptures scattered throughout.

There are several more **accommodation** options two or three miles away in **LOCHCARRON**, a pretty little village of whitewashed cottages stretched out along the northern shore of the loch. One of the best is *Rockvilla Hotel* (℡01520/722379, ⓦwww.rockvilla-hotel.co.uk; ❹), a small hotel in the centre of the village that serves moderately priced bar meals, real ales and good breakfasts using organic yoghurt, breads and local produce. There are numerous B&Bs to choose from, including the five-bedroom *Old Manse* (℡01520/722208, ⓦwww.theoldmanselochcarron.com; ❸), just off the road to Strome Castle. **Camping** is possible at the simple *Wee Campsite* (℡01520/722898; Easter to end Oct), above the village. Further down towards Strome Castle is the much-heralded **Lochcarron Weavers** (ⓦwww.lochcarronweavers.co.uk), housed in an old-fashioned timber-clad workshop, where you can watch weaving demonstrations. Another wet-weather option is the **Lochcarron Old Smiddy Heritage Centre** (April to mid-Oct Mon–Sat 8am–5.30pm, Sun noon–5.30pm; free; ℡01520/722108), a restored smithy and forge established in 1810 on the road between Strathcarron and Lochcarron, which houses a small exhibition and video on local history.

From here, a single-track road leads over the hillside to **Kishorn**, at the head of the loch of the same name. The wooden chalet of the 🏃 *Kishorn Seafood Bar* (℡01520/733240; Mon–Sat 10am–9pm, Sun noon–5pm) is worth a stop to indulge in **fresh local shellfish** or coffee, home-baking and bacon rolls.

Wester Ross

Wester Ross, the western seaboard of the old county of Ross-shire, is widely regarded as the most glamorous stretch of this coast. Here all the classic elements of Scotland's **coastal scenery** – dramatic mountains, sandy beaches, whitewashed crofting cottages and shimmering island views – come together in spectacular fashion. Settlements such as **Applecross** and the peninsulas north and south of

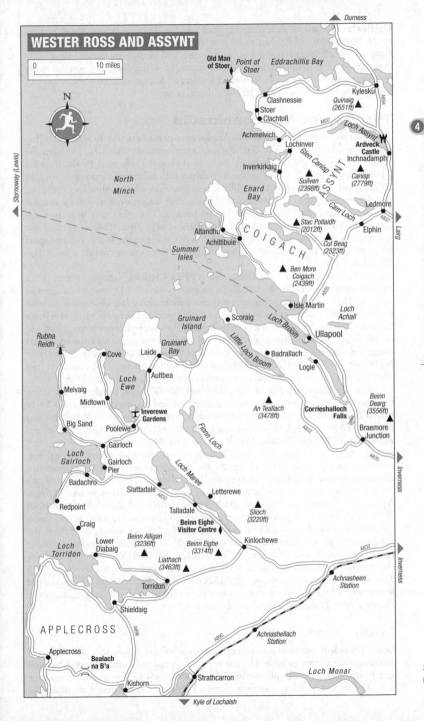

WESTER ROSS AND ASSYNT

0   10 miles

N

Durness

Old Man
of Stoer
*Point of
Stoer*
Eddrachillis Bay

Kylesku

Clashnessie
*Quinaig
(2651ft)*
Stoer
Clachtoll

Achmelvich

Lochinver
**Ardveck
Castle**
Inchnadamph

Loch Assynt

A837

*North
Minch*

Inverkirkaig

*Enard
Bay*

Suilven
(2398ft)

*Canisp
(2779ft)*

Glen Canisp

A S S Y N T

Cam Loch

Ledmore

A837

*Stac Pollaidh
(2012ft)*

C O I G A C H

Altandhu
Achiltibuie

*Summer
Isles*

*Cul Beag
(2523ft)*

Elphin

*Ben More
Coigach
(2439ft)*

A835

Isle Martin

*Loch
Achall*

*Gruinard
Island*

Scoraig

Loch Broom

Ullapool

*Rubha
Reidh*

Cove

Laide

*Gruinard
Bay*

Little Loch Broom

Badrallach

Logie

*Beinn
Dearg
(3556ft)*

Melvaig

Aultbea

*Loch
Ewe*

An Teallach
(3478ft)

**Corrieshalloch
Falls**

Braemore
Junction

A835

Midtown

**Inverewe
Gardens**

A832

Big Sand

Poolewe

Fionn Loch

Inverness

Gairloch

*Loch
Gairloch*

Gairloch
Pier

Loch Maree

Letterewe

Badachro

Slattadale

A832

Redpoint

Talladale

*Slioch
(3220ft)*

**Beinn Eighe
Visitor Centre**

Inverness

Craig

Lower
Diabaig

*Beinn Alligan
(3236ft)*

*Beinn Eighe
(3314ft)*

Kinlochewe

A832

*Loch
Torridon*

*Liathach
(3463ft)*

Achnasheen
Station

Torridon

Shieldaig

A896

A P P L E C R O S S

A890

Achnashellach
Station

Applecross

**Bealach
na B'a**

Loch Monar

Kishorn

Strathcarron

Kyle of Lochalsh

Stornoway (Lewis)

Laing

239

Gairloch maintain an endearing simplicity and sense of isolation. There is some tough but wonderful **hiking** to be had in the mountains around **Torridon** and **Coigach**, while **boat trips** and the prolific sea- and birdlife are another draw. The main settlement is the attractive fishing town of **Ullapool**, the port for ferry services to Stornoway in the Western Isles, and a pleasant enough place to use as a base, not least for its active social and cultural scene.

The Applecross peninsula

The most dramatic approach to the **Applecross peninsula** (the English-sounding name is a corruption of the Gaelic *Apor Crosan*, meaning "estuary") is from the south, up a classic glacial U-shaped valley and over the infamous **Bealach na Bà** ("Pass of the Cattle"). Crossing the forbidding hills behind Kishorn and rising to 2053ft, with a gradient and switchback bends worthy of the Alps, this route – a popular cycling piste – is hair-raising in places, but the panoramic views across the Minch to Raasay and Skye more than compensate. The other way in is from the north: a beautiful coast road that meanders slowly from Shieldaig on Loch Torridon, with tantalizing glimpses of the Skye Cuillin to the south. For transport between Strathcarron and Achasheen, calling at Applecross, contact Dial-A-Bus (℡01520/722205).

The sheltered, fertile coast around **APPLECROSS** village, where Irish missionary monk Maelrhuba founded a monastery in 673 AD, comes as a surprise after the bleakness of the approach: you can wander along lanes banked with wild iris and orchids, and explore beaches and rock pools. There's a small **Heritage Centre** (April–Oct Mon–Sat noon–4pm; Ⓦwww.applecrossheritage.org.uk) overlooking Clachan church and graveyard, and a number of **waymarked trails** along the shore – great for walking off a pub lunch. Local experts Applecross Mountain & Sea (℡01520/744394, Ⓦwww.applecross.uk.com), based at the entrance of the village, organize mountain expeditions and sea-kayaking.

The family-run *Applecross Inn* (℡01520/744262; ❻), right beside the sea, is the focal point of the community, with seven refurbished **rooms** upstairs, and a lively bar (with occasional ceilidh) that serves good, freshly prepared local seafood and produce (noon–9pm). A mile down the road, the excellent *Potting Shed Café and Restaurant* (℡01520/744440; March to end Oct Mon–Sat 11am–8.30pm, Sun 11am–4pm) is a culinary and visual delight, where the walled Victorian garden, woods and sea provide rich pickings for the chefs, who serve delicious dishes in a laid-back atmosphere. Fairly inexpensive in its daytime incarnation as a café, it's pricier in the evening; it operates a rickshaw service to take you to and from Applecross. There's an excellent **B&B** in the village: *Littlehill of My Heart* (℡01520/744432, Ⓦwww.applecrossaccommodation.com; ❹), with classy spacious rooms and a delicious breakfast. You'll also find several good B&Bs on the peninsula: *Tigh na Mara* (℡01520/744277; ❸) at Lonbain provides views of Raasay whilst, nearer Shieldaig, *Tigh a' Chracaich* (℡01520/755367, Ⓦwww .lochtorridon.net; ❸) sits in a small bay with spectacular views over Loch Torridon. *Applecross Campsite* (℡01520/744268, Ⓦwww.applecross.uk.com /campsite) is located as you come into the village from the pass; it features the cheery *Flower Tunnel* café/bar (daily from 9am).

Loch Torridon

Loch Torridon marks the northern boundary of the Applecross peninsula, its awe-inspiring setting enhanced by the appealingly rugged mountains of **Liathach** and **Beinn Eighe**, hulks of reddish 750-million-year-old Torridonian sandstone tipped by streaks of white quartzite. Some 15,000 acres of the massif are under the

Ordnance Survey Explorer map no. 433

With the support of Scottish Natural Heritage (SNH), large tracts of Torridon's Beinn Eighe National Nature Reserve are being replanted with native trees including birch, Scots pine and rowan. Good paths lead through the woodlands, but venture higher and conditions can be difficult, and the weather can change very rapidly. If you're relatively inexperienced but want to do the magnificent ridge walk along the **Liathach** (pronounced "lee-ach") massif, or the strenuous traverse of **Beinn Eighe** (pronounced "ben ay"), you can join a National Trust Ranger Service guided hike (July & Aug; Torridon Countryside Centre; ☎01445/791221).

For those confident to go it alone, one of many possible routes takes you behind Liathach and down the pass, **Coire Dubh**, to the main road in Glen Torridon. This covers thirteen miles and takes in superb landscapes: weather permitting, you can make the rewarding diversion up to the **Coire Mhic Fhearchair**, widely regarded as the most spectacular corrie in Scotland. Allow yourself the whole day.

Even in rough weather, the undulating, seven-mile hike up the coast from **Lower Diabaig**, ten miles northwest of Torridon village, to **Redpoint** is a rewarding one, and on a clear day the views across to Raasay and Applecross are wonderful. If you're staying in Shieldaig, the track that winds up the peninsula running north from the village makes a pleasant ninety-minute round walk. For any of these walks, ensure you are properly equipped with waterproofs, warm clothing and provisions.

protection of the National Trust for Scotland, which also looks after **Shieldaig Island**, where a heronry has been established among the tall Scots pines. The island lies in a sheltered bay off the prim but pretty village of **SHIELDAIG** ("herring bay") on the southern shore of Loch Torridon, where the popular Shieldaig Fete is held at the beginning of August every year.

There's an attractive small **hotel** and snug bar by the shore in the village, ⚘ *Tigh-an-Eilean* (☎01520/755251, ⓦwww.tighaneilean.co.uk; March–Oct; ⓞ), with live music every Friday in summer. The *Rivendell* B&B (☎01520/755250; ⓞ) is nearby and a simple **campsite** affords terrific loch views a little way up the hill. At **TORRIDON** village, at the east end of the loch, the main road heads inland through Glen Torridon, while the minor road runs through the village along the northern shore. At the road junction, past the Torridon Mountain Rescue post, a **Countryside Centre** (Easter to end Sept Mon–Sat 10am–5pm; £3) gives information on local geology, flora and fauna, plus advice on mountain walks.

On the south side of the loch stands one of the area's grandest **hotels**, the smart, rambling *Torridon* (☎01445/791242, ⓦwww.thetorridon.com; ⓞ), a Victorian building set amid well-tended lochside grounds. The hotel also runs the adjacent *Torridon Inn* (March–Oct; ⓞ), a cyclist- and walker-friendly modern farmstead conversion with neat twins and doubles and a moderately priced bar/bistro serving real ales, boar sausage and the like. Torridon Activities, run from the hotel, offers pursuits including hillwalking, mountain biking and sea-kayaking. Close to the Countryside Centre is a rather unsightly SYHA **hostel** (☎0870/004 1154, ⓦwww.syha.org.uk; March–Oct) and a council-run **campsite**.

Loch Maree

About eight miles north of Loch Torridon, **Loch Maree**, dotted with Caledonian-pine-covered islands, is one of the west's scenic highlights, best viewed from the A832 road that drops down to its southeastern tip through Glen Docherty. At the southeastern end of the loch, the A896 from Torridon meets the A832 from

Achnasheen at small **KINLOCHEWE** (Ⓦ www.torridon-mountains.com), a good base if you're heading into the hills. There's a twelve-bed **bunkhouse** as well as good meals at the *Kinlochewe Hotel* (Ⓣ 01445/760253, Ⓦ www.kinlochewehotel .co.uk; ❺). The corrugated-iron *Whistle Stop Café* is handy for breakfast, hot food and cakes, while Kinlochewe Store opposite the hotel contains the post office (which opens Mon–Sat 9–11am) and the basic *Teapot Café*, and sells outdoor kit including maps and camping gas.

The A832 skirts the southern shore of Loch Maree, passing the **Beinn Eighe Nature Reserve**, the UK's oldest wildlife sanctuary. Parts of the reserve are forested with Caledonian pinewood, which once covered the whole of the country, and it is home to pine martens, wildcats, buzzards and golden eagles. A mile north of Kinlochewe, the well-run **Beinn Eighe Visitor Centre** (Easter & May–Oct daily 10am–5pm) on the A832, informs visitors about the area's rare species. Outside, the "talking trails" provide an easy walk through the vicinity, while several interesting **walks** start from the car park, a mile north of the visitor centre. There's also a basic campsite here.

Loch Maree is surrounded by some of Scotland's finest **deerstalking** country: the remote, privately owned Letterewe Lodge on the north shore, accessible only by helicopter or boat, lies at the heart of a famous deer forest. In 1877, Queen Victoria stayed at the wonderfully sited *Loch Maree Hotel*, now an exclusive self-catering lodge. Just 100m away, set back from the loch and road amidst trees, *The Old Mill and Highland Lodge* (Ⓣ 01445/760271, Ⓦ www.theoldmillhighlandlodge .co.uk; ❽) is a pleasant if pricey place to **stay**.

Gairloch and around

GAIRLOCH spreads around the northeastern corner of the wide sheltered bay of Loch Gairloch. In summer it thrives as a low-key holiday resort, with several tempting sandy beaches and some excellent coastal walks within easy reach. The township is divided into pretty, distinct areas spread over nearly two miles of shoreline: to the south, in **Flowerdale Bay**, are the old pier and harbour; past the bank, at the turn-off to Melvaig, **Achtercairn** is the centre of Gairloch; and along the north side of the bay, on the road to Melvaig, are the strung-out crofts of **Strath**. The main supermarket and helpful **tourist office** (June–Sept daily; Oct–May Mon–Sat) are in Achtercairn, right by the **Gairloch Heritage Museum** (March–Sept daily 10am–5pm; Oct Mon–Sat 10am–1.30pm; £3; Ⓦ www.gairlochheritagemuseum .org), whose eclectic, appealing displays range from a mock-up of a croft house to an early knitting machine. Probably the most interesting section is the archive made by elderly locals – an array of photographs, maps, genealogies, lists of place names and taped recollections, mostly in Gaelic. The little whitewashed **Solas Gallery** (Ⓣ 01445/712626, Ⓦ www.solasgallery.co.uk) is worth a look for its displays of local ceramics and watercolours.

Gairloch has a good choice of **accommodation**, but you might prefer to stay out along the road north to Melvaig or south to Redpoint (see p.241). There are some good **B&Bs**: in Strath, try Miss Mackenzie's child-friendly *Duisary* (Ⓣ 01445/712252, Ⓦ www.duisary.freeserve.co.uk; April–Oct; ❶). At the southern edge of the village, just before the turn-off to Badachro, the atmospheric and tastefully furnished *Kerrysdale House* (Ⓣ 01445/712292, Ⓦ www .kerrysdalehouse.co.uk; ❷) is set back in its own lovely gardens. North of town you'll find the *Sands Holiday Centre* (Ⓣ 01445/712152, Ⓦ www.sandsholiday centre.co.uk) for **camping**.

For **food**, head for the harbour, where the *Old Inn* (Ⓦ www.theoldinn.net; ❺) offers moderately priced seafood on its bar menu, a very good range of Scottish real ales and snug rooms. There's also good-value lunch and evening fare at the

Harbour Lights Café; for **snacks**, try the bistro-style *Blueprint Café* across the road – where you'll also find the chip shop.

One leisurely way to explore the coast is on a wildlife-spotting **cruise**. There are several operators, but try the pier-based Gairloch Marine Life Centre & Cruises (Easter–Oct; from £10; ☎01445/712636, ⓦwww.porpoise-gairloch.co.uk), who run enjoyable trips across the bay in search of dolphins, seals and even the odd whale. They also deploy a mini-sub that sends underwater pictures back to the boat whilst a hydrophone picks up audio from the sea life. Take a cruise, go sea-angling or **rent a boat** for the day through the Gairloch Chandlery (☎01445/712458), at the pier, or go **pony trekking** with Gairloch Trekking Centre (☎01445/712652, ⓦwww.gairlochtrekkingcentre.co.uk; closed Thurs). From the car park on the north side of the Flowerdale river, a sheltered glen provides a scenic woodland walk: ask at the tourist office for directions. For bike rental, call ☎01445/712030.

Rubha Reidh and around

The area's real attraction is its beautiful **coastline**. To get to one of the most impressive stretches, head around the north side of the bay and follow the single-track B8021 to **BIG SAND**, which has a cleaner and quieter **beach** than the one in Gairloch, as well as an excellent **campsite** just above the beach (☎01445/712152). At Carn Dearg, just before Big Sand, a former hunting lodge is now an SYHA **hostel** (☎01445/712219, ⓦwww.syha.org.uk; April–Sept), spectacularly set on the edge of a cliff with views to Skye. The B8021, and the postbus from Gairloch, terminate at the tiny crofting hamlet of Melvaig, where a white-stone former Free Church provides a rustic setting for simple, hearty bar meals and a pint at the *Melvaig Inn* (Tues–Sun; ☎01445/771212, ⓦwww.melvaig-inn.co.uk).

From Melvaig, it's another three miles out to **Rubha Reidh** (pronounced "roo-a-ray"). You can stay at the headland's still operational *Rua Reidh Lighthouse* (☎01445/771263, ⓦwww.ruareidh.co.uk; ❶), which was built in 1910 and looks straight out to the Outer Hebrides. Comfortable accommodation options include a bunkhouse, double and family rooms (meals extra; book ahead in high season). Fran, the cheerful owner, can provide breakfast (£6) and a pre-booked evening meal (£15). Guided walking and climbing courses are also offered.

Around the headland from Rubha Reidh lies the secluded and beautiful **Camas Mòr** beach, a spot sought out by expert surfers. For a great half-day walk, follow the marked footpath inland (southeast) from here along the base of a sheer scarp slope, and past a string of lochans, ruined crofts and a remote wood to **MIDTOWN** on the east side of the peninsula, four miles north of Poolewe on the B8057. However, unless you leave a car at the end of the trail or arrange to be picked up, you'll have to walk or hitch back to Gairloch.

Badachro and Redpoint

Three miles south of Gairloch, a narrow single-track lane (built with the Destitution Funds raised during the nineteenth-century potato famine) winds west from the main A832, past wooded coves and inlets on its way south of the loch to **BADACHRO**, a sleepy former fishing village in a very attractive setting with a wonderful pub, the *Badachro Inn* (ⓦwww.badachroinn.com), right by the water's edge, where you can sit in the beer garden watching the boats come and go and tuck into quite pricey fresh seafood with a real ale. At the eastern edge of Badachro, secluded *Shieldaig Lodge Hotel* (☎01445/741250, ⓦwww.shieldaiglodge.com; ❸) has reasonable accommodation in a former Victorian shooting lodge. Accessed via a floating bridge and a short drive away, *Dry Island* is a great self-catering option (☎01445/741263, ⓦwww.dryisland.co.uk). The owner runs two-hour "creel trips" (£17.50) from his pier, giving you the chance to see octopus, prawns and lobster being hauled in. Evening fishing trips for mackerel can also be organized.

Beyond Badachro, the road winds for five more miles along the shore to **REDPOINT**, a straggling hamlet with beautiful beaches of peach-coloured sand and great views to Raasay, Skye and the Western Isles. It also marks the trailhead for the wonderful coast walk to Lower Diabaig (see box, p.241). Even if you don't fancy a full-blown hike, following the path a mile or so brings you to the exquisite **beach** hidden on the south side of the headland.

Poolewe and around

It's a fifteen-minute hop by bus over the headland from Gairloch to the trim little village of **POOLEWE**, which sits by a small bay at the sheltered southern end of Loch Ewe, where the (very short) River Ewe rushes down from Loch Maree. One of the area's best **walks** begins near here, signposted from the layby-cum-viewpoint on the main A832, a mile south of the village. It takes a couple of hours to follow the easy trail across open craggy moorland to the shores of **Loch Maree** (see p.241), and thence to the car park at Slattadale, seven miles southeast of Gairloch. If you reach the *Loch Maree Hotel* before 5pm (June–Sept Mon–Sat) you should be able to pick up the Wester bus from Inverness back to Gairloch and Poolewe.

The ten-mile drive along the small side-road running along the west shore of Loch Ewe leads to **COVE**, where you'll find an atmospheric cave that was used by the severe Presbyterian "Wee Frees" as a church into the twentieth century; it's a perilous scramble up, however, and there's little here to see other than the cave.

For **accommodation** Poolewe has a popular and well-equipped **campsite** (☎01445/781249; May–Oct), whilst the family-run and refurbished *Poolewe Hotel* (☎01445/781241, ⓦwww.poolewehotel.co.uk; ⑤) on the Cove road, serves seafood and game dinners. For a taste of luxury, relax in the sumptuous interior of the *Pool House Hotel* (☎01445/781272, ⓦwww.poolhousehotel.co.uk; ❸), which once belonged to Osgood MacKenzie (see below). At Aultbea, *Cartmel* (☎01445/731375, ⓦwww.cartmelguesthouse.com; ❸) is a welcoming 1970s four-bedroom guesthouse. In Poolewe itself, *The Bridge Cottage Café and Gallery*, in a neat white cottage opposite the post office, offers home-baking and tasty, freshly prepared snacks.

Inverewe Gardens

Half a mile across the bay from Poolewe on the A832, **Inverewe Gardens** (daily: April–May & Sept 10am–5pm; June–Aug 10am–6pm; Oct 10am–4pm Nov–March 10am–3pm; NTS; £8.50), a verdant oasis of foliage and riotously colourful flower collections, forms a vivid contrast to the wild, heathery crags of the adjoining coast. The gardens were the brainchild of **Osgood MacKenzie**, who inherited the surrounding twelve-thousand-acre estate from his stepfather, the laird of Gairloch, in 1862. Taking advantage of the area's famously temperate climate, Mackenzie collected plants from all over the world for his walled garden, which still forms the nucleus of the complex. Protected from Loch Ewe's corrosive salt breezes by a dense brake of Scots pine, rowan, oak, beech and birch trees, the fragile plants flourished on rich soil brought here as ballast on Irish ships to overlay the previously infertile beach gravel and sea grass. By the time MacKenzie died in 1922, his garden sprawled over the whole peninsula, surrounded by a hundred acres of woodland.

Thousands of visitors pour through here annually, but the place rarely feels overcrowded. Interconnected by a labyrinthine network of twisting paths and walkways, a few accessible by wheelchair, more than a dozen gardens feature exotic plant collections from as far afield as Chile, China, Tasmania and the Himalayas. Mid-May to mid-June is the best time to see the rhododendrons and azaleas, while the herbaceous garden reaches its peak in July and August, as does the wonderful Victorian vegetable and flower garden beside the sea. You'll need at least a couple of hours, particularly if you explore the Pinewood Trail and still leave time for the **visitor centre** (April–Sept daily 9.30am–5pm), which is the starting point for **guided walks**. There's also a pleasant **restaurant**.

Gruinard Bay and Little Loch Broom

At **LAIDE**, ten miles north of Poolewe, the road skirts the shores of **Gruinard Bay**, offering fabulous views and, at the inner end of the bay, some excellent sandy beaches. During World War II, the bay's **Gruinard Island** was used as a testing ground for biological warfare. After much protest, the Ministry of Defence had the island decontaminated and it was finally declared "safe" in 1990. As befits the stunning scenery, there are some lovely **accommodation** choices all along this stretch, including the pleasant *Gruinard Bay* campsite (℡01445/731225) and the welcoming *Old Smiddy Guest House* (℡01445/731696, ⓦwww.oldsmiddyguesthouse.co.uk; ④) on the main road in Laide.

Corrieshalloch Gorge

The road heads inland before joining the A835, the main Inverness–Ullapool road, at **Braemore Junction**, above the head of Loch Broom. Just nearby, and easily accessible from a layby on the A835, the spectacular 50m **Falls of Measach** plunge through the mile-long Corrieshalloch Gorge, formed by glacial melt-waters. You can overlook the cascades from a precarious observation platform, or from the impressive, wobbly Victorian suspension bridge that spans the chasm, whose 60m vertical sides are draped in wych elm, goat willow and bird cherry. The A835 from the head of Loch Broom to Ullapool is one of the so-called **Destitution Roads**, built to give employment to local people during the nineteenth-century potato famines.

Ullapool

ULLAPOOL (ⓦwww.ullapool.co.uk), the northwest's principal centre of population, was founded at the height of the herring boom in 1788 by the British Fisheries Society, on a sheltered arm of land jutting into Loch Broom. The grid-plan town is still an important fishing centre, though the **ferry** link to Stornoway on Lewis (see p.310) means that in high season it's swamped by visitors. You can make a day-long return ferry/bus visit (summer only Wed & Fri) to Lewis (departs Ullapool 9.30am and Stornoway at 7pm with Caledonian MacBrayne ℡01854/612358; £30.20). Though busy, Ullapool remains a hugely appealing place and a good base for exploring the northwest Highlands. Regular **buses** run from here to Inverness and Durness and there is a reasonable service north to Achiltibuie (Mon–Sat; ℡01463/222444) and southwest to Poolewe and Gairloch (Mon, Wed, Thurs & Sat; ℡01445/712255). Accommodation is plentiful and Ullapool is an obvious hideaway if the weather is bad, with cosy pubs and a lively **arts centre**, *The Ceilidh Place*.

Arrival and information

Forming the backbone of its grid plan, Ullapool's two main thoroughfares run parallel, with **Shore Street** on the lochside and **Argyle Street** further inland. **Buses** stop at the pier, in the town centre near the ferry dock, from where it's easy to get your bearings. The well-run **tourist office** (April–May Mon–Sat; June–Aug daily; Oct Mon–Fri; call ℡01854/612486 for winter opening hours) on Argyle Street offers an accommodation booking service.

Accommodation

Ullapool has all kinds of **places to stay**, including a couple of welcoming hostels and some decent guesthouses and B&Bs, though it's worth booking ahead to get any of the places listed below.

Hotels, guesthouses and B&Bs

The Ceilidh Place West Argyle St ☎01854/612103. Renowned for its live music and ceilidhs, the tastefully furnished interior of this charismatic place includes thirteen en-suite bedrooms, an excellent café/bar and bookshop specializing in Scottish literature, history and art. You can also call to reserve a bed in its small bunkhouse (❶), directly across the road. ❼

Dromnan Garve Rd ☎01854/612333, ⓦwww.dromnan.co.uk. Excellent B&B run by welcoming hosts, who serve up a hearty breakfast. Has lovely sea views, and from the dining area you can walk onto the patio or down to the shore. ❸

Ferry Boat Inn Shore St ☎01854/612366, ⓦwww.ferryboat-inn.com. Traditional inn right on the waterfront with a convivial atmosphere and reasonable food. ❺

Harbour Lights Hotel Garve Rd ☎01854/612222, ⓦwww.harbour-lights.co.uk. A modern, family-run hotel with nineteen comfortable en-suite bedrooms. ❸

Point Cottage 22 West Shore St ☎01854/612494, ⓦwww.pointcottage.co.uk. Rustic, very well-equipped B&B at the quieter end of the seafront. Guests can borrow OS maps that have been already marked up with walking routes. ❸

The Shieling Garve Rd ☎01854/612947, ⓦwww.thesheilingullapool.co.uk. Another friendly, comfortable guesthouse overlooking the loch, with

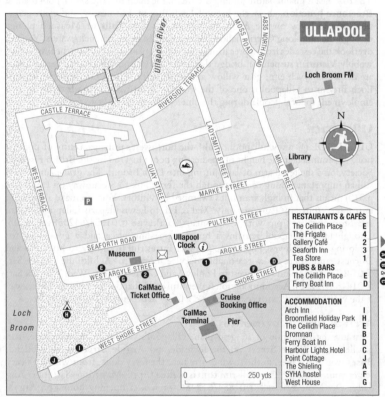

RESTAURANTS & CAFÉS
The Ceilidh Place	E
The Frigate	4
Gallery Café	2
Seaforth Inn	3
Tea Store	1

PUBS & BARS
The Ceilidh Place	E
Ferry Boat Inn	D

ACCOMMODATION
Arch Inn	I
Broomfield Holiday Park	H
The Ceilidh Place	E
Dromnan	B
Ferry Boat Inn	D
Harbour Lights Hotel	C
Point Cottage	J
The Shieling	A
SYHA hostel	F
West House	G

Walks and hikes around Ullapool

Ordnance Survey Explorer map nos. 439, 436 & 435

Ullapool lies at the start of several excellent **hiking trails**, ranging from sedate shoreside ambles to long and strenuous ascents of Munros. However, the weather here can change very quickly, so take the necessary precautions (see p.47). More detailed descriptions of the routes outlined below are available from the hostel on Shore Street; hostellers can also rent the relevant up-to-date OS maps – essential for the hill walks.

An easy **half-day ramble** begins at the north end of Quay Street: cross the walkway/footbridge here and follow the river bank on the far side left towards the sea. Walk past the golf course and follow the shoreline as best you can for around two miles until you reach a hilltop lighthouse, from where you gain fine views across the sea to the Summer Isles. Return the same way or via the main A835 road.

For a harder **half-day hike**, head north along Mill Street on the east edge of town to Broom Court retirement home, trailhead for the Ullapool hillwalk (look for the sign next to the electricity substation). A rocky path zigzags steeply up from the roadside to the summit of **Meall Mòr** (886ft), where there are great views of the area's major peaks. This is also a prime spot for botanists, with a rich array of plants and flowers, including two insect-eating species: sundew and butterwort. The path then drops sharply down the heather-clad northeast side of Meall Mòr into **Glen Achall**, where you turn left onto the surfaced road running past the limestone quarry; the main road back to Ullapool lies a further thirty minutes walk west.

A right turn where the path meets the road will take you through the **Rhidorroch** estate to Loch Achall and the start of a **two-day hike** along an old drovers' trail across the wilderness of the Highlands to **Croick** (see p.270). It should not be undertaken alone or without proper gear, and leave someone details of your route before setting off. Start off at East Rhidorroch Lodge, ignoring the suspension bridge and striking up the steep hill ahead onto open moorland. The halfway point is the small, well-maintained **Knockdamph bothy** by secluded Loch nan Daimh.

immaculate, spacious rooms (4 and 5 have the best views), superb breakfasts and a sauna. Free fishing for brown trout is also available. ❸
West House West Argyle St ☏01854/613126, ⓦwww.westhousebandb.co.uk. A former manse, centrally located and newly refurbished with four bright rooms. ❹

Hostel and campsite

Broomfield Holiday Park West Shore St ☏01854/612020. Large, good-value campsite, a 5min walk from town. Exposed to the wind off Loch Broom but offers great views and warm showers.
SYHA Hostel Shore St ☏01854/612254, ⓦwww.syha.org.uk. Busy hostel on the front, with internet access, laundry and lots of good information about local walks. March–Oct.

The Town

Day or night, most of the action in Ullapool centres on the **harbour**, which has an authentic and salty air, especially when the boats are in. By day, attention focuses on the comings and goings of the ferry, fishing boats and smaller craft, while, in the evening, yachts swing on the current, the shops stay open late, and customers from the *Ferry Boat Inn* line the sea wall. During summer, both the *Summer Queen* (☏01854/612472, ⓦwww.summerqueen.co.uk) and *Centaur* fast-rib boat (☏01854/633708, ⓦwww.sea-scape.co.uk) run wildlife cruises and trips to the uninhabited **Summer Isles** to view sea-bird colonies, grey seals, dolphins, porpoises and the occasional whale.

The only conventional attraction in town is the award-winning **museum**, in the old parish church on West Argyle Street (Easter to end Oct Mon–Sat 10am–5pm;

by prior arrangement in winter; ℡01854/612987; £3), where photographs, audiovisual and touch-screen displays provide an insight into life in a Highland community, including crofting, fishing, local religion and emigration. During the Clearances, Ullapool was one of the ports through which evicted crofters left to start new lives abroad.

Eating, drinking and entertainment

There are several good **pubs** in Ullapool; notably the *Ferry Boat Inn* (or "FBI"), where you can enjoy a pint of real ale at the lochside – midges permitting, and the *Arch Inn* on West Shore Street. **Live Scottish folk music** is a special feature at *The Ceilidh Place* and often at the *FBI*. The atmospheric *Ceilidh Place* also periodically holds art exhibitions.

Though the interior is hardly intimate, the busy *Seaforth Inn* on Quay Street serves terrific-value mains and starters, including a scrumptious fish pie. This busy bar/restaurant also hosts regular live-music performances, and there's an adjacent chip shop. Though pricier, *The Ceilidh Place* is another popular destination, offering lunch, snacks and dinners in a pleasant bistro area. On the shorefront, the *Frigate* is a good bet for coffee and sandwiches. For a no-frills option, tiny locals' favourite the *Tea Store* on Argyle Street (opposite the tourist information) serves up hearty, inexpensive breakfasts, home-baking and a refreshing cuppa. Nearby, *Gallery Café* on West Argyle Street, above an outdoor shop, provides all-day breakfasts, soup and sandwiches and has changing exhibitions of local landscape photography.

Ceilidhs

The **ceilidh** is essentially an informal, homespun kind of entertainment, the word being Gaelic for a "visit". In remote Highland communities, talents and resources were pooled, people gathering to play music, sing, recite poems and dance. The dances themselves are thought to be ancient in origin; the Romans wrote that the Caledonians danced with abandon round swords stuck in the ground, a practice echoed in today's formalized sword dance, where the weapons are crossed on the floor and a quick-stepping dancer skips over and around them.

Highland ceilidhs, fuelled by whisky and largely extemporized, must have been an intoxicating, riotous means of fending off winter gloom. Like much of clan culture, however, the traditions died or were forced underground after the defeat of the Highlanders at Culloden and the passing of the 1747 Act of Proscription, which forbade the wearing of the plaid and other expressions of Highland identity.

Ceilidhs were enthusiastically revived in the reign of tartan-fetishist Queen Victoria, and in the twentieth century became the preserve of the village hall and hotel ballroom, buoyed to some extent by the popularity of jaunty 1950s TV programmes such as *The White Heather Club*, which showed rather prim demonstrations of Scottish country dancing and made a star out of master accordionist Jimmy Shand. More recently, though, the ceilidh has thrown off some of these stale associations, with places such as *The Ceilidh Place* in Ullapool and the *Taybank Hotel* in Dunkeld (see p.148) restoring some of its spontaneous, infectious fun to a night of Scottish music and dancing. Whether performed by a band of skilled traditional musicians or in freer form by lively, younger players, ceilidh music is pretty irresistible, and it's quite common to find all generations gathering for an evening's entertainment. Ceilidh dances can look complex and often involve you being whirled breathlessly round the room, though in fact most of the popular ones, like the *Gay Gordons* and eightsome reel, are reasonably simple and are commonly explained or "called" beforehand by the bandleader.

Assynt

If you've come as far as Ullapool it really is worth continuing further north into the dramatic, remote and highly distinctive hills of **Assynt**, which marks the transition from Wester Ross into Sutherland. One of the least populated areas in Europe, this is a landscape not of mountain ranges but of extraordinary peaks, rising individually from the moorland. The area boasts some of the world's oldest rock formations, and occasional signs by the roadside highlight the whole area's considerable geological importance (W www.northwest-highlands-geopark.org.uk). It's an area of peaceful, slow backroads, which, after twisting past idyllic crofts, invariably end up at a deserted beach or windswept headland with superb clear-day views west to the Outer Hebrides. **Lochinver**, midway along the west coast and still an important fishing port, is the main settlement, though the crofting villages along the coast, like those around **Achiltibuie**, are more appealing. If you're keen to climb the mountains, head for **Inchnadamph**, which sits below the region's two Munros.

Coigach

Coigach (W www.coigach.com) is the peninsula immediately to the north of Loch Broom, accessible via a slow, winding, single-track road that leaves the A835 ten miles north of Ullapool, squeezing between the northern shore of Loch Lurgainn and the lower slopes of Cul Beag (2523ft) and craggy Stac Pollaidh (2012ft). To the southeast, the awesome bulk of Ben More Coigach (2439ft) presides over the district, which contains some spectacular coastal scenery. Coigach's main settlement is **ACHILTIBUIE**, an old crofting village scattered across the hillside above a series of beaches and rocks that taper into the Atlantic. A mile offshore lies Tanera Mor, the largest island of the **Summer Isles**. For **boat** trips round the isles, including some time ashore on Tanera Mor, *Hectoria* (T 01854/622315) usually runs twice a day from the Badentarbert pier at Achiltibuie (Easter–Oct; 3hr 30min; £22). Once on the island, you can buy "Summer Isles" stamps from the post office, rent kayaks or take a stroll.

The other attraction in the area is the **Achiltibuie Smokehouse** (T 01854/622353, W www.summerislesfoods.co.uk; free) at **ALTANDHU**, along the coast road west of Achiltibuie. Here you can see meat, fish and game being cured in the traditional way and buy some afterwards. Next to this, the *Am Fuaran* bar serves lunches, snacks and evening meals, including fresh hand-dived scallops, and like everywhere else along this stretch, enjoys terrific views.

For **accommodation**, the *Summer Isles Hotel* (T 01854/622282, W www .summerisleshotel.co.uk; Easter–Oct; ⑦) enjoys a perfect setting with views over the islands. It's also a memorable (if pricey) Michelin-starred spot for a seafood lunch or dinner. Of Achiltibuie's several **B&Bs**, *Dornie House* (T 01854/622271, E dorniehousebandb@aol.com; Easter–Nov; ①), halfway to Altandhu, is welcoming and provides huge breakfasts. Four miles west of the village there's a basic campsite at *Achnahaird Farm* (T 01854/622348; Easter–Sept).

There's also a beautifully situated twenty-bed SYHA **hostel** (T 01854/622482, W www.syha.org.uk; May–Sept), three miles southeast of Achiltibuie down the coast at **Achininver**, handy for accessing Coigach's mountain hikes. If you're experienced and can use a map and compass, you can walk the ten-mile path to the hostel from Ullapool.

Lochinver and around

The twisting, narrow road north from Achiltibuie through Inverkirkaig is unremittingly spectacular, threading its way through a tumultuous landscape of heaving valleys, moorland and bare rock, past the startling shapes of Cul Beag (2523ft), Cul Mor (2785ft) and the distinctive sugar-loaf **Suilven** (2398ft). You pass thick-walled, idyllic crofts and the start of several community woodland walking trails, before a sheltered bay heralds your arrival at **LOCHINVER**, sixteen miles north of Ullapool (although more than thirty by road). One of the busier fishing harbours in Scotland, it's a workaday and not very attractive place from where large trucks head off for the continent. The **tourist office** (April–Oct Mon–Sat, June–Sept also Sun; ℡01571/844330) in the excellent **Assynt Visitor Centre** gives an interesting rundown on the area's geology, wildlife and history and has a CCTV link to a nearby heronry. A handy leaflet, *Walks around Assynt*, is available from the tourist office, highlighting 31 low- and high-level walks.

Lochinver has a wide choice of good **B&Bs**. On the north side of the loch, *Davar* (℡01571/844501, ⓦwww.davar-lochinver.co.uk; March–Oct; ❷) is very welcoming, while you'll enjoy fine views and comfort in three-bedroom *Veyatie B&B* (℡01571/844424, ⓦwww.veyatie-scotland.co.uk; ❹) in Baddidarrach.

Walks in Coigach and Assynt

Ordnance Survey Explorer map no. 442

Of Coigach's and Assynt's spectacular array of idiosyncratic peaks, **Stac Pollaidh** (2012ft) counts as the most accessible and popular hike – so much so, in fact, that Inverpolly National Nature Reserve has had to extensively repair and re-route the main path up the mountain from the car park on the Achiltibuie road. The path now leads walkers around to the northern side of the hill before climbing steeply. You'll need a head for heights to explore the jagged summit ridge extensively, and this is one hill where you should turn back from bagging the summit if you feel uncertain doing some basic rock-climbing.

Suilven (2399ft), described by poet Norman McCaig as "one sandstone chord that holds up time in space", is the most memorable of the Assynt peaks to look at, though the ascent is a tough eight-hour outing, including the boggy five-mile walk to its base. From the A837 at Elphin, head round the north of Cam Loch then through the glen between Canisp and Suilven, until you pick up the path that aims for the saddle – Bealach Mor – in the middle of Suilven's summit ridge, from where the path to the top is straightforward. The return is by the same route, although at the saddle you could choose to turn southwest for the route to Inverkirkaig, while a descent down the northwestern side can lead either back to Elphin or west to Lochinver by way of Glen Canisp.

The highest peaks in Assynt are the neighbouring **Conival** and **Ben More Assynt**, often climbed for their status as Munros (see p.46), despite the fact that they're less distinctive than their neighbours, and are generally known for their rough harshness and bleak landscape. The route follows the track up Glen Dubh from Inchnadamph, staying to the north of the river as you aim for the saddle between Conival and the peak to the north, Beinn an Fhurain. Once on the ridge, turn southeast to climb to the top of Conival then turn east along a high, exposed ridge to the top of Ben More. The entire walk, including the return to Inchnadamph, takes five to six hours.

If you're looking for something less testing, there are some classic **coastal walks** immediately north of Lochinver. From **Baddidarrach**, opposite Lochinver village on the north side of the rivermouth, a path with fantastic views of the Assynt peaks leads over heather slopes to Loch Dubh and down to **Achmelvich** (a 1hr walk). From here there's a sporadically signposted but reasonable path to **Clachtoll** (about 2hr) past delightful sandy coves, grassy knolls, old water mills and rocks to clamber across at low tide. At Clachtoll there's a dramatic split rock (after which the crofting hamlet is named) and an Iron Age fort. More dramatic is the ninety-minute clifftop walk from Stoer lighthouse along to the famous stack, **The Old Man of Stoer** (220ft).

Closer to the tourist office, comfortable *Polcraig* (℡ 01571/844429, ⓔ cathelmac @aol.com; ❷) serves up fabulous breakfasts and can arrange fishing. Combining fine dining with a relaxed, upmarket stay, the beautifully appointed *Albannach Hotel* (℡ 01571/844407, Ⓦ www.thealbannach.co.uk; ❾; March–Dec; no children under 12) at Baddidarrach, an attractive nineteenth-century building set in a walled garden, offers sumptuous accommodation and memorable five-course dining based on croft-reared produce and fresh seafood; non-guests can dine for £49. Lochinver's most popular **food** halt is the ⚶ *Larder Riverside Bistro* on the main street, where the moderately priced fare includes excellent home-made pies such as wild boar, port and prune served with mash. Reasonably priced bar meals and a good selection of real ales are available at the *Caberfeidh* next door, which is also the most convivial place to head for a drink.

Inverkirkaig Falls

Approaching Lochinver from the south, the road bends sharply through a wooded valley where a signpost for **Falls of Kirkaig** marks the start of a long but gentle **walk** to the base of **Suilven** – the most distinctive mountain in Scotland, its huge sandstone dome rising above the heather boglands of Assynt. Serious hikers use the path to approach the mighty peak, but you can also follow it for an easy five-mile, three-hour (return) ramble, taking in a waterfall and a secluded loch. Just by the start of the trail but tucked away among the dark pine trees, **Achins Bookshop** must rate as the Highland's best-hidden nook. You can browse the shelves of heavyweight classics and local-interest titles, then head to the **coffee shop** for soup or home-baking. Fishing permits are also available here.

North of Lochinver

Heading **north** from Lochinver, there are two possible routes: the fast A837, which runs eastwards along the shore of Loch Assynt (see p.252) to join the north-bound A894, or the narrow, more scenic B869 **coast road** that locals dub the "Breakdown Zone", because its ups and downs claim so many victims during summer. Hugging the indented shoreline, this route offers superb views as well as a number of rewarding side-trips to beaches and dramatic cliffs.

Unusually, most of the land and lochs around here are owned by local crofters rather than wealthy landlords. Helped by grants and private donations, the **Assynt Crofters' Trust** (Ⓦ www.assyntcrofters.co.uk) made history in 1993 when it pulled off the first-ever community buyout of estate land in Scotland. Subsequent agreements have now given Little Assynt Estate over 1200 hectares of the Assynt hinterland to carefully nurture and manage. The Trust owns some of the lucrative fishing rights to the area, too, selling permits through local post offices and the Lochinver tourist office. The tourist office also sells permits for the lochs managed by the Assynt Angling Group on parcels of land to the south of the Assynt Crofters' Trust.

The first village worthy of a detour is **ACHMELVICH**, three miles northwest of Lochinver, where a tiny bay cradles a stunning white-sand beach lapped by startlingly turquoise water. There's a **campsite** and a basic 36-bed SYHA **hostel** (℡ 01571/844480, Ⓦ www.syha.org.uk; April–Sept) just behind the largest beach. However, there are plenty of equally seductive beaches up the coast, including one by the hamlet of Clachtoll, dominated by another beautiful bay with a basic campsite (Easter–Sept; ℡ 01571/855377, Ⓦ www.clachtollbeachcampsite.co.uk); nearby you'll find the former Clachtoll Salmon Station – now preserved by the Assynt Historical Society.

The side road that branches north off the B869 between **STOER** and **CLASH-NESSIE** ends abruptly by the automatic lighthouse at **Raffin**, Stevenson-built in

1870. You can continue for two miles along a boggy, slightly tricky track to the Point of Stoer, named after a colossal rock pillar, the **Old Man of Stoer**, which stands offshore, surrounded by sheer cliffs and splashed with guano from the sea-bird colonies that nest on its 200ft-high sides. Overlooking the Bay of Stoer is the wonderfully remote and snug *Stac Fada B&B* (℡0845/345 5349, Ⓦwww .stacfada.co.uk; ❷). Some five miles east of Clashnessie, the Drumbeg Stores is unexpectedly well stocked with some deli items, local food and good wine. Next door you can find rooms and a hearty salmon steak or steak and ale pie at the *Drumbeg Hotel* (℡01571/833236, Ⓦwww.drumbeghotel.co.uk; ❹), while just up the road is a small teagarden and craft shop.

Loch Assynt and around

The area east of Lochinver, traversed by the A837, centred on **Loch Assynt** and bounded by the gnarled peaks of the Ben More Assynt massif, is a wilderness of mountains, moorland, mist and scree. Dotted with lochs and lochans, it's also an angler's paradise, home to the only non-migratory fish in northern Scotland, the brown trout, and numerous other species, including the Atlantic salmon, sea trout, arctic char and ferox, a mysterious, cannibalistic strain of trout.

On a rocky promontory pushing out into Loch Assynt stand the jagged remnants of **Ardveck Castle** (free access), a MacLeod stronghold from 1597 that fell to the Seaforth Mackenzies after a siege in 1691. Previously, the famous general, the Marquis of Montrose, had been imprisoned here after his defeat at Carbisdale in 1650. The rebel duke, whom the local laird had betrayed to the government for £20,000 and four hundred bowls of sour meal, was eventually led away to be executed in Edinburgh, lashed back to front on his horse.

The displays within the grass-roofed, unstaffed **Knockan Crag** (Creag a' Chnocain; Ⓦwww.knockan-crag.co.uk) visitor centre, thirteen miles south of Loch Assynt on the A835 to Ullapool and part of the Inverpolly National Nature Reserve, outline what is one of the most important geological sites in the world. In 1859, the theory of thrust faults was developed by eminent geologist James Nicol, and two interpretive **trails** (one 15min, the other 1hr) show you how to detect the movement of rock plates in the nearby ancient cliffs.

Kylesku and around

At **KYLESKU**, 33 miles north of Ullapool on the A894, a long, curving road bridge sweeps over the mouth of lochs Glencoul and Glendhu. During World War II, these deep waters provided a secret training base for the brave crews of the x-craft mini-submarines. A small, poignant memorial stands in the car park at the northern end of the Kylesku road bridge.

The congenial 𝒜 *Kylesku Hotel* (℡01971/502231, Ⓦwww.kyleskuhotel.co.uk; March–Oct; ❺), by the water's edge above the old ferry slipway, has a welcoming bar with real ales where guests can feast on reasonably priced dishes including **fresh seafood**. Alternatively, *Newton Lodge* (℡01971/502070, Ⓦwww.newtonlodge.co.uk; ❺) is a modern, friendly and comfortable small **hotel** two miles south of Kylesku offering guests fine views over Loch Glencoul and the chance to spot seals on the shoreline. Statesman Cruises runs entertaining **boat trips** (March–Oct twice daily except Sat; round trip 2hr; ℡01971/502345; £15) from the jetty below the *Kylesku Hotel* to the 650ft **Eas-Coul-Aulin**, Britain's highest waterfall, located at the head of Loch Glencoul; otters, seals, porpoises and minke whales can occasionally be spotted along the way. You can get dropped off in the morning and/or picked up in the afternoon if you arrange it beforehand.

It's also possible to reach the waterfall **on foot**: a rough four-mile trail (3hr) leaves the A894 three miles south of Kylesku, skirting the south shore of Loch na Gainmhich (known locally as the "sandy loch") to approach the falls from above. Great care should be taken here as the path above the cliffs can get very slippery when wet; the rest of the route is also difficult to follow, particularly in bad weather, and should only be attempted by experienced, properly equipped and compass-literate hikers.

The far northwest coast

The Sutherland coastline north of Kylesku is a bridge too far for some, yet for others the stark, elemental beauty of the Highlands is to be found on the **far northwest coast** as nowhere else. Here, the peaks become more widely spaced and settlements smaller and fewer, linked by twisting single-track roads and shoreside footpaths that make excellent hiking trails. Places to stay and eat can be thin on the ground, particularly out of season.

Scourie and around

Ten miles north of Kylesku, the widely scattered crofting community of **SCOURIE**, on a bluff above the main road, surrounds a beautiful sandy beach whose safe bathing has made it a popular holiday destination for families; there's plenty to do for walkers and trout anglers, too. The Inverness to Durness bus service (Mon–Sat, via Lairg station) stops here. Scourie itself has some good **accommodation**, including the charming 🎄 *Scourie Lodge* (☎01971/502248, Ⓦ www.scourielodge.co.uk; March–Oct; ❺), an old three-bedroomed shooting retreat surrounded by trees on the north side of the sandy bay, with a lovely garden. There's a **campsite**, the modest *Scourie Caravan and Camping Park* (☎01971/502060; April–Sept) two minutes' walk away.

Even more remote is **UPPER BADCALL** village, three miles south of Scourie. The *Eddrachilles Hotel* (☎01971/502080, Ⓦ www.eddrachilles.com; ❹), a homely former 1700s manse hidden behind trees and just south of the turning to Upper Badcall, combines a warm welcome with comfortable rooms (the family room includes a separate bedroom for the kids), lunches and delicious three-course dinners in a rustic setting and the chance to enjoy great sea views while sampling one of the bar's 120 malt whiskies.

Tarbet and Handa Island

Visible just offshore to the north of Scourie, **Handa Island** is a huge chunk of red Torridon sandstone surrounded by sheer cliffs, carpeted with machair and purple-tinged moorland and teeming with sea birds. A **wildlife reserve** administered by the Scottish Wildlife Trust (Ⓦ www.swt.org.uk), the island supports one of the largest sea-bird colonies in northwest Europe. It's a real treat for ornithologists, with razorbills and guillemots breeding on its guano-covered cliffs during summer. From late May to mid-July, large numbers of puffins waddle comically over the turf-covered clifftops where they dig their burrows. Until the mid-nineteenth century, Handa supported a community of crofters, who survived on a diet of fish, potatoes and sea birds. The islanders, whose ruined cottages still cling to the slopes by the jetty, devised their own system of government, with a "queen" (Handa's oldest widow) and "parliament" (a council of men who met each morning to discuss the day's business). Uprooted by the 1847 potato famine, most of the villagers emigrated to Canada's Cape Breton.

Weather permitting, **boats** (☎07780/967800) leave for Handa throughout the day (Easter–Sept Mon–Sat 9.30am–2pm outbound; £10) from the tiny cove of **TARBET**, three miles northwest of the main road and accessible by postbus from Scourie, where there's a small car park and jetty. You're encouraged to make a donation towards Handa's upkeep. You'll need about three hours to follow the **footpath** around the island – an easy and enjoyable walk taking in the north shore's Great Stack rock pillar and some fine views across the Minch: a detailed route guide is featured in the SWT's free leaflet, available from the warden's office when you arrive. Camping is not allowed, and only volunteers and scientists for the nature reserve can use the small bothy. Tarbet's unexpected and delightful *Shorehouse* **restaurant** (☎01971/502251; Easter–Sept Mon–Sat), in a conservatory just above the jetty, serves delicious, moderately priced fresh seafood – some of it caught by the owner – as well as a good selection of home-made cakes and dessert.

Loch Laxford to Sandwood Bay

North of Scourie, the road sweeps inland through the starkest part of the Highlands, in which rocks piled on rocks, bog and water create an almost alien landscape, and the bare, stony coastline looks increasingly inhospitable. Here, on the Ardmore peninsula, an outdoor school was established in the 1960s by adventurer John Ridgway. Now, on an isolated sea loch, off **Loch Laxford**, his daughter Rebecca and her husband Will have set up Cape Adventure International (☎01971/521006, Ⓦwww.capeventure.co.uk), where you can get stuck into sea-kayaking, rock-climbing and land-yachting. They run residential courses and "castaway" weekends, and you can also join in the activities on a day-course.

At **RHICONICH** and under the shadow of **Foinaven** (2980ft), the comfortable *Rhiconich Hotel* (☎01971/521224, Ⓦwww.rhiconichhotel.co.uk; ❺) has the fishing rights to the local estate and will organize deerstalking, walking and birdwatching. A mile up the road, the B801 branches off to **KINLOCHBERVIE**, near which the welcoming *Old School Restaurant and Rooms* (☎01971/521383, Ⓦwww.oldschoolklb .co.uk; March–Oct; ❹) offers comfortable beds – including a cute separate en-suite single (£45) – and good-value evening meals. In Kinlochbervie itself, the eponymous *Kinlochbervie Hotel* (☎01971/521275, Ⓦwww.kinlochberviehotel .com; ❺) overlooks an incongruously huge fish market and modern concrete harbour from where trucks from all over Europe pick up cod and shellfish. There's a mobile bank, petrol pump and nearby shop; if you're in need of sustenance, try **fish and chips** at the *Fishermen's Mission* (Mon–Fri).

A single-track road continues northwest of Kinlochbervie through isolated **OLDSHOREMORE**, a working crofters' village scattered above a stunning white-sand beach (where you can camp rough), to **BLAIRMORE**, where a four-mile walk leads across peaty moorland to **Sandwood Bay**. After an unremarkable walk-in, the shell-white sandy **beach** at the end of the rough track is a breathtaking sight and one of the most beautiful in Scotland. Flanked by rolling dunes and lashed by fierce gales for much of the year, the dramatic leaning rock-stack to the south is said to be haunted by a bearded mariner – one of many sailors to have perished on this notoriously dangerous stretch of coast since the Vikings first navigated it over a millennium ago. Around the turn of the twentieth century, the beach, whose treacherous undercurrents make it unsuitable for swimming, also witnessed Britain's most recent recorded sighting of a **mermaid**. Turning back and past Blairmore at **SHEIGRA**, you can wild camp (there are no facilities) behind the beach.

It's possible to trek overland from Sandwood Bay north to Cape Wrath (see p.256), the northwestern tip of mainland Britain, a full day's walk away. If you're planning to meet the Cape Wrath minibus to Durness, contact them first since it won't run if the weather turns bad, leaving you stranded.

The north coast

Though a constant stream of sponsored walkers, caravans and tour groups makes it to the dull town of **John O'Groats**, surprisingly few visitors travel the whole length of the Highlands' wild **north coast**. Those who do, however, rarely return disappointed. Scotland's rugged northern shore is backed by barren mountains in the west, and by lochs and open rolling grasslands in the east. Mile upon mile of crumbling cliffs and sheer rocky headlands shelter bays whose perfect white beaches are nearly always deserted – they're also home to Scotland's best surfing waves (see p.50).

Though only a wee place, **Durness** is a good jumping-off point for rugged **Cape Wrath**, the windswept promontory at Scotland's northwest tip, which has retained an end-of-the-world mystique lost long ago by John O'Groats. Continuing east, **Loch Eriboll** is probably the most spectacular of the north-coast sea lochs, while Tongue, ten miles further east, enjoys the most attractive setting of the coast's small crofting villages. **Thurso**, the largest town on the north coast, is really only visited by those en route to Orkney. More enticing are the huge sea-bird colonies clustered in clefts and on remote stacks at **Dunnet Head** and **Duncansby Head**, to the east of Thurso.

Durness and around

Scattered around a string of sheltered sandy coves and grassy clifftops, **DURNESS** (ⓦ www.durness.org), the most northwesterly village on the British mainland, straddles the turning point on the main A838 road as it swings east from the peat bogs of the interior to the north coast's fertile strip of limestone machair. Durness village itself sits above its own sandy bay, Sango Sands, while half a mile to the east is **SMOO**, which used to be an RAF station. In between Durness and Smoo, the millennial village hall features a windblown and rather forlorn community garden that harbours a memorial commemorating the Beatle **John Lennon**, who came to Durness on family holidays and revisited in the 1960s with Yoko.

It's worth pausing at Smoo to see the 200ft-long **Smoo Cave**, a gaping hole in a sheer limestone cliff formed partly by the action of the sea and partly by the small burn that flows through it. Tucked away at the end of a narrow sheer-sided sea cove, the main chamber is accessible via steps from the car park by the A838. The much-hyped rock formations are less memorable than the short rubber-dinghy trip you have to make in the other two caverns, the whole experience enlivened after wet weather by a waterfall that crashes through the middle of the cavern. Twenty-minute walk/boat trips (May–Sept; £3) are run on request, weather permitting, by Colin Coventry (☎01971/511704).

A narrow road winds a mile or so northwest of Durness to **BALNAKIEL**, passing **Balnakiel Craft Village** en route. Disabuse yourself of any notion of quaint cottages, as the village is housed in a grim 1940s military base, transformed in the 1960s into a sort of industrial estate for arts and crafts. A dozen or so eclectic businesses (generally daily 10am–5.30pm) continue to function, including a print-makers and woodcarving studio and a pottery. The Loch Croispol bookshop runs a modest daytime café (☎01971/511777) whilst the nearby *Balnakeil Bistro* (March–Oct; ☎01971/511232) serves reasonably priced lunches and evening meals and sells crafts and books. At *Cocoa Mountain*, you can watch chocolates and truffles being made before sitting down in the bright modern café for a coffee or hot chocolate (☎01971/511233).

Balnakiel is also known for its **golf course** (£15), whose ninth and final hole involves a well-judged drive over the Atlantic; you can rent equipment from the clubhouse. The white-sand beach on the east side of **Balnakiel Bay** is stunning in any weather, but most spectacular on sunny days when the water turns to brilliant turquoise. For the best views, walk along the path that winds north through the dunes (pockmarked from naval bombing exercises) behind it; this eventually leads to **Faraid Head** – from the Gaelic *Fear Ard* (High Fellow) – where there's a very small colony of nesting puffins (ask the tourist office for directions). The fine views east to the mouth of Loch Eriboll and west to Cape Wrath make this round walk (3–4hr) the best in the Durness area.

Practicalities

Public transport is sparse; the key service is the Dearman Coaches link (May–Sept Mon–Sat 1 daily; also Sun in July & Aug) from Inverness via Ullapool, Lochinver and Scourie. The bus has a cycle carrier. Postbuses provide a more complicated year-round alternative and meet trains at Lairg; check schedules at the post office or the helpful Durness **tourist office** (March–April & Oct Mon–Sat; May–Sept daily; Nov–Feb Mon–Fri). This incorporates a small **visitor centre and ranger post** that features excellent panels detailing the area's history, geology, flora and fauna. Information about walks and cycle tracks, including guided ranger walks, can be sourced from here. Next to *Mackays* (see below), the old telephone exchange has been converted into **Surf Wrath** (℡07752/501333, ⓦwww .surfwrath.co.uk), where you can rent gear and book surfing and coasteering courses.

In terms of **accommodation**, ⌦ *Mackays Rooms and Restaurant*, at the western edge of the village, stands out for its welcoming personal touches and a daily-changing dinner menu (from 7pm) featuring locally sourced seafood, lamb and beef (book in advance, ℡01971/511202, ⓦwww.visitmackays.com; ⑤). The proprietor also runs the congenial and attractive *Lazy Crofter Bunkhouse* (℡01971/511202, ⓦwww.durnesshostel.com) next door. A shed-like SYHA **hostel** (℡01971/511264, ⓦwww.syha.org.uk; Easter–Sept), sits beside the Smoo Cave car park, a bleak half-mile east of the village. There are also a number of **B&Bs**, including *Glengolly B&B* in the village, which has two en-suite rooms in a working croft (℡01971/511255, ⓦwww.glengolly.com; ③). The **campsite** (℡01971/511222), on an exposed spot near the tourist office, has views over Sango Sands; close by is the local village **pub**. In addition to *Mackays*, the *Seafood Platter* (May–Sept; ℡01971/511215) on the eastern fringe of the village opposite the SYHA hostel is simple, tasty and moderately priced; it also does takeaway snacks.

Cape Wrath

An excellent day-trip from Durness begins two miles southwest of the village at **KEOLDALE**, where (tides and Ministry of Defence permitting) a foot-passenger **ferry** (daily: May, June & Sept 11am & 1.30pm; July & Aug 4 trips between 9.30am and 6.30pm; £5.50 return; ℡01971/511376 for ferry) crosses the spectacular Kyle of Durness estuary to link up with a **minibus** (May–Sept; £10 return; ℡01971/511343) that makes the forty-minute, fourteen-mile run out to **Cape Wrath**, the British mainland's most northwesterly point. Note that Garvie Island (An Garbh-eilean) is an air bombing range, and the military regularly close the road to Cape Wrath. The headland takes its name not from the stormy seas that crash against it for most of the year, but from the Norse word *hvarf*, meaning "turning place" – a throwback to the days when Viking warships used it as a navigation point during raids on the Scottish coast. These days, a Stevenson lighthouse warns ships away from the treacherous rocks; looking east to Orkney and west to the Outer Hebrides, it stands above the famous **Clo Mor cliffs**, the highest sea cliffs in Britain and a prime breeding site for sea birds.

Loch Eriboll

The road east of Durness passes several spectacular sandy bays en route to deep and sheltered **Loch Eriboll**, the north coast's most spectacular sea loch, where above the shoreline, high mountains accentuate the sense of wildness and isolation. Servicemen stationed here during World War II to protect passing Russian convoys nicknamed it "Loch 'Orrible", but it's wild and unspoilt; porpoises and otters are a common sight along the rocky shore, and minke whales occasionally swim in from the open sea.

Tongue to Thurso

There's great drama in the landscape between Tongue and Thurso, as the A836 – still single-track for some of the way – wends its way over bleak and often totally uninhabited rocky moorland, intercut with sandy sea lochs. Tiny little **Tongue** is pleasant enough, as is the settlement of **Bettyhill**, to the east, but the real reason to venture this far is to explore the countryside: **Ben Hope** (3040ft), the most northerly Munro, and the fascinating blanket bog of the **Flow Country** even further inland.

Tongue and around

The road takes a wonderfully slow and circuitous route around Loch Eriboll and east over the top of A' Mhoine moor to the pretty crofting township of **TONGUE**. Dominated by the ruins of **Castle Varrich** (Caisteal Bharraich), a medieval stronghold of the Mackays (3-mile return walk), the village is strewn above the east shore of the **Kyle of Tongue**, which you can cross either via a new causeway, or by following the longer and more scenic single-track road around its southern side. When the tide recedes, this shallow estuary becomes a mass of golden sand flats, superb on sunny days, with the sharp profiles of **Ben Hope** (3040ft) and **Ben Loyal** (2509ft) looming like twin sentinels to the south, and the Rabbit Islands a short way out to sea.

The best **accommodation** in Tongue is the nineteen-bedroom *Tongue Hotel* (T01847/611206, Wwww.tonguehotel.co.uk; April–Oct; ⑥), the plush former

---

Jacobites in the Kyle of Tongue

In 1746, the Kyle of Tongue was the scene of a naval engagement reputed to have sealed the fate of Bonnie Prince Charlie's **Jacobite rebellion**. In response to a plea for help from the prince, the King of France dispatched a sloop *Hazard* and £13,600 in gold coins to Scotland. However, the Jacobite ship was spotted by the English frigate HMS *Sheerness*, and fled into the Kyle, where it was forced aground. Pounded by English cannon fire, the Jacobite crew slipped ashore under cover of darkness in an attempt to smuggle the treasure to Inverness. The next morning, however, the rebels fell into an ambush laid by the anti-Jacobite MacKay clan, and began throwing the gold into **Lochan Hakel**, southwest of Tongue (most of it was recovered later). The prince instructed Lord Cromartie to send 1500 men north to rescue the treasure, but these too were defeated and taken prisoner; historians debate whether the missing men might have altered the outcome of the Battle of Culloden three weeks later. The local legend persists that cows still occasionally wander out of the loch's shallows with gold pieces stuck in their hooves.

hunting lodge of the Duke of Sutherland. The large and well-equipped SYHA **hostel** (℡01847/611789, ⓦwww.syha.org.uk), right beside the causeway a mile north of the village centre on the Kyle's east shore, is the best budget option. Over on the western side of the Kyle, five miles away from Tongue at **TALMINE**, a converted nineteenth-century church with great views out towards the Orkney Islands is the home of the popular *Cloisters* B&B (℡01847/601286, ⓦwww.cloistertal.demon.co.uk; ❷). There is also a very basic **campsite** opposite the sandy beach.

Bettyhill and around

Twelve miles east of Tongue, **BETTYHILL** is a major crofting village, set among rocky green hills. In Gaelic it was known as *Am Blàran Odhar* (Little Dun-coloured Field), but the origins of the English name are unknown; it was, however, definitely not named after Elizabeth, Countess of Sutherland, who presided over the Strathnaver Clearances. The story of those terrible times is told by local schoolchildren at the delightful and loyally maintained **Strathnaver Museum** (April–Oct Mon–Sat 10am–5pm; £2), housed in the old Farr church, east of the main village. Inside, you can see a reconstructed croft, some Pictish stones and a 3800-year-old early Bronze-Age beaker. The 24-mile Strathnaver Trail, running south from Bettyhill along the B873 to Altnaharra, highlights numerous historical sites from the Neolithic, Bronze and Iron Age periods.

A short stroll north of the church, sheltered **Farr beach** forms a splendid unbroken arc of pure white sand between the Naver and Borgie rivers. Even more visually impressive is the River Naver's narrow tidal estuary, to the west of Bettyhill, and **Torrisdale beach** (popular with surfers; access off the road to Borgie five miles west of Bettyhill), which ends in a smooth white spit that forms part of the **Invernaver Nature Reserve**. During summer, arctic terns nest here on the riverbanks, which are dotted with clumps of rare Scottish primrose, and you stand a good chance of spotting an otter or two.

In the museum car park, the small **tourist office** houses the basic *Café at Bettyhill* (closed Sun & weekdays in winter). Nearby, the *Farr Bay Inn*, known locally as the "FBI", also serves good meals. The *Bettyhill Hotel* (℡01641/521352, ⓦwww.bettyhill.info; ❷) offers good-value **rooms** and bar meals. Bettyhill's large campsite affords excellent bay views. Sheltered in woods four or five miles west of Bettyhill, the friendly, old-fashioned *Borgie Lodge Hotel* (℡01641/521332, ⓦwww.borgielodgehotel.co.uk; ❺) is a popular base for salmon- and sea-fishing.

Dounreay

As you move east from Bettyhill, the north coast changes dramatically as the hills on the horizon recede to be replaced by fields fringed with flagstone walls. It provides an incongruous setting for **Dounreay Nuclear Power Station** (ⓦwww.dounreay.com), a surreal collection of chimney stacks and box-like buildings, plus the famous golf-ball-shaped DFR (Dounreay Fast Reactor). Established in 1955, Dounreay pioneered the development of fast reactor technology and was the first in the world to provide mains electricity. The reactors themselves have long since closed, though Dounreay remains by the far the biggest employer on the north coast, with decommissioning of the 130-acre site estimated to last until 2033 and cost £2.9 billion.

The Flow Country

At a junction six miles before Dounreay, you can head forty miles or so south towards Helmsdale on the A897, through the **Flow Country**, whose name comes from *flói*, an Old Norse word meaning "marshy ground". This huge expanse of "blanket bog" is a valuable carbon sink and home to a wide variety

North-coast walking and cycling

Ordnance Survey Explorer map nos. 447 & 448

A pair of peaks rising up from the southern end of the Kyle of Tongue, Ben Hope and Ben Loyal offer moderate-to-hard walks, rewarded on a decent day by vast views over the harsh north coast and empty Sutherland landscape. **Ben Hope** (3040ft), which was given its name ("Hill of the Bay") by the Vikings, is the most northerly of Scotland's Munros. The best approach, a four-hour round-trip, is from the road that runs down the west side of Loch Hope. Start at a sheep shed by the roadside just under two miles beyond the southern end of Loch Hope, following the tributary of the stream that descends through an obvious break in the imposing-looking cliffline. Once on top of the cliffs, it's a relatively easy but inspiring walk along them to the summit.

Ben Loyal (2509ft), though lower, is a longer hike, at around six hours. To avoid the worst of the bogs, follow the northern spur from Ribigill Farm, a mile south of Tongue. At the end of the southbound farm-track, a path emerges; follow this up a steepish slope to gain the first peak on the ridge. It's not the summit, but the views are rewarding, and from here to the top the walking is easier.

For those looking for **shorter walks** or **cycles**, try tourist offices in the area for a leaflet entitled *The Forests of the Far North*, published by Forestry Commission Scotland (free). There are well-marked woodland trails at **Borgie Forest**, six miles west of Tongue, and **Truderscraig Forest** by Syre, twelve miles south of Bettyhill on the B871. Near the entrance to Borgie Forest is the *a'chraobh*, a spiral feature created using native trees and carved local stone. If you follow the signs to "**Rosal Pre-Clearance Village**", you'll find an area clear of trees with various ruins that stand as a memorial to the brutality of the Highland Clearances – fifteen families were evicted from here between 1814 and 1818. Various boards provide details about the way of life of the inhabitants in the eighteenth century before the upheavals, which saw them scattered to bleak coastal settlements or onto the emigration ships leaving for Canada and America.

of wildlife. At the train station at **FORSINARD**, fourteen miles south of Melvich and easily accessible from Thurso, Wick and the south by train, there is an RSPB **visitor centre** (April–Oct daily 9am–6pm; ☎01641/571225), with CCTV coverage of hen harriers nesting, and a **Peatland Centre**, which explains the wonders of peat.

To get to grips with the whole concept of blanket bog, of which eight square miles is currently being restored from forestry use to its natural state, take a leaflet and follow the mile-long **Dubh Lochan Trail** that's been laid out over the flagstones, through peat banks to some nearby black lochans. En route, you get to see bog asphodel, bogbean, sphagnum moss and the insect-trapping sundew and butterwort; you've also got a good chance of spotting greenshanks, golden plovers and hen harriers. The visitor centre runs twice-weekly guided walks (May to end July Tues & Thurs; 2–5pm; 3hr walk; £5) through the area. The *Forsinard Hotel* (☎01641/571221; ●), opposite the station, serves reasonable bar food, is popular with anglers and stalkers and runs hawking packages for guests. Right beside the RSPB centre, Sue Grimshaw's **B&B** (☎01641/571262; ●) offers guests a comfortable stay and tasty three-course evening meals (£13) made with local produce.

Thurso

Approached from the isolation of the west, **THURSO** feels like a metropolis. In reality, it's a relatively small service centre visited mostly by people passing

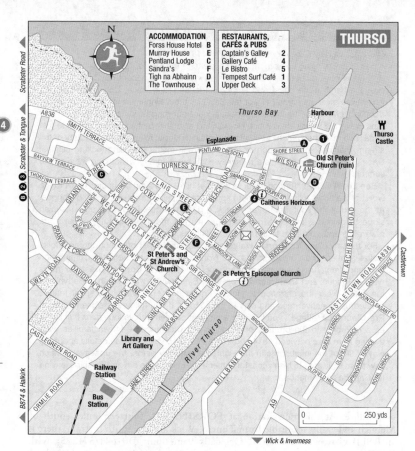

THURSO

ACCOMMODATION
Forss House Hotel   B
Murray House   E
Pentland Lodge   C
Sandra's   F
Tigh na Abhainn   D
The Townhouse   A

RESTAURANTS,
CAFÉS & PUBS
Captain's Galley   2
Gallery Café   4
Le Bistro   5
Tempest Surf Café   1
Upper Deck   3

through to the adjoining port of **Scrabster** to catch the ferry to Orkney or by increasing numbers of surfers attracted to the waves on the north coast.

Arrival and information

Trains from Inverness (all of which go via Wick) arrive at Thurso **train station**, adjacent to the **bus station**, both a ten-minute walk down Princes Street and Sir George's Street from the helpful riverside **tourist office** (April, May, June, Sept & Oct Mon–Sat; July & Aug daily). There's also an office at Caithness Horizons (see opposite). The **Scrabster ferry terminal** is a mile or so northwest of town, with regular buses from the train station in the morning, and from Olrig Street in the afternoon. For more on **ferries to Orkney** from Scrabster, Gills Bay and John O'Groats, see p.263.

If you're coming to **surf**, want a lesson, need to rent a board (£10/day) or simply want a coffee and home-baking before hitting the waves, ask at *Tempest Surf* on Riverside Road by Thurso harbour (☎01847/892500).

Accommodation

The nearest **campsite** (☎01847/805503) sits out towards Scrabster alongside the main road, though there are better views at Dunnet Bay (☎01847/821319) a few miles east (see opposite).

Forss House Hotel 3 miles west of Thurso on the A836 ☎01847/861201, ⓦwww.forsshousehotel .co.uk. Built in 1810, this thirteen-bedroom family-owned hotel offers an upmarket stay in spacious grounds. ❼

Murray House 1 Campbell St ☎01847/895759, ⓦwww.murrayhousebb.com. Central, comfortable and friendly and will rustle up a tasty three-course dinner for £15 per person. ❸

Pentland Lodge ☎01847/895103. Nine-bedroom B&B on the west side of Thurso offering comfort and views over Thurso Bay. ❺

Sandra's 24/26 Princes St ☎01847/894575, ⓦwww.sandras-backpackers.co.uk. A refurbished, clean and well-run place that's affiliated to the SYHA and owned by the popular chippie downstairs. All rooms are en suite and guests have free use of bikes and internet access. ❶

Tigh na Abhainn ☎01847/893443. B&B in an old house by the river serving the likes of kippers for breakfast. ❷

The Townhouse 2 Braehead House ☎01955/611291, ⓦwww.thesurfdirectory.co.uk. A smart two-bedroom self-catering option right by the sea, and popular with surfers.

The Town

The town's name derives from the Norse word *Thorsa*, literally "River of the God Thor", and in Viking times this was a major gateway to the mainland. Later, ships set sail from here for the Baltic and Scandinavian ports loaded with meal, beef, hides and fish. Much of the town, however, dates from the 1790s, when Sir John Sinclair built a large new extension to the old fishing port. The nearby Dounreay Nuclear Power Station ensured continuing prosperity after World War II, tripling the population when workers from the plant settled in Thurso.

Thurso's grid-plan streets boast some rather handsome Victorian architecture in the local, greyish sandstone. The main attraction is in the revamped Victorian Town Hall on the High Street, where **Caithness Horizons** (Mon–Sat 10am–6pm, Sun 11am–6pm; ⓦwww.caithnesshorizons.co.uk) comprises a museum, tourist office and café. The museum uses interactive technology and evocative old photos to explore local geology, history, farming and fishing, with treasures including a Bronze Age beaker and a Viking brooch. Downstairs there's a display on the decommissioning of Dounreay.

If you continue north up the High Street, you'll reach **Old St Peter's Church**, a substantial ruin with origins in the thirteenth century, and the old part of town, near the harbour.

Eating

Thurso has several good options for when you're feeling peckish.

Captain's Galley The Harbour, Scrabster ☎01847/894999, ⓦwww.captainsgalley.co.uk. A former ice-house and salmon bothy which now serves the best, most expensive seafood in the area; each day the menu details the boats the fish have come in on. Closed Sun & Mon.

Gallery Café Caithness Horizons museum. The museum's cheerful daytime café serves sandwiches, soup and home-baking, and has a kids' menu.

Le Bistro 2 Traill St ☎01847/893737. Popular option where the reasonably priced menu includes tradi-tional fare such as Cullen skink. Closed Sun & Mon.

Tempest Surf Café Riverside Rd. Inexpensive snacks by the harbour, and the place to warm up after a play in the waves.

The Upper Deck *The Ferry Inn*, Scrabster ☎01847/872814. The place to head for a huge (if pricey) steak, along with hearty seafood dishes and surf'n'turf classics.

Dunnet Head and the Castle of Mey

Thurso doesn't have much of a beach, so if you want to sink your toes into sand, head five miles east along the A836 to **Dunnet Bay**, a vast golden beach backed by huge dunes. One of the reef breaks here, known as "Thurso East", is regarded as one of Europe's finest, and the bay is popular with surfers even in the winter. At the northeast end of the bay, the new **Seadrift Visitor and Ranger Centre** (April–Sept Tues–Fri 2–5pm, Sat & Sun 2–6pm; free), near the excellent campsite, holds an exhibition about the area's sea birds, marine life and ecology amidst the sand dunes. You can also pick up information on good local history and nature walks, including a short self-guided trail into nearby **Dunnet Forest**.

To the north of the bay is the small village of **DUNNET**, where it's worth stopping in at **Mary-Ann's Cottage** (June–Sept Tues–Sun 2–4.30pm; £3), a farming croft vacated in 1990 by the then 93-year-old Mary-Ann Calder, whose grandfather had built the cottage, and maintained just as she left it, full of reminders of the three generations who lived and worked there over the last 150 years. For a welcoming **B&B**, try the *Dunnet Head B&B* at Brough, three miles south of Dunnet Head on the B855 and housed in the former post office (℡01847/851774, Ⓦwww.dunnethead.iberacal.com; ➋). The owners can advise on the archeology and wildlife in the area, including the chance to spot seals in the bay. The Thurso–John O'Groats bus stops near the B&B but you'll need to walk to the lighthouse.

Despite the publicity that John O'Groats customarily receives, mainland Britain's most northerly point is in fact **Dunnet Head**, north of Dunnet along

The Pentland Firth and Stroma

The Caithness coastline is a good place from which to view Orkney. Dividing the islands from the mainland is the infamous **Pentland Firth**, one of the world's most treacherous waterways. Only seven miles across, it forms a narrow channel between the Atlantic Ocean and North Sea, and for fourteen hours each day the tide rips through here from west to east at a rate of ten knots or more, flooding back in the opposite direction for the remaining ten hours. Combined with the rocky seabed and a high wind, this can cause deep whirlpools and terrifying 30- or 40-ft-high towers of water when the ebbing tide crashes across the reefs offshore. The latter, known as the "Bores of Duncansby", are the subject of many old mariners' myths from the time of the Vikings onwards. Ever-increasing numbers of oil tankers are braving the Pentland Firth to save time on the longer passage north of Orkney – an environmental catastrophe waiting to happen, according to locals.

Obstructing the flow of the Pentland Firth and, as a result, surrounded by turbulent seas, is **Stroma** (from the Norse *staum-øy* or "tidal stream"), a flat island visible a few miles north of Gills Bay, terminal for the Pentland Ferries to Orkney. Part of Caithness, and not counted as one of the nearby Orkney islands, Stroma had a population of well over three hundred in the late nineteenth century, which had dwindled to around eighty by the 1950s. To help stem the depopulation, a new harbour was constructed in 1955 at great expense. The contractors employed the locals as the workforce, paying such good wages that many of the islanders used the money to move to the mainland. Within a few years, just the lighthouse keepers remained, and nowadays only sheep make use of the buildings and the single road. John O'Groats Ferries (℡01955/611353, Ⓦwww.jogferry.co.uk) offers a leisurely afternoon **wildlife cruise**, which (depending on the tides) will take you round the sea-bird colonies and stacks of Duncansby Head or the seal colonies of Stroma (mid-June to Aug daily; 1hr 30min; £15). North Coast Marine Adventures (℡01955/611797, Ⓦwww.northcoast-marine-adventures.co.uk) offer rather more high-adrenaline thirty-minute trips (£15) in a rigid inflatable as well as sedate, hour-long wildlife tours (£20), but only Mr Simpson (℡01955/611394), who actually owns Stroma, will occasionally take groups on request across to the island in his boat (summer only).

the B855, which runs for four miles over bleak heather and bog to the tip of the headland, crowned with a Stevenson lighthouse. In early summer, puffins may be spotted on the impressive red cliffs whilst seals bathe off rocks below the weirdly eroded rock stacks. On a clear day you can see the whole northern coastline from Cape Wrath to Duncansby Head, and across the treacherous **Pentland Firth** to Orkney.

Roughly fifteen miles east of Thurso, just off the A836, lies the late Queen Mother's former Scottish home, the **Castle of Mey** (May–July & mid-Aug to Sept daily 10.30am–4pm; £9.50; ⓦwww.castleofmey.org.uk). It's a modest little place, hidden behind high flagstone walls, with great views north to Orkney and a herd of the Queen Mum's beloved Aberdeen Angus grazing out front. The original castle was a sixteenth-century Z-plan affair, owned by the earls of Caithness until 1889, and bought in a state of disrepair in 1952, the year her husband, George VI, died. The Queen Mum used to spend every August here, and it's unstuffy inside, the walls hung with works by local amateur artists (and watercolours by Prince Charles, who visits every August). There's a reasonable tearoom, or try nearby *Simply Unique* in Mey for traditional home-baking and coffee.

John O'Groats and around

Romantics expecting to find a magical meeting of land and water at **JOHN O'GROATS** (ⓦwww.visitjohnogroats.com) are invariably disappointed – sadly it remains an uninspiring tourist trap. The views north to Orkney are fine enough, but the village offers little more than a string of souvenir and craft shops and several refreshment stops thronged with coach parties. The village gets its name from the Dutchman, Jan de Groot, who obtained the ferry contract for the hazardous crossing to Orkney in 1496. The eight-sided house he built for his eight quarrelling sons (so that each one could enter by his own door) is echoed in the octagonal tower of the much-photographed but now vacant and dilapidated *John O'Groats Hotel*, which shares the same owners as Cornwall's *Land's End Hotel*, to and from which point walkers and cyclists make their epic journeys. Long overdue plans to redevelop the hotel seem to have stalled.

The **tourist office** (March–Oct daily) is by the car park. The working croft at *Bencorragh House* **B&B** (ⓣ01955/611449, ⓦwww.bencorraghhouse.com; March–Oct; ❷) provides farmhouse accommodation and spectacular views at Upper Gills near Canisbay, three miles southwest of John O'Groats. The small SYHA **hostel** (ⓣ01955/611761, ⓦwww.syha.org.uk; April–Oct) is in Canisbay itself. *Stroma View* **campsite** (ⓣ01955/611313; March–Sept), one mile along the Thurso road, is less exposed than the windswept but well-equipped *John O'Groats* site (ⓣ01955/611329). To **eat**, seek out the cosy, wood-furnished *School House Restaurant* (ⓣ01955/611714, ⓦwww.dinecaithness.co.uk; Wed–Sun). There are several **boat trips** to be had (see box opposite).

If you're disappointed by John O'Groats, press on a couple of miles further east to **Duncansby Head**, which, with its lighthouse, dramatic cliffs and well-worn coastal path, has a lot more to offer. The birdlife here is prolific, and south of the headland lie spectacular 200ft-high cliffs, cut by sheer-sided clefts known locally as *geos*, and several impressive sea-stacks.

The east coast

The **east coast** of the Highlands, between Inverness and Wick, is nowhere near as spectacular as the west, with gently undulating moors, grassland and low cliffs where you might expect sea lochs and mountains. Washed by the cold waters of the North Sea, it's markedly cooler, too.

While many visitors speed up the main A9 road through this region in a headlong rush to the Orkneys' prehistoric sites, those who dally will find a wealth of brochs, cairns and standing stones, many in remarkable condition. The area around the Black Isle and the Tain was a Pictish heartland, and has yielded important finds. Further north, from around the ninth century AD onwards, the **Norse** influence was more keenly felt than in any other part of mainland Britain, and dozens of Scandinavian-sounding names recall the era when this was a Viking kingdom.

Culturally and scenically, much of the east coast is more lowland than highland, and Caithness in particular evolved more or less separately from the Highlands, avoiding the bloody tribal feuds that wrought such havoc further south and west. Later, however, the nineteenth-century **Clearances** hit the region hard, as countless ruined cottages and empty glens show. Hundreds of thousands of crofters were evicted and forced to emigrate, or else take up fishing in one of the numerous herring ports established on the coast. The fishing heritage is a recurring theme along this coast, though there are only a handful of working boats scattered around the harbours today, and while oil has brought a transient prosperity to one or two, the area remains one of the country's poorest, reliant on sheep farming, fishing and tourism.

The one stretch of the east coast that's always been relatively rich is the **Black Isle**, just over the Kessock Bridge heading north out of Inverness, whose main village, **Cromarty**, is the region's undisputed highlight, with a crop of elegant mansions and appealing fishermen's cottages clustered near the entrance to the Cromarty Firth. In late medieval times, pilgrims, including James IV of Scotland, poured through here en route to the red-sandstone town of **Tain** to worship at the shrine of St Duthus, where the former sacred enclave has now been converted into one of the many "heritage centres" that punctuate the route north. Beyond **Dornoch**, a renowned golfing resort recently famous as the site of Madonna's wedding, the ersatz-Loire château **Dunrobin Castle** is the main tourist attraction, a monument as much to the iniquities of the Clearances as to the eccentricity of Victorian taste. The relatively flat landscapes of this northeast corner – windswept peat bog and farmland dotted with lochans and grey-and-white crofts – are a surprising contrast to the more rugged country south and west of here.

The Black Isle and around

Sandwiched between the Cromarty Firth to the north and the Moray and Beauly firths which separate it from Inverness to the south, the **Black Isle** is not an island at all, but a fertile peninsula whose rolling hills, prosperous farms and stands of deciduous woodland make it more reminiscent of Dorset or Sussex than the Highlands. It probably gained its name because of its mild climate: there's rarely frost, which leaves the fields "black" all winter; another explanation is that the name derives from the Gaelic word for black, *dubh* – a possible corruption of St Duthus (see p.268).

The Black Isle is littered with dozens of **prehistoric sites**, but the main incentive to make the detour east from the A9 is to visit the picturesque eighteenth-century town of **Cromarty**, huddled at the northeast tip of the peninsula. A string of villages along the south coast is also worth stopping off in en route, and one of them, Rosemarkie, has an outstanding small **museum** devoted to Pictish culture. Nearby Chanonry Point is among the best **dolphin-spotting** sites in Europe.

The southern Black Isle

Just across the Kessock Bridge from Inverness is a roadside lay-by that hosts a **tourist office** (Easter–Oct daily; ☎01463/731701), as well as a small **dolphin and seal centre** (June–Sept daily 9.30am–4.30pm; free), which offers the chance to observe (and listen to) the popular creatures.

Fortrose and Rosemarkie

FORTROSE, ten miles northeast of Inverness, is a quietly elegant village dominated by the beautiful ruins of an early thirteenth-century **cathedral** (daily 9.30am–5.30pm; free). Founded by King David I, it now languishes on a lovely green bordered by red-sandstone and colourwashed houses, where a horde of gold coins dating from the time of Robert III was unearthed in 1880.

There's a memorial plaque to the seer at nearby **Chanonry Point**, reached by a back road from the north end of Fortrose; the thirteenth hole of the golf course here marks the spot where he met his death. Jutting into a narrow channel in the Moray Firth (deepened to allow warships into the estuary during World War II), the point, fringed on one side by a beach of golden sand and shingle, is an excellent place to look for **dolphins** (see box, p.216).

ROSEMARKIE, a lovely one-street village a mile north of Fortrose at the opposite (northwest) end of the beach, is thought to have been evangelized by St Boniface in the early eighth century. The cosy **Groam House Museum** (May–Oct Mon–Sat 10am–5pm, Sun 2–4.30pm; Nov–April Sat & Sun 2–4pm; free; ⓦwww.groamhouse.org.uk), at the bottom of the village, displays fifteen intricately carved Pictish standing stones (among them the famous Rosemarkie Cross Slab) dating from as early as the eighth century AD and shows an informative video highlighting Pictish sites in the region. Good **bar food** in this area is available at the *Plough Inn*, just down the main street from the museum in Rosemarkie, and there's a branch of the Cromarty Bakery also on the main street.

To work up an appetite, head for the excellent **Learnie Red Rock Trails** (ⓦwww.HIMBA.org.uk) just four miles from Rosemarkie on the A832, where there are over ten miles of purpose-built mountain-bike track. Bikes can be rented in Cromarty.

Cromarty

According to legend, the twin headlands flanking the entrance to the **Cromarty Firth**, known as The Sutors (from the Gaelic word for shoemaker), were once a pair of giant cobblers who used to protect the Black Isle from pirates. Nowadays, however, the only giants in the area are the partially deconstructed oil rigs marooned in the estuary off Nigg and Invergordon like metal monsters marching out to sea. They form a surreal counterpoint to the web of tiny streets and chocolate-box workers' cottages of **CROMARTY**, the Black Isle's main settlement. The town, an ancient ferry crossing-point on the pilgrimage trail to St Duthus's shrine in Tain, lost much of its trade during the nineteenth century to places served by the railway; a branch line to the town was begun but never completed. Although a royal burgh since the fourth century, Cromarty didn't become a prominent port until 1772 when the entrepreneurial local landlord, George Ross, founded a hemp mill here, fuelling a period of prosperity during which Cromarty acquired some of Scotland's finest Georgian houses; these, together with the terraced fishers' cottages of the nineteenth-century herring boom, have left the town with a wonderful concentration of Scottish domestic architecture.

To get a sense of Cromarty's past, wander through the town's pretty streets to the **museum** housed in the old **Courthouse** on Church Street (April–Oct Sun–Thurs 10am–5pm; £2), which tells the history of the courthouse and town using audiovisuals and animated figures. You are also issued with an audio handset and a map for an excellent **walking tour** around the town. **Hugh Miller**, a nineteenth-century stonemason turned author, geologist, folklorist and Free Church campaigner, was born in Cromarty, and his **birthplace** (May–Sept Sun–Wed 1–5pm; NTS; £5.50), a thatched cottage on Church Street, has been restored to give an idea of what Cromarty must have been like in his day. There's also a wild garden and reading room.

Tucked-away **Cromarty Pottery** at 49 Shore St (Ⓦ www.cromarty-pottery .com) is well worth a peek, and otherwise Cromarty is simply a fascinating place just to wander around, and there's an excellent four-mile circular **walk** out to the south Sutor stacks. Pick up the route by leaving town to the east on Miller Road, and turning right when the lane becomes "The Causeway". For a simpler shoreline walk, turn left here, following the path to the water.

Dolphin- and other wildlife-spotting trips (2hr; £22) are offered locally by EcoVentures (Ⓣ 01381/600323, Ⓦ www.ecoventures.co.uk), who travel out through the Sutors to the Moray Firth in a powerful RIB. The tiny two-car **Nigg–Cromarty ferry** (June to end Sept daily 8am–6.15pm, until 7.15pm July and Aug; £2.50) is Scotland's smallest. Embark from the jetty near the lighthouse.

Practicalities

Buses run to Cromarty from Inverness Union Street, returning from Victoria Hall. During summer, **accommodation** is in short supply. The most upmarket option is the traditional *Royal Hotel* (Ⓣ 01381/600217, Ⓦ www.royalcromarty hotel.co.uk; ❺), down at the harbour, which has nicely furnished rooms overlooking the Firth. For **B&B**, try the modest but friendly *Trade Winds* in the Fishertown area (Ⓣ 01381/600430; ❷), *Gisborne B&B* (Ⓣ 01381/600376; ❸) on Marine Terrace, once the cottage hospital, or grand red-brick *Sydney House* (Ⓣ 01381/600451, Ⓦ www.sydneyhouse.co.uk; ❸).

For something **to eat**, the *Royal Hotel* specializes in seafood and the *Cromarty Arms* on Church Street is good for a pub lunch, but there are few more down-to-earth but satisfying restaurants in the Highlands than ⅉ *Sutor Creek* at 21 Bank St (Ⓣ 01381/600855, Ⓦ www.sutorcreek.co.uk; Wed–Sun 11am–late). It serves organic wines, delicious seafood and fresh pizza cooked in a wood-fired oven, though the imaginative toppings are local and seasonal rather than conventionally Italian. Further up the road at the *Cromarty Bakery* (closed Sun) you'll find tasty home-bakes, fresh breads such as spinach and walnut, and whisky cake.

For **bike rental** (£12/half-day, £20/day) to tackle the Learnie Trails (see p.265) or for a cycle tour, contact the friendly operator of MBHI (Ⓣ 07780/940342, Ⓦ www.mbhi.co.uk) just along from *Cromarty Bakery* at 5 Bank St.

Dingwall and the Cromarty Firth

Most traffic nowadays takes the upgraded A9 north from Inverness, bypassing the small market town of **DINGWALL** (from the Norse *thing*, "parliament", and *vollr*, "field"), a royal burgh since 1226. Once a port, it was left high and dry when the river receded during the nineteenth century, and today it has succumbed to the curse of British provincial towns and acquired an ugly business park and character-less pedestrian shopping street. However, there are two handy late-night petrol stations. Dingwall's only real claim to fame is that it was the birthplace of Macbeth, whose family occupied the now ruined castle on Castle Street. You're unlikely to want to hang around here for long – for somewhere pleasant to stay move onto Strathpeffer or push on north.

Strathpeffer

STRATHPEFFER, a mannered and leafy Victorian spa town four miles west of Dingwall, complete with Victorian street lamps and surrounded by wooded hills, is pleasant enough but does suffer from a high density of coach parties. During its heyday, this was a renowned European **health resort** reached by the tongue-twisting Strathpeffer Spa Express train from Aviemore. A recent face-lift has seen the town's attractive grand hall transformed into a performing arts centre, the Strathpeffer Pavilion (ⓦ www.strathpefferpavilion.org), and the nearby **Upper Pump Room** (April–Sept Mon–Sat 10am–6pm, Sun 2–5pm; donation) converted into a visitor centre, where displays and videos tell the history of the resort. You can sample three waters drawn from five different wells, which were supposed to treat all manner of ailments – most of today's visitors, however, find the sulphurous-smelling liquid more masochistic than medicinal.

Also making the most of the Victorian theme, the **Highland Museum of Childhood** (Easter–Oct Mon–Sat 10am–5pm, until 7pm July & August, Sun

---

Walks around Strathpeffer

Ordnance Survey Explorer map no. 437
From the former youth hostel at the southern end of Strathpeffer, a two- to three-hour walk leads to the remains of a vitrified Iron-Age fort at **Knock Farril**. The first part of the walk follows woodland trails; rather less than a mile further on, turn up onto the ridge above you and follow it in a northeasterly direction along the crest of the hill known as the Cat's Back. Past some fine old Scots pines, the trees begin to thin out, and as you reach the hill fort great views of the Cromarty Firth begin to show to the east. Before you get to the ridge, look out for the unusual **Touchstone Maze**, which was built as a local arts project in 1992 and includes around eighty stones set in circles representing the major rock types from around the Highlands. A path also leads directly to the maze from near the old train station in Strathpeffer. When you reach the fort, it is possible to pick up a minor road and continue along the ridge to Dingwall, from where there are buses back to Strathpeffer. A shorter route drops back down from Knock Farril to the main road and back to the village that way.

A little further out of the village, two miles north of Contin on the main A835 to Braemore, are the **Rogie Falls**. Well signposted, it's only a short walk from the car park to the spot where you can see the Black Water come frothing down a long stretch of rocks and mini-gorges, in one place plunging down a 25ft drop. Salmon leap upriver in summer, particularly at the fish ladder built to offer an alternative route up the toughest of the rapids. A suspension bridge over the river leads to some waymarked forest trails, including a five-mile loop to **View Rock**, at a point only 160ft above sea level, but which has great views of the local area.

The most ambitious hike in this area is up **Ben Wyvis**, a huge mass of mountain clearly seen from Inverness. The high point is Glas Lethad Mor (3432ft), which means, rather prosaically, "Big Greenish-Grey Slope". The most common route is through Garbat Forest, leaving the road just south of Garbat itself, staying on the north bank of the Allt a'Bhealaich Mhoir stream to get onto the southwestern end of the long summit ridge at the minor peak of An Cabar.

2–5pm; £2.50; @www.highlandmuseumofchildhood.org.uk) is located at the restored Victorian train station half a mile east of the main square. The museum looks at growing up in the Highlands, from home- and school-life to folklore and festivals, with some well-displayed photographs, display cabinets with toys and games and a colourful series of commissioned murals. In other parts of the station are a pleasant café and a woodworking craftshop.

Strathpeffer is within striking distance of the bleak **Ben Wyvis**, helping make it a popular base for walkers. One of the best hikes in the area is up the hill of Cnoc Mor, where the vitrified Iron-Age hill fort of **Knock Farril** affords superb panoramic views to the Cromarty Firth and the surrounding mountains.

Buses run regularly between Dingwall and Strathpeffer, dropping passengers in the square. **Tourist information** is available in the front section of Upper Pump Room (see p.267 for opening hours). The large **hotels** in the village are very popular with bus tours, so it's better to opt for **B&B** such as upmarket *Craigvar* (☎01997/421622, @www.craigvar.com; ❹), which overlooks the square, or luxurious Edwardian villa *Linnmhor House* on Park Road (☎01997/420072, @www.linnmhor-house.co.uk; ❺). For **food**, the moderately priced *Red Poppy* in the Pavilion (☎01997/423332; Tues–Sat 11am–9pm) serves up reasonable lunches and dinners and the *Richmond Hotel* is a pleasant dinner haunt with a cosy bar serving real ale. Anyone with a sweet tooth might enjoy paying a visit to *Maya* on Main Street, just across from the Pump Room, an attractive café and chocolate shop (Tues–Sat 10am–5pm) with a viewing window through to the production area where you can sometimes see the Belgian proprietor at work. There's also an excellent **bike** shop right on the Square, Square Wheels (☎01997/421000, @www.squarewheels.biz; closed Mon), which rents out bikes and offers good advice on some great local routes.

The Dornoch Firth and around

North of the Cromarty Firth, the hammer-shaped **Fearn peninsula** can still be approached from the south by the ancient ferry crossing from Cromarty to Nigg, though to the north the link is a more recent causeway over the **Dornoch Firth**, the inlet which marks the northern boundary of the peninsula. On the southern edge of the Dornoch Firth, the A9 bypasses the quiet town of **Tain**, probably best known as the home of Glenmorangie whisky. Inland, at the head of the firth, there's not much to the village of **Bonar Bridge**, but fans of unusual hostels travel from far and wide to spend a night with the ghosts at the duchess of Sutherland's imposing former home, **Carbisdale Castle**. Further inland, the lonely village of **Lairg** is a connection point between west and east coasts, with roads spearing through the glens from northwest Sutherland and the railway making a laboured detour in from the east coast.

Back on the coast, on the north side of the Dornoch Firth, the neat town of **Dornoch** itself, long known for its impressive cathedral and well-manicured golf courses, found renewed fame in 2000 as the venue for an outbreak of Madonna-mania, when it hosted the pop star's wedding to Guy Ritchie.

Tain

The peninsula's largest settlement is **TAIN**, reputedly Scotland's oldest Royal Burgh and an attractive if old-fashioned small town of grand whisky-coloured sandstone buildings, notably the castle-like early eighteenth-century Tolbooth. It was the birthplace of **St Duthus**, an eleventh-century missionary who inspired great devotion in the Middle Ages. His miracle-working relics were enshrined in a sanctuary here in the eleventh century, and in 1360 St Duthus Collegiate Church was built. It was subsequently visited annually by James IV, who usually arrived here fresh from the arms of his mistress, Janet Kennedy, whom he had conveniently installed in nearby Moray. A good place to get to grips with the peninsula's past is the revamped **Tain Through Time** exhibition (April–Oct Mon–Sat 10am–5pm; £3.50), which makes creative use of three old buildings around the church and graveyard, leading you round using an audioguide. The ticket price also includes a walking tour of the town and neighbouring **museum** (£1.50 museum only) on Castle Brae (just off the High Street), housing an interesting display of the much-sought-after work of the Tain silversmiths, along with mediocre archeological finds and clan memorabilia. Also on Castle Brae, **Brown's Gallery** (T01862/893884, Wwww.brownsart.com) shows contemporary Scottish art in a light-filled gallery. Tain's other main attraction is the **Glenmorangie whisky distillery**, where the highly rated malt is produced (shop Mon–Fri 9am–5pm, June–Aug also Sat 10am–4pm & Sun noon–4pm; tours Mon–Fri 10.30am–3.30pm, Sat 10.30am–2.30pm, Sun 12.30–2.30pm; £2.50; T01862/892477 Wwww.glenmorangie.com); it lies beside the A9 on the north side of town. Booking is recommended for the tours.

For **accommodation**, the *Carnegie Lodge Hotel* (T01862/894039, Wwww.carnegiehotel.co.uk; ④) on Viewfield Road, tucked away behind a housing estate on the west side of the A9 from the main part of Tain, looks and feels a bit like a golf clubhouse but offers decent and reasonably priced rooms. The more modest *Golf View House* (T01862/892856, Wwww.golf-view.co.uk; Feb–Nov; ③), three minutes' drive south of the town centre on Knockbreck Road, offers comfortable B&B and lovely views to the Dornoch Firth. The best option for simple but filling **food** in Tain is cheery *Sunflowers Café* on the High Street. Otherwise, there's Scottish-based fare in the bistro at the *Carnegie Lodge Hotel*, while the *Royal Hotel* (T01862/892013; ⑤), a lovely sandstone building at the western end of the main street, does reasonably priced bar meals.

Portmahomack

Unless you're making use of the Cromarty–Nigg ferry, not many people visit the Fearn peninsula to the east of Tain. It has a couple of delightful discoveries, however, including the green, windswept village of **PORTMAHOMACK**, which huddles around a curving sandy beach. On the edge of the village, ongoing archeological digs by the **Tarbat Discovery Centre** (daily: April & Oct 2–5pm; May–Sept 10am–5pm; £3.50) have unearthed original Pictish sculpted artefacts, suggesting the area around the twelfth-century church was highly significant to the Picts. From Portmahomack, narrow roads run through fertile farmland to the gorse-covered point at **Tarbat Ness**, where there's a lighthouse – one of the highest in Britain. A good seven-mile **walk** starts here (2–3hr round trip): head south from Tarbat Ness for three miles, following the narrow passage between the foot of the cliffs and the foreshore, until you get to the hamlet of Rockfield. A path leads past a row of fishermen's cottages from here to Portmahomack, then joins the tarmac road running northeast back to the lighthouse. Further south on the peninsula there are impressive Pictish **standing stones** at Hilton and at Shandwick, while near Fearn village the unexpectedly well-groomed Anta factory shop (April–Dec Mon–Sat 9.30am–5.30pm, Sun 11am–5pm; Wwww.anta.co.uk) sells attractive though still pricey modern tweed and tartan fabrics, as well as pottery. There's a nice wee **café** inside.

In Portmahomack, the *Oystercatcher* on Main Street (T01862/871560, Wwww.the-oystercatcher.co.uk; closed Mon & Tues; pre-booking advised) is one of the

restaurant highlights of this stretch of the east coast, serving a big selection of sumptuous seafood dishes. For **accommodation**, there's a small double (④) and a larger en-suite double (④) above the restaurant. For boat trips from the harbour to fish or spot dolphins, call ☎01862/871257.

Bonar Bridge and around

Before the causeway was built across the Dornoch Firth, traffic heading along the coast used to skirt west around the estuary, crossing the Kyle of Sutherland at the uninspiring village of **BONAR BRIDGE**. In the fourteenth and fifteenth centuries, the village harboured a large iron foundry. Ore was brought across the peat moors of the central Highlands from the west coast on sledges, and fuel for smelting came from the oak forest draped over the northern shores of the nearby kyle. However, James IV, passing through here on his way to Tain, was shocked to find the forest virtually clear-felled and ordered that oak saplings be planted in the gaps. Now hemmed in by spruce plantations, the beautiful ancient woodland east of Bonar Bridge dates from this era.

West of the village on the road towards Croik is one of Scotland's most intriguing accommodation options: exclusive and remote **Alladale Lodge** (☎01863/755338, ⓦwww.alladale.com; ⑨). The lodge itself and two equally luxurious stone bothies sit in a vast hunting estate owned by Paul Lister, an entrepreneur turned conservationist who aims to return the land to its pristine natural state. A high-profile plan to reintroduce predators such as wolves and bears has run up against stiff opposition and legal obstacles, but in the meantime a serious programme of reforestation is underway. Excellent ranger tours for guests explain the complexities of land management, and you can undertake a range of other outdoor activities, including shooting your very own stag. Book in advance to stay at the lodge; casual visits are not welcome.

CROIK itself is well worth a detour for its humble little **church**, which vividly illuminates the tragedy of the Clearances. Evicted from their homes in 1845, ninety villagers from Glencalvie took shelter in the churchyard, scratching poignant messages on the east window of the church that can still be deciphered.

Carbisdale Castle

Towering high above the River Shin, three miles northwest of Bonar Bridge, the daunting neo-Gothic profile of **Carbisdale Castle** overlooks the Kyle of Sutherland, as well as the battlefield where the gallant Marquis of Montrose was defeated in 1650, finally forcing Charles II to accede to the Scots' demand for Presbyterianism. The castle was erected between 1906 and 1917 for the dowager Duchess of Sutherland, following a protracted family feud.

Designed in three distinct styles (to give the impression it was added to over a long period of time), Carbisdale was eventually acquired by a Norwegian shipping magnate in 1933, and finally gifted, along with its entire contents and estate, to the SYHA, which has turned it into what must be one of the most opulent **hostels** in the world, full of white Italian-marble sculptures, huge gilt-framed portraits, sweeping staircases and magnificent drawing rooms alongside standard facilities such as self-catering kitchens, games and TV rooms and thirty dorms, including some four-bed family rooms (☎01549/421232, ⓦwww.syha.org.uk; March–Oct). You can tuck into a hearty three-course dinner at the hostel's restaurant for £11.50 before wandering the supposedly haunted corridors in search of ghosts. Bring a bike to take advantage of the several miles of **mountain-biking trails** in the nearby Balblair and Carbisdale woods. The best way to get here by public transport is to take a **train from Inverness** to nearby Culrain station, which lies within half a mile of the castle. Citylink buses (minimum 4 daily) stop in Tain, from where Macleod's Coaches buses (Mon–Sat 3 daily; 20min; ℡01408/641354) run as far as **Ardgay**, three miles from Carbisdale Castle.

Lairg and around

North of Bonar Bridge, the A836 parallels the River Shin for eleven miles to **LAIRG**, a bleak and scattered settlement at the eastern end of lonely **Loch Shin**. On fine days, the vast wastes of heather and deergrass surrounding the village can be beautiful, but in the rain it becomes a deeply depressing landscape. Lairg is predominantly a transport hub, and there's nothing much to see in town. The Ferrycroft Countryside Centre and **tourist office**, on the west side of the river (daily; ℡01549/402160), is friendly and helpful, and has a good free display on the woodlands and history of the area; the on-site ranger (℡01549/402638) can offer advice on local wildlife and walks.

Four miles south of Lairg, the **Falls of Shin** in Achany Glen are one of the best places in Scotland to see **salmon** leaping on their upstream migration; there's a viewing platform and a moderately priced restaurant (Ⓦwww.fallsofshin.co.uk) by the car park catering to bus parties. The new adventure playground also enables children to let off steam. Lairg hosts an annual lamb sale every August, one of the largest such one-day markets in Europe, when over 30,000 animals from all over the north of Scotland are bought and sold.

Lairg's train station is a mile south of town on the road to Bonar Bridge; buses stop right on the lochside. Should you want to **stay**, *Ambleside* B&B (℡01549/402130, Ⓦwww.amblesidelairg.co.uk; ❷) offers good views, as does the grander *Park House* (℡01549/402208, Ⓦwww.parkhousesporting.com; ❺) on Station Road, overlooking Loch Shin, which is a welcoming spot if you're planning walking, fishing or cycling in the area. Guests can also enjoy dinner here. Alternatively, you'll find six comfortable en-suite rooms and reasonable **bar food** at the *Highland Hotel* (℡01549/402243; ❺) next to the post office. You can also pitch a tent at *Dunroamin Caravan and Camping Park* (℡01549/402447, Ⓦwww.lairgcaravanpark.co.uk) in the village.

Dornoch

DORNOCH, a genteel and appealing town eight miles north of Tain, lies on a flattish headland overlooking the **Dornoch Firth**. Surrounded by sand dunes and blessed with an exceptionally sunny climate by Scottish standards, it's a middle-class holiday resort, with solid Edwardian hotels, trees and flowers in profusion, and miles of sandy beaches giving good views across the estuary to the Fearn peninsula. The town is also renowned for its championship **golf course** (℡01862/810219 ext 185), Scotland's most northerly first-class course. Dornoch was the scene for Scotland's most prestigious rock'n'roll wedding of recent times, when Madonna married Guy Ritchie at nearby **Skibo Castle** and had her son baptized in Dornoch cathedral. *Skibo*, an exclusive, private hotel used as a hideaway by the world's rich and powerful, is just to the west of Dornoch. Only members of the hugely expensive Carnegie Club (Ⓦwww.carnegieclub.co.uk) or their guests, however, will get anywhere near the place.

Dating from the twelfth century, Dornoch became a royal burgh in 1628. Among its oldest buildings, which are all grouped round the spacious square, the exquisite **cathedral** was founded in 1224 and built of local sandstone. The original building was horribly damaged by marauding Mackays in 1570, and much of what you see today was restored by the Countess of Sutherland in 1835, though her worst Victorian excesses were removed in the twentieth century, when the interior stonework was returned to its original state. The vaulted roof is particularly appealing; the stained-glass windows in the north wall were later additions, endowed by the expat Andrew Carnegie. Opposite, the fortified sixteenth-century **Bishop's Palace**, a fine example of vernacular architecture with stepped gables and towers, has been refurbished as a hotel (see below). Next door, the castellated **Old Town Jail** is home to a series of upmarket craft shops under the banner Jail Dornoch, while tucked in behind the *Castle Hotel* is the local **Historylinks Museum** (April, May & Oct Mon–Fri 10am–4pm; June–Sept daily 10am–4pm; Nov–March Wed & Thurs only; Ⓦwww.historylinks.org.uk; £2), which tells the story of Dornoch, from local saints and golfers to Madonna herself.

Practicalities

The council-run **tourist information** office (Easter to end Sept Mon–Fri, June–Sept also Sat, July & Aug also Sun; Ⓣ01862/810594;) is based in the sheriff courthouse right next to the *Castle Hotel*. There's no shortage of **accommodation**: *Tordarroch B&B* (Ⓣ01862/810855; March–Oct; ❷) offers good value and has a great location opposite the cathedral, as does the friendly *Trevose* (Ⓣ01862/810269; March–Sept; ❷), which is swathed in roses. The fifteenth-century *Dornoch Castle Hotel* (Ⓣ01862/810216, Ⓦwww.dornochcastlehotel.com; ❻), in the Bishop's Palace on the Square, has a decent restaurant and a cosy, old-fashioned bar with an 11ft-wide fireplace, though the revamped interior doesn't live up to the buttressed, turreted facade. The *Caravan Park* (Ⓣ01862/810423, Ⓦwww.dornochcaravans .co.uk; April–Oct) is attractively set between the manicured golf course and the vegetation of the sand dunes that fringe the beach; it also offers **camping**.

Expensive gourmet meals are available at the *2 Quail* **restaurant** (Ⓣ01862/811811; May–Sept Tues–Sat; Oct–April Fri & Sat) on Castle Street, which also has tasteful rooms (❼); otherwise, try *Luigi's* on Castle Street, for familiar but decent Italian-style snacks and meals, and the *Dornoch Patisserie* on the High Street for delicious cakes.

North to Wick

North of Dornoch, the A9 hugs the coastline for most of the sixty or so miles to **Wick**, the principal settlement in the far north of the mainland. Perhaps the most important landmark in the whole stretch is the **Sutherland Monument** near Golspie, erected in memory of the first duke of Sutherland, the landowner who oversaw the eviction of thousands of his tenants during the Clearances. The bitter memory of those times resonates through most of the small towns and villages on this stretch, including **Brora**, **Dunbeath**, **Lybster** and the gold-prospecting village of **Helmsdale**. With sites dotted around recalling Iron Age settlers and Viking rule, many of these settlements also hark back to the days of a thriving fishing trade, none more so than the main town of Wick, once the busiest herring port in Europe.

Golspie and around

Ten miles north of Dornoch on the A9 lies the straggling red-sandstone town of **GOLSPIE**, whose status as an administrative centre does little to relieve its dullness. It does, however, boast an eighteen-hole golf course and a sandy beach, while half a mile further up the coast the **Big Burn** has several rapids and waterfalls that can be seen from an attractive **woodland trail** beginning at the *Sutherland Arms Hotel*. Notably, Golspie village is also the jumping-off point for the brilliant

Highland Wildcat (mountain-bike) Trails (Ⓦwww.highlandwildcat.com) within the forested hills half a mile to the west. The (colour-coded) trails include a huge descent from the summit of Ben Bhraggie to sea level and a ride past the statue of the Duke of Sutherland.

Dunrobin Castle

Mountain-bikers aside, the main reason to stop in Golspie is to look around **Dunrobin Castle** (April, May, Sept & early Oct Mon–Sat 10.30am–4.30pm, Sun noon–4.30pm; June–Aug daily 10.30am–5.30pm; £8.50), overlooking the sea a mile north of town. Approached via a long tree-lined drive, this fairy-tale confection of turrets and pointed roofs – modelled by the architect Sir Charles Barry (designer of London's Houses of Parliament) on a Loire château – is the seat of the infamous Sutherland family, at one time Europe's biggest landowners, with a staggering 1.3 million acres, and the principal driving force behind the Clearances in this area. The castle is on a correspondingly vast scale, boasting 189 furnished rooms, of which the tour takes in only seventeen. Staring up at the pile from the midst of its elaborate **formal gardens**, it's worth remembering that such extravagance was paid for by uprooting literally thousands of crofters from the surrounding glens.

The castle's opulent **interior** is crammed full of fine furniture, paintings (including works by Landseer, Allan Ramsay and Sir Joshua Reynolds), tapestries and *objets d'art*. The attractive gardens are pleasant to wander around, and it's worth diverting through them to get to Dunrobin's unusual **museum**, housed in an eighteenth-century building at the edge of the garden. Inside, hundreds of disembodied animals' heads and horns peer down from the walls, alongside other more macabre appendages, from elephants' toes to rhinos' tails.

Conveniently – though not too surprisingly, considering the duke built the railway – the castle has its own **train** station (summer only) on the main Inverness–Wick line.

The Sutherland Monument

Approaching Golspie, you can't miss the 100ft-high **monument** to the first duke of Sutherland, which peers proprietorially down from the summit of the 1293ft-high **Beinn a'Bhragaidh** (Ben Bhraggie). An inscription cut into its base recalls that the statue was erected in 1834 by "a mourning and grateful tenantry [to] a judicious, kind and liberal landlord". Unsurprisingly, there's no reference to the fact that the duke, widely regarded as Scotland's own Josef Stalin, forcibly evicted 15,000 crofters from his million-acre estate – a fact which, in the words of one local historian, makes the monument "a grotesque representation of the many forces that destroyed the Highlands". A campaign to have the statue smashed and scattered over the hillside has largely died down.

It's worth the stiff **climb** to the top of the hill (round trip 1hr 30min) for the wonderful views south along the coast past Dornoch to the Moray Firth and west towards Lairg and Loch Shin. The path is steep and strenuous in places, however, and there's no view until you're out of the trees, about twenty minutes from the top. Head up Fountain Road about halfway along Golspie's main street; after crossing the railway line and pass (or park at) Rhives Farm steading. From here, follow the Beinn a'Bhragaidh footpath (BBFP) signs along the path into the woods.

Loch Fleet and Rogart

Just to the south of Golspie, the A9 fringes **Loch Fleet**, a tidal estuary harbouring some delicate coastal and woodland vegetation, as well as a range of birdlife including greylag geese and arctic terns, and sealife such as seals and otters. Four miles northwest of Loch Fleet on the A839 to Lairg is one of Scotland's most unusual and imaginative **hostels**, ⚡ *Sleeperzzz.com* (☎01408/641343, ⓦwww .sleeperzzz.com), where you can stay in one of three first-class railway carriages parked in a siding beside the station on the Inverness–Thurso line in the tiny settlement of **ROGART**. Each of the comfortable compartments has a bunk bed on one side and the original seats on the other, while the two end compartments are used as a kitchen and common room. A small reduction is offered to those making their journey by train or bicycle. The owners have free **mountain bikes** available to explore the local countryside, and the place stands a hundred yards from a convivial local **pub**, the *Pittentrail Inn*, where the bar/bistro serves moderately priced evening meals.

Helmsdale and around

Eleven scenic miles north along the A9 from Golspie, **HELMSDALE** (ⓦwww .helmsdale.org) is an old herring port, founded in the nineteenth century to house the evicted inhabitants of Strath Kildonan, which lies behind it. Today, the main draw in the sleepy, steadily rejuvenating village is the attractively designed **Timespan Heritage Centre** beside the river (Easter–Oct Mon–Sat 10am–5pm, Sun noon–5pm; £4; ☎01431/821327). It's an ambitious venture for a place of this size, the refurbished museum telling the local story of Viking raids, witchburning, Clearances and fishing through high-tech displays, sound effects and an audiovisual programme. The story of the Kildonan Gold Rush Trail uses 21st-century GPS technology: visitors are issued with an interactive hand-held audiovisual device for a self-guided tour (1hr 30min; £6 deposit) of the nearby Baile an Or gold-prospecting area. The centre also has an art gallery, café and geology garden.

There's no official tourist office in town, but you'll pick up local information at the very friendly Strath Ullie Crafts on the harbour (☎01431/821402). At the end of Dunrobin Street is the ⚡ *Bridge Hotel* (☎01431/821100, ⓦwww.bridgehotel .net; ❻), a pleasantly grand and comfortable **hotel** with wood-panelling, big open fireplaces and two large aquariums holding freshly caught live lobsters – available at the discerning *Green Stag* restaurant; the *Red Lobster* restaurant is less formal. There are several good-value **B&Bs**, including *Broomhill House* on Navidale Road (☎01431/821259, ⓦwww.blancebroomhill.com; ❶), which has bedrooms in a turret added to the former croft by a miner who struck it lucky in the Kildonan gold rush. Evening meals are also available. Alternatively, try Mrs McDonald at *Customs House* on the harbour, which offers terrific views and a great breakfast (☎01431/821648 and 821643; ❶). There's also a small SYHA-affiliated ⚡ **youth hostel** (☎01431/821636, ⓦwww.helmsdalehostel.co.uk; April–Oct; family room ❶), beside the A9 as it climbs north up from the harbour; it's located in a sensitively converted gymnasium, with high ceilings and a wood-burning stove.

If you're looking for somewhere to **eat** in Helmsdale, the seasonal game and seafood on the menu of the *Green Stag* in the *Bridge Hotel* won't disappoint, though your eye may well be drawn to the bizarre *Mirage* restaurant (ⓦwww.lamirage .org) on Dunrobin Street. The late former proprietor of the *Mirage* became something of a local celebrity, modelling herself on the romantic novelist Barbara Cartland. Under new owners, the furnishings remain suitably garish, including a lampshade with fishnet tights round the stand and framed photographs of visiting personalities covering the walls. There's a long menu, which includes large helpings of fish and chips. *Gilbert's* antique shop and tearoom on Dunrobin Street is terrific for cakes, while *Timespan's* bright daytime café looks onto its beautiful herbaceous garden and the bridge.

Dunbeath and around

Just north of Helmsdale, the A9 begins its long haul up the **Ord of Caithness**. This steep hill used to form a pretty impregnable obstacle, and the desolate road still gets blocked during winter snowstorms. Once over the pass, the landscape changes dramatically, as heather-clad moors give way to miles of treeless green grazing lands, peppered with derelict crofts and latticed by long dry-stone walls. As you come over the pass, look out for signs to the ruined village of **Badbea**, reached via a ten-minute walk from the car park at the side of the A9. Built by tenants cleared from nearby Ousdale, the settlement now lies deserted, although its ruined hovels show what hardship the crofters had to endure: the cottages stood so near the windy cliff-edge that children had to be tethered to prevent them from being blown into the sea.

DUNBEATH, hidden at the mouth of a small strath twelve miles north of Ord of Caithness, was another village founded to provide work in the wake of the Clearances. The local landlord built a harbour here in 1800, at the start of the herring boom, and the settlement briefly flourished. The novelist Neil Gunn was born here, in one of the terraced houses under the flyover that now swoops above the village; you can find out more about him at the **Dunbeath Heritage Centre** (Easter–Oct daily 10am–5pm; Nov–March Mon–Fri 11am–3pm; £2). The staff can advise you on several good walks along the Highland River of Gunn's novel; his other famous book, *The Silver Darlings*, was also set on this coastline. The best of the handful of modest **B&Bs** here is *Tormore Farm* (℡01593/731240; May–Oct; ❶), a large farmhouse with three comfortable rooms, half a mile north of the harbour on the A9.

Just north of Dunbeath is the simple but moving **Laidhay Croft Museum** (Easter–Oct daily 10am–5pm; £2), housed in a long thatched croft, which has a lovely tearoom and offers a useful perspective on the sometimes over-romanticized life of the Highlander before the Clearances. A little further up the coast, the **Clan Gunn Heritage Centre and Museum** (June–Sept Mon–Sat 11am–1pm & 2–4pm; £2.50) is mainly a place for members of the Clan Gunn and its septs (branches), although it also doles out a bit more local history and a few titbits for those on the trail of **Neil Gunn**.

Lybster and around

The final stretch of road before Wick gives great views out to the sea and the oil rigs on the horizon. The planned village of **LYBSTER** (pronounced "libe-ster"), established at the height of the nineteenth-century herring boom, once had two hundred-odd boats working out of its harbour: now there are just a handful. The **Water Lines** heritage centre by the harbour (May to mid-Oct daily 11am–5pm; £2.50) is an attractive place, with CCTV footage of sea birds on the nearby cliffs and modern displays about the "silver darlings" and the fishermen that pursued them; there's a snug café downstairs. There's not much else to see here apart from the harbour; the upper town is a grim collection of grey pebble-dashed bungalows centred on a broad main street.

The **Grey Cairns of Camster**, seven miles due north, are one of the most memorable sights on the northeast coast. Surrounded by bleak moorland, these two enormous reconstructed prehistoric burial-chambers, originally built four or five thousand years ago, were immaculately designed, with corbelled dry-stone roofs in their hidden chambers, which you can crawl into through narrow passageways. More extraordinary ancient remains lie at **East Clyth**, two miles north of Lybster on the A99, where a path leads to the "**Hill o'Many Stanes**". Some two hundred boulders stand in the ground here, forming 22 parallel rows that run north to south; no one has yet worked out what they were used for, although archeological studies have shown there were once six hundred stones in place. A fourteen-mile track waymarked as a cycle path leads between the two sites, entering the forest at a car park half a mile south of the Camster Cairns and emerging near the single-track road which passes the Hill o'Many Stanes and connects with the A99.

Another relatively unknown historic site in the area is the **Whaligoe staircase**, ten miles north of Lybster on the A99 at the north end of the village of Ulbster. The stairway, which has 365 steps constructed out of the distinctive local slab stone, leads steeply down from the side of the house beside the car park to a natural harbour surrounded by cliffs. At the bottom you'll see a few remnants of the harbour used by herring fishermen in the last century, as well as vast numbers of sea birds, including cormorant, skua and puffin; the daunting climb back up is made a little bit easier by the thought that, unlike the women of Ulbster, you don't have a creel full of herring to carry all the way to the top. The stairway is steep and uneven for much of the way down, so be particularly careful if the steps are wet. To get to the stairway, turn off towards the sea at the junction signposted on its landward side to the "Cairn o'Get".

Wick

Originally a Viking settlement named *Vik* (meaning "bay"), **WICK** has been a royal burgh since 1589. It's actually two towns: Wick proper, and **Pultneytown**, immediately south across the river, a messy, rather run-down community planned by Thomas Telford in 1806 for the British Fisheries Society to encourage evicted crofters to take up fishing. Wick's heyday was in the mid-nineteenth century, when it was the busiest herring port in Europe, with a fleet of over 1100 boats, exporting tons of fish to Russia, Scandinavia and the West Indian slave plantations. Robert Louis Stevenson described it as "the meanest of man's towns, situated on the baldest of God's bays", and though redevelopment of the harbour is under way, including the installation of pontoons and facilities for yachts, something of that down-at-heel atmosphere remains. If you're here for a few hours, scout out the huge area around the harbour in Pultneytown where builders and redevelopers are steadily transforming the rows of fishermen's cottages, derelict net-mending sheds, stores and cooperages. It all gives an insight into the sheer scale of the former fishing trade.

Walks and cycles around Wick

Ordnance Survey Explorer map no. 450

There's a good **clifftop walk** to the dramatic fifteenth-to-seventeenth-century ruins of **Sinclair** and **Girnigoe castles**, rising steeply from a needle-thin promontory three miles north of Wick, which functioned as a single stronghold for the earls of Caithness. In 1570 the fourth earl, suspecting his son of trying to murder him, imprisoned him in the dungeon here until he died of starvation. From the tiny fishing village of **Staxigoe**, head north from the harbour to Field of Noss farm and follow the line of the cliffs, where you'll encounter all sorts of sea birds, including puffins. At Noss Head lighthouse, head along the access road to a car park, where a path leads out to the castles on the north-facing coastline. **Cycling** is a good way to get to the castles: the roads near Noss Head are flat and straight, though you should think twice about setting off if the wind is too strong.

A longer ride (a 14-mile two-way trip) is along the backroads southwest of Wick through Newton Row and Tannach to the short archeological walking-trail at the **Loch of Yarrows**, which includes remains of a lochside broch, a hilltop fort and chambered cairns.

The town's story is told in the loyally volunteer-maintained **Wick Heritage Centre** in Bank Row, Pultneytown (Easter–Oct Mon–Sat 10am–5pm; Ⓦwww .wickheritage.org; £3), which contains a fascinating, jumbled array of artefacts from the old fishing days, including fully rigged boats, original boat models, the old Noss Head lighthouse light and a huge photographic collection dating from the 1880s. The other visitor attraction nearby is the fairly simple **Pulteney Distillery** (Mon–Fri 10am–1pm & 2–4pm; tours at 11am & 2pm or by arrangement; £4, includes discount voucher; Ⓣ01955/602371) on Huddart Street, a few blocks back from the sea. Much is made here of the maritime character of both the distillery and the whisky – the coopers who made barrels for the distillery, for example, also made them for storing cured herrings bound for Russia and Germany.

The **train** station and **bus** stops are next to each other immediately south and west of the bridge that crosses the River Wick in the centre of town. Frequent local buses run to Thurso and up the coast to John O'Groats. Wick also has an **airport** (Ⓣ01955/602215), a couple of miles to the north, with direct flights to and from Edinburgh and Aberdeen.

In Macallans's menswear shop on the High Street (Mon–Sat 9am–5.30pm; Ⓣ01955/602547), you'll find the small **tourist office**. The best of the **hotels** is *Mackay's*, on the south side of the river in the town centre (Ⓣ01955/602323, Ⓦwww.mackayshotel.co.uk; ❺), while reasonable **B&B** options include *Quayside*, 25 Harbour Quay (Ⓣ01955/603229, Ⓦwww.quaysidewick.co.uk; ❹), and *The Clachan*, 13 Randolph Place on South Road (Ⓣ01955/605384, Ⓦwww.theclachan.co.uk; ❸). Five miles towards Thurso is seventeenth-century *Bilbster House* (April–Oct, in winter by prior arrangement; Ⓣ01955/621212; ❷), a lovely eighteenth-century manor house with walled gardens.

Good **eating** options don't abound, though the moderately priced *Bord de l'Eau* (Ⓣ01955/604400; closed Mon) on Market Street, which runs along the north side of the river, offers a reasonable menu of classic French standards.

Travel details

Trains

Fort William to: Arisaig (Mon–Sat 3–4 daily, Sun 1–2 daily; 1hr 10min); Glenfinnan (Mon–Sat 3–4 daily, Sun 2–4 daily; 35min); Mallaig (Mon–Sat 3–4 daily, Sun 2–4 daily; 1hr 25min).
Inverness to: Cromarty (Mon–Sat 9 daily, 2 on Sun; 55min); Dingwall (Mon–Sat 3–4 daily, Sun 1–2 daily; 25min); Helmsdale (Mon–Sat 3 daily, 2 on Sun; 2hr 20min); Kyle of Lochalsh (Mon–Sat 3–4 daily, Sun 1–2 daily; 2hr 40min); Lairg (Mon–Sat 3 daily, 2 on Sun; 1hr 40min); Plockton (Mon–Sat 3–4 daily, Sun 1–2 daily; 2hr 15min); Thurso (Mon–Sat 3 daily, 2 on Sun; 3hr 25min); Wick (Mon–Sat 3 daily, 2 Sun; 3hr 45min).
Kyle of Lochalsh to: Dingwall (Mon–Sat 3–4 daily, Sun 1–2 daily; 2hr); Inverness (Mon–Sat 3–4 daily, Sun 1–2 daily; 2hr 40min); Plockton (Mon–Sat 3–4 daily, Sun 1–2 daily; 15min).

Thurso to: Dingwall (Mon–Sat 4 daily, 2 on Sun; 3hr); Inverness (Mon–Sat 4 daily, 2 on Sun; 3hr 20min); Lairg (Mon–Sat 4 daily, 2 on Sun; 1hr 50min); Wick (Mon–Sat 3 daily, 2 on Sun; 35min).
Wick to: Dingwall (Mon–Sat 4 daily, 2 on Sun; 3hr 30min); Inverness (Mon–Sat 4 daily, 2 on Sun; 4hr); Lairg (Mon–Sat 4 daily, 2 on Sun; 2hr 20min).

Buses

Fort William to: Acharacle (Mon–Sat 1–2 daily; 1hr 30min); Inverness (5 daily; 2hr 15min); Kilchoan (1–2 daily on request only from Acharacle; 3hr 35min); Mallaig (Mon–Fri 3 daily; 1hr 20min).
Gairloch to: Inverness (Mon–Sat 1 daily; also ScotBus 1 daily Mon–Sat, June–Sept only; 2hr 45min); Ullapool (1 daily Mon, Wed, Thurs & Sat). To Redpoint and Melvaig only Dial-a-bus service Ⓣ01445/712255.

Inverness to: Durness (Mon–Sat 1 daily; 2hr 40min; also bike bus, May to end Sept Mon–Sat 1 daily, also July & Aug 1 on Sun); Thurso (4–5 daily; 3hr 35min); Wick (Mon–Fri 4 daily, Sat & 3 on Sun; 2hr 55min).

Kyle of Lochalsh to: Fort William (3 daily; 1hr 50min); Glasgow (3 daily; 5hr); Inverness (3 daily; 2hr).

Lochinver to: Inverness (May–end Sept 1 daily; plus July & Aug 1 on Sun; 3hr 10min); Ullapool (2 daily;1hr).

Thurso to: Inverness (4–5 daily; 3hr 30min); John O' Groats (Mon–Fri 4 daily, Sat 3 daily; 1hr); Wick (Mon–4 on Sun; 35min).

Ullapool to: Durness (May–end Sept Mon–Sat 1 daily; also July & Aug 1 on Sun; 3hr); Inverness (Mon–Sat 2 daily; 1hr 30min).

Wick to: John O' Groats (Mon–Sat; 4 daily 50min).

Ferries

To Lewis: Ullapool–Stornoway (Mon–Sat 2 daily; 2hr 45min).

To Mull: Kilchoan–Tobermory (Mon–Sat 7 daily; also May–Aug 5 on Sun; 35min); Lochaline–Fishnish (Mon–Sat every 50min, Sun hourly; 15min).

To Orkney: Gill's Bay–St Margaret's Hope (3 daily; 45min); John O'Groats–Burwick (passengers only; 2–4 daily; 40min); Scrabster–Stromness (2–3 daily; 90min).

To Skye: Glenelg–Kylerhea (every 15–30min; 15min); Mallaig–Armadale (Mon–Sat 8 daily; also mid-May to mid-Sept Sun at least 4 daily; 30min).

Mallaig to the Small Isles: Canna (Mon, Wed, Fri, Sat 1 daily; 2hr 30min); Eigg (Mon, Thurs, Sat 1 daily; 1hr 15min; Muck (Tues, Thurs, Fri, Sat 1 daily; 2hr 5min); Rùm (Mon, Wed, Fri, Sat 1 daily; 1hr 20min).

To Nigg from Cromarty: May–Oct, daily from 8am and every 30min until 6pm.

Flights

Wick to: Aberdeen (Mon–Fri 4 daily; 35min); Edinburgh (Mon–Fri 1 daily; 1hr 10min).

Skye and the
Small Isles

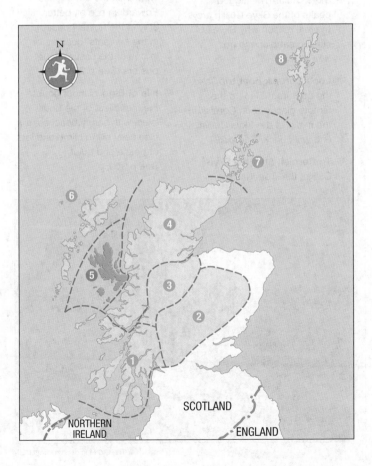

CHAPTER 5 # Highlights

* **Isle of Raasay** Just off the coast of Skye, Raasay is well off the beaten track, yet offers a wide variety of outdoor pursuits, from windsurfing to hillwalking. See p.285

* **Skye Cuillin** The jagged peaks of the Skye Cuillin are the real reason why Skye is still a great place to go. See p.287

* **Loch Coruisk boat trip** Take the boat from Elgol to the remote glacial Loch Coruisk in the midst of the Skye Cuillin, and walk back. See p.287

* **Trotternish** After the Skye Cuillin, the Trotternish peninsula is the most distinctive landscape on Skye, with its basalt intrusions and massive landslides. See p.293

* **Kinloch Castle, Isle of Rùm** Visit the outrageous Edwardian pile or, better still, stay in the hostel housed in the servants' quarters or in one of the castle's four-posters. See p.298

* **Isle of Eigg** Without doubt the friendliest of the Small Isles, with sandy beaches, a nice easy hill to climb and lots of peace and quiet. See p.300

▲ The Old Man of Storr, Trotternish

Skye and the Small Isles

S ome say the **Isle of Skye** was named after the Old Norse word for "cloud" (*skuy*), earning itself the Gaelic moniker *Eilean a' Cheò* (Island of Mist). Yet, despite the unpredictability of the weather, tourism has been an important part of the island's economy for over a century, since the railway reached Kyle of Lochalsh in 1897. From here, it was a brief boat trip across to Skye, and the Edwardian bourgeoisie was soon swarming over to walk its mountains, whose beauty had been proclaimed by the Victorians. Since the building of the Skye Bridge, the island has been busier than ever, and at the height of the summer the roads are crammed with coach tours, minibuses and caravans. Yet Skye is a deceptively large island, and you'll get the most out of it – and escape the worst of the crowds – if you take the time to explore its more remote corners.

The Clearances saw an estimated 30,000 indigenous *Sgiathanachs* (pronounced "ski-anaks") emigrate in the mid-nineteenth century; today, the population is just over 9000. Tourism is now by far the island's biggest earner and has attracted hundreds of incomers from the rest of Britain over the last couple of decades. Nevertheless, Skye remains the most important centre for **Gaelic culture** and language outside the Western Isles. Over a third of the population is fluent in Gaelic, the Gaelic college on Sleat is the most important in Scotland, and the Free Church (see p.308) maintains a strong presence. A good way of finding out what's going on in the region is to read the weekly *West Highland Free Press*, a refreshingly vociferous campaigning newspaper published in Broadford.

One way to avoid the crowds on Skye is to head off to the so-called **Small Isles** – the improbably named **Rùm**, **Eigg**, **Muck** and **Canna** – to the south. Each with a population of less than a hundred, they are easily accessible by ferry from Mallaig and Arisaig, though with limited accommodation available, a visit requires forward planning.

Skye

Jutting out from the mainland like a giant butterfly – *sgiath* means "winged" – the bare and bony promontories of **Skye** (An t-Eilean Sgiathanach) fringe a deeply indented coastline. The island's most popular destination is the **Cuillin** ridge, whose jagged peaks dominate the island during clear weather; to explore

SKYE & THE SMALL ISLES

them at close quarters you'll need to be a determined walker. More accessible but equally dramatic are the rock formations of the **Trotternish** peninsula, in the north. And if you're determined to escape the summer crush, shuffle off to the little-visited **Isle of Raasay**, off Skye's east coast. Of the two main settlements, **Portree** is the only one with any charm, and a useful base for exploring the Trotternish.

Most visitors reach Skye via the **Skye Bridge,** which sweeps across the sea from Kyle of Lochalsh, itself linked to Inverness by train. The more scenic approach is via **Armadale** on the Sleat peninsula, linked by **ferry** with Mallaig, at the end of the train line from Fort William. A third option is to arrive at **Kylerhea** via the tiny **car ferry** (Easter–Oct) which leaves from Glenelg, south of Kyle of Lochalsh. If you're heading for the Western Isles, it's 57 miles from Armadale and 49 miles from Kyleakin to **Uig**, from which ferries leave for Tarbert on Harris and Lochmaddy on North Uist.

Skye has several **campsites**, and numerous **hostels** or bunkhouses – all of which recommend advance bookings, particularly in July and August – along with plenty of B&Bs and a string of pricey, but excellent **hotels**. If you're travelling by **public transport**, it's worth knowing that a Skye Roverbus ticket is available (£6 for one day; £15 for three). Services do peter out in the more remote areas, and many close down on Sundays.

Sleat

Ferries from Mallaig (see p.232) connect with the **Sleat** (pronounced "Slate") **peninsula**, Skye's southern tip, an uncharacteristically fertile area known as "The Garden of Skye". The CalMac ferry terminal is at **ARMADALE** (Armadal), an elongated hamlet stretching along the wooded shoreline. If you've time to kill waiting for the ferry, take a look at the huge variety of Scottish and Irish knitwear on offer at Ragamuffin by the pier; if you need a bite **to eat**, pop into *The Shed* next door, which does a great seafood pizza (eat-in or takeaway).

There are several good **accommodation** options in neighbouring Ardvasar, from the traditional, whitewashed *Ardvasar Hotel* (☎01471/844223, ⓦwww .ardvasarhotel.com; ❼) which has a good restaurant specializing in local seafood and a lively bar, to *Morar* (☎01471/844378, ⓦwww.accommodation-on-skye .co.uk; ❹), a modern crofthouse B&B, just beyond the hotel, with superb sea views and an indoor swimming pool. There's also the *Flora MacDonald Hostel* (☎01471/844272, ⓦwww.skye-hostel.co.uk; ❷), two miles or so up the road to Broadford, a converted barn run by locals, with cheap bunks in mixed dorms, and a lodge with a double, triple and quad. **Bike rental** is available from the local petrol station (☎01471/844249), close to the pier; **boat trips** operate from Armadale with Sea fari (☎01471/833316, ⓦwww.seafari.co.uk).

A little further along the A851, past the youth hostel, you'll find one of the best attractions on the island, the **Armadale Castle Gardens** (April–Oct daily 9.30am–5.30pm; £6.95; ⓦwww.clandonald.com). Within the handsome forty-acre gardens lies the shell of the MacDonalds' neo-Gothic castle, a café and a library for those who want to chase up their ancestral Donald connections. The gardens' slick, purpose-built **Museum of the Isles** has a good section on the Jacobite period and its aftermath, featuring a few Bonnie Prince Charlie objects and a couple of cannonballs fired at the castle by HMS *Dartmouth*, sent by William and Mary to shell the castle, which "sent them scampering to the hills" (those who surrendered were hanged). There's also one or two top-notch works of art: a splendid portrait of a young, theatrical Glengarry (on whom Walter Scott modelled the hero of the Waverley novels) by Angelika Kaufmann, and a portrait of his more conventional brother, MacDonell, by Henry Raeburn.

Sabhal Mòr Ostaig to Isleornsay

A couple of miles up the road in an old MacDonald farm is the splendid white **Sabhal Mòr Ostaig** (☎01471/844373, ⓦwww.smo.uhi.ac.uk), a modern Gaelic-medium college that's part of the university of the Highlands and Islands. For those interested in Gaelic, the college bookshop is always worth a browse, and the college regularly puts on exhibitions and live gigs. Six miles further on is **ISLEORNSAY** (Eilean Iarmain), a secluded little village of whitewashed cottages that was once Skye's main fishing port. The views out across the bay are wonderful, overlooking a necklace of seaweed-encrusted rocks and the tidal **Isle of Ornsay**, which sports a trim lighthouse built by Robert Louis Stevenson's father.

One of the loveliest parts of the Sleat peninsula, however, is the west coast: take the fiercely winding single-track road over to the scattered settlement of **TARSKAVAIG**, with its little sandy beach looking out over to the Small Isles. Further up the coast, the stony, seaweedy beach at **TOKAVAIG** is overlooked by the ruined Dunscaith Castle and boasts views over the entire Cuillin range – this, and neighbouring **ORD**, with a pleasant sandy beach, are the two best places on the whole of Skye from which to view the mountains in fine weather.

The best place **to stay** is at *Ord House* (T 01471/855212, W www.ord-house .co.uk ⑤), a lovely Georgian house in Ord, set in its own grounds, overlooking the Cuillin and the Small Isles. Another luxury option is *Hotel Eilean Iarmain* (T 01471/833332, W www.eilean-iarmain.co.uk; ⑤), a Victorian hotel in Isleornsay, whose bar and **restaurant** serves great seafood. Another couple of miles brings you to the turning for *Kinloch Lodge Hotel* (T 01471/833333, W www .claire-macdonald.com/kinloch-lodge; ⑨), an old hunting lodge owned by Lord Macdonald of Macdonald, with Michelin-starred food guaranteed by wife Claire whose cookery books are internationally famous. Book ahead for lunch (from around £30), afternoon tea (from £15) or dinner (from £55); the setting is superb, the staff are very welcoming, and, if you're staying, you'll find the rooms decked out in standard country house hotel style – all stays are dinner, bed and breakfast.

Kyleakin and Kylerhea

Built in 1995, the **Skye Bridge** was once the most expensive toll bridge in Europe, and no cheaper than the ferry it replaced. Protests and non-payment eventually persuaded the Scottish government to buy the bridge in 2004 and abolish the tolls. Strictly speaking there are, in fact, two bridges, with an island in the middle, **Eilean Bàn**, whose lighthouse cottages were briefly the home of author and naturalist Gavin Maxwell. One of the houses is now a museum and can be visited, along with the lighthouse, on a guided tour (£6); numbers are limited and must be booked in advance through the **Bright Water Visitor Centre** (phone for times; T 01599/530040, W www.eileanban.org) in nearby Kyleakin.

Most folk don't actually bother to stop in the old ferry port of **KYLEAKIN** (pronounced "ka*la*kin", with the stress on the second syllable), which has now become something of a backpackers' hangout. If you're looking for a party atmosphere, *Saucy Mary's* (T 01599/534845, W www.saucymarys.com) is the **hostel** to head for; otherwise, snuggle down at the cosy *Dun Caan Hostel* (T 01599/534087, W www.skyerover.co.uk). You can grab a bite to eat at *Harry's* and **bike rental** is available from the hostels.

In the summer, you can still go "over the sea to Skye" by taking the community-run **car ferry** (Easter–Sept; W www.skyeferry.co.uk) which sets off every quarter or half-hour from Glenelg and takes just five minutes to reach **KYLERHEA** (pronounced "kile-ray"), a peaceful little place some four miles down the coast from Kyleakin. From here you can walk half an hour up the coast to the Forestry Commission **Otter Hide**, where, if you're lucky, you may be able to spot one of these elusive creatures.

Broadford

From the west, there's no avoiding the island's second-largest village, charmless **BROADFORD** (An t-Àth Leathann), strung out along the main road. Despite its rather unlovely appearance, Broadford makes a useful base for exploring the southern half of Skye, and has one of the island's best wet-weather retreats, the unusual **Skye Serpentarium** (Easter–June & Sept–Oct Mon–Sat 10am–5pm; July & Aug daily; £2.50; Ⓦ www.skyeserpentarium.org.uk), housed in an old mill by the main road heading east out of town. There are over fifty animals on display, all of them abandoned or rescued, ranging from tiny tree frogs to large iguanas and there's usually a snake you can handle.

Broadford's **tourist office** (Easter–June & Sept–Oct Mon–Sat only; July & Aug daily; Ⓣ 0845/225 5121) is by the 24-hour garage on the main road, where there's a laundry, small shop and bureau de change. At the west end of the village there's a bank, a bakery, a café and a post office. The SYHA **hostel**, on the west shore of Broadford Bay (Ⓣ 0870/004 1106, Ⓦ www.syha.org.uk; March–Oct), is no beauty, but it's clean and well-equipped. There's a surfeit of **B&Bs**, but a couple stand out from the crowd: *Berabhaigh* (Ⓣ 01471/822372, Ⓦ www.isleofskye.net /berabhaigh; March–Oct; ❸), 3 Lime Park, a spotlessly clean, whitewashed Victorian house close to the centre of the village, run by a very hospitable couple; and ⚘ *Tigh an Dochais* (Ⓣ 01471/820022, Ⓦ www.skyebedbreakfast.co.uk; ❺), a striking piece of contemporary architecture as well as a very comfortable guesthouse, with stunning views across Broadford Bay (binoculars provided). If you want a bite **to eat**, try the justifiably popular *Creelers Seafood Restaurant* (Ⓣ 01471/822281, Ⓦ www.skye-seafood-restaurant.co.uk; closed Sun) at the south end of the bay. **Bike rental** is available from the SYHA hostel and *Fairwinds* (Ⓣ 01471/822270), on the road to Elgol. *Skyak Adventures* (Ⓣ 01471/820002; Ⓦ www.skyakadventures.com), based outside Broadford at Lower Breakish, run **sea-kayaking** trips.

Isle of Raasay

I will wait for the birch wood
Until it comes up by the cairn,
Until the whole ridge from Beinn na Lice
Will be under its shade.

If it does not, I will go down to Hallaig,
To the Sabbath of the dead,
When the people are frequenting,
Every single generation gone.

They are still in Hallaig,
MacLeans and MacLeods,
All who were there in the time of Mac Gille Chaluim
The dead have been seen alive.

The men lying on the green
At the end of every house that was,
The girls a wood of birches,
Straight their backs, bent their heads.

from *Hallaig* by Sorley MacLean

Despite lying less than a mile offshore, the long, hilly island of **Raasay** (Ratharsair) sees surprisingly few visitors. For much of its history, Raasay was the property of a branch of the staunchly Jacobite MacLeods of Lewis, and the island sent 100 men and 26 pipers to Culloden, as a consequence of which it was practically destroyed by government troops in the aftermath of the 1745 uprising. Bonnie Prince Charlie spent a miserable night in a "mean low hut" on Raasay during his flight and swore to replace the burnt turf cottages with proper stone houses (he never did). When the MacLeods were finally forced to sell up in 1843, the Clearances started in earnest, a period of the island's history immortalized by Raasay poet Sorley MacLean (Somhairle MacGill-Eain). In 1921, seven ex-servicemen and their families from the neighbouring isle of **Rona** (see box below) illegally squatted crofts on Raasay, and were imprisoned, causing a public outcry. As a result, both islands were bought by the government the following year. Rona now has one permanent resident while Raasay's population stands at around two hundred, many of them members of the Free Presbyterian Church. Strict observance of the Sabbath is the most obvious manifestation for visitors, who should respect the islanders' feelings.

The ferry docks in Churchton Bay, near **INVERARISH**, the island's tiny village set within thick woods on the southwest coast. If your time is limited there are several walks in these woods: you can follow the miners' trail, which traces the route of the railway constructed to carry iron ore to the jetty, built by German POWs in 1914. You will also see the ruins of a once grand Georgian mansion, **Raasay House**, built by the MacLeods in the late 1740s, and all but ruined a few years later by government troops. The place was run as an outdoor centre (see also "Practicalities", opposite) until a fire gutted it in 2009. The grounds slope down to a tiny **harbour**, overlooked by two weathered stone mermaids stuck on top of the remains of a battery armed in the Napoleonic era with several cannons. The house's stable clock stopped on the day in 1914 when 36 men of Raasay went to war – only 14 returned. Also in the grounds, there are Pictish symbol stones and the charming ruined thirteenth-century chapel of St Moluag.

The interior of Raasay is starkly barren, a rugged and rocky terrain of sandstone in the south and gneiss in the north, with the most obvious feature being the curiously truncated basalt cap on top of **Dun Caan** (1456ft), where Boswell "danced a Highland dance" on his visit to the island with Dr Johnson in 1773 – you may feel like doing the same if you're rewarded with a clear view over to the Cuillin and the Outer Hebrides. The trail to the top of the peak is fairly easy to follow, a splendid five-mile trek up through the forest and along the burn behind Inverarish. The quickest return is made down the northwest slope of Dun Caan, but – by going a couple of miles further – you can get back to the ferry along the path by the southeast shore, passing the abandoned crofters' village of Hallaig, whose steep incline led mothers to tether their children to stakes to prevent them rolling onto the shore.

If you want to explore the north of the island you need a fine day to appreciate the views across to the Cuillin, Portree and the Trotternish peninsula. Where the road dips to the east coast the stark remains of fifteenth-century **Brochel Castle** stand overlooking the shore. The last two miles of the road to Arnish is known as **Calum's Road**: in the 1960s the council refused to extend the road to the village, so Calum MacLeod decided to build it himself. It took him ten years, and by the time he'd finished he and his wife were the only people left in the village. You can walk on a boggy path to the north end and on to **Eilean Tigh** at low tide, or

Isle of Rona

To the north of Raasay is the **Isle of Rona** (Ⓦwww.isleofrona.com) – sometimes called South Rona to distinguish it from North Rona (see p.316) – ancestral home of the family of Billy Graham, the American evangelist. Since 1943, the only permanent inhabitants have been the lighthouse keepers, NATO personnel and now, the manager, who lives at above the sheltered harbour of Acairseid Mhòr (Bug Harbour). You can camp with permission, there's a **bunkhouse**, three self-catering cottages, and you can even get dinner, bed and breakfast at *Rona Lodge*; phone ☏07831/293963 for more information on how to reach the island.

there's a shorter walk on to **Eilean Fladday**, which is also tidal. Raasay is rich in flora and fauna, and it's at the north end that you're more likely to see a golden eagle, snipe, orchids and perhaps the unique Raasay vole.

Practicalities

The CalMac **ferry** departs for Raasay from Sconser (Mon–Sat 8–10 daily, 2 on Sun; 25min). Many visitors go for the day, since there's plenty to do within walking distance of the pier – you could stay in Sconser at *Loch Aluinn* (℡01478/650288, Ⓦwww.isleofskye.net/loch-aluinn; March–Oct; ③), a good modern crofthouse **B&B** by the shore. If you do take a car, be warned, there's no petrol on the island. A rough track cuts up the steep hillside from the village to Raasay's isolated but beautifully placed SYHA **hostel** (℡01478/660240, Ⓦwww .syha.org.uk; mid-May to mid-Sept). Accommodation is also available at *Allt Arais* (℡01478/660237, Ⓦwww.allt-arais.co.uk; ③), a modern **B&B**, with free wi-fi and a large lounge with great views over the bay. *Raasay Outdoor Centre* is currently being run out of *Borodale House* (℡01478/660266, Ⓦwww.raasay-house.co.uk), the former Estate Manager's House, while Raasay House is out of action. The centre's activity programme includes everything from sailing and kayaking to climbing and hillwalking, and includes optional accommodation in one of their twelve en-suite rooms. There's a restaurant and a café serving good local food.

The Cuillin and the Red Hills

For many people, the **Cuillin** (An Cuiltheann), whose sharp snowcapped peaks rise mirage-like from the flatness of the surrounding terrain, are Skye's *raison d'être*. When the clouds finally disperse, they are the dominating feature of the island, visible from every other peninsula on Skye. There are basically three approaches to the Cuillin: from the south, by foot or by boat from Elgol; from the *Sligachan Hotel* to the north; or from Glen Brittle to the west of the mountains. Glen Sligachan is one of the most popular routes, dividing as it does the granite of the round-topped **Red Hills** (sometimes referred to as the Red Cuillin) to the east from the dark, coarse-grained jagged-edged gabbro of the real Cuillin (sometimes referred to as the Black Cuillin) to the west. With some twenty Munros between them, these are mountains to be taken seriously, and many routes through the Cuillin are for experienced climbers only (for more on safety, see p.47).

Elgol, Loch Coruisk and Glen Sligachan

The road to **ELGOL** (Ealaghol), fourteen miles southwest of Broadford at the tip of the Strathaird peninsula, is one of the most dramatic on the island, leading right into the heart of the Red Hills and then down a precipitous slope, with a stunning view from the top down to Elgol pier. On the way you pass the ruins of a pre-Reformation church and graveyard at Kilchrist, where there are also traces of marble quarries which flourished for a while, employing Belgian experts and running the marble on a small railway to Broadford pier. Further down the road at Torrin you'll see the modern quarry with its white gleaming gash in the hillside.

The chief reason for visiting Elgol is to take a boat across Loch Scavaig to a jetty near the entrance of **Loch Coruisk** (*Coire Uisg* or "cauldron of waters"). An isolated, glacial loch, this needle-like shaft of water, nearly two miles long but only a couple of hundred yards wide, lies in the shadow of the highest peaks of the Cuillin, a wonderfully overpowering landscape. The journey takes about an hour and passengers are dropped off to spend time ashore. Two boats offer the trip (Easter–Oct; £12.50–14 one-way): the *Bella Jane* (℡0800/731 3089, Ⓦwww .bellajane.co.uk) and the *Misty Isle* (℡01471/866288, Ⓦwww.mistyisleboattrips .co.uk; Mon–Sat only).

Ordnance Survey Explorer map no. 411

For many walkers and climbers, there's nowhere in Britain to beat **the Cuillin**. The main ridge is just eight miles long, but with its immediate neighbours it is made up of over thirty peaks, twelve of them Munros, including the most difficult of the lot, the Inaccessible Pinnacle. Those intent on doing a complete traverse of the Cuillin ridge usually start at **Gars-bheinn**, at the southeastern tip, and finish off at **Sgùrr nan Gillean** (3167ft), descending on the famous *Sligachan Hotel* for a well-earned pint. The entire journey takes a minimum of sixteen hours, which either means a very long day, or two days and a bivouac. A period of settled weather is pretty much essential, and only experienced walkers and climbers should attempt it. Before setting out on any of the walks below, you should not only take note of all the usual safety precautions, but should also be aware of the fact that **compasses** are unreliable in the Cuillin, due to the magnetic nature of the rocks. If you want to hire a guide, or take a course in mountain climbing and walking, contact Skye Guides (℡01471/822116; ⓦwww.skyeguides.co.uk).

If you're based in Glenbrittle, one of the easiest walks is the five-mile round trip from the campsite up **Coire Làgan**, to a crystal-cold lochan squeezed in among the sternest of rockfaces. If you simply want to bag one or two of the peaks, there are several corries that provide relatively straightforward approaches to the most central Munros. From the SYHA hostel, a path heads west along the southern bank of the stream that tumbles down from the **Coire a' Ghreadaidh**. From the corrie, you can climb up to An Dorus, the most obvious gap in the ridge ahead, from which you can either ascend **Sgùrr a' Mhadaidh** (3012ft), to the north, or **Sgùrr a' Ghreadaidh** (3192ft) to the south. Alternatively, before you reach Coire a' Ghreadaidh, you can head south to the Coir' an Eich, from which you can easily climb **Sgùrr na Banachdaich** (3166ft) via its western ridge. To the south of the youth hostel, the road crosses another stream, with another path along its southern banks. This path heads west past the impressive **Eas Mòr** (Great Waterfall), before heading up to the **Coire na Banachdich**. The pass above the corrie is the main one over to Loch Coruisk, but also gives access to Sgùrr Dearg, best known for its great view of the **Inaccessible Pinnacle** or "In-Pin" (3235ft), Scotland's most difficult Munro to conquer, since it requires considerable rock-climbing skills. Back at Eas Mòr, paths head off for Coire Làgan, by far the most popular corrie thanks to its steep sides and tiny lochan. A laborious slog up the Great Stone Chute is the easiest approach if you want to reach the top of **Sgùrr Alasdair** (3258ft).

Walkers use the boat simply to get to Loch Coruisk, from where you can hike amidst the Red Hills, or over the pass into **Glen Sligachan**. Alternatively, you can walk round the coast to the sandy bay of **Camasunary**, over two miles to the east – a difficult walk that involves a tricky river-crossing and negotiating "The Bad Step", an overhanging rock with a thirty-foot drop to the sea – and either head north to Glen Sligachan, continue south three miles along the coast to Elgol or continue east to the Am Màm shoulder, for a stunning view of mountains and the islands of Soay, Rùm and Canna. From Am Màm, the path leads down to the Elgol road, joining it just south of Kirkibost.

If you want a bite to eat, there's a coffee shop, or the excellent seafood **restaurant** in *Coruisk House* (℡01471/866330, ⓦwww.seafood-skye.co.uk; April–Oct; ⑤), which also offers **B&B** in its bright and cheerful rooms. Alternatively, head for *Rowan Cottage* (℡01471/866287, ⓦwww.rowancottage-skye.co.uk; March–Oct; ③), a lovely B&B a mile or so east in Glasnakille. For walkers and climbers, by far the most popular place to stay is the roadside **campsite** and the secluded **bunkhouse** (℡01478/650204, ⓦwww.sligachan.co.uk; April–Oct) **run** by the

Sligachan Hotel on the A87, at the northern end of Glen Sligachan. The hotel's huge *Seamus Bar* serves food for weary walkers until 11pm, and quenches their thirst with its own real ales, and often has live bands.

Glen Drynoch and Glen Brittle

Three miles along the A863 to Dunvegan, halfway along **Glen Drynoch**, *Bla Bheinn* B&B (T01478/640269, Wwww.blabheinn.co.uk; ④) makes a good little base for attacking the Cuillin from the north. Further on, a turning signed "Carbost and Portnalong" leads to the entrance to stony **Glen Brittle**, edging the most spectacular peaks of the Cuillin. At the foot of the glen, idyllically situated by the sea, is the village of **GLENBRITTLE**. Climbers and serious walkers tend to congregate at the SYHA **hostel** (T01478/640278, Wwww.syha.org.uk, April–Sept) or the beautifully situated, but basic, **campsite** (T01478/640404; April–Oct), a mile or so further south behind the wide sandy beach at the foot of the glen. Both the hostel and the campsite have grocery stores, the only ones for miles. From Glen Brittle, a score of **hiking** trails lead east into the **Cuillin** (see box opposite).

Minginish

If the Cuillin has disappeared into the mist for the day, you could while away an afternoon exploring the nearby **Minginish** peninsula, to the north of Glen Brittle. One wet-weather activity is to take a guided tour of the **Talisker whisky distillery** (April-June Mon–Sat 9.30am–5pm, July-Aug Mon–Sat 9.30am–5pm, Sun 11am–5pm; Nov–March Mon–Fri 10am–5pm; £5), which produces a very smoky, peaty single malt. Skye's only distillery, Talisker is situated on the shores of Loch Harport at **CARBOST** (and not, confusingly, at the village of Talisker itself, which lies on the west coast of Minginish).

Without your own transport, Minginish is not that convenient as a base for exploring Skye. Nevertheless, there are several year-round **bunkhouses** in Carbost and **PORTNALONG**, a couple of miles north: the *Waterfront Bunkhouse* is next to (and owned by) the *Old Inn* in Carbost (T01478/640205, Wwww.carbost.f9.co .uk), which does good bar meals; the *Croft Bunkhouse* (T01478/640254, Wwww .skyehostels.com), with family rooms, heated wigwams and **camping**, is signposted just before you get to Portnalong; while the simple, cheap and clean *Skyewalker Independent Hostel* (T01478/640250, Wwww.skyewalkerhostel.com) is in a converted school building beyond Portnalong, en route to Fiskavaig – it also has a campsite, shop and an excellent café bar that welcomes passers-by. Another option is the friendly *Taigh Ailean Hotel* (T01478/640271, Wwww.taigh-ailean-hotel.co .uk; ⑤), which serves good meals in the evening, or the *Ullinish Country Lodge* (T01470/572214, Wwww.theisleofskye.co.uk; ⑦), a **hotel** which overlooks Portnalong from the north – to get there head eight miles up the A863 to Dunvegan and follow the signs. The building itself dates back to the mid-eighteenth century and has lots of character – you can sleep in a super-king-size half-tester bed in the room once occupied by Dr Johnson – and the hotel also offers delicious three-course dinners for around £40 a head.

Dunvegan, Duirinish and Waternish

After the Portnalong and Glen Brittle turning, the A863 slips across bare rounded hills to skirt the bony sea cliffs and stacks of the west coast twenty miles or so north to **DUNVEGAN** (Dùn Bheagain). It's an unimpressive place, strung out along the east shore of the sea loch of the same name, though it does make quite a good base for exploring two interesting peninsulas: **Duirinish** and **Waternish**.

Dunvegan Castle

Dunvegan's chief tourist-trap is **Dunvegan Castle** (Easter to Oct daily 10am–5pm; £8, gardens only £6; ⓦ www.dunvegancastle.com), which sprawls on top of a rocky outcrop, to the north of the village, between the sea and several acres of beautifully maintained gardens. Seat of the Clan MacLeod since the thirteenth century, the present greying, rectangular fortress, with its uniform battlements and dummy pepper-pots, dates from the 1840s. Inside, you don't get a lot of castle for your money, but there are three famous items worth seeking out. The most intriguing is the battered remnants of the **Fairy Flag** in the pretty pink drawing room; this yellow silken flag from the Middle East may have been the battle standard of the Norwegian king Harald Hardrada, who had been the commander of the imperial guard in Constantinople. Hardrada died trying to seize the English throne at the Battle of Stamford Bridge in 1066, after which his flag was allegedly carried back to Skye by his Gaelic boatmen. MacLeod family tradition asserts that the flag was the gift of a fairy (see Fairy Bridge, opposite), blessed with the power to protect the clan in times of danger on no more than three occasions – as late as World War II, MacLeod pilots carried pictures of it for luck. The other two items are **Rory Mor's Horn**, a drinking vessel made from the horn of a mad bull and capable of holding half a gallon, which each new chief still has to drain at one draught "without setting down or falling down"; and the **Dunvegan Cup**, made of bog oak covered in medieval silver filigree, and believed to have been given to Rory Mor by the O'Neils of Ulster in return for his help against England. Among the Jacobite mementoes are a lock of hair and cream waistcoat belonging to Bonnie Prince Charlie (whom the MacLeods, in fact, fought against) and Flora MacDonald's corsets. Below stairs, there's a "virtual" consumptive in the dungeon, and an interesting display on the remote archipelago of St Kilda (see p.320), long the fiefdom of the MacLeods.

From the jetty outside the castle there are regular seal-spotting **boat trips** out along Loch Dunvegan, as well as longer and less-frequent sea cruises to the small islands of Mingay, Isay and Clett, which were cleared of the last crofters in 1860.

Duirinish and Glen Dale

The hammerhead **Duirinish peninsula** lies to the west of Dunvegan, much of it inaccessible to all except walkers prepared to scale or skirt the area's twin flat-topped basalt peaks: Healabhal Bheag (1600ft) and Healabhal Mhòr (1538ft). The mountains are better known as **MacLeod's Tables**, for legend has it that the MacLeod chief held an open-air royal feast on the lower of the two for James V.

The main areas of habitation lie to the north, along the western shores of Loch Dunvegan, and in the broad green sweep of **Glen Dale** (ⓦ www.glendale-skye .org.uk), attractively dotted with white farmhouses and dubbed "Little England" by the locals, due to its high percentage of incomers searching for a better life. Glen Dale's current predicament is doubly ironic given its history, for it was here in 1882 that local crofters staged a rent strike against their landlords, the MacLeods. Five locals – who became known as the "Glen Dale Martyrs" – were given two-month prison sentences, and eventually, in 1904, the crofters became the first owner-occupiers in the Highlands. All this, and a great deal more about crofting, is told through fascinating contemporary news-cuttings at **Colbost Croft Museum** (Easter–Oct daily 10am–6.30pm; £1.50), in a restored black-house, four miles up the road from Dunvegan. A guide is usually on hand to answer questions, the peat fire smokes all day, and there's a restored illegal whisky-still round the back.

Just off the road to **BORRERAIG** is **Borreraig Park** (daily 10am–6pm; £2), which tells the story of the MacCrimmons, hereditary pipers to the MacLeod chiefs for three centuries, until they were sent packing in the 1770s. The plaintive sounds of the *piobaireachd* of the MacCrimmons, the founding family of Scottish piping, fill this museum, a sound as melancholy as the sight of dusty, worm-eaten rat skeletons and artefacts from a lost way of life.

If you've got kids, you might like to pay a visit to the **Toy Museum** (Mon–Sat 10am–6pm; £3; ⓦwww.toy-museum.co.uk), in **GLENDALE** itself, which has everything from early Meccano sets to a fully equipped mini-crofters' kitchen, plus innumerable Sasha dolls and Star Wars toys. Beyond Glendale, a bumpy road leads to Ramasaig, and beyond for another five miles to the deserted village of Lorgill where, on August 4, 1830, life came to an end when every crofter was ordered to board the *Midlothian* in Loch Snizort to go to Nova Scotia or go to prison (those over the age of 70 were sent to the poorhouse). As a result of such Clearances, the west coast of Duirinish is mostly uninhabited now. For walkers, though, it's a great area to explore, with blustery but easy footpaths leading to the dramatically sited lighthouse on **Neist Point**, Skye's most westerly spot, which features some fearsome sea cliffs, and wonderful views across the sea to the Western Isles. Alternatively, you could head north for the sheer thousand-foot cliffs of **Biod an Athair** (Cliff of the Sky) near Dunvegan Head, though there's no path, and it's a bit of a slog.

Waternish

Waternish is a thin and little-visited peninsula north of Dunvegan. It's not as spectacular as either Duirinish or Trotternish, but it provides equally good views over to the Western Isles on a clear day. To reach the peninsula, you must cross the **Fairy Bridge** (Beul-Ath nan Tri Allt or "Ford of the Three Burns"), at the junction of the B886, where legend has it that the fourth MacLeod clan chief was forced to say farewell to his fairy wife as she had to return to her kind – her parting gift was the Fairy Flag (see opposite).

STEIN, looking out over Loch Bay and over to the Western Isles, is Waternish's prettiest village. Descending from the heights, you eventually reach a row of whitewashed cottages built in 1787 by the British Fisheries Society. The place never really took off and was more or less abandoned within a couple of generations. Today, however, it's quite a lively place, particularly the sixteenth-century *Stein Inn*, which is well worth a visit (see p.292).

At the end of the road that runs along the west of the peninsula is **Trumpan Church**, an evocative medieval ruin on a clifftop looking out to the Western Isles. This peaceful site was the scene of one of the bloodiest episodes in Skye history, when, in a revenge attack in 1578, the MacDonalds of Uist set fire to the church while numerous MacLeods were attending a service inside. Everyone perished except one young girl, who escaped by squeezing through a window, severing one of her breasts in the process. She raised the alarm, and the rest of the MacLeods rallied and, bearing the Fairy Flag (see opposite), attacked the MacDonalds as they were launching their galleys. Every MacDonald was slaughtered and their bodies were thrown in a nearby dyke. In the churchyard, along with two medieval gravestones, you can also see the **Trial Stone**, a four-foot-high pillar with a hole drilled in it. Anyone accused of a crime was blindfolded and had to attempt to put their finger in it: success meant innocence, failure signified death.

Practicalities

The area around Dunvegan is a useful alternative base to Portree, as it has a **tourist office** (Easter–Oct daily; ☎0845/225 5121), on the road to the castle, and several good **accommodation** options in the surrounding countryside. Beyond Glendale, ⚘ *Carter's Rest* (☎01470/511272, ⓦwww.cartersrestskye.co.uk; ⑤) is a spotless, high-quality modern B&B that serves excellent food. In the opposite direction, along the A863 to Bracadale, you'll find the *Old Byre* (Wwww.theoldbyre.net; ❸), a cosy converted farmhouse B&B in Roskill, and *Roskhill House* (T01470/521317, Wwww.roskhillhouse.co.uk; ❸) – confusingly a further four miles down the road in Ose – once the village post office, now a lovely B&B with a log fire and free wi-fi. There are a couple of excellent lochside **campsites**: one at Loch Greshornish, a mile north of Edinbane on the A850 (April to mid-Oct; T01470/582230, Wwww.skyecamp.com), and another on Loch Dunvegan (April–Oct; T01470/521531, Wwww.kinloch-campsite.co.uk), five minutes' walk from Dunvegan on the road to Colbost.

The most famous **restaurant** in the area is the *Three Chimneys* (T01470/511258, Wwww.threechimneys.co.uk; ❾), next door to the Colbost Croft Museum, which serves sublime three-course meals at around £55 a head – the restaurant also has six fabulous rooms at the adjacent *House Over-By* which cost around £300 for dinner, bed and breakfast for two. A great **place to stay**, with welcoming fires and good **pub food**, is the sixteenth-century ⚓ *Stein Inn* (T01470/592362, Wwww.steininn.co.uk; ❹) in Stein – next door is the much pricier *Lochbay Seafood Restaurant* (T01470/592235, Wwww.lochbay-seafood-restaurant.co.uk; Easter–Oct Tues–Fri only), where you'll need to book ahead. Without doubt, the best place to eat in Dunvegan is *The Old School* (March–Dec eve only; T01470/521421), whose excellent food belies its appearance from outside – try the Stornoway black pudding starter or the local langoustines. Otherwise, all the hotels do dinner and, on a more modest scale, there is a snug **café** attached to *Dunvegan Bakery*.

Portree

Although referred to by the locals as "the village", **PORTREE** is the only real town on Skye, with a population of around two thousand. It's also one of the most attractive fishing ports in northwest Scotland, its deep, cliff-edged harbour filled with fishing boats and circled by multicoloured restaurants and guesthouses. Originally known as *Kiltaraglen*, it takes its current name – some say – from *Port Rìgh* (Port of the King), after the state visit James V made in 1540 to assert his authority over the chieftains of Skye.

Information and accommodation

Portree's **tourist office** (April–Oct daily; Nov–March Mon–Fri only), just off Bridge Street, will book **accommodation** for you – useful if you haven't booked ahead, and you can go online here. Portree has a couple of centrally located **hostels**, but you're better off going to nearby Staffin or Uig. By contrast, Torvaig **campsite** (T01478/611849, Wwww.portreecampsite.co.uk; April–Oct) is well kept, with a friendly owner, and lies a mile and a half north of town off the A855 Staffin road.

Ben Tianavaig 5 Bosville Terrace T01478/612152, Wben-tianavaig.co.uk. The best B&B in the centre of town, with charming hosts, views over the harbour, and free wi-fi. ❸
Cuillin Hills Hotel 10min walk out of town along the northern shore of the bay T01478/612003, Wcuillinhills-hotel-skye.co.uk. Rooms are spacious and comfortable at this secluded hotel, with splendid views over the harbour and reasonably priced bar snacks. ❾
Gràsmhor Woodend T01478/611664, Wwww.grasmhor.co.uk. Modern B&B sitting

in splendid isolation a couple of miles out of Portree along the single-track road to Bracadale. Very welcoming hosts, and bright and cheerful rooms, with great views. ❷
Medina Coolin Hills Gardens T01478/612821, Wmedinaskye.co.uk. Well-run and attractive bungalow B&B, with tasty breakfasts, in a quiet spot near the *Cuillin Hills Hotel*. ❹
Peinmore House Two miles south of Portree T01478/612574, Wpeinmorehouse.co.uk. Wonderful old manse set in its own grounds, with a walled garden and sun-trap courtyard. Rooms are

spacious and kitted out with modern furnishings; the lounge is a wonderful 30ft "long room". **⑥**

Skeabost House Five miles northwest of Portree ☎01470/532202, ⓦskeabostcountryhouse.com. Late-Victorian pile which offers the life of a country gent in the main building, with an original billiard room and, outdoors, fishing, golf and extensive gardens – just don't take a room in the modern annexe. Open March–Oct. **⑧**

Viewfield House ☎01478/612217, ⓦviewfieldhouse.com. For old-school Scots Baronial style, it's hard to beat this hotel on the southern outskirts of town, which has been in the hands of the MacDonalds for over two hundred years, and has a real Victorian air, with stuffed polecats and antiques. Open mid-April to mid-Oct. **⑦**

The Town

The **harbour** is well worth a stroll, with its attractive pier built by Thomas Telford in the early nineteenth century. Fishing boats still land a modest catch, some of which is sold through Anchor Seafoods (Tues–Fri only) at the end of the pier. The harbour is overlooked by **The Lump**, a steep and stumpy peninsula with a flagpole on it that was once the site of public hangings on the island, attracting crowds of up to five thousand; it also sports a folly built by the celebrated Dr Ban, a visionary who wanted to make Portree into a second Oban. Up above the harbour is the spick-and-span town centre, spreading out from **Somerled Square**, built in the late eighteenth century as the island's administrative and commercial centre, and now housing the bus station and car park. The **Royal Hotel** on Bank Street occupies the site of the McNab's Inn where Bonnie Prince Charlie took leave of Flora MacDonald (see p.425), and where, 27 years later, Boswell and Johnson had "a very good dinner, porter, port and punch"; it also hosts the annual Accordion and Fiddle Festival in May.

A mile or so out of town on the Sligachan road is the **Aros Centre** (daily 9am–5.30pm; ☎01478/613750, ⓦwww.aros.co.uk), where you can view a live RSPB webcam centred on sea eagles' nests and an audiovisual roam around the island (£4). Aros's most useful function is that it hosts gigs and contains a **cinema**, a modern exhibition space, a licensed bar and a popular café, and there's a special play area for small kids, plus some easy waymarked forest walks.

Eating, drinking and activities

There's a surfeit of **places to eat** in Portree, all aimed at the tourist trade. The best solution is to head for ⚘*Café Arriba*, a truly relaxing place to eat at the top of the road down to the harbour, with an array of imaginative dishes for under £10. For decent seafood, *Sea Breezes* (☎01478/613611; closed Mon), on the harbour, is excellent, but you'll have to book ahead; for good **fish and chips**, pop to the chippy a few doors down. As for **pubs**, the bar of the *Pier Hotel* on the quayside is the fishermen's drinking hole, and the *Tongadale* on Wentworth Street is a lively, convivial place. Currently the most popular evening venue by far, though, is the *Isles Inn* on Somerled Square, which has excellent **bar meals**, a real fire and occasional live music.

For **bike rental**, go to Island Cycles (☎01478/613121; closed Sun) below The Green. Day or half-day **boat trips** leave the pier for daily excursions to Raasay and Rona (☎07798/743858, ⓦwww.skyeboat-trips.co.uk); **diving** can be organized through Dive-and-Sea the Hebrides in Lochbay, towards Dunvegan (☎01470/592219, ⓦwww.dive-and-sea-the-hebrides.co.uk).

Trotternish

Protruding twenty miles north from Portree, the **Trotternish peninsula** boasts some of the island's most bizarre scenery, particularly on the east coast, where volcanic basalt has pressed down on the softer sandstone and limestone underneath, causing massive landslides. These, in turn, have created sheer cliffs, peppered with outcrops of hard, wizened basalt, which run the full length of the peninsula. These pinnacles and pillars are at their most eccentric in the **Quiraing**, above Staffin Bay, on the east coast. Trotternish is easily explored with your own transport, but the Flodigarry Circular bus service #57A and #57C gives access to almost all the coast.

The east coast

The first geological eccentricity on the **Trotternish** peninsula, six miles north of Portree along the A855, is the **Old Man of Storr**, a distinctive column of rock, shaped like a willow leaf, which, along with its neighbours, is part of a massive landslip. Huge blocks of stone still occasionally break off the cliff face of the Storr (2358ft) above, and slide downhill. At 165ft, the Old Man is a real challenge for climbers; less difficult is the half-hour trek up the footpath to the foot of the column from the woods beside the car park.

Five miles further north, there's another turn-off to the **Lealt Falls**, at the head of a gorge which spends most of its day in shadow (and is home to a fiendish collection of midges). Walking all the way down to the falls is fairly pointless, but the views across to Raasay and Rona from the first stage of the path are spectacular (weather permitting). The coast here is worth exploring, however, especially the track leading to **Rubha nam Brathairean** (Brothers' Point), where the Glasgow provision boat used to put in, and where fossil hunters can also follow the road that turns off at Dunans down to the end and try their luck on the beach at low tide.

Another car park a few miles up the road gives access to **Kilt Rock**, whose tubelike, basaltic columns rise precipitously from the sea, set amongst sea cliffs dotted with nests for fulmar and kittiwake. There is a spectacular waterfall which drops 300ft to the sea, and a small loch by the car park alive with wildlife. Close by, near the turn-off to Elishader, is the **Staffin Museum** (by appointment ✆01470/562321), a converted byre which contains a private collection of the area's remarkable fossil finds, including a dinosaur legbone discovered here in the 1990s, megalosaurus footprints and several large ammonites.

Over the brow of the next hill, the wonderful amphitheatre of **Staffin Bay** is spread out before you, dotted with whitewashed and "spotty" houses. **STAFFIN** itself is a lively, largely Gaelic-speaking community where crofts have been handed down the generations. A single-track road cuts across the peninsula from the north end of the bay, allowing access to the **Quiraing**, a spectacular forest of mighty pinnacles and savage rock formations. There are two car parks: from the first, beside a cemetery, it's a steep half-hour climb to the rocks; from the second, on the saddle, it's a longer, but more gentle traverse. Once you're in the midst of the rocks, you should be able to make out the Prison to your right, and the 120-foot Needle, to your left; the Table, a great sunken platform where locals used to play shinty, lies above and beyond the Needle, another fifteen-minute scramble up the rocks; legend also maintains that a local warrior named Fraing hid his cattle there from the invading Norsemen.

Practicalities

Most **accommodation** choices on the east coast enjoy fantastic views out over the sea. Just beyond the Lealt Falls there's the very welcoming and comfortable *Glenview* Hotel (✆01470/562248, ⓦglenview-skye.co.uk; ❼), with an excellent restaurant. Or for half the price, you can stay at *Hallaig Guest House* (✆01470/562250, ⓦwww.hallaig.com; ❸), a comfortable, modern B&B in Marishadder, along the dead-end road to Garros. There's also a **campsite** (✆01470/562213, ⓦwww.staffincampsite.co.uk; April–Sept) south of Staffin

Bay. In fine weather, you can enjoy good bar snacks on the castellated terrace of the stylish *Flodigarry Country House Hotel*, three miles up the coast from Staffin. Behind the hotel (and now part of it) is the cottage where local heroine Flora MacDonald lived, and had six of her seven children, from 1751 to 1759. You can **camp** or stay at the neat and attractive *Dun Flodigarry* **hostel** (℡01470/552212, ⓦwww.hostelflodigarry.co.uk), a couple of minutes' walk away.

Duntulm and Kilmuir

Beyond Flodigarry, at the tip of the Trotternish peninsula, by the road to Shulista, a public footpath leads past the ruins of a cleared hamlet to the spectacular sea-stacks of **Rubha Hunish**, the most northerly point on Skye. A couple of miles further along the A855 lies **DUNTULM** (Duntuilm), whose heyday as a major MacDonald power base is recalled by the shattered remains of a headland fortress abandoned in 1732 after a clumsy nurse dropped the baby son (and future clan chief) from a window onto the rocks below; on these same rocks, it is said, can be seen the keel marks of Viking longships. *Duntulm Castle Hotel* (March–Nov) is close by, and offers pub food along with wonderful views across the Minch to the Western Isles.

Heading down the west shore of the Trotternish, it's two miles to the **Skye Museum of Island Life** (Easter–Oct Mon–Sat 9.30am–5pm; £2.50; ⓦwww .skyemuseum.co.uk), an impressive cluster of thatched blackhouses on an exposed hill overlooking Harris. The museum, run by locals, gives a fascinating insight into a way of life that was commonplace on Skye a hundred years ago. The blackhouse, housing the ticket office, is much as it was when it was last inhabited in 1957, while the two houses to the east contain interesting snippets of local history. Behind the museum in the cemetery up the hill are the graves of **Flora MacDonald** and her husband. Thousands turned out for her funeral in 1790, creating a procession a mile long – indeed, so widespread was her fame that the original family mausoleum fell victim to souvenir hunters and had to be replaced. The Celtic-cross headstone is inscribed with a simple tribute by Dr Johnson, who visited her in 1773: "Her name will be mentioned in history, if courage and fidelity be virtues, mentioned with honour."

If you want an antidote to folk history, pop into **MacCurdie's Exhibition**, just before the turn-off to Heribusta, in **KILMUIR**, a mile or so to the south. It's an unattended museum full of spoof artefacts and pseudo-proverbs such as "It's easier to extract a Mars bar from the gullet of a seagull than to clean your shoes with a blade of grass." The land around Kilmuir used to be called the "Granary of Skye", since every inch was cultivated: even St Columba's Loch, where there are still indistinct remains of beehive cells and a chapel, was drained and the land eagerly reclaimed by crofters.

Uig

Four miles south of Kilmuir is **UIG** (Ùige), which curves its way round a dramatic, horseshoe-shaped bay, and is Skye's chief ferry port for the Western Isles. Most folk are just passing through, but if you've time to kill, there's a lovely, gentle **walk** up Glen Uig, better known as the **Faerie Glen**, at the east end of the bay. Uig's **campsite** is on a sloping field very close to the pier (℡01470/542714, ⓦwww.uig-camping-skye.co.uk) and offers **bike rental**. By contrast, the SYHA **hostel** (℡0870/004 1155; April–Sept) is a twenty-minute walk away, high up on the south side of the village, with exhilarating views over the bay. If you need to stay near the ferry terminal, *Harris Cottage* (℡01470/542243, ⓦwww.harris -cottage.co.uk; April–Oct; ❶) is an inexpensive **B&B** a short walk from the pier. If you're staying more than one night, head for *Woodbine House* (℡01470/542243,

@ www.skyeactivities.co.uk; April–Oct; ❸), a luxurious Victorian house just under a mile from the pier, tastefully furnished by a couple who also run boat trips from Uig. The *Pub at the Pier* offers basic **pub food**, and serves beers from the nearby **brewery**.

The Small Isles

The history of the **Small Isles**, which lie to the south of Skye, is typical of the Hebrides: early Christianization, followed by Norwegian rule, ending in 1266 when the islands fell into Scottish hands. Their support for the Jacobites resulted in hard times after the failed 1745 rebellion, but the biggest problems came with the introduction of the **potato** in the mid-eighteenth century. The consequences were as dramatic as they were unforeseen: the success of the crop and its nutritional value – when grown in conjunction with traditional cereals – eliminated famine at a stroke, prompting a population explosion. In 1750, there were a thousand islanders, but by 1800 their numbers had almost doubled.

At first, the problem of overcrowding was camouflaged by the **kelp** boom; the islanders were employed, and the islands' owners made a fortune, gathering and burning local seaweed to sell for use in the manufacture of gunpowder, soap and glass. But the economic bubble burst with the end of the Napoleonic Wars and, to

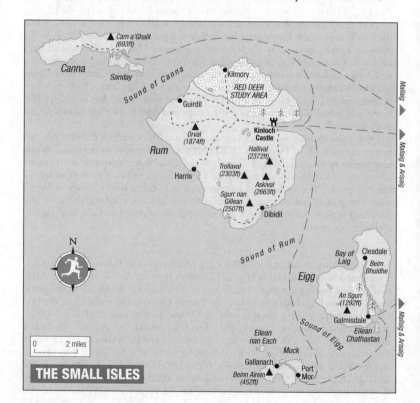

CalMac run ferries to the Small Isles year round (except Sun) from Mallaig (☎01687/462403, ⓦwww.calmac.co.uk). Day-trips are possible to each of the islands on certain days, and to all four islands on Saturdays, if you catch the 7.30am ferry.

From late April to late September, the **Sheerwater**, run by Arisaig Marine (☎01687/450224, ⓦwww.arisaig.co.uk), operates a daily service to Rùm, Eigg or Muck. This is a much more pleasant way to get there, not least because if any marine mammals are spotted en route, the boat will pause for a bit of whale-watching. Day-trips are possible to Eigg on most days, allowing four to five hours ashore, and to Rùm and Muck on a few days, allowing two to three hours ashore – advance booking is advisable.

With careful studying of both CalMac and Sheerwater timetables, you should be able to organize a visit to suit you, especially as Arisaig and Mallaig are linked by railway. Be warned, however, that boats to the Small Isles are frequently cancelled in bad weather, so be prepared to spend longer than you planned.

maintain their profit margins, the owners resorted to drastic action. The first to sell up was Alexander MacLean, who sold Rùm as grazing land for **sheep**, got quotations for shipping its people to Nova Scotia, and gave them a year's notice to quit. He also cleared Muck to graze cattle, as did the MacNeills on Canna. Only on Eigg was some compassion shown: the new owner, a certain Hugh MacPherson, who bought the island from the Clanranalds in 1827, actually gave some of his tenants extended leases.

Since the Clearances, each of the islands has been bought and sold several times, though only **Muck** is now privately owned by the benevolent laird, Lawrence MacEwen. **Eigg** was bought by the islanders themselves in 1997, putting an end to more than 150 years of property speculation. The other islands were bequeathed to national agencies: **Rùm**, by far the largest and most-visited of the group, possessing a cluster of formidable volcanic peaks and the architecturally remarkable Kinloch Castle, passed to the Nature Conservancy Council (now Scottish Natural Heritage) in 1957; and **Canna**, in many ways the prettiest of the isles, with its high basalt cliffs, has been in the hands of the National Trust for Scotland since 1981.

Accommodation on the Small Isles is limited and requires **forward planning** at all times of year; formal public transport is nonexistent, but the locals will usually oblige if you have heavy baggage to shift.

Rùm

Like Skye, **Rùm** (ⓦwww.isleofrum.com) is dominated by its Cuillin, which, though only reaching a height of 2663ft at the summit of Askival, rises up with comparable drama straight from the sea in the south of the island. The majority of the island's twenty or so inhabitants now live in **KINLOCH**, overlooking the large bay on the sheltered east coast, and most are employed by Scottish Natural Heritage (SNH), who run the island as a National Nature Reserve. SNH have been reintroducing native woodland to the island, overseeing a long-term study of the large red-deer population, which features annually on BBC's *Autumnwatch*, and have reintroduced **white-tailed (sea) eagles**, which have since mostly abandoned Rùm in favour of neighbouring islands. You can learn more about the history of the island, and its flora and fauna, in the small **museum** near the old pier.

Kinloch Castle

Rùm's chief formal attraction is **Kinloch Castle** (March-Oct guided tours coincide with the ferry; £6; Ⓦwww.kinlochcastle.co.uk), a squat red-sandstone edifice fronted by colonnades and topped by crenellations and turrets, which dominates the village of Kinloch. Completed at enormous expense in 1900 – the red sandstone was shipped in from Dumfriesshire, and the soil for the gardens from Ayrshire – and now in need of some serious restoration, its interior is a perfectly preserved example of Edwardian decadence, "a living memorial of the stalking, the fishing and the sailing, the tenantry and plenty of the days before 1914". From the galleried hall, with its tiger rugs, stags' heads and giant Japanese incense burners, to the "Extra Low Fast Cushion" of the Soho snooker table in the Billiard Room, the interior is packed with nick-nacks and technical gizmos accumulated by **Sir George Bullough** (1870–1939), the spendthrift son of self-made millionaire Sir John Bullough, who bought the island as a sporting estate in 1888. As such, it was only really used for a few weeks each autumn, during the "season", yet employed an island workforce of one hundred all year round. Bullough's guests were woken at eight each morning by a piper; later on, an orchestrion, an electrically driven barrel-organ (originally destined for

---

Sir George Bullough

Scotland has had more than its fair share of eccentric rich landlords, but few come close to **Sir George Bullough** (1870–1939), heir to a fortune accumulated by his ancestors' Lancashire textile machinery factories. Educated at Harrow, George inherited his fortune at the age of just 21 – he was on a two-year world tour, at the time, allegedly to keep him away from his young stepmother, with whom he enjoyed a rather "close relationship". In 1899, at the time of the Second Boer War, Bullough, at his own expense, converted his recently acquired 221ft steam yacht, *Rhouma*, to a hospital ship, and sailed it to South Africa. He was rewarded with a knighthood, and in 1903 went on to marry Monique Lily de la Pasture (aka Monica), once she had divorced her husband Charles Charrington.

Meanwhile, in 1897, work had began on George Bullough's ultimate dream: his very own Scottish castle. For three years, 300 men were employed to build **Kinloch Castle** on Rùm – or, as George preferred it to be known, "Rhum" – and paid an extra shilling a week to wear Rùm tartan kilts; smokers were also given a daily bonus of twopence "to keep the midges away". The castle's heyday was the **Edwardian era**, when Rùm was fitted out with every mod con money could buy: it was double-glazed, centrally heated, was the first place in Scotland to be lit by electricity (after Glasgow) and the first private house in Scotland to have an internal telephone system. There was a nine-hole golf course, a bowling green, a huge walled garden, with fourteen green-houses producing exotic fruit for the guests, and six domed palm-houses, alive with hummingbirds (they died when the heating broke down and can now be found stuffed in the house), and fitted with heated pools stocked with giant turtles and alligators, though these were eventually removed at the insistence of the terrified staff. There were twelve full-time gardeners and fourteen full-time roadmen, whose job it was to keep Rùm's roads carefully raked so that George and his chums could race their sports cars across the island. In the bay, the Bulloughs would moor *Rhouma*, whose band would come ashore to play from the ballroom's minstrels' gallery.

The outbreak of World War I signalled the end of the world of opulence in which the Bulloughs had excelled. Sir George was elevated to the baronetcy in 1916, after having loaned £50,000 interest-free to the government, but after the war he and the family visited Rùm less and less. The house was barely used when Sir George died of a heart attack while playing golf in France in 1939. Lady Bullough eventually sold Rùm in 1957; she died ten years later, and was buried, along with her husband, in the **Bullough Mausoleum** on Rùm.

Balmoral), crammed in under the stairs, would grind out an eccentric mixture of pre-dinner tunes – *The Ride of the Valkyries* and *Ma Blushin' Rosie* among others (a demo is included in the tour). The ballroom has a sprung floor, the library features a gruesome photographic collection from the Bulloughs' world tours, but the *pièce de résistance* has to be Bullough's **Edwardian bathrooms**, whose baths have hooded walnut shower-cabinets, fitted with two taps and four dials, which allow the bathers to fire high-pressure water at their bodies from every angle.

The rest of the island

For those with limited time or energy, there are two gentle waymarked **trails**, both of which start from Kinloch, and take around two hours to complete. If you're heading out into the hills, you must fill in route cards and pop them into the *White House* (☎01687/462026), where the reserve manager can give useful advice. They also occasionally offer **guided walks** around the island, including a night-time hike to see the shearwaters on the slopes of Hallival.

The island's best beach is at **KILMORY**, to the north (5hr return), where students get eaten alive by midges while studying red deer. When the island's human head-count peaked at 450 in 1791, the hamlet of **HARRIS** on the southwest coast (6hr return) housed a large crofting community – all that remains now are several ruined blackhouses and the extravagant **Bullough Mausoleum**, built by Sir George to house the remains of his father in the style of a Greek Doric temple, overlooking the sea. This is, in fact, the second one to be

---

Hiking in the Rùm Cuillin

Ordnance Survey Explorer map no. 397

Rùm's **Cuillin** may not be as famous as Skye's, but if the weather's fine there are equally exhilarating **hiking** possibilities. Whatever route you choose, be sure to take all the usual safety precautions, described on p.47.

The most popular walk is to traverse most or part of the **Cuillin Ridge**, which takes between eight and twelve hours round-trip from Kinloch. The most frequent route is up past the old dams to Coire Dubh, and then on to the saddle of Bealach Bairc-mheall. From here, you can either climb Barkeval itself, to the west, or go straight for **Hallival** (2372ft) to the southeast, which looks daunting but is no more than a mild rock scramble. South of Hallival, the ridge is grassy, but the rocky north ridge of **Askival** (2663ft) needs to be taken quite carefully, sticking to the east side for safety. Askival is the highest mountain on Rùm, and if you're thinking of heading back, or the weather's closing in, Glen Dibidil provides an easy means of descent, after which you can follow the track back to Kinloch.

To continue along the ridge, head west to the double peak of **Trollaval** (or Trallval), the furthest of which is the highest. The descent to Bealach an Fhuarain is steep, after which it's another scramble to reach the top of **Ainshval** (2562ft). Depending on the time and weather, you can continue along the ridge to **Sgùrr nan Gillean**, descend via Glen Dibidil and take the coastal path back to Kinloch, or skip the Sgurr and go straight on to the last peak of the ridge, **Ruinsival**, descend via the Fiachanis basin to Harris, and then slog it back to Kinloch along the road.

On your walks, look out for the island's **native ponies**, which feed mainly in Kilmory Glen and Kinloch Glen, and are used for the stag cull in July; the **Highland cattle**, who live in Harris, except during July and August, when they're moved to Guirdil; and the multicoloured **wild goats**, which stick to the coastal areas between Kilmory, Harris and Dibidil. However, if you want to see the **Manx shearwater**, which nest in burrows on the slopes of Hallival, you'll need to be there around dusk or dawn, as this is the only time the birds return to their nests – SNH organize regular night-time hikes to go and see the birds.

constructed here: the first was lined with Italian-marble mosaics, but when a friend remarked that it looked like a public lavatory Bullough had it dynamited and the current Neoclassical one erected.

Practicalities

Until Rùm passed into the hands of the SNH, it was known as the "Forbidden Isle" because of its exclusive use as a sporting estate for the rich; nowadays, visitors are made very welcome by the SNH staff. Day-trips are possible more or less daily in the summer (see p.297). *Kinloch Castle* was a luxury hotel until the 1990s, and still lets one of its (non-en-suite) four-poster rooms (❷), but it's mainly run as an independent **hostel** (☎01687/462037), with dormitories in the old servants' quarters – advance booking is essential. Wild camping is permitted, and there are two simple mountain **bothies** (three nights maximum stay), in Dibidil, on the southeast coast, and Guirdil, on the northwest coast, plus a basic community **campsite** with hot showers on the foreshore near the old pier.

Wherever you're staying, you can use the hostel kitchen, have a drink in the castle bar, and eat in the hostel's licensed **bistro**, which serves full breakfasts (£7), offers packed lunches (£5) and tasty three-course evening meals (£15) – advance booking essential. There is also a small shop/off-licence/post office on the north side of the bay. Bear in mind that Rùm is the wettest of the Small Isles, and is known for having some of the worst **midges** (see p.45) in Scotland – come prepared for both. Note that overnight visitors cannot bring dogs, but day-trippers can.

Eigg

Eigg (ⓦwww.isleofeigg.org) is easily spotted across the sea, since the island is mostly made up of a basalt plateau 1000ft above sea level, and a great stump of columnar pitchstone lava, known as An Sgurr, rising out of the plateau another 290ft. It's also by far the most vibrant, populous and welcoming of the Small Isles, with a real, strong sense of community amongst the seventy-odd islanders who bought the island back in 1997 (along with the local council and the Scottish Wildlife Trust). The buyout ended Eigg's unhappy history of private ownership, most notoriously with the Olympic bobsleigher and gelatine heir Keith Schellenberg, and the anniversary is celebrated every year with an all-night ceilidh on the weekend nearest to June 12.

Ferries arrive at the modern causeway, which juts out into **Galmisdale Bay**, in the southeast corner of the island, where **An Laimhrig** (The Anchorage), the island's community centre, stands, housing a shop, post office, licensed tearoom and information centre. If time is limited, you could simply head through the woods to the gardens of the nearby **Lodge**, the former laird's house. With the island's great landmark, **An Sgurr** (1292ft), watching over you wherever you go, many folk feel duty-bound to climb it, and enjoy the wonderful views over to Muck and Rùm. The easiest approach is to take the path that skirts the summit to the north, and ascend from the saddle to the west (3–4hr return).

Many visitors head off to **CLEADALE**, the main crofting settlement in the north of the island, where the beach, known as Camas Sgiotaig, or the **Singing Sands**, is comprised of quartz, which squeaks underfoot when dry (hence the name). The steep climb up to the ridge of **Ben Bhuidhe**, to the east, is hard going underfoot, but worth it for the views across to Rùm and Skye. A large colony of **Manx shearwater** nests in burrows around the base of Ben Bhuidhe; to view the birds, you need to be there just after dusk.

If you're just here for the day, make sure you pop into the **tearoom** by the causeway, which has a lovely terrace looking out to sea. A great place **to stay** is

🏛 *Kildonan House* (☎01687/482446, Ⓦwww.kildonanhouseeigg.co.uk; full board ❻), an eighteenth-century, wood-panelled house beautifully situated on the north side of Galmisdale Bay, with good home-cooking. Alternatively, you can stay in the north of the island at *Lageorna* (☎01687/482405, Ⓦwww .lageorna.com; full board ❼), a beautifully designed modern house in Cleadale, with free wi-fi and a **restaurant** (Easter–Sept) that offers delicious lunches and evening meals to residents and nonresidents. *Glebe Barn* (☎01687/482417) is a very comfortable **bunkhouse** a mile from the pier, and wild **camping** is possible at Galmisdale Bay and at Sue Hollands' organic croft in Cleadale (☎01687/482480, Ⓔsuehollands@talk21.com), plus there's a **yurt** for hire in the middle of the island (☎01687/460317). A minibus and **bike rental** are usually available – ask locally for details.

Muck

Smallest and most southerly of the Small Isles, **Muck** (Ⓦwww.isleofmuck.com) is low-lying, mostly treeless and extremely fertile, and as such shares more characteristics with the likes of Coll and Tiree (see p.94) than its nearest neighbours. Its name derives from *muc*, the Gaelic for "pig" – or, as some would have it, *muc mara*, "sea pig" or porpoise, which abound in the surrounding waters – and has long caused much embarrassment to generations of lairds who preferred to call it the "Isle of Monk", because it had briefly belonged to the medieval church.

PORT MÓR, the village on the southeast corner of the island, is where visitors arrive and where most of the thirty or so residents live. The prominent memorial in the local graveyard commemorates two islanders and a visiting student who were drowned shooting shags near Eilean nan Each (Horse Island). A road, just over a mile in length, connects Port Mór with the island's main farm, **GALLANACH**, which overlooks the rocky seal-strewn skerries on the north side of the island. The nicest sandy beach is Camas na Cairidh, to the east of Gallanach. Despite being only 452ft above sea-level, it really is worth climbing **Beinn Airein**, in the southwest corner of the island, for the 360-degree panoramic view of the surrounding islands; the return journey from Port Mór takes around two hours.

You can **stay** with one of the MacEwen family, who have owned the island since 1896, at *Port Mór House* (☎01687/462365; full board ❻); the rooms are pine-clad and enjoy great views, and the food is delicious (nonresidents welcome). Alternatively, there are a couple of B&Bs, including *Godag House* (☎01687/462371; full board ❺), halfway between Port Mór and Gallanach, or you can try the island's seven-bed **bunkhouse** (☎01687/462042), a characterful, wood-panelled bothy heated by a Raeburn stove. You can also hire the island **yurt** (☎01687/462362; May–Sept), or **camp rough** – ask at the *Green Shed* (☎01687/462990; June–Aug) in Port Mór. The only shop on the island, the *Green Shed* is essentially a craft shop, which springs into life when day-trippers arrive, and also sells seasonal vegetables and serves evening meals on request.

Canna

Measuring a mere four miles by one, and with just a handful of full-time residents, **Canna** is run as a single farm and bird sanctuary by the National Trust for Scotland (NTS). The island enjoys the best harbour in the Small Isles, a horn-shaped haven at its southeastern corner protected by the tidal island of Sanday, linked to Canna by a road bridge. For visitors, the chief pastime is walking: from the dock it's about a mile across a grassy basalt plateau to the bony sea-cliffs of the north shore, which rise to a peak around Compass Hill – so called because its high metal content distorts compasses – in the northeastern corner of the island, from where you get great views across to Rùm and Skye. The cliffs of the buffeted western half of the island are a breeding ground for both Manx shearwaters, razorbills and puffins. Some seven miles offshore stands **Hyskeir** (Òigh-sgeir) a curious mass of stone columns sticking up 30ft above the water.

With permission from the NTS, you may **camp rough** on Canna, though you need to bring your own supplies, as there's no real shop to speak of. There's also a traditional bell **tent** for hire sleeping five (℡01687/460166, ⓦcannafolk.co.uk; April–Oct), tucked away in some woodland. *Tighard*, a substantial, red sandstone, Victorian house half a mile from the jetty, is the island's only **guesthouse** (℡01687/462474, ⓦwww.peaceofcanna.co.uk; ➍); the rooms are spacious, with glorious views, and they'll cook you dinner when the restaurant's not working. The **restaurant**, *Gille Brighde* (℡01687/460164, ⓦwww.cannarestaurant.com; Tues–Sat only), offers lunch and dinner with the emphasis on local produce where possible. Note that Canna is not on the national grid; **electricity** is powered by diesel generators, which are switched off between midnight and 6am.

Travel details

Trains

Fort William to: Mallaig (4–5 daily; 1hr 20min).
Glasgow (Queen St) to: Mallaig (Mon–Sat 3 daily, 1 on Sun; 5hr 10min).
Inverness to: Kyle of Lochalsh (Mon–Sat 4 daily, 1–2 on Sun; 2hr 30min).

Buses

Mainland
Glasgow to: Broadford (3 daily; 5hr 30min); Portree (3 daily; 6hr 15min); Uig (2 daily; 6hr 50min).
Kyle of Lochalsh to: Broadford (Mon–Sat hourly; 25min); Kyleakin (Mon–Sat hourly; 10min); Portree (Mon–Sat 5 daily, 2 on Sun; 1hr).

Skye
Armadale to: Broadford (Mon–Sat 5 daily, 2 on Sun; 35min); Portree (Mon–Sat 5 daily, 2 on Sun; 1hr 20min); Sligachan (Mon–Sat 5 daily, 2 on Sun; 1hr).
Broadford to: Elgol (Mon–Fri 4 daily, 2 on Sat; 45min); Kyleakin (hourly; 15min); Portree (Mon–Sat 5–10 daily; 40min); Sligachan (Mon–Sat 5 daily, 2 on Sun; 20min).
Dunvegan to: Glendale (school days 2–3 daily; 30min).
Portree to: Carbost (Mon–Fri 3 daily, 1 on Sat; 40min); Duntulm (Mon–Sat 4–5 daily; 55min); Dunvegan (Mon–Sat 3–4 daily; 45min); Glen Brittle (Mon–Fri 2 daily; 50min); Staffin (Mon–Sat 4–5 daily; 35min); Uig (Mon–Sat 7–8 daily, 3 on Sun; 30min).

Ferries

Summer timetable only
To Canna: Eigg–Canna (Mon & Sat; 2hr 30min); Mallaig–Canna (Mon, Wed, Fri & Sat; 2hr.30min–3hr 50min); Muck–Canna (Sat; 1hr 35min); Rùm–Canna (Mon, Wed, Fri & Sat; 55min).
To Eigg: Canna–Eigg (Mon & Sat; 2hr 15min); Mallaig–Eigg (Mon, Thurs, Sat; 1hr 15min–2hr 25min); Muck–Eigg (Sat; 35min); Rùm–Eigg (Mon; 1hr–3hr 30min).
To Muck: Eigg–Muck (Tues, Thurs & Sat; 35min); Mallaig–Muck (Tues, Thurs, Fri & Sat; 1hr 40min–4hr 20min); Rùm–Muck (Tues & Sat; 2hr 45min).
To Raasay: Sconser–Raasay (Mon–Sat 8–10 daily, 2 on Sun; 25min).
To Rùm: Canna–Rùm (Mon, Wed, Fri & Sat; 55min); Eigg–Rùm (Mon & Sat; 1hr–3hr 30min); Mallaig–Rùm (Mon, Wed, Fri & Sat; 1hr 20min–2hr 30min); Muck–Rùm (Sat; 1hr 10min).
To Skye: Glenelg–Kylerhea (Easter–Oct daily every 20min; 5min); Mallaig–Armadale (Mon–Sat 8–9 daily, 4–6 Sun; 30min).

The Western Isles

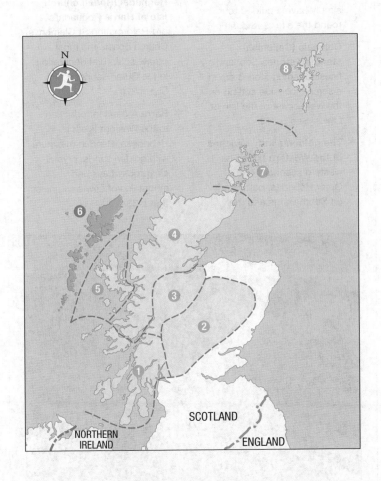

CHAPTER 6

Highlights

✳ **Gearrannan (Garenin), Isle of Lewis** A crofting village of painstakingly restored thatched blackhouses: you can stay in the hostel, or simply have a guided tour round the site. See p.318

✳ **Calanais (Callanish) standing stones** Scotland's finest standing stones are in a serene lochside setting on the west coast of the Isle of Lewis. See p.319

✳ **The golden sandy beaches of the Western Isles** The western seaboard of the Outer Hebrides, particularly on South Harris and the Uists, is strewn with stunning, deserted beaches backed by flower-strewn machair. See p.325

✳ **Roghadal (Rodel) church, Isle of Harris** Roghadal's pre-Reformation St Clement's Church boasts the most ornate sculptural decoration in the Outer Hebrides. See p.326

✳ **Barra** A great introduction to the Western Isles: a Hebridean island in miniature, with golden sands, crystal-clear rocky bays and mountains of Lewisian gneiss. See p.334

▲ Restored blackhouse, Gearrannan

The Western Isles

B
eyond Skye, across the unpredictable waters of the Minch, lie the wild and windy Outer Hebrides or Outer Isles, now officially known as the **Western Isles** (Ⓦ www.visithebrides.com). A 130 mile-long archipelago stretching from Lewis and Harris in the north to the Uists and Barra in the south, the islands appear as an unbroken chain when viewed from across the Minch – hence their other nickname, the Long Isle. In reality there are more than two hundred islands, although only a handful are actually inhabited, with the islands' total population just under 27,000. This is truly a land on the edge, where the turbulent seas of the Atlantic smash up against a geologically complex terrain whose coastline is interrupted by a thousand sheltered bays and, in the far west, a long line of sweeping sandy beaches. The islands' interiors are equally dramatic, veering between flat, boggy, treeless peat moor and bare mountain tops soaring high above a host of tiny lakes, or lochans.

However, the most significant difference between the Western Isles and the rest of the Hebrides is that the islands' fragile economy is still mainly concentrated around crofting, fishing and weaving, and the percentage of incomers is fairly low. In fact, the Outer Hebrides remain the heartland of **Gaelic** culture, with the language spoken by the majority of islanders, though its everyday usage remains under constant threat from the national dominance of English. Its survival is, in no small part, due to the efforts of the Western Islands Council, the Scottish parliament, and the influence of the Church in the region: the Free Church and its various offshoots in Lewis, Harris and North Uist, and the Roman Catholic Church in South Uist and Barra.

Lewis and Harris form two parts of the same island. The interior of the northernmost part, **Lewis**, is mostly peat moor, a barren and marshy tract that gives way abruptly to the bare peaks of **North Harris**. Across a narrow isthmus lies **South Harris**, with wide beaches of golden sand trimming the Atlantic in full view of the rough boulder-strewn mountains to the east. Across the Sound of Harris, to the south, a string of tiny, flatter isles – **North Uist**, **Benbecula**, **South Uist** – linked by causeways, offer breezy beaches, whose fine sands front a narrow band of boggy farmland, which, in turn, is mostly bordered by a lower range of hills to the east. Finally, tiny **Barra** contains all the above landscapes in one small Hebridean package.

In contrast to their wonderful surroundings, villages in the Western Isles are rarely very picturesque in themselves, and are usually made up of scattered, relatively modern crofthouses dotted about the elementary road system. **Stornoway**, the only real town in the Outer Hebrides, rarely impresses. Many visitors, walkers and nature-watchers forsake the main settlements altogether and retreat to secluded cottages, simple hostels and B&Bs.

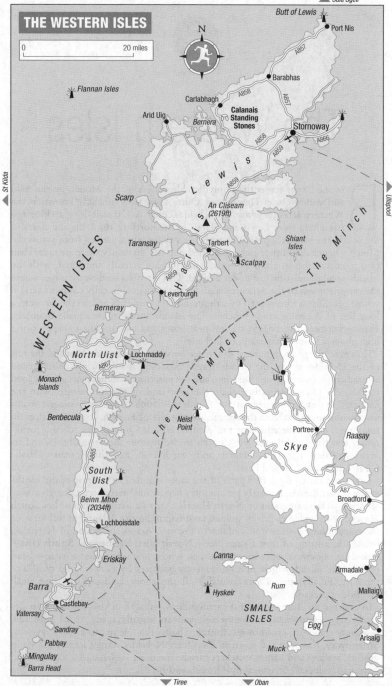

THE WESTERN ISLES

N

0   20 miles

Sula Sgeir

Butt of Lewis

Port Nis

A857

Flannan Isles

Barabhas

A858

Carlabhagh

Calanais
Standing
Stones

A857

Arid Uig

Bernera

Stornoway

St Kilda

A858

A866

A859

L e w i s

Ullapool

Scarp

An Cliseam
(2619ft)

Taransay

Tarbert

Shiant
Isles

H a r r i s

Scalpay

T h e   M i n c h

A859

Leverburgh

WESTERN ISLES

Berneray

North Uist

Lochmaddy

A867

T h e   L i t t l e   M i n c h

Uig

Monach
Islands

Benbecula

Neist
Point

Portree

Raasay

A865

S k y e

South
Uist

Beinn Mhor
(2034ft)

Broadford

A87

Lochboisdale

Eriskay

Canna

Armadale

Barra

Hyskeir

Rum

Mallaig

Castlebay

Vatersay

SMALL
ISLES

Eigg

Sandray

Pabbay

Arisaig

Muck

Mingulay

Barra Head

Tiree   Oban

Gaelic in the Western Isles

All Ordnance Survey maps and many **road signs** are exclusively in **Gaelic**, a difficult language to the English-speaker's eye, with complex pronunciation (see p.437), though the English names sometimes provide a rough pronunciation guide. If you're driving, it's a good idea to pick up a bilingual Western Isles **map**, available at most tourist offices. We've put the Gaelic first in the text, with the English equivalent in brackets, to try to familiarize readers with their (albeit variable) spellings – the only exceptions are in the names of islands and ferry terminals, where we've stuck to the English names (with the Gaelic in brackets), partly to reflect CalMac's own policy.

Some history

The Western Isles were first settled by Neolithic farming peoples in around 4000 BC. They lived along the coast, where they are remembered by scores of remains, from passage graves through to stone circles – most famously at **Calanais** (Callanish) on Lewis. Viking colonization gathered pace from 700 AD onwards – as evidenced by the islands' place names, the majority of which are of Norse, not Gaelic, origin – and it was only in 1266 that the islands were returned to the Scottish Crown. James VI (and I of England), a Stuart and a Scot, though no Gaelic-speaker, was the first to put forward the idea of clearing the Hebrides, though it wasn't until after the Jacobite uprisings, in which many Highland clans disastrously backed the wrong side, that the **Clearances** began in earnest.

The isolation of the Outer Hebrides exposed them to the whims and fancies of merchants and aristocrats who caught "island fever" and bought them up. From the mid-eighteenth century onwards, the land and its people have been sold to the highest bidder. Some proprietors have been well-meaning, but insensitive – like **Lord Leverhulme**, who had no time for crofting and wanted to turn Lewis into a centre of the fishing industry in the 1920s. Others have simply been autocratic – such as **Colonel Gordon of Cluny**, who bought Benbecula, South Uist, Eriskay and Barra, and forced the inhabitants onto ships bound for North America at gunpoint. Almost everywhere crofters were driven from their ancestral homes, robbing them of their particular sense of place. Today, memorials and cairns dot the landscape commemorating the often violent struggle which accompanied this period.

Visiting the Western Isles

There are scheduled **flights** from Glasgow, Edinburgh, Inverness and Aberdeen to Stornoway on Lewis, and to Barra and Benbecula (see p.338). Be warned: weather conditions are notoriously changeable, making flights prone to delay and cancellation. On Barra, the other complication is that you land on the beach, so the timetable is adjusted with the tides. CalMac **car ferries** run from Ullapool to Stornoway; from Uig, on Skye, to Tarbert (Mon–Sat only) and Lochmaddy (daily); and from Oban to South Uist and Barra, via Coll and Tiree (Thurs only).

A series of causeways makes it possible to drive from one end of the Western Isles to the other with just two interruptions – the **ferry** from Harris to Berneray, and from Eriskay to Barra. The islands boast a decent **bus** service, though there are no buses on Sundays. **Bike rental** is also available, but the wind makes cycling something of a challenge – head south to north to catch the prevailing wind.

Many of the islands' **hostels** occupy remote locations on or near the coast. Several of them are run by the Gatliff Hebridean Hostels Trust or GHHT (🌐www.gatliff.org.uk) – none take advanced bookings, so get there early to be sure of a bed; each hostel has hot water, a simple kitchen and space outside for camping. The islands' **B&Bs** and **guesthouses** are often better value than the

Religion in the Western Isles

It is difficult to overestimate the importance of **religion** in the Western Isles, which are divided – with very little enmity – between the **Catholic** southern isles of Barra and South Uist, and the **Protestant** islands of North Uist, Harris and Lewis. Church attendance is higher here than anywhere else in Britain and in fact, Barra, Eriskay and South Uist are the only parts of Britain where Roman Catholics are in a majority, and where you'll see statues of the Madonna by the roadside. In the Presbyterian north, the creed of **Sabbatarianism** is very strong. Here, Sunday is the Lord's Day, and pretty much the whole community (irrespective of their degree of piety) stops work – shops close, pubs close, garages close and there's very little public transport. It's advisable for visitors to check whether it's OK to arrive at or leave their accommodation on a Sunday, to avoid causing offence.

The main area of division is, paradoxically, within the Protestant Church itself. Scotland is unusual in that the national church, the **Church of Scotland**, is Presbyterian (ruled by the ministers and elders of the church) rather than Episcopal (ruled by bishops). At the time of the main split in the Presbyterian Church – the so-called **1843 Disruption** – a third of its ministers left the Church of Scotland, protesting at a law that allowed landlords to impose ministers against parishioners' wishes, and formed the breakaway **Free Church of Scotland** – sometimes referred to as the "**Wee Frees**", though this term is also used for members of the Free Presbyterian Church of Scotland. Since those days there have been several amalgamations and reconciliations with the Church of Scotland, as well as further splits, some as recently as the year 2000.

The various brands and subdivisions of the Presbyterian Church may appear trivial to outsiders, but to the churchgoers of Lewis, Harris and North Uist (as well as much of Skye and Raasay) they are still keenly felt. In part, this is due to social and cultural reasons: Free Church elders helped organize resistance to the Clearances, and the Wee Frees have contributed greatly to preserving the **Gaelic language**. A Free Church service is a memorable experience – there's no set service or prayer book and no hymns, only biblical readings, psalm singing and a sermon; the pulpit is the architectural focus of the church, not the altar, and communion is taken only on special occasions. If you want to attend a service, the Free Church on Kenneth Street in Stornoway has one of the largest Sunday-evening congregations in the UK, with up to 1500 people attending.

hotels, and allow you to meet the locals – bed numbers are limited though, so it's always best to book in advance.

The Gulf Stream ensures a mild but moist climate, though you can expect the **strong Atlantic winds** to blow in rain on two out of every three days even in summer – the upside is that means few problems with midges. Lastly, a good way to get acquainted with local life is to read the **local papers**: the old-fashioned *Stornoway Gazette* and, in particular, the weekly *West Highland Free Press*, a refreshingly vociferous campaigning paper, published in Broadford on Skye, but covering events in the whole of the Western Isles and Highland region.

Lewis (Leodhas)

Shaped rather like the top of an ice-cream cone, **Lewis** is the largest and by far the most populous of the Western Isles. Nearly half of the island's 18,500 inhabitants – two-thirds of the archipelago's total population – live in the crofting and fishing villages strung out along the northwest coast, between **Calanais** and

Port Nis, in one of the most densely populated rural areas in the country. On this coast you'll also find the islands' best-preserved **prehistoric remains** – Dùn Charlabhaigh and the Calanais standing stones – as well as a smattering of ancient crofters' houses in various stages of abandonment. The landscape is mostly flat peat bog – hence the island's name, derived from the Gaelic *leogach* (marshy) – but the shoreline is more dramatic especially around Rubha Robhanais (Butt of Lewis), the island's rocky northernmost tip, near Port Nis. The other half of the island's population live in **Stornoway**, on the east coast, the only real town in the Western Isles. To the south, where Lewis is physically joined with Harris, the land rises to over 1800ft, providing an exhilarating backdrop for the excellent beaches that pepper the isolated western coastline around **Uig**.

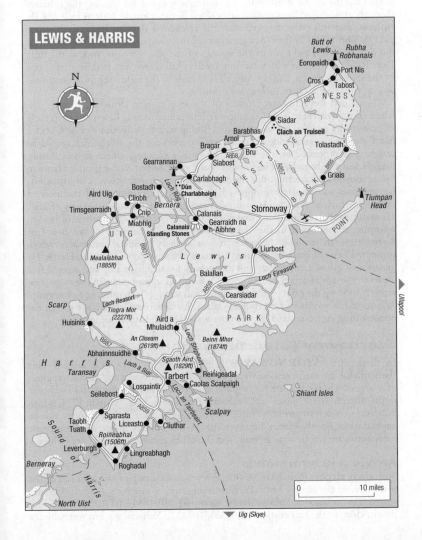

Some history

After Viking rule ended in 1266, Lewis became a virtually independent state, ruled over by the **MacLeod clan** for several centuries. King James VI, however, had other ideas: he declared the folk of Lewis to be "void of religion", and attempted to establish a colony, as in Ulster, by sending Fife Adventurers to attack Lewis. They were met with armed resistance by the MacLeods, so, in retaliation, James VI granted the lands to their arch rivals, the MacKenzies of Kintail. The MacKenzie chiefs – the Earls of Seaforth – chose to remain absentee landlords until 1844, when they sold Lewis to **Sir James Matheson**, who'd made a fortune from pushing opium on the Chinese. Matheson invested heavily in the island's infrastructure, though, as his critics point out, he made sure he recouped his money through tax or rent. He was relatively benevolent when the island was hit by potato famine in the mid-1840s, but ultimately opted for solving the problem through eviction and emigration. His chief factor, Donald Munro, was utterly ruthless, and was only removed after the celebrated Bernera Riot of 1874 (see p.319). The 1886 Crofters' Act greatly curtailed the power of the Mathesons; it did not, however, right any of the wrongs of the past. Protests, such as the Pairc Deer Raid of 1887, in which starving crofters killed two hundred deer from one of the sporting estates, and the Aignish land raids of the following year, continued against the Clearances of earlier that century.

When **Lord Leverhulme**, founder of the soap empire Unilever, acquired the island (along with Harris) in 1918, he was determined to drag Lewis out of its cycle of poverty by establishing an integrated fishing industry. To this end he founded MacFisheries, a nationwide chain of retail outlets for the fish which would be caught and processed on the islands: he built a cannery, an ice factory, roads, bridges and a light railway; he bought boats, and planned to use spotter planes to locate the shoals of herring. But the dream never came to fruition. Unfortunately, Leverhulme was implacably opposed to the island's centuries-old tradition of crofting, which he regarded as inefficient and "an entirely impossible way of life". He became involved in a long, drawn-out dispute over the distribution of land to returning ex-servicemen, the "land fit for heroes" promised by the Board of Agriculture. In the end, however, it was actually financial difficulties which prompted Leverhulme to pull out of Lewis in 1923 and concentrate on Harris. He generously gifted Lews Castle and Stornoway to its inhabitants and offered free crofts to those islanders who had not been involved in land raids. In the event, few crofters took up the offer – all they wanted was security of tenure, not ownership. Whatever the merits of Leverhulme's plans, his departure left a huge gap in the non-crofting economy, and between the wars thousands more emigrated.

Stornoway (Steòrnabhagh)

In these parts, **STORNOWAY** is a buzzing metropolis, with around nine thousand inhabitants, a one-way system, a pedestrian precinct and all the trappings of a large town. It's a centre for employment, a social hub for the island and home to the Western Isles Council or **Comhairle nan Eilean Siar**, set up in 1974, which has done so much to promote Gaelic language and culture and to stem the tide of anglicization. For the visitor, however, the town is unlikely to win any great praise – aesthetics are not its strong point, and the urban pleasures on offer are limited.

Arrival and information

Stornoway **airport** (☎01851/707400, ⓦwww.hial.co.uk) is four miles east of the town centre: the hourly bus takes fifteen minutes, or else it's a £5 taxi ride into town. The octagonal CalMac **ferry terminal** (☎01851/702361) is on South Beach, close to the **bus station** (☎01851/704327). You can get bus timetables, a map of the town, a parking disc and other useful information from the **tourist office**, near North Beach at 26 Cromwell St (April to mid-Oct Mon–Sat only; mid-Oct to March Mon–Fri only; ℡01851/703088). **Bike rental** is available from Hebridean Cycles, 67 Kenneth St (℡01851/704025, ⓦwww.hebrideancycles .co.uk; closed Sun); **car rental** from Mackinnon Self-Drive, (℡01851/702984, ⓦwww.mackinnonselfdrive.co.uk), who will deliver locally for free.

Accommodation

Away from the town's hotels, Stornoway's **accommodation** choices have improved dramatically in recent years, but prices remain high. The only **hostel** is the *Heb Hostel* (℡01851/709889, ⓦwww.hebhostel.co.uk; breakfast included), a clean, centrally located and friendly, converted terrace house at 25 Kenneth St. If you're **camping**, it's better to camp away from Stornoway, unless you need to stay near town, in which case *Laxdale Holiday Park* (℡01851/703234, ⓦwww.laxdale holidaypark.com) lies a mile or so along the road to Barabhas, on Laxdale Lane; the

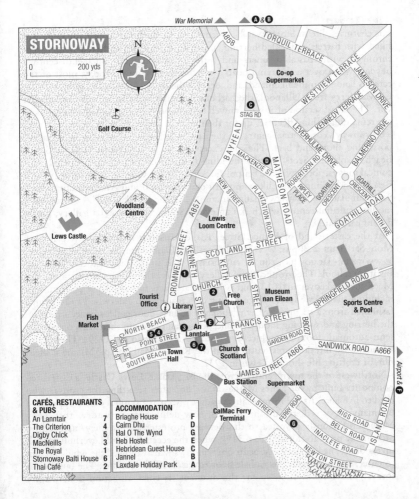

CAFÉS, RESTAURANTS & PUBS

An Lanntair	7
The Criterion	4
Digby Chick	5
MacNeills	3
The Royal	1
Stornoway Balti House	6
Thai Café	2

ACCOMMODATION

Brighe House	F
Cairn Dhu	D
Hal O The Wynd	G
Heb Hostel	E
Hebridean Guest House	C
Jannel	B
Laxdale Holiday Park	A

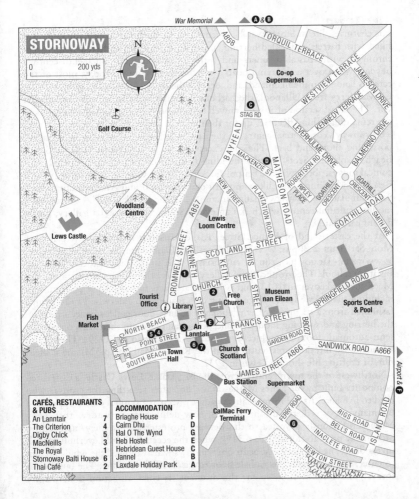

well-equipped campsite has holiday caravans (short breaks available), a self-catering bungalow and a purpose-built **bunkhouse**, as well as a nice sheltered spot for tents.

Braighe House 20 Braighe Rd ☎01851/705287, ⓦwww.braighehouse.co.uk. Forget the town's hotels, if you've got the budget, then spend the night at this faultless modern guesthouse, overlooking the sea, just outside town beside the airport. ⑥

Cairn Dhu 18a Matheson Rd ☎01851/701611, ⓦwww.lewisapartments.co.uk. Superbly equipped contemporary apartment, with free wi-fi, in a Victorian villa on the town's nicest leafy street. ⑥

Hal O The Wynd 2 Newton St ☎01851/706073, ⓦwww.halothewynd.com. Reliable, inexpensive town centre B&B in an old townhouse, conveniently situated directly opposite the ferry terminal. ②

Hebridean Guest House 61 Bayhead St ☎01851/702268, ⓦwww.hebrideanguesthouse .co.uk. A whole range of smartly refurbished, en-suite rooms on offer here, including a couple of self-catering apartments. ⑤

Jannel 5 Stewart Drive ☎0800/634 3270, ⓦwww.jannel-stornoway.co.uk. A short walk from the town centre, this B&B is run by a delightful landlady, and offers five spacious, immaculate rooms, with free wi-fi. ④

The Town

For centuries, life in Stornoway has focused on its **harbour**, whose quayside was filled with barrels of pickled herring, and whose deep and sheltered waters were thronged with coastal steamers and fishing boats in their nineteenth-century heyday, when over a thousand boats were based at the port. Today, most of the catch is landed on the mainland, and, despite the daily comings and goings of the CalMac ferry from Ullapool, the harbour is a shadow of its former commercial self. The nicest section of it is Cromwell Street Quay, by the tourist office, where the remaining fishing fleet ties up for the night.

Stornoway's commercial centre, to the east, is little more than a string of unprepossessing shops and bars. The one exception is the old **Town Hall** on South Beach, a splendid Scots Baronial building from 1905, its rooftop peppered with conical towers, above which a central clocktower rises. One block east along South Beach, and looking rather like a modern church, you'll find **An Lanntair** (Mon–Sat 10am–late; free; ⓦwww.lanntair.com) – Gaelic for "lantern" – Stornoway's modern cultural centre, which has an events space, cinema and a gallery, plus a decent café/bar.

At the eastern end of Francis Street is the **Museum nan Eilean** (April–Sept Mon–Sat 10am–5.30pm; Oct–March Tues–Fri 10am–5pm, Sat 10am–1pm; free; ⓦwww.cne-siar.gov.uk), run by enthusiastic staff in the old Victorian Nicolson Institute school. The ground-floor gallery explores the island's history until the MacKenzie takeover in 1613, and is full of artefacts found during peat cutting, including silver jewellery, a large Viking dish made from alderwood and a plaque fashioned from a fragment of whalebone. The first-floor gallery concentrates on the herring and weaving industries and houses an old loom shed with one of the semi-automatic looms introduced by Lord Leverhulme in the 1920s. There's also a blackhouse interior, press cuttings on the Rocket Mail (see p.324) and a silent film of crofting life shot on Lewis in 1937.

Northwest of the town centre, across the bay, stands **Lews Castle**, a castellated pomposity built by Sir James Matheson in 1863 after resettling the crofters who used to live here. As the former laird's pad, it is seen as a symbol of old oppression by many: it was here, in the house's now-defunct conservatory, that Lady Matheson famously gave tea to the Bernera protesters, when they marched on Stornoway prior to rioting (see p.319); when the eccentric Lord Leverhulme took up residence, he had unglazed bedroom windows which allowed the wind and rain to enter, and gutters in the asphalt floor to carry off the residue. The building is forever under renovation, so for the moment its chief attraction is its mature

Wild Scotland

From wintering wildfowl to cliff-breeding summer sea birds, Scotland is a year-round top wildlife destination – all you need is a bit of patience and a pair of binoculars. While the region's vast tracts of moorland and forest support a relatively small human population, they harbour a surprisingly healthy quota of mammals and birds. Herds of red deer roam the hillsides, while buzzards and eagles patrol the skies. Out at sea, the west coast, in particular, is one of the best places in the world to spot marine mammals, from the humble porpoise to the humungous humpback whale.

Nesting gannets, Westray, Orkney ▲

Puffins, Treshnish Isles ▼

Eagles to ospreys

The bird most visitors are keen to see, is the golden eagle, whose wingspan can reach over seven feet. Yet, with only around 400 pairs in the Highlands and Islands, you're more likely to see a buzzard. Larger (and easier to spot) is the white-tailed eagle or "fish eagle", reintroduced to the Inner Hebrides in the 1970s. After forty years' absence, the osprey returned of its own accord in the 1950s, and over 100 pairs now breed across the Highlands.

Scotland's most distinctive bird is now one of the rarest in the country. The capercaillie was eradicated in Scotland in 1785, but re-introduced in the following century. It's an unexpectedly large, turkey-like bird, which has a flamboyant, communal courting display known as

Top six for twitchers

▶▶ **Ospreys** Loch Garten, Speyside. The best place to spot this rare, fish-eating summer visitor. See p.176.

▶▶ **Capercaillie lek** Abernethy Forest, Strathspey. An early start in April and May is necessary to see the capercaillie's fierce mating rituals. See p.176.

▶▶ **Wintering wildfowl** Isle of Islay. Thousands of barnacle and white-fronted geese fly from Greenland to winter here. See p.123.

▶▶ **Puffins** Mull, Orkney and Shetland. Scotland's favourite sea bird is at its most abundant in the northern isles, but can also be seen in the Treshnish Isles off Mull. See p.87.

▶▶ **Storm petrels** Mousa Broch, Shetland. Watch thousands of storm petrels return to their nests at dusk. See p.393.

▶▶ **Red-throated divers** Isle of Eday, Orkney. The hide overlooking Mill Loch is home to several pairs of nesting red-throated divers. See p.372.

a "lek". Capercaillie are confined to the last remaining native pine forest in the Highlands, as are the crested tit and the parrot-like Scottish crossbill – the UK's only endemic bird species.

Scotland is also big on sea birds from streamlined fish-eating divers, which nest in isolated pairs on inland lochs but go fishing at sea, to cliff-breeding colonies. The most spectacular sight, though, are the remote cliffs that attract vast colonies of gannets, puffins, guillemots, razorbills, fulmars, shags and kittiwakes, or the isolated colonies of Manx shearwaters on Rùm or the storm petrels on Mousa in Shetland.

▲ Male capercaillie

Red in tooth and claw

Scotland's largest wild mammal, the red deer, can be easily seen by road or rail travellers in the Highlands and Islands. So too can the country's most popular (albeit domesticated) mammal, the shaggy auburn Highland cow, designed for the country's snowy climate. Another favourite is the diminutive Shetland pony, which still roams semi-wild in its remote homeland.

Scotland once boasted a much wider variety of mammals, from wolves to elk, most of which had disappeared by the mid-eighteenth century. A semi-wild herd of reindeer has since returned to the Cairngorms and the beaver has been reintroduced to the forests of Argyll. A healthy population of otters exists in the west and north, but they can prove remarkably elusive, and are easily confused with mink, a fugitive from fur farms that causes merry havoc in the wild. Even more difficult to spot are the wildcat and pine marten.

▲ Red stag

▼ Highland cow

Female grey seal ▲

Dolphin watching off Skye ▼

Carnivorous sundew ▼

Salmon and seals

Ninety-nine percent of Scottish salmon spend their life in offshore fish farms. Nevertheless, you can still see wild salmon leaping waterfalls in June and July en route to their ancestral gravel breeding grounds at Pitlochry in Perthshire (see p.153). Scotland also has the world's second-largest seal population, mostly grey seals, but also (the rarer) common seal, both easy to encounter in bays and harbours across the country. To catch a glimpse of other sea mammals, you need to take to the water. The easiest cetacean to spot is the porpoise, but dolphins and whales are also frequent summer visitors – head for the Moray Firth (see p.216) or the Isle of Mull (see p.85).

Pinecones and peat bogs

Although fifteen percent of Scotland is covered by forest, away from Rothiemurchus (see p.171) you'll rarely spot a native Scots pine, once the backbone of the Caledonian Forest, a vast mosaic of birch, willow, alder, elm, ash and oak. An incredible three-quarters of the country is uncultivated peat bog, rock and heather, which turns the hillsides purple in late summer. These boggy areas support specialized plants such as butterwort and the sundews, which gain nutrients by trapping midges. Scotland abounds in lichens and mosses, some found nowhere else in Britain. While the thistle is commonly associated with Scotland, the national flower is the Scottish bluebell (aka the harebell). Equally characteristic are introduced species such as the rhododendron and azalea which flourish in the damp, frost-free climate on the west coast.

The Iolaire disaster

Of the 6200 men from the Western Isles who served in [...]
– the highest casualty rate per capita in the British Empir[...]
1919, in the single most terrible tragedy to befall Lewis, ano[...]
530 servicemen were gathered at Kyle of Lochalsh to return hor[...]
families on the mailboat. As there were so many of them, an ext[...]
into service, the **Iolaire**, originally built as a luxury yacht in 1881. [...]
7.30pm heavily overloaded, carrying 284 men, young men and veterans,[...]
relatives, to cross the Minch. In the early hours of the morning as [...]
approached Stornoway harbour, she struck a group of rocks called Blastan [...]
(Beasts of Holm). In the darkness, it was impossible for those on board to see [...]
they were in fact only twenty yards from the shore.

One man, a boatbuilder from Nis (Ness), a village that was to lose 21 men that
night, fought his way ashore with a lifeline which saved the lives of forty others.
Another was saved by clinging to the mast for seven hours, but he lost his elder
brother, who'd postponed his return so that they could come back together. Another
man, when on active service, had spent 36 hours in the sea, the sole survivor of his
torpedoed ship; now he drowned within sight of his home. Every village in Lewis lost
at least one returning loved one, and this, together with the losses in the war and the
mass emigration that followed, cast a shadow over life on Lewis for many years. It
was the worst peacetime shipping disaster in home waters that century. There's a
monument at Rubha Thuilm (Holm Point), overlooking the rocks, and the ship's bell
is in the Museum nan Eilean in Stornoway.

wooded grounds, a unique sight on the Western Isles, for which Matheson had to
import thousands of tons of soil from the mainland. Hidden in amongst the trees
is the **Woodland Centre** (Mon–Sat 10am–5pm; free), which has a straightforward
exhibition on the history of the castle and the island upstairs, and a decent **café**
serving soup, salads and cakes downstairs.

If you enter or exit Stornoway via Willowglen Road (A858), you'll see the
town's giant **War Memorial** – the islands suffered a higher proportion of casual-
ties than anywhere else in the Empire – a castle tower set high above the town
amidst gorse bushes, and a good place to take in the sprawl that is Stornoway.

Eating, drinking and nightlife

Fish and chips are as popular as ever in Stornoway, but the choice of cafés and
restaurants has improved enormously over the last few years. Wherever you decide
to eat, be sure to sample the local **black puddings** (or the white and fruit ones) –
the best ones are made to a secret family recipe by local butcher, Charles MacLeod,
who has his HQ at Ropework Park (℡01851/702445, ⊛www.charlesmacleod
.co.uk). As for **pubs**, *MacNeills* on Cromwell Street (closed Sun) is the liveliest
central pub, with a mixed clientele of keen drinkers. *The Criterion*, a tiny wee pub
on Point Street (closed Sun), is another option. There's a regular programme of
gigs and films at An Lanntair, and in mid-July, the annual **Hebridean Celtic
Festival** (⊛www.hebceltfest.com) hits town, with a festival tent in Lews Castle
grounds, and events right across Lewis and Harris.

An Lanntair Kenneth St ℡01851/703307,
⊛www.lanntair.com. Stylish café/restaurant
in the An Lanntair arts centre which does decent
sandwiches and lighter dishes during the day, as
well as more imaginative stuff in the evening. Free
wi-fi. Closed Sun.

Digby Chick 5 Bank St ℡01851/700026, ⊛www
.digbychick.co.uk. Smart, modern, buzzy little bistro
with a real emphasis on using local produce.
Sandwiches available at lunchtimes or two courses
for around £10; three-course dinners for under
£25. Closed Sun.

rries are the real thing and the service great, but
e real boon is that it serves food until at least
pm and on Sun.

ai Café 27 Church St ☏01851/701811. Despite
e name, this is actually a restaurant, serving
thentic Thai food. No licence so bring your own
ttle. Closed Sun.

s east coast, north of Stornoway – an
ellent golden beaches and marks the
ess.

wnership of Lewis is recalled by the
nd-raiders, situated by Griais Bridge,
ulme's plans came unstuck: he wanted
three big farms, which would provide
milk for the workers of his fish-canning factory; the local crofters just wanted to
return to their traditional way of life. Such was Leverhulme's fury at the land-
raiders from Griais (Gress) and nearby Col (Coll), a mile to the south, that, when
he offered to gift the crofts of Lewis to their owners, he made sure the offer didn't
include Griais and Col. The stone-built memorial is a symbolic croft split asunder
by Leverhulme's interventions.

Further north, beyond Tolastadh (Tolsta), is probably the finest of the coast's
sandy **beaches**, Gheardha (Garry), and the beginning of the footpath to Ness.
Shortly after leaving the bay, the path crosses the **Bridge to Nowhere**, built by
Leverhulme as part of an unrealized plan to forge a new road right along the east
coast to Ness. A little further along the track, there's a fine waterfall on the
Abhainn na Cloich (River of Stones). The makeshift road peters out, but a
waymarked path continues for another ten miles via the old sheiling village of
Diobadail, to Ness (see opposite). It's very boggy, and badly churned up in places
due to its popularity with local quad-bikers, so make sure you've got proper
footwear.

If you're in search of a cuppa, try the **café** at *Coll Pottery* back in Col. Surprisingly,
for such a little-visited part of Lewis, there are two exceptional **accommodation**
options. *Broad Bay House* (☏01851/820990, ⓦwww.broadbayhouse.co.uk; ⑧)
has raised the bar exponentially both in terms of standards and price, with quality
furnishings, patio doors leading to private decking areas, free wi-fi in every room
and exceptionally good home cooking. The alternative is *Crowberry*
(☏01851/605004, ⓦwww.crowberry.co.uk; ⑤), a luxuriously plush B&B, just
north of Col, with spacious rooms kitted out with all mod cons, including
free wi-fi.

The road to Barabhas (Barvas)

The A857 crosses the vast, barren **peat** bog (see box opposite) that occupies most
of the interior of Lewis, an empty, undulating wilderness riddled with stretch-
marks formed by peat cuttings and pockmarked with freshwater lochans. The
whole area was once covered by forests, but these disappeared long ago, leaving a
smothering deposit of peat that continues to serve as a valuable energy resource,
with each crofter being assigned a slice of the bog.

Twelve miles across the peat bog the road approaches the west coast of Lewis and
divides, heading southwest towards Calanais, or northeast through **BARABHAS**

World War I, around 1000 died
e. Yet, on **New Year's Day**
her 208 perished. Some
ne to Lewis and their
a boat was called
the boat left at
friends and
the boat
hulm
hat

Peat

One of the characteristic features of the landscape of the Highlands and Islands is **peat** (*mòine*) – and nowhere is its presence more keenly felt than on Lewis. Virtually the whole interior of the island is made up of one, vast blanket bog, scarred with lines of peat banks old and new, while the pungent smell of peat smoke hits you as you pass through the villages. Essentially, peat is made up of dead vegetation that has failed to rot completely because the sheer volume of rainfall has caused the soil acidity to reach a level that acts as a preservative. In other words, organic matter – such as sphagnum moss, rushes, sedges and reeds – is dying at a faster rate than it is decomposing. This means, of course, that peat is still (very slowly) forming in certain parts of Scotland, at around an inch or less every fifty years. In the (mostly treeless) islands, peat provided an important source of fuel, and the cutting and stacking of peats in the spring was part of the annual cycle of crofting life. Peat cutting remains embedded in the culture, and is still practised on a large scale particularly in the Hebrides and Shetland. It's a social occasion as much as anything else, which heralds the arrival of the warmer, drier days of late spring.

Great pride is taken in the artistry and neatness of the peat banks and stacks. In some parts, the peat lies up to thirty feet deep, but peat banks are usually only cut to a depth of around six or seven feet. Once the top layer of turf has been removed, the peat is cut into slabs between two and four peats deep, using a traditional *tairsgeir* (pronounced "tushkar"). Since peat is ninety percent water in its natural state, it has to be carefully "lifted" in order to dry out. Peats tend to be piled up either vertically in "rooks", or crisscrossed in "windows"; either way the peat will lose three quarters of its water content, and shrink by about a quarter. Many folk wonder how on earth the peat can dry out when it seems to rain the whole time, but the wind helps, and eventually a skin is formed that stops any further water from entering the peats. After three or four weeks, the peats are skilfully "grieved", rather like the slates on a roof, into round-humped stacks or onto carts that can be brought home. Traditionally, the peat would be carried from the peat banks by women using "creels", baskets that were strapped on the back. Correctly grieved peats allow the rain to run off, and therefore stay dry for a year or more outside the croft.

(Barvas), which has a handy shop. Just beyond Barabhas, a signpost points to the pleasant **Morven Gallery** (Easter–Sept Tues–Sat 10.30am–5pm; free; Ⓦwww .morvengallery.com), which hosts exhibitions by local artists and photographers and has a handy café, serving great coffee, where you can hole up during bad weather. Three miles further up the road, you pass the twenty-foot monolith of **Clach an Truiseil**, the first of a series of prehistoric sights between the crofting and weaving settlements of **Baile an Truiseil** (Ballantrushal) and **Siadar** (Shader).

Ness (Nis)

The main road continues through a string of densely populated, fervently Presbyterian villages, that make up **NESS** (Nis), at the northern tip of Lewis. Ness has the highest percentage of Gaelic speakers in the country, at over 75 percent, but the locals are perhaps best known for their annual culling of young gannets on Sula Sgeir (see box, p.316). These scattered settlements have none of the photogenic qualities of Skye's whitewashed villages: the churches are plain and unadorned; the crofters' houses relatively modern and smothered in grey pebble-dash rendering or harling; the stone cottages and enclosures of their forebears often lie half-abandoned in the front garden; a rusting assortment of discarded cars and vans store peat bags and the like.

For an insight into the social history of the area, take a look inside Ness Heritage Centre or **Comunn Eachdraidh Nis** (March–Oct Mon–Fri 10am–4pm; Nov–Feb

Mon–Fri noon–4pm; ⓦ www.c-e-n.org; £2), on the left as you pass through **TABOST** (Habost). The museum, housed in an unlikely-looking building, contains a huge collection of photographs, but its prize possession is a diminutive sixth- or seventh-century cross from the Isle of Rona (see box, p.286), decorated with a much-eroded nude male figure, and thought by some to have been St Ronan's gravestone; you can have tea and coffee here too.

Offshore islands

Though three men dwell on Flannan Isle
To keep the lamp alight,
As we steer'd under the lee, we caught
No glimmer through the night.

Flannan Isle by Wilfred Wilson Gibson

On December 15, 1900, a passing ship reported that the lighthouse on the **Flannan Isles** 21 miles west of Aird Uig on Lewis, was not working. The lighthouse had been built the previous year by the Stevenson family (including the father and grandfather of author Robert Louis Stevenson). Gibson's poem goes on to recount the arrival of the relief boat from Oban on Boxing Day, whose crew found no trace of the three keepers. More mysteriously still, a full meal lay untouched on the table, one chair was knocked over, and only two oilskins were missing. Subsequent lightkeepers doubtless spent many lonely nights trying in vain to figure out what happened, until the lighthouse went automatic in 1971.

Equally famous, but for different reasons, is the tiny island of **Sula Sgeir**, 41 miles north of the Butt of Lewis. Every August, the men of Ness (known as Niseachs) have set sail from Port Nis to harvest the young gannet or guga that nest in their thousands high up on the islet's sea cliffs. It's a dangerous activity, but boiled gannet and potato are a popular Lewis delicacy (the harvest has to be strictly rationed), and there's no shortage of volunteers for the annual cull. For the moment, the Niseachs have a licence to harvest up to two thousand birds, and Scottish Natural Heritage and the RSPB have accepted the cull as sustainable.

Somewhat incredibly, the island of **Rona** (sometimes referred to as North Rona), ten miles east of Sula Sgeir, was inhabited on and off until the nineteenth century, despite being less than a mile across. The island's St Ronan's Chapel is one of the oldest Celtic Christian ruins in the country. St Ronan was, according to legend, the first inhabitant, moving here in the eighth century with his two sisters, Miriceal and Brianuil, until one day he turned to Brianuil and said, "My dear sister, it is yourself that is handsome, what beautiful legs you have." She apparently replied that it was time for her to leave the island, and made her way to neighbouring Sula Sgeir where she was later found dead with a shag's nest in her ribcage.

Clearly visible from the ferry to Lewis and Harris, the **Shiant Islands** (ⓦ www.shiant isles.net), whose name translates as "the enchanted islands", sit in the middle of the Minch, five miles off the east coast of Lewis. Inhabited on and off until the beginning of the last century, the islands were bought by the author Compton MacKenzie in 1925, and then sold on to the publisher, Nigel Nicolson, whose family still own them. The Shiants have wonderful cliffs of fluted basalt columns that shelter thousands of sea birds, including puffin, in the breeding season.

There's a wide choice of **boat trips** offered locally, including to some of the islands mentioned above: try Sea Trek (☎ 01851/672464, ⓦ www.seatrek.co.uk), based in Uig, or Kilda Cruises in Leverburgh (☎ 01859/502060, ⓦ www.kildacruises.co.uk) – prices start at around £35 per person for a short RIB wildlife cruise to £180 for a day-trip to St Kilda (see p.320). For longer trips around the islands, contact Island Cruising (☎ 01851/672381, ⓦ www.island-cruising.com), based in Uig.

The road terminates at the fishing village of **PORT NIS** (Port of Ness), with a tiny harbour and lovely golden beach. Shortly before you reach Port Nis, a minor road heads two miles northwest to the hamlet of **EOROPAIDH** (Europie) – pronounced "Yor-erpee". Here, by the road junction that leads to the Butt of Lewis, the simple stone structure of **Teampull Mholuaidh** (St Moluag's Church) stands amidst the runrig fields, which now act as sheep runs. Thought to date from the twelfth century, when the islands were still under Norse rule, but restored in 1912 (and now used once a month by the Scottish Episcopal Church for sung Communion), the church features a strange south chapel with only a squint window connecting it to the nave. In the late seventeenth century, the traveller Martin Martin noted: "They all went to church…and then standing silent for a little time, one of them gave a signal…and immediately all of them went into the fields, where they fell a drinking their ale and spent the remainder of the night in dancing and singing, etc." Church services aren't what they used to be.

From Eoropaidh, a narrow road twists to the bleak and blustery northern tip of the island, **Rubha Robhanais** – well-known to devotees of the BBC *Shipping Forecast* as the **Butt of Lewis** – where a redbrick lighthouse sticks up above a series of sheer cliffs and stacks, alive with kittiwakes, fulmars and cormorants, with skuas and gannets feeding offshore; it's a great place for spotting marine mammals. The lighthouse is closed to the public, and there's no way down to the sea, but backtrack half a mile or so, and there's a path down to the tiny sandy bay of **Port Sto**, a more sheltered spot for a picnic than the Butt itself. From Eoropaidh, you can also gain access to the dunes and machair of the nearby coastline that stretches for two or three miles to the southwest.

Practicalities

Accommodation is available at *Loch Beag* (℡01851/810405, ⓦwww.lochbeag.co .uk; ❸), a typically dour-looking B&B on the road to Butt of Lewis, run by a very friendly local couple, or at *Galson Farm* (℡01851/850492, ⓦwww.galsonfarm .co.uk; ❹), an attractive converted eighteenth-century farmhouse in Gabhsann Bho Dheas (South Galson), which offers dinner, bed and breakfast, and runs a six-bunk **bunkhouse** close by. The best place to **eat** is *Port Beach House* (℡01851/810000; closed Sun), in Port Nis, with great views out to sea, and locally caught fish and seafood on the menu. There are few shops (other than mobile ones) in these parts, so it's as well to stock up in Stornoway before you set out. The *Cross Inn* in Cros (Cross) is about the only **pub** in the area, but look out for any **live music** or other events going on at Taigh Dhonnchaidh (ⓦwww.taighdhonnchaidh.com), an arts and music centre in Tabost.

Westside (An Toabh Siar)

Heading southwest from the crossroads near Barabhas brings you to the **Westside**, where several villages meander down towards the sea. In **ARNOL**, the remains of numerous blackhouses lie abandoned by the roadside; at the north end of the village, no. 42 is the **Arnol Blackhouse** (Mon–Sat: April–Sept 9.30am–5.30pm; Oct–March 9.30am–4.30pm; HS; £2.50). The house has been very carefully preserved to show exactly how a true blackhouse, or *taigh-dubh*, would have been. The dark interior is lit and heated by a small peat fire, kept alight in the central hearth of bare earth; smoke drifts up through the thatch, helping to keep out the midges and turn the heathery sods and oat-straw thatch itself into next year's fertilizer. The animals would have slept in the byre, separated only by a low partition, while potatoes and grain were stored in the adjacent barn. The old woman who lived here moved out very reluctantly in 1964, only after the council agreed to build a house with a byre for her animals (the building now houses the ticket office). Across the road is a ruined blackhouse, abandoned in 1920 when the family moved into no. 39, the white house, or *taigh-geal*, next door. A little beyond the blackhouse, a path leads down to **Loch na Muilne**, where you've a good chance of spotting the very rare red-necked phalarope (May–Aug).

A mile or so west, in **BRAGAR**, it's difficult to miss the stark arch formed by the jawbone of a blue whale, washed up on the nearby coast in 1920. The spear sticking through the bone is the harpoon, which only exploded when the local blacksmith was trying to remove it, badly injuring him. Two miles on, at **SIABOST** (Shawbost) – home to the main Harris Tweed mill in the Outer Hebrides – there's a tiny **museum** in the **Old School Centre** (April–Sept Mon–Sat 11am–4pm; free), across the road from the local school. The exhibits – most of them donated by locals – include a rare Lewis brick from the short-lived factory set up by Lord Leverhulme. The grass field of the *Eilean Fraoich* **campsite** (℡01851/710504, ⓦwww.eileanfraoich.co.uk; April–Oct) is located behind the old village church.

Just outside Siabost, to the west, there's a sign to the newly restored **Norse Mill and Kiln**. It's a ten-minute walk over a small hill to the two thatched bothies beside a little stream; the nearer one's the kiln, the further one's the horizontal mill. Mills and kilns of this kind were common in Lewis up until the 1930s, and despite the name are thought to have been introduced here from Ireland as early as the sixth century.

Gearrannan (Garenin)

The landscape becomes less monotonous as you approach the parish of **CARLA-BHAGH** (Carloway), with its crofthouses, boulders and hillocks rising out of the peat moor. A mile-long road leads off north to the beautifully remote coastal settlement of **GEARRANNAN** (Garenin). Here, rather than re-create a single museum-piece blackhouse as at Arnol, a whole cluster of nine thatched crofters' houses – the last of which was abandoned in 1974 – have been restored and put to a variety of uses. As an emsemble, they also give a great impression of what a **Baile Tughaidh**, or blackhouse village (May–Sept Mon–Sat 9.30am–5.30pm; £2.50), must have been like. The first house you come to houses the ticket office and **café**, serving cheap and cheerful fare during the day. The second house has been restored to its condition at the time of abandonment, so there's electric light, but no running water, lino flooring, but a peat fire and box beds – and a weaving machine in the byre. The third house has interpretive panels and a touch-screen computer telling the history of the village and the folk who lived there. Next door, there are toilets and opposite is the GHHT **hostel** (ⓦwww.gatliff.org.uk); several others have been converted into **self-catering** houses (ⓦwww.gearrannan.com). A waymarked path leads four miles east to Dail Beag (Dalbeg), affording spectacular views along the coast and passing two lovely, **sandy bays** – a mile beyond is a restored Norse Mill and Kiln. In the opposite direction, it's a mile and a half along the cliffs to Laimisiadair lighthouse.

Just beyond Carlabhagh village, **Dùn Charlabhaigh** perches on top of a conspicuous rocky outcrop overlooking the sea. Scotland's west coast is strewn with over five hundred **brochs**, or fortified towers, but this is one of the best preserved, its dry-stone circular walls reaching a height of more than 30ft on one side. The broch consists of two concentric walls, the inner one perpendicular, the outer one slanting inwards, the two originally fastened together by roughly hewn flagstones, which also served as lookout galleries reached via a narrow stairwell. The only entrance to the roofless inner yard is through a low doorway set beside a crude and cramped guard cell. As at Calanais (see opposite), there have been all sorts of theories about the purpose of the brochs, which date from between 100

BC and 100 AD; the most likely explanation is that they were built to provide protection from Roman slave-traders.

Calanais (Callanish)

Overlooking the sheltered, islet-studded waters of Loch Ròg, on the west coast, are the islands' most dramatic prehistoric ruins, the **Calanais standing stones**. These monoliths – nearly fifty slabs of gnarled and finely grained gneiss up to 15ft high – were transported here between 3000 and 1500 BC, but their exact function remains a mystery. No one knows for certain why the ground plan resembles a colossal Celtic cross, nor why there's a central burial chamber. It's likely that such a massive endeavour was prompted by the desire to predict the seasonal cycle upon which these early farmers were entirely dependent, and indeed many of the stones are aligned with the positions of the sun and the stars. Whatever the reason for their existence, there's certainly no denying the powerful primeval presence, not to mention sheer beauty, of the stones.

To the south of the stones, the **Calanais Visitor Centre** (April–Sept Mon–Sat 10am–9pm; Oct–March Wed–Sat 10am–4pm; museum £2.50; ⓦwww.callanish visitorcentre.co.uk) serves straightforward snacks and has a small museum on the site, exploring the theories about the stones. If you want to commune with standing stones in solitude, head for the smaller circles in more natural surroundings a mile or two southeast of Calanais, around Gearraidh na h-Aibhne (Garynahine).

There are several good **places to stay** near the stones: try *Eshcol* (☎01851/621771, ⓦwww.eshcol.com; March–Oct; ⑤), a large, modern and very well-run guesthouse, or *Leumadair* (☎01851/612706, ⓦwww.leumadair.co.uk; ④), another purpose-built guesthouse owned by a very friendly Lewis couple, who have a pet hawk. Eating out options are limited, but both guesthouses offer dinner.

Bernera (Bearnaraigh)

Dividing Loch Ròg in two is the island of Great Bernera, usually referred to simply as **Bernera**. Joined to the mainland since 1953 via a narrow bridge that spans a small sea channel, Bernera is a rocky island, dotted with lochans, fringed by a few small lobster-fishing settlements and currently owned by Comte Robin de la Lanne Mirrlees, the Queen's former herald, who also claims the title, Prince of Incoronata (an area of former Yugoslavia gifted to the count by King Peter II).

Bernera has an important place in Lewis history due to the **Bernera Riot** of 1874, when local crofters successfully defied the eviction orders delivered to them by the landlord, Sir James Matheson. In truth, there wasn't much of a riot, but three Bernera men were arrested and charged with assault. The crofters marched on the laird's house, Lews Castle in Stornoway, and demanded an audience with Matheson, who claimed to have no knowledge of what his factor, Donald Munro, was doing. In the subsequent trial, Munro was exposed as a ruthless tyrant, and the crofters were acquitted. A stone-built cairn now stands as a memorial to the riot, at the crossroads beyond the central settlement of **BREACLEIT** (Breaclete), which sits beside one of the island's many lochs. Here, you'll find the **Bernera Museum** (May–Sept Mon–Fri noon–4pm; £1.50), housed in the local community centre. There's a small exhibition on lobster fishing, a St Kilda mailboat and a mysterious 5000-year-old Neolithic stone tennis-ball, and you can trace your ancestry.

Much more interesting is the replica **Iron Age House** (for times contact the tourist office) that has been built above a precious little bay of golden sand beyond the cemetery at **BOSTADH** (Bosta), three miles north of Breacleit – follow the signs "to the shore". In 1992, gale-force winds revealed an entire late Iron Age or Pictish settlement hidden under the sand; due to its exposed position, the site has been refilled with sand, and a full-scale mock-up built instead, based on the "jelly baby" houses – after the shape – that were excavated. Inside, the house is incredibly spacious, and very dark, illuminated only by a central hearth and a few chinks of sunlight. If the weather's fine and you climb to the top of the nearby hills, you should get a good view over the forty or so islands in Loch Ròg, and maybe even the Flannan Isles (see p.316) on the horizon.

Uig (Uuige)

It's a long drive along the partially upgraded B8011 to the remote region of **Uig**, one of the areas of Lewis that suffered really badly from the Clearances. The landscape here is hillier, and more dramatic than elsewhere, a combination of myriad islets, wild cliff scenery and patches of pristine golden sand.

At the crossroads to **MIABHAIG** (Miavaig), you have a choice of either heading straight for the Uig Sands (see below), or veering off the main road, and heading along a dramatic little road northeast to **CLIOBH** (Cliff). The Atlantic breakers that roll onto the beach below the village are often spectacular, but make it unsafe for swimmers, who should continue another mile to **CNÌP** (Kneep), to the southeast of which is **Tràigh na Beirghe**, a glorious strand of shell sand, backed by dunes and machair, where there's a small, primitive **campsite** (mid-April to mid-Sept; ℡01851/672265).

The other route from Miabhaig is to continue along the main road through the narrow canyon of Glèann Bhaltois (Glen Valtos) to **TIMSGEARRAIDH** (Timsgarry), which overlooks **Uig Sands** (Tràigh Uuige), the largest and most prized of all the golden strands on Lewis, where the sea goes out for miles at low tide; the best access point is from the car park near the cemetery in Eadar Dha Fhadhail. It was here in 1831 that a local cow rubbed itself against a sandbank and stumbled across the **Lewis Chessmen**, 78 twelfth-century Viking chesspieces carved from walrus ivory that now reside in Edinburgh's Royal Museum of

St Kilda

Britain's westernmost island chain is the NTS-owned **St Kilda** (Hiort) archipelago (ⓦwww.kilda.org.uk), roughly forty miles from its nearest landfall, Griminish Point on North Uist. Dominated by the highest cliffs and sea stacks in Britain, Hirta, St Kilda's main island, was occupied on and off for two thousand years, with the last 36 Gaelic-speaking inhabitants evacuated at their own request in 1930. Immediately after evacuation, the island was bought by the Marquess of Bute, to protect the island's millions of puffins, gannets, petrels and other sea birds. In 1957, having agreed to allow the army to build a missile-tracking radar station here linked to South Uist, the marquess bequeathed the island to the NTS. St Kilda is one of only two dozen **UNESCO World Heritage Sites** with a dual status reflecting its natural and cultural significance. Despite its inaccessibility, several thousand visitors make it out here each year; if you get to land, you can see the museum, send a postcard and enjoy a drink at the army's pub, the *Puff Inn*. Several companies offer **boat day-trips** for around £180 per person (see p.316). Between mid-May and mid-August, the NTS organizes volunteer **work parties**, which either restore and maintain the old buildings or take part in archeological digs – for more information, contact the NTS (℡0844/493 2100, ⓦwww.nts.org.uk). For the armchair traveller, the best general book on St Kilda is Tom Steel's *The Life and Death of St Kilda*, or else there's the classic 1937 film *The Edge of the World* by Michael Powell (which was actually shot on Foula in Shetland).

Scotland and the British Museum in London. You can see replicas of the chessmen in the **Uig Museum** (Mon–Fri noon–5pm; Ⓦwww.ceuig.com; £1), housed in Uig School in Timsgearraidh. As well as putting on some excellent temporary exhibitions, the museum has bits and bobs from blackhouses and is staffed by locals, who are happy to answer any queries you have; there's also a welcome **tearoom** in the adjacent nursery during the holidays.

There are several idyllic **places to stay** overlooking the Uig Sands, the most intriguing being *Baile na Cille* (Easter–Oct; ⓉO1851/672242, Ⓦwww.bailenacille .co.uk; ❺), a chaotic kind of place, run by an eccentric couple, who are very welcoming to families and dogs and dish up wonderful set-menu dinners for £30 a head. The best B&B in the area is *Suainaval* (ⓉO1851/672386, Ⓦwww.suainaval .com; ❹), in Cradhlastadh (Crowlista), run by a truly welcoming couple.

An entirely different (but equally unusual) experience is to stay at *Gallen Head* (ⓉO1851/672474, Ⓦwww.gallanheadhotel.co.uk; ❹), housed in the old RAF station in **AIRD UIG**, three miles north of Timsgearraidh. The concrete buildings themselves are something of an eyesore, but the hotel has been tastefully converted inside and the position, overlooking a rocky inlet, is spectacular.

To the west of the Uig Sands is the tiny settlement of **MANGURSTADH** (Mangersta), and a coastline of spectacular stacks and cliffs. A mile or so to the north, the old RAF radio station on the headland of **Aird Mòr** is the chosen site for a new **St Kilda Centre** (Ⓦwww.ionadhiort.org), which will tell the fascinating story of the remote archipelago (see opposite), and – on fine days – afford views of it.

Harris (Na Hearadh)

Harris, whose name derives from the Old Norse for "high land", is much hillier, more dramatic and much more immediately appealing, its boulder-strewn slopes descending to aquamarine bays of dazzling, white sand. The shift from Lewis to Harris is almost imperceptible, as the two are, in fact, one island, the "division" between them embedded in a historical split in the MacLeod clan, lost in the mists of time. The border was also, somewhat crazily, a county boundary until 1975, with Harris lying in Invernessshire, and Lewis belonging to Ross and Cromarty. Nowadays, the dividing line is rarely marked even on maps; for the record, it comprises Loch Reasort in the west, Loch Shìphoirt (Loch Seaforth) in the east, and the six miles in between. Harris itself is more clearly divided by a minuscule isthmus, into the wild, inhospitable mountains of **North Harris** and the gentler landscape and sandy shores of **South Harris**.

Along with Lewis, Harris was purchased in 1918 by **Lord Leverhulme**. In contrast to Lewis, though, Leverhulme and his ambitious projects were broadly welcomed by the people of Harris. His most grandiose plans were drawn up for Leverburgh (see p.326), but he also purchased an old Norwegian whaling station in Bun Abhain Eadara in 1922, built a spinning mill at Geocrab and began the construction of four roads. Financial difficulties, a slump in the tweed industry and the lack of market for whale products meant that none of the schemes was a wholehearted success, and when he died in 1925 the plug was pulled on all of them by his executors.

Since the Leverhulme era, unemployment has been a constant problem in Harris. Crofting continues on a small scale, supplemented by the Harris tweed industry, though the main focus of this has, in fact, shifted to Lewis. Fishing continues on **Scalpay**, while the rest of the population gets by on whatever employment is available: roadworks, crafts, hunting and fishing and, of course, the one growth

Harris tweed

Far from being a picturesque cottage industry, as it's sometimes presented, the production of **Harris tweed** is vital to the local economy, with a well-organized and unionized workforce. Traditionally the tweed was made by women, from the wool of their own sheep, to provide clothing for their families, using a 2500-year-old process. Each woman was responsible for plucking the wool by hand, washing and scouring it, dyeing it with lichen, heather flowers or ragwort, carding (smoothing and straightening the wool, often adding butter to grease it), spinning and weaving. Finally the cloth was dipped in stale urine and "waulked" by a group of women, who beat the cloth on a table to soften and shrink it whilst singing Gaelic waulking songs. Harris tweed was originally made all over the islands, and was known simply as *clò mór* (big cloth).

In the mid-nineteenth century, Catherine Murray, **Countess of Dunmore**, who owned a large part of Harris, started to sell surplus cloth to her aristocratic friends; she then sent two sisters from Srannda (Strond) to Paisley to learn the trade. On their return, they formed the genesis of the modern industry, which continues to serve as a vital source of employment, though demand (and therefore employment levels) can fluctuate wildly as fashions change. To earn the official **Harris Tweed Authority (HTA)** trademark of the Orb and the Maltese Cross – taken from Lady Dunmore's coat of arms – the fabric has to be hand-woven on the Outer Hebrides from 100 percent pure new Scottish wool, while the other parts of the manufacturing process must take place only in the local mills.

The main centre of production is actually now in Siabost, in Lewis, where the wool is dyed, carded and spun. In the last few decades, there has been a revival of traditional tweed-making techniques, with several small producers following old methods, using indigenous plants and bushes to dye the cloth: yellow comes from rocket and broom; green from heather; grey and black from iris and oak; and, most popular of all, reddish brown from crotal, a flat grey lichen scraped off rocks.

industry, tourism. There's a regular **bus** connection between Stornoway and **Tarbert**, and an occasional service which circumnavigates South Harris (see also "Travel details" on p.337).

Tarbert (An Tairbeart)

Sheltered in a green valley on the narrow isthmus, **TARBERT** is the largest place on Harris and a wonderful place to arrive by boat. The port's mountainous backdrop is impressive, and the town is attractively laid out on steep terraces sloping up from the dock. It boasts Harris's only **tourist office** (April to mid-Oct Mon–Sat only; also open to greet the evening ferry), close to the ferry terminal. The office can arrange modest, inexpensive B&B **accommodation** and has a full set of bus timetables, but its real value is as a source of information on local walks.

If you're looking for **accommodation** close to the ferry terminal, *Rockview Bunkhouse* (☎01859/502626), on Main Street, is a possibility, but it's best to book ahead as there's no warden on-site. There's a very good local **B&B**, *Tigh na Mara* (☎01859/502270, ⓦwww.tigh-na-mara.co.uk; ❸), just up the Scalpay road, or the long-established *Harris Hotel* (☎01859/502154, ⓦwww.harrishotel.com; ❺), five minutes' walk from the harbour. Two miles back up the road to Stornoway is the *Ardhasaig Hotel* (☎01859/502500, ⓦwww.ardhasaig.co.uk; ❻), idyllically located overlooking West Loch Tarbert and the mountains of North Harris – the food is locally sourced and superbly prepared with dinner costing around £40 a head.

Other options for **food** include the *Isle of Harris Inn* (closed Sun), next door to the *Harris Hotel*, which has a short seafood specials menu worth perusing. Alternatively, head for the very pleasant *First Fruits* **tearoom** (April–Sept; closed Sun), behind the tourist office, housed in an old stone-built cottage and serving real coffee, home-made cakes, toasties and so forth, plus evening meals (Thurs–Sat; booking essential; ☎01859/502439). **Fish and chips** are dispensed by *Ad's Take-Away* (April–Oct; closed Sun), next to the hostel.

North Harris (Ceann a Tuath na Hearadh)

Mountainous **North Harris** was run like some minor feudal fiefdom until 2003, when the locals managed to buy the land for a knock-down £2 million. If you're coming from Stornoway on the A859, it's a spectacular introduction to Harris, its bulging, pyramidal mountains of gneiss looming over the dramatic fjord-like **Loch Shiphoirt** (Loch Seaforth). From **AIRD A' MHULAIDH** (Ardvourlie), you weave your way over a boulder-strewn saddle between mighty **Sgaoth Aird** (1829ft) and An Cliseam or the **Clisham** (2619ft), the highest peak in the Western Isles. This bitter terrain, littered with debris left behind by retreating glaciers, offers but the barest of vegetation, with an occasional cluster of crofters' houses sitting in the shadow of a host of pointed peaks, anywhere between 1000ft and 2500ft high.

Other than self-catering cottages, the only place to stay in this area is the GHHT **hostel** (ⓦwww.gatliff.org.uk), in the lonely coastal hamlet of **REINIGEADAL** (Rhenigdale), until the 1990s only accessible by foot or boat. Nowadays, there's a basic bus service, though this must be booked in advance (☎01859/502871). To reach the hostel on foot, walk east from Tarbert along the wonderfully undulating road to Caolas Scalpaigh (Kyles Scalpay). After a couple of miles, watch for the sign marking the start of the path which threads its way for three miles over the rocky landscape to Reinigeadal. It's a magnificent hike, with superb views out along the coast and over the mountains, but you'll need to be properly equipped (see p.47) and should allow three hours for the one-way trip.

A high-flying, single-track bridge, erected in 1997, spans Loch an Tairbeairt to the island of **Scalpay** (Scalpaigh) – from the Norse *skalp-ray* (the island shaped like a boat), off the east coast of Harris. Traditionally, Scalpay is the place where Bonnie Prince Charlie tried unsuccessfully to get a boat to take him back to France after the defeat at Culloden. On a good day, it's a pleasant and fairly easy three-mile hike along the island's north coast to the **Eilean Glas** lighthouse, which looks out over to Skye. This was the first lighthouse to be erected in Scotland, in 1789, though the present Stevenson-designed granite tower dates from 1824.

The road to Huisinis (Hushinish)

The only other road on North Harris is the winding, single-track B887, which clings to the northern shores of Loch a Siar (West Loch Tarbert), and gives easy access to the awesome mountain range of the (treeless) Forest of Harris to the north. Immediately as you turn down the B887, you pass through **Bun Abhàinn Eadarra** (Bunavoneadar), where some Norwegians established a short-lived whaling station – the slipways and distinctive redbrick chimney can still be seen. Seven miles further on, the road takes you through the gates of **Abhainnsuidhe Castle** (pronounced "avan-soo-ee"), designed by David Bryce in Scottish Baronial style in 1865 for the Earl of Dunmore, and right past the front door, much to the annoyance of the castle's successive owners. As it is, you have time to admire the lovely salmon-leap waterfalls and pristine castle grounds.

It's another five miles to the end of the road at the small crofting community of **HUISINIS** (Hushinish), where you are rewarded with a south-facing beach of shell sand that looks across to South Harris. A slipway to the north of the bay serves the nearby island of **Scarp**, a hulking mass of rock rising to over 1000ft, once home to more than two hundred people and abandoned as recently as 1971 (it's now a private holiday hideaway). The most bizarre moment in its history – and the subject of the 2002 film *The Rocket Post* – was undoubtedly in 1934,

Walking in North Harris

Ordnance Survey Explorer map no. 456

Harris is great walking country. The crowds that flock to the Skye Cuillin are absent, there are no Munro-baggers, and the landscape is wonderfully lunaresque. It's also one of the largest continuously mountainous regions in the country, made up of ancient **Lewisian gneiss**, among the oldest rocks in the world formed some three thousand million years ago. As always, if you're walking, you should take note of safety precautions (see p.47), and be particularly conscious of the weather conditions, which can change rapidly in these parts.

As the highest mountain in the Western Isles, Clisham or **An Cliseam** (2619ft) is an obvious objective for walkers, and can be easily climbed from the parking space on the A859, where the road crosses the Abhainn Mhàraig. There isn't a path as such, but if you follow the river, and approach the mountain from its southeast ridge, an ascent should be fairly straightforward (2–3hr return). Clisham forms part of a horseshoe ridge that extends from Mullach an Langa in the northwest to Tomnabhal in the east. In order to climb the whole ridge, you're better off starting off from near where the A859 crosses the Abhainn Scaladail, just before Aird a Mhulaidh. There's an old drovers' road, half a mile before the bridge, which heads south, skirting Caisteal Ard and Cleit Ard; from the track you get a gentle approach to the southeastern ridge of Tomnabhal. At the other end of the ridge, you can return to Aird a' Mhulaidh, via Loch Mhisteam and the Abhainn Scaladail. The entire circuit of the ridge should take around five hours. If you're based in Tarbert and don't have your own transport, it's roughly an hour's walk to Bun Abhainn Eadarra.

If weather conditions are poor, there are several low-level walks that nevertheless take you through the heart of the mountains of North Harris. None of them are circular, so you need to study the bus timetables carefully or backtrack. The first route takes the aforementioned path from Bun Abhainn Eadarra, and then continues up to Loch a' Sgàil, and, over the narrow pass into **Glen Langadale**, from which a path eventually heads east to the A859 just north of Aird a' Mhulaidh, a total distance of eight miles (4hr). A longer and more rewarding ten-mile walk (5–6hr) is along **Gleann Mhiabhaig** via Loch Scourst and Loch Bhoisimid, and then east to the A859 just north of Aird a' Mhulaidh; an interesting detour can also be made to Gleann and Loch Stuladail, which are surrounded by crags. The most impressive low-level walk, however, is along **Gleann Ulladail**, where Loch Ulladail is overlooked by the rocky headland of Sron Ulladail. There's a decent path all the way from the dam on the B887, just before Abhainn Suidhe, to Loch Ulladail, a distance of under five miles; the return journey takes four to five hours. If you've energy, and the weather's good, you can use the above low-level walk as a return route, after climbing the ridge of peaks that starts with Cleiseabhal in the south, and ends with Ullabhal in the north.

Unfortunately, the Reinigeadal GHHT hostel is too far east to use as a base for any of these walks. However, you can console yourself by climbing the nearby peak of **Tòdun** (1732ft), which can be easily approached along its north or south ridge. The return trip will probably only take a couple of hours, so for a longer day's hike you could aim for a circuit of the trio of mountains further west: Sgaoth Iosal (1740ft), Sgaoth Aird (1829ft) and Gillaval Glas (1544ft).

when the German scientist **Gerhardt Zucher** conducted an experiment at sending mail by rocket. Zucher made two attempts at launching his rocket from Scarp, but the letter-laden missile exploded before it even got off the ground, and the idea was shelved.

South Harris (Ceann a Deas na Hearadh)

The mountains of **South Harris** are less dramatic than in the north, but the scenery is equally breathtaking. There's a choice of routes from Tarbert to the ferry port of **Leverburgh**, which connects with North Uist: the east coast, known as **Na Baigh** (The Bays), is rugged and seemingly inhospitable, while the **west coast** is endowed with some of the finest stretches of golden sand in the whole of the archipelago, buffeted by the Atlantic winds.

The Bays (Na Baigh)

Paradoxically, most people on South Harris live along the harsh eastern coastline of **The Bays** rather than the more fertile west side. But not by choice – they were evicted from their original crofts to make way for sheep-grazing. Despite the uncompromising lunar landscape – mostly bare grey gneiss and heather – the crofters managed to establish "lazybeds" (small labour-intensive, raised plots between the rocks fertilized by seaweed and peat), a few of which are still in use even today. The narrow sea lochs provide shelter for fishing boats, while the interior is speckled with freshwater lochans, and the whole coast is now served by the endlessly meandering **Bays Road**, often wrongly referred to as the "Golden Road", though this, in fact, was the name given to the sideroad to Scadabhagh (Scadabay), coined by a local councillor who disapproved of the expense.

There are only a few **places to stay** along the coast, the most obvious being *No.5 Hostel* (℡01851/511255, ⓦwww.number5.biz; April–Nov), a converted cottage three miles south of Tarbert in Drinisiadar (Drinishader). The best **campsite** is at 🏕 *Lickisto Blackhouse* (℡01851/530485, ⓦwww.freewebs.com/vanvon), four miles south of Tarbert in Liceasto (Lickisto) – there's fresh bread and eggs available and a peat fire to warm you in the blackhouse. If you're looking for somewhere to stop and have home-made soup, baguettes and cakes, head for the popular *Skoon* **café** and art gallery in Geocrab, which also has internet access (ⓦwww.skoon .co.uk; April–Sept Tues–Sat; Oct–March Fri & Sat).

The west coast

The main road from Tarbert into South Harris snakes its way west for ten miles across the boulder-strewn interior to reach the coast. Once there, you get a view of the most stunning **beach**, the vast golden strand of **Tràigh Losgaintir**. The road continues to ride above a chain of sweeping sands, backed by rich **machair**, that stretches for nine miles along the Atlantic coast. In good weather, the scenery is particularly impressive, foaming breakers rolling along the golden sands set against the rounded peaks of the mountains to the north and the islet-studded turquoise sea to the west – and even on the dullest day the sand manages to glow beneath the waves. A short distance out to sea is the island of **Taransay** (Tarasaigh), which once held a population of nearly a hundred, but was abandoned as recently as 1974. Day-trips are possible from Horgabost beach (April–Oct Mon–Fri; £20; ℡01859/550260, ⓦwww.visit-taransay.com).

Beul-na-Mara (℡01859/550205, ⓦwww.beulnamara.co.uk; ❹) is a very good modern **B&B** in Seiilebost, overlooking the sands of Tràigh Losgaintir. A few miles further south, in Na Buirgh (Borve), is a lovely, tastefully converted

Victorian crofthouse, *Pairc an t-Srath* (☎01859/550386, ⓦwww.paircant-srath
.co.uk; ❻), which also serves up excellent three-course dinners for £35 a head.
Beyond lies **Sgarasta** (Scarista), where one of the first of the Hebridean Clearances
took place in 1828, when thirty families were evicted and their homes burnt.

There's a particularly magnificent stretch of machair, by the golden sands close
to the village of **TAOBH TUATH** (Northton), a lovely spot overlooked by the
round-topped hill of Chaipabhal at the southwesternmost tip of the island. Taobh
Tuath itself is no picture postcard, with the exception of the **MacGillivray
Centre** (open all year at any time), whose modern design was inspired by the
Hebridean blackhouse; clearly, though, the building won the accolades and not
the centre, which contains only a tiny bit of information on the naturalist William
MacGillivray (1796–1852), after whom it's named, and a little on crofting and
machair. There's more information on local geology, flora and fauna to be found
at **Seallam!** (Mon–Sat 10am–5pm; £2.50; ⓦwww.seallam.com), on the main
road, a useful centre for eager ancestor-hunters, but also providing interest for
kids, literally at their level.

Leverburgh (An t-Ob)

From Taobh Tuath the road veers to the southeast to trim the island's south shore,
eventually reaching the sprawling settlement of **LEVERBURGH** (An t-Ob).
Named after Lord Leverhulme, who planned to turn the place into the largest
fishing port on the west coast of Scotland, it's the terminal for the CalMac **car
ferry** service to Berneray and the Uists. The hour-long journey across the skerry-
strewn Sound of Harris is one of Scotland's most tortuous ferry routes, with the
ship taking part in a virtual slalom-race to avoid numerous hidden rocks – it's also
a great crossing from which to spot sea birds and sea mammals.

For **accommodation**, *Grimisdale* (☎01859/520460, ⓦwww.grimisdale.co.uk; ❻;
March–Nov) is the luxury option; a modern guesthouse with loch views from most
rooms and free wi-fi. A cheaper option is *Sorrel Cottage* (☎01859/520319, ⓦwww
.accommodationisleofharris.co.uk; ❸), a converted crofthouse a mile back towards
Taobh Tuath from Leverburgh, that also offers **bike rental**, or the quirky, timber-
clad 🔱 *Am Bothan* (☎01859/520251, ⓦwww.ambothan.com), a luxurious, very
welcoming **bunkhouse** close to the ferry. On the north side of the bay is the *An
Clachan* co-op store which houses a small **information office**. For some local
seafood, home-made cakes and the usual comfort **food**, head for *The Anchorage*
(closed Sun), a lively bar and restaurant, by the ferry slipway, that has great views and
the occasional live-music night.

Roghadal (Rodel)

A mile or so from Rubha Reanais (Renish Point), the southern tip of Harris, is the
old port of **ROGHADAL** (Rodel), where a smattering of ancient stone houses lies
among the hillocks. Down by the old harbour where the ferry from Skye used to
arrive, you'll find the *Rodel Hotel* (☎01859/520210, ⓦwww.rodelhotel.co.uk; ❻),
a solid, stone-built, family-run hotel originally erected in 1781.

On top of one of the grassy humps, with sheep grazing in the graveyard, is
St Clement's Church (Tur Chliamainn), burial place of the MacLeods of Harris
and Dunvegan in Skye. Dating from the 1520s – in other words pre-Reformation,
hence the big castellated tower (which you can climb) – the church was saved from
ruination in the eighteenth century, and fully restored in 1873 by the countess of
Dunmore. The bare interior is distinguished by its wall tombs, notably that of the
founder, Alasdair Crotach (also known as Alexander MacLeod), whose heavily
weathered effigy lies beneath an intriguing backdrop and canopy of sculpted reliefs
depicting vernacular and religious scenes – elemental representations of, among

others, a stag hunt, the Holy Trinity, St Michael and the devil, and an angel weighing the souls of the dead. Look out, too, for the *sheila-na-gig* halfway up the south side of the church tower; unusually, she has a brother displaying his genitalia, below a carving of St Clement on the west face.

North Uist (Uibhist a Tuath)

Compared to the mountainous scenery of Harris, **North Uist** – seventeen miles long and thirteen miles wide – is much flatter and for some comes as something of an anticlimax. Over half the surface area is covered by water, creating a distinctive peaty-brown lochan-studded "drowned landscape". Most visitors come here for the trout-and-salmon-fishing and the deerstalking, both of which (along with poaching) are critical to the survival of the island's economy. Others come for the smattering of prehistoric sites, the birds, or the sheer peace of this windy isle and the solitude of North Uist's vast sandy beaches, which extend – almost without interruption – along the north and west coasts.

There are two **car ferry** services to North Uist: from Leverburgh on Harris to Berneray, from where there are regular **buses** to Lochmaddy, the principal village on the east coast; and from Uig on Skye to Lochmaddy itself. Public transport is pretty good but there's no service on Sundays.

Lochmaddy (Loch nam Madadh) and around

Despite being situated on the east coast, some distance away from any beach, the ferry port of **LOCHMADDY** – "Loch of the Dogs" – makes a good base for exploring the island. Occupying a narrow, bumpy promontory and overlooked by the brooding mountains of Lì a Tuath (North Lee) and Lì a Deas (South Lee) to the southeast, it's difficult to believe that this sleepy settlement was a large herring port as far back as the seventeenth century.

The only thing to keep you in Lochmaddy is **Taigh Chearsabhagh** (Mon–Sat 10am–5pm; free), a converted eighteenth-century merchant's house, now home to a vibrant community arts centre, with a simple airy café, post office, shop and excellent museum, which puts on some seriously innovative exhibitions. Taigh Chearsabhagh was one of the prime movers behind the commissioning of a series of seven sculptures dotted about the Uists. Ask at the arts centre for directions to the ones in and around Lochmaddy, the most interesting of which is the **Both nam Faileas** (Hut of the Shadow), 1km north of the town. The hut is an ingenious dry-stone, turf-roofed camera obscura built by sculptor Chris Drury that projects the nearby land, sea and skyscape onto its back wall – take time to allow your eyes to adjust to the light. On the way back keep a look out for otters, who love the tidal rapids hereabouts.

Lochmaddy has the island's only **bank** and **tourist office** (April to mid-Oct Mon–Sat only; open to greet the evening ferry; ☎01876/500321), near the quayside, which has local bus and ferry timetables and can help with **accommodation**. In Lochmaddy itself, you can stay at the cherry-red, purpose-built *Tigh Dearg* (☎01876/500700, ⓦwww.tighdearghotel.co.uk; ➐), whose stylish modernity is pretty much unique on the Uists; guests get free use of the hotel's gym, sauna and steam room and there's free wi-fi. Back towards the main road, there's *Redburn House* (☎01876/500301, ⓦwww.redburnhouse.com; ➌), a nicely renovated Victorian house, and in the opposite direction, the *Uist Outdoor Centre* (☎01876/500480, ⓦwww.uistoutdoorcentre.co.uk; March to mid-Dec), which

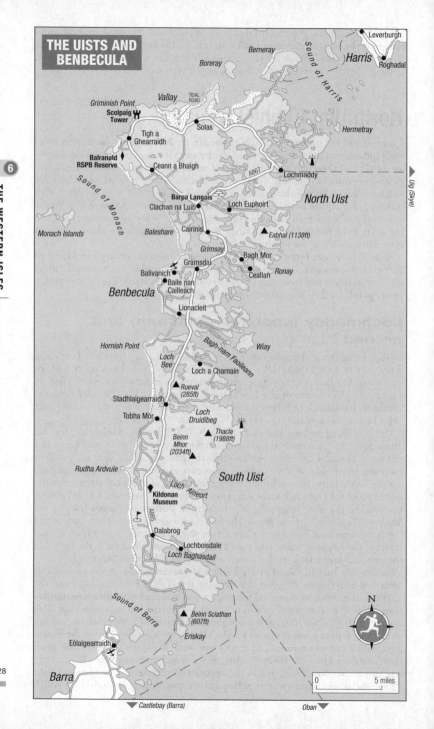

THE UISTS AND
BENBECULA

Leverburgh

Sound of Harris

Harris

Roghadal

Berneray

Boreray

Hermetray

Valley

TIDAL
ROAD

Griminish Point

Scolpaig
Tower

Solas

Tigh a
Ghearraidh

Balranald
RSPB Reserve

Ceann a Bhaigh

Sound of Monach

A867

Lochmaddy

Uig (Skye)

Barpa Langais

North Uist

Clachan na Luib

Loch Euphoirt

Baleshare

Cairinis

Eabhal (1138ft)

Monach Islands

Grimsay

Bagh Mor

Balivanich

Gramsdal

Ronay

Baile nan
Cailleach

Ceallan

Benbecula

Lionacleit

Hornish Point

Bagh nam Faoileann

Wiay

Loch
Bee

Loch a Charnain

Rueval
(285ft)

Stadhlaigearraidh

Loch
Druidibeg

Tobha Mòr

Thacla
(1988ft)

Beinn
Mhor
(2034ft)

South Uist

Rudha Ardvule

Loch Aineort

Kildonan
Museum

Dalabrog

A865

Lochboisdale

Loch Baghasdail

Sound of Barra

N

Beinn Sciathan
(607ft)

Eriskay

Eòlaigearraidh

Barra

0   5 miles

Castlebay (Barra)

Oban

has **hostel** accommodation and offers activities ranging from sea-kayaking to rock climbing for residents and nonresidents alike.

Tigh Dearg serves delicious, quite elaborate **food** in the bar and restaurant, while the *Lochmaddy Hotel*, whose bar is the local **social centre**, serves pretty standard bar meals; if you're looking for something a bit more special, you'll need to head for *Langass Lodge* (see below). There is a small **general store**, but the island's largest supermarket is eight miles away in Solas.

Nearby Neolithic sites

Several prehistoric sites lie in the vicinity of Lochmaddy. The most remarkable is **Barpa Langais**, a huge, chambered burial cairn a short walk from the A867, seven barren miles southwest. The stones are visible from the road and, unless the weather's good, it's not worth making a closer inspection as the chamber has collapsed and is now too dangerous to enter. A mile further down the A867, a sideroad leads off to *Langass Lodge* (℡01876/580285, ⓌＷwww.langasslodge.co.uk; ❻), a venerable **hotel** with a stylish modern extension, whose restaurant and bar serve excellent local seafood. Beside the hotel, a rough track leads to the small stone circle of **Pobull Fhinn** (Finn's People), which enjoys a much more picturesque location overlooking a narrow loch. The circle covers a large area and, although the stones are not that huge, they occupy an intriguing amphitheatre cut into the hillside. For those interested in wildlife, the RSPB runs **otter walks** (May–Aug Wed 10am; £5; booking essential ℡01876/560287), which set off from the car park at *Langass Lodge*. Three miles northwest of Lochmaddy along the A865 you'll find **Na Fir Bhreige** (The Three False Men), three standing stones which, depending on your legend, mark the graves of three spies buried alive or three men who deserted their wives and were turned to stone by a witch.

Berneray (Bhearnaraigh)

The ferry connection with Harris leaves from the very southeastern point of **Berneray** (Ⓦwww.isleofberneray.com), a low-lying island immediately to the north of North Uist and connected to the latter via a causeway. Two miles by three, with a population of just over a hundred, the island has a superb three-mile-long sandy beach on the west and north coast, backed by rabbit-free dunes and machair. The **Nurse's Cottage** (June–Aug Mon–Fri 11am–3pm; £1), just past the harbour, has a small historical display on the island. Berneray boasts a wonderful GHHT **hostel** (Ⓦwww.gatliff.org.uk), which occupies a pair of thatched black-houses in a lovely spot by a beach, beyond Loch a Bhàigh and the main village. Alternatively you can follow in Prince Charles's footsteps and stay (and help out) at "Splash" MacKillop's *Burnside Croft* **B&B** (℡01876/540235; ❸), in Borgh (Borve), overlooking the machair and dunes, and enjoy "storytelling evenings"; bike rental is also available. *The Lobster Pot* **tearoom** (and shop) on the main road, near the ferry terminal, serves toasties and soup and simple early evening meals (closed Sun).

The coastal road via Solas (Sollas)

The A865, which skirts the northern and western shoreline of North Uist for more than thirty miles, takes you through the most scenic sections of the island. Once you've left the boggy east coast and passed the turning to Berneray and the Harris ferry, the road reaches the parish of **SOLAS** (Sollas), which stands at the centre of a couple of superb tidal strands – sea green at high tide, golden sand at low tide – backed by large tracts of machair that are blanketed with wild flowers in summer. A new memorial opposite the local co-op recalls the appallingly brutal

Clearances undertaken by Lord MacDonald of Sleat in Solas. Visible across the nearby sandy strand is the tidal island of **Vallay** (Bhalaigh), on which stands the ruined mansion of wealthy textile manufacturer and archeologist Erskine Beveridge – check tide times before setting out.

Beyond Solas, the rolling hills that occupy the centre of North Uist slope down to the sea. Here, in the northwest corner of the island, you'll find **Scolpaig Tower**, a castellated folly on an islet in Loch Scolpaig, erected as a famine-relief project in the nineteenth century – you can reach it, with some difficulty, across stepping stones. A tarmac track leads down past the loch and tower to Scolpaig Bay, beyond which lies the rocky shoreline of **Griminish Point**, the closest landfall to St Kilda (see box, p.320), clearly visible on the horizon in fine weather, looming like some giant dinosaur's skeleton emerging from the sea.

Roughly three miles south of Scolpaig Tower, through the sand dunes, is the **Balranald RSPB Reserve** where, if you're lucky, you should be able to encounter corncrakes, once common throughout the British countryside, but now among the country's rarest birds. Unfortunately, the birds are very good at hiding in long grass, so you're unlikely to see one; however, the males' loud "craking" is relatively easy to hear from May to July throughout the Uists and Barra. In fact, there are usually one or two making a loud noise right outside the RSPB **visitor centre**, from which you can pick up a leaflet outlining a two-hour walk along the headland, marked by posts. A wonderful carpet of flowers covers the machair in summer, and there are usually corn bunting and arctic tern inland, and gannet, Manx shearwater and skua out to sea.

A couple of miles down the main road from Balranald, the *Claddach Kirkibost Centre* has an excellent **café** in a conservatory with sea views, which uses local produce and has internet facilities (Mon–Fri 11am–5pm). Half a mile further on, you can get peat-smoked salmon and other seafood delights by the roadside from the *Hebridean Smokehouse* (closed Sun).

Clachan to Grimsay (Griomasaigh)

At **CLACHAN NA LUIB**, by the crossroads with the A867 from Lochmaddy, there's a post office and general store; the nearby *Carinish Inn* serves as the local **pub** and offers the usual bar meals. Offshore, to the southwest, lie two flat, tidal, dune and machair islands, the largest of which is **Baleshare** (Baile Sear), with its fantastic three-mile-long beach, connected by causeway to North Uist. In Gaelic the island's name means "east village", its twin "west village" having disappeared under the sea during a freak storm in the fifteenth or sixteenth century. The storm also isolated the **Monach Islands** (also known by their old Norse name of Heisker or Heisgeir in Gaelic), once joined to North Uist at low tide, now eight miles out to sea. The islands, which are connected with each other at low tide, were inhabited until the 1930s, when the last remaining families moved to Solas in North Uist. **Accommodation** options include *Moorcroft Holidays* (℡01876/580305, Ⓦmoorcroftholidays.com), an exposed, but very well-equipped **campsite** (and bunkhouse), overlooking the sea just south of Carinis (Carinish), or you can stay on Baleshare at *Bagh Alluin* (℡01876/580370, Ⓦwww.jacvolbeda.co.uk; ❸), a secluded, modern **B&B** with fantastic views over the island.

For a superb overview of North Uist's watery landscape, it's a boggy, but relatively straightforward climb up Baleshare's highest hill, **Eabhal** (1138ft). The best starting-point is the end of the B894 to Loch Euphoirt: skirt round the east side of Loch Obasaraigh and approach the summit from the northeast (return trip 3–4hr).

On leaving North Uist the main road squeezes along a series of single-track causeways, built by the military in 1960, that cross the tidal rapids separating

North Uist from Benbecula. The causeways trim the west edge of **Grimsay** (Griomasaigh), a peaceful, little-visited, rocky island that's really quite pretty, especially around **BAGH MOR** (Baymore). The main source of employment is fishing for langoustine, lobster and the like, which takes place at the modern pier in **CEALLAN** (Kallin), where you can usually buy some shellfish on Saturday mornings. Ceallan is also home to the **Grimsay Boatshed** (Mon–Sat 9am–4pm; free), where there's a display of old and new Grimsay Boats, the clinker-built open boats that were perfectly designed for negotiating the local watery labyrinth. For a **place to stay** on Grimsay, look no further than *Ardnastruban House* (T01870/602452; ❷), a B&B run by a very welcoming couple, close to the causeways.

Benbecula (Beinn na Faoghla)

Blink and you could miss the pancake-flat island of **Benbecula** (put the stress on the second syllable), sandwiched between Protestant North Uist and Catholic South Uist. Most visitors simply trundle along the main road that cuts across the middle of the island in less than five miles – not such a bad idea, since the island is scarred from the postwar presence of the Royal Artillery, who once made up half the local population. Economically, of course, the area benefited enormously from the military presence, though the impact on the environment and the local Gaelic culture (with so many English-speakers around) was less positive.

The legacy of Benbecula's military past is only too evident in the depressing, barracks-like housing developments of **BALIVANICH** (Baile a Mhanaich), the grim, grey capital of Benbecula in the northwest. The only reason to come here at all is if you happen to be flying into or out of **Benbecula airport** (Wwww .hial.oc.uk), need an ATM, the laundry (behind the bank) or a supermarket. There's no tourist office and no real need **to stay** here, but if you've time to kill, you could head down to *MacGillivray's*, a long-established, old-fashioned shop selling everything from local tweeds to books, within easy walking distance of the airport, on the road to North Uist. If you need a bite to eat, there's just *Stepping Stone*, a purpose-built **café/restaurant** which serves up chips with everything during the day, and tries a bit harder (and charges more) in the evenings.

If you're passing along the west side of the island, pop into Baile nan Cailleach, better known as the **Nunton Steadings** (Mon–Sat 10am–5pm; Wwww .nuntonsteadings.co.uk), an unusual three-sided eighteenth-century farm building with a cobbled courtyard, and a small belltower (used to call the workers in from the fields), that hosts occasional exhibitions and gigs, has free wi-fi and houses a **café**. The only secondary school (and public swimming pool) on the Uists and Benbecula is **Sgoil Lionacleit** at **LIONACLEIT** (Liniclate), in the south of the island. The school is home to a small **Museum nan Eilean** (Mon–Sat only; phone for times; T01870/602864), which puts on temporary exhibitions on the history of the islands, as well as occasional live music and other events.. For **accommodation**, close to the school, there's *Shell Bay Campsite* (T01870/602447; April–Oct) and *Lionacleit Guest House* (T01870/602176, Wwww.lionacleit-guesthouse.com; ❷), a very comfortable modern crofthouse. More secluded and picturesque, though, is *Kyles Flodda* (T01870/603145, Wwww.kylesflodda.com; ❺), a beautifully converted Victorian B&B halfway down the dead-end road to Caolas Fhlodaigh (Kyles Flodda), in the north of the island.

South Uist (Uibhist a Deas)

To the south of Benbecula, the island of **South Uist** (Ⓦ www.southuist.com) is the largest and most varied of the southern chain of islands. The west coast boasts some of the region's finest machair and beaches – a necklace of gold and grey sand strung twenty miles from one end to the other – while the east coast features a ridge of high mountains rising to 2034ft at the summit of Beinn Mhòr. Whatever you do, don't make the mistake of simply driving down the main A865 road, which runs down the centre of the island like a backbone. To reach the beaches (or even see them), you have to get off the main road and pass through the old crofters' villages that straggle along the west coast; to climb the mountains in the east, you need a detailed 1:25,000 Explorer map, in order to negotiate the island's maze of lochans. The only blot on South Uist's landscape is the old Royal Artillery missile range, which dominates the northwest corner of the island.

Rueval to Kildonan

The Reformation never took a strong hold in South Uist (or Barra), and the island remains Roman Catholic, as is evident from the various roadside shrines and the slender modern Madonna, *Our Lady of the Isles*, that stands by the main road below the small hill of **Rueval**, known to the locals as "Space City" for its forest of aerials and giant "golf balls", which help track missiles launched by the nearby MOD range.

One of the best places to gain access to the sandy shoreline is at **TOBHA MÒR** (Howmore), a pretty little crofting settlement with a fair number of restored houses, many still thatched, including one distinctively roofed in brown heather. A GHHT **hostel** (Ⓦ www.gatliff.org.uk) occupies one such house near the village church, from where it's an easy walk across the flower-strewn machair to the gorgeous beach. Close by the hostel are the shattered, lichen-encrusted remains of no fewer than four medieval churches and chapels, and a burial ground now harbouring just a few scattered graves. The sixteenth-century **Clanranald Stone**, carved with the arms of the clan who ruled over South Uist from 1370 until 1839, used to lie here. It's now displayed in the nearby Kildonan Museum (see below), after it was stolen in 1990 and removed to London by a Canadian artist, Lawren Maben. It took three months before anyone noticed it had disappeared. Five years later, it was discovered by the artist's father in a bedsit near Euston station, as he sorted out his son's belongings, following his "death by misadventure".

There's much more besides the aforementioned stone at the **Taigh-tasgaidh Chill Donnain** – or **Kildonan Museum** (April–Oct daily 10am–5pm; £2; Ⓦ www.kildonanmuseum.co.uk), on the main road five miles south of Tobha Mòr. Mock-ups of Hebridean kitchens through the ages, two lovely box-beds and an impressive selection of old photos are accompanied by a firmly unsentimental yet poetic written text on crofting life in the last two centuries. Among the more unusual exhibits is a pair of ornamental shoes made of deer hooves. The museum also runs a café serving sandwiches and home-made cakes, and has a choice of historical videos for those really wet and windy days. A little to the south of the museum, the road passes a cairn that sits amongst the foundations of **Flora MacDonald**'s childhood home; she was born nearby, but the house no longer stands.

Apart from the hostel, there's the *Orasay Inn* (Ⓣ 01870/610298, Ⓦ www .orasayinn.co.uk; ⑤), a modern **hotel** off the road to Loch a Charnain (Lochcarnan); the rooms are pretty standard, but the location is peaceful and the breakfasts are good – if you're hoping for a bar meal, it's best to book ahead. Just south of

Rueval, there's *Kinloch* (℡01870/620316, Ⓦwww.kinlochuist.com; ❹), a fine modern **B&B**, run by a keen angler, sheltered by trees and overlooking a fresh-water loch. **Bike rental** (and repair) is available from Rothan Cycles (℡01870/620283, Ⓦwww.rothan.com), on the main road in Tobha Mòr (Howmore).

Lochboisdale (Loch Baghasdail) and around

LOCHBOISDALE occupies a narrow, bumpy promontory on the east coast, but, despite being South Uist's chief settlement and ferry port, has only very limited facilities. If you're arriving here late at night on the boat from Oban (or from Barra or Tiree), you should try to book accommodation in advance; otherwise, head for the **tourist office** (Easter–Oct Mon–Sat only; open for an hour to meet the ferry; ℡01878/700286); next door is a useful coin-operated shower and toilet block (daily 9am–6pm). The town's only **hotel**, the *Lochboisdale* does decent **bar meals**, occasionally featuring local seafood. For **accommodation**, there are several small, perfectly friendly **B&Bs** within comfortable walking distance of the dock: one of the best (and nearest) being *Brae Lea House* (℡01878/700497, Ⓦwww.braelea.co.uk; ❷). There's a bank in Lochboisdale, but the shops are pretty limited; the nearest supermarket is three miles west in Dalabrog (Daliburgh), where you'll also find the *Uist Bunkhouse* (℡01878/700566, Ⓦwww.uistbunkhouse.co.uk; ❶), which offers singles, doubles and family rooms as well as bunks. Another place you could happily hole up in is the *Polochar Inn* (℡01878/700215, Ⓦwww.polocharinn.com; ❹), eight miles from Lochboisdale, right on the south coast overlooking the Sound of Barra, and with its own sandy beach close by; the rooms all have sea views, and on the ground floor is a genuine **pub**, serving decent bar meals.

Eriskay (Eiriosgaigh)

Famous for its patterned jerseys and a peculiar breed of pony, originally used for carrying peat and seaweed, the barren, hilly island of **Eriskay** is connected to the south of South Uist by a causeway, built in 2001. The island, which measures just over two miles by one, and shelters a small fishing community of about 150, makes an easy day-trip from South Uist.

For a small island, Eriskay has had more than its fair share of historical headlines. The island's main beach on the west coast, Coilleag a Phrionnsa (Prince's Cockle Strand), was where **Bonnie Prince Charlie** landed on Scottish soil on July 23, 1745 – the sea bindweed that grows here to this day is said to have sprung from the seeds Charles brought with him from France. The prince, as yet unaccustomed to hardship, spent his first night in a local blackhouse and ate a couple of flounders, though he apparently couldn't take the peat smoke and chose to sleep sitting up rather than endure the damp bed.

Eriskay's other claim to fame came in 1941 when the 8000-ton **SS Politician** or "*Polly*" as it's fondly known, sank on its way from Liverpool to Jamaica, along with its cargo of bicycle parts, £3 million in Jamaican currency and 264,000 bottles of whisky, inspiring Compton MacKenzie's book, and the Ealing comedy (filmed on Barra in 1948), *Whisky Galore!* (released as *Tight Little Island* in the US). The real story was somewhat less romantic, especially for the 36 islanders who were charged with illegal possession by the Customs and Excise officers, 19 of whom were found guilty and imprisoned in Inverness. The ship's stern can still be seen at low tide northwest of Calvay Island in the

Sound of Eriskay, and one of the original bottles (and lots of other related memorabilia) can be viewed at *Am Politician*, the island's purpose-built pub near the two cemeteries on the west coast, which offers an extensive bar menu and great views out to sea.

Built in 1903, in a vaguely Spanish style on raised ground above the harbour, is the Roman Catholic **St Michael's Church**. Its most striking features are the bell, which sits outside the church and comes from the World War I battle cruiser *Derfflinger*, the last of the scuttled German fleet to be salvaged from Scapa Flow (see p.356), and the altar, which is made from the bow of a lifeboat. From the church, it's a short walk to the **community centre** (Mon–Sat 11am–3pm), which serves tea and snacks in summer, and sells jumpers and occasionally hosts exhibitions. The walk (2hr return from the village) up to the island's highest point, **Ben Sciathan** (607ft), is well worth the effort on a clear day, as you can see the whole island, plus Barra, South Uist, and across the sea to Skye, Rùm, Coll and Tiree. On the way up or down, look out for the diminutive Eriskay ponies, which roam free on the hills but tend to graze around Loch Crakavaig, the island's freshwater source.

Apart from a couple of self-catering options, the only way to stay here is to **camp rough** (with permission). CalMac runs a **car ferry to Barra** (4–5 daily; 40min) from the southwest coast of Eriskay.

Barra (Barraigh)

Just four miles wide and eight miles long, **Barra** (Ⓦ www.isleofbarra.com) is like the Western Isles in miniature. It has sandy beaches, backed by machair, mountains of Lewisian gneiss, prehistoric ruins, Gaelic culture and a laid-back, welcoming Catholic population of just over 1300. Like some miniature feudal island state, it was ruled over for centuries, with relative benevolence, by the MacNeils. Unfortunately, however, the family sold the island in 1838 to Colonel Gordon of Cluny, who had also bought Benbecula, South Uist and Eriskay. The colonel deemed the starving crofters "redundant", and offered to turn Barra into a state penal colony. The government declined, so the colonel called in the police and proceeded with some of the cruellest forced Clearances in the Hebrides. In 1937, the 45th chief of the MacNeil clan bought back most of the island, and in 2003 gifted the estate to the Scottish government.

Castlebay (Bàgh a Chaisteil)

The only settlement of any size is **CASTLEBAY** (Bàgh a Chaisteil), which curves around the barren rocky hills of a beautiful wide bay on the south side of the island. It's difficult to imagine it now, but Castlebay was a herring port of some significance in the nineteenth century, with up to four hundred boats in the harbour and curing and packing factories ashore. Barra's religious allegiance is immediately announced by the large Catholic church, Our Lady, Star of the Sea, which overlooks the bay; to underline the point, there's a *Madonna and Child* on the slopes of **Sheabhal** (1260ft), the largest peak on Barra, and a fairly easy hike from the bay.

As its name suggests, Castlebay has a castle in its bay, the picturesque medieval islet-fortress of Caisteal Chiosmuil, or **Kisimul Castle** (April–Sept daily 9.30am–5.30pm; HS; £4.70), ancestral home of the MacNeil clan. The castle burnt down in the eighteenth century, but when the 45th MacNeil chief – conveniently enough, a wealthy American and trained architect – bought the

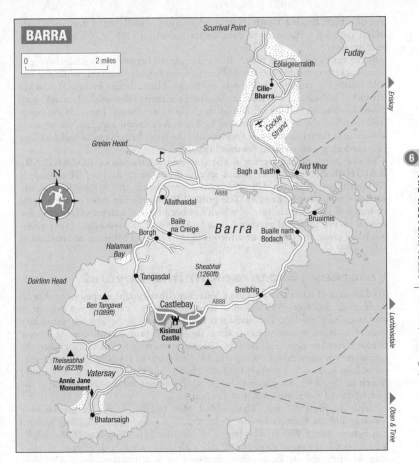

island back in 1937, he set about restoring the castle. There's nothing much to see inside, but the whole experience is fun – head down to the slipway at the bottom of Main Street, where the HS ferryman will take you over (weather permitting; ☎01871/810313).

To learn more about the history of the island, and about the postal system of the Western Isles, it's worth paying a visit to the Barra Heritage Centre, known as **Dualchas** (March, April & Sept Mon, Wed & Fri 10.30am–4.30pm; May–Aug Mon–Sat 10.30am–4.30pm; £2; ⓦwww.barraheritage.com), on the road that leads west out of town; the museum also has a handy **café** serving soup, toasties and cakes.

North to Cockle Strand and Eòlaigearraidh

If you head north from Castlebay, basically you have a choice of taking the west- or the east-coast road. The west-coast road takes you past the island's finest sandy beaches, particularly those at **Halaman Bay** and near the village of Allathasdal (Allasdale). The east-coast road winds its way in and out of various rocky bays, one of which, **Bàgh a Tuath** (Northbay), shelters a small fishing fleet and a little island sporting a statue of St Barr, better known as Finbarr, the island's Irish patron saint.

At the north end of the island, Barra is squeezed between two sandy bays: the dune-backed west side takes the full force of the Atlantic breakers, while the east side boasts the crunchy shell sands of Tràigh Mhòr, better known as **Cockle Strand**. The beach is also used as the island's **airport** (ⓦ www.hial.co.uk), with planes landing and taking off according to the tides, since at high tide the beach (and therefore the runway) is covered in water. As its name suggests, the strand is also famous for its cockles and cockleshells, the latter being used to make harling (the rendering used on most Scottish houses).

To the north of the airport is the scattered settlement of **EÒLAIGEAR-RAIDH** (Eoligarry), which boasts several sheltered sandy bays. Here, too, is **Cille-Bharra** (St Barr's Church), burial ground of the MacNeils (and the author Compton MacKenzie). The ground lies beside the ruins of a medieval church and two chapels, one of which has been rerofed to provide shelter for several carved medieval gravestones and a replica of an eleventh-century rune-inscribed cross, the original of which is in the National Museum of Scotland in Edinburgh.

Vatersay (Bhatarsaigh) and beyond

To the south of Barra is the island of **Vatersay** (Bhatarsaigh), shaped rather like an apple core, and since 1991 linked to its neighbour by a causeway – a mile or so southwest of Castlebay. The island is divided into two peninsulas connected by a slender isthmus, whose dunes feature the **Annie Jane Monument**, a granite needle erected to commemorate the 350 emigrants who lost their lives when the *Annie Jane* ran aground off Vatersay in 1853 en route to Canada. The main settlement (also known as Vatersay) has little charm, but it does have a lovely **sandy beach** to the south; another fine beach, visible from Castlebay, is situated at the eastern end of the northern half of the island.

Climb up the chief hill, **Theiseabhal Mòr** (623ft), to get an overview of Vatersay and the Bishop's Isles to the south, all of which were inhabited up until just before World War II. The largest of the islands is **Mingulay** (Miùghlaigh), which once had a population of 160 and with its large sea-bird colonies, spectacular sea cliffs and stacks, is often compared to St Kilda (see box, p.320). The crofters of Mingulay began a series of land raids on Vatersay from 1906 and by 1912 the island had been abandoned, with none of the publicity later given to St Kilda. The most southerly of the Western Isles is Berneray (Bearnaraigh) – not to be confused with the Berneray north of North Uist – best known for its lighthouse, **Barra Head**, which stands on cliffs over 620ft high. For details of boat trips to the island, phone Barra Fishing Charters (below).

Practicalities

There are two **ferry terminals** on Barra: from Eriskay, you arrive at an uninhabited spot called Aird Mhòr, on the northeast of the island; from Oban, Lochboisdale or Tiree, you arrive at the main terminal in Castlebay itself. Barra Car Hire (℗01871/890313) will deliver **cars** to either terminal or the airport, and Barra Cycle Hire (℗01871/810284) will do the same with **bikes**. There's also a fairly decent **bus** service, which does the rounds of the island (Mon–Sat). Barra's **tourist office** (April–Oct Mon–Sat only; open to greet the ferry; ℗01871/810336) is situated on Main Street in Castlebay just round from the pier, and can help book accommodation, though it's as well to book in advance for B&Bs and hotels. Guided **sea-kayaking** is available from the *Dunard Hostel* (see below), and those interested in a **boat trip** to any of the islands around Barra, including **Mingulay**, should phone Donald (℡01871/890384, ⓦwww.barrafishingcharters.com) or enquire at the tourist office.

For **accommodation** in Castlebay itself, the *Castlebay Hotel* (℡01871/810223, ⓦwww.castlebay-hotel.co.uk; ⑤) is the more welcoming of the town's two options. For a cheaper alternative, try *Tigh-na-Mara* (℡01871/810304, ⓦwww.tighnamara-barra.co.uk; April–Oct; ③), a Victorian guesthouse a couple of minutes' walk from the pier, overlooking the sea, or *Dunard Hostel* (℡01871/810443, ⓦwww.dunardhostel.co.uk), a relaxed, family-run place just west of the ferry terminal in Castlebay. The best option on Barra is the old church in Bagh a Tuath (Northbay), now home to the *Heathbank Hotel* (℡01871/890266, ⓦwww.barrahotel.co.uk; ⑤), a comfortable hotel and local watering hole.

On Main Street, the *Kisimul* **café** (closed Sun) serves breakfast all day, and specializes in cheap-and-cheerful Scottish fry-ups and Asian food. For fancier fare, head to the *Castlebay Hotel*'s cosy **bar**, which regularly has cockles, crabs and scallops on its menu, and good views out over the bay. The aforementioned *Heathbank Hotel* serves good bar meals. **Films** are occasionally shown on Saturday evenings at the local school – look out for the posters – where there is also a swimming pool (Tues–Sun), library and sports centre, all of which are open to the general public.

Travel details

Buses

Lewis/Harris

Information at ⓦwww.cne-siar.gov.uk/travel.

Stornoway to: Arnol (Mon–Sat 6–8 daily; 35min); Barabhas (Mon–Sat 6–9 daily; 25min); Calanais (Mon–Sat 4–6 daily; 40min); Carlabhagh (Mon–Sat 5–6 daily; 45min); Gearrannan (Mon–Sat 3–4 daily; 1hr); Great Bernera (Mon–Sat 4 daily; 1hr); Leverburgh (Mon–Sat 4–5 daily; 2hr); Port Nis (Mon–Sat 6–8 daily; 1hr); Siabost (Mon–Sat 5–6 daily; 45min); Tarbert (Mon–Sat 5 daily; 1hr); Tolsta (Mon–Sat hourly; 40min); Uig (Mon–Sat 4 daily; 1hr–1hr 30min).

Tarbert to: Huisinis (schooldays Mon–Fri 3–4 daily; school holidays Tues & Fri 3 daily; 45min); Leverburgh (Mon–Sat 6–8 daily; 45min–1hr); Leverburgh via the Bays (Mon–Sat 2–4 daily; 1hr); Rhenigdale (Mon–Sat 2 daily; 30min); Scalpay (Mon–Sat 4–6 daily; 20min).

Uists & Benbecula

Balivanich to: Eriskay (Mon–Sat 5–7 daily; 1hr 30min); Lochboisdale (Mon–Sat 7–9 daily; 1hr).

Berneray to: Balivanich (Mon–Sat 5–7 daily; 1hr 15min); Eriskay (Mon–Sat 4 daily; 3hr); Lionacleit (Mon–Sat 6–8 daily; 1hr 15min); Lochboisdale (Mon–Sat 6 daily; 2hr 15min); Lochmaddy (Mon–Sat 9 daily; 25min); Solas (4–5 daily; 30min)

Lochboisdale to: Eriskay (Mon–Sat 7 daily; 35min).

Lochmaddy to: Balivanich (Mon–Sat 6 daily; 45min–2hr); Balranald (Mon–Sat 3 daily; 50min); Lochboisdale (Mon–Sat 6 daily; 1hr 30min).

Barra

Castlebay to: airport/ferry for Eriskay (Mon–Sat 4–6 daily; 35–45min); Vatersay (Mon–Sat 4–5 daily; 20min).

Ferries

Summer timetable only.

To Barra: Eriskay–Barra (5 daily; 40min); Lochboisdale–Castlebay (Mon, Tues & Thurs; 1hr 30min); Oban–Castlebay (1 daily; 4hr 50min); Tiree–Castlebay (Thurs; 3hr).

To Harris: Berneray–Leverburgh (3–4 daily; 1hr); Uig–Tarbert (Mon–Sat 1–2 daily; 1hr 45min).

To Lewis: Ullapool–Stornoway (Mon–Sat 2–3 daily, 1 on Sun; 2hr 45min).
To North Uist: Leverburgh–Berneray (3–4 daily; 1hr); Uig–Lochmaddy (1–2 daily; 1hr 40min).
To South Uist: Castlebay–Lochboisdale (daily except Sat; 1hr 40min); Oban–Lochboisdale (Tues, Thurs, Sat & Sun; 5hr 20min–6hr 30min).

Flights

Aberdeen to: Stornoway (Mon–Fri 1daily; 1hr).
Benbecula to: Barra (Mon–Fri 1 daily; 20min); Stornoway (Mon–Fri 2 daily; 30min).

Edinburgh to: Stornoway (Mon–Fri 2 daily, Sat & 1 on Sun; 1hr 5min).
Glasgow to: Barra (Mon–Sat 2–3 daily; 1hr 10min); Benbecula (Mon–Fri 2 daily, Sat & 1 on Sun; 55min); Stornoway (Mon–Fri 3–4 daily, Sat & Sun 1–2 daily; 1hr 10min).
Inverness to: Stornoway (Mon–Fri 3 daily, Sat & 1 on Sun; 40min).

7

Orkney

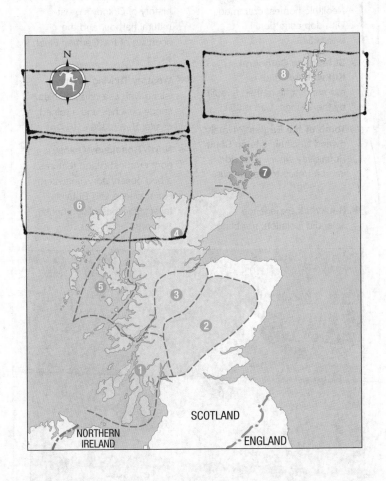

CHAPTER 7

Highlights

* **Maes Howe** Orkney's – and Europe's – finest Neolithic chambered tomb. See p.347

* **Skara Brae** Mesmerizing Neolithic homes, crammed with domestic detail. See p.348

* **St Magnus Cathedral, Kirkwall** Beautiful red-sandstone cathedral built by the Vikings. See p.354

* **Tomb of the Eagles** Privately owned Neolithic site on South Ronaldsay where you slide in on a trolley to view inside. See p.360

* **Rackwick** Experience splendid isolation, rumbling rocky beach and the famous Old Man of Hoy. See p.361

* **Scapa Flow Visitor Centre** Learn about the wartime history of Orkney's great natural harbour and the scuttling of the German Fleet. See p.363

* **Westray** Thriving Orkney island with sea-bird colonies, sandy beaches and a ruined castle. See p.368

* **North Ronaldsay** Orkney's northernmost island features a bird observatory, seaweed-eating sheep and Britain's tallest land-based lighthouse. See p.377

▲ Puffins and razorbill, Westray

Orkney

Orkney is a captivating and fiercely independent archipelago made up of seventy or so mostly low-lying islands, with a population of less than twenty thousand. The locals tend to refer to themselves first as Orcadians, regarding Scotland as a separate entity, and proudly flying their own flag. For an Orcadian, the **Mainland** invariably means the largest island in Orkney rather than the rest of Scotland, and throughout their distinctive history they've been linked to lands much further afield, principally Scandinavia.

Orkney has two chief settlements: **Stromness**, an attractive old fishing town on the far southwestern shore, and the capital, **Kirkwall**, which stands at the dividing point between East and West Mainland. The Mainland is relatively heavily populated and farmed throughout, and is joined by causeways to a string of southern islands, the largest of which is **South Ronaldsay**. The island of **Hoy**, the second largest in the archipelago, south of Mainland, presents a superbly dramatic landscape, with some of the highest sea cliffs in the country. Hoy, however, is atypical: Orkney's smaller, much quieter **northern islands** are low-lying, elemental but fertile outcrops of rock and sand, scattered across the ocean.

Rolling out of the sea "like the backs of sleeping whales" (George Mackay Brown), the Orkney isles offer excellent coastal **walking**, abundant birdlife and beautiful sweeping white-sand beaches. The main cultural celebration is the week-long **St Magnus Festival** (Ⓦ www.stmagnusfestival.com), a superb arts festival. July is peppered with several island regattas, followed by numerous agricultural shows, culminating in the County Show held in the middle of August in Kirkwall. To find out **what's on** (and what the weather's going to be like), tune in to Radio Orkney on 93.7FM, and buy yourself a copy of one of the local newspapers, *The Orcadian* or *Orkney Today*, both of which come out on a Thursday.

Some history

Orkney lay athwart a great sea-way
from Viking times onwards, and its lore
is crowded with sailors, merchants, adventurers,
pilgrims, smugglers, storms and sea-changes.
The shores are strewn with wrack, jetsam,
occasional treasure.

George Mackay Brown

Small communities began to settle in the islands around 4000 BC, and **Skara Brae** on the Mainland is one of the best-preserved Stone Age settlements in Europe. Elsewhere the islands are scattered with chambered tombs and stone circles, a tribute to the well-developed religious and ceremonial practices taking place here from around 2000 BC. More sophisticated **Iron Age** inhabitants built fortified

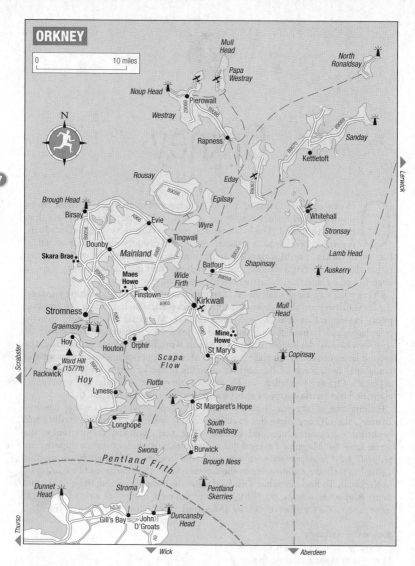

ORKNEY

0   10 miles

N

Mull
Head

North
Ronaldsay

Papa
Westray

Noup Head
Pierowall

Westray

Rapness

Sanday

Kettletoft

Rousay

Eday

Egilsay

Whitehall

Brough Head
Birsay

Evie

Wyre

Stronsay

Dounby

Tingwall

Mainland

Skara Brae

Balfour

Shapinsay

Lamb Head

Maes
Howe

Wide
Firth

Auskerry

Finstown

Kirkwall

Stromness

Mull
Head

Graemsay

Mine
Howe

Hoy

Houton

Orphir

St Mary's

Copinsay

Ward Hill
(1577ft)

Scapa
Flow

Rackwick

Hoy

Lyness

Flotta

Burray

St Margaret's Hope

Longhope

South
Ronaldsay

Swona

Burwick

Brough Ness

Pentland Firth

Dunnet
Head

Stroma

Pentland
Skerries

Gill's Bay

John
O'Groats

Duncansby
Head

Scrabster

Thurso

Lerwick

Wick

Aberdeen

villages incorporating stone towers known as brochs, the finest of which is the **Broch of Gurness**. Later, **Pictish** culture spread to Orkney and the remains of several early Christian settlements can be seen, the best at the **Brough of Birsay**. Around the ninth century, settlers from Scandinavia arrived and the islands became **Norse** earldoms, forming an outpost of a powerful, expansive culture. The last of the Norse earls was killed in 1231, but they had a lasting impact on the islands, leaving behind not only their language but also Kirkwall's great medieval **St Magnus Cathedral**.

After Norse rule, the islands became the preserve of **Scottish earls**, who exploited and abused the islanders, although a steady increase in sea trade did offer some chance of escape. French and Spanish ships sheltered here in the sixteenth century, and the ships of the **Hudson's Bay Company** recruited hundreds of Orcadians to work in the Canadian fur trade. The islands were also an important staging-post in the **whaling industry** and the herring boom, which drew great numbers of small Dutch, French and Scottish boats. The choice of **Scapa Flow**, Orkney's natural harbour, as the Royal Navy's main base brought plenty of money and activity during both world wars, and left the clifftops dotted with gun emplacements and the sea bed scattered with wrecks – which these days make for wonderful diving opportunities.

After the war, things quietened down somewhat, although since the mid-1970s the large **oil terminal** on the island of Flotta, the establishment of the Orkney Islands Council (OIC), combined with EU development grants, have brought surprise windfalls, stemming the exodus of young people. Meanwhile, many disenchanted southerners have become "ferryloupers" (incomers), moving to Orkney in search of peace and the apparent simplicity of island life.

Arrival

Orkney is connected to the Scottish mainland by several **car ferry** routes. Pentland Ferries (℡01856/831226, ⓦwww.pentlandferries.co.uk) operates catamarans from **Gills Bay**, near John O'Groats (linked by bus to Wick and Thurso) to **St Margaret's Hope** on South Ronaldsay (3 daily; 1hr). Services to **Stromness** from **Scrabster** (2–3 daily; 1hr 30min), which is connected to nearby Thurso by shuttle bus, are run by Northlink Ferries (℡0845/600 0449, ⓦwww.northlink ferries.co.uk), which also operates ferries to **Kirkwall** from **Aberdeen** (4 weekly; 6hr) and from **Lerwick** in Shetland (3 weekly; 5hr 30min).

John O'Groats Ferries (℡01955/611353, ⓦwww.jogferry.co.uk) runs a **passenger ferry** from **John O'Groats** to **Burwick** on South Ronaldsay (May & Sept 2 daily; June–Aug 4 daily; 40min), its departure timed to connect with the arrival of the Orkney Bus from Inverness; there's also a free shuttle service from Thurso train station for certain sailings. The ferry is small and, except in fine weather, is recommended only for those with strong stomachs.

Direct **flights** on British Airways serve Kirkwall airport from Sumburgh in Shetland, Inverness, Aberdeen, Edinburgh and Glasgow.

Island transport

Bus services (ⓦwww.stagecoachbus.com) on the Orkney Mainland are infrequent, and skeletal on Sundays – a free timetable is available from the tourist office. On the smaller islands, a minibus usually meets the ferry and will take you to your destination. **Cycling** is not a bad option if the weather holds, since there are few steep hills and distances are modest, though the wind can make it hard going. If your time is limited, you could join one of the informative **tours** by the likes of Wildabout Orkney Tours (March–Oct; ℡01856/877737, ⓦwww.wildabout orkney.com) which cover the chief sights on the Mainland, or one of the island-specific tours detailed in the text.

Getting to the other islands from the Mainland isn't difficult, though it's expensive: Orkney Ferries (℡01856/872044, ⓦwww.orkneyferries.co.uk) operates all **ferry routes** and it's essential to book your ticket well in advance. If you're taking a car on any of the ferries, book your ticket well in advance. There are **flights** from Kirkwall to most of the outer isles, operated by Loganair (℡01856/872494, ⓦwww.loganair.co.uk), using an eight-seater plane, with discounted fares to North Ronaldsay and Papa Westray and between the islands, if you stay over. Travel between individual islands by sea or air isn't straightforward, but careful study of timetables may reduce the need to travel via Kirkwall. It's worth enquiring from Orkney Ferries about their **additional Sunday sailings** in summer, which often make useful inter-island connections.

Stromness

STROMNESS has to be one of the most enchanting ports at which to arrive by boat, its picturesque waterfront a procession of tiny sandstone jetties and slate roofs nestling below the green hill of Brinkies Brae. As one of Orkney's main points of arrival, Stromness is a great introduction, and one that's well worth spending a day exploring, or using as a base in preference to Kirkwall. Its natural sheltered harbour (known as Hamnavoe) must have been used in Viking times, but the town itself only really took off in the eighteenth century when the **Hudson's Bay Company** made Stromness its main base from which to make the long journey across the North Atlantic, and crews from Stromness were also hired for herring and whaling expeditions – and, of course, press-ganged into the Royal Navy.

By 1842, the town boasted forty or so pubs, and reports circulated of "outrageous and turbulent proceedings of seamen and others who frequent the harbour". The **herring boom** brought large numbers of small boats to the town, along with thousands of young women who gutted, pickled and packed the fish in barrels. Things got so rowdy by World War I that the town voted in a referendum to ban the sale of alcohol, leaving Stromness dry from 1920 until 1947. Nowadays, Stromness is very quiet, though it remains an important fishing port and **ferry terminal** and is the focus of the popular four-day **Orkney Folk Festival** (Ⓦ www .orkneyfolkfestival.com), held at the end of May.

Information and accommodation

Stromness's modern ferry terminal also houses the **tourist office** (March–Oct daily; Ⓣ01856/850716, Ⓦ www.visitorkney.com). **Accommodation** is surprisingly thin on the ground. The venerable Victorian *Stromness Hotel* – the town's first – has seen better days, and you're better off heading for the *Miller's House and Harbourside Guest House*, 13 John St (Ⓣ01856/851969, Ⓦ www.millershouseorkney.com; ❸), in the town's oldest property (and a nearby annexe), or the nearby former harbourmaster's house, *45 John Street* (Ⓣ01856/850949, Ⓦ www.45johnstreet.co.uk; ❸). There's a choice of **hostels**: the *Hamnavoe*, 10a North End Rd (Ⓣ01856/851202, Ⓦ www .hamnavoehostel.co.uk), is no beauty from the outside, but inside it's all spotlessly clean and well equipped; *Brown's* (Ⓣ01856/850661, Ⓦ www.brownshostel.co.uk) is a family-run place, right in the centre of town on Victoria Street, with bunk beds in very small, shared rooms. There's also a **campsite** (Ⓣ01856/873535; May to mid-Sept) in a superb (though extremely exposed) setting a mile south of the ferry terminal at Point of Ness. **Bike rental** is available from Orkney Cycle Hire, 54 Dundas St (Ⓣ01856/850255, Ⓦ www.orkneycyclehire.co.uk), near the museum.

The Town

Stromness has a few reminders of its trading heyday, starting with the **Warehouse**, situated diagonally opposite the new ferry terminal – though it may not look like it, the building was constructed in the 1760s. More eye-catching is the **Stromness Hotel**, a tall and imposing sandstone building behind the Warehouse; during World War II, Gracie Fields sang from its balcony, when it served as the headquarters of the Orkney and Shetland Defence ("OS Def").

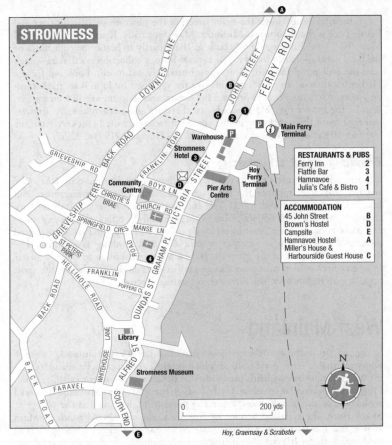

STROMNESS

RESTAURANTS & PUBS
Ferry Inn   2
Flattie Bar   3
Hamnavoe   4
Julia's Café & Bistro   1

ACCOMMODATION
45 John Street   B
Brown's Hostel   D
Campsite   E
Hamnavoe Hostel   A
Miller's House &
  Harbourside Guest House C

Hoy, Graemsay & Scrabster

Unlike Kirkwall, the old town of Stromness – famously described by Sir Walter Scott as "a dirty, straggling town" – still hugs the shoreline, its one and only street, a narrow winding affair, built long before the advent of the motor car, still paved with great flagstones and fed by a tight network of alleyways or closes. The central section, which begins at the *Stromness Hotel*, is known as **Victoria Street**, though in fact it takes on several other names – Graham Place, Dundas Street, Alfred Street and South End – as it threads its way southwards. On the east side of the street the houses are gable-end-on to the waterfront, and originally each one would have had its own pier, from which merchants would trade with passing ships.

The warehouse on the first of the old jetties, on Victoria Street, now forms half of the **Pier Arts Centre** (Mon–Sat 10.30am–5pm; Ⓦwww.pierartscentre.com; free); the other half is a modern glass-and-steel structure which offers views of the harbour framed like pictures. The galley has always featured a remarkable collection of twentieth-century British art, mostly by members of the Cornish school such as Barbara Hepworth, Ben Nicholson, Terry Frost, Patrick Heron, Eduardo Paolozzi and the self-taught Alfred Wallis, but has now also acquired contemporary works, many by northern and Scandinavian artists, which continue the marine themes of the original collection.

Ten minutes' walk down the main street, at the junction of Alfred Street and South End, is the **Stromness Museum** (May–Sept daily 10am–5pm; Oct–April Mon–Sat 11am–3.30pm; £3.50), built in 1858, partly to house the collections of the local natural-history society. The natural-history collection is still here – don't miss the pull-out drawers of birds' eggs, butterflies and moths. Look out for the Halkett cloth boat, an early inflatable like the one used by John Rae, the Stromness-born Arctic explorer, whose fiddle, octant and shotgun are also on display. Amidst the beaver furs and model boats, there are also numerous salty artefacts gathered from shipwrecks, including some barnacle-encrusted crockery from the German High Seas Fleet that was sunk in Scapa Flow in 1919 (see p.357).

Eating and drinking

Stromness has only a few **places to eat**, starting with the daytime-only *Julia's Café and Bistro* situated opposite the ferry terminal, with a sunny conservatory and imaginative meals for under £10. The *Hamnavoe Restaurant*, at 35 Graham Place (April–Sept; ☏01856/850606; Tues–Sun eve only), offers the town's most ambitious cooking, concentrating on local produce such as grilled sole or peppered monkfish – main courses start at around £15 and booking is essential. The downstairs *Flattie Bar* of the *Stromness Hotel* is a congenial place to warm yourself by a real fire or (depending on the season) sit outside with a **drink**; the most popular pub is, however, the *Ferry Inn*, opposite the terminal.

West Mainland

Stromness sits in the southwesternmost corner of the **West Mainland** – west of Kirkwall, that is – the great bulk of which is fertile, productive farmland, fenced off into a patchwork of fields used either to produce crops or for cattle-grazing. Fringed by spectacular coastline, particularly in the west, West Mainland is littered with some of the island's most impressive prehistoric sites, such as the village of **Skara Brae**, the standing **Stones of Stenness**, the chambered tomb of **Maes Howe** and the **Broch of Gurness**, as well as one of Orkney's best preserved medieval castles at **Birsay**. Despite the intensive farming, there are some areas that are too barren to cultivate, and the high ground and wild coastline include several interesting **wildlife reserves**.

Stenness

The parish of **Stenness**, northeast of Stromness along the main road to Kirkwall, slopes down from Ward Hill (881ft) to the lochs of Stenness and Harray; the first is tidal, the second is Orkney's most famous freshwater trout loch. The two lochs are separated by a couple of promontories, now joined by a short causeway that may well have been a narrow isthmus around 3000 BC, when it stood at the heart of Orkney's most important Neolithic ceremonial complex, centred on the burial chamber of **Maes Howe**.

The Stones of Stenness and the Ring of Brodgar

The most visible part of the complex between lochs Stenness and Harray is the **Stones of Stenness**, originally a circle of twelve rock slabs, now just four, the tallest of which is a real monster at over 16ft, though it's more remarkable for its incredible thinness. A broken table-top lies within the circle, which is surrounded by a much-diminished henge (a circular bank of earth and a ditch) with a couple of entrance causeways.

Westray & Papa Westray ▲   Sanday ▲

Costa Head   Rousay

Brough of Birsay

Brough Head

Earl's Palace   BIRSAY

Marwick Head

Twatt

Kirbuster

Evie ● Broch of Gurness

Tingwall

Egilsay   Eday

Eynhallow Sound

Wyre

Stronsay ▲

Dounby

SANDWICK   HARRAY

RANDALL   Gairsay

Finstown

Ness of Ork

Broch of Borroughston

Skara Brae

Mill Dam

Shapinsay

Balfour

Lerwick ▶

Maes Howe

Yesnaby Castle

Stones of Stenness

Wideford Hill (740ft)

Kirkwall

Rerwick Head

Mull Head

Aberdeen ▶

Stromness

STENNESS

Ward Hill (881ft)

Mainland

Loch of Harray

Loch of Stenness

Loch of Kirbister

Scapa Bay

ORPHIR

Houton

Mine Howe

DEERNESS

HOLM

St John's Head

Hoy

Graemsay

Old Man of Hoy

Ward Hill (1577ft)

Rackwick

Dwarfie Stane

Cava

Waulkmill Bay

Scapa Flow

St Mary's

Glimps Holm

Lamb Holm

Rose Ness

Hoy

Fara

Oil Terminal

Lyness

Flotta

Burray Village

Burray

Melsetter House

Hackness Tower

Longhope

Swithra

Cantick Head

Tor Ness

South Walls

St Margaret's Hope

Grim Ness

South Ronaldsay

N

Pentland Firth

Swona

Burwick

Halcro Head

Brough Ness

Tomb of the Eagles

0   4 miles

MAINLAND AND HOY

◀ Scrabster

▼ Gill's Bay   ▼ John O'Groats

Less than a mile to the northwest, past the awesome **Watch Stone** which stands beside the road, at over 18ft in height, you reach another stone circle, the **Ring of Brodgar**, a much wider circle dramatically sited on raised ground. Here there were originally sixty stones, 27 of which now stand; of the henge, only the ditch survives. For both the Stones of Stenness and the Ring of Brodgar, it's best to go early (or late) in the height of summer, so as to avoid the coach parties – or coincide with one of the guided tours (June–Aug Wed & Fri 1pm; free).

Maes Howe

There are several quite large burial mounds visible to the south of the Ring of Brodgar, but these are entirely eclipsed by one of the most impressive Neolithic burial chambers in Europe, **Maes Howe** (April–Sept daily 9.30am–5pm; Oct–March Mon–Sat 9.45am–4.30pm; HS; £5.20; ☎01856/761606), which lies less than a mile northeast of the Stones of Stenness. Dating from around 3000 BC, its excellent state of preservation is partly due to the massive slabs of sandstone it was constructed from, the largest of which weighs over thirty tons. To visit the tomb, you must first buy a **timed ticket** for a guided tour, either over the phone or direct from the nineteenth-century meal mill by the main road, which houses the **ticket office**, toilets and interpretive display on the ground floor.

You enter the **central chamber** down a low, long passage, one wall of which is comprised of a single immense stone. Once inside, you can stand upright and admire the superb masonry of the lofty corbelled roof. Remarkably, the tomb is aligned so that the rays of the winter solstice sun hit the top of the Barnhouse Stone, half a mile away, and reach right down the passage of Maes Howe to the ledge of one of the three cells built into the walls of the tomb. When Maes Howe was opened in 1861, it was virtually empty, thanks to the work of generations of grave-robbers, who had left behind only a handful of human bones. The Vikings entered in the twelfth century, probably on their way to the Crusades, leaving large amounts of runic graffiti, some of which are cryptographic twig runes, cut into the walls of the main chamber and still clearly visible today. They include phrases such as "Many a beautiful woman has stooped in here, however pompous she might be", and "These runes were carved by the man most skilled in runes in the entire western ocean", to the more prosaic "Thor and I bedded Helga".

Practicalities

Given the density of prehistoric sites around Stenness, and its central position on the Mainland, it's not a bad area in which to base yourself. For **accommodation** look no further than the carefully converted *Mill of Eyrland* (T01856/850136, Wwww.millofeyrland.co.uk; ❹), in a delightful setting by a mill stream on the A964 to Orphir; it's filled with wonderful antiques, old mill machinery plus all mod cons, and serves enormous breakfasts. Alternatively, you could stay at the excellent *Holland House* (T01856/771400, Wwww .hollandhouseorkney.co.uk; ❺), a former manse halfway along the A986 to Dounby, that's tastefully furnished and serves up very good breakfasts. The **bar meals** at the *Merkister Hotel*, on the northeastern shore of the Loch of Harray, are popular with the locals and visiting anglers.

Skara Brae and around

North of Stromness, the parish of Sandwick contains the best known of Orkney's prehistoric monuments, **Skara Brae** (April–Sept daily: 9.30am–5.30pm; Oct–March Mon–Sat 9.30am–4.30pm; HS; £6.70), beautifully situated beside the white curve of the Bay of Skaill. Here, the extensive remains of a small Neolithic fishing and farming village, dating back to 3000 BC, were discovered in 1850 after a fierce storm ripped off the dunes covering them. The village is amazingly well preserved, its houses huddled together and connected by narrow passages, which would originally have been covered over with turf. The houses themselves consist of a single, spacious living room, filled with domestic detail, including dressers, fireplaces, built-in cupboards, beds and boxes, all ingeniously constructed from slabs of stone.

The **visitor centre** houses an excellent 🍴 **café/restaurant**, where you can also get takeaway sandwiches to order. If you want to, you can take in the small introductory **exhibition**, with a few replica finds, and some hands-on stuff for kids. You then proceed to a full-scale replica of House 7 (the best-preserved house), complete with a fake wood and skin roof. It's all a tad neat and tidy, with fetching uplighting – rather than dark, smoky and smelly – but it gives you the general idea, and makes up for the fact that, at the site itself, you can only look down on the houses from the outer walls. A short video, in the little building at the far end of the site, helps put the site in context.

In the summer months, your ticket also covers entry to nearby **Skaill House**, an extensive range of buildings 300yd inland, home of the laird of Skaill. The original house was a simple two-storey block, built for Bishop George Graham in the 1620s, but it has since been much extended. The house's prize possession is Captain Cook's dinner service from the *Resolution*, which was delivered after Cook's death when the *Resolution* and the *Discovery* sailed into Stromness in 1780. The bedroom of the last occupant of the house, Mrs Kathleen Scarth, has been left as it was when she died in 1991, and is filled with old frocks, an ostrich-feather fan and a "twist and slim exerciser".

The other good reason for exploring the area around Skara Brae are the cliffs either side of the Bay of Skaill, which provide some of the most spectacularly rugged **coastal walks** on Orkney's Mainland. At **Yesnaby**, to the south, the sandstone cliffs have been savagely eroded into stacks and geos by the force of the Atlantic. Come here during a westerly gale and you'll see the waves sending sea spray shooting over the wartime buildings and the neighbouring fields. As a result, the clifftops support a unique plantlife, which thrives on the salt spray, including the rare, and very small, purple Scottish primrose, which flowers in May and from July to late September. The walk south along the coast from here is exhilarating: the Old Man of Hoy is visible in the distance and, after a mile and a half, you come to West Mainland's own version of the Old Man, known as Yesnaby Castle.

Practicalities

With only infrequent bus connections, you really need your own transport to reach Skara Brae. **Accommodation** options are limited; try *Hyval Farm* (T01856/841522, Wwww.hyval.co.uk; April–Oct; ②), a working beef farm within walking distance of Skara Brae. For really delicious **food** with a good view, head for the bright and cheerful *Appie's Tea Room* (April–Oct only; closed Sat; Wwww.pamfarmer.co.uk), signed off the A967, with home-made cakes and soups and mouthwatering veggie options made with local produce.

Birsay and around

Occupying the northwest corner of the Mainland, the parish of **BIRSAY** was the centre of Norse power in Orkney for several centuries before Kirkwall got its cathedral. Today a tiny cluster of homes is gathered around the imposing sandstone ruins of the **Earl's Palace**, which was built in the late sixteenth century by Robert Stewart, Earl of Orkney, using the forced labour of the islanders, who weren't even given food and drink for their work. By all accounts, it was a "sumptuous and stately dwelling", built in four wings around a central courtyard, its upper rooms decorated with painted ceilings and rich furnishings; surrounding the palace were flower and herb gardens, a bowling green and archery butts. The palace appears to have lasted barely a century before falling into rack and ruin; the crumbling walls and turrets retain much of their grandeur, although inside there is little remaining domestic detail. However, its vast scale makes the Earl's Palace in Kirkwall seem almost humble in comparison.

Brough of Birsay

Just over half a mile northwest of the palace is the **Brough of Birsay** (mid-June to Sept daily 9.30am–5.30pm; HS; £3.20), a substantial Pictish settlement on a small tidal island only accessible two hours either side of low tide. Stromness and Kirkwall tourist offices have the tide times and Radio Orkney broadcasts them (93.7FM; Mon–Fri 7.30–8am). On the island, there's a small ticket office, where you can see a few artefacts gathered from the site, including a game made from whalebone and an antler pin. Coastal erosion over the last eight centuries means that some of the site has disappeared off the side of the low cliffs, and concrete sea defences are currently in place to try and stem the tide.

The focus of the village was – and still is – the sandstone-built twelfth-century **St Peter's Church**, which stands higher than the surrounding buildings; the stone seating along the walls is still in place, and there are a couple of semicircular recesses for altars, and a semicircular apse. The church is thought to have stood at the centre of a monastic complex – the foundations of a courtyard and outer buildings can be made out to the west. Close by is a large complex of Viking-era buildings, including several houses, a sauna and some sophisticated stone drains.

The Brough of Birsay is a popular day-trip, partly due to the fun of dodging the tides, but few folk bother to explore the rest of the island, whose gentle green slopes, when viewed from the mainland, belie the dramatic, rugged cliffs that characterize the rest of the coastline. In winter, sea spray from the waves crashing against the cliffs can envelop the entire island. In summer, the cliffs are home to various sea birds, including a few puffins, making the half-mile walk to the island's castellated **lighthouse** and back along the northern coastline well worth the effort. If you make it out here, spare a thought for the lighthouse keepers who used to man the **Sule Skerry** lighthouse – the most isolated in Britain – which lies on a piece of bare rock just visible some 37 miles out to sea, and whose only contact with the outside world was via carrier pigeon.

Barony Mills

Half a mile southeast of the palace, up the burn, is the **Barony Mills** (May–Sept daily 10am–1pm & 2–5pm; free), Orkney's only working nineteenth-century water mill. The mill specializes in producing traditional stoneground beremeal, essential for making bere bannocks. Bere is a four-kernel barley crop with a very short growing season perfectly suited for the local climate and was once the staple diet in these parts. The miller on duty will give you a guided tour and show you the machinery going through its paces, though milling only takes place in the autumn.

Marwick Head

The best of Birsay's coastal scenery lies to the south of Birsay Bay around **Marwick Head**. The headland itself is clearly visible thanks to the huge castellated tower of the **Kitchener Memorial**, raised by the people of Orkney to commemorate the Minister of War, Lord Kitchener, who drowned along with all but 12 of the 655 men of the 11,000-ton cruiser HMS *Hampshire* when the ship struck a mine just off the coast on June 5, 1916. There has been much speculation about the incident over the years, due to the fact that Kitchener was on a secret mission to Russia to hold talks with the Tsar. A German spy claimed to have sabotaged and sunk the ship, and rumours abounded that Kitchener had been deliberately sent to his death (he was extremely unpopular at the time). In reality, it appears to have been a simple case of naval incompetence: the weather forecast of severe northwesterly gales was ignored, as were the reports of submarine activity in the area. Marwick Head is also popular with nesting sea birds in the summer, with numerous fulmar, kittiwake, guillemot and razorbill in residence on the 200-foot cliffs; at that time, the sight and smell are quite overwhelming.

Kirbuster and Corrigall farm museums

Lying between the Loch of Boardhouse and the Loch of Hundland, the **Kirbuster Farm Museum** (March–Oct Mon–Sat 10.30am–1pm & 2–5pm, Sun 2–7pm; free) offers an interesting insight into life on an Orkney farmstead in the mid-nineteenth century. Built in 1723, the farm is made up of a typical, though substantial, collection of flagstone buildings, with its own, very beautiful, garden. Ducks, geese and sheep wander around the grassy open yard, which is entered through a whalebone archway. Despite being inhabited until as late as 1961, the farm has retained its firehoose, in which the smoke from the central peat fire is used to dry fish fillets, and before drifting up towards a hole in the ceiling; the room even retains the old neuk-beds, simple recesses in the stone walls, which would have originally been lined with wood.

If you've enjoyed your time at Kirbuster – and kids almost certainly will – then it's definitely worth visiting **Corrigall Farm Museum** (same times), another eighteenth-century farmstead some five miles southeast of Kirbuster, beyond Dounby in the parish of Harray. There are lovely views west and south from the honeysuckle-draped shop, as well as hens and sheep scampering around the farmyard. Be sure to check out the well-preserved flagstone byre, and the stable, which has a characteristic beehive-shaped kiln for drying grain at one end.

Practicalities

The best **accommodation** in Birsay is at *Linkshouse* (℡01856/721221, ⓦwww .ewaf.co.uk; ❸), an attractive, stone-built, Edwardian B&B with a bit of character close to Birsay village itself. There's also the large, refurbished Birsay Outdoor Centre (April–Sept; ℡01856/873535 ext 2415), a **hostel** and **campsite**, half a mile south of the Barony Mills. The nearest watering hole is the bar of the *Barony Hotel*, overlooking the Loch of Boardhouse, to the southeast of Birsay village. For **food**, head for the *Birsay Tea Room* just south of the village: it has a superb view of the Brough (binoculars provided) and offers light snacks and home-made cake.

Evie and the Broch of Gurness

The village and parish of **EVIE**, on the north coast, look out across the turbulent waters of Eynhallow Sound towards the island of Rousay. Its chief draw is the **Broch of Gurness** (April–Sept daily 9.30am–5.30pm; HS; £4.70), the best-preserved broch on an archipelago replete with them, still surrounded by a remarkable complex of later buildings. As at Birsay, the sea has eaten away half the site, but the broch itself, dating from around 100 BC, still stands, its walls reaching a height of 12ft in places, its inner cells still intact. The compact group of homes clustered around the broch has also survived amazingly well, with much of their original and ingenious stone shelving and fireplaces still in place. The best view of the site is from the east, where you can clearly make out the "main street" leading towards the broch. The **visitor centre** is also worth a quick once-over, especially for those with kids, who will enjoy using the quernstone corn grinder. The broch is clearly signposted from Evie, the road skirting the pristinely white **Sands of Evie**, a perfect picnic spot in fine weather.

Practicalities

One of the most secluded **accommodation** options on the Mainland is the artfully decorated ⚘ *Woodwick House* (℡01856/751330, ⓦwww.woodwickhouse .co.uk; ❹), southeast of the main village, which provides an excellent breakfast; some rooms have shared, slightly ancient bathrooms, but the residents' lounge has a real fire and the wooded grounds are delightful (and feature a seventeenth-century doocot). At the other end of the scale, you can stay in the simple *Eviedale* **campsite** (April–Oct; ℡01856/751270, ⓦwww.creviedale.orknet.co.uk) situated in a sheltered spot right by the junction of the road to Dounby.

Orphir

The southern shores of the West Mainland, overlooking Scapa Flow, are much gentler than the rest of the coastline, and have fewer of Orkney's premier-league sights. However, if you've time to spare, or you're heading for Hoy from the car ferry terminal at Houton, there are a couple of points of interest in the neighbouring parish of **ORPHIR**. Here, beside the parish cemetery, you'll find the **Orkneyinga Saga Centre** (daily 9am–5pm; free), containing a small exhibition with a fifteen-minute audiovisual show which gives you a taste of the *Orkneyinga Saga*, the bloodthirsty Viking tale written around 1200 AD by an unnamed Icelandic author, which described the conquest of the Northern Isles by the Norsemen. The **Earl's Bu** at Orphir features in the saga as the home of Earl Thorfinn the Mighty, Earl Paul and his son, Håkon, who ordered the murder of Earl (later St) Magnus on Egilsay (see p.367). The foundations of what is presumed to have been the Earl's Bu have been uncovered just outside the cemetery gates, while inside the cemetery is a section of the round church, built by Håkon after his pilgrimage in penance to Jerusalem.

Kirkwall

Initial impressions of **KIRKWALL**, Orkney's capital, are not always favourable. It has nothing to match the picturesque harbour of Stromness, and its residential sprawl is far less appealing. However, it does have one great redeeming feature – its sandstone cathedral, without doubt the finest medieval building in the north of Scotland. In any case, if you're staying any length of time in Orkney you're more or less bound to find yourself in Kirkwall at some point, as it's home to the islands' better-stocked shops, including the only large supermarket, and is the departure point for most of the ferries to Orkney's northern isles.

Part of the reason for Kirkwall's disappointing waterfront is that today's harbour is a largely modern invention; in the mid-nineteenth century, the shoreline ran along Junction Road, and before that it was flush with the west side of Broad Street. Nowadays, the town is very much divided into two main focal points: the old harbour, at the north end of the town, where visiting yachts moor and the small inter-island ferries come and go all year round; and the flagstoned **main street**.

Arrival and information

Northlink **ferries** from Shetland and Aberdeen (and all cruise ships) dock at the Hatston terminal, a mile northwest of town; a shuttle bus will take you into Kirkwall (or to Stromness if you prefer). Kirkwall **airport** is three miles southeast of town on the A960; a bus (Mon–Sat every 30min–hourly, 9 on Sun; 15min) will take you to the **bus station** (aka Kirkwall Travel Centre) on West Castle Street. For **bike rental** head for Cycle Orkney, Tankerness Lane (T01856/875777, Wwww.cycleorkney.com; closed Sun).

Despite the **main street** taking four different names – Bridge Street, Albert Street, Broad Street and Victoria Street – as it winds through the town, orientation is easy with the prominent spire of St Magnus Cathedral clearly marking the town centre. The helpful **tourist office** (April–Sept daily; Oct–March Mon–Sat only; T01856/872856, Wwww.visitorkney.com) is in Kirkwall Travel Centre, by the bus station.

Accommodation

Kirkwall has plenty of small **B&Bs**, and a host of fairly bland **hotels**, but, unless you have to, there's really no reason to base yourself here rather than head out into Orkney's wonderful countryside.

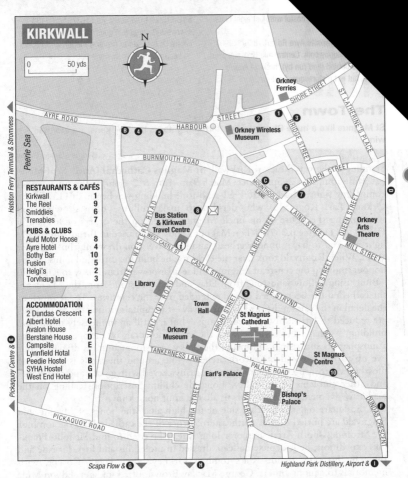

KIRKWALL

0 — 50 yds

RESTAURANTS & CAFÉS
Kirkwall 1
The Reel 9
Smiddies 6
Trenabies 7

PUBS & CLUBS
Auld Motor Hoose 8
Ayre Hotel 4
Bothy Bar 10
Fusion 5
Helgi's 2
Torvhaug Inn 3

ACCOMMODATION
2 Dundas Crescent F
Albert Hotel C
Avalon House A
Berstane House D
Campsite E
Lynnfield Hotal I
Peedie Hostel B
SYHA Hostel G
West End Hotel H

Hatston Ferry Terminal & Stromness

Peerie Sea

AYRE ROAD

HARBOUR STREET

Orkney Ferries

SHORE STREET

ST CATHERINE'S PLACE

BRIDGE STREET

Orkney Wireless Museum

BURNMOUTH ROAD

MOUNTHOOLIE LANE

GARDEN STREET

QUEEN STREET

Orkney Arts Theatre

GREAT WESTERN ROAD

Bus Station & Kirkwall Travel Centre

WEST CASTLE ST

ALBERT STREET

LAING STREET

KING STREET

MILL STREET

CASTLE STREET

THE STRYND

SCHOOL PLACE

Library

JUNCTION ROAD

Town Hall

BROAD STREET

St Magnus Cathedral

Orkney Museum

TANKERNESS LANE

PALACE ROAD

St Magnus Centre

Earl's Palace

VICTORIA STREET

WATERGATE

Bishop's Palace

DUNDAS CRESCENT

PICKAQUOY ROAD

Pickaquoy Centre &

Scapa Flow &

Highland Park Distillery, Airport &

ORKNEY | Kirkwall

Hotels and B&Bs

2 Dundas Crescent 13 Palace Rd ⊕01856/872249, Ⓦwww.twodundas.co.uk. Situated just behind the cathedral, this former manse is a grand, and taste-fully decorated, Victorian house. ④

Albert Hotel Mounthoolie Lane ⊕01856/876000, Ⓦwww.alberthotel.co.uk. Great central location, lively bar (with disco attached) and contemporary furnishings: this is Kirkwall's trendiest hotel. ⑥

Avalon House Carness Rd ⊕01856/876665, Ⓦwww.avalon-house.co.uk. Modern B&B run efficiently by a very welcoming couple, and situated a 20min coastal walk from the town centre. ③

Berstane House A mile and a half southeast of town down Berstane Rd ⊕01856/876277, Ⓦwww.berstane.co.uk. The B&B rooms and self-catering flats are a steal at this handsome Victorian pile, set

in its own wooded grounds with sea views – best with your own transport. ①

Lynnfield Hotel Holm Rd ⊕01856/872505, Ⓦwww.lynnfieldhotel.com. Small, recently renovated eight-room hotel in a quiet spot a mile or so out of town near the distillery – the new owners have an excellent pedigree and the food is superb. ⑥

West End Hotel 14 Main St ⊕01856/872368, Ⓦwww.westendkirkwall.co.uk. Orkney's first hospital is now a good, old-fashioned hotel in a quiet street, a few minutes' walk south of the centre. ⑤

Hostels and campsites

Peedie Hostel Ayre Houses ⊕01856/875477, Ⓦpeediehostel.yolasite.com. Centrally located overlooking the old harbour and out to sea, this is a

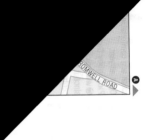

SYHA Hostel Old Scapa Rd ☎0870/004 1133,
Ⓦwww.syha.org.uk. A good 10min walk out of the
centre on the road to Orphir – friendly enough, but
no beauty outside or in. April–Oct.

ode Island Red that gathers her chickens… under her

George Mackay Brown

Standing at the very heart of Kirkwall, **St Magnus Cathedral** (April–Sept Mon–Sat 9am–6pm, Sun 2–5pm; Oct–March 9am–1pm & 2–5pm) is the town's most compelling sight. This beautiful red-sandstone building was begun in 1137 by the Orkney Earl Rognvald, who decided to make full use of a growing cult surrounding the figure of his uncle Magnus, killed on the orders of his cousin Håkon in 1117 (see p.367). When Magnus's body was buried in Birsay, a heavenly light was said to have shone overhead, and his grave soon drew pilgrims from far afield. When Rognvald took over the earldom, he built the cathedral in his uncle's honour, moving the centre of religious and secular power from Birsay to Kirkwall.

Built using yellow sandstone from Eday and red sandstone from the Mainland, the cathedral has been added to and extended over the centuries. Today much of the detail in the soft sandstone has worn away – the capitals around the main doors are reduced to artistically gnarled stumps – but it's still an immensely impressive building, its shape and style echoing the great cathedrals of Europe. Inside, the atmosphere is surprisingly intimate, the bulky sandstone columns drawing your eye up to the exposed brickwork arches, while around the walls is a series of mostly seventeenth-century tombstones, many carved with a skull and crossbones and other emblems of mortality, alongside chilling inscriptions calling on the reader to "Remember death waits us all, the hour none knows".

In the square pillars on either side of the high altar, the bones of Magnus and Rognvald are buried. In the southeastern corner of the cathedral lies the tomb of the Stromness-born Arctic explorer John Rae, who tried to find Sir John Franklin's expedition; he is depicted asleep, dressed in moleskins and furs, his rifle and Bible by his side. Beside Rae's tomb is Orkney's own Poets' Corner, with memorials to, among others, George Mackay Brown, Eric Linklater, Edwin Muir and Robert Rendall (who was also an eminent conchologist). Another poignant monument is the one to the dead of HMS *Royal Oak*, which was torpedoed in Scapa Flow in 1939 with the loss of 833 men (see p.356).

The Bishop's Palace and Earl's Palace

South of the cathedral are the ruined remains of the **Bishop's Palace** (April–Sept daily 9.30am–5.30pm; HS; £3.70), traditional residence of the Bishop of Orkney from the twelfth century. It was here that the Norwegian king Håkon died in 1263 on his return from defeat at the Battle of Largs. Most of what you see now, however, dates from the time of Bishop Robert Reid, founder of Edinburgh University, in the mid-sixteenth century. The walls still stand, as does the tall round tower in which the bishop had his private chambers; a narrow spiral staircase takes you to the top for a good view of the cathedral and across Kirkwall's rooftops.

The ticket for the Bishop's Palace also covers entry to the neighbouring **Earl's Palace** – better preserved and a lot more fun to explore – built by the infamous

Orcadian wedding traditions

If you're passing through Kirkwall, particularly during the summer, you may come across a bunch of locals sitting in the back of a truck, banging drums and pots and pans and drinking alcohol. What you are witnessing is the strange local custom known as **"the Blackening"**. Not for the faint-hearted (nor the politically correct), the blackening takes place in the build-up to a wedding. The groom's "friends" hire a lorry and ambush him, strip him naked and then tar and feather him. They then set off on a tour of the town, possibly a pub-crawl, and often a dip in the sea. No one knows the origin of the Blackening, though the din may have originally been made to ward off evil spirits. Occasionally, you may even see a bride subjected to the same humiliations.

Earl Patrick Stewart around 1600 using forced labour. With its grand entrance, fancy oriel windows, dank dungeons, massive fireplaces and magnificent central hall, it has a confident solidity, and is one of the finest examples of Renaissance architecture in Scotland. The roof may be missing, but many domestic details remain, including a set of toilets and the stone shelves used by the clerk to do his filing. Earl Patrick enjoyed his palace for only a very short time before he was imprisoned and charged with treason. The earl might have been acquitted, but he foolishly ordered his son, Robert, to organize an insurrection; he held out four days in the palace against the Earl of Caithness, before being captured, sent to Edinburgh and hanged there; his father was beheaded at the same place five weeks later.

The museums

Opposite the cathedral stands the sixteenth-century **Tankerness House** (Mon–Sat 10.30am–5pm; free), a former home for the clergy. now home to the **Orkney Museum**. A couple of rooms have been restored to how they would have been in 1820, when the building was a private home for the Baikie family. The rest houses some of the islands' most treasured finds, among the more unusual of which are a witch's spell box, and a lovely whalebone plaque from a Viking boat grave discovered on Sanday. On a warm summer afternoon, the museum **gardens** are thick with the buzz of bees and vibrantly coloured flora. In wet weather, you can stay inside and watch a video of the traditional Orkney ball game, **The Ba'**, played at Christmas and New Year. Beginning at 1pm at the Mercat Cross outside the cathedral, the "Uppies" and the "Doonies" attempt to get the ba' (ball) into the other's goal (a wall to the south and the harbour respectively). There's no restriction on numbers, and the game can take hours – spectators (and participants) rarely get a glimpse of the ball, which is usually stuck tight in a heaving, steaming scrum of men.

At the harbour end of Junction Road, at Kiln Corner, you can browse around the tiny **Orkney Wireless Museum** (April–Sept Mon–Sat 10am–4.30pm, Sun 2.30–4.30pm; £3; Ⓦ www.owm.org.uk), a single room packed to the roof with every variety of antique radio equipment you can imagine. The museum is particularly strong on technical flotsam from the two world wars, and there's even a working crystal set which you can listen to.

Out of the centre

Further afield, a mile or so south along the A961 to South Ronaldsay, is the **Highland Park distillery** (April & Sept Mon–Fri 10am–5pm hourly tours; May–Aug Mon–Sat 10am–5pm, Sun noon–5pm hourly tours; Oct–March Mon–Fri

Scapa Flow

Apart from a few oil tankers, there's very little activity in the great natural harbour of **Scapa Flow**, yet for the first half of the twentieth century, the Flow served as the main base of the Royal Navy, with over a hundred warships anchored here at any one time. The coastal defences required to make Scapa Flow safe to use as the country's chief naval headquarters were considerable and many are still visible all over Orkney, ranging from half-sunk blockships to the **Churchill Barriers** (see p.358) and the gun batteries that pepper the coastline. Unfortunately, these defences weren't sufficient to save **HMS Royal Oak** from being torpedoed by a German U-boat in October 1939 (see opposite), but they withstood several heavy German air raids during the course of 1940. Ironically, the worst disaster the Flow has ever witnessed was self-inflicted, when **HMS Vanguard** sank on July 9, 1917, after suffering an internal explosion, killing 843 crew and leaving only two survivors.

Scapa Flow's most celebrated moment in naval history, however, was when the entire **German High Seas Fleet** was interned here immediately after World War I. A total of 74 ships, manned by several thousand German sailors, was anchored off the isle of Cava awaiting the outcome of the Versailles Peace Conference. At around noon on Midsummer's Day 1919, believing either that the majority of the German fleet was to be handed over, or that hostilities were about to resume, the commanding officer, Admiral von Reuter, ordered the fleet to be scuttled. By 5pm, every ship was beached or had sunk and nine German sailors had lost their lives, shot by outraged British servicemen. The British government was publicly indignant, but privately relieved since the scuttling avoided the diplomatic nightmare of dividing up the fleet between the Allies.

Between the wars, the largest **salvage operation** in history took place in Scapa Flow, with the firm of Cox & Danks alone raising 26 destroyers, one light cruiser, four battlecruisers and two battleships. Despite this, seven large German ships – three battleships and four light cruisers – remain on the sea bed of Scapa Flow, along with four destroyers and a U-boat. Although the remaining vessels can only be salvaged on a piecemeal basis, their pre-atomic-era steel is still extremely valuable as it is radiation-free and is in great demand in the space and nuclear industries. Scapa Flow is also considered one of the world's greatest dive sites. Scapa Scuba (T01856/851218, W www.scapascuba.co.uk), based in Stromness, offers one-to-one **scuba-diving** tuition for all abilities. If you don't want to get your feet wet, Dawn Star II (T01856/876743, W www.orkneyboattrips.co.uk) will take you close to the Admiralty buoys and give you a history tour of the harbour; tours begin at St Mary's.

1–5pm, tours at 2 & 3pm; £6; T01856/874619, W www.highlandpark.co.uk). It's been in operation for more than two hundred years, and still has its own maltings, although it was closed during World War II, when the army used it as a food store and the huge vats served as communal baths. You can decide for yourself whether the taste still lingers by partaking of the customary dram after one of the regular guided tours of the beautiful old buildings.

If the weather happens to be unusually good and you're moved to consider a swim, do as the locals do and head one mile south of town on the B9148 to **Scapa Bay**, Kirkwall's very own sandy beach. Briefly a naval headquarters at the outbreak of World War I, Scapa's pier is now used by the council tugs and pilot launches servicing the oil tankers out in Scapa Flow. Visible from the beach is the green Admiralty wreck buoy marking the position of **HMS Royal Oak**, torpedoed by a German U-boat on October 14, 1939, with the loss of 833 men (out of a total crew of around 1400). A small display shed at the eastern end of the bay tells the full story, and has photos of the wreck (still an official war grave) as it looks today.

Eating, drinking and entertainment

Kirkwall has a smattering of decent **food** options. The best **place** in town is *Smiddies*, 21 Albert St (01856/875576), which has a great deli and daytime café on the ground floor and a licensed **restaurant** upstairs serving imaginative dishes using Orkney produce, such as spoots (razorfish). Another option is *Helgi's*, 14 Harbour St (①01856/879293), a popular new **pub** on the harbourfront which serves filling bar food. Of the town's **hotels** the *Kirkwall*, on Harbour Street, is definitely the best option, as it offers **bar meals** at lunch time and a very good à la carte menu in the evening. *The Reel*, near the cathedral, is a laid-back café run by the musical Wrigley Sisters, serving great coffee, sandwiches and cakes, and offering free wi-fi and occasional live music. The alternative is *Trenabies* on Albert Street, a cosy café with booths, that's a classic Kirkwall institution.

Kirkwall has its very own **nightclub**, *Fusion*, on Ayre Road, which caters for all musical tastes and occasionally stages live gigs. The liveliest **pub** is the *Torvhaug Inn* at the harbour end of Bridge Street; another good place to try is the *Bothy Bar* in the *Albert Hotel*, which sometimes has live music, as does *The Auld Motor Hoose*, on Junction Road. The *Ayre Hotel* has regular Orkney Accordion & Fiddle Club nights on Wednesdays – ask at the tourist office or check the *Orcadian* listings for the latest.

Kirkwall's **Pickaquoy Leisure Centre** (Ⓦwww.pickaquoy.com) – known locally as the "Picky" – is a short walk west of the town centre, up Pickaquoy Road past the supermarket. It now serves as one of the town's main large-scale venues, and also contains the New Phoenix **cinema** (①01856/879900). Kirkwall's chief cultural bash is the week-long **St Magnus Festival** (Ⓦwww.stmagnus festival.com), a superb arts festival based in Kirkwall and held in the middle of June. For many of the locals, though, the most important event is the agricultural **County Show** held in the middle of August in Kirkwall.

East Mainland and South Ronaldsay

Southeast from Kirkwall, the narrow spur of the **East Mainland** juts out into the North Sea and is joined, thanks to the remarkable Churchill Barriers, to several smaller islands, the largest of which are **Burray** and **South Ronaldsay**. As with the West Mainland, the land here is heavily farmed, but it contains few of Orkney's more famous sights. Nevertheless, there are some good coastal walks to enjoy, an unusual new Iron-Age site to explore at **Mine Howe** and, at the **Tomb of the Eagles**, one of the most enjoyable and memorable of Orkney's prehistoric sites.

East Mainland

The northern side of the **East Mainland** consists of three exposed peninsulas that jut out like giant claws. The most intriguing is Deerness (see p.358), the eastern-most one, but before you reach it you should pay a quick visit to the Iron-Age mound of **Mine Howe** (May & Sept Tues & Fri 11am–3pm; June–Aug daily 10am–4pm; £3.50), just off the A960, beyond the airport. Originally Mine Howe would have been a large mound surrounded by a deep ditch, but only a small section has been excavated. At the top of the mound a series of steps leads steeply down to a half-landing, and then plunges down even deeper to a small chamber some twenty feet below the surface. Visitors don a hard hat and grab a torch, before heading underground. The whole layout is unique and has left archeologists baffled, though, naturally, numerous theories have been put forward, from execution by ritual drowning to a temple to the god of the underworld. Mine Howe's relationship to the nearby mound and broch of Longhowe remains a mystery too. A survey has revealed a ditch encompassing the site, beyond which are signs of a settlement, probably of Pictish origin.

The easternmost peninsula of **Deerness** is joined to the Mainland only by a narrow, sandy isthmus. Its northeastern corner, around the sea cliffs of **Mull Head**, boasts a large colony of nesting sea birds from May to August, including fulmars, kittiwakes, guillemots, razorbills and puffins, plus, inland, arctic terns that swoop and screech threateningly. The only way to reach Mull Head is to walk from the car park, located a mile or so to the south. A short walk east of the car park will bring you to **The Gloup**, an impressive collapsed sea-cave, the name of which stems from the Old Norse *gluppa*, or "chasm"; the tide still flows in and out through a natural arch, making strange gurgling noises. Half a mile north is the **Brough of Deerness**, a grassy promontory whose narrow land-bridge has collapsed, and which is now accessible only via a precipitous path; the ruins are thought to have once been a Norse or Pictish monastic site.

Visible across the sea to the north are Auskerry and Stronsay and, to the southeast, the uninhabited island of **Copinsay**, with its lighthouse perched on yet more sea-bird-infested cliffs; boat trips are possible – ask at the tourist office. If you want to stay in Deerness, head for *Northfield* (☎01856/741353, ⓦwww .orkneybedandbreakfast.com; ❸), a great modern farmhouse **B&B**, with exposed oak timber beams, tasteful furnishings, free wi-fi and sea views out to Copinsay.

The Churchill Barriers and Italian Chapel

The southeastern corner of Orkney Mainland is connected to the islands of Lamb Holm, Burray and South Ronaldsay by four causeways known as the **Churchill Barriers**, built during World War II as anti-submarine barriers. The Admiralty (of which Churchill presided over at the time) were only prompted into action by the sinking of the battleship HMS *Royal Oak* on October 14, 1939. Despite the presence of blockships, deliberately sunk during World War I in order to close off the eastern approaches, one German U-boat captain managed to get through and torpedo the *Royal Oak*, before returning to a hero's welcome in Germany. He claimed to have acquired local knowledge while fishing in the islands before the war. As you cross the barriers – don't cross them during high winds – you can still see the blockships, rusting away, an eerie reminder of Orkney's important wartime role.

The barriers – an astonishing feat of engineering when you bear in mind the strength of Orkney tides – were an incredibly expensive undertaking, costing an estimated £2.5 million. Special camps were built on the uninhabited island of Lamb Holm, in order to accommodate the 1700 men involved in the project, 1200 of whom were Italian POWs. The camps have long since disappeared, but the Italians left behind the extraordinary **Italian Chapel** (daily dawn–dusk; free) on **Lamb Holm**. This, the so-called "Miracle of Camp 60", must be one of the greatest adaptations ever, made from two Nissen huts, concrete, barbed wire and parts of a rusting blockship. It has a great false facade, and colourful trompe-l'oeil decor, lovingly restored by the chapel's principal architect, Domenico Chiocchetti, in 1960.

Burray

If you're travelling with children, you may like to stop off on the island of **Burray** in order to visit the **Orkney Fossil and Heritage Centre** (April–Sept daily 10am–4pm; £3.50; ⓦwww.orkneyfossilcentre.co.uk), housed in a converted farm on the main road across the island. Most of the fossils on display downstairs have been found locally, so they tend to be of fish and sea creatures, since Orkney was at the bottom of a tropical sea in Devonian times. The UV room, where the rocks reveal their iridescent colours, is a particular favourite with kids. Upstairs, there's a lot of wartime memorabilia, books to read, a rocking horse to play on and a comfy chair and binoculars with which to spot the birdlife down by the shore; the museum also has a café.

BURRAY VILLAGE, on the south coast of the island, expanded in the nineteenth century during the boom years of the herring industry, but was badly affected by the sinking of the blockships during World War I. The two-storey warehouse, built in 1860 in order to cure and pack the herring, has since been converted into the *Sands Hotel*, where you can sink a pint by the seashore.

South Ronaldsay

At the southern end of the barriers is low-lying **South Ronaldsay**, the largest of the islands linked to the Mainland and, like the latter, rich farming country. It was traditionally the chief crossing-point to the Scottish mainland, as it's only six miles across the Pentland Firth from Caithness. Today, car **ferries** arrive at St Margaret's Hope, and there's a small passenger ferry between John O'Groats and Burwick, on the southernmost tip of the island (see p.343 for details).

St Margaret's Hope

The main settlement on South Ronaldsay is **ST MARGARET'S HOPE**, which local tradition says takes its name from Margaret, the Maid of Norway and daughter of the king of Norway, who is thought to have died here at the age of 8 in November 1290. As the granddaughter of Alexander III, Margaret had already been proclaimed queen of Scotland and was on her way to marry the English prince Edward (later Edward II), thereby unifying the two countries. Today, St Margaret's Hope – or "The Hope", as it's known locally (from the Norse *hyop* meaning "bay") – is a pleasing little gathering of stone-built houses overlooking a sheltered bay, and is by far the best base from which to explore the area. As is obvious from the architecture, and the piers, The Hope was once a thriving port. Nowadays, despite the presence of the Pentland Ferries terminal, it remains a very peaceful place.

The village smithy on Cromarty Square has been turned into a **Smiddy Museum** (May & Sept daily 2.30–4.30pm; June–Aug Mon–Fri 11am–1pm & 2–4pm, Sat & Sun noon–4pm; free), particularly fun for kids who enjoy getting hands-on with the old tools, drills and giant bellows. There's also a small exhibition on the annual **Boys' Ploughing Match**, in which local boys compete with miniature hand-held ploughs. The competition, which is taken extremely seriously by all those involved, happens on the third Saturday in August, at the beautiful golden beach at the **Sands O'Right** in Hoxa, a couple of miles west of The Hope. At the same time a **Festival of the Horse** takes place, with the local children, mostly girls, dressing up in spectacular costumes and harnesses. A further attraction is the **Orkney Marine-Life Aquarium** (Easter–Oct daily 10am–6pm; £5; Ⓦwww.orkneymarinelife.co.uk), a mile or so east of The Hope, off the A961. The tanks are housed in the back of an articulated trailer, and feature native sea-creatures from lobsters and octopuses to the iridescent Cuckoo Wrasse.

If you just want a pint, head for the *Murray Arms* **pub** on Back Road. If you want **to stay** in St Margaret's Hope itself you can stay at ⚜ *The Creel* (Ⓣ01856/831311, Ⓦwww.thecreel.co.uk; ⓺) on the harbourfront, with a view over the bay, and one of the best **restaurants** in Scotland serving three-course dinners for around £30.

There's also a backpackers' **hostel** nearby (☎ 01856/831225, ⓦorkneybackpackers .com; ❶), with singles, doubles and family rooms available. More spacious rooms are available from *Roeberry House* (☎01856/831228, ⓦwww.roeberryhouse.com; ❺), a substantial Victorian mansion, boasting spectacular views, in Hoxa. On the eastern side of South Ronaldsay, a mile and a half from the war memorial on the main road, an organic farm called *Wheems* (April–Oct; ☎01856/831556, ⓦwww.wheems organic.co.uk), has a **self-catering bothy** (sleeping 8) for hire, and a field for **camping**, with all the usual facilities, plus a communal yurt.

The Tomb of the Eagles

One of the most enjoyable archeological sights on Orkney is the Isbister chambered cairn at the southeastern corner of South Ronaldsay, known as the **Tomb of the Eagles** (daily: March 10am–noon; April–Oct 9.30am–5.30pm; Nov–Feb by appointment; £6.50; ☎01856/831339, ⓦwww.tomboftheeagles .co.uk). The cairn was discovered and excavated by a local farmer, Ronald Simison of Liddle, who still owns it, so a visit here makes a refreshing change from the usual interpretive centre. First off, you get to look round the family's private museum of prehistoric artefacts; this is the original hands-on museum, so visitors can actually touch and admire the painstaking craftsmanship of Neolithic folk, and examine a skull. Next you get a brief guided tour of a nearby Bronze-Age **burnt mound**, which is basically a Neolithic rubbish dump, beside which there was a large trough, where joints of meat were boiled by throwing in rocks from the fire. Finally you get to walk out to the **chambered cairn**, by the cliff's edge, where human remains were found alongside talons and carcasses of sea eagles. To enter the cairn, you must lie on a trolley and pull yourself in using an overhead rope – something that's guaranteed to put a smile on every visitor's face. The cairn's clifftop location is spectacular, and walking along the coast in either direction is rewarding: south to the sea inlet of Ham Geo, or north to Halcro Head and beyond to Wind Wick Bay, where seals and their pups can be seen in the autumn.

If you're looking for **accommodation** in the southern part of South Ronaldsay, *Eastward Guest House* (☎01856/831551, ⓦwww.eastwardhouse.com; ❷) is a B&B full of character a couple of miles north of Burwick, housed in a tastefully converted former church.

Hoy

Hoy, Orkney's second-largest island, rises sharply out of the sea to the southwest of the Mainland. The least typical Orkney island, but certainly the most dramatic, its north and west sides are made up of great glacial valleys and mountainous moorland rising to over 1500ft, dropping into the sea off red sandstone cliffs, and forming the landmark sea stack known as the **Old Man of Hoy**. The northern half of Hoy, though a huge expanse, is virtually uninhabited, with just the village of Hoy opposite Stromness, and the cluster of houses at **Rackwick** nestling dramatically in a bay between the cliffs. Meanwhile, most of Hoy's four hundred or so residents live on the gentler, more fertile land in the southeast, in and around the villages of **Lyness** and **Longhope**. This part of the island is littered with buildings dating from the two world wars, when Scapa Flow served as the main base for the Royal Navy (see p.357).

Two **ferry services** run to Hoy: a passenger ferry **from Stromness** to Moaness Pier, by Hoy village (Mon–Fri 4–5 daily, Sat & 2 on Sun; 25min; ☎01856/850624), which also serves the small island of Graemsay; and the roll-on/roll-off car ferry

from Houton on the Mainland to Lyness (Mon–Fri 6–8 daily, Sat & Sun 2–4 daily; 35min–1hr; ☎01856/811397), which sometimes calls in at the oil-terminal island of Flotta (see p.362), and begins and ends its daily schedule at Longhope. There's a seasonal Hoy Hopper **bus service** (mid-May to mid-Sept Wed–Fri only), which departs from Kirkwall Travel Centre, and is integrated with the ferries.

Hoy village to Rackwick

Much of Hoy's magnificent landscape is made up of rough grasses and heather, which harbour a cluster of arctic plants and a healthy population of mountain hares, as well as a wide variety of birdlife. Walkers arriving at Moaness Pier, near the tiny village of **HOY**, and heading for Rackwick (1hr 30min), should take the well-marked footpath that goes past Sandy Loch and along the large open valley beyond. On the western side of this valley is the narrow gully of **Berriedale**, which supports Britain's most northerly native woodland, a huddle of birch, hazel and honeysuckle.

The single-track road to Rackwick travels along another valley to the south. En route, duckboards head across the heather to the **Dwarfie Stane**, Orkney's most unusual chambered tomb, cut from a solid block of sandstone and dating back to 3000 BC. The sheer effort that must have been involved in carving out this tomb, with its two side-cells, is staggering and, as you crawl inside, the marks of the tools used by the Neolithic builders on the ceiling are still visible. The tomb is also decorated with copious Victorian graffiti, the most interesting of which is to be found on the northern exterior, where Major Mouncey, a former British spy in Persia and a confirmed eccentric who dressed in Persian garb, carved his name backwards in Latin, and also carved in Persian the words "I have sat two nights and so learnt patience".

RACKWICK is an old crofting and fishing village squeezed between towering sandstone cliffs on the west coast. In an area once quite extensively cultivated, Rackwick went into a steady decline in the middle of the twentieth century: its school closed in 1953 and the last fishing boat put to sea in 1963. Electricity finally arrived in 1980 but these days only a few of the houses are inhabited all year round (the rest serve as holiday homes), though the savage isolation of the place has provided inspiration to a number of artists and writers, including Orkney's George Mackay Brown, who wrote "When Rackwick weeps, its grief is long and forlorn and utterly desolate". A small farm building beside the hostel serves as a tiny **museum** (open any time; free), with a few old photos and a brief rundown of Rackwick's rough history. Take the time, too, to stroll down to the sandy beach, backed by giant sandstone pebbles washed smooth by the sea, which make a thunderous noise when the wind gets up.

The Old Man of Hoy

Despite its isolation, Rackwick has a steady stream of walkers and climbers passing through it en route to the **Old Man of Hoy**, a great sandstone column some 450ft high, perched on an old lava flow which protects it from the erosive power of the sea. The Old Man is a popular challenge for rock-climbers, and a 1966 ascent, led by the mountaineer Chris Bonington, was the first televised climb in Britain. The well-trodden footpath from Rackwick is an easy three-mile walk (3hr round trip) – the great skuas will dive-bomb you only during the nesting season – and gives the reward of a great view of the stack. The surrounding cliffs provide ideal rocky ledges for the nests of thousands of sea birds, including guillemot, kittiwake, razorbill, puffin and shag.

Continuing north along the clifftops, the path peters out before **St John's Head** which, at 1136ft, is one of the highest sea cliffs in the country and mostly too sheer even for nesting sea birds. Another, safer, option is to hike to the top of **Ward Hill** (1577ft), the highest mountain in Orkney, from which on a fine day you can see the whole archipelago laid out before you.

Practicalities

There are only a few basic places to stay in North Hoy. There are two council-run, SYHA-affiliated **hostels**, housed in converted schools (book via ☏01856/873535 ext 2415, ⓦhostelsorkney.co.uk): the *Hoy Centre* (open all year) in Hoy village is large and modern, with all rooms en suite, while *Rackwick Hostel* (April–Sept) has just eight beds but is in Rackwick village itself. You can also **camp** behind *Rackwick Hostel*, or beside the basic heather-thatched *Burnside Bothy* (☏01856/791316) by the beach. Be warned, that North Hoy is probably the worst place on Orkney for midges. The nearest shop is in Longhope (see opposite), so it's best to take your supplies with you if you're staying overnight. If you've just come for a day-trip, the *Beneth'hill Café* (☏01856/851116; May–Sept only) is a short walk from Moaness Pier, a really friendly, simple **café** serving up cullen skink, fresh local crab, home-made puddings and proper coffee – they'll even do you a packed lunch and an evening meal on a Friday.

Lyness and Longhope

Along the sheltered eastern shore of Hoy, high moorland gives way gradually to a gentler environment similar to that on the rest of Orkney. Hoy defines the western boundary of Scapa Flow, and **LYNESS** played a major role for the Royal Navy during both world wars. Most of the old wartime buildings have been cleared away, but the harbour and hills around Lyness are still scarred with scattered concrete structures that once served as hangars and storehouses, and are now used as barns and cowsheds. Among these are the remains of what was – incredibly – the largest cinema in Europe, but perhaps the most unusual building is the monochrome Art-Deco facade of the old **Garrison Theatre**, on the main road south of Lyness, now a private home. Lyness also has a large **naval cemetery**, where many of the victims of the various disasters that have occurred in the Flow,

Flotta

It comes as something of a shock when you first catch sight of the 223-foot flare stack that rises like a giant Bunsen burner from the oil-terminal island of **Flotta**, east of Hoy in Scapa Flow. However, it's also a testament to the success of the local council, which, in confining the **oil industry** to **Flotta**, has minimized the impact it's had on the community. That said, it's difficult to underestimate the significance of the discovery of North Sea oil on Orkney, less in terms of providing well-paid jobs, but more in pumping money into the local economy. Ten percent of Britain's oil production passes through Flotta, and supertankers from all over the world remain a constant, slightly menacing sight in Scapa Flow.

It may seem perverse to visit an island dominated by an oil terminal, but Flotta does have one or two points of interest, and is very easily accessible, with frequent car ferries from both Hoy and the Mainland. Like Lyness, Flotta was an important naval base during both world wars, and there are a lot of wartime relics dotted over the island, including gun and rocket batteries, a signal station, and the huge ruin of an old YMCA, built in local stone during World War I. For a panoramic **view** of the island, and the whole of Scapa Flow, climb up West Hill (190ft), Flotta's highest point.

such as the sinking of the *Royal Oak* (see p.356), now lie, alongside a handful of German graves.

The old oil pumphouse, which still stands opposite the Lyness ferry terminal, has been turned into the **Scapa Flow Visitor Centre** (mid-May to Sept Mon–Fri 9am–4.30pm, Sat & Sun 10.30am–4pm; Oct to mid-May Mon–Fri 9am–4.30pm; Ⓦ www.scapaflow.co.uk; free), a fascinating insight into wartime Orkney – even the **café** has an old NAAFI feel about it. As well as the usual old photos, torpedoes, flags, guns and propellers, there's a paratrooper's folding bicycle, and a whole section devoted to the scuttling of the German High Seas Fleet and the sinking of the *Royal Oak*. The pumphouse itself retains much of its old equipment – you can even ask for a working demo of one of the oil-fired boilers – used to pump oil off tankers moored at Lyness into sixteen tanks, and from there into underground reservoirs cut into the neighbouring hillside. On request, an audiovisual show on the history of Scapa Flow is screened in the sole surviving tank, which has incredible acoustics. You can also wander over to the Romney Hut, where Admiral von Reuter's *Chefboot* resides along with engines from the old wartime railway, and to the Air-Raid Shelter beyond.

Melsetter House

The finest architecture on Hoy is to be found at **Melsetter House** (Thurs & Sun by appointment; Ⓣ 01856/791352), four miles southwest of Lyness, overlooking the deep inlet of North Bay. Originally built in 1738, it was bought by Thomas Middlemore, heir to a Birmingham leather tycoon, who commissioned Arts and Crafts architect William Lethaby to transform the house in 1898. The owners will happily take you round a handful of the thoroughly lived-in rooms in the house itself, all of which are simply decorated with white wood panelling, floral plasterwork and William Morris–style fabrics, and leave you to wander freely around the house's very beautiful grounds. Don't miss the little **Chapel of St Margaret and St Colm** that Lethaby fashioned from the Melsetter's outhouses, which features some characteristic symbolic touches, and four tiny, stained-glass windows by, among others, Ford Madox Brown and Burne-Jones.

South Walls

East of Melsetter House, a causeway built during World War II connects Hoy with **South Walls** (pronounced "Wås"), a fertile tidal island which is more densely populated with farms and homes than Hoy. Along the north coast is the main settlement of **LONGHOPE**, an important safe anchorage even today. The **Longhope Lifeboat** capsized in strong gale-force winds in 1969 on its way to the aid of a Liberian freighter. The entire eight-man crew was killed, leaving seven widows and ten fatherless children; the crew of the freighter, by contrast, survived. There's a moving memorial to the men – six of whom came from just two families – in **Kirkhope churchyard** on the road to Cantick Head Lighthouse. Just up the road before the causeway is the **Longhope Lifeboat Museum** (by appointment via Ⓦ www.longhopelifeboat.org.uk) which houses the *Thomas McCunn*, a lifeboat in service from 1933 to 1962 and still launched for high days and holidays.

Longhope's strategic importance during the Napoleonic Wars is evident at the Point of Hackness, where the **Hackness Martello Tower** (April–Oct daily 9.30am–5.30pm; HS; £4.20) stands guard over the entrance to the bay, with a matching tower on the opposite promontory of Crockness. Built in 1815, these two circular sandstone Martello towers are the northernmost in Britain, and were built to protect merchant ships from American and French privateers. You enter Hackness Tower via a steep ladder connected to the upper floor, where nine men and one officer shared the circular room. Originally a portable ladder would have been used and retracted, making the place pretty much impregnable: the walls are up to 9ft high on the seaward side, and the tower even had its own water supply. Overlooking the bay at the nearby **Hackness Battery**, positioned closer to the shore, yet more cannon were trained on the horizon.

Practicalities

The most outstanding **accommodation** on Hoy is ☀ *Wild Heather* B&B (☎01856/791098, ⓦwww.wildheatherbandb.co.uk; ❷), in Lyness, just beyond the naval cemetery. It's a converted mill with just two en-suite rooms, both with sea views, and a lovely breakfast conservatory – they'll offer dinners, too, if required. In Longhope itself, there's the small, welcoming *Stromabank Hotel* (☎01856/701494, ⓦwww.stromabank.co.uk; ❸), a nicely converted old schoolhouse, which also does good bar **food** in the evening (closed Thurs). There's just one shop by the pier in Longhope.

Shapinsay

Just a few miles northeast of Kirkwall, **Shapinsay** is the most accessible of Orkney's northern isles. A gently undulating grid-plan patchwork of rich farmland, it's a bit like an island suburb of Kirkwall, which is clearly visible across the bay. Its chief landmark is **Balfour Castle**, an imposing baronial pile designed by David Bryce and completed in 1848 by the Balfour family of Westray, who had made a small fortune in India the previous century. The Balfours died out in 1960 and the castle was bought by a Polish cavalry officer, Captain Tadeusz Zawadski, whose family ran the place for many years as a hotel – nowadays, it's an exclusive-use holiday retreat.

The Balfours reformed the island's agricultural system and rebuilt **BALFOUR** village (previously known as Shoreside), a neat and disciplined cottage development, to house their estate workers. The family's grandiose efforts in estate management have left some appealingly eccentric relics. Melodramatic fortifications around the harbour include the huge and ornate **Gatehouse**, which now serves as the local pub. There's also a stone-built coal-fired **Gasometer**, which once supplied castle and harbour with electricity and, southwest of the pier, the castellated **Dishan Tower**, a seventeenth-century doocot that was converted into a saltwater toilet in Victorian times. The old smiddy, halfway along the village street, houses the **Shapinsay Heritage Centre** (May–Sept Mon–Fri 11am–4.30pm, Sat & Sun 11am–6pm; free), where you can learn everything you ever wanted to know about the island, before availing yourself of its excellent café.

There are one or two points of interest beyond the castle and village. One mile north of the village is the small **Mill Dam**, a breeding ground for black-headed gulls, with a hide to the west from which you can also look down on wigeon, teal, shoveller and (if you're really lucky) pintail. The **east coast** from the Bay of Linton to the Foot of Shapinsay has the most interesting cliffs and sea caves and is backed by the only open moorland on the island. On the far northeastern peninsula is Shapinsay's most striking ancient monument, the **Broch of Burroughston**, a well-preserved strongly fortified Iron-Age broch with the substantial remains of living quarters within, a bar hole to make fast the door, and a guard-cell. This bit of the coast is also a good spot for watching **seals** sunning themselves on the nearby rocks. The finest stretch of sandy beach is at the sweeping curve of **Sandgarth Bay**, in the southeast.

Practicalities

Less than thirty minutes from Kirkwall by **ferry** (4–5 daily), Shapinsay is an easy day-trip, but if you wish to stay, **B&B** is available at the whitewashed *Hilton Farmhouse* (T01856/711239, W www.hiltonorkneyfarmhouse.co.uk; ④), which also has a restaurant in the conservatory (booking ahead essential) and offers optional full board. Even if you're just coming for the day, it's worth popping into *The Smithy* (May–Sept; T01856/711722), the wonderfully cosy licensed **café** below the heritage centre, which serves delicious food.

Rousay, Egilsay and Wyre

Just over half a mile from the Mainland's northern shore, the hilly island of **Rousay** (W www.visitrousay.co.uk) is one of the more accessible northern isles as well as being home to a number of intriguing prehistoric sites. The group of a dozen or so houses above the ferry terminal is the only settlement of any size, but a single road runs around the edge of the island, connecting a string of small farms which make use of the more cultivable coastal fringes. Many visitors come on a day-trip, as it's easy enough to reach the main points of archeological interest on the south coast by foot from the ferry terminal.

Rousay's diminutive neighbours, **Egilsay** and **Wyre**, contain a few medieval attractions of their own, which can either be visited on a day-trip from Rousay itself, or from the mainland.

Trumland House to the Knowe of Yarso

Despite its long history of settlement, Rousay is today home to little more than two hundred people (many of them incomers), as this was one of the few parts of Orkney to suffer Highland-style Clearances, initially by George William Traill at Quandale in the northwest. His successor and nephew, Lieutenant General Traill-Burroughs, built a wall to force crofters onto a narrow coastal strip and eventually provoked so much distress and anger that a gunboat had to be sent to restore order. You can learn about the history and wildlife of the island from the well laid out display-room of the **Rousay Heritage Centre** housed in the back of the ferry waiting room.

It was the aforementioned Burroughs who built **Trumland House**, the forbidding Jacobean-style pile designed by David Bryce in 1873, and hidden in the trees half a mile northwest of the ferry terminal. The house is currently undergoing much-needed restoration, as are the **gardens**, which can be visited (May–Sept Mon–Fri 10am–5pm; £1.50). The road west from Trumland House is bordered over the next couple of miles by a trio of intriguing prehistoric cairns, starting with **Taversoe Tuick**, discovered by workers during the building of a Victorian viewpoint. Dating back to 3500 BC, it's remarkable in that it exploits its sloping site by having two storeys, one entered from the upper side and one from the lower. A little further west is the **Blackhammar Cairn**, which is more promising inside than it looks from the outside. You enter through the roof via a ladder; the long interior is divided into "stalls" by large flagstones, rather like the more famous cairn at Midhowe (see p.366). Finally, there's the **Knowe of Yarso**, another stalled cairn dating from the same period that's a stiff climb up the hill from the road, but worth it, if only for the magnificent view. The remains of 29 individuals were found inside, with the skulls neatly arranged around the walls; the bones of 36 deer were also buried here.

A footpath sets off from beside the Taversoe Tuick tomb into the **RSPB reserve** that encompasses a large section of the nearby heather-backed hills, the highest of

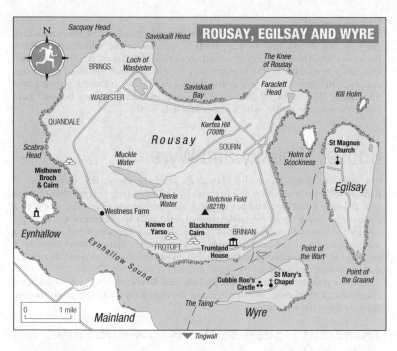

ORKNEY | Rousay, Egilsay and Wyre

which is **Blotchnie Field** (821ft). This high ground offers good hillwalking, with superb panoramic views of the surrounding islands, as well as excellent bird-watching. If you're lucky, you may well catch a glimpse of merlins, hen harriers, short-eared owls and red-throated divers, although the latter are more widespread just outside the reserve on one of the island's three freshwater lochs, which also offer good trout-fishing.

Midhowe Cairn and Broch

The southwestern side of Rousay is home to the most significant and impressive of the island's archeological remains, strung out along the shores of Eynhallow Sound, which runs between the island and the Mainland. Most lie on the mile-long **Westness Walk** that begins at Westness Farm, four miles west of the ferry terminal. This scramble along the shore is rewarded with a kaleidoscope of history, with remains of an Iron Age cairn, a Viking farm, a post-Reformation church, a medieval tower, and crofts from which the tenants were evicted in the nineteenth century. At the end stands the **Midhowe Cairn**, which comes as something of a surprise, both for its immense size – it's known as "the great ship of death" and measures nearly 100ft in length – and for the fact that it's now entirely surrounded by a stone-walled barn with a corrugated roof. Unfortunately, you can't actually explore the roofless communal burial chamber, dating back to 3500 BC, but only look down from the overhead walkway. The central corridor, 25yd long, is partitioned with slabs of rock, with twelve compartments on each side, where the remains of 25 people were discovered in a crouched position with their backs to the wall.

A couple of hundred yards beyond Midhowe Cairn is Rousay's finest archeological site, **Midhowe Broch**, whose compact layout suggests that it was originally built as a sort of fortified family house, surrounded by a complex series of ditches and ramparts. These are now partially obscured by later houses, many of which have shelving and stairs still intact. The broch itself looks as though it's about to slip into the sea: it was obviously shored up with flagstone buttresses back in the Iron Age, and has more recently been given extra sea defences by Historic Scotland. The interior of the broch, entered through an impressive doorway, is divided into two separate rooms, each with its own hearth, water tank and quernstone, all of which date from the final phase of occupation around the second century AD.

From Midhowe Broch you get a good view of the nearby small island of **Eynhallow**, which is surrounded by the most ferocious tides. The island was cleared in 1851, at which point it was discovered that one of the houses was in fact a converted church, possibly part of a monastery, dating back to at least the twelfth century. Beyond Midhowe, a walk along the clifftops will take you past the impressive scenery around **Scabra Head**, where numerous sea birds nest in summer. Inland, the heathland of Quandale and Brings provides yet more bird-watching, with arctic terns and arctic skuas in abundance. To the north is a fine sandy beach at Saviskaill Bay, where seals hang out.

Practicalities

Rousay makes a good day-trip from the Mainland, with regular **car ferry** sailings from Tingwall (30min), linked to Kirkwall by buses. Most ferries also call in at Egilsay and Wyre, but some need to be booked the day before at the Tingwall ferry terminal (℡01856/751360). A **bus service** works (on request ℡01856/821360) every Thursday, or there are **minibus tours** available on demand (℡01856/821234; £16.50), which connect with ferries and last between five and seven hours.

Accommodation on Rousay is limited. If you want to be near the ancient sites, your best bet is the **hostel** at *Trumland Farm* (℡01856/821252), a working organic farm half a mile or so west of the terminal. As well as a couple of dorms, you can also camp here, and they offer **bike rental**. The *Taversoe*, further along the road, offers unpretentious accommodation (℡01856/821325, ⓦtaversoe hotel.co.uk; ❸) and does good bar meals (April–Oct daily; Nov–March Wed–Sun only). *The Pier* **pub**, right beside the terminal, serves bar meals at lunchtime and will make up some fresh crab sandwiches if you phone in advance (℡01856/821359). Don't arrive expecting to be able to buy yourself many provisions, though, as Marion's Shop, the island's main general store, is in the northeastern corner of the island.

Egilsay and Wyre

Egilsay, the largest of the low-lying islands sheltering close to the eastern shore of Rousay, makes for an easy day-trip. The island is dominated by the ruins of **St Magnus Church**, with its distinctive round tower, venue for Egilsay's ever more popular summer solstice celebrations. Built around the twelfth century in a prominent position in the middle of the island, probably on the site of a much earlier version, the roofless church is the only surviving example of the traditional round-towered churches of Orkney and Shetland. It is possible that it was built as a shrine to Earl (later Saint) Magnus, who arranged to meet his cousin Håkon here in 1117, only to be treacherously killed on Håkon's orders by the latter's cook, Lifolf. A cenotaph marks the spot where the murder took place, about a quarter of a mile southeast of the church. Egilsay is almost entirely inhabited by incomers, and a large slice of the island's farmland is managed by the RSPB in a vain attempt to encourage corncrakes. If you're just here for the day, walk due east from the ferry terminal to the coast, where there's a beautiful sandy bay overlooking Eday.

The tiny, neighbouring island of **Wyre**, to the southwest, directly opposite Rousay's ferry terminal, is another possible day-trip, and is best known for **Cubbie Roo's Castle**, the "fine stone fort" and "really solid stronghold" mentioned in the *Orkneyinga Saga*, and built around 1150 by local farmer Kolbein Hruga. The castle gets another mention in *Håkon's Saga*, when those inside successfully withstood all attacks. The outer defences have survived well on three sides of the castle, which has a central keep, with walls to a height of around six feet, its central water-tank still intact. Close by the castle stands **St Mary's Chapel**, a roofless twelfth-century church founded either by Kolbein or his son, Bjarni the Poet, who was Bishop of Orkney. Kolbein's permanent residence or **Bu** is recalled in the name of the nearby farm, the Bu of Wyre, where the poet **Edwin Muir** (1887–1959) spent his childhood, described in detail in his autobiography. To learn more about Muir, Cubbie Roo or any other aspect of Wyre's history, pop into the **Wyre Heritage Centre**, near the chapel. If you walk to the very western tip of Wyre, known as **The Taing**, you're pretty much guaranteed to see large numbers of grey and common **seals** basking on the rocks.

Westray

Although exposed to the full force of the Atlantic weather in the far northwest of Orkney, **Westray** (Ⓦwww.westraypapawestray.com) shelters one of the most tightly knit, prosperous and independent island communities. Old Orcadian families still dominate every aspect of life, giving the island a strong individual character. Fishing, farming and tourism are the mainstays of the economy, and there's a fairly stable population of around six hundred. The landscape is very varied, with sea cliffs and a trio of hills in the west, and rich low-lying pastureland and sandy bays elsewhere. However, given that distances are fairly large – it's about twelve miles from the ferry terminal in the south to the cliffs of Noup Head in the far northwest – and that the boat from Kirkwall takes nearly an hour and a half, Westray is an island that repays a longer stay, especially as there's lots of good accommodation and the locals are extremely welcoming and genuinely interested in visitors.

Pierowall and around

The main village and harbour is **PIEROWALL** set around a wide bay in the north of the island, eight miles from the Rapness ferry terminal on the island's southernmost tip. Pierowall is a place of some considerable size, relatively speaking, with a school, several shops and a bakery (Orkney's only one off the Mainland). The village's **Westray Heritage Centre** (May–Sept Mon 11.30am–5pm, Tues–Sat 10am–noon & 2–5pm, Sun 1.30–5.30pm; £2.50) is a very welcoming wet-weather retreat, and a great place to gen up on (and with any luck catch a glimpse of) the Westray Wife or **Orkney Venus**, a remarkable, miniature Neolithic female figurine found in 2009 in the dunes to the northwest of Pierowall.

The island's most impressive ruin is the colossal sandstone hulk of **Noltland Castle**, which stands above the village half a mile west up the road to Noup Head. This Z-plan castle, pockmarked with over seventy gun loops, was begun around 1560 by Gilbert Balfour, a shady character from Fife, who was Master of the Household to Mary, Queen of Scots, and was implicated in the murder of her husband, Lord Darnley, in 1567. Mary was deposed before she could make her planned visit to Noltland, and Balfour, having joined an unsuccessful uprising in favour of the exiled queen, was forced to flee to Sweden. There he was found

WESTRAY AND PAPA WESTRAY

Mull Head

Papa
Westray

North Hill
(157ft)

Fowl Craig

Bow Head

St Boniface Kirk

AIKERNESS

Holm of
Aikerness

Knap of
Howar

Holland
House

Holm of Papa

RACKWICK

Papa Sound

Loch of
St Tredwell

Noup Head

Grobust

LINKS

Noltland
Castle

Pierowall

Vest Ness

Head of Moclett

Bis Geos

The
Barn

Knucker Hill
(370ft)

Gallo Hill
(355ft)

Westray

SKELWICK

Fitty Hill
(557ft)

MIDBEA

Bay of
Tuquoy

Inga Ness

Cross
Kirk

Castle
O'Burrian

Stanger
Head

Berst Ness

Skerry of
Wastbust

RAPNESS

Skea Skerries

Holm of
Faray

0   2 miles

Wart Holm   Point of
Huro

Kirkwall

guilty of plotting to murder the Swedish king and was executed in 1576. Somewhat miraculously, the Balfour family managed to hold on to Noltland (and Westray), eventually shifting their seat to Shapinsay (see p.364). To explore the castle, you must first pick up the key, which hangs outside the back door of the nearby farm. The most striking features of the interior are the huge, carved stone newel at the top of the grand, main staircase, and the secret compartments built into the sills of two of the windows.

The sea cliffs

The northwestern tip of Westray rises up sharply, culminating in the dramatic sea cliffs of **Noup Head**, which are particularly spectacular when a good westerly swell is up. During the summer months the guano-covered rock ledges are packed with over 100,000 nesting guillemots, razorbills, kittiwakes, fulmars and puffins: a truly awesome sight, sound and smell. The open ground above the cliffs, which is grazed by sheep, is superb maritime heath and grassland, carpeted with yellow, white and purple flowers, and a favourite breeding-ground for arctic tern and arctic skua.

The four-mile coastal walk along the top of Westray's red-sandstone cliffs from Noup Head south to Inga Ness is thoroughly recommended, as is a quick ascent of **Fitty Hill** (557ft), Westray's highest point. Also in the south of the island is the tiny **Cross Kirk** which, although ruined, retains an original Romanesque arch, door and window. It's right by the sea, and on a fine day the nearby sandy beach is a lovely spot for a picnic, with views over to the north side of Rousay. The sea cliffs in the southeast of the island around **Stanger Head** are not quite as spectacular as at Noup Head, but it's here that you'll find **Castle o'Burrian**, a sea stack that was once an early Christian hermitage. It's now the best place on Westray at which to see **puffins** nesting; there's even a signpost to the puffins from the main road.

Practicalities

Westray is served by car **ferry** from Kirkwall (2–3 daily; 1hr 25min; ☎01856/872044), or you can **fly** from Kirkwall (Mon–Sat 2 daily, 1 on Sun; 15min). **Guided tours** of the island by minibus can be arranged with Westråk (☎01857/677777, ⓦwww.westrak.co.uk), who will meet you at the ferry, and also offer **bike rental**. A **minibus** (May–Sept; at other times phone ☎01857/677758) also meets the ferry and connects with the Papa Westray ferry at Gill Pier in Pierowall; book a seat for the bus on the ferry.

As for **accommodation**, the *Pierowall Hotel* (☎01857/677472, ⓦwww.pierowall hotel.co.uk; ❸), the social hub of Pierowall itself, is unpretentious and very welcoming – the cheaper rooms have shared facilities. Alternatively, you can get top-notch, good-value **B&B** at *No. 1 Broughton* (☎01857/677726, ⓦwww .no1broughton.co.uk; ❸), a renovated mid-nineteenth-century house on the south shore of the bay, with a lovely conservatory and a sauna, or at *The Old Manse* (☎01857/677578, ⓦwww.bandbwestray.co.uk; ❷) in the heart of Pierowall. Westray is positively spoilt for **hostels**. If you want superb sea views and splendid isolation, head for ⭐ *Bis Geos* (☎01857/677420, ⓦwww.bisgeos.co.uk), a traditional Orcadian croft, on the road to Noup Head, that's been beautifully renovated inside. If you want to be closer to civilization, head for ⭐ *The Barn* (☎01857/677214, ⓦwww.thebarnwestray.co.uk), an old farm at the southern edge of Pierowall; it's luxurious inside, with family rooms and twins available (❸), has a small **campsite** adjacent to it and a games room and genuinely friendly hosts.

The *Pierowall Hotel* has a popular bar and a well-justified reputation for excellent **fish** fresh off the boats (much of it you're unlikely to have heard of) – they serve it up deep fried with chips or you can take it away to cook yourself. The island has a couple of **tearooms**, too: *Wheeling Steen* (closed Sun) café/gallery is over by the airfield in the north of the island, while Westråk tour company runs the *Haf Yok* café in Pierowall itself.

Papa Westray

Across the short Papa Sound from Westray is the island of **Papa Westray**, known locally as "Papay" (ⓦwww.papawestray.co.uk). With a population hovering around seventy, Papay has had to fight hard to keep itself viable over the last couple of decades, helped by a hefty influx of outsiders. With one of Orkney's

best-preserved Neolithic settlements, and a large nesting sea-bird
Papay is worthy of a stay in its own right or an easy day-trip from its

As the name suggests – *papøy* is Old Norse for "priest" – the island
medieval pilgrimage centre, focused on a chapel dedicated to **St Tred**
is now reduced to a pile of rubble on a promontory on the loch of the
just inland from the ferry terminal. St Tredwell (Triduana) was a pl
local girl who gouged out her eyes and handed them to the eighth-century Pictish
king Nechtan when he attempted to rape her. By the twelfth century, the chapel
had become a place of pilgrimage for those suffering from eye complaints.

Holland House and the west coast

The island's visual focus is **Holland House**, occupying the high central point of the
island and once seat of the local lairds, the Traill family, who ruled over Papay for
three centuries. The main house, with its crow-stepped gables, is still in private hands,
but the current owners are perfectly happy for visitors to explore the old buildings of
the home farm, on the west side of the road, which include a kiln, a doocot and a
horse-powered threshing mill. An old bothy for single male servants, decorated with
red horse-yokes, has even been restored and made into a small **museum** (open
anytime; free), filled with bygone bits and bobs, from a wooden flea-trap to a box bed.

A road leads down from Holland House to the western shore, where Papay's prime
prehistoric site, the **Knap of Howar**, stands overlooking Westray. Dating from
around 3500 BC, this Neolithic farm building makes a fair claim to being the oldest-
standing house in Europe. It's made up of two roofless buildings, linked by a little
passageway; one has a hearth and copious stone shelves, and is thought to have been
some kind of storehouse. Half a mile north along the coast from the Knap of Howar
is **St Boniface Kirk**, a pre-Reformation church that has recently been restored.
Inside, it's beautifully simple, with a bare flagstone floor, dry-stone walls, a little
wooden gallery and just a couple of surviving box pews. The church is known to
have seated at least 220, which meant they would have been squashed in, fourteen to
a pew. In the surrounding graveyard there's a Viking **hogback grave**, decorated
with carvings in imitation of the wooden shingles on the roof of a Viking longhouse.

North Hill and the east coast

The northern tip of the island around **North Hill** (157ft) is now an RSPB reserve.
During the breeding season you're asked to keep to the coastal fringe, where razorbills, guillemots, fulmars, kittiwakes and puffins nest, particularly around Fowl
Craig on the east coast, where you can also view the rare Scottish primrose, which
flowers in May and from July to late September. If you want to explore the
interior of the reserve, which plays host to one of the largest arctic tern colonies
in Europe as well as numerous arctic skuas, contact the warden (℡01857/644240;
April–Aug Tues, Thurs & Sat), who conducts regular escorted walks.

If you're here for more than a day, it's worth considering renting a boat to take
you over to the **Holm of Papay**, an islet off the east coast. Despite its tiny size,
the Holm boasts several Neolithic chambered cairns, one of which, occupying the
highest point, is extremely impressive. Descending into the tomb via a ladder, you
enter the main rectangular chamber, which is nearly 70ft in length, with no fewer
than twelve side-cells, each with its own lintelled entrance. To arrange a boat,
contact the Community Co-operative (see p.372).

Practicalities

Papay is an easy day-trip from Westray, with a **passenger ferry** service from Gill
Pier in Pierowall (3–6 daily; 25min), which also takes bicycles. On Tuesdays, the

erry goes from Kirkwall to Papa Westray via North Ronaldsay, which means takes over four hours; on Fridays, the **car ferry** from Kirkwall to Westray continues on to Papa Westray; at other times, you have to catch a **bus** to connect with the Papa Westray ferry from Pierowall. The bus should be booked ahead, whilst on the Westray ferry (T01857/677758); it accepts a limited number of bicycles. Papay is also connected to Westray by the **world's shortest scheduled flight** – two minutes in duration, or less with a following wind. You can also fly direct from Kirkwall to Papa Westray (Mon–Sat 2–3 daily, 1 on Sun; 25min) for a special return fare of £20 if you stay overnight.

Papay's Community Co-operative (T01857/644321) has a **minibus**, which will take you from the pier to wherever you want on the island, and can arrange a "Peedie Package" tour (peedie means small in Orkney dialect). The Co-op also runs a shop, a two-room, sixteen-bed **hostel** and the *Beltane House* **B&B** (❸), all housed within the old estate-workers' cottages at Beltane, east of Holland House. There's one other B&B, *School Place* (T01857/644268, ✉sonofhewitj@aol.com; ❸), in the island's former school, right in the centre of the island. *Beltane House* opens its "bar cupboard" every Saturday night from 8pm, with **bar meals** available – a great way to meet the locals.

Eday

A long, thin island at the centre of Orkney's northern isles, **Eday** (Wwww .visiteday.com) shares more characteristics with Rousay and Hoy than with its immediate neighbours, dominated as it is by a great block of heather-covered upland, with farmland confined to a narrow strip of coastal ground. However, Eday's hills have proved useful in their own way, providing huge quantities of peat, which has been exported to the other peatless northern isles for fuel, and was even, for a time, exported to various whisky distillers. Eday's yellow sandstone has also been extensively quarried, and was used to build the St Magnus Cathedral in Kirkwall.

Eday is sparsely inhabited, with a population of around 120, the majority of them incomers, and there's no real village as such. The ferry terminal is at the south end of the island, whereas the chief points of interest (and most of the amenities) are all in the northern half of the island, about four miles away. The island is almost divided in two by its thin waist, flanked on either side by sandy bays, between which lies the airfield (known as London Airport). Eday has a large resident population of whimbrels, which nest around Flaughton Hill (328ft), a mile or so to the south. A mile or so north of the airport, you'll find the **Eday Heritage Centre** (daily: April–Oct 9am–6pm; free). As well as historical displays, there's information on the island's new tidal energy testing centre, as well as a café/bar.

Less than a mile further north, near the post office, petrol pump and community shop, there's a bird hide by the road, looking south over **Mill Loch**, where several pairs of **red-throated divers** regularly breed. Clearly visible on the other side of the road is the fifteen-foot **Stone of Setter**, Orkney's most distinctive standing-stone, weathered into three thick, lichen-encrusted fingers. The stone clearly held centre stage in the Neolithic landscape, and is visible from the other nearby prehistoric sites. From here, passing the less spectacular Braeside and Huntersquoy chambered cairns en route, you can climb the hill to reach Eday's finest, the **Vinquoy Chambered Cairn**, which has a similar structure to that of Maes Howe. You can crawl into the tomb through the narrow entrance: a skylight inside lets light into the main, beehive chamber,

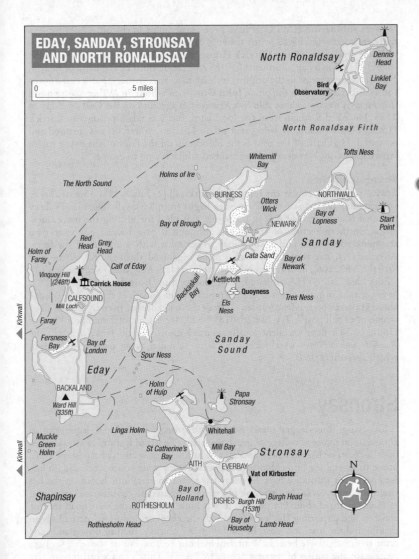

EDAY, SANDAY, STRONSAY AND NORTH RONALDSAY

0   5 miles

North Ronaldsay   Dennis Head

Bird Observatory   Linklet Bay

North Ronaldsay Firth

Whitemill Bay   Tofts Ness

The North Sound   *Holms of Ire*

BURNESS   NORTHWALL

Otters Wick   Bay of Lopness   Start Point

Bay of Brough   NEWARK

LADY   *Sanday*

Holm of Faray

Red Head   Grey Head

Cata Sand   Bay of Newark

Vinquoy Hill (248ft)   **Carrick House**

Calf of Eday

Kettletoft

Quoyness

CALFSOUND

Backaskaill Bay

Els Ness

Tres Ness

Mill Loch

Kirkwall

Faray

Fersness Bay   Bay of London

Sanday Sound

Spur Ness

Eday

BACKALAND

Holm of Huip   Papa Stronsay

Ward Hill (335ft)

Kirkwall

Muckle Green Holm

Linga Holm   Whitehall

St Catherine's Bay   Mill Bay   *Stronsay*

AITH   EVERBAY   **Vat of Kirbuster**

Shapinsay

Bay of Holland

ROTHIESHOLM   DISHES   Burgh Hill (153ft)   Burgh Head

Rothiesholm Head   *Bay of Houseby*   Lamb Head

N

---

now home to some lovely ferns, but not into the four side-cells. From the cairn, you can continue north to the viewpoint on the summit of **Vinquoy Hill** (248ft), and on to the very northernmost tip of the island, where lie the dramatic red-sandstone sea cliffs of **Red Head**, where guillemots, razorbills, puffins and other sea birds nest in summer.

To the west of Vinquoy Hill is the **Red House Croft Restoration Project**, where you can explore the evocative remains of a large nineteenth-century farm (June–Sept Tues–Fri 10am–5pm, Sat & Sun by appointment; free; ☎01857/622217); there's a tearoom with a limited menu of food available (ring for evening meal). Perhaps the most unusual attraction is at the former North School, almost opposite the shop, where several internal sections of the Cold

War-era **submarine** HMS *Otter* have been reassembled in the old school hall – a truly eerie experience (call in any time; ℡01857/622225; free).

Visible on the east coast is **Carrick House**, the grandest home on Eday (late June to mid-Sept Sun by appointment; ℡01857/622260). Built by the Laird of Eday in 1633, it was extended in the original style by successive owners, but is best known for its associations with the pirate **John Gow** – on whom Sir Walter Scott's novel *The Pirate* is based – whose ship *The Revenge* ran aground on the **Calf of Eday** in 1725. He asked for help from the local laird, but was taken prisoner in Carrick House, before eventually being sent off to London, where he was tortured and executed. Highlight of the tour is the bloodstain on the floor of the living room, where John Gow was detained and stabbed whilst trying to escape.

Practicalities

Eday is served by regular **car ferry** from Kirkwall (2–3 daily; 1hr 15min–2hr) or you can do a day-trip on the Wednesday **flight** from Kirkwall. The island's **ferry** terminal is at Backaland pier in the south, not ideal for visiting the more interesting northern section of the island, although if you haven't got your own transport you should find it fairly easy to get a lift with someone off the ferry. Alternatively, **car rental** and **taxis** can be organized through J&J by the pier (℡01857/622206); he also runs **minibus tours** (May–Aug Mon, Wed & Fri; £12).

Eday has an SYHA-affiliated, community-run **hostel** (℡01857/622283, Ⓦwww.syha.org.uk), situated in an exposed spot just north of the airport – phone ahead as there's no resident warden. There's also a handful of friendly **B&Bs**, all of which offer full board. Try **Blett** (℡01857/622248; ❹), a crofthouse near Carrick House, which does excellent locally-sourced meals. If you fancy a drink, the *Roadside Public House*, overlooking the ferry terminal, is an evening-only **pub**, which also offers B&B.

Stronsay

A low-lying, three-legged island, **Stronsay** is strongly agricultural, its interior an almost uninterrupted collage of green pastures. The island features few real sights, but the coastline has enormous appeal: a beguiling combination of sandstone cliffs, home to several sea-bird colonies, interspersed with wide white sands and (in fine weather) clear turquoise bays. Stronsay has seen two economic booms in the last three hundred years. The first took place in the eighteenth century, and employed as many as three thousand people; it was built on collecting vast quantities of seaweed and exporting the **kelp** for use in the chemical industry, particularly in making iodine, soap and glass. In the following century, **fishing** on a grand scale came to dominate life here, as Whitehall harbour became one of the main Scottish centres for the curing of herring caught by French, Dutch and Scottish boats. By the 1840s, up to four hundred boats were working out of the port, attracting hundreds of women herring-gutters. By the 1930s, however, the herring stocks had been severely depleted and the industry began a long decline.

WHITEHALL, in the north of the island, is the only real village on Stronsay, made up of rows of stone-built fishermen's cottages set between two large piers. Wandering along the tranquil, rather forlorn harbourfront today, you'll find it hard to believe that the village once supported five thousand people in the fishing industry during the summer season, as well as a small army of coopers, coal merchants, butchers, bakers, several Italian ice-cream parlours and a cinema. It was said that, on a Sunday, you could walk across the decks of the boats all the way to **Papa Stronsay**, the tiny island that shelters Whitehall from the north, on which a

Papa Stronsay

Clearly visible from the harbourfront at Whitehall is the tiny island of **Papa Stronsay**. The island features in the *Orkneyinga Saga* (see p.430) as the place where Earl Rognvald Brusason was murdered by Earl Thorfinn Sigurdarson. Later, during the herring boom, it was home to no fewer than five fish-curing stations. As the name suggests, the island is thought originally to have been a **monastic retreat**, a theory given extra weight by the discovery of an eighth-century chapel during recent excavations. In 2000, the island was bought by **Transalpine Redemptorist monks**, who had broken with the Vatican over their refusal to stop celebrating Mass in Latin. They have subsequently built themselves the multi-million-pound Golgotha Monastery, with a creamery for making their Monastery Cheese. Since 2008, they have been accepted into the Roman Catholic Church and have been renamed the **Sons of the Most Holy Redeemer**. The black-robed monks are happy to take visitors across to (and around) the island by boat, by prior arrangement (T01857/616389).

new monastery has been built (see box above). The old fish market by the pier houses a small **museum**, with a few photos and artefacts from the herring days – ask at the adjacent café for access.

If the weather's fine, you can choose which of the island's many arching, dazzlingly white beaches to relax on. The most dramatic section of coastline, featuring great, layered slices of sandstone, lies in the southeast corner of the island. Signposts show the way to Orkney's biggest and most dramatic natural arch, the **Vat of Kirbuster**. Before you reach the arch there's a seaweedy, shallow pool in a natural sandstone amphitheatre, where the water is warmed by the sun, and kids and adults can safely wallow: close by is a rocky inlet for those who prefer colder, more adventurous swimming. You'll find progressively more nesting sea birds, including a few puffins, as you approach **Burgh Head**, further along down the coast. Meanwhile, at the promontory of **Lamb Head**, there are usually loads of seals, a large colony of arctic terns, and good views out to the lighthouse on the outlying island of **Auskerry**, to the south.

Practicalities

Stronsay is served by a regular car **ferry** service from Kirkwall to Whitehall (2–3 daily; 1hr 40min–2hr), and **flights**, also from Kirkwall (Mon–Fri 2 daily, 1 on Sat; 25min). There's no bus service, but D.S. Peace (T01857/616335) operates taxis and offers **car rental**.

Of the few **accommodation** options, a good choice is the *Stronsay Fish Mart* **hostel** (T01857/616386) in the old fish market by the pier, with a well-equipped kitchen, washing machine and comfortable bunk-bedded rooms. The pub opposite is the nicely refurbished *Stronsay Hotel* (T01857/616213, Wwww.stronsayhotel orkney.co.uk; ❹), which once boasted the longest bar in the north of Scotland. The **hotel** does good pub **food** – try the seafood taster – but otherwise you'll need to bring your own supplies and make use of the island's two shops.

Sanday

Sanday (Wwww.sanday.co.uk), though the largest of the northern isles, and the most populous after Westray, is also the most insubstantial, a great low-lying, drifting dune strung out between several rocky points. The island's sweeping aquamarine bays and vast stretches of clean white sand are the finest in Orkney, and in dry, clear weather it's a superb place to spend a day or two. The sandy soil is, in fact, very fertile, and the island remains predominantly agricultural even today, holding its very own agricultural show each year at the beginning of August.

The island has a long history as a shipping hazard, with many wrecks smashed against its shores, although the construction of the **Start Point Lighthouse** in 1802 on the island's exposed eastern tip reduced the risk for seafarers. Shipwrecks were, in fact, not an unwelcome sight on Sanday, as the island has no peat, and driftwood was the only source of fuel other than cow dung – it's even said that the locals used to pray for shipwrecks in church. The present Stevenson lighthouse, which dates from 1870, now sports very natty vertical black-and-white stripes. It actually stands on a tidal island, accessible only either side of low tide, so ask locally for the tide times before setting out (it takes an hour to walk there and back). Better still, phone and arrange a tour (℡01857/600341), which allows you to climb to the top of the lighthouse.

The shoreline supports a healthy seal, otter and wading bird population, and behind the splendid sandy beaches are stretches of beautiful open machair and grassland, thick with wild flowers during the spring and summer. The entire coastline presents the opportunity for superb walks, with particularly spectacular sand dunes to the south of the vast, shallow, tidal bay of **Cata Sand**. Sanday is also rich in archeology, with hundreds of mostly unexcavated sites including cairns, brochs and burnt mounds. The most impressive is **Quoyness Chambered Cairn**, on the fertile farmland of Els Ness peninsula. The tomb, which dates from before 2000 BC, has been partially reconstructed, and rises to a height of around thirteen feet. The imposing, narrow entrance, flanked by high dry-stone walls, would originally have been roofed for the whole of the way into the thirteen-foot-long main chamber, where bones and skulls were discovered in the six small side-cells.

Lastly, Sanday's **Orkney Angora** craft shop (℡01857/600421, ⓦwww .orkneyangora.co.uk) is in Upper Breckan in the parish of Burness. The owner will usually oblige with a quick look and a stroke of one of the comically long-haired albino rabbits that supply the wool. Close by is the stone tower of an old windmill, which belonged to the neighbouring farmstead and house of **Scar**, where you can still see the chimney from the farm's old steam-powered meal mill.

Practicalities

Ferries to Sanday arrive at Loth Pier, at the southern tip of the island, and are met by the **minibus** (℡01857/600769), which will take you to most points. The airfield is in the centre of the island and there are regular **flights** to Kirkwall (Mon–Fri 2 daily, 1 on Sat; 10min). The fishing port of **Kettletoft** is where ferries used to dock, and where you'll find the island's two **hotels** – the *Belsair* and the *Kettletoft* – both of which do decent pub food and have free wi-fi. There's a good choice of **B&Bs**: *Marygarth Manse* (℡01857/600467, ⓦwww.bedandbreakfast -orkney.co.uk; ❷) is a nicely modernized nineteenth-century former manse near the Bay of Brough, while *Ladybank* (℡01857/600339; ❷), another converted manse, is close to the airfield. If you're on a budget, *Ayre's Rock* (℡01857/600410, ⓦwww.ayres-rock-sanday-orkney.co.uk) is a great place to stay: a well-equipped **hostel** and **campsite** overlooking the bay, with washing and laundry facilities, a chip shop (Tues & Sat) and bike rental.

North Ronaldsay

North Ronaldsay – or "North Ron" as it's fondly known [...] northerly island (𝕎 www.northronaldsay.com). Separated fr[...] treacherous waters of the North Ronaldsay Firth, it has a uni[...] phere, brought about by its extreme isolation. Measuring just [...] and rising only 66ft above sea level, the island is almost ove[...] enormity of the sky, the strength of wind and the ferocity of th[...] that its very existence seems an act of tenacious defiance. Desp[...] conditions, North Ronaldsay has been inhabited for centuries, and continues to be heavily farmed, from old-style crofts whose roofs are made from huge local flagstones. With no natural harbours and precious little farmland, the islanders have been forced to make the most of what they have, and **seaweed** has played an important role in the local economy. During the eighteenth century, kelp was gathered here, burnt in pits and sent south for use in the chemicals industry.

The island's **sheep** are a unique, tough, goatlike breed, who feed mostly on seaweed, giving their flesh a dark tone and a rich, gamey taste, and making their thick wool highly prized. A high **dry-stone dyke**, completed in the mid-nineteenth century and running the thirteen miles around the edge of the island, keeps them off the farmland, except during lambing season, when the ewes are allowed onto the pastureland. North Ronaldsay sheep are also unusual in that they can't be rounded up by sheepdogs like ordinary sheep, but scatter far and wide at some considerable speed. Instead, once a year the islanders herd the sheep communally into a series of **dry-stone "punds"** near Dennis Head, for clipping and dipping, in what is one of the last acts of communal farming practised in Orkney.

The most frequent visitors to the island are ornithologists, who come in considerable numbers to clock the rare migrants who land here briefly on their spring and autumn migrations. The peak times of year for migrants are from late March to early June, and from mid-August to early November, although there are also many breeding species which spend the spring and summer here, including gulls, terns, waders, black guillemots, cormorants and even the odd corncrake. As on Fair Isle (see p.396), there's a permanent **Bird Observatory**, in the southwest corner of the island, who can give advice as to what birds have recently been sighted.

Holland House – built by the Traill family, who bought the island in 1727 – and the two lighthouses at **Dennis Head** are the only features to interrupt the flat horizon. The attractive, stone-built **Old Beacon** was first lit in 1789, but the lantern was replaced by the huge bauble of masonry you now see as long ago as 1809. The **New Lighthouse** (May–Sept Sun noon–5.30pm; at other times by appointment; £4; ☎01857/633257), designed by Alan Stevenson in 1854 half a mile to the north, is the tallest land-based lighthouse in Britain, rising to a height of over 100ft. There's an exhibition on the lighthouse in one of the keepers' cottages, as well as a café. You can also climb to the top of the lighthouse, don white gloves (to protect the brass) and admire the view – on a clear day you can see Fair Isle, and even Sumburgh and Fitful Head on Shetland.

Practicalities

The **ferry** from Kirkwall to North Ronaldsay runs just once a week (usually Fri; 2hr 40min), though day-trips are possible on occasional Sundays between late May and early September (phone ☎01856/872044 for details). Your best bet is to catch a **flight** from Kirkwall (Mon–Sat 3 daily, 2 on Sun; 15min): if you stay the night on the island, you're eligible for a bargain £20 return fare. A **minibus** usually meets the ferries and planes (☎01857/633244) and will take you off to the lighthouse. You can **stay** at the ecofriendly *Bird Observatory* (☎01857/633200, 𝕎 www.nrbo.f2s.com),

.n-suite guest room or in a **hostel** bunk bed; the observatory's *Obscafé* is
.ub/restaurant and serves decent meals. Accommodation is also available at
, a B&B in the northeast of the island (☎01857/633244, ⓔmuir886
.tinternet.com; ❸). The *Burrian Inn*, to the southeast of the war memorial, is the
island's small **pub**, and does hot food. **Bike rental** can be organized: phone
☎01857/633257.

Travel details

Buses on Orkney Mainland

Kirkwall to: Birsay (Mon–Fri 2 daily; 45min);
Burwick (5 daily; 40–55min); Deerness (Mon–Fri 5
daily, 3 on Sat; 30min); Evie (Mon–Sat 4–5 daily;
30min); Houton (Mon–Fri 5 daily, 3 on Sat;
20–40min); Kirkwall Airport (Mon–Sat every
30min–hourly, 9 on Sun; 15min); Skara Brae
(June–Aug Mon–Fri 2 daily; 1hr 15min); St Margaret's Hope (Mon–Sat hourly; 30min); Stromness
(Mon–Sat hourly, 6 on Sun; 30min); Tingwall
(Mon–Fri 4 daily, 2 on Sat; 30–40min).
Stromness to: Skara Brae (Mon–Fri & Sun 3–4
daily; 20min); Tingwall (Wed & Fri 2 daily; 1hr).

Ferries to Orkney

Summer timetable only.
Aberdeen to: Kirkwall (4 weekly; 6hr).
Gills Bay to: St Margaret's Hope (3 daily; 1hr).
John O'Groats to: Burwick (passengers only;
2–4 daily; 40min).
Lerwick to: Kirkwall (3 weekly; 5hr 30min).
Scrabster to: Stromness (2–3 daily; 1hr 30min).

Inter-island ferries

Summer timetable only.
To Eday: Kirkwall–Eday (2–3 daily; 1hr
15min–2hr).
To Egilsay: Tingwall–Egilsay (3–4 daily; 50min–1hr
45min).

To Flotta: Houton–Flotta (Mon–Fri 4 daily, Sat &
Sun 2–3 daily; 45min–1hr).
To Hoy: Houton–Lyness (Mon–Fri 6–8 daily, Sat &
Sun 2–4 daily; 35min–1hr); Stromness–Hoy
(passengers only; Mon–Fri 4–5 daily, Sat & 2 on
Sun; 25min).
To North Ronaldsay: Kirkwall–North Ronaldsay
(Fri; 2hr 40min).
To Papa Westray: Kirkwall–Papa Westray (Tues &
Fri; 2hr 15min); Pierowall (Westray)–Papa Westray
(passengers only; 3–6 daily; 25min).
To Rousay: Tingwall–Rousay (5–6 daily; 30min).
To Sanday: Kirkwall–Sanday (2 daily; 1hr 25min).
To Shapinsay: Kirkwall–Shapinsay (4–5 daily;
25min).
To Stronsay: Kirkwall–Whitehall (2–3 daily; 1hr
40min–2hr).
To Westray: Kirkwall–Westray (2–3 daily; 1hr
25min).
To Wyre: Rousay–Wyre (5–7 daily; 10–20min).

Inter-island flights

Kirkwall to: Eday (Wed; 8–26min); North Ronaldsay
(Mon–Sat 3 daily, 2 on Sun; 15min); Papa Westray
(Mon–Sat 2–3 daily, 1 on Sun; 15–25min); Sanday
(Mon–Fri 2 daily, 1 on Sat; 10min); Stronsay
(Mon–Fri 2 daily, 1 on Sat; 25min); Westray
(Mon–Sat 2 daily, 1 on Sun; 15min).

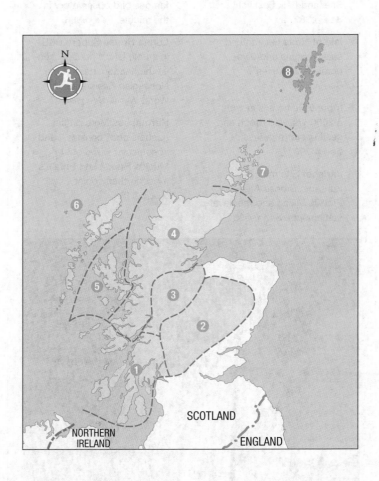

8

Shetland

N

NORTHERN
IRELAND

SCOTLAND

ENGLAND

CHAPTER 8

Highlights

✳ **Traditional music** Catch some local music at the weekly Simmer 'n Sessions in Lerwick, or the annual Shetland Folk Festival. See p.389

✳ **Isle of Noss** Guaranteed seals, puffins and dive-bombing "bonxies". See p.390

✳ **Mousa** Remote islet with a 2000-year-old broch and nesting storm petrels. See p.393

✳ **Jarlshof** Site mingling Iron Age, Bronze Age, Pictish, Viking and medieval settlements. See p.395

✳ **Fair Isle** Magical little island halfway between Shetland and Orkney, with a lighthouse at each end and a world-famous bird observatory in the middle. See p.396

✳ **Lunna House** Superb B&B in an old laird's house, used as the headquarters of the Norwegian Resistance in World War II. See p.404

✳ **Hermaness** More puffins, gannets and "bonxies", and spectacular views out to Muckle Flugga and Britain's most northerly point. See p.413

▲ Shetland folk band, Fiddler's Bid

8

Shetland

Shetland is, in nearly all respects, a complete contrast with Orkney. Orkney lies within sight of the Scottish mainland, whereas Shetland lies beyond the horizon. Most maps plonk the islands in a box somewhere off Aberdeen, but in fact they're a lot closer to Bergen in Norway than Edinburgh, and to the Arctic Circle than Manchester. With little fertile ground, Shetlanders have traditionally been crofters rather than farmers, often looking to the sea for an uncertain living in fishing and whaling or the naval and merchant services. The 20,000 or so islanders tend to refer to themselves as Shetlanders first, and, with the Shetland flag proudly and widely displayed, they regard Scotland as a separate and quite distant entity. As in Orkney, the "Mainland" is the one in their own archipelago, not the Scottish mainland.

Most folk come here for the unique wildlife and **landscape**, a product of the struggle between rock and the forces of water and ice that have, over millennia, tried to break it to pieces. Smoothed by the last glaciation, the coastline's crust of cliffs with caves, blowholes and stacks, testifies to the continuing battle with the weather. Inland (a relative term, since you're never more than three miles from the sea), the treeless terrain is a barren mix of moorland, often studded with peaty lochs.

Whatever else you do in Shetland you're sure to find yourself, at some point or other, in the capital, **Lerwick**, a busy port and the only town of any size. Many parts of Shetland can be reached from here on a day-trip. **South Mainland**, a narrow finger of land that runs some 25 miles from Lerwick to **Sumburgh Head**, is an area rich in archeological remains, including the Iron Age **Mousa Broch** and the ancient settlement of **Jarlshof**. A further 25 miles south of Sumburgh Head is the remote but thriving **Fair Isle**, synonymous with knitwear and exceptional birdlife. The **Westside** of Mainland is bleaker and more sparsely inhabited, as is **North Mainland**. A mile off the west coast, **Papa Stour** boasts some spectacular caves and stacks; much further out are the distinctive peaks and precipitous cliffs of the remote island of **Foula**. Shetland's three **North Isles** bring Britain to a dramatic, windswept end: **Yell** has the largest population of otters in Shetland; **Fetlar** is home to the rare red-necked phalarope; north of **Unst**, there's nothing until you reach the North Pole.

It's impossible to underestimate the influence of the **weather** in these parts. In winter, gales are routine and Shetlanders take even the occasional hurricane in their stride, marking a calm fine day as "a day atween weathers". Even in the summer months, more often than not, it will be windy and rainy; though, as they say in the nearby Faroes, you can have all four seasons in one day. The wind-chill factor is not to be taken lightly, and there is often a dampness or drizzle in the air, even when it's not actually raining. Of course, there are some good spells of dry, sunny weather (which often brings in sea mist) from May to September, but it's the

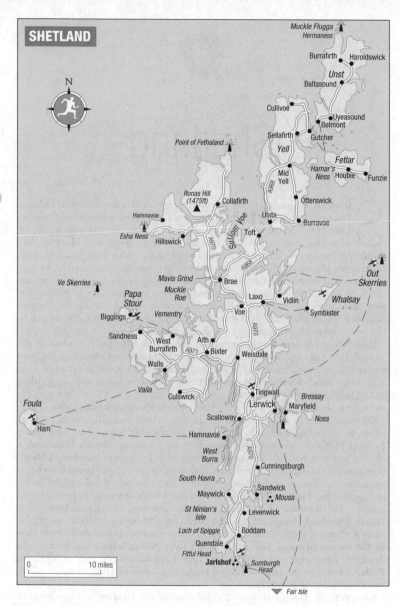

simmer dim, the twilight which lingers through the small hours at this latitude, which makes Shetland summers so memorable.

Some history

Since people first began to explore the North Atlantic, Shetland has been a stepping stone on routes between Britain, Ireland and Scandinavia, and people have lived here since **prehistoric times**, certainly from about 3500 BC. The **Norse settlers** began to

Shetland ponies, sheep and sheepdogs

Shetland is famous for its diminutive **ponies**, but it is still a surprise to find so many of the wee beasts on the islands. Traditionally they were used exclusively as pack animals (although a ninth-century carving on Bressay shows a hooded priest riding a very small pony), and their tails were essential for making fishing nets. During the Industrial Revolution, Shetland ponies were exported to work in the mines in England, since they were the only animals small enough to cope with the low galleries. Shetlands then became the playthings of the English upper classes (the Queen Mother was patron of the Shetland Pony Stud Book Society) and they still enjoy the limelight at the Horse of the Year show. You can see them in action at the annual **Shetland Pony Show** in August, or visit a Shetland pony **stud** near Tingwall airport (℡01595/840330, ℠www.trondraandgottponies.co.uk).

It's not just the ponies that are small on Shetland either; the **sheep** are also less substantial than their mainland counterparts. Thought to be descended from those brought by the Vikings, their wool comes in a wide range of colours, is very fine and is used to make the famous "Fair Isle" patterns and shawls so gossamer-thin that they can be passed through a wedding ring. To round up Shetland's small sheep, an even smaller **sheepdog** was bred, crossed with rough-coated collies. These dogs are now recognized as a separate breed, called "shelties", known for their gentleness and devotion as well as their working characteristics of agility and obedience. Their coat is distinctive, being long, straight and rough over a dense furry undercoat – perfect for Shetland weather.

arrive from about 800 AD, and established Shetland first as part of the Orkney earldom, ruling it directly from Norway after 1195. The Vikings left the islands with a unique cultural character, most evident today in the place names and in the **dialect**, which contains many words from **Norn**, the language spoken here until the nineteenth century (for more on Norn, see p.437). Shetland was never part of the Gaelic-speaking culture of Highland Scotland, and the later Scottish influence is essentially a Lowland one.

In 1469, Shetland followed Orkney in being **mortgaged to Scotland**, King Christian I of Norway being unable to raise the dowry for the marriage of his daughter, Margaret, to King James III. The Scottish king annexed Shetland in 1472 and the mortgage was never redeemed. Though Shetland retained links with other North Sea communities, religious and administrative practice gradually became Scottish, and **mainland lairds** set about grabbing what land and power they could. The economy soon fell increasingly into the hands of **merchant lairds**; they controlled the fish trade and the tenants who supplied it through a system of truck, or forced barter. It wasn't until the 1886 Crofters' Act and the simultaneous rise of **herring fishing** that ordinary Shetlanders gained some security. However, the boom and the prosperity it brought were short-lived and the economy soon slipped into depression.

During the two world wars, thousands of naval, army and air force personnel were drafted in and some notable relics, such as huge coastal guns, remain. **World War II** also cemented the old links with Norway, Shetland playing a remarkable role in supporting the Norwegian Resistance (see box, p.391). Since the 1970s, the **oil industry** has provided a substantial income, which the Shetland Islands Council (SIC) have wisely reinvested in the community, building roads, improving housing and keeping the price of ferry tickets down. The oil boom days are over, though, and **tourism** is slowly beginning to play a more important role in the economy. For the moment, however, comparatively few travellers make it out here, and those that do are as likely to be Faroese or Norwegian as British.

Böds

With only one SYHA hostel in Shetland, it's worth knowing about the islands' unique network of **camping böds** (April–Oct). Traditionally, a böd was a small building beside the shore, where fishermen used to house their gear and occasionally sleep; the word was also applied to trading posts established by Hanseatic merchants. Today, the tourist board uses the term pretty loosely: none of the places they run is strictly speaking a böd, ranging instead from stone-built cottages to weatherboarded sail lofts. To stay at a böd, you must **book in advance** (℡01595/694688, ⓦwww.camping-bods.com), as there are no live-in wardens. All but one of the böds has a solid fuel stove, and all have toilets and a kitchen (though not necessarily hot water, a stove or any cooking utensils), and bunk beds with mattresses. If you're on a camping trip, they're a great way to escape the wind and rain; they're also good value, at around £6–8 per person per night. **Camping rough** is also possible in Shetland, with the landowner's permission, but make sure you're fully equipped for the Shetland wind.

Arrival and island transport

NorthLink Ferries (℡0845/600 0449, ⓦwww.northlinkferries.co.uk) operates a daily overnight **car ferry** from **Aberdeen** to Lerwick, either direct (12hr) or via Kirkwall (14hr). Flybe (℡0870/850 9850) runs direct **flights** from several airports in Scotland to Sumburgh airport, 25 miles south of Lerwick. There are **inter-island flights** from Tingwall airport, five miles west of Lerwick, to Fair Isle, Out Skerries (via Whalsay on request), Papa Stour and Foula; some Fair Isle flights leave from Sumburgh airport. One-way fares from Tingwall to Foula or Fair Isle are around £35; be sure to book well in advance through Directflight (℡01595/840246), as they're ten-seater planes, and be prepared for the flight to be cancelled due to the weather. To reach Tingwall airport, there's a dial-a-ride taxi service (£1.70), which must be booked a day in advance (℡01595/745745).

Public transport is pretty good in Shetland, with **buses** fanning out from Lerwick to just about every corner of Mainland, and even via ferries across to Yell and Unst. Various **tours** are also available from specialists such as Shetland Wildlife (℡01950/422483, ⓦwww.shetlandwildlife.co.uk). Given the price of bringing a car on the ferry to Shetland, it's worth considering **car rental** once on the islands: Bolts Car Hire (℡01595/693636, ⓦwww.boltscarhire.co.uk) or Star Rent-a-Car (℡01595/692075, ⓦwww.starrentacar.co.uk) all have vehicles available at Sumburgh airport and Lerwick. **Cycling** are hard going due to the almost constant wind.

The council-run **inter-island ferries** are excellent: journey times are mostly less than half an hour, and fares are kept very low. It's also possible to take **boat trips** for pleasure, to explore the coastline and spot birds, seals, porpoises, dolphins and whales; operators include Shetland Wildlife (see above), Seabirds and Seals (℡07595/540224, ⓦwww.seabirds-and-seals.com) and Tom Jamieson from Sandwick for the Broch of Mousa (℡01950/431367, ⓦwww.mousa.co.uk). The more adventurous should contact Sea Kayak Shetland (℡01595/840272, ⓦwww.seakayakshetland.co.uk).

Lerwick

LERWICK is home to about seven thousand people, just under a third of the islands' population, and is very much the focus of Shetland's commercial life. All year, its sheltered **harbour** at the heart of the town is busy with ferries, fishing boats, oil-rig supply vessels and a variety of more specialized craft including seismic-survey and naval vessels from all round the North Sea. In summer, the quayside comes alive with local pleasure craft, visiting yachts, cruise liners, historic vessels such as the restored *Swan* and the occasional tall sailing ship. Behind the old harbour is the compact town centre, made up of one long main street, Commercial Street; from here, narrow lanes, known as "**closses**", rise westwards to the late Victorian new town.

Leir Vik ("Muddy Bay") was established in the seventeenth century to cater for the **Dutch** herring fleet, which brought in as many as 20,000 men. It was burnt down in 1614 and 1625 by the jealous and disapproving folk of Scalloway, and again in 1702 by the French fleet. During the nineteenth century, with the presence of ever-larger Scottish, English and Scandinavian boats, it became a major **fishing** centre, and whalers called to pick up crews on their way to the northern hunting grounds. Business was from the jetties of buildings known as **lodberries** (from the Old Norse for "loading rock"), several of which survive beyond the *Queen's Hotel*. **Smuggling** was part of the daily routine, and secret tunnels – some of which still exist – connected the lodberries to illicit stores. Lerwick expanded in the Victorian era, and the large houses and grand public buildings established then still dominate, notably the landmark **Town Hall**. Another period of rapid growth began during the oil boom of the 1970s, with the farmland to the southwest disappearing under a suburban sprawl, the town's northern approaches becoming an industrial estate.

Arrival and information

Lerwick's **ferry terminal** lies in the north harbour, about a mile from the town centre. **Flying** into Sumburgh airport, you can take one of the regular buses to Lerwick or take a taxi (around £25). **Buses** stop on the Esplanade, by the old harbour, or at the Viking Bus Station on Commercial Road, north of the town centre. **Bike rental** is available from Grantfield Garage (℡01595/692709, ⓦwww.grantfield-garage.co.uk), on Commercial Road, between the town centre and the ferry terminal.

The **tourist office**, at the Market Cross on Commercial Street (April–Oct Mon–Fri 9am–5pm, Sat & Sun 10am–4pm; Nov–March Mon–Fri 9am–5pm; ℡01595/669343), is a good source of information, and will book accommodation for a small fee.

Accommodation

Shetland's best **hotels** are not to be found in Lerwick – the town's **B&Bs** and **guesthouses** are usually better value for money, and will allow you to get closer to Shetland life.

The SYHA **hostel** (April–Sept; ℡01595/692114, ⓦwww.syha.org.uk) at Isles-burgh House on King Harald Street, offers unusually comfortable surroundings and has family rooms, a café, free wi-fi and laundry facilities. The *Clickimin* **campsite** (May–Sept; ℡01595/741000) enjoys the excellent facilities of the neighbouring leisure centre, but its sheltered suburban location, west of the town centre, is far from idyllic.

Hotels, guesthouses and B&Bs

Aald Harbour 7 Church Rd ℡01595/690870. Situated just a minute's stroll from the harbour, this is a well-run B&B with modern furnishings and very welcoming hosts. **③**

Brentham House 7 Harbour St ℡01595/460201, ⓦwww.brenthamhouse.co.uk. Spacious, newly furnished rooms in a Victorian, bay-fronted terrace; no reception, and no proper breakfast – you pick the keys up from *Baroc*, the bar a couple of doors down. **④**

Fort Charlotte Guest House 1 Charlotte St ☎01595/692140, ⊛www.fortcharlotte.co.uk. Small guesthouse with a great central location (by the fort), good-sized rooms and a friendly proprietor. ❸

Seafield Farm Off Sea Rd ☎01595/693853. A very friendly B&B in a huge modern farmhouse overlooking the sea, a mile or so southwest of town and therefore best for those with their own transport. ❷

Westhall Lower Sound ☎01595/694247, ⊛www .bedandbreakfastlerwick.co.uk. A splendid Victorian mansion, known locally as the "Sheriff's Hoose", set in its own grounds a mile or so southwest of town overlooking a bay. Rooms are spacious, the breakfasts are immense and there's free wi-fi. ❺

The Town

Lerwick's attractive main street is the narrow, winding, flagstone-clad **Commercial Street**, set back one block from the Esplanade. The street's buildings exhibit a mixed bag of architectural styles, from the powerful neo-Baroque of the Bank of Scotland at no. 117 to the plainer houses and old lodberries at the south end, beyond the *Queen's Hotel*. Here, you'll find **Bain's Beach**, a small, hidden stretch of golden sand that's one of the prettiest spots in Lerwick. Further south lie the Victorian Anderson Homes and the Anderson High School, the latter's ornate, Franco-Scottish towers and dormers now unfortunately rather lost among later additions. Both were the gift of **Arthur Anderson** (1792–1868), co-founder of the Peninsular and Oriental Steam Navigation Company (P&O), for more on whom see p.388.

The Street's northern end is marked by the towering walls of **Fort Charlotte** (daily: June–Sept 9am–10pm; Oct–May 9am–4pm; free), which once stood directly above the beach. Begun for Charles II in 1665 during the wars with the Dutch, the fort was attacked and burnt down by the Dutch fleet in August 1673. In the 1780s it was repaired and given its name in honour of George III's queen. Since then, it's served as a prison and a Royal Navy training centre; it's now open

Up Helly-Aa

On the last Tuesday in January, whatever the weather, Lerwick's new town is the setting for the most spectacular part of **Up Helly-Aa**, the largest of several fire festivals held in Shetland from January to March. Around nine hundred torchbearing participants, all male and all in extraordinary costumes, march in procession behind a grand Viking longship. The annually appointed Guizer Jarl and his "squad" appear as Vikings and brandish shields and silver axes; each of the forty or so other squads is dressed for their part in the subsequent entertainment, perhaps as giant insects, space invaders or ballet dancers. Their circuitous route leads to the King George V Playing Field where, after due ceremony, all the torches are thrown into the longship, creating an enormous bonfire. A firework display follows, then the participants, known as "guizers", set off in their squads to do the rounds of more than a dozen "halls" (including the Town Hall) from around 8.30pm in the evening until 8am the next morning, performing some kind of act – usually a comedy routine – at each.

Up Helly-Aa dates from Victorian times, when it was introduced to replace the much older Christmas tradition of rolling burning tar-barrels through the streets, a practice banned in 1874. Seven years later a torchlight procession took place, which eventually developed into a full-blown Viking celebration, known as "Up Helly-Aa". Although this is essentially a community event with entry to halls by invitation only, visitors are welcome at the Town Hall – contact the tourist office well in advance. To catch some of the atmosphere of the event, check out the Up Helly-Aa exhibition in the **Galley Shed** on St Sunniva Street (mid-May to mid-Sept Tues 2–4pm & 7–9pm, Fri 7–9pm, Sat 2–4pm; £3), where you can see a full-sized longship, costumes, shields and photographs.

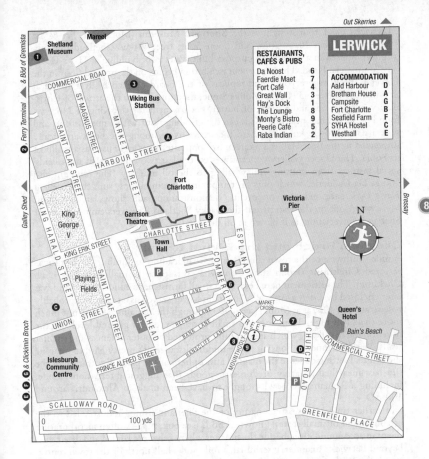

to the public, except on rare occasions when it's used by the Territorial Army, and affords good views across Bressay Sound.

Although the narrow lanes or **closses** that connect the Street to Hillhead are now a desirable place to live, it's not so long ago that they were regarded as slum-like dens of iniquity, from which the better-off escaped to the Victorian new town laid out to the west on a grid plan. The steep stone-flagged lanes are fun to explore, each one lined by tall houses with trees, fuchsias, flowering currants and honeysuckle pouring over the garden walls. If you look at the street signs, you can see that all the closses have two names: their former ones and their current titles, chosen in 1845 by the Police Commissioners – Reform, Fox and Pitt, reflecting the liberal political culture of the period – or derived from the writings of Sir Walter Scott.

Hillhead, up in the Victorian new town, is dominated by the splendid **Town Hall** (Mon–Thurs 9am–5pm, Fri 9am–4pm; free), a Scottish Baronial monument to civic pride, built by public subscription. Visitors are free to wander round the building (providing there are no functions going on), to admire the wonderful stained-glass windows in the main hall, which celebrate Shetland's history, and to climb the castellated central tower that occupies the town's highest point.

Lerwick's chief tourist sight is the **Shetland Museum** (Mon–Wed, Fri & Sat 10am–5pm, Thurs 10am–7pm, Sun noon–5pm; free; ⓦwww.shetland-museum .org.uk), housed in a wonderful purpose-built waterfront building at Hay's Dock, off Commercial Road. The permanent exhibition begins on the ground floor in the Lower Gallery, where you'll find replicas of the hoard of Pictish silver found at St Ninian's Isle (see p.394); the Monks Stone, thought to show the arrival of Christianity in Shetland; and a block of butter, tax payment for the King of Norway, found preserved in a peat bog. Kids can try grinding flour with a quern stone, and visit a dark "trowie knowe" where the trows live. Among the boats artistically suspended in the Boat Hall is a sixareen (see opposite) amazingly used as a mailboat to Foula. The Upper Gallery concentrates on the last two centuries of the islands' social history, from knitting and whaling to the oil industry. The museum also houses Da Gadderie, which puts on temporary art exhibitions, runs the excellent *Hay's Dock* café and puts on events, demonstrations and shows archive films. Meanwhile, out on the waterfront, the wacky Shetland Receivers emit snippets of Shetland conversation, as if blown in on the wind.

Clickimin Broch and the Böd of Gremista

A mile southwest of the town centre on the road leading to Sumburgh, the much-restored **Clickimin Broch** stands on what was once a small island in Loch Clickimin. The settlement here began as a small farmstead around 700 BC and was later enclosed by a defensive wall. The main tower served as a castle and probably rose to around 40ft, as at Mousa (see p.393), though the remains are now not much more than 10ft high. There are two small entrances, one at ground level and the other on the first floor, which are carefully protected by outer defences and smaller walls. With the modern housing in the middle distance, it's pretty hard to imagine the original setting or sense the magical atmosphere of the place. Excavation of the site has unearthed an array of domestic goods that suggest international trade, including a Roman glass bowl thought to have been made in Alexandria around 100 AD.

In earlier times, the seasonal nature of the Shetland fishing industry led to the establishment of small stores, known as **böds** (see box, p.384), often incorporating sleeping accommodation, beside the beaches where fish were landed and dried. Just beyond Lerwick's main ferry terminal, a mile and a half north of the town centre, stands the **Böd of Gremista** (May–Sept Tues–Sat 10am–1pm & 2–5pm; free), the birthplace of **Arthur Anderson** (1792–1868). Though almost lost among the surrounding industrial estate, the building has been completely restored and the displays explore Anderson's life as beach boy (helping to cure and dry fish), naval seaman, businessman, philanthropist, Shetland's first native MP and founder of Shetland's first newspaper, the *Shetland Journal*. Built at the end of the eighteenth century for Anderson's father, the ground floor was originally used as an office and fish-curing station, while the trader and his family resided permanently upstairs.

Eating

Shetland produces a huge harvest of fresh fish from the surrounding seas, and has its own celebrated local delicacy, *reestit* mutton: steeped in brine, then air-dried, it's the base for a potato soup cooked around New Year. Unfortunately, the **food** on offer in many of Lerwick's hotels and pubs doesn't always live up to its potential. It's not even possible to assemble a decent picnic without resorting to a visit to the supermarket, situated a mile southwest of town, or the one on the way to the ferry terminal.

Daytime cafés

Faerdie-Maet Commercial St (by the post office). Cosy café serving generously filled rolls, as well as cakes, teas, real cappuccino and good ice cream. Closed Sun.

Peerie Café Esplanade. Funky designer shop/gallery/café in an old lodberry, with a good range of cakes, soup and sandwiches, and what is probably Britain's northernmost latte. Closed Sun.

Restaurants

Fort Café 2 Commercial St. Lerwick's best fish-and-chip shop, situated below Fort Charlotte: take away or eat inside in the small café. Closed Sun lunch.

Hay's Dock Shetland Museum, Hay's Dock ☎01595/741569, ⒲www.haysdock.co.uk.

Bright, modern, licensed café/restaurant in the museum, with a great view over the north bay, and a short but imaginative menu of local dishes, filled bannocks and cakes. Closed Mon & Sun eve.

Great Wall Viking Bus Station ☎01595/693988. A Chinese/Thai restaurant located above the bus station. Highly rated by the locals.

Monty's Bistro 5 Mounthooly St ☎01595/696555. Unpretentious place serving inexpensive and delicious meals and snacks at lunchtimes, and accomplished contemporary cooking in the evening, with friendly service. Closed Sun & Mon.

Raba Indian Restaurant 26 Commercial Rd ☎01595/695585. A consistently excellent curry-house, with cheerful, efficient service and reasonable prices.

Drinking, nightlife and entertainment

The friendliest **pub** is the upstairs bar in *The Lounge*, up Mounthooly Street, where local musicians often do sessions. The Garrison Theatre (☎01595/692114), by the Town Hall, shows occasional **films** as well as putting on theatre productions, comedy acts and live gigs. There are also **informal sessions** over the summer held regularly in various venues on the islands including *The Lounge* and *Da Noost*, two pubs on Commercial Street.

Traditional music features very strongly in Shetland life, with the emphasis firmly on instrumental – particularly fiddle – music. For details of **what's on**, listen in to BBC Radio Shetland, 92.7 FM (Mon–Fri 5.30pm), visit ⒲www.shetland-music.com, or buy the *Shetland Times* on Fridays (⒲www.shetlandtoday.co.uk) from any newsagent or the excellent Shetland Times **bookshop**, opposite the post office on Commercial Street. There are numerous music festivals throughout the summer, starting in late April with the excellent four-day **Shetland Folk Festival** (☎01595/694757, ⒲www.shetlandfolkfestival.com), which embraces a wide range of musical styles, with concerts and dances in every corner of the islands. The season finishes in mid-October with the **Accordion and Fiddle Festival** (⒲www.shetland accordionandfiddle.com). To pick up a CD of traditional Shetland music, head for High Level Music, up the steps by the chemist's on the Market Cross.

Another Shetland passion is **boating and yachting**, and regattas take place most summer weekends, in different venues throughout the islands. The sport of **yoal racing** has a big following, too, and teams from different districts compete passionately in sixareens, large six-oared boats which replaced yoals as the backbone of Shetland's fishing fleet. If you plan ahead, you could take a trip on the *Swan* (☎01595/697406, ⒲www.swantrust.com), a restored wooden **sailing ship**, which undertakes trips from one to nine days' long. Alternatively, the replica Viking longship, *Dim Riv* (☎07970/864189, ⒲www.dimriv.co.uk), takes passengers on regular trips around Bressay Sound.

Bressay and Noss

Shielding Lerwick from the full force of the North Sea is the island of **Bressay**, dominated at its southern end by the conical Ward Hill (744ft) – "da Wart" – and accessible on an hourly car and passenger ferry from Lerwick (takes 5min). At the end of the nineteenth century, Bressay had a population of around eight hundred, due mostly to the prosperity brought by the Dutch herring fleet; now less than four hundred people live here. If you've time to kill before the ferry, go for a pint in the nearby hotel and pub *Maryfield House*, or pop into the **Bressay Heritage Centre** (May–Sept Tues, Wed, Fri & Sat 10am–4pm, Sun 11am–5pm; free), by the ferry terminal in **MARYFIELD**, where the local history group puts on temporary exhibitions. A Bronze Age **burnt mound** – essentially a pile of discarded rocks and charcoal used in fires – has been reconstructed next to the centre. A short distance to the north lies **Gardie House**, built in 1724 and, in its Neoclassical detail, one of the finest of Shetland's laird houses, where the likes of Sir Walter Scott and minor royalty once stayed, and now home to the Lord Lieutenant of Shetland.

In 1917, convoys of merchant ships would gather in Bressay Sound before travelling under naval escort across the Atlantic. Huge World War I gun batteries at Score Hill on Aith Ness in the north, and on Bard Head in the south, were constructed, and now provide a focus for a couple of interesting cliff and coastal walks. Another fine walk can be made to **Bressay Lighthouse**, three miles south of the ferry terminal at Kirkibuster Ness, built by the Stevensons in the 1850s.

Noss

The chief reason most visitors pass through Bressay is to visit the tiny but spectacular island of **Noss** – the name means "a point of rock" – just off Bressay's eastern shore. Sloping gently into the sea at its western end, and plunging vertically from over 500ft at its eastern end, Noss has the dramatic and distinctive outline of a half-sunk ocean liner. The island was inhabited until World War II but is now a nature reserve and sheep farm, partly managed by Scottish Natural Heritage, who operate an RIB as a **ferry** from Bressay (May–Aug Tues, Wed & Fri–Sun 11am–5pm; £3 return; phone ⓣ0800/107 7818 before setting off). The ferry departs from the landing stage two miles from Maryfield – an easy stroll or short journey on bikes rented in Lerwick beforehand. Another way to see Bressay and Noss is to join one of the **boat trips** that set out from Lerwick: try Seabirds and Seals (mid-April to mid-Sept; £40; ⓣ07595/540224, ⓦwww.seabirds-and-seals.com).

On the island, the old farmhouse, or Haa of Gungstie, contains a small **visitor centre** (open whenever the ferry is operating), where the warden will give you a quick briefing and a free map. Nearby is a sandy beach, perfect for a picnic in fine weather, while behind the Haa is a **Pony Pund**, a square stone enclosure built for the breeding of Shetland ponies. A stud was established here in the late nineteenth century, when the Marquis of Londonderry needed ponies to replace the women and children who had been displaced by new laws from his coal mines in County Durham. The animals were specially bred to produce "as much weight as possible and as near the ground as it can be got". The stud was closed in 1899, and superseded by English studs able to meet the demand at lower cost. There are no ponies on Noss today, but it's said that the influence of the breeding programme can still be seen in those roaming other parts of Shetland.

As Noss is only one mile wide, it's easy enough to do an entire circumference of the island in one day. If you do, make sure you keep close to the coast, since otherwise the great skuas (locally known as "bonxies") will dive-bomb you. The most memorable feature of Noss is its eastern coastline of cliffs, rising to a peak at the massive **Noup** (500ft), from which can be seen vast colonies of cliff-nesting gannets, puffins, guillemots, shags, razorbills and fulmars: a truly wonderful sight and one of the highlights of Shetland. Another feature visible on the walk is the **Holm of Noss**; until 1864, it was connected to the main island by an extraordinary device called a cradle, a sort of basket suspended on ropes which was intended to allow access for the grazing of sheep. The Foula man who allegedly installed it in the seventeenth century is said to have died when, preferring to climb back down the cliffs, he fell.

Central Mainland

The districts of Tingwall and Weisdale, plus the old capital of **Scalloway**, make up the **Central Mainland**, an area of minor interest in the grand scheme of things, but one that is very easy to reach from Lerwick. In fine weather, it's a captivating mix of farms, moors and lochs, and includes Shetland's only significant woodland. The area also holds strong historical associations, with the Norse parliament at **Law Ting Holm**, unhappy memories of Earl Patrick Stewart's harsh rule at Scalloway and nineteenth-century Clearances at Weisdale.

Scalloway

Approaching **SCALLOWAY** from the shoulder of the steep hill to the east known as the **Scord**, there's a dramatic view over the town and the islands to the south and west. Once the capital of Shetland, Scalloway's importance waned through the eighteenth century as Lerwick, just six miles to the east, grew in trading success and status. Nowadays, Scalloway is fairly sleepy, though its prosperity, always closely linked to the fluctuations of the fishing industry, has recently been given a boost with investment in fish-processing factories, and in the impressive North Atlantic Fisheries College on the west side of the busy harbour.

In spite of modern developments nearby, Scalloway is dominated by the imposing shell of **Scalloway Castle**, a classic fortified tower-house built with forced labour in 1600 by the infamous Earl Patrick Stewart, and thus seen as a powerful symbol of oppression. Stewart, who'd succeeded his father Robert to the Earldom of Orkney and Lordship of Shetland in 1592, held court in the castle and gained a reputation for

The Shetland Bus

The story of the **Shetland Bus** – the link between Shetland and Norway that helped to sustain the Norwegian Resistance through the years of Nazi occupation – is quite extraordinary. Under threat of attack by enemy aircraft or naval action, small Norwegian fishing boats set out from Shetland to run arms and resistance workers into lonely fjords. The trip took at least 24 hours and on the return journey boats brought back Norwegians in danger of arrest by the Gestapo, or those who wanted to join Norwegian forces fighting with the Allies. For three years, through careful planning, the operation was remarkably successful: instructions to boats were passed in cryptic messages in BBC radio broadcasts. Local people knew what was going on, but the secret was generally well kept. In total, 350 refugees were evacuated, and more than 400 tons of arms, large amounts of explosives and 60 radio transmitters were landed in Norway.

Originally established at **Lunna** in the northeast of the Mainland, the service moved to **Scalloway** in 1942, partly because the village could offer good marine engineering facilities at Moore's Shipyard on Main Street, where a plaque records the morale-boosting visit of the Norwegian Crown Prince Olav. Many buildings in Scalloway were pressed into use to support the work: explosives and weapons were stored in the castle. **Kergord House** in Weisdale was used as a safe house and training centre for intelligence personnel and saboteurs. The hazards, tragedies and elations of the exercise are brilliantly described in David Howarth's book, *The Shetland Bus*; their legacy today is a heartfelt closeness between Shetland and Norway.

enhancing his own power and wealth through the calculated use of harsh justice, frequently including confiscation of assets. He was eventually arrested and imprisoned in 1609, not for his ill-treatment of Shetlanders, but for his aggressive behaviour toward his fellow landowners; his son, Robert, attempted an insurrection and both were executed in Edinburgh in 1615. The castle was used for a time by Cromwell's army, but had fallen into disrepair by 1700 and is nowadays in the hands of Historic Scotland. The castle itself is well preserved and fun to explore; if the door is locked, the key can be borrowed from the *Scalloway Hotel*.

On Main Street, the small **Scalloway Museum** (May–Sept Mon–Sat 10am–noon & 2–4.30pm; free), run by volunteers, holds a few local relics. It also explains the importance of fishing and tells the story of the **Shetland Bus** (see box, p.391), a memorial for which stands along the harbour at Mid Shore.

Scalloway has very little **accommodation** apart from the *Scalloway Hotel* (℡01595/880444, ⓦwww.scalloway-hotel.com; ❸), on the harbourfront, whose bar acts as the local pub, and serves delicious bar **food**. Alternatively, you can stay at the wood-clad *Windward* B&B (℡01595/880769, ⓦwww.accommodation -shetland.co.uk/; ❷), at the far western end of the bay, close to the North Atlantic Fisheries College (ⓦwww.nafc.ac.uk). The college also runs *Da Haaf* (℡01595/880747), a daytime coffee bar (Mon–Fri only) serving toasted paninis and pasties and a restaurant (Wed–Fri lunch, Thurs & Fri eve) specializing in a wide range of fresh fish, simply prepared, with broad harbour views to enjoy.

Trondra and Burra

Southwest of Scalloway – and connected to the Mainland by a bridge since 1971 – is the island of **Trondra**, where you can visit a working crofthouse, situated in a lovely spot in the centre of the island. Pick up a leaflet and a bucket of feed for the hens from the barn, and head off along the **Croft Trail**, which takes you to see the ducks, down to the shore (a good picnic spot), over to a restored watermill and then through a field of orchids, buttercups and other flowers.

Further south, the Burra Bridge connects Trondra with the twin islands of East and West **Burra**, which have some beautiful beaches and some fairly gentle coastal walks. West Burra has the largest settlement in the area, **HAMNAVOE**, unique among Shetland villages in having been planned by the local landlord as a fishing port. Just south of Hamnavoe, a small path leads down from the road to the white sandy beach at **Meal**. At the southern end of West Burra, at **Banna Minn**, there's another fine beach, with excellent walking nearby on the cliffs of Kettla Ness, linked to the rest of West Burra only by a sliver of tombolo.

East Burra, joined to West Burra at the middle like a Siamese twin, ends at the hamlet of **HOUSS**, distinguished by the tall, ruined laird's house or Haa. From the turning place outside the cattlegrid, continue walking southwards, following the track to the left, down the hill and across the beach, and after about a mile you'll reach the deserted settlement of **Symbister**, inhabited until the 1940s. You can now see ancient field boundaries and, just south of the ruins, a **burnt mound**. Half a mile further south, the island ends in cliffs, caves and wheeling fulmars. From there, the islet of **South Havra**, topped by the ruins of Shetland's only **windmill**, is just to the southwest. Once supporting a small fishing community, the islet was abandoned by the last eight families in 1923; it was such a perilous existence that children as well as animals had to be tethered to prevent them from falling over the cliffs.

Tingwall and Weisdale

TINGWALL, the name for the loch-studded, fertile valley to the north of Scalloway, takes its name from the **Lawting** or Althing (from *thing*, the Old Norse for "parliament"), in existence from the eleventh to the sixteenth century, where local people and officials gathered to make or amend laws and discuss evidence. The Lawting was situated at **Law Ting Holm**, the small peninsula at the northern end of Loch Tingwall that was once an island linked to the shore by a causeway. Although structures on the holm have long since vanished, there's an information board which helps in visualizing the scene. At the southwest corner of the loch, a seven-foot **standing stone** by the roadside is said to mark the spot where, after a dispute at the Lawting in 1389, Earl Henry Sinclair killed his cousin and rival, Marise Sperra, together with seven of his followers.

Just north of the loch is **Tingwall Kirk**, unexceptional from the outside, but preserving its simple late eighteenth-century interior. In the burial ground, there's a dank, turf-covered **burial aisle** from the old medieval church that was demolished in 1788. Inside are several very old gravestones, including one to a local official called a *Foud* – a representative of the king – who died in 1603.

The parish of **WEISDALE**, five miles northwest of Tingwall, is notable primarily for **Weisdale Mill** (Tues–Sat 10.30am–4.30pm, Sun noon–4.30pm; free), situated up the B9075 from the head of Weisdale Voe. Built for milling grain in 1855, this is now an attractively converted arts centre, housing the small, beautifully designed **Bonhoga Gallery**, in which touring and local exhibitions of painting, sculpture and other media are shown. There's also a very pleasant **café**, serving soup, scones and snacks in the south-facing conservatory overlooking the stream.

South Mainland

Shetland's **South Mainland** is a long, thin finger of land, only three or four miles wide but 25 miles long, ending in the cliffs of **Sumburgh Head** and **Fitful Head**. It's a beautiful area with wild undulating landscapes, lots of good green farmland, fabulous views out to sea and the mother of all brochs on the island of **Mousa**, just off the east coast. The most concentrated points of interest are at the southern end of the peninsula, with its sea bird colonies, crofting museum, and **Jarlshof**, Shetland's most impressive archeological treasure.

Mousa

Halfway down the east coast of South Mainland, the island of **Mousa** boasts the most amazingly well-preserved broch in the whole of Scotland. Rising to more than 40ft, and looking rather like a Stone-Age cooling tower, **Mousa Broch** has a remarkable presence, and features in both *Egil's Saga* and the *Orkneyinga Saga*, contemporary chronicles of Norse exploration and settlement. In the former, a couple eloping from Norway to Iceland around 900 AD take refuge in it after being shipwrecked, while in the latter the broch is besieged by an Earl Harald Maddadarson when his mother is abducted and brought here from Orkney by Erlend the Young, who wanted to marry her. The broch's low entrance-passage leads through two concentric walls to a central courtyard, divided into separate beehive chambers. Between the walls, a rough (very dark) staircase leads to the top parapet; a torch is provided for visitors.

A small **passenger ferry** runs to Mousa either from Aithsvoe in Cunningsburgh or Leebotten in Sandwick (April to mid-Sept; 25min; £13 return; ☎01950/431367, ⓦwww.mousaboattrips.co.uk). Mousa is only a mile wide, but if the weather's not too bad it's easy enough to spend the whole day here. For a start, there are usually lots of grey and common **seals** sunning themselves on the rocks at the southeastern corner of the island, plus black guillemots (or "tysties" as they're known locally) breeding along the low-lying coast, and arctic tern colonies inland. Thousands of **storm petrels** breed around the broch, fishing out at sea during the day and only returning to the nests after dark. The ferry runs special late-night trips (late May to mid-July Wed & Sat weather permitting), setting off in the "simmer dim" twilight around 11pm. Even if you've no interest in the storm petrels, which appear like bats as they flit about in the half-light, the chance to explore the broch at midnight is worth it alone.

In Hoswick, a mile or so southwest of Leebotton, is **Hoswick Visitor Centre** (May–Sept Mon–Sat 10am–5pm, Sun 11am–5pm; free), with a fantastic collection of vintage radios, and a permanent exhibition on crofting, haaf fishing, whaling, and the copper and iron mines beyond Sand Lodge. The Betty Mouat story (see opposite) is also told here and there's a café serving cakes, tea and coffee.

St Ninian's Isle to Quendale

Halfway down the South Mainland, a road leads across to **BIGTON**, on the west coast. From the village, a signposted track leads down to a spectacular sandy causeway, or **tombolo**, leading to **St Ninian's Isle**. The tombolo – a concave strip of shell sand with Atlantic breakers crashing on either side – is usually exposed; you can walk over to the island, where there are the ruins of a church probably dating from the twelfth century and built on the site of an earlier, Pictish, one. The site was excavated in the 1950s and **treasure**, a hoard of 28 objects of Pictish silver, was found hidden in a larch box beneath a slab in the earlier building's floor; the larch probably came from the European mainland, as it didn't grow in Britain at that time. The treasure included bowls, a spoon and brooches and is thought to date from around 800 AD; it may have been hastily hidden during a Norse raid. Replicas are in the Shetland Museum in Lerwick and the originals can be seen in the Museum of Scotland in Edinburgh.

South of Bigton, the coast is attractive: cliffs alternate with beaches and the vivid greens and yellows of the farmland contrast with black rocks and a sea which may be grey, deep blue or turquoise. The **Loch of Spiggie**, which used to be a sea inlet, attracts large autumn flocks of some two hundred whooper swans; it's pretty quiet the rest of the year, though you've a chance of spotting red-throated divers. A track leads from the east side of the loch to a long, reasonably sheltered sandy beach known as the **Scousburgh Sands** or Spiggie Beach.

Over on the east coast, a back road winds around to the **Crofthouse Museum** (mid-April to Sept daily 10am–1pm & 2–5pm; free) in Southvoe. Housed in a fairly well to do thatched croft built around 1870, the museum tries to re-create the feel of late nineteenth-century crofting life, with a peat fire, traditional box beds and so forth. Adjacent to the living quarters is the byre for the cows and tatties, and the kiln for drying the grain. Crofting was mostly done by women in Shetland, while the men went out haaf fishing for the laird. Down by the nearby burn, there's also a restored, thatched horizontal mill.

A few miles south of the Loch of Spiggie lies **QUENDALE**, overlooking a sandy south-facing bay. The village contains the beautifully restored full-size **Quendale Watermill** (mid-April to mid-Oct daily 10am–5pm; £2; ⓦwww .quendalemill.shetland.co.uk), built in the 1860s but not in operation since the early 1970s. You can explore the interior and watch a short video of the mill working, and there's a tearoom attached. Not far from Quendale, near the head of the rocky inlet of Cro Geo, on the other side of Garths Ness, lies a rusting ship's bow, all that remains of the **Braer oil tanker** that ran onto the rocks here on January 5, 1993, a wild Tuesday morning etched in the memory of every

Shetlander. Although the *Braer* released twice the quantity of oil spilt even by the *Exxon Valdez* in Alaska, the damage was less serious than it might have been, due to the oil being churned and ultimately cleansed by huge waves driven by hurricane-force winds which, unusually even for Shetland, blew for most of January.

Sumburgh

Shetland's southernmost parish is known as **DUNROSSNESS** or "The Ness", a rolling agricultural landscape (often likened to that of Orkney), dominated from the west by the great brooding mass of Fitful Head (929ft). The main road leads to **SUMBURGH**, whose **airport** is busy with helicopters and aircraft shuttling to and from the North Sea oilfields, as well as passenger services, and **GRUTNESS**, the minuscule **ferry terminal** for Fair Isle.

Extending the airport revealed a vast Iron-Age archaological site known as **Old Scatness Broch & Iron Age Village** (May–Sept Mon–Thurs & Sun 10am–5pm; £4). At the centre of the site are the remains of an Iron Age broch, surrounded by a settlement of interlocking wheelhouses – so called because of their circular groundplan. Visits of the site are led by costumed guides, who will take you around the ongoing dig and inside two of the wheelhouses that have been either partially or wholly reconstructed.

In the nearby village of Scatness itself is **Betty Mouat's Cottage** (now a camping böd). Betty Mouat was quite a character. In January 1886, at the age of 60, she set off for Lerwick in the smack *Columbine*, crewed by three local men. A storm swept the skipper overboard and the other two jumped in to try to rescue him; they failed, the skipper drowned and the two men, though they survived, lost contact with the smack. Betty and her boat were battered by the storm for nine days and nights, finally running ashore north of Ålesund in Norway. Astonishingly, she survived this experience, existing on some milk which she had with her. She returned to Shetland to become a celebrity, living into her nineties.

The Mainland comes to a dramatic end at **Sumburgh Head** (262ft), which rises sharply out of the land only to drop vertically into the sea. The **lighthouse**, on the top of the cliff, was built by Robert Stevenson in 1821, and the road up to the lighthouse is the perfect site for watching nesting sea birds such as kittiwakes, fulmars, shags, razorbills and guillemots, not to mention gannets diving for fish. This is also the easiest place in Shetland to get close to **puffins**: during the nesting season (May to early Aug), you simply need to look over the western wall, just before you enter the lighthouse complex, to see them arriving at their burrows a few yards below with beakfuls of sand eels or giving flying lessons to their offspring.

Jarlshof

Of all the archeological sites in Shetland, **Jarlshof** (April–Sept daily 9.30am–5.30pm; HS; £4.70) is the largest and most impressive. What makes Jarlshof so amazing is the fact that you can walk right into a house built 1600 years ago, which is still intact to above head height. The site is big and confusing, scattered with the ruins of buildings dating from the Stone Age to the early seventeenth century. The name, which is misleading as it is not primarily a Viking site, was coined by Sir Walter Scott, who decided to use the ruins of the Old House in his novel *The Pirate*. However, it was only at the end of the nineteenth century that the Bronze Age, Iron Age and Viking settlements you see now were discovered, after a violent storm ripped off the top layer of turf.

The Bronze Age smithy and Iron Age dwellings nearest the entrance, dating from the second and first millennia BC, are nothing compared with the cells which cluster around the **broch**, close to the sea. Only half of the original broch survives, and its courtyard is now an Iron-Age aisled roundhouse, with stone piers. However, it's difficult to distinguish the broch from the later Pictish **wheelhouses** which now surround it. Still, it's all great fun to explore, as you're free to roam around the cells, checking out the in-built stone shelving, water tanks, beds and so on. Inland lies the maze of grass-topped foundations marking out the **Viking longhouses**, from the ninth century AD. Towering over the whole complex are the ruins of the laird's house, built by Robert Stewart, Earl of Orkney and Lord of Shetland, in the late sixteenth century, and the **Old House of Sumburgh**, built by his son, Earl Patrick.

South Mainland practicalities

There are some excellent **accommodation** choices in the South Mainland, starting with ⚓ *Mucklehus* (☎01950/422370, ⓦwww.mucklehus.co.uk; ❸), a lovely B&B in a former Master Mariner's house built in 1890 near the beach in Levenwick, eighteen miles south of Lerwick; the rooms are small, but stylish and there's free wi-fi. A little further south, there's the *Spiggie Hotel* (☎01950/460409, ⓦwww.thespiggiehotel.co.uk; ❻), which has a lively bar serving real ales and a **restaurant** with great views over the Loch of Spiggie and out to Foula; both serve very reasonably priced and well-presented dishes. And a stone's throw from the *Spiggie* is the comfortable modern B&B, *Setterbrae* (☎01950/460468, ⓦwww.setterbrae.co.uk; ❸). There's also a **camping böd**, *Betty Mouat's Cottage* (book ahead on ☎01595/694688, ⓦwww.camping-bods.com; April–Oct), in Scatness, close to the airport. Also at Levenwick is a small, terraced **campsite** run by the local community (May–Sept; ☎01950/422207), with hot showers, a tennis court and a superb view over the east coast.

Fair Isle

Fair Isle (ⓦwww.fairisle.org.uk) – just three miles by one and a half – is marooned in the sea halfway between Shetland and Orkney and very different from both. The weather reflects its isolated position: you can almost guarantee that it'll be windy, though if you're lucky your visit might coincide with fine weather – what the islanders call "a given day". At one time Fair Isle's population was not far short of four hundred, but Clearances forced emigration from the middle of the nineteenth century. By the 1950s, the population had shrunk to 44, and evacuation of the island was seriously considered. **George Waterston**, who'd bought the island and set up a bird observatory in 1948, passed it into the care of the NTS in 1954 and rejuvenation began. Today Fair Isle supports a vibrant community of around seventy.

The north end of the island rises like a wall, while the Sheep Rock, a sculpted stack of rock and grass on the east side, is another dramatic feature. The croft land and the island's scattered (exclusively white) houses are concentrated in the south, but the focus for many visitors is the **Bird Observatory**, a large building just above the sandy bay of North Haven, where the ferry from Shetland Mainland arrives, with an exhibition on the island past and present. It's one of the major European centres for ornithology, and its work in watching, trapping, recording and ringing birds goes on all year. Fair Isle is a landfall for a huge number and range of migrant birds during the spring and autumn passages. Migration routes converge here and more than 345 species, including many rarities, have been noted. As a result, Fair Isle is a haven for twitchers, who descend on the island in

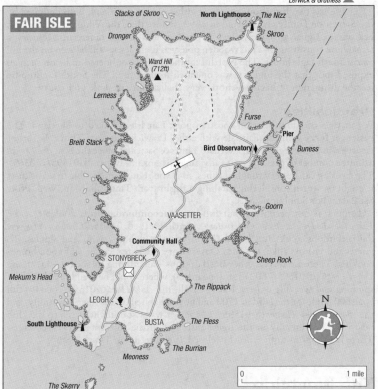

planes and boats whenever a major rarity is spotted; for more casual birders, however, there's also plenty of summer resident birdlife to enjoy. The high-pitched screeching that fills the sky above the airstrip comes from hundreds of **arctic terns**, and arctic skuas can also be seen here. Those in search of **puffins** should head for the cliffs around Furse, while to find gannets aim for the spectacular **Stacks of Scroo**.

Fair Isle is, of course, even better known for its **knitting** patterns, still produced with great skill by the local knitwear cooperative; from time to time there are displays at the Community Hall, by the island school (usually on a Monday, or when a cruise ship calls by). If the Hall is closed, then you'll have to make do with the samples on display at the island's **museum** (Mon 2–4pm, Wed 10.30am–noon, Fri 2–3.30pm; ☎01595/760244; free), which is named after George Waterston and situated next door to the island's Methodist chapel. Particularly memorable are stories of shipwrecks; in 1868 the islanders undertook a heroic rescue of all 465 German emigrants aboard the *Lessing*. More famously, the *El Gran Grifón*, part of the retreating Spanish Armada, was lost here in 1588 and three hundred Spanish seamen were washed up on the island. Food was in such short supply that fifty died of starvation before help could be summoned from Shetland. The idea that the islanders borrowed all their patterns from the shipwrecked Spanish seamen is nowadays regarded as a patronizing myth.

Fair Isle has two **lighthouses**, one at either end of the island, both designed by the Stevenson family and erected in 1892. Before that, the Vikings used to light beacons to signal an enemy fleet advancing, and in the nineteenth century a semaphore consisting of a tall wooden pole was used; it can still be seen on the hill above South Lighthouse. The North Lighthouse was considered to be on such an exposed spot that the foghorn was operated from within. The South Lighthouse has the distinction of having a short, very challenging, six-hole golf course.

Practicalities

For matters of administration and transport, Fair Isle is linked to Shetland. The passenger **ferry** connects Fair Isle with either Lerwick (alternate Thurs; 4–5hr) or Grutness in Sumburgh (Tues, alternate Thurs & Sat; 3hr); since the boat only takes a limited number of passengers, it's advisable to book in advance (℡01595/760363). The crossing can be very rough at times, so if you're at all susceptible to seasickness it might be worth considering catching a **flight** from Tingwall (Mon, Wed, Fri & Sat 2 daily) or Sumburgh (Sat).

Camping is not permitted, but full-board **accommodation** is available at the *Fair Isle Lodge & Bird Observatory* (April–Oct; ℡01595/760258, Ⓦwww .fairislebirdobs.co.uk; full board ❻), in en-suite doubles/twins and singles. To guests and visitors alike, the Bird Observatory offers tea, coffee and good home-cooking. There are several other **B&B** options – all offering full board – including *Upper Leogh* (℡01595/760248; full board ❺), where you'll be well looked after by spinning and weaving expert, Kathy Coull, the *Auld Haa* (℡01595/760349; full board ❻), built for the laird in 1700 and now inhabited by an American family, and the *South Light House* (℡01595/760355, Ⓦwww.southlightfairisle.co.uk; full board ❺), not literally in the lighthouse, but in the adjacent keepers' cottages. There is a shop/post office nearby (closed Tues afternoon, Thurs & Sun).

The Westside

The western Mainland of Shetland – known as the **Westside** – stretches west from Weisdale and Voe to Sandness. Although there are some important archeological remains and wildlife in the area, its greatest appeal lies in its outstanding **coastal scenery** and walks. Cut by several deep voes, the coastline is very varied; aside from dramatic cliffs, there are intimate coves and some fine beaches, as well as, just offshore, the stunning island of **Papa Stour**.

Bixter and around

Having left Weisdale, the first settlement you come to on the A971 is **TRESTA**, at the head of Sandsound Voe. If you're keen on plants, it's worth having a peek round **Lea Gardens** (March–Oct Wed & Sat 11am–8pm, Sun 2–6pm; just knock at other times), where German-born Rosa Steppanova has put a great deal of energy into her cottage garden, growing a huge variety of plants that enjoy the moist, frost-free Shetland climate.

On the north coast, a dead-end road leads to **Vementry**, also, confusingly, the name of the nearby island that boasts the best-preserved **heel-shaped cairn** in Shetland, right on top of the highest hill, Muckle Ward (298ft). There are also two excellently preserved **six-inch guns** from World War I on Swarbucks Head, in the north of the island. To reach the island, try Victor Gray (℡01595/810378, Ⓦwww.stmagnusbay.shetland.co.uk) or enquire at Lerwick tourist office (see p.385).

In the south, on the picturesque Sandsting peninsula, there are two beautiful terracotta-coloured **sandy bays** at **REAWICK**, and excellent **coastal walks** to be had along the coast around Westerwick and Culswick, past red-granite cliffs, caves and stacks. There's also a **camping böd** (book ahead on ☎01595/694688, ⓦwww.camping-bods.com; April–Oct) and **campsite** at **SKELD**, by the pier and marina in the sheltered Skelda Voe, between Reawick and Westerwick.

Three miles southwest of **Bixter**, the chief crossroads for the area, lies the finest Neolithic structure in the Westside, dubbed the **Staneydale Temple** by the archeologist who excavated it because it resembled a temple on Malta. Whatever its true function, it was twice as large as the surrounding oval-shaped houses (now in ruins) and was certainly of great importance, perhaps as some kind of community centre. The horseshoe-shaped foundations measure more than 40ft by 20ft internally, with immensely thick walls, still around 4ft high, whose roof would have been supported by spruce posts (two postholes can still be clearly seen). To reach the temple, take the path marked out by black-and-white poles across the moorland for half a mile from the road.

Walls and Sandness

Once an important fishing port, **WALLS** (pronounced *waas*), appealingly set round its harbour, is now a quiet village which comes alive once a year in the middle of August for the Walls Agricultural Show, the biggest farming bash on the island. If you're just passing by, you might like to stop by the **bakery and tearoom**, but Walls also has several good **accommodation** options: the nicely restored *Voe House* (book ahead on ☎01595/694688, ⓦwww.camping-bods.com; April–Oct), the largest **camping böd** on Shetland, with its own peat fire, and the wonderfully welcoming *Skeoverick* (☎01595/809349; ❶), a lovely modern crofthouse B&B which lies a mile or so north of Walls. The only **guesthouse** in the area is 🥢 *Burrastow House* (☎01595/809307, ⓦwww.burrastowhouse.co.uk; ❺), beautifully situated about three miles southwest of Walls; parts of the house date back to 1759, and have real character, others are more modern. With fresh Shetland ingredients and a French chef, the cooking is superb.

A short distance across the sea lies the island of **Vaila**, from where in 1837 Lerwick philanthropist Arthur Anderson operated a fishing station in an unsuccessful attempt to break down the system of fishing tenures under which tenants were forced to fish for the landlords under pain of eviction. The ruins of Anderson's fishing station still stand on the shore, but the most conspicuous monument is **Vaila Hall**, the largest laird's house on Shetland, originally built in 1696, but massively enlarged by a wealthy Yorkshire mill-owner, Herbert Anderton, who bought the island in 1893. Anderton also restored the island's ancient watchtower of Mucklaberry Castle, built a Buddhist temple (now sadly in ruins), and had a cannon fired whenever he arrived on the island. The island is currently owned by Dorota Rychlik, an equally eccentric Polish émigré and her husband, Richard Rowland. They welcome visitors, who should make a point of popping into the Whalehouse at Cloudin, where they'll find the 42ft skeleton of a young male **sperm whale** – nicknamed "Bony Dick" – who washed up on the island in 2000. Enquire at *Burrastow House* about transport.

At the end of a long winding road across an undulating, uninhabited, boulder-strewn landscape, you eventually reach the fertile scattered crofting settlement of **SANDNESS** (pronounced "saaness"), which you can also reach by walking along the coast from Walls past the dramatic Deepdale and across Sandness Hill. It's an oasis of green meadows in the peat moorland, with a nice beach, too. The modern **Jamieson's Spinning Mill** at Sandness (Mon–Fri 8am–5pm; free) is the only one on Shetland producing pure Shetland wool; the factory welcomes visitors, and you can watch how workers take the fleece and then wash, card and spin the exceptionally fine Shetland wool into yarn.

Papa Stour

A mile offshore from Sandness is the rocky island of **Papa Stour**, created out of volcanic lava and ash, which has subsequently been eroded into some of the most impressive coastal scenery in Shetland. In good weather, it makes for a perfect day-trip, but in foul weather or a sea mist it can certainly appear pretty bleak. Its name, which means "big island of the priests", derives from its early Celtic Christian connections, and the island was home, in the eighteenth century, to people who were mistakenly believed to have been lepers (though it seems more likely they were suffering from vitamin deficiency). The land is fertile, and in the nineteenth century Papa Stour supported a community of three hundred, but by the early 1970s there was a population crisis. With just sixteen inhabitants, and no children, the islanders made appeals for new blood to revive the fragile economy and managed to stage a dramatic recovery, releasing croft land to young incomers. Papa Stour was briefly dubbed "the hippie isle". A new harbour and ro-ro ferry in 2005 gave the island some hope, but the school is currently closed and the population down to single figures.

Papa Stour's main settlement, **BIGGINGS**, lies in the east near the pier, and it was here that excavation in the early 1980s revealed the remains of a thirteenth-century Norse house or **"Stofa"**, thought to have belonged to the future King Haakon V of Norway. In 2008, the house was partially reconstructed, and there's an explanatory panel explaining the significance of the stofa. The chief reason to come to Papa Stour, however, is to go **walking**; to reach the best of the coastal scenery, head for the far west of the island. From **Virda Field** (285ft), the highest point, in the far northwest, you can see the treacherous rocks of **Ve Skerries**, three miles or so northwest off the coast, where a lighthouse was erected as recently as

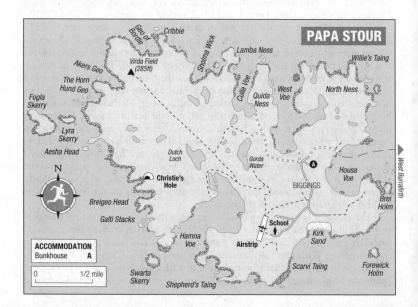

1979. The couple of miles of coastline from here southeast to Hamna Voe has some of the island's best stacks, blowholes and natural arches. The most spectacular is **Kirstan's Hole**, a gloup or partly roofed cleft, which extends far inland from the cliff line, and where shags nest on precipitous ledges. Other points of interest include a couple of defunct horizontal click-mills, below Dutch Loch, and the remains of a "meal road", so called because the workmen were paid in oatmeal or flour. In addition, several pairs of red-throated divers regularly breed on inland lochs such as Gorda Water.

Practicalities

The **ferry** runs from West Burrafirth, five miles or so north of Walls on the Westside to the east coast of Papa Stour (Mon & 1 on Sun, Wed, Fri & Sat 2 daily; 45min; ☎01957/722259) – book in advance, and reconfirm the day before departure. There are **flights** from Tingwall every Tuesday, and a day-trip is feasible; tickets cost around £40 return. The only place to stay is the small, clean, friendly **bunkhouse** (☎01595/873227, ⓦwww.hurdibackhostel.co.uk; April–Sept) at Hurdiback, near the pier, where you can also camp. There's no shop, but the hostel can help with getting supplies. Alternatively, you can stay with the Leasks at *Snarraness House* (☎01595/809375, ⓦwww.shetlandknitwear.com; ❷), a nicely renovated B&B with great sea views, in **West Burrafirth**, the ferry terminal for Papa Stour.

Foula

Separated from the nearest point on Shetland's Mainland by about fourteen miles of often turbulent ocean, **Foula** is without a doubt the most isolated inhabited island in the British Isles. Seen from the Mainland, its distinctive mountainous form changes subtly, depending upon the vantage point, but the outline is unforgettable. Its western **cliffs**, the second highest in Britain after those of St Kilda, rise at **The Kame** to some 1220ft above sea level; a clear day at The Kame offers a magnificent panorama stretching from Unst to Fair Isle. On a bad day, the exposure is complete and the cliffs generate turbulent blasts of wind known in Shetland as "flans", which rip through the hills with tremendous force.

Foula has been inhabited since prehistoric times, and the people here take pride in their separateness from Shetland, cherishing local traditions such as the observance of the **Julian calendar** (officially dropped in Britain in 1752), where Old Yule is celebrated on January 6 and New Year doesn't arrive until January 13. The folk of Foula were still using Norse **udal law** in the late seventeenth century, seemingly unaware that it had been superseded by Scots law in the rest of the country. Foula was also the last place that **Norn**, the old Norse language of Orkney and Shetland, was spoken as a first language, in the eighteenth century. Likewise, the island's isolation meant that more of the Shetland dialect survived here than elsewhere; in the late nineteenth century, Foula's people provided an enormous amount of information on the dialect and its roots in Norn for a study undertaken by the Faroese philologist Jakob Jakobsen. Foula's population, which peaked at around two hundred at the end of the nineteenth century, today numbers around thirty.

Arriving on Foula, you can't help but be amazed by the sheer size of the island's immense, bare mountains, whose summits are often hidden in cloud, known on the Mainland as "Foula's hat". The gentler eastern slopes provide good crofting land, and plentiful peat, and it is along this "green belt" that the island's population is scattered. The island, whose name is derived from the Old Norse for "bird island", also provides a home for a quarter of a million **birds**. Arctic terns wheel overhead at the airstrip, red-throated divers can usually be seen on the island's smaller lochs, while fulmars, guillemots, razorbills, puffins and gannets cling to the rock ledges. However, it is the island's colony of **great skuas** or "bonxies" that you can't fail to notice. From the edge of extinction a century ago, bonxies are now thriving, with an estimated 3000 pairs on Foula, making it the largest colony in the world. During the nesting season, they attack anyone who comes near. Although their dive-bombing antics are primarily meant as a threat, they can make walking across the moorland interior fairly stressful: the best advice is to hold a stick above your head or stick to the road and the coast.

Practicalities

Be sure to book and reconfirm your journey by **ferry** (Tues, Thurs & Sat; 2hr; ☎07881/823732, ⓦwww.atlanticferries.co.uk), which departs from Walls (or Scalloway) and arrives at Ham, in the middle of Foula's east coast. Day-trips are not possible on the regular ferry, but Cycharters (☎01595/696598, ⓦwww.cycharters.co.uk) do boat trips on Wednesdays. There are also regular **flights** from Tingwall (Mon & Tues 1 daily, Wed & Fri 2 daily); tickets cost around £50 return. From mid-April to October, Foula has its own resident part-time ranger, who usually greets new arrivals and offers local advice; it's also possible to arrange for guided walks (☎01595/753233, ⓦwww.foulaheritage.org.uk). The only **accommodation** on Foula is *Leraback* (☎01595/753226, ⓦwww.originart.com/leraback/leraback.html; ❹), a B&B near Ham, which does full board only; they

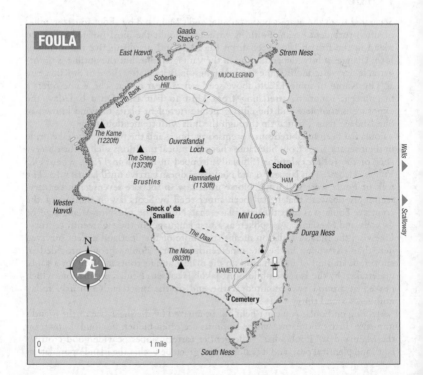

Many people come to Foula intent on viewing the island's famous cliffs – though in actual fact they are very difficult to appreciate except from the air or the sea. If the weather's fine, though, it's worth climbing to the top of **The Sneug** (1373ft), for the views stretching from Unst to Fair Isle. From the airstrip, climb up the southeast ridge of **Hamnafield** (1130ft), and then continue along the ridge of Brustins to The Sneug itself. From The Sneug, drop down to **The Kame** (1220ft), Foula's sheer cliff, the best view of which is from Nebbiefield, to the south. Return via Da Nort Bank to Soberlie Hill, from where you can pick up the island's road. All in all, it's only a walk of five or six miles, but it'll take three to four hours. If you're coming from the ferry at Ham, it's probably best to do the circuit in reverse, which is no bad thing, as the climb from Soberlie Hill up Da Nort Bank is one of the most exhilarating on the island, as the edge of the hill is an ever-increasing vertical drop.

There are other, more gentle walks possible on Foula, too. The coastal scenery to the north of the island, beyond Mucklegrind, features several stacks and natural arches, with the waves crashing over skerries, and seals sunning themselves. One of the easiest places to spot sea birds is from beyond the graveyard in Biggings, past Hametoun. The nearby hill of **The Noup** (803ft) is a relatively easy climb, compared to The Sneug, and, if you descend to the northwest, brings you to **Sneck o' da Smallie**, where there's a narrow slit in the cliffs, some 200ft high. You can return to the airstrip by heading back down the valley known as The Daal, although the bonxies are pretty thick on the ground. All Foula's cliffs are potentially lethal, especially in wet weather, and all the usual safety precautions should be taken (see p.47).

will collect you from the airstrip or pier. The island's one road runs along the eastern side of the island, and is used by Foula's remarkable fleet of clapped-out vehicles. There's no shop on the island so bring your own supplies.

North Mainland

The **North Mainland**, stretching more than thirty miles north from the central belt around Lerwick, is wilder than much of Shetland, with almost relentlessly bleak moorland and some rugged and dramatic coastal scenery. It is all but split in two by the isthmus of Mavis Grind: to the south are the districts of Delting, home to Shetland's oil terminal (Sullom Voe) and the area's largest town (Brae), Lunnasting (gateway to the islands of Whalsay and Out Skerries) and Nesting; to the north is the remote region of Northmavine, which boasts some of the most scenic cliffs in Shetland.

Voe and Lunnasting

If you're travelling north, you're bound to pass by **VOE**, as it sits at the main crossroads of the North Mainland: to the east, the road leads to Vidlin and Laxo, ferry terminals for Whalsay and Out Skerries; to the northeast, the road cuts across to Toft, where the ferry departs for Yell; to the northwest, it continues on to Brae and Northmavine. If you stay on the main road, it's easy to miss the picturesque old village, a tight huddle of homes and workshops down below the road around the pier (and signposted "Lower Voe"). Set at the head of a deep, sheltered, sea loch, Voe has a Scandinavian appearance, helped by the presence of the **Sail Loft**, painted in a rich, deep red. The building was originally used by fishermen and whalers for storing their gear; later, it became a knitwear workshop, and it was here that woollen jumpers were knitted for Edmund Hillary's 1953 Mount Everest expedition. Today, the building has been converted into a large **camping böd** (book ahead on ☎01595/694688, ⓦwww.camping-bods.com; April–Oct); it has hot showers and a kitchen, but limited heating. Across the road, the old butcher's is now the *Pierhead Restaurant & Bar* (☎01806/588332): the cosy wood-panelled **pub** has a real fire, occasional live music and offers a good bar menu, a longer version of which is on offer in the upstairs restaurant, featuring local mussels and the odd catch from the local fishing boats.

LAXO, the ferry terminal for Whalsay (see p.406), lies two miles east of Voe. If you continue along the B9071 past the village, you'll pass **The Cabin** (April–Sept Tues, Thurs, Sat & Sun 1–5pm; ☎01806/577232; free), a modern barn packed to the rafters with wartime memorabilia. You can try on some of the uniforms and caps or pore over the many personal accounts of the war written by locals. Three miles or so further north past Vidlin, the departure point for the Out Skerries (see p.408), is 🏃**Lunna House** (☎01806/577311, ⓦwww.lunnahouse.co.uk; ❹), set above a sheltered harbour nine miles northeast of Voe. Originally built in 1660, the house is best known as the headquarters of the Shetland Bus during World War II (see p.391). It's now a wonderful **place to stay**: the bedrooms, though not en suite, have lovely views and you get a top-class breakfast.

Down the hill from Lunna House lies the little whitewashed **Lunna Kirk**, built in 1753, with a simple tiny interior including a carved hexagonal pulpit. Among its more peculiar features is a "lepers' squint" on the outside wall, through which those believed to have the disease could participate in the service without risk of infecting the congregation; there was, however, no leprosy here, the outcasts in fact suffering from a hereditary, non-infectious skin condition brought on by malnutrition. In the graveyard, several unidentified Norwegian sailors, torpedoed by the Nazis, are buried.

Brae and Sullom Voe

BRAE, a sprawling settlement that still has the feel of a frontier town, was expanded in some haste in the 1970s to accommodate the workforce for the **Sullom Voe Oil Terminal**, just to the northeast. During World War II Sullom Voe was home to the Norwegian Air Force and a base for RAF seaplanes. Although the oil terminal, built between 1975 and 1982, has passed its production peak, it's still the largest of its kind in Europe. Brae may not, at first sight, appear to be somewhere to spend the night, but it does boast one of Shetland's better **hotels**, *Busta House* (☎01806/522506, ⓦwww.bustahouse.com; ❻), a lovely laird's house with stepped gables that has been tastefully enlarged over the last four hundred years and which sits across the bay of Busta Voe from the modern sprawl of Brae. Even if you're not staying the night here, it's worth coming for afternoon tea in the Long Room, for a stroll around the lovely wooded grounds, or for a drink and a **bar meal** in the hotel's pub-like bar. A cheaper alternative is the modern crofthouse **B&B** of *Westayre* (☎01806/522368, ⓦwww.westayre.shetland.co.uk; ❸), beyond Busta, overlooking a red sandy bay on the peaceful island of Muckle Roe, which is linked to the mainland by a bridge. Brae's other **food** option is *Frankie's* (☎01806/522700, ⓦwww.frankies fishandchips.com), a very popular fish and chip café with an attractive interior and views over Busta Voe.

Northmavine

Northmavine, the northwest peninsula of North Mainland, is unquestionably one of the most picturesque areas of Shetland, with its often rugged scenery, magnificent coastline and wide-open spaces. The peninsula begins a mile west of Brae at **Mavis Grind**, a narrow isthmus at which it's said you can throw a stone from the Atlantic to the North Sea, or at least to Sullom Voe.

Hillswick

HILLSWICK, the main settlement in the area, was once a centre for deep-sea or haaf fishing, and later a herring station. Down by the harbour, **Da Böd** was founded by a Hanseatic merchant in 1684, later became Shetland's oldest pub and is now a seal and wildlife sanctuary and occasional weekend café (☏01806/503348). In 1900, the North of Scotland, Orkney & Shetland Steam Navigation Company built the **St Magnus Hotel** to house their customers, importing it in the form of a timber kit from Norway. Despite various alterations over the years, it still stands overlooking St Magnus Bay, rather magnificently clad in black timber-framing and white weatherboarding.

If you're looking for a decent **B&B** in the vicinity, head for *Almara* (☏01806/503261, ⓦwww.almara.shetland.co.uk; ❸), a mile or two back down the road in Upper Urafirth, which will present you with good food, a family welcome and excellent views. The nicest sandiest **beach** to collapse on is on the west side of the Hillswick isthmus, overlooking Dore Holm (see below), a short walk across the fields from the hotel.

Esha Ness

Just outside Hillswick, a sideroad leads west to the exposed headland of **Esha Ness** (pronounced "*Ay*sha Ness"), celebrated for its splendid coastline views. Spectacular red-granite **cliffs**, eaten away to form fantastic shapes by the elements, are spread out before you as the road climbs away from Hillswick: in the foreground are the stacks known as **The Drongs** off the Ness of Hillswick, while in the distance the Westside and Papa Stour are visible. You can enjoy great views of the Drongs from *Braewick* **café** (☏01806/503345, ⓦwww.eshaness.moonfruit.com), five miles along the road to Esha Ness, which serves sandwiches and toasties, plus fancier fare in the evening; the adjacent **campsite** is pretty exposed but you can always book into one of the four wooden wigwams if the wind gets too much.

A mile or so south off the main road is the **Tangwick Haa Museum** (Easter–Sept daily 11am–5pm; free), housed in a seventeenth-century building, which, through photographs, old documents and fishing gear, tells the often moving story of this remote corner of Shetland and its role in the dangerous trade of deep-sea fishing and whaling. Kids and adults alike will also enjoy the shells and the Shetland wool and sand samples. Visible half a mile offshore to the south is **Dore Holm** or the "Drinking Horse", an impressive island with a natural arch.

Just before it finally peters out, the road divides, with the southern branch leading to the remains of **Stenness fishing station**, which was once one of the most important haaf fishing stations in Shetland. The remains of a few of the böds used by the fishermen are still visible along the sloping pebbly beach where they would dry their catch. At the peak of operations, in the early nineteenth century, as many as eighteen trips a year were made in up to seventy open, six-oared boats, known as "sixareens", to the fishing grounds thirty or forty miles to the west. A Shetland folk song, *Rowin' Foula Doon*, recalls how the crews rowed so far west that the island of Foula began to sink below the eastern horizon.

The northern branch of the road ends at the **Esha Ness Lighthouse**, a great place to view the red-sandstone cliffs, stacks and blowholes of this stretch of coast. A useful information board at the lighthouse details some of the dramatic geological features here and, if the weather's a bit rough, you should be treated to some spectacular crashing waves. One of the features to beware of at Esha Ness are the blowholes, some of which are hidden far inland. The best example is the **Holes of Scraada**, a partly roofed cleft where the sea suddenly appears 300yd inland from the cliff line. The incredible power of the sea can be seen in the various giant boulder fields above the cliffs: these **storm beaches** are formed by rocks torn from the cliffs in storms and deposited inland.

One of the few places to stay in Esha Ness is *Johnnie Notions* **camping böd** (book ahead on ☎01595/694688, ⓦwww.camping-bods.com; April–Oct; no electricity), up a turning north off the main road, in the hamlet of **HAMNAVOE**. The house was originally the birthplace of Johnnie "Notions" Williamson (1740–1803), a man of many talents, including blacksmithing and weaving, whose fame rests on his work in protecting several thousand of the population against smallpox using a serum and a method of inoculation he'd invented himself, to the amazement of the medical profession. He used a scalpel to lift a flap of skin without drawing blood, then placed the serum he'd prepared underneath, dressing it with a cabbage leaf and a bandage.

Ronas Hill

North of Ronas Voe, by the shores of Colla Firth, an unmarked road leads up **Collafirth Hill**, topped by the crumbling remains of a NATO radio station. The natural landscape is much more impressive, with tremendous views on a clear day, and a foreground of large, scattered stones with hardly any vegetation. Though the walk isn't quite as straightforward as it looks, scale and distance being hard to judge in this setting, Collafirth Hill is the easiest place from which to approach the rounded contours of **Ronas Hill**, Shetland's highest point (1475ft). The climb, with no obvious path, is exhausting but rewarding (4hr round trip; be aware of the safety precautions on p.47): from the top you can look west to one of the most beautifully sculpted parts of the Shetland coast, as the steep slope of the hill drops down to the arching sand-and-shingle beach called the **Lang Ayre**, south and east over all of the Mainland, north along the coast of Yell, or out into the daunting expanse of the Atlantic. Also at the summit, among subarctic vegetation and block-fields of granite boulders formed by intense frost and wind, is a Neolithic or Bronze Age **chambered cairn**, one of the best preserved in Shetland and useful as a shelter from the wind.

Whalsay and Out Skerries

The island of **Whalsay**, known in Shetland as the "Bonnie Isle", is a friendly community of over a thousand, devoted almost entirely to fishing. The islands' crews operate a very successful pelagic fleet of immense super-trawlers which can fish far afield in all weathers and catch a wide range of species. The island is, in addition, extremely fertile, but crofting takes second place to fishing here; there are also plentiful supplies of peat, which can be seen in spring and summer, stacked neatly to dry out above huge peat banks, ready to be bagged for the winter.

Ferries from the Mainland arrive at the island's chief town, **SYMBISTER**, in the southwest, whose harbour is usually dominated by the presence of several of the island's sophisticated, multi-million-pound purse-netters, some over 180ft long; you'll also see smaller fishing boats and probably a few "foureens", which the locals race regularly in the summer months. Across the busy harbour from the ferry berth stands the tiny grey-granite **Pier House** (Mon–Sat 9am–1pm & 2–5pm, Sun 2–4pm; free), the key for which resides in the shop opposite. This picturesque little building, with a hoist built into one side, is thought to have been a Hanseatic merchants' store, and contains a good display on how the Germans traded salt, tobacco, spirits and cloth for Whalsay's salted, dried fish from medieval times until the eighteenth century; close by is the Harbour View house that is thought to have been a Hanseatic storehouse or booth. On a hill overlooking the town is the imposing Georgian mansion of **Symbister House**, built in grey granite and boasting a Neoclassical portico. It was built in the 1830s at great expense by the laird Robert Bruce, not because he wanted to live on Whalsay but, so the story goes, because he wanted to deprive his heirs of his fortune. Since 1960, it has served as the local school, though you can still see the old doocot behind the house, and various outbuildings in the Midden Court, one of which houses an **exhibition** (June–Sept Wed & Fri–Sun 2–5pm; Oct–May Wed 7–9pm; free) on the history of the island.

About half a mile east of Symbister at the hamlet of **SODOM** – an anglicized version of Sudheim, meaning "South House" – is **Grieve House** (now a camping böd; see p.384), the modest former home of celebrated Scots poet, writer and republican **Hugh MacDiarmid** (1892–1978), born Christopher Grieve in the Borders town of Langholm. He stayed here from 1933 until 1942, writing about half of his output, including much of his best work: lonely, contemplative poems honouring fishing and fishermen, with whom he sometimes went out to sea. Estranged from his first wife and family and with a drink problem, MacDiarmid, practically broken, had sought temporary relief in Shetland. At first, he seems to have fallen in love with the islands, but poor physical and mental health, exacerbated (if not caused) by chronic poverty, dogged him. Eventually, unwillingly conscripted to work in a Glasgow munitions factory, he left with his new wife and young son, never to return.

Although the majority of folk live in or around Symbister, the rest of Whalsay – which measures roughly two miles by eight – is quite evenly and fairly densely populated. Of the prehistoric remains, the most notable are the two **Bronze Age houses** on the northeastern coast of the island, half a mile south of Skaw, known respectively as the "Benie Hoose" and "Yoxie Biggins". The latter is also known as the "Standing Stones of Yoxie", due to the use of megaliths to form large sections of the walls, many of which still stand. The houses were clearly used over a very long period, as over 1800 tools were discovered in the Benie Hoose; the community also built the nearby chambered tomb.

Practicalities

Car ferries run regularly to Whalsay from Laxo on the Mainland (℡01806/566259; 30min) – book ahead if you have a car. In bad weather, especially southeasterly gales, the service operates from Vidlin instead. There are also request-only **flights** from Tingwall (Mon, Wed & Thurs; ℡01595/840246); day-trips are only possible on Thursdays. The only accommodation is at the **camping böd** of *Grieve House* in Sodom (book ahead on ℡01595/694688, ⓦwww.camping-bods.com; April–Oct; no electricity). The house has lovely views overlooking Linga Sound, but is hidden from the main road, so ask for directions at the shop on the brow of the hill along the road to the Loch of Huxter. A little further along the road is the *Oot Ower Lounge*, an agreeable **pub** (Fri–Sun only) overlooking the loch, and pretty much the only place to eat and drink on the island (Chinese evening meals Sat only or by arrangement; ℡01806/566658), and somewhere you're welcome to **camp**. The island also has an eighteen-hole **golf course**, near the airstrip in Skaw, in the northeast, several shops, and a **leisure centre** with an excellent swimming pool close to the school in Symbister.

Out Skerries

Lying four miles out to sea, off the northeast tip of Whalsay, the **Out Skerries** ("Oot Skerries" or plain "Skerries" as the locals call them), consist of three tiny low-lying rocky islands, Housay, Bruray and Grunay, the first two linked by a bridge, with a population of around seventy. That people live here at all is remarkable, and that it is one of Shetland's most dynamic communities is astonishing, its affluence based on fishing from a superb, small natural harbour sheltered by all three islands, and on salmon farming in a nearby inlet. There are good, if short, walks, with a few prehistoric remains, but the majority of visitors are divers exploring the wreck-strewn coastline, and ornithologists who come here when the wind is in the east, in the hope of catching a glimpse of rare migrants.

The Skerries' jetty and airstrip are both on the middle island of **Bruray**, which also boasts the Skerries' highest point, Bruray Wart (173ft), an easy climb, and one which brings you up close to the islands' ingenious spiral-channel collection system for rainwater, which can become scarce in summer. The easternmost island, **Grunay**, is now uninhabited, though you can clearly see the abandoned lighthouse-keepers' cottages on the island's chief hill; despite appearances, the Stevenson-designed lighthouse itself sits on the outlying islet of Bound Skerry. The largest of the Skerries' trio, **Housay**, has the most indented and intriguing coastline, to which you should head if the weather's fine. En route, make sure you wander through the Battle Pund stone circle, a wide ring of boulders in the southeastern corner of the island.

Ferries to and from Skerries leave from Vidlin on the Mainland (Mon & Fri–Sun; 1hr 30min) and Lerwick (Tues & Thurs; 2hr 30min), but day-trips are only possible from Vidlin (Fri–Sun). Make sure you book your journey by 5pm the previous evening (☎01806/515226), or the ferry might not run. You can take your car over, but, with less than a mile of road to drive along, it's not worth it. There are also regular **flights** from Tingwall (Mon, Wed & Thurs), with day-trips possible on Thursdays. There is a shop, and a shower/toilet block by the pier, and **camping** is permitted, with permission. Alternatively, you can stay in *Rocklea* (☎01806/515228, ⓦwww.rockleaok.co.uk; ❸), a friendly modern **B&B** on Bruray run by Mrs Johnson, who offers optional full board.

The North Isles

Many visitors never make it out to Shetland's trio of remote **North Isles**, which is a shame, as the ferry links are frequent and inexpensive, and the roads fast. Certainly, there is no dramatic shift in scenery: much of what awaits you is the familiar Shetland landscape of undulating peat moorland, dramatic coastal cliffs and silent glacial voes. However, with Lerwick that much further away, the spirit of independence and self-sufficiency in the North Isles is much more keenly felt. **Yell**, the largest of the three, is best known for its vast otter population, but is otherwise often overlooked. **Fetlar**, the smallest of the trio, is home to the rare red-necked phalarope, but **Unst** has probably the widest appeal, partly as the most northerly landmass in the British Isles, but also for its nesting sea bird population. Note that **public transport** on all three islands is very limited, and that often it's necessary to book your journey the day before to ensure that the service runs.

Yell

Historically, **Yell** hasn't had good write-ups. The writer Eric Linklater described it as "dull and dark", while the Scottish historian Buchanan claimed it was "so

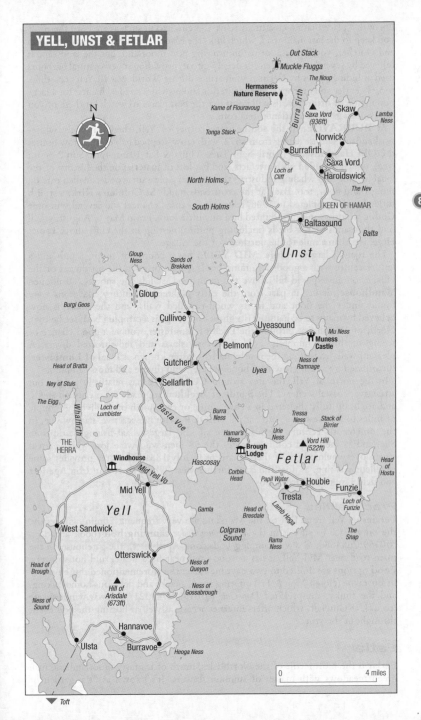

YELL, UNST & FETLAR

N

Out Stack

Muckle Flugga

The Noup

Hermaness
Nature Reserve

Burra Firth

Kame of Flouravoug

Saxa Vord
(936ft)

Skaw

Lamba
Ness

Tonga Stack

Norwick

Burrafirth

Saxa Vord

North Holms

Loch of
Cliff

Haroldswick

The Nev

South Holms

KEEN OF HAMAR

Baltasound

Balta

Unst

Gloup
Ness

Sands of
Brekken

Gloup

Burgi Geos

Cullivoe

Uyeasound

Mu Ness

Muness
Castle

Belmont

Head of Bratta

Gutcher

Uyea

Ness of
Ramnage

Ney of Stuis

Sellafirth

The Eigg

Basta Voe

Burra
Ness

Tressa
Ness

Stack of
Birrier

Whalfirth

Loch of
Lumbister

Hamar's
Ness

Brough
Lodge

Urie
Ness

Vord Hill
(522ft)

THE
HERRA

Windhouse

Hascosay

Fetlar

Head
of Hosta

Mid Yell Vo

Corbie
Head

Papil Water

Houbie

Mid Yell

Tresta

Funzie

West Sandwick

Yell

Gamla

Head of
Bresdale

Lamb Hoga

Loch of
Funzie

Colgrave
Sound

Rams
Ness

The
Snap

Otterswick

Ness of
Queyon

Head of
Brough

Ness of
Gossabrough

Hill of
Arisdale
(673ft)

Ness of
Sound

Hannavoe

Ulsta

Burravoe

Heoga Ness

0   4 miles

Toft

uncouth a place that no creature can live therein, except such as are born there". If you keep to the fast main road, which links the island's two ferry terminals of Ulsta and Gutcher, you'll pass a lot of uninspiring peat moorland, but the landscape is relieved by several voes, which cut deeply into it, providing superb natural harbours used as hiding places by German submarines during World War II. Yell's coastline, too, is gentler and greener than the interior and provides an ideal habitat for a large population of **otters**; locals will point out the best places to watch for them or you can contact Ⓦwww.shetlandotters.com.

At **BURRAVOE**, in the southeastern corner of Yell, there's a lovely white-washed laird's house dating from 1672, with crow-stepped gables, that now houses the **Old Haa Museum** (April–Sept Tues–Thurs & Sat 10am–4pm, Sun 2–5pm; free), which is stuffed with artefacts, and has lots of material on the history of the local herring and whaling industry; there's a very pleasant wood-panelled café on the ground floor, too. Back at the crossroads stands **St Colman's Kirk**, a stylish little church completed in 1900, featuring an apsed chancel and several winsome Gothic windows and surmounted by a tiny little spire. From May to August, you'll find thousands of **sea birds** (including puffins) nesting in the cliffs above Ladies Hole, less than a mile to the northeast of the village.

The island's largest village, **MID YELL**, has a couple of shops, a pub and a leisure centre with a good swimming pool. A mile or so to the northwest of the village, on an exposed hill above the main road, stands the spooky, abandoned **Windhouse**, dating in part from the early eighteenth century; skeletons were found under the floor and in its wood-panelled walls, and the house is now believed by many to be haunted (its ghost-free lodge is a camping böd; see below). North of Windhouse, around the Loch of Lumbister, you've a good chance of seeing merlins, whimbrels, golden plovers, skuas and red-throated divers. A pleasant walk leads along the nearby narrow gorge known as **Daal of Lumbister**, surrounded by a lush growth of honeysuckle, wild thyme and moss campion.

In the north of Yell, the area around **CULLIVOE** has relatively gentle, but attractive, coastal scenery. The **Sands of Brekken** are made from crushed shells, and are beautifully sheltered in a cove a mile or two north of Cullivoe. A couple of miles to the west, the road ends at **GLOUP**, with its secretive, narrow voe. In the nineteenth century, this was one of the largest haaf-fishing stations in Shetland; a memorial commemorates the 58 men who were lost when a great storm overwhelmed six of their sixareens in July 1881. This area provides some excellent walking, as does the coast further west, where there's an Iron Age fort and field system at **Burgi Geos**.

Practicalities

Ferries to Yell from Toft on the Mainland are very frequent (20min). Currently, the only place to **stay** is in the *Windhouse Lodge* **camping böd** (book ahead on ℡01595/694688, Ⓦwww.camping-bods.com; April–Oct), the gatehouse on the main road near Mid Yell; it has a wood- and peat-fired heater and hot showers. **Food** options are limited to two daytime cafés: the aforementioned museum café in Burravoe (closed Mon & Fri) offering soup, snacks and delicious home-baking, and the funky, camp, *Wind Dog Café* (℡01957/744321, Ⓦwww.winddogcafe .co.uk), at Gutcher, which offers internet access, as well as hosting the odd event throughout the year.

Fetlar

Fetlar is the most fertile of the North Isles, much of it grassy moorland and lush green meadows with masses of summer flowers. It's known as "the garden of

Shetland", though that's pushing it a bit, as it's still, relatively speaking, an unforgiving, treeless landscape. Around nine hundred people once lived here and there might well be more than a hundred now were it not for the activities of **Sir Arthur Nicolson**, who in the first half of the nineteenth century cleared many of the people at forty days' notice to make room for sheep. Nicolson's architectural tastes were rather more eccentric than some other local tyrants; his rotting but still astonishing **Brough Lodge**, a rambling castellated composition built in stone and brick in the 1820s, can be seen a mile or so south of the ferry terminal, and owes something – perhaps an apology – to Gothic, Classical and maybe even Tudor styles. Nicolson is also responsible for the nearby round-tower folly, which was built with stone taken from the abandoned crofthouses.

Today Fetlar's population lives on the southern and eastern sides of the island. At the main settlement, **HOUBIE**, in the centre of the island on the south coast, there's a rather less adventurously styled laird's house called Leagarth, with an impressive conservatory, built by Fetlar's most famous son, Sir William Watson Cheyne (1852–1932), who, with Lord Lister, pioneered antiseptic surgery. You can learn more about Cheyne's colourful life from the nearby **Fetlar Interpretive Centre** (May–Sept Mon–Fri 11am–3pm, Sat & Sun 1–4pm; £2; Ⓦwww.fetlar .com), a welcoming museum with information on Fetlar's outstanding birdlife and the archeological excavations that took place near Houbie. Fetlar also shelters Britain's most northerly religious community, the Society of Our Lady of the Isles, based in the modern lodge on the edge of the cliffs at Aith Ness, to the southeast of Houbie.

Much of the northern half of the island around Fetlar's highest point, **Vord Hill** (522ft), is now an RSPB Reserve (mid-May to mid-July: phone for access Ⓣ01957/733246). As well as harbouring important colonies of arctic skuas and whimbrels, Fetlar is perhaps best known for having harboured Britain's only breeding pair of **snowy owls**, which bred on Stackaberg, to the southwest of Vord Hill, from 1967 to 1975. Fetlar is also one of very few places in Britain where you'll see the graceful **red-necked phalarope** (late May–early Aug): the birds are unusual in that the female does the courting and then leaves the male in charge of incubation. A hide has been provided overlooking the marshes (or mires) to the east of the **Loch of Funzie** (pronounced "Finny"); the loch itself is also a good place at which to spot the phalaropes, and is a regular haunt of red-throated divers.

If you're just looking for a nice sandy bay in which to relax, then head for **Tresta**, on the south coast, which boasts a beautiful, sheltered beach of golden sand, with the freshwater loch of Papil Water immediately behind it. Of the archeological remains on Fetlar, perhaps the most remarkable is the **Funzie Girt** or Finnigirt, an ancient stone boundary of uncertain date, which divides the island into two. Its southern end has been destroyed, but it is well preserved on the western and northern slopes of **Vord Hill** (see above). Fetlar also offers some great coastal walks along its jagged shores, which are punctuated by an enormous number of natural arches. The cliffs are particularly impressive on Lamb Hoga, the higher moorland peninsula to the southwest, where storm petrels return to their nests at night.

Practicalities

Ferries to Fetlar (25–40min) depart regularly from both Gutcher on Yell and Belmont on Unst, and dock at **Hamar's Ness**, three miles northwest of Houbie. There's a dial-a-ride **bus service** on Fetlar (Mon–Sat 3–4 daily) – to use it you must book your journey the day before (Ⓣ01595/745745). If you do have a car, bear in mind that there's no petrol station on Fetlar, so fill up before you come across. **Accommodation** is in short supply, so book ahead either at *Gord*

(☎01957/733227, ✉nicboxall@btinternet.com; ④), the comfortable modern house attached to the island shop in Houbie, which does dinner, bed and breakfast, or at the **camping böd** in Aithbank (book ahead on ☎01595/694688, ⓦwww .camping-bods.com; April–Oct), a cosy wood-panelled cottage, a mile east of Houbie. The folk at *Gord* also run the *Garths* **campsite** (☎01957/733227; May–Sept), a simple field just to the west of Houbie, with toilets, showers and drying facilities. The post office, shop and **café** (closed Thurs & Sun) are all in one building in the middle of Houbie.

Unst

Much of **Unst** (ⓦwww.unst.org) is rolling grassland – a blessed relief for some after the peaty moorland of Yell – but the coast is more dramatic: a fringe of cliffs relieved by some beautiful sandy beaches. As Britain's most northerly inhabited island, there is a surfeit of "most northerly" sights, which is fair enough, given that many visitors only come here in order to head straight for Hermaness, to see the sea birds and look out over Muckle Flugga and the northernmost tip of Britain, to the North Pole beyond. The island's population recently plummeted to around six hundred due to the closure of the local RAF radar base at Saxa Vord, which used to employ a third of the population.

Uyeasound and Baltasound

On the south coast of the island, not far from the ferry terminal, is **UYEASOUND**, with Greenwell's Booth, an old Hanseatic merchants' warehouse by the pier, sadly now roofless. Further east lie the ruins of **Muness Castle**, a diminutive defensive structure, with matching bulging bastions and corbelled turrets at opposite corners. The castle was built in 1598 by the Scots incomer, Laurence Bruce, stepbrother and chief bullyboy of the infamous Earl Robert Stewart, and probably designed by Andrew Crawford, who shortly afterwards built Scalloway Castle for Robert's son, Patrick. The inscription above the entrance asks visitors "not to hurt this vark aluayis", but the castle was sacked by Danish pirates in 1627 and never really re-roofed. A little to the north is a vast sandy beach, backed by the deserted crofting settlement of Sandwick.

Unst's main settlement is **BALTASOUND**, five miles north, whose herring industry used to boost the local population of around five hundred to as much as ten thousand during the fishing season. As you leave Baltasound, heading north, be sure to take a look at **Bobby's bus shelter** (ⓦwww.unstbusshelter .shetland.co.uk), an eccentric, fully furnished, award-winning Shetland bus shelter on the edge of the town.

From Baltasound, the main road crosses a giant boulder field of serpentine, a greyish-green, occasionally turquoise rock found widely on Unst, that weathers to a rusty orange. The **Keen of Hamar**, east of Baltasound, and clearly signposted from the main road, is one of the largest expanses of serpentine debris in Europe, and is home to an extraordinary array of plantlife. It's worth taking a walk on this barren, exposed, almost lunar landscape that's thought to resemble what most of northern Europe looked like at the end of the last Ice Age. With the help of one of the SNH leaflets (kept in a box by the stile), you can try and identify some of the area's numerous rare and minuscule plants, including Norwegian sandwort, frog orchid, moonwort and the mouse-eared Edmondston's chickweed, which flowers in June and July and is found nowhere else in the world.

Haroldswick and Hermaness

Beyond the Keen of Hamar, the road drops down into **HAROLDSWICK**, where near the shore you'll find the **Unst Boat Haven** (May–Sept daily 11am–5pm; £2), displaying a beautifully presented collection of historic boats with many tools of the trade and information on fishing. If you want to learn about other aspects of Unst's history, head for the nearby **Unst Heritage Centre** (May–Sept daily 11am–5pm; £2), housed in the old school building by the main crossroads. Less than a mile north of Haroldswick is **SAXA VORD** (also confusingly the name of the nearby hill), home to the eyesore former. **Saxa Vord RAF base**, now containing a restaurant, bar and hostel, and a chocolate factory (Mon–Sat 11.30am–5pm, Sun 1–4pm; free), where there's also an exhibition on the history of the RAF on Unst. The former base is also now home to Britain's most northerly brewery, the **Valhalla Brewery**, source of the Shetland Ales you see around the islands, which welcomes visits by appointment (℡01957/711658, Ⓦwww.valhallabrewery.co.uk).

Beyond Saxa Vord, a road (unsuitable for vehicles) continues for another couple of miles before ending at Skaw, with a beautiful beach and the very last house in Britain. Northwest from Haroldswick, a road leads to the head of **Burra Firth**, a north-facing inlet surrounded by cliffs and home to Britain's most northerly golf course. It is guarded to the east by the hills of **Saxa Vord** (936ft), Unst's highest point, topped by several Ministry of Defence installations. To the west of Burra Firth lies the bleak headland of **Hermaness**, now a National Nature Reserve and home to more than 100,000 nesting sea birds. There's an excellent **visitor centre** in the former lighthouse-keepers' shore station, where you can pick up a leaflet showing the marked routes across the heather, which allow you access into the reserve. Whatever you do, stick to the path so as to avoid annoying the vast numbers of nesting great skuas.

From Hermaness Hill, you can look down over the jagged rocks of the wonderfully named Vesta Skerry, Rumblings, Tipta Skerry and **Muckle Flugga**, the latter providing the dramatic setting for a lighthouse. Few sites could ever have presented as great a challenge to the builders, who erected it in 1858. Beyond Muckle Flugga is **Out Stack**, the most northerly bit of Britain, where Lady Franklin landed in 1849 in order to pray (in vain, as it turned out) for the safe return of her husband from his expedition to discover the Northwest Passage, undertaken four years previously. The views from here are inevitably marvellous, as is the birdlife; there's a huge gannetry on one of the stacks, and puffins burrow all along the clifftops. The walk down the west side of Unst towards Westing is one of the finest in Shetland: if the wind's blowing hard, the seascape is memorably dramatic.

Practicalities

Ferries shuttle regularly across Bluemull Sound from Gutcher on Yell over to **BELMONT** on Unst (℡01957/722259; 10min). By far the most unusual **accommodation** is *Buness House* (℡01957/711315, Ⓦwww.users.zetnet.co.uk/buness -house; ❼), a seventeenth-century Haa in Baltasound still owned and run by the eccentric Edmondstons (of chickweed fame). Another very good bet is *Prestegaard* (℡01957/755234, Ⓔprestegaard@postmaster.co.uk; ❷), a modest Victorian B&B with just a couple of rooms in Uyeasound, where there's also the very handy *Gardiesfauld* (℡01957/755279, Ⓦwww.gardiesfauld.shetland.co.uk; April–Sept), a clean and modern **hostel** near the pier which allows **camping**, and offers **bike rental**. *Northern Lights* (closed Mon) is a spacious, bistro-style **café**, with views across the bay, by Unst Boat Haven in Haroldswick, while the *Skibhoul Café & Stores* has the odd "chip night" and will fill your flask. There are no decent options for dinner so book this at your accommodation or plan to self-cater. Nevertheless, wherever you stay, you should book yourself in for dinner or self-cater, rather than resort to the bar food at the *Baltasound Hotel*.

Travel details

Buses

Shetland Mainland
Lerwick to: Brae (Mon–Fri 5 daily, 3 on Sat; 45min); Hamnavoe (2–3 daily; 30min); Hillswick (Mon–Sat 1–2 daily; 1hr 40min); Laxo (Mon–Sat 1 daily; 40min); Levenwick (Mon–Sat 6–8 daily, 4 on Sun; 30min); Sandwick (Mon–Fri 8–10 daily, 6 on Sat, 4 on Sun; 25min); Scalloway (Mon–Sat hourly, 2 on Sun; 25min); Sumburgh Airport (Mon–Sat 5–6 daily, 4 on Sun; 45min); Tingwall (Mon–Fri 7 daily, Sat 4 daily; 10min); Toft (Mon–Sat 3–4 daily; 45–55min); Vidlin (Mon–Sat 2 daily; 45min); Voe (Mon–Fri 5 daily, 3 on Sat; 35min); Walls (Mon–Sat 1–4 daily; 45min).

Unst
Baltasound to: Haroldswick (Mon–Sat 3–4 daily; 10min).
Belmont to: Baltasound (Mon–Sat 1–3 daily; 20min); Uyeasound (Mon–Sat 1–3 daily; 5min).

Yell
Mid Yell to: Gutcher (Mon–Sat 2–5 daily, 1 on Sun in school term; 20min).
Ulsta to: Burravoe (Mon–Sat 1 daily; 15min); Gutcher (Mon–Sat 2–5 daily, 1 on Sun in school term; 25min).

Ferries to Shetland

Summer timetable only.
Aberdeen to: Lerwick (daily; 12hr).
Kirkwall (Orkney) to: Lerwick (3–4 weekly; 6hr).

Inter-island ferries

Summer timetable only.
To Bressay: Lerwick–Bressay (Mon–Sat every 30min–1hr, Sun every 1hr–1hr 30min; 7min).
To Fair Isle: Lerwick–Fair Isle (alternate Thurs; 4–5hr); Grutness–Fair Isle (Tues, alternate Thurs & Sat; 3hr).
To Fetlar: Belmont (Unst) and Gutcher (Yell)–Hamar's Ness (Mon–Sat 7–9 daily, 5 on Sun; 25–40min).
To Foula: Scalloway–Foula (alternate Thurs; 3hr 30min); Walls–Foula (Tues, alternate Thurs & Sat; 2hr).
To Out Skerries: Lerwick–Skerries (Tues & Thurs; 2hr 30min); Vidlin–Skerries (1 on Mon, Fri–Sun 3 daily; 1hr 30min).
To Papa Stour: West Burrafirth–Papa Stour (Mon & 1 on Sun, Wed, Fri & Sat 2 daily; 40min).
To Unst: Gutcher (Yell)–Belmont (every 30min–1hr; 10min).
To Whalsay: Laxo–Symbister (every 45min–1hr 15min; 30min).
To Yell: Toft–Ulsta (every 30min–1hr; 20min).

Inter-island flights

Summer timetable only.
Sumburgh to: Fair Isle (Sat; 15min).
Tingwall to: Fair Isle (Mon, Wed, Fri & Sat 2 daily; 25min); Foula (Mon & Tues 1 daily, Wed & Fri 2 daily; 15min); Out Skerries, calling at Whalsay on request (Mon & Wed 1 daily, Thurs 2 daily; 20min); Papa Stour (Tues 2 daily; 10min).

Contexts

Contexts

History

I t's hard to look at a landscape in the Scottish Highlands and Islands and not have a sense of the stories from history swirling around, from the ancient Stone Age settlers whose dwellings and stone circles are still so well preserved around the Northern and Western Isles, to the empty villages and lonely glens depopulated during the Clearances. Unusually for Europe, the history of the region is dominated more by the wildness of the sea and harshness of the landscape than the politics of London or Paris, and even Edinburgh has often felt distant, another landscape, another language and another difficult journey away.

Prehistoric Scotland

Scotland's first inhabitants were Mesolithic **hunter-gatherers**, who arrived as the last Ice Age retreated around 8000 BC. They lived initially in the area south of Oban, where heaps of animal bones and shells have been excavated in the caves on the Mull of Kintyre and on the plains north of Crinan. From here there is evidence of their moving onto the islands of Arran, Jura, Rùm, Skye and Lewis, where the damp and relatively warm coastal climate would have been preferable to the harsher inland hills and glens. Around 4500 BC, **Neolithic farming peoples** from the European mainland began moving into Scotland. To provide themselves with land for their cereal crops and grazing for their livestock, they cleared large areas of upland forest, usually by fire, and in the process created the characteristic moorland landscapes of much of modern Scotland. These early farmers established permanent settlements, some of which, like the well-preserved village of **Skara Brae** on Orkney, were near the sea, enabling them to supplement their diet by fishing and to develop their skills as boatbuilders. The Neolithic settlements were not as isolated as was once imagined: geological evidence has, for instance, revealed that the stone used to make axeheads found in the Hebrides was quarried in Northern Ireland.

Settlement spurred the development of more complex forms of religious belief. The Neolithic peoples built large chambered burial mounds or **cairns**, such as Maes Howe in Orkney (see p.347) and the Clava Cairns near Inverness (see p.214). This reverence for human remains suggests a belief in some form of afterlife, a concept that the next wave of settlers, the **Beaker people**, certainly believed in. They built the mysterious **stone circles**, thirty of which have been discovered in Scotland. Such monuments were a massive commitment in terms of time and energy, with many of the stones carried from miles away, just as they were at Stonehenge in England. The best-known Scottish circle is that of **Calanais** (Callanish) on the Isle of Lewis (see p.319), where a dramatic series of monoliths (single standing stones) form avenues leading towards a circle made up of thirteen standing stones. The exact function of the circles is still unknown, but many of the stones are aligned with the position of the sun at certain points in its annual cycle, suggesting that the monuments are related to the changing of the seasons.

The Beaker people also brought the **Bronze Age** to Scotland. New materials led directly to the development of more effective weapons, and the sword and the shield made their first appearance around 1000 BC. Agricultural needs plus new weaponry added up to a state of endemic warfare as villagers raided their neighbours to steal livestock and grain. The Bronze Age peoples responded to the danger by developing a range of defences, among them the spectacular **hillforts**, great earthwork defences, many of which are thought to have been occupied from around 1000 BC and remained in use throughout the Iron Age, sometimes far longer. Less spectacular but equally practical were the **crannogs**, smaller settlements built on artificial islands constructed of logs, earth, stones and brush, such as those found on Loch Tay (see p.151).

Conflict in Scotland intensified in the first millennium BC as successive waves of **Celtic** settlers, arriving from the south, increased competition for land. Around 400 BC, the Celts brought the technology of **iron** with them. These fractious times witnessed the construction of hundreds of **brochs** or fortified towers. Concentrated along the Atlantic coast and in the Northern and Western Isles, the brochs were dry-stone fortifications (built without mortar or cement) often over 40ft in height. Some historians claim they provided protection for small coastal settlements from the attentions of Roman slave-traders. Much the best-preserved broch is on the Shetland island of **Mousa** (see p.393); its double walls rise to about 40ft, only a little short of their original height. The Celts continued to migrate north almost up until Julius Caesar's first incursion into Britain in 55 BC.

At the end of the prehistoric period, immediately prior to the arrival of the Romans, Scotland was divided among a number of warring Iron-Age tribes, who, apart from the raiding, were preoccupied with wresting a living from the land, growing barley and oats, rearing sheep, hunting deer and fishing for salmon. The Romans were to write these people into history under the collective name Picti, or **Picts**, meaning "painted people", after their body tattoos.

The Romans

The **Roman conquest** of Britain began in 43 AD, almost a century after Caesar's first invasion. By 80 AD the Roman governor Agricola felt secure enough in the south of Britain to begin an invasion of the north, building a string of forts along the southern edge of the Highlands and defeating a large force of Scottish tribes at Mons Graupius. Precisely where this is remains a puzzle for historians, though most place it somewhere in the northeast, possibly on the slopes of Bennachie, near Inverurie in Aberdeenshire. The long-term effect of his campaign, however, was slight. Work on a major fort – to be the base for 5000 – at Inchtuthill, north of Perth on the Tay, was abandoned before it was finished, and the legions withdrew south. In 123 AD **Emperor Hadrian** decided to seal the frontier against the northern tribes and built **Hadrian's Wall**, which stretched from the Solway Firth to the Tyne and was the first formal division of the mainland of Britain. Twenty years later, the Romans again ventured north and built the **Antonine Wall** between the Clyde and the Forth, a clear statement of the hostility they perceived to the north. This was occupied for about forty years, but thereafter the Romans, frustrated by the inhospitable terrain of the Highlands, largely gave up their attempt to subjugate the north, and instead adopted a policy of containment.

The Dark Ages

In the years following the departure of the Romans in 410 AD, the population of Scotland changed considerably. By 500 AD there were four groups of people, or nations, dominant in different parts of the country. The **Picts** occupied the Northern Isles, the north and the east as far south as Fife. Today their settlements can be generally identified by place names with a "Pit" prefix, such as Pitlochry, and by the existence of carved symbol stones, like those found at Aberlemno in Angus. To the southwest, between Dumbarton and Carlisle, was a population of **Britons**. Many of the Briton leaders had Roman names, which suggests that they were a Romanized Celtic people, possibly a combination of tribes maintained by the Romans as a buffer between the Wall and the northern tribes, and peoples pushed west by the Anglo-Saxon invaders landing on the east coast. Both the Britons and the Picts spoke variations of P-Celtic, from which Welsh, Cornish and Breton developed.

On the west coast, to the north and west of the Britons (in what is now Argyll), lived the **Scotti**, Irish-Celtic invaders who would eventually give their name to the whole country. The first Scotti arrived in the Western Isles from Ireland in the fourth century AD, and about a century later their great king, Fergus Mor, moved his base from Antrim to Dunadd, near Lochgilphead, where he founded the Kingdom of Dalriada. The Scotti spoke Q-Celtic, the precursor of modern Scottish Gaelic. On the east coast, the Germanic **Angles** had sailed north along the coast to carve out an enclave around Dunbar in East Lothian.

Within three centuries, another non-Celtic invader was making significant incursions. From around 795 AD, **Norse** raids began on the Scottish coast and Hebrides, soon followed by the arrival of settlers, mainly in the Northern Isles and along the Caithness and Sutherland coastline. In 872 AD, the king of Norway set up an earldom in **Orkney**, from which **Shetland** was also governed, and for the next six centuries the Northern Isles took a path distinct from the rest of Scotland, becoming a base for raiding and colonizing much of the rest of Britain and Ireland – and a link in the chain that connected the Faroes, Iceland, Greenland and, more tenuously, North America.

The next few centuries saw almost constant warfare among the different groups. The main issue was land, but this was frequently complicated by the need of the warrior castes, who dominated all of these cultures, to exhibit martial prowess. Military conquests did play their part in bringing the peoples of Scotland together, but the most persuasive force was **Christianity**. Many of the Britons had been Christians since Roman times and it had been a Briton, St Ninian, who conducted the first missionary work among the Picts at the end of the fourth century. Attempts to convert the Picts were resumed in the sixth century by St Columba, who, as a Gaelic-speaking Scot, demonstrated that Christianity could provide a bridge between the different tribes.

Columba's establishment of the island of **Iona** (see p.90) as a centre of Christian culture opened the way for many peaceable contacts between the Picts and Scotti. Intermarriage became commonplace, so much so that the king of the Scotti, Kenneth MacAlpine, who united Dalriada and Pictland in 843, was the son of a Pictish princess – the Picts traced succession through the female line. Similarly, MacAlpine's creation of the united kingdom of **Alba**, later known as **Scotia**, was part of a process of integration rather than outright conquest, though it was the Scots' religion, Columba's Christianity and their language (Gaelic) that were to dominate the merger, allowing many aspects of Pictish life, including their language, to fall forgotten and untraceable into the depths of history. Kenneth and his successors gradually extended the frontiers of their kingdom by marriage and force of arms until, by 1034, almost all of what we now call Scotland – on the mainland, at least – was under their rule.

The Middle Ages

By the time of his death in 1034, **Malcolm II** was recognized as the king of Scotia. He was not, though, a national king in the sense that we understand the term, as under the Gaelic system kings were elected from the *derbfine*, a group made up of those whose great-grandfathers had been kings. The chosen successor, supposedly the fittest to rule, was known as the tanist (*tànaiste*). By the eleventh century, however, Scottish kings had become familiar with the principle of heredity, and were often tempted to bend the rules of tanistry. Thus, Malcolm secured the succession of his grandson **Duncan** by murdering a potential rival tanist. Duncan, in turn, was killed by **Macbeth** near Elgin in 1040. Macbeth was not, therefore, the villain of Shakespeare's imagination, but simply an ambitious Scot of royal blood acting in a relatively conventional way.

The victory of **Malcolm III**, known as Canmore (Bighead), over Macbeth in 1057 marked the beginning of a period of fundamental change in Scottish society. Having avenged his father Duncan, Malcolm III, who had spent the previous seventeen years at the English court, sought to apply to Scotland a range of ideas he had brought back with him. He and his heirs established a secure dynasty based on succession through the male line and introduced **feudalism** into Scotland, a system that was diametrically opposed to the Gaelic system, which rested on blood ties: the followers of a Gaelic king were his kindred, whereas the followers of a feudal king were vassals bought with land. The Canmores successfully feudalized much of southern and eastern Scotland by making grants to their Norman, Breton and Flemish followers; they preferred to make their capital in Edinburgh, and in these regions, Scots – a northern version of Anglo-Saxon – pushed out Gaelic as the lingua franca. They also began to reform the **Church**, a development started with the efforts of Margaret, Malcolm III's second wife, who, though English, had been brought up in Hungary, and brought Scottish religious practices into line with those of the rest of Europe, for which she was eventually canonized.

The policies of the Canmores laid the basis for a **cultural rift** in Scotland between the Highland and Lowland communities. Factionalism between various chiefs tended to distract the Highland tribes from their widening differences with the rulers to the south, while the ever-present Viking threat also served to keep many of the clans looking to the west and north rather than the south.

In 1098, a **treaty** between Edgar, King of Scots, and Magnus Bareleg, King of Norway, ceded sovereignty of all the islands to the Norwegians – Magnus even managed to include Kintyre in his swag by being hauled across the isthmus at Tarbet sitting in a boat, thus proving it an "island", as it could be circumnavigated. In practice, however, power in this Viking kingdom of *Súðreyjar* (Southern Islands) was in the control of local chiefs, lieutenants of a king on the Isle of Man who was himself subordinate to the king of Norway. By marrying the daughter of one of the Manx kings and skilful raiding of neighbouring islands, **Somerled**, King of Argyll, established himself and his successors as Lords of the Isles. Their natural ally was to the Scottish rather than the Norwegian king, and when **Alexander III** (1249–86), Scotland's strongest king in two centuries, sought to buy back the Hebrides from King Hákon of Norway in 1263, the offended Norwegian king sent a fleet of 120 ships to teach the Scots a lesson and drag the islands back into line. Initially the bullying tactics worked, but the fleet lingered too long, was battered by a series of autumnal storms, and retreated back to Orkney in disarray following a skirmish with Alexander's army at the **Battle of Largs** on the Clyde coast. While in Orkney, King Hákon died, and three years later the **Treaty of Perth** of 1266 returned the Isle of Man and the Hebrides to Scotland in exchange for an annual rent.

In 1286 **Alexander III** died, and a hotly disputed succession gave Edward I, King of England, an opportunity to subjugate Scotland. In 1291 Edward presided over a conference where the rival claimants to the Scottish throne presented their cases. Edward chose **John Balliol** in preference to Robert the Bruce, his main rival, and obliged John to pay him homage, thus turning Scotland into a vassal kingdom. Bruce refused to accept the decision, thereby continuing the conflict, and in 1295 Balliol renounced his allegiance to Edward and formed an alliance with France – the beginning of what is known as the "**Auld Alliance**". In the conflict that followed, the Bruce family sided with the English, Balliol was defeated and imprisoned, and Edward seized control of almost all of Scotland.

Edward had shown little mercy during his conquest of Scotland – he had, for example, had most of the population of Berwick massacred – and his cruelty seems to have provoked a truly national resistance. This focused on **William Wallace**, a man of relatively lowly origins from southwest Scotland who forged an army of peasants, lesser knights and townsmen that was fundamentally different to the armies raised by the nobility. Figures like Balliol, holding lands in England, France and Scotland, were part of an international aristocracy for whom warfare was merely the means by which they struggled for power. Wallace, by contrast, led proto-nationalist forces drawn from both Lowlands and Highlands determined to expel the English from their country. Probably for that very reason Wallace never received the support of the nobility and, after a bitter ten-year campaign, he was betrayed and executed in London in 1305.

With Wallace out of the way, feudal intrigue resumed. In 1306 **Robert the Bruce**, the erstwhile ally of the English, defied Edward and had himself crowned king of Scotland. Edward died the following year, but the unrest dragged on until 1314, when Bruce decisively defeated a huge English army under Edward II at the **Battle of Bannockburn**. At last Bruce was firmly in control of his kingdom, and in 1320 the Scots asserted their right to independence in a successful petition to the pope, now known as the **Declaration of Arbroath**.

In the years following Bruce's death in 1329, the Scottish monarchy gradually declined in influence. The last of the Bruce dynasty died in 1371, to be succeeded by the "Stewards", hence **Stewarts**. The reign of **James IV** (1488–1513), the most

The Highland clans

The term "**clan**", as it is commonly used to refer to the quasi-tribal associations found in the Highlands of Scotland, only appears in its modern usage in the sixteenth century. In theory, the clan bound together blood relatives who shared a common ancestor, a concept clearly derived from the ancient Gaelic notion of kinship. But in practice many of the clans were of non-Gaelic origin – such as the Frasers, Sinclairs and Stewarts, all of Anglo-Norman descent – and it was the mythology of a common ancestor, rather than the actuality, that cemented the clans together. Furthermore, clans were often made up of people with a variety of surnames, and there are documented cases of individuals changing their names when they swapped allegiances. At the upper end of Highland society was the clan chief (who might have been a minor figure, like MacDonald of Glencoe, or a great lord, like the Duke of Argyll, head of the Campbells), who provided protection for his followers: they would, in turn, fight for him when called upon to do so. Below the clan chief were the chieftains of the septs, or sub units of the clan, and then came the tacksmen, major tenants of the chief to whom they were frequently related. The tacksmen sublet their land to tenants, who were at the bottom of the social scale. The Highlanders wore a simple belted plaid wrapped around the body – rather than the kilt – and not until the late seventeenth century were certain tartans roughly associated with particular clans. The detailed codification of the tartan was produced by the Victorians, whose romantic vision of Highland life originated with George IV's visit to Scotland in 1822, when he appeared in an elaborate version of Highland dress, complete with flesh-coloured tights (for more on tartan, see p.210).

talented of the early Stewarts, ended in a terrible defeat for the Scots – and his own death – at the **Battle of Flodden Field**.

Meanwhile, the shape of modern-day Scotland was completed when the Northern Isles were gradually wrested from Norway. In 1469, a marriage was arranged between Margaret, daughter of the Danish king, Christian I, and the future **King James III** (1460–88) of Scotland. Short of cash for her dowry, Christian mortgaged Orkney to Scotland in 1468, followed by Shetland in 1469; neither pledge was ever successfully redeemed. The laws, religion and administration of the Northern Isles became Scottish, though their Norse heritage is still very evident in place names, dialect and culture. Meanwhile, the MacDonald Lords of the Isles had become too unruly for the more unified vision of James IV, and in 1493 the title reverted to the Crown. It still remains there: the current Lord of the Isles is Prince Charles.

The religious wars

In many respects the **Reformation** in Scotland was driven as much by the political intrigue of the reign of **Mary, Queen of Scots** (1542–67), as it was by religious conviction. Although in later years the hard-line Presbyterianism of the Highlands and Hebrides would triumph over political expediency, the revolutionary thinking of **John Knox** and his Protestant die-hards initially made little impact in the north. If some of the Lowland lords were still inclined to see religious affiliation as a negotiable tool in the quest for power and influence, the loyalty – if not, perhaps, the piety – of many of the Highland chiefs to both their monarch and the Catholic faith was much more solid.

James VI (1567–1625), who in 1603 also became James I of England, disliked Presbyterianism because its quasi-democratic structure – particularly the lack of royally appointed bishops – appeared to threaten his authority. In 1610 he restored the Scottish bishops, leaving a legacy that his son, **Charles I** (1625–49), who was raised in Episcopalian England, could not handle. He provoked the **National Covenant**, a religious pledge that committed the signatories to "labour by all means lawful to recover the purity and liberty of the Gospel as it was established and professed".

Charles declared all the "**Covenanters**" to be rebels, a proclamation endorsed by his Scottish bishops. The Covenanters, well financed by the Kirk, assembled a proficient army under Alexander Leslie. In desperation, Charles summoned the English Parliament, the first for eleven years, hoping it would pay for an army. But the decision was a disaster and Parliament was much keener to criticize his policies than to raise taxes. In response Charles declared war on Parliament in 1642.

The major conflicts of the ensuing **Civil War** were mostly confined to England. In Scotland, the English Parliamentarians made an uneasy alliance with the Covenanters, who ruled over Scotland until 1650. During this period, the power of the Presbyterian Kirk grew considerably: laws were passed establishing schools in every parish and, less usefully, banning trade with Catholic countries. The only effective opposition to the theocratic state came from the **Marquis of Montrose**, who had initially supported the Covenant but lined up with the king when war broke out. Montrose was a gifted campaigner whose army was drawn from the Highlands and Islands, where the Kirk's influence was still weak, and included a frightening rabble of islanders and Irishmen under the inspiration of Colonsay chief Alasdair MacDonald, or **Colkitto**, whose appetite for the fray was fed by Montrose's willingness to send them charging into battle at the precise moment they could inflict most damage. For a golden year Montrose's army roamed the Highlands undefeated, scoring a number of brilliant tactical victories over the Covenanters, but the reluctance of his troops to stay south of the Highland Line made it impossible for him to capitalize on his successes and, as the clansmen dispersed with the spoils of victory back to their lands, Montrose was left weak and exposed. Unfailingly loyal to a king who was unwilling to take the same risks for his most gifted general, Montrose was eventually captured and executed in 1650.

Many English Parliamentarians suspected the Scots of hankering for the return of the monarchy, a suspicion confirmed when, at the invitation of the earl of Argyll, the future **Charles II** came back to Scotland in 1650. To regain his Scottish kingdom, Charles was obliged to renounce his father and sign the Covenant, two bitter pills taken to impress the population. In the event, the "Presbyterian restoration" was short-lived. Cromwell invaded, defeated the Scots at Dunbar and forced Charles into exile. Until the Restoration of 1660, Scotland was united with England and governed by seven commissioners. The Restoration brought bishops back to the Kirk, integrated into an essentially Presbyterian structure of Kirk sessions and presbyteries. Over three hundred clergymen, a third of the Scottish ministry, refused to accept the reinstatement of the bishops and were edged out of the Church and forced to hold open-air services, called **Conventicles**, which Charles did his best to suppress.

When **James VII** (James II of England), whose ardent Catholicism caused a Protestant backlash in England, was forced into exile in France in 1689, the throne passed to **Mary**, his Protestant daughter, and her Dutch husband, **William of Orange**. In Scotland there was a brief flurry of opposition to William when **Graham of Claverhouse**, known as "Bonnie Dundee", united the Jacobite clans against the government army at the **Battle of Killiekrankie**, just north of Pitlochry. However, the inspirational Claverhouse was killed on the point of claiming a famous victory, and again the clans, leaderless and unwilling to press south, dissipated and the threat passed. William and Mary quickly consolidated their position, restoring the full Presbyterian structure in Scotland and abolishing the bishops, though they chose not to restore the political and legal functions of the Kirk, which remained subject to parliamentary control. It was sufficient, however, to bring the religious wars to a close, essentially completing the Reformation in Scotland and establishing a platform on which political union would be built.

The Union

One thing that lingered, however, was Highland loyalty to the Stewart line, something both William and the political pragmatists saw as a significant threat. In 1691, William offered pardons to those Highland chiefs who had opposed his accession, on condition that they took an oath of allegiance by New Year's Day 1692. Alastair Maclain, one of the MacDonalds of Glencoe had turned up at the last minute, but his efforts to take the oath were frustrated by the king's officials, who were determined to see his clan, well known for their support of the Stewarts, destroyed. In February 1692, Captain Robert Campbell of Glenlyon quartered his men with the MacDonalds of Glencoe and, two weeks later, in the middle of the night, his troops acted on their secret orders, turned on their hosts and carried out the infamous **Massacre of Glencoe**. Thirty-eight MacDonalds died, and the slaughter caused a national scandal, especially among the clans, where "murder under trust" – killing those offering you shelter – was considered a particularly heinous crime.

The situation in Scotland was further complicated by the question of the succession. Mary died without leaving an heir and, on William's death in 1702, the crown passed to her sister **Anne**, James VII's second daughter, who was also childless. In response, the English Parliament secured the Protestant succession by passing the **Act of Settlement**, which named the Electress Sophia of Hanover, a granddaughter of James VI (I), as the next in line to the throne. The Act did not, however, apply in Scotland, and the English feared that the Scots would invite James Edward Stewart, the son of James VII (II) by his second wife, back from France to be their king. Consequently, Parliament appointed commissioners charged with the consideration of "proper methods towards attaining a union with Scotland". The project seemed doomed to failure when the Scottish Parliament passed the **Act of Security**, in 1703, stating that Scotland would not accept a Hanoverian monarch unless they had first received guarantees protecting their religion and their trade.

Nevertheless, despite the strength of anti-English feeling, the Scottish Parliament passed the **Act of Union** by 110 votes to 69 in 1707. Some historians have explained the vote in terms of bribery and corruption, but there were other factors. Scottish politicians were divided between the Cavaliers – Jacobites (supporters of the Stewarts) and Episcopalians – and the Country party, whose presbyterian members dreaded the return of the Stewarts more than they disliked the Hanoverians. To the Highlands and Islands, however, the shift of government four hundred miles further south from Edinburgh, itself distant enough for many, was to make relatively little difference to their lives for the best part of the rest of the century.

The country that was united with England in 1707 contained three distinct cultures: in south and east Scotland, they spoke Scots; in Shetland, Orkney and the far northeast, the local dialect, though Scots-based, contained elements of Norn (Old Norse); in the rest of north and west Scotland, including the Hebrides, Gaelic was spoken. These linguistic differences were paralleled by different forms of social organization and customs. The people of north and west Scotland were mostly pastoralists, moving their sheep and cattle to Highland pastures in the summer, and returning to the glens in the winter. They lived in single-room dwellings, heated by a central peat fire and sometimes shared with livestock, and in hard times they would subsist on cakes made from the blood of their live cattle mixed with oatmeal. Highlanders supplemented their meagre income by raiding their clan neighbours and the prosperous Lowlands, whose inhabitants regarded their northern compatriots with a mixture of fear and contempt. This was the background for the exploits of Scotland's very own Robin Hood character, **Rob Roy**, for more on whom see p.143.

The Jacobite uprisings

When James VII (II) was deposed, he had fled to France, where he planned the reconquest of his kingdom with the support of the French king. When James died in 1701, the hopes of the Stewarts passed to his only son, James Edward Stewart, the "Old Pretender" ("Pretender" in the sense of having pretensions to the throne; "Old" to distinguish him from his son Charles, the "Young Pretender"). James's followers became known as **Jacobites**, derived from Jacobus, the Latin equivalent of James. After the accession to the British throne of the Hanoverian George I, son of Sophia, Electress of Hanover, it sparked the **Jacobite uprising of 1715**: its timing appeared perfect. Scottish opinion was moving against the Union, which had failed to bring Scotland any tangible economic benefits. The English had also been accused of bad faith when, contrary

Bonnie Prince Charlie

Prince Charles Edward Stuart – better known as **Bonnie Prince Charlie** or "The Young Pretender" – was born in 1720 in Rome, where his father, "The Old Pretender", claimant to the British throne (as the son of James VII), was living in exile with his Polish wife. At the age of 25, with no knowledge of Gaelic, an imperfect grasp of English and a strong attachment to the Catholic faith, the prince set out for Scotland with two French ships, disguised as a seminarist from the Scots College in Paris. He arrived on the Hebridean island of **Eriskay** (see p.333) on July 23, 1745, with just seven companions, and was immediately implored to return to France by the clan chiefs, who were singularly unimpressed by his lack of army. Charles was unmoved and went on to raise the royal standard at **Glenfinnan** (see p.229), thus signalizing the beginning of the **Jacobite Uprising**. He only attracted less than half of the potential 20,000 clansmen who could have marched with him, and promises of support from the French and English Jacobites failed to materialize. Nevertheless, after a decisive victory over government forces at the **Battle of Prestonpans**, near Edinburgh, Charles made a spectacular advance into England, getting as far as Derby. London was in a state of panic: its shops were closed and the Bank of England, fearing a run on sterling, slowed withdrawals by paying out in sixpences. But Derby was as far as Charles got. On December 6, threatened by superior forces, the Jacobites decided to retreat to Scotland against Charles's wishes. Pursued back to Scotland by the Duke of Cumberland, he won one last victory, at Falkirk, before the final disaster at **Culloden** (see p.213) in April 1746.

The prince spent the following five months in hiding, with a price of £30,000 on his head, and literally thousands of government troops searching for him. He certainly endured his fair share of cold and hunger whilst on the run, but the real price was paid by the Highlanders themselves, who risked their lives (and often paid for it with them) by aiding and abetting the prince. The most famous of these was, of course, 23-year-old **Flora MacDonald**, whom Charles first met on South Uist in June 1746. Flora was persuaded – either by his looks or her relatives, depending on which account you believe – to convey Charles "over the sea to Skye", disguised as an Irish servant girl by the name of Betty Burke. She was arrested just seven days after parting with the prince in Portree, and held in the Tower of London until July 1747. She went on to marry a local man, had seven children, and in 1774 emigrated to America where her husband was taken prisoner during the American War of Independence. Flora returned to Scotland and was reunited with her husband on his release; they resettled in Skye and she died at the age of 68.

Charles eventually boarded a ship back to France in September 1746, but, despite his promises – "for all that has happened, Madam, I hope we shall meet in St James's yet" – never returned to Scotland, nor did he ever see Flora again. After mistreating a string of mistresses, he eventually got married at the age of 52 to the 19-year-old **Princess Louise of Stolberg-Gedern** in an effort to produce a Stuart heir. They had no children, and she eventually fled from his violent drunkenness; in 1788, a none-too-"bonnie" Prince Charles died in the arms of his illegitimate daughter in Rome. Bonnie Prince Charlie became a legend in his own lifetime, but it was the Victorians who really milked the myth for all its sentimentality, conveniently overlooking the fact that the real consequence of 1745 was the virtual annihilation of the Highland way of life.

to their pledges, they attempted to impose their legal practices on the Scots. Neither were Jacobite sentiments confined to Scotland. There were many in England who toasted the "King across the water" and showed no enthusiasm for the new German ruler. In September 1715, the fiercely Jacobite John Erskine, Earl of Mar, raised the Stewart standard at Braemar Castle. Just eight days later, he captured Perth, where he gathered an army of over 10,000 men, drawn mostly from the Episcopalians of northeast Scotland and from the Highlands. Mar's rebellion took the government by surprise. They had only 4000 soldiers in Scotland, under the Duke of Argyll, but Mar dithered until he lost the military advantage. The **Battle of Sheriffmuir** in November was indecisive, but by the time the Old Pretender arrived the following month 6000 veteran Dutch troops had reinforced Argyll. The rebellion disintegrated rapidly and James slunk back to exile in France in February 1716.

Though better known, the **Jacobite uprising of 1745**, led by James's dashing son, Charles Edward Stewart (Bonnie Prince Charlie), had even less chance of success than the 1715 rising. In the intervening thirty years, the Hanoverians had consolidated their hold on the English throne, Lowland society had become uniformly loyalist and access into the Highlands for both trade and internal peacekeeping had been vastly improved by the military roads built by General Wade. Even among the clans, regiments such as the Black Watch were recruited, which drew on the Highlanders' military tradition, but formed part of the government's standing army. Despite a promising start to his campaign, Charles met his match at the **Battle of Culloden**, near Inverness, in April 1746, the last set-piece battle on British soil, and the last time a claymore-wielding Highland charge would be set against organized ranks of musket-bearing troops, and the last time a Stewart would take up arms in pursuit of the throne. As with so many of the other critical points in the campaign, the Jacobite leadership at Culloden was divided and ill-prepared. When it came to the fight, the Highlanders were in the wrong place, exhausted after a forced overnight march, and seriously outnumbered and outgunned. They were swept from the field, with over 1500 men killed or wounded compared to Cumberland's 300 or so. After the battle, many of the wounded Jacobites were slaughtered, an atrocity that earned Cumberland the nickname "Butcher".

In the aftermath of the uprising, the wearing of tartan, the bearing of arms and the playing of bagpipes were all banned. Rebel chiefs lost their land and the Highlands were placed under military occupation. Most significantly, the government prohibited the private armies of the chiefs, thereby effectively destroying the clan system. Within a few years, more Highland regiments were recruited for the British army, and by the end of the century thousands of Scots were fighting and dying for their Hanoverian king against Napoleon.

The Highland Clearances

Once the clan chief was forbidden his own army, he had no need of the large tenantry that had previously been a vital military asset. Conversely, the second half of the eighteenth century saw the Highland **population increase** dramatically after the introduction of the easy-to-grow and nutritious potato. Between 1745 and 1811, the population of the Outer Hebrides, for example, rose from 13,000 to 24,500. The clan chiefs adopted different policies to deal with the new situation. Some encouraged emigration, and as many as 6000 Highlanders left for the Americas between 1800 and 1803 alone. Other landowners saw the economic advantages of developing alternative forms of employment for their tenantry, mainly fishing and kelping. **Kelp** (brown seaweed) was gathered and burnt to produce soda ash, which was used in the manufacture of soap, glass and explosives. There was a rising market for soda ash until the 1810s, with the price increasing from £2 a ton in 1760 to £20 in 1808, making a fortune for some landowners and providing thousands of Highlanders with temporary employment. Fishing for **herring** – the "silver darlings" – was also encouraged, and new harbours and coastal settlements were built all around the Highland coastline. Other landowners developed **sheep runs** on the Highland pastures, introducing hardy breeds like the black-faced Linton and the Cheviot. But extensive sheep-farming proved incompatible with a high peasant population, and many landowners decided to clear their estates of tenants, some of whom were forcibly moved to tiny plots of marginal land, where they were to farm as **crofters**.

The pace of the **Highland Clearances** accelerated after the end of the Napoleonic wars in 1815, when the market price for kelp, fish and cattle declined, leaving sheep as the only profitable Highland product. The most notorious Clearances took place on the estates of the Countess of Sutherland, who owned a million acres in northern Scotland. Between 1807 and 1821, around 15,000 people were thrown off her land, evictions carried out with considerable brutality. A potato famine followed in 1846, forcing large-scale emigration to America and Canada and leaving the huge uninhabited areas found in the region today.

The crofters eked out a precarious existence, but they hung on throughout the nineteenth century, often by taking seasonal employment away from home. In the 1880s, however, a sharp downturn in agricultural prices made it difficult for many crofters to pay their rent. This time, inspired by the example of the Irish Land League, they resisted eviction, forming the **Highland Land League** or **Crofters' Party**, and taking part in direct action protests, in particular land occupations or **land raids** as they became known. In 1886, in response to the social unrest, Gladstone's Liberal government passed the **Crofters' Holdings Act**, which conceded three of the crofters' demands: security of tenure, fair rents to be decided independently, and the right to pass on crofts by inheritance. But Gladstone did not attempt to increase the amount of land available for crofting, and shortage of land remained a major problem until the **Land Settlement Act** of 1919 made provision for the creation of new crofts. Nevertheless, the population of the Highlands continued to fall into the twentieth century, with many of the region's young people finding city life more appealing.

The world wars

Depopulation of an all-too-familiar kind was present in the early decades of the twentieth century, with Highland regiments at the vanguard of the British Army's infantry offensives in both the Anglo-Boer wars at the start of the century and **World War I**. The months after hostilities ended also saw one of the most remarkable spectacles in Orkney's long seafaring history, when 74 vessels from the German naval fleet, lying at anchor in **Scapa Flow** having surrendered to the British at the armistice, were scuttled by the skeleton German crews that remained aboard (see p.357).

The same harbour was immediately involved in **World War II**, when a German U-boat breached the defences around Orkney in October 1939 and torpedoed HMS *Royal Oak*, with the loss of 833 men (see p.356). Many more ships and lives were lost in the waters off the Hebrides during the hard-fought Battle of the Atlantic, when convoys carrying supplies and troops were constantly harried by German U-boats. Various bases were established in the Highlands and Islands, including a flying-boat squadron at Kerrera, by Oban, with Air Force bases on Islay, Benbecula, Tiree and Lewis, and a Royal Naval anchorage at Tobermory; on the mainland, commandos were trained in survival skills and offensive landings in the area around lochs Lochy and Arkaig, near Fort William. Though men of fighting age again left the Highlands to serve in the forces, the war years were not altogether bleak, as the influx of servicemen ensured a certain prosperity to the places where they were based, and the need for the country to remain self-sufficient meant that farms and crofts – often worked by the women and children left behind – were encouraged to keep production levels high.

Even before the war, efforts had been made to recognize the greater social and economic needs of the Highlands and Islands with the establishment of the **Highlands and Islands Medical Service**, a precursor to the National Health Service introduced by the first postwar Labour government. Other agencies were set up in the 1940s, including the **North of Scotland Hydro Electric Board** and the **Forestry Commission**, both of which were tasked to improve the local infrastructure and create state-sponsored employment.

The contemporary Highlands and Islands

After Britain joined the EEC in 1972, the Highlands and Islands were identified as an area in need of special assistance and, in harness with the **Highlands and Islands Development Board**, significant investment was made in the area's infrastructure, including roads, schools, medical facilities and harbours. European funding was also used to support the increased use and teaching of **Gaelic**, and the encouragement of Gaelic broadcasting, publishing and education. At the same time there was renaissance of Gaelic culture across Scotland as a whole, from the annual National Mod (see p.42) to the nationwide success of folk-rock bands such as Runrig and Capercaillie, with the result that the indigenous language and culture of the Highlands and Islands, while still vulnerable, is as healthy now as it has been for a century.

The strength of cultural identity – even in its more clichéd forms – has always been a vital aspect of the Highlands and Islands' attraction as a tourist destination. **Tourism** remains the dominant industry in the region, despite the furrowed brows of, on the one hand, businesses vulnerable to dips in numbers and spending, and on the other, conservationists concerned by the impact of increased numbers. The main traditional industries, **farming** and **fishing**, continue with European support to struggle against European competition, while others, such as **whisky** and **tweed making**, remain prominent in certain pockets although they have never, in fact, been large-scale employers. Few of the region's new industries have quite fulfilled the initial hopes raised of them, but most remain to contribute to the economic diversity of the region. **Forestry**, for example, has seen large tracts of the Highlands planted, more sensitively now than in the past; North Sea **oil** has brought serious economic benefits not just to the northeast coast but also to Orkney and Shetland; **salmon farming** has become widespread, tainting many otherwise idyllic west-coast scenes, but long accepted as a vital part of numerous coastal communities. The new growth industry is **alternative energy**, most controversially large "wind farms", but also schemes to harness tidal and wave energy. More unequivocally positive is the emergence of **"cyber-crofting"** – essentially the operation of internet-based businesses or services from remoter areas. The possibilities thrown up by the communications revolution have also led to the establishment of the **University of the Highlands**, with various colleges linked to each other and to outlying students by networked computers.

As remote living is made more viable, however, it is not just the indigenous population who benefit, and **immigration** into the Highlands now matches the long-term trend of emigration, with Inverness ranking as one of the fastest-growing urban areas in Britain. The incomers – invariably called "white settlers" – are now an established aspect of Highland life, often providing economic impetus in the form of enthusiastically run small businesses, though their presence can still rankle in the intimate lives of small communities. Any prejudicial control from outside the region is looked on suspiciously, not least in the question of **land ownership**, which remains one of the keys to Highland development – some would say the most important of all. Some of the largest Highland estates continue to be owned and managed from afar, with little regard to local needs or priorities; two-thirds of the private land in Scotland is owned by a mere 1250 people, many of them aristocrats or foreign nationals. However, the success of groups of crofters in buying estates in Assynt and Knoydart, as well as the purchase of the islands of Eigg and Gigha by their inhabitants, hints at a gradual broadening of land ownership.

With so many unique issues to tackle, it is perhaps not surprising that the Highlands and Islands have always maintained an independent and generally restrained voice in Scottish **politics**. Despite the unshakable Scottishness of the region, it has remained largely ambivalent to the surges of nationalism seen in other parts of the country. Even **devolution** was long regarded with scepticism by Highlanders and Islanders for the likelihood of any Scottish Parliament being dominated by the politics of the Central Belt. Now that it has arrived, however, with the **Scottish Parliament** firmly established in Edinburgh, the demands for a more sensitive and understanding handling of the issues that matter to the Highlands and Islands have justifiably grown. After centuries of what has often seemed like ostracism from the rest of Scotland, the Highlands and Islands have good reason to believe that they are now partners in the dance.

Books

Out-of-print titles are indicated as o/p – these should be easy to track down in secondhand bookshops; 🏃 indicates titles that merit a special recommendation.

History, politics and culture

🏃 **Neal Ascherson** *Stones Voices.* Intelligent, thought-provoking ponderings on the nature of Scotland and the road to devolution from Scots-born *Observer* journalist, interspersed with personal anecdotes.

🏃 **Joni Buchanan** *The Lewis Land Struggle.* A history of crucial encounters between the crofters of Lewis and their various landlords, written from the crofters' point of view using contemporary sources.

🏃 **Tom Devine** *The Scottish Nation 1700–2000.* Best post-Union history from the last Scottish Parliament to the new one.

Diana Henderson *Highland Soldier: A Social History of the Highland Regiments 1820–1920.* Detailed history of the ten Highland regiments and the lives of their officers and men.

W.S. Hewison *This Great Harbour Scapa Flow.* Very straightforward and readable, quick rundown of Scapa Flow's history and its wartime role, written by an ex-serviceman and *Orcadian* journalist.

🏃 **David Howarth** *The Shetland Bus.* Wonderfully detailed story of the espionage and resistance operations carried out from Shetland by British and Norwegian servicemen, written by someone who was directly involved.

Roger Hutchinson *The Soap Man.* The intriguing tale of Lord Leverhulme who bought Lewis and Harris and tried to impose his benevolent despotism on them.

Fitzroy Maclean *Bonnie Prince Charlie.* Very readable and more or less definitive biography of Scotland's most romantic historical figure written by the "real" James Bond.

🏃 **Orkneyinga Saga** Probably written about 1200 AD, this is a Norse saga which sheds light on the connection between Norway and the Northern Isles, still felt strongly today; contains history of the early earls of Orkney, and is, incidentally, a stirring, bloodthirsty thriller.

🏃 **John Prebble** *Glencoe, Culloden* and *The Highland Clearances.* Emotive and subjective accounts of key events in Highland history which are very readable.

Guides and picture books

George Mackay Brown *Portrait of Orkney.* A personal account by the famous Orcadian poet of the island, its history and way of life, illustrated with photographs and drawings.

Derek Cooper *Skye.* A gazetteer and guide, and an indispensable mine of information; although first written in 1970, it has been revised where necessary.

Sheila Gear *Foula, Island West of the Sun.* An attempt to convey what it is like to live far out in the sea on an island of savage beauty.

James Shaw Grant *Discovering Lewis & Harris*. Anecdotal and informative book by former editor of the *Stornoway Gazette*.

Hamish Haswell-Smith *The Scottish Islands*. An exhaustive and impressive gazetteer with maps and absorbing information on all the Scottish islands. Filled with attractive sketches and paintings, the book is breathtaking in its thoroughness and lovingly gathered detail.

Mairi Hedderwick *Eye on the Hebrides*. The author of the Katie Morag children's books knows the Hebrides well, and with her enchanting watercolours takes you to meet all sorts of people in an affectionate look at the islands.

Charles Maclean *St Kilda*. Traces the social history of the island, from its earliest beginnings to the seemingly inevitable end of the community, with moving compassion.

Magnus Magnusson *Rùm: Nature's Island*. A detailed history of Rùm from earliest times up to its current position as a National Nature Reserve.

Memoirs and travelogues

Mike Cawthorne *Hell of a Journey*. If you want a harrowing armchair experience, trace this man's journey through the Highlands on foot in winter.

Jim Crumley *Gulfs of Blue Air – A Highland Journey*. Recent travelogue mixed with nature notes and references to Scottish poets such as MacCaig and Mackay Brown. *Among Islands* is superbly illustrated, taking you to the outer fringes of islands from Shetland to St Kilda in poetic mood.

David Duff (ed) *Queen Victoria's Highland Journals*. The daily diary of the Scottish adventures of "Mrs Brown" – Victoria's writing is detailed and interesting without being twee, and she lovingly conveys her affection for Deeside and the Highlands.

Elizabeth Grant of Rothiemurchus *Memoirs of a Highland Lady*. Hugely readable recollections, written with wit and perception at the beginning of the eighteenth century, charting the social changes in Edinburgh, London and particularly Speyside.

Peter Hill *Stargazing*. Engaging account of being a tyro lighthouse-keeper on three of Scotland's most famous lighthouses: Pladda, Ailsa Craig and Hyskeir.

Samuel Johnson & James Boswell *A Journey to the Western Isles of Scotland* and *The Journal of a Tour to the Hebrides*. Lively accounts of a famous journey around the islands taken by the noted lexicographer Dr Samuel Johnson, and his biographer and friend.

Alasdair Maclean *Night Falls on Ardnamurchan*. First published in 1984 and recently reprinted, this is a classic story of the life and death of the Highland community in which the author grew up.

Iain Mitchell *Isles of the West*; *Isle of the North*. In the first book, Mitchell sails round the Inner Hebrides, talking to locals and incomers, siding with the former, caricaturing the latter, and, with a fair bit of justification, laying into the likes of the RSPB and SNH. *Isles of the North* gives Orkney and Shetland the same treatment, before heading off to Norway to find out how it can be done differently.

Edwin Muir *Scottish Journey*. A classic travelogue written in 1935 by the troubled Orcadian writer on his return to Scotland from London.

F.G. Rea *A School on South Uist*. As an Englishman who was headmaster of a South Uist school from 1890 to 1913, Rea looks with a fresh eye at the life around him and notices details which native Hebridean writers often take for granted.

Sir Walter Scott *The Voyage of the Pharos*. In 1814 Scott accompanied Stevenson senior on a tour of the northern lighthouses, visiting Shetland, Orkney, the Hebrides and even nipping across to Ireland; he wrote a lively diary of their adventures, which included dodging American privateers.

Fiction

George Mackay Brown *Beside the Ocean of Time*. A child's journey through the history of an Orkney island, and an adult's effort to make sense of the place's secrets in the late twentieth century. *Magnus* is his retelling of the death of St Magnus, with parallels for modern times.

George MacDonald Fraser *The General Danced at Dawn*; *The Sheikh and the Dustbin*. Touching and very funny collections of short stories detailing life in a Highland regiment after World War II.

Lewis Grassic Gibbon *Sunset Song*; *Cloud Howe*; *Grey Granite*. This trilogy, known as *A Scots Quair* and set in northeast Scotland, has become a classic, telling the story of the conflict in one man's life between Scottish and English culture.

Neil M. Gunn *The Silver Darlings*. Probably Gunn's most representative and best-known book, evocatively set on the northeast coast and telling the story of the herring fishermen during the great years of the industry. Other examples of his romantic, symbolic works include *The Lost Glen*, *The Silver Bough* and *Wild Geese Overhead*.

Eric Linklater *The Dark of Summer*. Set on the Faroes, Shetland, Orkney (where the author was born) and in theatres of war, this novel exhibits the best of Linklater's compelling narrative style, although his comic *Private Angelo* is better known.

Compton MacKenzie *Whisky Galore*. Comic novel based on a true story of the wartime wreck of a cargo of whisky off Eriskay. Full of predictable stereotypes, but still funny.

Anne Macleod *The Dark Ship*. A gripping love story set on the Isle of Lewis against the background of two world wars.

Naomi Mitchison *The Bull Calves*. Written during World War II, but set in 1747, this comment on the after-effects of war is wrapped in a historical setting. *Lobster on the Agenda*. Written in 1952, this book closely mirrors contemporary life in Kintyre where Mitchison lived, with its community trying to look forward while hampered by the prejudices of the past.

Neil Munro *The Complete Edition of the Para Handy Tales*. Engaging and witty stories relating the adventures of a Clyde puffer captain as he more or less legally steers his grubby ship up and down the west coast. Despite a fond – if slightly patronizing – view of the Gaelic mind, they are enormous fun.

Sir Walter Scott *The Pirate*. Inspired by stories of Viking raids and set in Orkney and Shetland, this novel was very popular in Victorian times.

Iain Crichton Smith *Consider the Lilies*. Poetic lament about the Highland Clearances by Scotland's finest bilingual (English and Gaelic) writer.

Children's fiction

Rowena Farre *Seal Morning*. An absorbing account of a young girl growing up on a remote croft in the Highlands towards the beginning of the last century and the wildlife she adopted. Eight-year-olds and upwards will love it and so will adults.

Mairi Hedderwick *Katie Morag and the Two Grandmothers*. One of the many delightful stories of a little girl and the trouble she gets into on the West Coast island of Struay, beautifully illustrated by the author. Suitable for reading to under-5s.

Gavin Maxwell *Ring of Bright Water*. Heart-warming true tale of a relationship with three otters. Suitable for 7-year-olds upwards.

Stephen Potts *Hunting Gumnor*. A haunting story set on a Scottish island, both an adventure and a fantasy, which affirms the values of island life and the creatures that live there. For 10-year-olds upwards.

Robert Louis Stevenson *Kidnapped*. A thrilling historical adventure set in the eighteenth century, every bit as exciting as the better-known *Treasure Island*.

Poetry

George Mackay Brown *Selected Poems 1954–1992*. Brown's work is as haunting, beautiful and gritty as the Orkney islands which inspire it. The most recent collection, *Travellers* – compiled after his death – is work either previously unpublished or appearing only in newspapers and periodicals.

Robert Burns *Selected Poems*. Scotland's most famous bard. Immensely popular all over the world, his best-known works are his earlier ones, including *Auld Lang Syne* and *My Love is Like a Red, Red Rose*.

Crawford & Imlah *The New Penguin Book of Scottish Verse*. A historical survey of Scottish verse and its many languages, from St Columba to Don Paterson.

Norman MacCaig *Selected Poems*. This selection includes some of the best work from this important Scottish poet, whose deep love of nature and of the Highland landscape is always evident. *Norman MacCaig: A Celebration*, an anthology written for his 85th birthday, includes work by more than ninety writers, including Ted Hughes and Seamus Heaney.

Sorley Maclean (Somhairle Macgill-Eain) *From Wood to Ridge: Collected Poems*. Written in Gaelic, his poems have been translated into bilingual editions all over the world, dealing as they do with the sorrows of poverty, war and love.

Edwin Morgan *New Selected Poems*. A love of words and their sounds is evident in Morgan's poems, which are refreshingly varied and often experimental. He comments on the Scottish scene with shrewdness and humour.

Edwin Muir *Collected Poems*. Muir's childhood on Orkney at the turn of the twentieth century remained with him as a dream of paradise from which he was banished to Glasgow. His poems are passionately concerned with Scotland.

Iain Crichton Smith *Collected Poems*. Born on the Isle of Lewis, Iain Crichton Smith wrote with feeling, and sometimes bitterness, in both Gaelic and English, of the life of the rural communities, the iniquities of the Free Church, the need to revive Gaelic culture and the glory of the Scottish landscape.

Outdoor pursuits and wildlife

Dave Brown & Ian Mitchell *Mountain Days and Bothy Nights*. A slim but highly entertaining volume describing the characters and experiences of modern-day hill-climbing.

Hamish Brown *Hamish's Mountain Walk* and *Climbing the Corbetts*. The best of the travel narratives about walking in the Scottish Highlands.

George Hendry *Midges in Scotland*. Everything you ever wanted to know about *Culicoides impunctatus* – a strangely satisfying read on warm, damp nights in the Highlands.

Philip Lusby & Jenny Wright *Scottish Wild Plants*. Beautifully produced book about the rarer plants of Scotland, their discovery and their conservation, produced in conjunction with the Royal Botanic Gardens of Edinburgh.

Michael Madders & Julia Welstead *Where to Watch Birds in Scotland*. Region-by-region guide with maps, details on access and habitat, and notes on what to see when.

Ralph Storer *100 Best Routes on Scottish Mountains*. A compilation of the best day-walks in Scotland, including some of the classics overlooked by the Munroing guides.

C

Language

Language

Language

L anguage is a thorny, complex and often highly political issue in Scotland. If you're not from Scotland yourself, you're most likely to be addressed in a variety of **English**, spoken in a Scottish accent. Even then, you're likely to hear phrases and words that are part of what is known as Lowland Scottish or **Scots**, which is now officially recognized as a distinct language in its own right. To a lesser extent, **Gaelic**, too, remains a living language, particularly in the *Gàidhealtachd* or Gaelic-speaking areas of the northwest Highlands, the Western Isles, parts of Skye and a few scattered Hebridean islands. In Orkney and Shetland, the local dialect of Scots contains many words carried over from **Norn**, the Old Norse language spoken in the Northern Isles from the time of the Vikings until the eighteenth century.

Scots

Scots began life as a northern branch of Anglo-Saxon, emerging as a distinct language in the Middle Ages. From the 1370s until the Union in 1707, it was the country's main literary and documentary language. Since the eighteenth century, however, it has been systematically suppressed to give preference to English.

Robbie Burns is the most obvious literary exponent of the Scots language, which he referred to as "Lallans", as did Robert Louis Stevenson, but there was a revival in the last century led by poets such as Hugh MacDiarmid. Only very recently has Scots enjoyed something of a renaissance, getting itself on the Scottish school curriculum in 1996, and achieving official recognition as a distinct language in 1998. Despite these enormous political achievements, many people (rightly or wrongly) still regard Scots as a dialect of English.

For more on the Scots language, visit Ⓦ sco.wikipedia.org.

Gaelic

Scottish **Gaelic** (*Gàidhlig*, pronounced like "garlic") is one of only four Celtic languages to survive into the modern age (Welsh, Breton and Irish are the other three). Manx, the old language of the Isle of Man, died out early last century, while Cornish was finished as a community language way back in the eighteenth century. Scottish Gaelic is most closely related to Irish and Manx – hardly surprising, since Gaelic was introduced to Scotland from Ireland around the third century BC. Some folk still argue that Scottish Gaelic is merely a dialect of its parent language, Irish, and indeed the two languages remain more or less mutually intelligible. From the fifth to the twelfth centuries, Gaelic enjoyed an expansionist phase, gradually becoming the national language, thanks partly to the backing of the Celtic Church in Iona.

Since then Gaelic has been in steady decline. Even before Union with England, power, religious ideology and wealth gradually passed into non-Gaelic hands. The royal court was transferred to Edinburgh and an Anglo-Norman legal system was put in place. The Celtic Church was Romanized by the introduction of foreign clergy and, most importantly of all, English and Flemish merchants colonized the new trading towns of the east coast. In addition, the pro-English attitudes held by the Covenanters led to strong anti-Gaelic feeling within the Church of Scotland from its inception.

The two abortive Jacobite rebellions of 1715 and 1745 furthered the language's decline, as did the Clearances that took place in the Gaelic-speaking Highlands from the 1770s to the 1850s, which forced thousands to migrate to central Scotland's new industrial belt or emigrate to North America. Although efforts were made to halt the decline in the first half of the nineteenth century, the 1872 Education Act gave no official recognition to Gaelic, and children were severely punished if they were caught speaking the language in school.

The 2001 census put the number of Gaelic speakers at under 60,000 (just over one percent of the population), the majority of whom live in the *Gàidhealtachd*, though there is thought to be an extended Gaelic community of perhaps 250,000 who have some understanding of the language. Since the 1980s, great efforts have been made to try to save the language, including the introduction of bilingual primary and nursery schools, a huge increase in the amount of broadcasting time given to Gaelic-language and Gaelic-music programmes, and the establishment of highly successful Gaelic colleges such as Sabhal Mòr Ostaig (Ⓦ www.smo .uhi.ac.uk).

Gaelic grammar and pronunciation

Gaelic is a highly complex tongue, with a fiendish, antiquated **grammar** and, with only eighteen letters, an intimidating system of spelling. **Pronunciation** is easier than it appears at first glance – one general rule to remember is that the **stress** always falls on the first syllable of a word. The general rule of syntax is that the verb starts the sentence whether it's a question or not, followed by the subject and then the object; adjectives generally follow the word they are describing.

Short and long vowels

Gaelic has both short and long vowels, the latter being denoted by an acute or grave accent.

a as in cat; before nn and ll, as in cow

à as in bar

e as in pet

é like rain

i as in sight

í like free

o as in pot

ò like enthral

ó like cow

u like scoot

ù like loo

Vowel combinations

Gaelic is littered with diphthongs, which, rather like in English, can be pronounced in several different ways depending on the individual word.

ai like cat, or pet; before dh or gh, like street

ao like the sound in the middle of colonel

ei like mate

ea like pet, or cat, and sometimes like mate; before *ll* or *nn*, like in cow

èa as in hear

eu like train, or fear

ia like fear

io like fear, or shorter than street

ua like wooer

Consonants

The consonants listed below are those that differ substantially from the English.

b at the beginning of a word as in big; in the middle or at the end of a word, like the *p* in pair

bh at the beginning of a word like the *v* in **v**an; elsewhere it is silent

c as in **c**at; after a vowel it has aspiration *before* it

ch always as in lo**ch**, *never* as in **ch**urch

cn like the *cr* in **cr**owd

d like the *d* in **d**og, but with the tongue pressed against the back of the upper teeth; at the beginning of a word or before e or i, like the *j* in **j**am; in the middle or at the end of a word, like the *t* in ca**t**; after i, like the **ch** in chur**ch**

dh before and after a, o or u is an aspirated *g*, rather like a gargle; before e or i, like the *y* in **y**es; elsewhere silent

fh usually silent; sometimes like the *h* in **h**ouse

g at the beginning of a word, as in **g**et; before e, like the *y* in **y**es; in the middle or end of a word, like the *ck* in so**ck**; after i, like the **ch** in lo**ch**

gh at the beginning of a word as in **g**et; before or after a, o or u rather like a gargle; after i sometimes like the *y* in ga**y**, but often silent

l after i and sometimes before e like the *l* in lot; elsewhere, a peculiarly Gaelic sound produced by flattening the front of the tongue against the palate

mh like the *v* in **v**an

p at the beginning of a word as in **p**et; elsewhere it has aspiration *before* it

rt pronounced as **sht**

s before e or i, like the *sh* in **sh**ip; otherwise as in English

sh before a, o or u, like the *h* in **h**ouse; before e, like the **ch** in lo**ch**

t before e or i, like the **ch** in **ch**urch; in the middle or at the end of a word it has aspiration *before* it; otherwise as in English

th at the beginning of a word, like the *h* in **h**ouse; elsewhere, and in the word *thu*, silent

Gaelic phrases and vocabulary

The choice is limited when it comes to **teach-yourself Gaelic** courses, but the BBC *Can Seo* cassette and book is perfect for starting you off. Drier and more academic is *Teach Yourself Gaelic*, which is aimed at bringing beginners to working competence. *Everyday Gaelic* by Morag MacNeill is the best phrasebook around. You can do some self-learning on the Gaelic section of the BBC website Ⓦwww .bbc.co.uk, or order learning materials from Ⓦwww.smo.uhi.ac.uk.

Basic words and greetings

yes	tha
no	chan eil
hello	hallo
how are you?	ciamar a tha thu?
fine	tha gu math
thank you	tapadh leat
welcome	fàilte
come in	thig a-staigh
good day	latha math
goodbye	mar sin leat
goodnight	oidhche mhath
who?	cò?
where is...?	càit a bheil...?
when?	cuine?
what is it?	dé tha ann?

morning	madainn
evening	feasgar
day	là
night	oidhche
here	an seo
there	an sin
this way	mar seo
that way	mar sin
tomorrow	a-màireach
tonight	a-nochd
cheers	slàinte
yesterday	an-dé
today	an-diugh
tomorrow	maireach
now	a-nise
hotel	taigh-òsda
house	taigh

story	sgeul	7	seachd
song	òran	8	ochd
music	ceòl	9	naoi
book	leabhar	10	deich
tired	sgìth	11	aon deug
pound/s (sterling)	not/aichean	20	fichead
food	lòn	21	aon ar fhichead
bread	aran	30	deug ar fhichead
water	uisge	40	dà fhichead
milk	bainne	50	lethcheud
beer	leann	60	trì fichead
wine	fion	100	ceud
whisky	uisge beatha	1000	mìle
post office	post oifis	Monday	Diluain
Edinburgh	Dun Eideann	Tuesday	Dimàirt
Glasgow	Glaschu	Wednesday	Diciadain
America	Ameireaga	Thursday	Diardaoin
Ireland	Eire	Friday	Dihaoine
England	Sasainn	Saturday	Disathurna
London	Lunnain	Sunday	Didòmhnaich/ La na Sàbaid

Some useful phrases

How much is that?	Dè tha e 'cosg?
What's your name?	Dè 'n t-ainm a th'ort?
Excuse me	Gabh mo leisgeul
What time is it?	Dé am uair a tha e?
I'm thirsty	Tha am pathadh orm
I'd like a double room	'Se rùm dùbailte tha mi'giarraigh
Do you speak Gaelic?	A bheil Gàidhlig agad?
What is the Gaelic for ...?	Dé a' Ghàidhlig a tha ... air?
I don't understand	Chan eil mi 'tuigsinn
I don't know	Chan eil fhios agam
That's good	'S math sin
It doesn't matter	'S coma
I'm sorry	Tha mi duilich

Numbers and days

1	aon
2	dà/dhà
3	trì
4	ceithir
5	còig
6	sia

Gaelic geographical and place-name terms

The purpose of the list below is to help with place-name derivations from Gaelic and with more detailed map-reading. For a list of place names derived from Norse, see p.442.

river	abhainn
field	ach or auch, from achadh ail, aileach
rock	
Scotland	Alba
ridge	aonach
a point of land or height	ard, ardan or arden, from àird
dwelling	aros
stream	ault, from allt
brake or clump of trees	bad
bay	bagh
town, village	bal or bally, from baile
mountain pass	balloch, from bealach
white, fair	ban
summit	bàrr
small	beg, from beag
mountain	ben, from beinn
field or battlefield	blair, from blàr

pile of stones	cairn, from càrn	head	ken or kin, from ceann
bay, harbour	camas	hill	knock, from cnoc
hill	cnoc	narrow strait	kyle, from caolas
wood or forest	coll or colly, from coille	hollow	lag
		site of an old ruin	larach
a spit or point jutting into the sea	corran	grey	liath
		lake	loch
round hollow in mountainside, whirlpool	corrie, from coire	round hill	meall
		hill	mon, from monadh
rock, crag	craig, from creag	large, great	more, from mór
bold hill	cruach	round mountain	ord
ridge	drum, from druim	bracken	rannoch, from raineach
black	dubh	promontory	ross, from ros
fort	dun or dum, from dùn	promontory	rubha
island	eilean	sea rock	sgeir
waterfall	ess, from eas	sharp point	sgurr
white	fin, from fionn	nose, prow or promontory	sron
short	gair or gare, from geàrr	broad valley	strath, from srath
rough	garv, from garbh	isthmus	tarbet, from tairbeart
cove	geodha	house	tigh
valley	glen, from gleann	land	tir or tyre, from tìr
goat	gower or gour, from gabhar	hill, castle	torr
		shore	tràigh
meadow or island	inch, from innis	shelter	uig
river mouth	inver, from inbhir	water	uisge

Norn (Orkney and Shetland)

Between the tenth and seventeenth centuries, the chief language of Orkney and Shetland was **Norn**, a Scandinavian tongue close to modern Faroese and Icelandic. After the end of Norse rule, and with the transformation of the church, the law, commerce and education, Norn gradually lost out to Scots and English, eventually petering out completely in the eighteenth century. Today, Orkney and Shetland have their own dialects, and individual islands and communities within each group have local variations. The **dialects** have a Scots base, with some Old Norse words; however, they don't sound strongly Scottish, with the Orkney accent – which has been likened to the Welsh one – especially distinctive. Listed below are some of the words you're most likely to hear, including some birds' names and common elements in place names.

Norn phrases and vocabulary

guillemot	aak	large	muckle
storm petrel	alan	hollow place where a boat is drawn up	noost
beach	ayre		
farm	bister	puffin	norie
fisherman's store	böd		(or tammie-norie)
great skua	bonxie	steep headland	noup
rubbish	bruck	small	peerie/peedie
heath rush	burra	small dry-stone enclosure for growing cabbages	plantiecrub
sheepfold	crö		(or plantiecrö)
rod-fishing from small boats	eela		
incomer (Orkney)	ferrylouper	enclosed, cultivated common land	quoy
four-oared boat	fourareen	tide race	roost
party or festival	foy	common grazing land	scattald
coastal inlet	geo		
blowhole, behind a cliff face, where spray is blasted out from the cave below (from Old Norse *glup*, a throat)	gloup	gap or pass in a ridge of hills	scord
		farm	setter
		dark grey	shaela
		summer twilight	simmer dim
		six-oared boat	sixern/sixareen
laird's house	haa	gannet	solan
deep-sea fishing. Lit. "heave" (Shetland)	haaf	incomer (Shetland)	soothmoother
		Norse law designating land as a freehold without any charter or feudal-type arrangement	udal
hand-knitted shawl	hap		
mound	howe		
ridge of hills	kame		
basket	kishie		
seagull	maa	sea inlet	voe
headland	mool	rowing boat used for fishing (Shetland)	yoal
brown	moorit		
tiny	mootie		

Glossary

Auld Old.

Aye Yes.

Bairn Baby.

Bannock Flat, unleavened bread traditionally made from oats or barley.

Baronial see "Scottish Baronial".

Ben Hill or mountain.

Blackhouse Thick-walled traditional dwelling.

Bonnie Pretty.

Bothy Primitive cottage or hut; farmworker's or shepherd's mountain shelter.

Brae Slope or hill.

Brig Bridge.

Broch Circular prehistoric stone fort.

Burn Small stream or brook.

Byre Shelter for cattle; cottage.

Cairn Mound of stones.

CalMac Caledonian MacBrayne ferry company.

Carse Riverside area of flat alluvium.

Ceilidh (pronounced "kay-lee"). Social gathering involving dancing, drinking, singing and storytelling.

Central Belt The densely populated strip of central Scotland between the Forth and Clyde estuaries, incorporating the conurbations of Edinburgh, Glasgow and Stirling.

Clan Extended family.

Clearances Policy adopted by late eighteenth- and early nineteenth-century landowners to evict tenant crofters in order to create space for more profitable sheep-grazing. Families cleared from the Highlands were often put on emigrant ships to North America or the colonies.

Clootie well A cloot is a cloth or rag; the well was festooned with these and folk would drink three sips and circle the well for good luck.

Corbett A mountain between 2500ft and 3000ft high.

Corbie-stepped Architectural term; any set of steps on a gable.

Covenanters Supporters of the Presbyterian Church in the seventeenth century.

Crannog Celtic lake or bog dwelling.

Croft Small plot of farmland with house, common in the Highlands.

Crow-stepped Same as corbie-stepped.

Dirk A long dagger.

Dolmen Grave chamber.

Doocot Dovecot.

Dram Literally, one-eighth of a fluid ounce. Usually refers to any small measure of whisky.

Dun Fortified mound.

Episcopalian A church which has bishops in its organisational structure.

First-foot The first person to enter a household after midnight on Hogmanay (see below).

Firth A wide sea inlet or estuary.

Gabbro Igneous basalt-like rock formed by molten lava and found in the Northwest Highlands of Scotland.

Gàidhealtachd Gaelic-speaking area.

Gillie Personal guide used on hunting or fishing trips.

Glen Deep, narrow mountain valley.

Harling Limestone and gravel mix used to cover buildings.

Henge Circular ditch with a bank.

Hogmanay New Year's Eve.

Howe Valley.

Howff Meeting place; pub.

HS Historic Scotland, a government-funded heritage organization.

Ken Knowledge; understanding.

Kilt Knee-length tartan skirt worn by Highland men.

Kirk Church.

Laird Landowner; aristocrat.

Lallans Scots language.

Law Rounded hill.

Links Grassy coastal land; coastal golf-course.

Loch Lake.

Lochan Little loch.

Mac/Mc These prefixes in Scottish surnames derive from the Gaelic, meaning "son of". In Scots "Mac" is used for both sexes. In Gaelic "Nic" is used for women: *Donnchadh Mac Aodh* is Duncan MacKay, *Iseabail Nic Aodh* is Isabel MacKay.

Machair Sandy, grassy, lime-rich coastal land, generally used for grazing.

Manse Official home of a Presbyterian minister.

Munro A mountain over 3000ft high.

Munro-bagging The sport of trying to climb as many Munros as possible.

Neuk Corner.

NTS The National Trust for Scotland, a heritage organization.

Peel Fortified tower, built to withstand Border raids.

Pend Archway or vaulted passage.

Presbyterian The form of church government used in the official (Protestant) Church of Scotland, established by John Knox during the Reformation.

RIB Rigid Inflatable Boat.

RSPB Royal Society for the Protection of Birds.

Runrig A common form of land tenure in which separate ridges are cultivated by different occupiers under joint agreement.

Sassenach Derives from the Gaelic *Sasunnach*, meaning literally "Saxon"; used by Scots to describe the English.

Scottish Baronial Style of architecture favoured by the Scottish landowning class featuring crow-stepped gables and round turrets.

Sept Branches of clans: often septs have a different surname to the clan name.

Sheila na gig Female fertility symbol, usually a naked woman displaying her vulva.

Shieling Simple huts or shelters used by shepherds during summer grazing.

Shinty Stick-and-ball game played in the Highlands, with similarities to hockey.

Smiddy Smithy.

SNH Scottish Natural Heritage, a government-funded conservation body.

SNP Scottish National Party.

Sporran Leather purse worn in front of, or at the side of, a kilt.

Tartan Check-patterned woollen cloth, particular patterns being associated with particular clans.

Tatties Potatoes.

Thane A landowner of high rank; the chief of a clan.

Tombolo A spit of sand connecting an island to the mainland.

Trews Tartan trousers.

Wee Small.

Wee Frees Followers of the Free Presbyterian or Free Church of Scotland.

Wynd Narrow lane.

Yett Gate or door.

FAIR FARES from
NORTH SOUTH TRAVEL

Our great-value air fares cover the world, from Abuja to Zanzibar and from Zurich to Anchorage. North South Travel is a fund-raising travel agency, owned by the NST Development Trust.

ALL our profits go to development organisations.

Call 01245 608 291 (or +44 1245 608 291 if outside UK) to speak to a friendly advisor. Your money is safe (ATOL 5401). For more information, visit northsouthtravel.co.uk. Free Rough Guide of your choice for every booking over £500.

EVERY FLIGHT A FIGHT AGAINST POVERTY

www.roughguides.com

nformation on over 25,000 destinations around the world

- **Read** Rough Guides' trusted travel info
- **Access** exclusive articles from Rough Guides authors
- **Update** yourself on new books, maps, CDs and other products
- **Enter** our competitions and win travel prizes
- **Share** ideas, journals, photos & travel advice with other users
- **Earn** points every time you contribute to the Rough Guide community and get rewards

Small print and

Index

A Rough Guide to Rough Guides

Published in 1982, the first Rough Guide – to Greece – was a student scheme that became a publishing phenomenon. Mark Ellingham, a recent graduate in English from Bristol University, had been travelling in Greece the previous summer and couldn't find the right guidebook. With a small group of friends he wrote his own guide, combining a highly contemporary, journalistic style with a thoroughly practical approach to travellers' needs.

The immediate success of the book spawned a series that rapidly covered dozens of destinations. And, in addition to impecunious backpackers, Rough Guides soon acquired a much broader and older readership that relished the guides' wit and inquisitiveness as much as their enthusiastic, critical approach and value-for-money ethos.

These days, Rough Guides include recommendations from shoestring to luxury and cover more than 200 destinations around the globe, including almost every country in the Americas and Europe, more than half of Africa and most of Asia and Australasia. Our ever-growing team of authors and photographers is spread all over the world, particularly in Europe, the US and Australia.

In the early 1990s, Rough Guides branched out of travel, with the publication of Rough Guides to World Music, Classical Music and the Internet. All three have become benchmark titles in their fields, spearheading the publication of a wide range of books under the Rough Guide name.

Including the travel series, Rough Guides now number more than 350 titles, covering: phrasebooks, waterproof maps, music guides from Opera to Heavy Metal, reference works as diverse as Conspiracy Theories and Shakespeare, and popular culture books from iPods to Poker. Rough Guides also produce a series of more than 120 World Music CDs in partnership with World Music Network.

Visit www.roughguides.com to see our latest publications.

Rough Guide credits

Text editor: Andy Turner and Ann-Marie Shaw
Layout: Sachin Tanwar
Cartography: Jasbir Sandhu
Picture editor: Sarah Cummins
Production: Erika Pepe
Proofreader: Susanne Hillen
Cover design: Nicole Newman, Dan May
Photographer: Helena Smith
Editorial: **London** Keith Drew, Edward Aves,
Alice Park, Lucy White, Jo Kirby, James Smart,
Natasha Foges, Róisín Cameron, James Rice,
Emma Beatson, Emma Gibbs, Kathryn Lane,
Monica Woods, Mani Ramaswamy, Harry Wilson,
Lucy Cowie, Alison Roberts, Lara Kavanagh,
Eleanor Aldridge, Ian Blenkinsop, Joe Staines,
Matthew Milton, Tracy Hopkins; **Delhi** Madhavi
Singh, Jalpreen Kaur Chhatwal, Jubbi Francis
Design & Pictures: **London** Scott Stickland,
Dan May, Diana Jarvis, Mark Thomas, Nicole

Newman, Emily Taylor; **Delhi** Umesh Aggarwal,
Ajay Verma, Jessica Subramanian, Ankur Guha,
Pradeep Thapliyal, Anita Singh, Nikhil Agarwal,
Sachin Gupta
Production: Rebecca Short, Liz Cherry,
Louise Daly
Cartography: **London** Ed Wright, Katie Lloyd-
Jones; **Delhi** Rajesh Chhibber, Ashutosh Bharti,
Rajesh Mishra, Animesh Pathak, Swati Handoo,
Deshpal Dabas, Lokamata Sahu
Marketing, Publicity & roughguides.com:
Liz Statham
Digital Travel Publisher: Peter Buckley
Reference Director: Andrew Lockett
Operations Coordinator: Becky Doyle
Publishing Director (Travel): Clare Currie
Commercial Manager: Gino Magnotta
Managing Director: John Duhigg

Publishing information

This sixth edition published May 2011 by
Rough Guides Ltd,
80 Strand, London WC2R 0RL
11, Community Centre, Panchsheel Park,
New Delhi 110017, India

Distributed by the Penguin Group

Penguin Books Ltd,
80 Strand, London WC2R 0RL

Penguin Group (USA)
375 Hudson Street, NY 10014, USA

Penguin Group (Australia)
250 Camberwell Road, Camberwell,
Victoria 3124, Australia

Penguin Group (NZ)
67 Apollo Drive, Mairangi Bay, Auckland 1310,
New Zealand

Rough Guides is represented in Canada by
Tourmaline Editions Inc. 662 King Street West,
Suite 304, Toronto, Ontario M5V 1M7

Cover concept by Peter Dyer.

Typeset in Bembo and Helvetica to an original
design by Henry Iles.

Printed in Singapore
© Rob Humphreys and Donald Reid
Maps © Rough Guides
No part of this book may be reproduced in any
form without permission from the publisher except
for the quotation of brief passages in reviews.
464pp includes index
A catalogue record for this book is available from
the British Library
ISBN: 978-1-84836-715-9
The publishers and authors have done their best
to ensure the accuracy and currency of all the
information in **The Rough Guide to Scottish
Highlands and Islands**, however, they can
accept no responsibility for any loss, injury, or
inconvenience sustained by any traveller as a
result of information or advice contained in the
guide.

3   5   7   9   8   6   4   2

Help us update

We've gone to a lot of effort to ensure that the
sixth edition of **The Rough Guide to Scottish
Highlands and Islands** is accurate and up-to-
date. However, things change – places get
"discovered", opening hours are notoriously
fickle, restaurants and rooms raise prices or lower
standards. If you feel we've got it wrong or left
something out, we'd like to know, and if you can
remember the address, the price, the hours, the
phone number, so much the better.

Please send your comments with the subject
line "**Rough Guide Scottish Highlands and
Islands Update**" to ©mail@uk.roughguides.com.
We'll credit all contributions and send a copy of
the next edition (or any other Rough Guide if you
prefer) for the very best emails.
    Find more travel information, connect with
fellow travellers and book your trip on ⓦwww
.roughguides.com

Acknowledgements

The authors would like to thank the National Trust for Scotland, Historic Scotland, VisitScotland, Andrew Deeprose at CalMac and Andy and Annie for their careful and patient editing.

Rob Humphreys would also like to thank: Alasdair Enticknap and Jane Dubrowski for dispatches from Islay and Jura, Val & Gordon for exploring the byways of the Borders and Skye,

Val for getting away against the odds to our old stamping grounds, Sara for holding the fort back in Yorkshire and to Kate for hostelling and camping at the wrong time of year.

Helena Smith would also like to thank: David at the Lismore Museum for his help, and my parents, Angela and Grahame, for running the best B&B in the whole of Scotland.

Readers' letters

Thanks to everyone who took the trouble to write in with amendments and additions. Apologies for any misspellings or omissions.

Paul Adderley, Anne Benner, Anthony Bradbury, Jacky Bright, Nancy Brinton, John & Freda Cammack, Margaret Eden, Max Garrone, Shana Goldberg, Emma Harbour, Pat Jeffers, Chris Keeling, Sally MacDonald, Alistair & Solveig McCleery, Jenny MacKay, Raymond Maxwell, Karin MacKinnon, Rachel Pepa, Jane Richards, Jonard Rood, Jane Rooth, Patsy Thompson, Philip Ward, Annie Warwick, Heather White, Sinead Williams, David Wood, Wendy Wood.

ROUGH
GUIDES

SMALL PRINT

Photo credits

All photos © Rough Guides except the following:

Title page
Red deer stag in snow © Niall Benvie/Corbis

Full page
Sanna Bay, Ardnamurchan peninsula © Joe Cornish/Photolibrary

Introduction
Puffin, Shetland © David Tipling/Alamy
Rubha Reidh lighthouse, near Gairloch, Skye © Simon Butterworth/Photolibrary
Man in kilt at the Highland Games © Daniel Boschung/Corbis
Loch Lomond © nagelestock.com/Alamy
Walking Glen Lyon, Perthshire © Niall Benvie/Getty
Eilean Donan Castle, Loch Duich © Peter Adams/JAI/Corbis
Winter road near Loch Tay © Gary Cook/Alamy
Scottish thistle, Cairngorms © Duncan Shaw/Photolibrary

Things Not to Miss
01 Dawn on Ben Eighe, Wester Ross © Malcolm MacGregor/John Warburton-Lee Photography Ltd/Corbis
04 West Highland Railway © Christophe Boisvieux/Corbis
05 Killer whale © Hugh Harrop/Alamy
07 Mousa Broch © David Robertson/Alamy
09 Kinloch Castle © WildCountry/Corbis
10 Skiing, Cairngorms © Rob Penn/Axiom
11 Highland dancing © Steven Vidler/Eurasia Press/Corbis
12 Red squirrel, Caledonian Forest © Chris Gomersall/Alamy
14 Tobermory © Macduff Everton/Getty
16 Shetland Folk Festival © Dave Donaldson/Alamy
17 Hikers, Glen Coe © Paul Harris/Getty
18 Flying over Orkney © Simon Price/Alamy
19 Jarlshof © Gallo Images/Getty
20 St John's Cross, Iona © Michael Nicholson/Corbis

21 South Harris beaches © Patrick Dieudonne/Robert Harding/Corbis
24 Geese, Islay © Mike Read/Alamy
25 Loch Shiel and Glenfinnan Monument © Derek Croucher/Alamy
27 Skye Cuillin © Gavin Hellier/JAI/Corbis
28 Isle of Eigg © Robert Harding Picture Library Ltd/Alamy

The great outdoors colour section
Stob Ban © Travel Ink/Getty
Buchaille Etive, Glen Coe © Kathy Collins/Getty
Road sign © Duncan Hale-Sutton/Alamy
Mountain biking, Great Glen © John James/Alamy
Sea-kayaking, Staffa © Alan Payton/Alamy
Ice climbing, Aonach Mhòr © Paul Harris/Photolibrary
Windsurfers and the Tiree Wave Classic © TNT Magazine/Alamy

Wild Scotland colour section
Golden eagle © Laurie Campbell/Getty
Gannet nest on Westray, Orkney © Graham Uney/Alamy
Puffins © Frans Lanting/Corbis
Male capercaillie © Niall Benvie/Corbis
Red stag © Niall Benvie/Corbis
Highland cow © Jason Hoksing/Getty
Female grey seal © Niall Benvie/Corbis
Dolphins watching © Specialist Stock/Corbis
Carnivorous sundew © Naturfoto Honal/Corbis

Black and whites
p.60 Whisky barrels © Macduff Everton/Corbis
p.132 Shinty match © Russell Cheyne/Reuters/Corbis
p.188 Commando Memorial © Dave Porter/Alamy
p.222 Stac Pollaidh. Ben More Assynt massif © Ashley Cooper/Corbis
p.280 The Old Man of Storr, Isle of Skye © Alan Novelli/Alamy
p.340 Puffins and razorbill, Orkney © Gareth McCormack/Alamy

ROUGH GUIDES

Index

Map entries are in colour.

INDEX

453

D

I

INDEX

Map symbols

maps are listed in the full index using coloured text

▬▬▪	International boundary	☰	Stately home
▬▬▬	Chapter division boundary	♛	Castle
▬▬▬	Motorway	●	Museum
▬▬▬	Pedestrianized street	♟	Gardens
▬▬	Road	⚔	Battlefield
▪▪▪▪▪	Track	⛺	Campsite
⊔⊔⊔⊔	Steps	◉	Accommodation
▪▪▪▪▪	Footpath	P	Parking
▬▬	Wall	ⓘ	Tourist office
▬◆▬	Railway	✉	Post office
●▪▪▪●	Cable car	🍾	Whisky distillery
▬▬	Coastline/river	⚐	Skiing
▬ ▬	Ferry route	⚑	Golf course
◆	Point of interest	🏊	Swimming Pool
▲	Peak	)(	Bridge
⚘	Viewpoint	⌂	Abbey
⅔	Rocks	⌂	Monastery
🐦	Lighthouse	⌇	Chapel
✈	Domestic airport	▬	Building
✈	International airport	╬	Church
⚑	Waterfall	⊞	Cemetery
⌂	Cave	▦	Park
∴	Ruins/archeological site	森	Forest
⌂	Cairn(s)	⋮	Beach
/|\\	Hill shading		

Ordnance Survey data © Crown copyright and database rights 2011

MAP SYMBOLS

So now we've told you about the things not to miss, the best places to stay, the top restaurants, the liveliest bars and the most spectacular sights, it only seems fair to tell you about the best travel insurance around

👤 WorldNomads.com
keep travelling safely

Recommended by Rough Guides

www.roughguides.com
MAKE THE MOST OF YOUR TIME ON EARTH

ROUGH GUIDES